Housing in the Ancient Mediterranean World

One of the greatest benefits of studying the ancient Greek and Roman past is the ability to utilize different forms of evidence, in particular both written and archaeological sources. The contributors to this volume employ this evidence to examine ancient housing, and what might be learned of identities, families and societies, but they also use it as a methodological locus from which to interrogate the complex relationship between different types of sources. Chapters range from the recreation of the house as it was conceived in Homeric poetry, to the decipherment of a painted Greek *lekythos* to build up a picture of household activities, to the conjuring of the sensorial experience of a house in Pompeii. Together, they present a rich tapestry which demonstrates what can be gained for our understanding of ancient housing from examining the interplay between the words of ancient texts and the walls of archaeological evidence.

J. A. BAIRD is Professor of Archaeology at Birkbeck College. She is the author of *The Inner Lives of Ancient Houses* (2014) and *Dura-Europos* (2018), and co-editor of *Ancient Graffiti in Context* (2011).

APRIL PUDSEY is Reader in Roman history at Manchester Metropolitan University. She has published widely on ancient childhood, family, and demography including *Demography and the Graeco-Roman World* (with C. Holleran, 2011) and *A Social Archaeology of Roman and Late Antique Egypt* (with E. Swift and J. Stoner, 2021).

Housing in the Ancient Mediterranean World

Material and Textual Approaches

Edited by

J. A. BAIRD
Birkbeck College, University of London

APRIL PUDSEY
Manchester Metropolitan University

CAMBRIDGE
UNIVERSITY PRESS

University Printing House, Cambridge CB2 8BS, United Kingdom

One Liberty Plaza, 20th Floor, New York, NY 10006, USA

477 Williamstown Road, Port Melbourne, VIC 3207, Australia

314–321, 3rd Floor, Plot 3, Splendor Forum, Jasola District Centre, New Delhi – 110025, India

103 Penang Road, #05–06/07, Visioncrest Commercial, Singapore 238467

Cambridge University Press is part of the University of Cambridge.

It furthers the University's mission by disseminating knowledge in the pursuit of
education, learning, and research at the highest international levels of excellence.

www.cambridge.org
Information on this title: www.cambridge.org/9781108845267
DOI: 10.1017/9781108954983

© Cambridge University Press 2022

First published 2022

A catalogue record for this publication is available from the British Library.

Library of Congress Cataloging-in-Publication Data
Names: Baird, J. A., 1978– editor. | Pudsey, April, editor.
Title: Housing in the ancient Mediterranean world : material and textual approaches / Edited by J. A. Baird,
    Birkbeck College, University of London, April Pudsey, Manchester Metropolitan University.
Description: New York : Cambridge University Press, 2022. | Includes index.
Identifiers: LCCN 2021053899 (print) | LCCN 2021053900 (ebook) | ISBN 9781108845267 (hardback) |
    ISBN 9781108949972 (paperback) | ISBN 9781108954983 (epub)
Subjects: LCSH: Dwellings–Mediterranean Region–History. | Housing–Mediterranean Region–History. |
    Building materials–Mediterranean Region–History. | Architecture, Ancient–Mediterranean Region–History. |
    Mediterranean Region–History. | BISAC: HISTORY / Ancient / General
Classification: LCC GT175 .H72 2022 (print) | LCC GT175 (ebook) | DDC 392.3/6091822–dc23/eng/20220104
LC record available at https://lccn.loc.gov/2021053899
LC ebook record available at https://lccn.loc.gov/2021053900

ISBN 978-1-108-84526-7 Hardback

Contents

Figures

Tables

Contributors

Professor Penelope Allison is based in the School of Archaeology and Ancient History at the University of Leicester. Her research focuses on household archaeology and consumption approaches to artefacts. Her books include: *The Archaeology of Household Activities* (1999); *Pompeian Households: An Analysis of the Material Culture* (2004); *People and Spaces in Roman Military Bases* (2013); and *Who Came to Tea at the Old Kinchega Homestead?* (2020).

Professor Richard Alston is a historian of the Roman Empire and its reception and has worked on various themes from the settlement history of Byzantine Egypt to Foucault's understanding of Rome. His work focuses on the individual in history and operates in the intersections between political and social philosophy and ancient history.

Professor J. A. Baird is Professor of Archaeology in the Department of History, Classics and Archaeology at Birkbeck College. Her most recent book is *Dura-Europos*, published in Bloomsbury's *Archaeological Histories* series in 2018. Her book on the housing of Dura-Europos, *The Inner Lives of Ancient Houses*, was published by Oxford University Press in 2014.

Dr Crysta Kaczmarek completed her PhD in Archaeology at the University of Leicester in 2016, having written a thesis on settlement patterns, identity and social strategies in Thessaly during the Roman period. Her current research interests focus on continuing investigations of different social strategies employed during periods of change.

Dr Maeve McHugh is a Lecturer in Classical Archaeology, Department of Classics, Ancient History and Archaeology, University of Birmingham. She researches the lived experience of rural non-elite communities in the Greek world, to learn more about the interrelationships between physical, social and cultural landscapes. Her 2017 monograph *The Ancient Greek Farmstead* used archaeological and historical data to reconstruct the role that farmsteads played in supporting agriculture as an economic and communal activity.

Professor Caspar Meyer teaches archaeology at the Bard Graduate Center in New York. His interests range from archaeological visualization and digital heritage to the possibilities which artefacts and landscapes offer in shaping social experiences. He is the author of *Greco-Scythian Art and the Birth of Eurasia: From Classical Antiquity to Russian Modernity* (Oxford, 2013).

Dr Janett Morgan is an independent scholar researching ancient Greek material culture and its reception. She has published *The Classical Greek House* (2010) and *Greek Perspectives on the Achaemenid Empire: Persia through the Looking Glass* (2016), as well as articles on gender, religion, Achaemenid art, and 'Etruscan' ware in 19th-century Wales.

Lisa Nevett is Professor of Classical Archaeology at the University of Michigan, Ann Arbor (ed. 2017) and *An Age of Experiment: Classical Archaeology Transformed (1976–2014)* (co-ed with James Whitley). She is co-director of the Olynthos Project, a multidisciplinary archaeological research project focusing on the city of Olynthos in northern Greece, in the field 2014–19 and now under publication.

Dr Hannah Platts is Senior Lecturer in Ancient History and Archaeology at Royal Holloway, University of London, and specializes in Roman domestic space and is author of *Multisensory Living in Ancient Rome: Power and Space in Roman Houses* (2019). Connected with this interest in sensory research, in 2017 she collaborated on an Arts and Humanities Research Council project entitled *Sensations of Roman Life*, which recreated a Roman residence with sounds and smells in virtual reality.

Dr April Pudsey of Manchester Metropolitan University is a Roman social historian who has published widely on ancient childhood, family, fertility and mortality, with particular focus on Graeco-Roman Egypt. She works with Greek and Coptic papyrological texts, and material culture, to shine a light on the lives of those often neglected by historical record.

Professor Amy C. Smith is a specialist in the art of ancient Greece, with particular interests in ceramics, political and religious iconography, museum collections histories and digital classics. Since her PhD studies at Yale, she has worked in museums, uniting her enthusiasms for antiquity and material cultures.

Simon Speksnijder is a PhD candidate in Ancient History at the University of Groningen. His dissertation, provisionally titled 'Eating and greeting in Roman society', examines the role of daily interactions in shaping social relationships and hierarchies in the Roman world.

Dr Inge Uytterhoeven is Associate Professor at Koç University. She obtained her PhD in Archaeology from KU Leuven in 2003. She has published extensively on Hellenistic, Roman and late antique housing, public architecture, and urbanism in Anatolia and the Eastern Mediterranean, including her book *Hawara in the Graeco-Roman Period: Life and Death in a Fayum Village* (Leuven 2009).

Dr Emily Varto is Associate Professor in Ancient Greek History in the Department of Classics at Dalhousie University. Much of her research focuses on early Iron Age Greek kinship, and the relationship between state and family in early Greece. She is editor of Brill's *Companion to Classics and Early Anthropology* (2018).

Dr Katerina Volioti is Associate Lecturer at the School of Humanities, University of Roehampton. She has published extensively on the materiality of Greek vases. Her research has appeared in leading peer-reviewed journals and edited volumes (e.g., Routledge 2011 and 2017).

Acknowledgements

This volume is based on the conference 'Between Words and Walls: Material and Textual Approaches to Ancient Housing' held in August 2013 in London. That conference was only possible due to the generous support of the Department of History, Classics and Archaeology at Birkbeck College, University of London, for which we remain grateful. The editors are grateful also to John Arnold, Serafina Cuomo, Catharine Edwards, Lesley McFadyen and Daniel Stewart, for providing vital support and encouragement during that conference and in the time since.

That original conference included papers which do not appear here, including that of Barbara Tsakirgis, who sadly passed away in 2019 and whose work on Greek households continues to shape how we think about them. Included in this volume are scholars who did not present at the original conference, but whose attendance prompted invitations to contribute, including Caspar Meyer, Hannah Platts and Richard Alston. The editors are grateful to them, and to all the contributors, for bearing with the long gestation of the volume (due in part to a non-metaphorical gestation by one of the editors and the relocation, twice, of the other: we hope the delay caused by our own households to the publication of the households in this volume is forgivable). We are grateful also for the sage direction of the anonymous referees whose comments strengthened the volume immeasurably, although they are not to blame for any issues which remain. More than anyone else, though, we are grateful to Michael Sharp at Cambridge University Press, who expertly shepherded this volume with incredible patience and wisdom.

Introduction

Between Words and Walls: Material and Textual Approaches
to Housing in the Graeco-Roman World

RICHARD ALSTON, J. A. BAIRD AND APRIL PUDSEY

This collection begins from a methodological problem familiar to all who
have worked on the housing of the ancient world. That problem centres on
the relationship between the diverse texts that have come down to us from
antiquity, documentary and literary, and the archaeology of Classical
settlements. In relation to housing, the problem is a special instance of
the sometimes fraught disciplinary relationship between Classical archaeology and Classical history, which goes back to the formation of the
modern academic disciplines, and the more particular issue of a perceived
gap between the material world and the textual world.[1] Texts and archaeology rarely tell the same story.

From the 18th century onwards, there was an increased availability and
understanding of material remains. Classical archaeology brought together
aesthetic interests, focused on art and architecture, but 'early' archaeology
also aimed itself at resolving questions derived from the literary material
(see the historiographical elements in the studies of Varto, Morgan and
Allison in the volume). From Schliemann's discoveries of Troy and
Mycenae to the investigations at Pompeii, texts often determined patterns
of excavation and how that material evidence was interpreted.

Until the late 19th century, history was very much focused on the
political and the event, while social history was a minor discipline.[2] The
hegemony of political history created a problem for archaeology; Classical
archaeology proved poor at providing evidence of particular events and
thus the narratives emerging from archaeological material were difficult to
reconcile with mainstream historical studies. Nevertheless, expeditionary
and excavation decisions were determined largely by the interest in the
political on the one hand and the aesthetic on the other, and so concentrated on major public buildings and monuments at those sites perceived to
be of civic importance. Even today, if one wanders across major Classical
urban sites, such as Corinth or the Athenian Agora or Rome, it is the major
civic buildings, the temples, the meeting places, the basilicas, that is,
especially the monuments, to which one's attention is directed. In so many

urban centres, the Campanian cities preserved by Vesuvius being an exception, the archaeology of housing is either invisible or hidden away. Archaeology's role as 'handmaiden to history' determined its agendas.[3]

Texts retained their primacy in understandings of the Classical world even after cultural and economic history came to challenge the hegemony of the history of the event.[4] With regard to household spaces, as various contributors to this volume show (Varto, Morgan, Speksnijder), historians and archaeologists sought to discover physical traces of the spaces and material artefacts represented in their texts.[5] The perceived presence or absence of such traces allowed them in some cases, particularly for Archaic periods, to argue about the realities depicted in those texts.[6] It also provided illustrative material for the social and political structures understood from the texts: archaeology was used to confirm what was already 'known' from historical sources.[7]

The hegemony of the textual heavily influenced the development of study of the ancient domestic, and indeed the very notion of 'the domestic' as Meyer's contribution to the volume demonstrates. Textual hegemonies encouraged a practice of labelling material remains and creating typologies thereof which drew heavily on textual resources (Speksnijder, in this volume), sometimes to the exclusion of material, archaeological, realities.[8] This was a particularly tempting tactic for work on the Roman world for which Vitruvius could be mined for a wealth of labels and architectural descriptions.[9] But such labelling created an epistemic circle: the use of Vitruvian labels for spaces in the archaeological record allowed the labels in the textual record to be given material form, which in turn confirmed the labels applied to the archaeological record. Consequently, archaeologists applied a vocabulary derived from Vitruvius to the spaces on which they worked with a presumption that the spaces in the texts (often very poorly described, or described with other purposes in mind) were identical to the spaces on the ground; historians saw the spaces on the ground as confirmation of the societal models they were developing from the texts. Practitioners of both disciplines ignored the leap of faith that such an epistemic circle required. In both cases, particular methodological concerns which are almost innate to the disciplinary areas (the 'elite' nature of texts; the difficulties of deriving social meaning from material form) were set aside.

For Greece, which does not have an associated treatise on architectural forms, the same process followed from the excavation of significant numbers of domestic structures, as at Olynthus and Priene.[10] The interpretation of the archaeological remains needed a vocabulary and a taxonomy. That taxonomy, as Morgan (in this volume) shows, employed a vocabulary that was derived from Classical Greek. Consequently, the labels themselves gave the impression that the taxonomy was drawn from Classical texts, that it was part of a Classical Greek world view, and that there was thus a very close relationship between texts and walls that was simply uncovered by the scholars. In reality, of course, archaeologists educated in and deeply familiar with the Classical texts invented the taxonomic system. Baird points to a similar dynamic in the study of Durene housing. Consequently, the taxonomies had embedded within them similar epistemic relationships to texts in Italy, Greece, Egypt and Syria.[11]

This process of labelling also had the unfortunate consequence of reinforcing the primacy of the texts. In the 'Roman' instances, historians and archaeologists found ways of interpreting the social significance of those spaces through the textual record.[12] Archaeology remained subservient to the tropes and narratives of the historians. For the Roman world, narratives of aristocratic decline, luxury and the rise of 'insurgent' social groups, such as freedmen and a bourgeoisie, were written into the domestic architecture of Pompeii.[13] For the 'Greek' world, such labels encouraged historians to write into the very fabric of the house perceived features of 'Greek' society (normally derived from Athenocentric texts) such as the spatial segregation of women, homosociability, and democratic egalitarianism.[14] Hellenistic variation from this model fitted within a trope of Classical decline and cultural contact with non-Greeks.[15]

Methodologically, as Allison has forcibly argued, such scholarly endeavours took scholarship on the house to an unfortunate location.[16] In the first instance, the relationship between archaeological–architectural taxonomies and the labels drawn from texts tended not to be treated critically.[17] Nuances of textual description were lost. There was, for instance, no perceived need to entertain the possibility that Vitruvius was not describing an everyday reality of 'Roman' or 'Greek' housing, since Vitruvian models could be seen in the archaeology. Whereas, Varro and other didactic writers of the late Republican and Augustan period could be seen as engaged in a form of cultural creation, and thus treated more cautiously and critically.[18] Further, the words in texts tended to be treated as descriptive architectural terms, associated with built forms, and through analogy with modern architectural plans were divested of any ideological value or contentious content. Yet, almost every contribution in this volume stresses the flexibility of spatial use and that the function of the spaces within the house was likely to have been varied and subject to adaptation (see summaries below), related not only to the built environment but to activities and objects. As a consequence, we need not necessarily think of the words in ancient texts as referring to closely defined and regulated architectural forms rather than to the function the space was performing at a particular moment.[19] As Morgan (in this volume), for example, polemically argues, the labelling of rooms by architectural features to which function is then associated misrepresents the nuanced descriptions of spaces that we see in our literary material. Indeed, the tendency in our sources is the reverse: rooms seems to have been identified by function rather than by architectural features. One may also note, in advance of the discussion below, that the modern bourgeois house operates with a high degree of functional separation, which is often clearly reflected in the architecture, and this tendency of scholars to universalize Western bourgeois experience has been a pervasive feature of much social history.

Furthermore, seeing the house through such labels constrains archaeological interpretation.[20] Allison's work on the domestic archaeology of Pompeii in particular argues for the employment of archaeological techniques and interpretative strategies familiar from non-Classical archaeological studies.[21] Her work (notably Allison 2004) poses the challenge of how can we understand the urban houses of Campania if we start from the archaeology rather than from the texts, and in the coda to this volume she argues once more for detailed attention to be paid to archaeological data. The rigour with which the archaeology is treated needs, in Allison's view (in this volume), to be matched by the rigour with which texts, especially literary texts, are treated.

The problems of interpretation are not, however, limited to the methodological. As Alston and Meyer (both in this volume) argue in very different ways, the interpretation of domestic architecture has embedded within it complex cultural assumptions about the 'home'.[22] Meyer examines the representation of domestic archaeology in three museum displays. These displays offered to reconstruct elements of domestic life, very much against contemporary preferences for taxonomic displays of artefacts. There seems to have been a need on the part of the museums to construct an image of 'everyday life', presumably in part to connect visitor to object and culture.

'Everyday life' is a difficult term. In a non-theorized way, it offers a descriptive insight into forms of low or popular culture.[23] These cultural forms can be distinguished from the products of high artistic cultures on display elsewhere in the museums, but also from the deeds and thoughts of 'the great men', who exercise hegemony over historical narratives. Once more, Classical archaeology, in forms other than art history, is deployed to provide a narrative secondary to that of the perceived major fields of historical and literary analysis. This is not just a narrative from a century ago: anyone who visited the 2013 British Museum exhibition, *Life and Death in Pompeii and Herculaneum* (British Museum, London, 28 March–29 September, 2013) will have experienced that same emphasis on 'the everyday' the centrepiece of which was a reimagining of a Pompeian house.[24]

Within these models of the everyday, certain assumptions are offered. Invariably, these everydays are bourgeois. They offer us an image of Rome and Greece that is familiar to middle-class audiences. In the British Museum exhibition, the 'Roman house' was notable in its familiarity, explicit in drawing connections to contemporary middle-class Italian mores and startlingly liberal social values, particularly in regard to gender, especially in the depiction of a slave society. It even safely concentrated the erotica in the bedroom.

The reconstruction of this everyday also tends to provide a history for women, normally 'respectable' women.[25] For moderns, gender construction is deeply intertwined with an understanding of the domestic, and Meyer shows how modern norms and assumptions about domesticity and sexuality inflected the understanding of artefacts and spaces.[26] If the history and archaeology of women is to be a history and archaeology of the domestic, a history of an unproblematic everyday separated from the mainstreams of cultural, social and political history, then it simply maintains and repositions familiar, heavily gendered and repressive tropes of social and historical analysis.

Of course, some of this investigative focus on the female and the domestic derives from textual material, such as the much-quoted section of Lysias 1, but for eastern Mediterranean lands there is a clear replication of Orientalist tropes and explicit or implicit anachronistic parallels with much later societies.[27] More generally, seeing the domestic as somehow more closely related to female histories replicates modern notions of the domestic as predominantly female space and particular forms of gender politics. Such assumptions carry over into understandings of social class (through norms of respectability) and ethnic identity (for which the woman is seen as a carrier; see Alston in this volume). But imagined continuities between the Classical and more modern Mediterranean gender constructions tend to depict the house as fundamentally unchanging and representative of 'Mediterranean' sexualities or honour/shame cultures that are seen fundamentally as ahistorical.[28]

Such understandings of 'the everyday' can be traced back to the essentialist discourses around the formation of the nation state in the late

18th and 19th centuries and to the related perception of fundamental divisions between public and private realms that led to the 19th-century cult of bourgeois domesticity.[29] As Alston (in this volume) argues, within structuralist anthropology the domestic has been seen as the primary location of acculturation and even a microcosm of cultural value and identity. If the public was the realm of change, the private was the realm of continuity (and resistance). If national values were embedded in a remote past and a cultural inheritance, that past needed to be located not in the ever-changing public sphere, but in the resistant and culture-producing private.

'Seeing' the house as cultural or national signifier changes the sorts of questions that we ask of the evidence, determining what we 'look' for in ancient household structures and how we conceptualize difference between housing cultures.[30] The axis of private and public, for instance, which has been so influential in studies of Roman housing,[31] is a way of thinking about how the communal is integrated in the private and how the domestic becomes political.[32] It is also a way of thinking about difference between the 'Roman experience' and the 'modern experience': in weakening the separation of public and private, the Roman domestic sphere becomes more closely integrated into the dynamics of public culture and its histories than contemporary bourgeois domestic culture (supposedly). For the more private 'Greek' house, by contrast, the dynamics are reversed and the boundaries between public and private spheres maintained. The results may be different, but the theoretical presumptions are the same.[33]

One consequence of such a perception is to see the house as the producer of a form of cultural identity and to focus attention on any aspects of domestic cultures which seem exogenous to a community.[34] Structuralist or essentialist analyses are notoriously ahistorical and find accounting for change, especially change generated within societies, difficult. If cultures are set and timeless and cultural values are embedded within the everyday of the house, it follows that changes in that everyday structure are likely a response to influences external to the local culture. As Baird has pointed out, much of the historiography of the Middle East has been shaped around an obsession with cultural origins and identities.[35] The narratives that historians of culture have deployed have, for the Classical world, focused on the degree to which a culture has retained local values or adopted exogenous characteristics. For historians of imperial phases of Mediterranean history, notably the Hellenistic and Roman imperial periods, Hellenization and Romanization have been defining issues. For Classical archaeologists, taxonomic debates around artefacts and architectural features have ultimately revolved around this question of cultural origins. The narratives spun around household archaeologies have been shaped by this essentialist rhetoric.[36] The ideal type of the 'Greek' or 'Roman' or 'Syrian' or 'Egyptian' house is driven by an assumption that there was a unitary and long-lasting 'Greek' or 'Roman' or 'Syrian' or 'Egyptian' culture.[37]

One response to the problems outlined here could be to sever the tie between words and walls. One could start afresh and examine the words without thinking about the archaeology, and the walls without regard to the texts. Arguably, one could consider the separate 'data' sets, as Allison describes them, separately. We could, as Speksnijder's analysis of 'vestibu-lum'(the word) or the *vestibulum* (the architectural feature) might encourage us to do, narrow our definitions so that those aristocratic residences in the city of Rome, as understood from Vitruvius, were seen as an entirely separate category to those of the Campanian cities. One might, as Morgan (2010) and Nevett (1999) suggest, emphasize the variety and mutability of housing from the 'Greek world', wherever and whenever that may have been, and thereby render diverse the category of the 'Greek' house', consequently undermining meanings underlying a 'national' typology.

But, of course, these are somewhat artificial techniques and one may doubt whether such mental discipline is even possible. One has undoubtedly to be critical of the way in which words used to describe architecture in one area of the ancient Mediterranean might inform our understanding of archaeological spaces in another part, and aware of the methodological and theoretical issues that are involved. Even with documentary evidence that can be closely associated with the archaeology, there are significant problems in the translation between document and space. But with the fragmentary and difficult evidence at our disposal, we need to use all that we can to understand the house and its meanings.

The key shift is not so much methodological as theoretical: we need to change the questions. If we reject the epistemological understandings associated with the nation state and bourgeois historiography as outlined above, then issues of typology and taxonomy and the meaningful content of spatial labels, ancient or modern, become much less important. Instead of seeing housing as representative of a culture, we get to ask a more basic question about how the house functioned within a culture and created cultural value. Specifically, we can ask about the cultural value of particular houses in particular settlements at particular times. Instead of thinking about the house in terms of the macro-level narratives of empires and peoples and their relationships with ethnic culture, we can focus on the workings of power and the making of cultures within specific communities. The commitment, then, is to the microhistories, or object biographies, of houses and settlements.[38] Such histories may play into narratives of widespread cultural change or integration in or resistance to imperial forms, but will inevitably give more focus to immediate and local social, economic, environmental, cultural and political influences.[39] It is those influences which structured the 'everyday' lives of the inhabitants of the houses studied in this volume. This commitment to microhistories, in whatever form, is the guiding thread through this collection.

The benefits of such an approach can be seen in the chapters in this volume. The authors restore temporality and histories to their houses. Volioti uses the notion of a biography of things to think about *lekythoi* within the Greek cultural context. Baird applies the same notion to the Durene houses, whose 'biographies' might stretch over generations. Instead of seeing the house as a cultural symbol or as productive of a form of ethnic identity, we can situate the house in its particular conditions of production in which the everyday struggles to get by and maintain status are played out. Pudsey and Baird both focus on the familial and the complex interrelationship between the structures of family and its places.[40] The house emerges not just as having its own biography, but as offering us insight into the familial histories of those who resided within it. Family and household are also depicted as non-fixed groups, shifting in composition and interests, needs and abilities through their life courses. These familial entities are interrelated in complex ways, or as Baird puts it, 'entangled' in the physical forms of the houses. We can become more sensitive to variation, as Pudsey and Uytterhoeven show, for houses both within a single rural community (Tebtynis) and to variation between urban and rural settlement. Baird shows that although the Durene houses have marked similarities, they also have differences. But if we can, as outsiders, identify differences within the limited remains and documentation available to us, we can be certain that to members of the community themselves, likely hypersensitive to social nuance and sociocultural markers, such differences must have been very clear.

Such microhistories allow us to interpret houses within the social and economic structures of those local communities. The chapters associate shifts in house forms with changes in economic activities over the long term (Nevett; McHugh) and see its symbolic functions within a changing historical and cultural context (Varto and also Nevett). They are sensitive to the particular needs and desires of the residents (Alston; Platts) and how particular communities used the domestic as means of negotiating status and identity (Kaczmarek). We can assess the needs of economic production (Alston; McHugh) in shaping the distribution of residences across the environment and the forms that those residences took. We can rethink housing design, paying attention to senses other than the visual (Platts) and functions beyond the symbolic. But we can also reframe our understanding of the symbolism of the house and the domestic, paying due regard to the values written into spaces in particular ritual contexts (Smith) and the emotional engagement with house (Varto) and its symbolic objects (Volioti) which must in part derive from a shared experience of living within that space (Baird).

Alston's contribution attempts to think through the problem of domestic space starting from a fundamental question about the relationships between space and society. Deploying insights from spatial theorists and political philosophers, he focuses on the micro-dynamics of household formation. If we assume, as he suggests, that the primary desire and requirement of the domestic community was for social reproduction, ensuring the continuity of individuals and families from year to year and generation to generation, then any household must have had an interest in controlling the economic resources necessary for maintaining itself to an appropriate status, controlling the household's labour resources and its productive and reproductive capacities, and negotiating and asserting status with persons and institutions external to the household. Social reproduction depended upon maintaining a level of control in the family and in negotiating relationships with wider societal powers. Households could not be in any meaningful sense autarkic since they must always have engaged in the wider community. Households must, however, have always been multiple, composed of individual agents whose interests and desires were not necessarily aligned: one need only imagine discussions around the forming of new conjugal relations. Yet, the multiplicity of agents does not open the way to anarchy. To negotiate one's path through society, one needed to follow social codes and convention and to find modes of communication and cooperation. The built environment becomes the enabling structure and symbolic representation of these needs and desires and it is in terms of those needs and desires that we can interpret those spaces. In a number of brief case studies, he argues that we might explain evident change, such as the development of villa culture in Italy, and seeming continuities, such as the rural housing types in Syria, through an interplay of desires, resources and power. The culture of villas, for example, can be seen as a coming together of an extreme desire for individual power and the concentration of economic, cultural and political resources in the hands of a small and immensely privileged elite: what happens if when we look at one of the many fantastic 4th-century CE villa mosaics, we see them not as aesthetics, but as representations of massive social inequality? Through such an approach, Alston argues, we can explain the villa's cultural association with sexual excess and tyranny. In the Syrian examples, Alston links the house form to the modes of economic production and familial and societal reproduction. He embeds the house in particular needs and desires to concentrate and control household resources of land and labour. In contrast to the notion of the everyday deployed above, Alston's view of the everyday is of a field of contestation and competition, ordered, but subject to economic, ideological and political modifications.[41] There was more than one way of exploiting a particular environment and ensuring that a family survived from generation to generation, and it was the politics of the everyday that ensured that particular modes were followed and, sometimes, adapted. It was the everyday negotiation of these complex social requirements that gave shape to the histories of the domestic communities, and to understand those histories we need to return to the individual agents who acted within those households.

We can see a similar interplay of desires and needs in Pudsey's analysis of the houses of Tebtynis. Her focus is on the dynamics of family, dynamics which are only visible through the documentary material, and their interplay with housing. She shows how families (however defined) managed their marital strategies to ensure that their particular households maintained the means by which to survive and continue from generation to generation. She argues that there was a flexibility in the arrangements of domestic space that allowed a negotiation of complex tenurial arrangements. The Egyptian partible inheritance system empowered multiple agents within a household, which must have given rise to a need to negotiate within a household of mutually dependent individuals. Gender dynamics were likely influenced by female control of economic resources and the normative residency of a wife in the house of her husband's family. Since the management of the household/house depended on economic and social resources, it seems likely, as Pudsey suggests, that different dynamics applied in different types of settlement: the houses and households of Tebtynis were likely different, when taken as a group, than the houses and households of nearby Ptolemais Euergetis, the regional capital.

Uytterhoeven similarly argues for a level of diversity in the housing of the Fayum villages. Although many of the sites were poorly excavated and even more poorly published in the early years of the 20th century, more recent and smaller-scale archaeological investigation has allowed

Uytterhoeven to identify 'elite' residence within the villages, which at Tebtunis at least is marked through a different architectural style. Although some of the Fayumic villages were seemingly controlled, or at least heavily influenced, by powerful estate holders in the Ptolemaic period, by the early Roman period the villages seem to have been relatively egalitarian, in economic terms, judging from the ample tax and other documentation from the Roman Fayum, especially when compared with other contemporary Mediterranean communities.[42] But even within a relatively egalitarian community, social competition (the play of social desires) can be seen in the archaeology. One might imagine that status competition was manifested through other markers of status within a rural community which are less easily recognized in an archaeological record, such as holding priesthoods, leadership positions within the community, even in such things as dress and furnishings (see Smith, in this volume), but houses were also a way in which social competition and identity within the community were manifest.

Baird follows a similar pathway. Her investigation finds evidence of relationships in the houses of Dura-Europos. Relationships are, by their very nature, open to individual agency and are formed within social dynamics of power, including those of gender and age. It is those relationships which 'make up a household', but, as she shows, those relationships were 'entangled' with house structures. It was in those houses that the many everyday negotiations and celebrations and cooperations and, no doubt, arguments and disputes and feuds took place. We can detect in both the archaeology and the textual material divisions within houses consequent on tenurial division. But tenurial division was also a division of family and households and we may wonder quite how such a division would, in the everyday organization of the household(s), have worked. As Baird argues, the consequence of such a division was not to make a new house and erase the 'biography' or the memory of the old house, but to leave memories of the house as it was (and how it could again be).[43] One imagines that the memories of rituals, events, and the structuring of relationships was entangled within that structure and that the house, in whatever formation, operated as a 'place of memory'. Present in the imagined community of the house were the later divided residences but also the earlier united house and the consequent restructurings of the familial ties. The house as structured then reflected the complex processes of household formation and social reproduction over generations which were economic and social, but also engaged in the memories and relationships of the various inhabitants.

Such complexities can be seen in the way in which the cult of the *Lares compitalia* operated on Delos. As Kaczmarek shows, the 'Romans' in the Delian community established status and cultural identity through the worship of the cult. Moving between domestic cult and public cult, a connection was made between the Romans within this particularly hetero-geneous community. The domestic elements of the cult brought the public and communal aspects of identity into the domestic sphere. In a commu-nity of immigrants and traders, establishing those connections and asserting identity were socially and economically necessary, more so because it seems likely that a significant number of the inhabitants of the houses were freed persons, who had an extreme need to assert status and identity in the community. The houses or, in this specific case, the use of cults associated with the houses responded to the needs and desires of the residents through a community context, and it is a story we can only tell through the association of the archaeology and epigraphy.

The contribution which focuses most closely on the productive capaci-ties and functions of housing is McHugh's study of rural 'farmsteads'. McHugh focuses initially on an archaeological problem. Since most 'farms' are identified through survey archaeology rather than through excavation, how do we establish what we are looking at when we find a scatter of material in a rural context? If we use the term 'farm', do we know what sort of architectural structure or socioeconomic institution we are discussing? There are, of course, a variety of possible settlements that might generate a cluster of building materials and ceramics in the rural environment and a variety of possible ways in which the rural environment could be settled, managed and exploited. By using GIS analysis and through a consideration of the road network, McHugh shows that the 'farms' were closely related to transport routes. She concludes that her archaeological traces of farms correspond reasonably closely to the situation and operation of the farm described in Lysias 1: relatively easy to access from the city and relatively close to other agricultural structures. The economic integration of the farm into wider economic networks, certainly those of the city, would seem to mirror a social integration of urban and rural.

Speksnijder looks to the flexibility and functionality of housing. Starting with a conventional problem of identification (what might the *vestibula* discussed in Vitruvius have been and can we find such structures in the archaeological record?), his investigation explores the particular needs and requirements of different social groups within Rome and how those needs and requirements might have been met through architectural forms. His identification of the *vestibulum* as a waiting area for those calling on aristocratic families provides a social practice which the structure served. But that social practice was limited to the leading families of the city. The consequence was that the structure that supported that social practice would also be limited in distribution to the houses of a particular socio-political group. It was, of course, to this group that Vitruvius' work was primarily addressed and it is therefore no surprise that the *vestibulum* seems more significant in Vitruvius than it does in the archaeology.

Morgan similarly focuses on flexibility and difference, but this time within Greek houses. She argues that the textual material shows that houses were extremely flexible spaces in which each space could perform multiple functions. Consequently, the house could be reordered to meet the changing needs and desires of the community, and thus what we see in the archaeology is not the house itself, but the framework in which the house was lived and experienced. Rooms could be adapted and even repurposed to become workshops. Morgan suggests that this flexibility undermines any definition of the house as built space, since what made the house was functionality not architecture.

It is that very flexibility that meant that the symbolic value of housing needed to be transmitted in different ways that were context-dependent. Smith considers the use of textiles within the house. Although precision is difficult and of course the archaeological evidence for textiles is slim, Smith employs epigraphic, iconographic and literary evidence to show that a house would be replete with soft furnishings, from pillows and cushions to coverings. Given the technologies available, textiles must have been a visible and tangible display of status and wealth. They must have notably influenced the aesthetic of the house. Her key example though comes from the marriage ceremony. She argues from the iconographic evidence that the textile references in the accounts of marriage relate not so much to the covering and uncovering of the bride as to the marriage bed: it was the bed and its associated decoration that came to symbolize the conjugal bond and to represent the spaces of marriage. And it was in the marriage rituals that the space was displayed. The shift in focus is from the person of the bride to the status and wealth of the husband. Such an approach adds to our understanding of the cultural resonance of the domestic space, but is arguably also transformational. When we read of the marital chamber or the bed in our literary material, we have to reimagine the significance of such spaces and furniture in symbolic association with the marriage cere-mony and the display of male power and wealth. If Smith is right, we need to rethink the anthropology of marriage customs and how we understand what was at stake in the formation of marital alliances.

Nevett also traces this symbolic value of housing, but in a very different way. Her analysis locates changes in housing in shifting cultural and economic circumstances. But those changes generate a history of housing, probably better described as a cultural memory, on which basis Demosthenes seems to aim to create and exploit a political nostalgia for more egalitarian and democratic times. She identifies different housing traditions in Macedon and Athens and traces the development of a more regal form in Macedon. But if the palatial structures of Macedon did not follow fixed plans, neither did the houses of Athens. Nevett relates the changes in Athens to economic developments: people, especially richer people, were getting richer and this was reflected in their housing. But it is the combination of these changes that gives the housing cultural and political resonance. Nevett reinterprets Demosthenes' complaints about grand houses (as opposed to grand public buildings) as reflecting a decline in citizen values. But in the light of these perceived trends in housing, we can see that Demosthenes was using housing to suggest that the new aristocracy of Athens was somehow un-Athenian, more related to those North Greeks. Consequently, we see housing used as a signifier of political identity and political value, but also as a marker of a conservative and nostalgic vision of the democratic community. Like so many appeals to collective memory, Demosthenes was employing a cultural memory to marginalize his political opponents. The power of Demosthenes' image is to turn a relatively abstract idea and ideological complaint into the concrete realities of everyday life in the city; he makes the political differences between the rich and powerful and the 'ordinary' citizen visible and associates those differences with cultural value. As a process of labelling it works, presumably, because it gives significance to the built environment. It is strictly speaking irrelevant whether that significance was intended by the builders and owners of the houses since the meaning is imposed on the pre-existing structures by Demosthenes. Nevett turns on its head the idea that archaeology should be understood in light of texts, instead using archaeological evidence to provide a contextual framework through which to understand texts on the relationship between Greece and Macedon in the 4th century BCE and the workings of political symbolism in Demosthenic Athens.

Varto also sees the development of housing in the Archaic period as reflecting changing economic circumstances, but for a much earlier period. As the economy developed, houses became larger and more sophisticated; they developed spaces for storage and other economic functions. As in other periods, we can see changes in the house in response to economic resources and needs. Varto shows that the initial drive to investigate early

Greek housing came from the philologists' desire to find material evidence that would confirm or deny the reality of the Homeric world. This quest was unsuccessful: the archaeology and poetry made uneasy bedfellows. But she sees the value of the poetry as providing insight into the emotional values invested in the house. In the phrase conventionally translated as 'in the halls' she finds not a reference to some sort of heroic period architecture but a metonym for domestic values. Such 'halls' cease to have architectural significance, but become a way of thinking about what we might call 'home'.

Volioti approaches the same question, looking for the emotional investment in space. She finds it not in a phrase or language, but in the representation of *lekythoi*, a distinctive form of oil jar that is frequently represented in funerary contexts. She establishes an object biography for the *lekythoi*, from Attic production to everyday use to funerary contexts. She shows that the jar comes to be representative of domesticity. It is the investment of domestic value, of the everyday of the household, in a jar that accounts for its funerary use. But if we reverse the analysis, we can see that domesticity in itself comes to be associated with consumption and perhaps also commensality. Volioti offers us insight into the entanglement of the domestic and the objects of the everyday.

The symbolic values invested in the house point us in the way of the poetic disciplines of psychogeography, tracing the subtle cultural investments in domestic spaces.[44] These are, as many of the contributors show, spaces of feelings, memories and relationships, as well as spaces of production, reproduction, power and status. Platts asks the question what it might feel like to be in a Roman villa, specifically the villa of Diomedes. Excavated in the 18th century, we have to work mostly with the walls rather than with detailed artefactual records. Platts rejects the reductionist analyses of access plans and the emphasis on sight and bumping into people. She thinks about noise and smells, the multisensory world of the villa. And that multisensory experience is surely also part of the distinctiveness of the house and how meanings and memories are generated for the residents. In such luxurious residences, the owner could manipulate the sensory engagement of the residents both with the external world (audible perhaps more than visible), but also we need to imagine the sensory experience within the household, what was heard, what was smelled, and how luxury might be generated in various parts of the house through the control of sensory stimuli.

Finally, Meyer's contribution takes us back to the problems of presentation and understanding. By looking at the way in which the domestic is presented in museums, he warns us against easy assumptions and methodological laziness. In a rather different way to Allison's concluding response to the papers, Meyer also makes an appeal to intellectual rigour, to really look at the evidence that we are considering and ask what it depicts. He considers the way in which a modern understanding of the domestic feeds into a reading of iconographic material depicting women and assumptions about those depictions. His analysis problematizes the nature of domesticity and the evidence we use to talk about it.

All the contributions are wary of fixity in our understanding of ancient houses. We see houses as flexible spaces, allowing their inhabitants to respond to their varying needs and desires. Houses are seen as having cycles and histories, following the cycles and histories of their residents. Baird and Pudsey think of families in terms of life courses, and to a great extent houses also had their life courses. The parallels between family histories and house histories are instructive, but also reflective of a symbolic association of family/household and house. Houses make households visible in the archaeological record. Houses can be metonymic for family. Houses contain all those feelings, hopes, desires and memories. They are foci of production, reproduction and, indeed, consumption. They are locations of loyalty and community. The chapters herein look to expose the working of power within the household, and the ways in which economic and political constraints shaped the households and houses. In each case, we are looking at microhistories, histories of the everyday (in the critical sense) through which local societies and social individuals are formed. Those microhistories take into account the symbolic and emotional value of the houses, again not as symbolic of belonging to a wider cultural identity, but in the complex interplay of family and community, tradition, development and memory. To access the complexity of the house and household, we need to understand the walls and the words.

Notes

1 The fraught relationship between the disciplines has itself been a topic of discussion; see e.g. the discussion in contributions to Sauer 2004; on the relationship between written and material evidence in Roman houses, Allison 2001 marks a key shift.
2 Arguably, the major change in the writing of ancient history came in the 20th century and resulted from the influences of the *Annales* movement, on which see the useful introductory essay, Clark 1985, Harsgor's 1978 review article, and the short book of Burke 1990 (and note 4).
3 Andrén 1998.

4 For the shift towards 'structural' history, see the pioneering work of the
   Annales school (note 2 above). Particularly influential for scholarship of
   antiquity remain Bloch 1939 and Braudel 1966. More recent work in ancient
   history influenced by the *Annales* school (though they denied they were a
   school) includes Bagnall 1995 and Horden and Purcell 1999, with further
   references. On archaeology and microhistory, Mímisson and Magnússon
   2014, and on the nature of the archaeological event, Lucas 2008. On
   structuralist histories of event and archaeology, Bintliff 1991; on the
   relationship between ancient material culture and narratives of the past,
   Bassi 2011.

5 Dyson 2006. For a survey of the historiography of Campanian houses, see
   Wallace-Hadrill 2007.

6 Varto, Chapter 1, this volume; Carandini 1986; Cristofani 1990.

7 Dyson 1995.

8 Allison 1999a shows that this influence on the textual was not limited to the
   description of architectural forms.

9 Studies of Vitruvius have shifted the reading of *De architectura* considerably in
   recent years, e.g. the contributions in Cuomo and Formisano 2016.

10 See the reports of the pioneering excavations in Wiegand and Schrader 1904;
   Robinson 1930; 1946; Robinson and Graham 1938.

11 On the use of terminology from ancient sources for labelling rooms within
   archaeological structures e.g. Husson 1983; Alston 1997; Leach 1997; Baird
   2007; Carucci 2012.

12 As famously and controversially in the groundbreaking article of Wallace-
   Hadrill 1988 (but also Richardson 1988: 382–90). See the balanced discussion
   of this essay and its approaches in Nevett 2010: 89–95. For discussions of such
   approaches, see Goldberg 1999 and for the historiography of Greek housing,
   and Allison 1999b and 2001 for Roman housing.

13 For Pompeii, the changes in the archaeology of the city in the later 1st century
   BCE are sometimes attributed to the values of veteran colonists: see Zanker
   1998: 61–77; for the Claudian period (Zanker 1998: 192–99) for the rise of the
   middle classes and freedmen and their influence on domestic architecture
   (cf. Maiuri 1929: 1942; Castrén 1975: 85–124) and perceived as an urban
   'crisis', see the discussion of Mouritsen 1997 and the detailed refutation of
   Mouritsen 1988.

14 For finding women's spaces in the Greek house, see the influential article of
   Walker 1983, with more critical discussion from Nevett 1995; 2011; and
   Davidson 2011. See also Cohen 1989, who links the discussion of female
   seclusion to Mediterraneanist and national rhetorics. See further below. More
   generally, see discussions in Nevett 1999 and Morgan 2010. For democratic
   values, see Nevett (Chapter 6, this volume) and Hoepfner and Schwanner 1994.

15 See, for example, Trümper's (1998: 132) discussion of change in Delian houses

16 Allison 2001; see also the discussion in Nevett 2010: 3–21.

17 See the useful summary account in Allison 2007.

18 See Wallace-Hadrill 1997.

19 Among many other discussions, see Leach 1997 and Riggsby 1997. Alston 1997 discusses the labelling of space on a graphic representation of a house (*P.Oxy.* 24.2406). He notes that the space was labelled '*atreion*', but that the space looked very unlike the modern category of the *atrium*. The point was not, as has been suggested, to imply that the ancient label was wrong, but to show issues with the modern typology. Notably, this unique document, which is the only house plan we have from Roman Egypt on papyrus, also provides us with a unique papyrological usage of 'atreion' for house architecture.

20 Berry 1997 shows that the distribution of artefacts in rooms in Pompeii shows that they were multifunctional. For the Greek house, see also Jameson 1990a; 1990b.

21 See, in particular, her analysis of datasets for artefacts in Pompeian residences in Allison 2004.

22 For the modern invention of 'home', see Chakrabarty 1997; Spencer-Wood 1999; Tosh 1999; Davidoff and Hall 2002; Hall and Rose 2006; Hall 2007.

23 As in the 'popular' Quennell and Quennell 1952 or Cowell 1961; Webster 1969.

24 Roberts 2013.

25 There is an extensive literature on how respectability in the 19th century focused on female behaviours. See, *exempli gratia*, Stoler 1995; Stoler and Cooper 1997; Cooper 2005; Hall 2007. See also the essays in Helly and Reverby 1992 and Ardener 1993.

26 Walkowitz 1992 shows how the social life of the 19th-century city was constructed around poles of gender and respectability. See also Gunn 2007.

27 See the critical discussions of Cohen 1989; Davidson 2011; and Nevett 2011. For misrepresentations of the seclusion of women in Islamic culture, see Lewis 2004; Noorani 2010; Fay 2012. For use of Islamic nomenclature (including *harem*) for housing spaces in Roman Syria, Baird 2007.

28 See the cogent critique offered by Herzfeld 1987 of approaches such as that of Blok 1974, 2001; Goody 1983; and Gilmore 1986. For Classics, see the discussion of Cairns 2011.

29 As shown by Tosh 1999. Habermas 1991 sees this period as marking the emergence of the 'public sphere'. For the emergence of national cultures, see Smith 2004; Anderson 2006; Gellner 2008. For a particular instance of national invention, see Jusdanis 1991; 2001.

30 For a discussion of the power relations engaged in a reduction of cultures to tableaux, see Mitchell 1991: 19–31.

31 Particularly influential were Thébert 1987 and Wallace-Hadrill 1988. See also Hales 2003 and Speksnijder 2015 on the sociocultural implications of the public–private divide in housing.

32 See this assumption in Zanker 1998: 5, in which limited differentiation of housing is seen as representative of democratic values. Compare the limited

differentiations in houses in Dura (Baird, in this volume) and Roman Egypt (Uttyerhoeven, in this volume) which do not seem particularly inspired by democratic ideologies.

33 Davidson 2011; Nevett 2011.

34 For Pompeii, see, *exempli gratia*, Zanker 1998: 9–15, on the Pompeian house as a display of Roman identity.

35 Baird 2014: 31–33.

36 See Wallace-Hadrill 2007 for a summary discussion of the historiographic issues around Campanian housing, which maintains as key issues cultural identity and cultural labels.

37 See Wallace-Hadrill's (2015) discussion of the Roman house, which reflects his rethinking of the conception of Roman culture (2008). His argument is that the Roman house is distinctive in its borrowings from other cultural traditions, notably the Greek, and in its *luxuria*. Alston (this volume) however argues we might endeavour towards a narrative of villa housing which entirely avoids 'ethnic' labels. For housing in the Roman provinces, the bibliography is vast, but compare the more traditional studies of Smith 1997 and Ellis 2000, with the more cautious Boozer 2010; 2011; 2012; 2014. Hales 2003 sees the house as a means of displaying a Roman identity; Baird 2014 sees 'Roman' most useful in a chronological or hegemonic sense. The 'Greek' house is an extremely diverse concept, see essays in Ault and Nevett 2005.

38 Kopytoff 1986; Gosden and Marshall 1999.

39 This argument is given further detail in Alston forthcoming in a discussion focused on Egyptian village housing.

40 For such approaches to houses in the ancient Near East utilizing textual evidence and archaeological plans, Baker 2010.

41 By contrast to the anglophone traditions of the 'everyday', French traditions have been more theorized and complex, closely connected to understandings of social theory. See, notably, de Certeau 1984; Lefebvre 1991; 2004; Highmore 2002.

42 See Bowman 1985; Bagnall 1992. Egypt in the Roman period probably saw a progressive concentration of wealth. See also Alston 2001 and Banaji 2001.

43 Compare the discussions of house division in Roman Egypt in Pudsey (Chapter 9 in this volume) and Alston (forthcoming). For places of memory, Nora 1997.

44 On psychogeographic approaches to the Roman world, see, most recently, Fitzgerald and Spentzou 2018.

References

Allison, P. M. (1999a). Labels for ladles: interpreting the material culture of Roman households. In P. M. Allison, ed., *The Archaeology of Household Activities*. London and New York: Routledge, 57–77.

(1999b). Introduction. In P. M. Allison, ed., *The Archaeology of Household Activities*. London and New York: Routledge, 1–18.

(2001). Using the material and written sources: turn of the millennium approaches to Roman domestic space. *American Journal of Archaeology* 105, 181–208.

(2004). *Pompeian Households: An Analysis of the Material Culture*. Los Angeles: Cotsen Institute of Archaeology.

(2007). Domestic spaces and activities. In J. J. Dobbins and P. W. Foss, eds., *The World of Pompeii*. London and New York: Routledge, 269–78.

Alston, R. (1997). Houses and households in Roman Egypt. In. R. Laurence and A. Wallace-Hadrill, eds., *Domestic Space in the Roman World: Pompeii and Beyond*. Portsmouth, RI: Journal of Roman Archaeology, 25–39.

(2001). The population of Late Roman Egypt and the end of the Ancient world. In W. Scheidel, ed., *Debating Roman Demography*. Leiden, Boston and Köln: Brill, 161–204.

(forthcoming). Modes of production and reproduction in Egyptian villages. In C. Barrett and J. C. Carrington, eds., *Households in Context: Dwelling in Ptolemaic and Roman Egypt*. Ithaca, NY: Cornell University Press.

Anderson, B. (2006). *Imagined Communities: Reflections on the Origin and Spread of Nationalism*. London and New York: Verso.

Andrén, A. (1998). *Between Artifacts and Texts: Historical Archaeology in Global Perspective*. New York: Plenum Press.

Ardener, S. (ed.) (1993). *Women and Space: Ground Rules and Social Maps*, 2nd ed. Oxford: Berg.

Ault, B. A. and Nevett, L. C. (eds.) (2005). *Ancient Greek Houses and Households: Chronological, Regional, and Social Diversity*. Philadelphia: University of Pennsylvania Press.

Bagnall, R. (1992). Landholding in Late Roman Egypt: the distribution of wealth. *Journal of Roman Studies* 82, 128–49.

(1995). *Reading Papyri, Writing Ancient History*. London: Routledge.

Baird, J. A. (2007). The bizarre bazaar: early excavations in the Roman East and problems of nomenclature. In B. Croxford, N. Ray, R. Roth and N. White, eds., *TRAC'06: Theoretical Roman Archaeology Conference Proceedings*, Oxford: Oxbow, 34–42.

(2014). *The Inner Lives of Ancient Houses: An Archaeology of Dura-Europos*. Oxford: Oxford University Press.

Baker, H. D. (2010). The social dimensions of Babylonian domestic architecture in the Neo-Babylonian and Achaemenid periods. In J. Curtis and S. J. Simpson, eds., *The World of Achaemenid Persia. History, Art and Society in Iran and the Ancient Near East*. London: I.B. Tauris, 179–94.

Banaji, J. (2001). *Agrarian Change in Late Antiquity: Gold, Labour, and Aristocratic Dominance*. Oxford: Oxford University Press.

Bassi, K. (2011). Seeing the past/reading the past. *Image & Narrative* 12, 29–50.

Berry, J. (1997). The conditions of domestic life in Pompeii in AD 79: a case-study of Houses 11 and 12, Insula 9, Region I. *Papers of the British School at Rome* 65, 103–25.

Bintliff, J. (1991). The contribution of an Annaliste/structural history approach to archaeology. In J. Bintliff, ed., *The Annales School and Archaeology*. Leicester: University of Leicester Press, 1–33.

Bloch, M. (1939). *La société féodale: La formation des liens de dépendance*. Paris: Albin Michel.

Blok, A. (1974). *The Mafia of a Sicilian Village, 1860–1960: A Study of Violent Peasant Entrepreneurs*. Oxford: Basil Blackwell.

  (2001). *Honour and Violence*. Malden, MA: Polity.

Boozer, A. L. (2010). Memory and microhistory of an Empire: domestic contexts in Roman Amheida, Egypt. In D. Borić, ed., *Archaeology and Memory*. Oxford: Oxbow, 138–57.

  (2011). Forgetting to remember in the Dakleh Oasis, Egypt. In M. Bommas, ed., *Cultural Memory and Identity in Ancient Societies*. London: Continuum, 109–26.

  (2012). Globalizing Mediterranean identities: the overlapping spheres of Egyptian, Greek and Roman worlds at Trimithis. *Journal of Mediterranean Archaeology* 25.2, 219–42

  (2014). *Amheida II: A Late Romano-Egyptian House in the Dakhla Oasis: Amheida House B2*. New York: New York University Press.

Bowman, A. (1985). Landholding in the Hermopolite Nome in the fourth century A.D. *Journal of Roman Studies* 75, 137–63.

Braudel, F. (1966). *La Méditerranée et le monde méditerranéen à l'époque de Philippe II*, 2nd ed. Paris: Librairie Armand Colin.

Burke, P. (1990). *The French Historical Revolution: The Annales School, 1929–89*. Cambridge: Polity.

Cairns, D. (2011). Honour and shame: modern controversies and ancient values. *Critical Quarterly* 53, 23–41.

Carandini, A. (1986). Domus e insulae sulla pendice settentrionale del Palatino. *Bullettino della Commissione Archeologica comunale di Roma* 91, 263–78.

Carucci, M. (2012). The construction/deconstruction of the cubiculum: an example from the villa of maternus at Carranque (Spain). *Oxford Journal of Archaeology* 31, 213–24.

Castrén, P. (1975). *Ordo populusque Pompeianus: Polity and Society in Roman Pompeii*. Rome: Bardi.

Chakrabarty, D. (1997). The difference – deferral of a colonial modernity: public debates on domesticity in British Bengal. In F. Cooper and A. L. Stoler, eds., *Tensions of Empire. Colonial Cultures in a Bourgeois World*, Berkeley: University of California Press, 373–405.

Clark, S. (1985). The Annales Historians. In Q. Skinner ed., *The Return of Grand Theory in the Human Sciences*. Cambridge: Cambridge University Press, 177–98.

Cohen, D. (1989). Seclusion, separation, and the status of women in Classical Athens. *Greece & Rome* 36, 3–15.

Cooper, F. (2005). Postcolonial studies and the study of History. In A. Loomba, ed., *Postcolonial Studies and Beyond*. Durham, NC: Duke University Press, 401–22.

Cowell, F. R. (1961). *Everyday Life in Ancient Rome*. London: B.T. Batsford.

Cristofani, M. (ed.). 1990. *La grande Roma dei Tarquini*, Rome: "L'Erma" di Bretschneider.

Cuomo, S. and Formisano, M., eds., 2016. *Vitruvius: Text, Architecture, Reception. Arethusa 49.2.* Baltimore: Johns Hopkins University Press, 121–391.

Davidoff, L. and Hall, C. (2002). *Family Fortunes: Men and Women of the English Middle Class, 1780–1850*. London: Routledge.

Davidson, J., (2011). Bodymaps: sexing space and zoning gender in Ancient Athens. *Gender & History* 23, 597–614.

de Certeau, M. (1984). *The Practice of Everyday Life*, trans. Steven Rendall. Berkeley, Los Angeles and London: University of California Press.

Dyson, S. L. (1995). Is there a text in this site? In D. B. Hall, ed., *Methods in the Mediterranean: Historical and Archaeological Views on Texts and Archaeology*. Leiden: Brill, 25–44.

(2006). *In Pursuit of Ancient Pasts: A History of Classical Archaeology in the Nineteenth and Twentieth Centuries*. New Haven: Yale University Press.

Ellis, S. P. (2000). *Roman Housing*. London: Duckworth.

Fay, M. A. (2012). *Unveiling the Harem: Elite Women and the Paradox of Seclusion in Eighteenth-Century Cairo*. Syracuse, NY: Syracuse University Press.

Fitzgerald, W. and Spentzou, E. (2018). *The Production of Space in Latin Literature*. Oxford: Oxford University Press.

Gellner, E. (2008). *Nations and Nationalism*, 2nd ed. Ithaca, NY: Cornell University Press.

Gilmore, D. (ed.) (1986). *Honor and Shame and the Unity of the Mediterranean*. Washington, DC: American Anthropological Association.

Goldberg, M. Y. (1999). Spatial and behavioural negotiation in Classical Athenian city houses. In P. M. Allison, ed., *The Archaeology of Household Activities*. London and New York: Routledge, 142–61.

Goody, J. (1983). *The Development of the Family and Marriage in Europe*. Cambridge: Cambridge University Press.

Gosden, C., and Marshall, Y. (1999). The cultural biography of objects. *World Archaeology* 31, 169–78.

Gunn, S. (2007). *The Public Culture of the Victorian Middle Class: Ritual and Authority in the English Industrial City 1840–1914*. Manchester and New York: Manchester University Press.

Habermas, J. (1991). *The Structural Transformation of the Public Sphere: An Inquiry into a Category of Bourgeois Society (translated by Thomas Burger with the assistance of Frederick Lawrence)*. Cambridge, MA: Polity.

Hales, S. (2003). *The Roman House and Social Identity*. Cambridge: Cambridge University Press.

Hall, C. (2007). Of gender and empire: reflections on the nineteenth century. In P. Levine, ed., *Gender and Empire*. Oxford: Oxford University Press, 46–75.

Hall, C. and Rose, S. O. (2006). Introduction: being at home with the empire. In C. Hall and S. O. Rose, eds., *At Home with the Empire: Metropolitan Culture and the Imperial World*. Cambridge: Cambridge University Press, 1–31.

Harsgor, M. (1978). Total History: the Annales school. *Journal of Contemporary History* 13: 1–13.

Helly, D. O. and Reverby, S. (eds.) (1992). *Gendered Domains: Rethinking Public and Private in Women's History*. Ithaca, NY: Cornell University Press.

Herzfeld, M. (1987). *Anthropology through the Looking-Glass: Critical Ethnography in the Margins of Europe*. Cambridge: Cambridge University Press.

Highmore, B. (2002). *The Everyday Life Reader*. London and New York: Routledge.

Hoepfner, W. and Schwander, E.-L. (1994). *Haus und Stadt im klassischen Griechenland*. Munich: Deutscher Kunstverlag.

Horden, P. and Purcell, N. (1999). *The Corrupting Sea: A Study of Mediterranean History*. Oxford: Wiley.

Husson, G. (1983). *Oikia: Le vocabulaire de la maison privée en Égypte d'après les papyrus grecs*. Paris: Publications de la Sorbonne.

Jameson, M. H. (1990a). Domestic space in the Greek city state. In S. Kent, ed., *Domestic Architecture and the Use of Space: An Interdisciplinary Cross-cultural Study*. Cambridge: Cambridge University Press, 92–113.

(1990b). Private space and the Greek city. In O. Murray and S. Price, eds., *The Greek City from Homer to Alexander*. Oxford: Clarendon Press, 171–95.

Jusdanis, G. (1991). *Belated Modernity and Aesthetic Culture: Inventing National Tradition: Inventing National Literature*. Minneapolis: University of Minnesota Press.

(2001). *The Necessary Nation*. Princeton and Oxford: Princeton University Press.

Kopytoff, I. (1986). The cultural biographies of objects: commoditization as process. In A. Appadurai, ed., *The Social Life of Things*. Cambridge: Cambridge University Press, 64–91.

Leach, E. W. (1997). *Oecus* on *Ibycus*: investigating the vocabulary of the Roman house. In S. E. Bon and R. Jones, eds., *Sequence and Space in Pompeii*. Oxford: Oxbow, 50–72.

Lefebvre, H. (1991). *Critique of Everyday Life, Volume 1: Introduction*. London and New York: Verso.

(2004). *Rhythmanalysis: Space, Time, and Everyday Life*. London and New York: Verso.

Lewis, R. (2004). *Rethinking Orientalism: Women, Travel and the Ottoman Harem.* London: Continuum.

Lucas, G. (2008) Time and archaeological event. *Cambridge Archaeological Journal* 18, 59–65.

Maiuri, A. (1929). *Pompeii.* Rome: Istituto geografico de Agostini.

(1942). *L'ultima fase edilizia di Pompei.* Rome: Istituto di studi romani. Mímisson, K. and Magnússon, S. G. (2014) Singularizing the past: the history and archaeology of the small and ordinary. *Journal of Social Archaeology* 14, 131–56.

Mitchell, T. (1991). *Colonising Egypt.* Berkeley: University of California Press.

Morgan, J. (2010). *The Classical Greek House.* Exeter: Bristol Phoenix Press.

Mouritsen, H. (1988). *Elections, Magistrates and Municipal Élite: Studies in Pompeian Epigraphy.* Rome: Analecta Romani Instituti Danici Suppl. 15.

(1997). Mobility and social change in Italian towns during the Principate. In H. Parkin, ed., *Roman Urbanism: Beyond the Consumer City.* London and New York: Routledge, 59–82.

Nevett, L. C. (1995). Gender relations in the Classical Greek household: the archaeological evidence. *Annual of the British School at Athens* 90, 363–81.

(1999). *House and Society in the Ancient Greek World.* Cambridge, Cambridge University Press.

(2010). *Domestic Space in Classical Antiquity.* Cambridge: Cambridge University Press.

(2011). Towards a female topography of the Ancient Greek city: case studies from Late Archaic and Early Classical Athens (c.520–400 BCE). *Gender & History* 23, 576–96.

Noorani, Y. (2010). Normative notions of public and private in early Islamic culture. In M. Booth, ed., *Harem Histories: Envisioning Places and Living Spaces.* Durham, N.C.: Duke University Press, 49–68.

Nora, P. (1997). *Les lieux de mémoire.* Paris: Gallimard.

Quennell, M. and Quennell, C. H. B. (1952). *Everyday Life in Roman Britain.* London: B.T. Batsford.

Richardson, L. (1988). *Pompeii: An Architectural History.* Baltimore: Johns Hopkins University Press.

Riggsby, A. M. (1997). 'Public' and 'private' in Roman culture: the case of the cubiculum. *Journal of Roman Archaeology* 10, 36–56.

Roberts, P. (2013). *Life and Death in Pompeii and Herculaneum.* London: British Museum Press.

Robinson, D. M. (1930). *Excavations at Olynthus II: Architecture and Sculpture: Houses and Other Buildings.* Baltimore: Johns Hopkins University Press.

(1946). *Excavations at Olynthus XII: Domestic and Public Architecture.* Baltimore: Johns Hopkins University Press.

Robinson, D. M. and Graham, J. W. (1938). *Excavations at Olynthus VIII: The Hellenic House. A Study of the Houses Found at Olynthus with a Detailed*

Account of Those Excavated in 1931 and 1934. Baltimore: Johns Hopkins University Press.

Sauer, E. W. (2004). The disunited subject. Human History's split into 'history' and 'archaeology'. In E. Sauer, ed., *Archaeology and Ancient History, Breaking Down the Boundaries*. London: Routledge, 17–45.

Smith, A. D. (2004). *The Antiquity of Nations*. Cambridge: Polity.

Smith, J. T. (1997). *Roman Villas: A Study in Social Structures*. London and New York: Routledge.

Speksnijder, S.A. (2015). Beyond 'public' and 'private': accessibility and visibility during salutations. In K. Tuori and L. Nissin, eds., *Public and Private in the Roman House and Society*. Portsmouth, RI: Journal of Roman Archaeology, 87–99.

Spencer-Wood, S. M. (1999). The world their household: changing meanings of the domestic sphere in the nineteenth century. In P.M. Allison, ed., *The Archaeology of Household Activities*. London: Routledge, 162–89.

Stoler, A. L. (1995). *Race and the Education of Desire: Foucault's History of Sexuality and the Colonial Order of Things*. Durham, NC, and London: Duke University Press.

Stoler, A. L. and Cooper, F. (1997). Between metropole and colony: rethinking a research agenda. In F. Cooper and A. L. Stoler, eds., *Tensions of Empire: Colonial Cultures in a Bourgeois World*. Berkeley: University of California Press, 1–56.

Thébert, Y. (1987). Private life and domestic architecture in Roman Africa. In *A History of Private Life, Volume I: From Pagan Rome to Byzantium*. London: Harvard University Press, 313–409.

Tosh, J. (1999). *A Man's Place: Masculinity and the Middle Class Home in Victorian England*. New Haven and London: Yale University Press.

Trümper, M. (1998). *Wohnen in Delos: eine baugeschichtliche Untersuchung zum Wandel der Wohnkultur in hellenistischer Zeit*. Rahden: Leidorf.

Walker, S. (1983). Women and housing in Classical Greece: the archaeological evidence. In A. Cameron and A. Kuhrt, eds., *Images of Women in Antiquity*, London: Routledge, 81–91.

Walkowitz, Judith R. (1992). *City of Dreadful Delight: Narratives of Sexual Danger in Late-Victorian London*. Chicago: University of Chicago Press.

Wallace-Hadrill, A. (1988). The social structure of the Roman house. *Papers of the British School at Rome* 56, 43–97.

(1997). Mutatio Morum: the idea of a cultural revolution. In T. Habinek and A. Schiesaro, eds., *The Roman Cultural Revolution*. Cambridge: Cambridge University Press, 3–22.

(2007). The development of the Campanian House. In J. J. Dobbins and P. W. Foss, eds., *The World of Pompeii*. London and New York: Routledge, 279–91.

(2008). *Rome's Cultural Revolution*. Cambridge: Cambridge University Press.

(2015). What makes a Roman house a 'Roman house'? In K. Tuori and L. Nissin, eds., *Public and Private in the Roman House and Society*. Portsmouth, RI: Journal of Roman Archaeology, 177–86.

Webster, T. B. L. (1969). *Everyday Life in Classical Athens*. London: Harper Collins.

Wiegand, T. and Schrader, H. (1904). *Priene: Ergebnisse der Ausgrabungen und Untersuchungen in den Jahren 1895–1898*. Berlin: Georg Reimer.

Zanker, P. (1998). *Pompeii: Public and Private Life*, trans. D. L. Schneider. Cambridge, MA, and London: Harvard University Press.

1 | Kinship 'In the Halls'

Poetry and the Archaeology of Early Greek Housing

EMILY VARTO

> After a century of desperate scholarly attempts to reconstruct from
> Homer something that could be called, by a great effort of will, a
> Mycenaean palace, it must be obvious that the attempt
> was foredoomed.
>
> Moses I. Finley[1]

Responding to the critics of his *World of Odysseus*, Finley drew upon the
example of the Homeric house, or rather the search for the Homeric house,
to illustrate the futility of mining poetry to recover the Homeric world.[2] The
scholarship had been trying to find what could not be found. The palaces in
Homer, according to Finley, were uninformed creative visualizations of an
heroic past. In this, Finley criticized both the identification of the Homeric
world with the Mycenaean, as well as the tradition of searching for direct
parallels between the poetic world and archaeological material. Rather than
allowing archaeology to distance itself from textual or philological imperatives, the development of Aegean Bronze Age archaeology in the early part
of the 20th century was bound so intricately and enduringly to Homeric
poetry that it suffused the archaeological agenda and its methods until
Finley's time and beyond.[3] Homer truly looms throughout.[4] For this reason,
the Homeric house, that is, the house as it appears in Homeric poetry,
illustrates well the challenges and common pitfalls of combining archaeological evidence with textual sources, especially poetry.

Through most of the 20th century, the scholarship on the Homeric
house pressed archaeology into service of the textual material, using it
not only to illuminate a historical Homeric society, but also to explain
the poetry's origins, nature and date. In particular, the question of the
poetry's Mycenaean origins or setting dominated scholarship on the
Homeric house even beyond the translation of Linear B in the 1950s.
Archaeology and the Homeric house, however, largely parted ways in the
late 1960s, when Drerup published an influential study of Geometric
period houses. He described and sorted the archaeological remains of
houses into typologies by shape and number of rooms, instead of using
Homeric passages to comprehend them.[5] Freed from immediate

27

association with the Homeric house, the domestic architecture of early Greek communities could be studied apart from and without necessary reference, or deference, to the poetry.[6]

This estrangement intensified as more nuanced theories about Homer and history developed.[7] No longer is it so easy to find Homeric society in any one time or place, or even anywhere at all, outside of the epics. The Homeric world is now often thought to have not a historical basis but a *social background* in the early Iron Age, usually the 8th century BCE.[8] Some argue that the Homeric world has no historical basis at all, but is fictive, existing nowhere outside of a poetic imagination.[9] Even where it is argued that some of its elements are historical, Homeric society is often considered an amalgam at an 'epic distance' from the world in which it was performed.[10] New questions asked of material culture have also contributed to the estrangement. Early Greek domestic architecture is now usually studied to investigate problems not defined by (although not absent from) the poetry, like class and social structure, economics, politics and state formation, and gender.[11] In a 2010 chapter on houses in the early Iron Age, Nevett dismisses the Homeric epics as having 'limited relevance as sources of information about any aspect of Greek society at any single place and time' and containing 'ideas which are not always representative of a single contemporary reality.'[12] The Homeric house is out.

For all the debate and uncertainty about the Homeric epics, however, those who debate the nature of the epic world of Homer all seem to agree upon its importance *in* the early Iron Age.[13] Very rarely do ideas ever belong strictly to any one single contemporary reality; the burgeoning wealth of classical reception studies reveals how ideas thrive and have relevance beyond their original contexts. The epics reflect norms, ideals, worries and experiences that were significant when they were composed and performed, and continued to be significant for centuries after.[14] This is where their usefulness for the historian and archaeologist truly lies. As Osborne writes, 'The contribution which the Homeric and Hesiodic poems make to the historian rests not with any additional information which they provide on topics illuminated by the archaeologist, but with the evidence they give for ways of seeing the world, ways which archaeology can at best only dimly illuminate.'[15] The heroes inhabit a world of 8th-century Greek *imagining*, and that world gives us access to the thought of a historical culture. We may, therefore, as Morris suggests, approach poetry as a source for cultural history, alongside material culture.[16] In the context of housing, Nevett advocates for a similar approach for using textual evidence to understand Greek perceptions of domestic space (for example, the importance of orderliness or the symbolic value of the external appearance of a house).[17] My purpose here, therefore, is to contribute to the cultural history of the early Iron Age by examining cultural ideas about kinship and prosperity through poetry and domestic architecture.

In this chapter, I first present the history of the relationship between archaeology and the Homeric house to illustrate how Homer does loom throughout it all. I highlight the methodological issues that arise because of that influence and situate my approach to combining words and walls accordingly. In the second part, I employ this approach to investigate how the physical house was perceived and the importance the house had in early Greek kinship. To do this, I turn to the stock phrase *en megaroisi*, 'in the halls', used abundantly in early Greek poetry, especially Homeric poetry. A review of its uses in early Greek poetry suggests that in most cases the phrase should not be taken as an explicit reference to a specific structure or type of structure, but rather as a metonym in which the physical structure stands in for the household and the home. This is, perhaps, similar to how modern English employs 'home' to mean not just the physical house, but the ideas and feelings associated with the house (like kinship, familiarity and belonging). *En megaroisi* expresses not merely the physical house, but the conceptual household and its ongoing formation and success. In its metonymic use, the phrase reveals an important cultural idea, also observable in early Greek domestic architecture, in which kinship and prosperity are linked to the physical house. This association can be considered among other signs of developing social stratification from the early Iron Age into the Archaic period.

Archaeology and the Homeric House

The Dominance of the Mycenaean Question

In 1900, Myres published 'On the Plan of the Homeric House, with Special Reference to Mykenaian Analogies'. In this article, he combined evidence from Homeric poetry with recent Bronze Age archaeological discoveries to show that analogies for his poetry-based understanding of the layout and features of Odysseus' palace could be found in the palaces of Mycenae and Tiryns.[18] In part, the article aimed to describe the plan of the Homeric house, thereby illuminating the space in which the heroes lived and in which some actions of the poems occurred. Myres' greater purpose in turning to the archaeology, however, was to show that the plan devised from the poetry mapped onto Mycenaean palaces so well that Homeric poetry should indeed be dated to the late Bronze Age. Myres was tapping into a broader debate that had intensified in the late 19th century, following discoveries in Mycenaean and Minoan archaeology.[19] Schliemann's excavations at Troy, Mycenae and Tiryns had revived the question of the historicity of the *Iliad* and the *Odyssey*. Gladstone enthusiastically embraced the identification of a Mycenaean setting for Homeric poetry in his preface to Schliemann's *Mycenae*.[20] Everything in Homer, according to Gladstone, was Mycenaean; this was what the archaeology supposedly showed. There were detractors who questioned the historicity of the epics, but now they had to contend with the ever-expanding archaeology of the Bronze Age, which soon included the evidence of the Minoan palaces as well.[21] Detractors, like Jebb, now had to show how the archaeology did not fit with the poetry. Scholarship was therefore primarily concerned with what the new archaeological discoveries could contribute (or not) to understanding the origins, nature and date of the Homeric epics.[22]

The same concerns drove interest in the Homeric house. The problem of Odysseus' house, in particular, was part of this larger challenge to conventional scholarship. At the time, there were two competing proposed types for Odysseus' house.[23] After the excavations of Mycenae and Tiryns, Dörpfeld (following Schliemann) claimed that the Homeric house was of a Mycenaean or pre-Hellenic type.[24] This type was based particularly on the plan of the palace at Tiryns, thought by Dörpfeld and Middleton to be the best match for the palaces of the poetry on the basis of its layout. Mycenae and Athens were exemplars of this type too, but less perfect. That the Homeric house was the Mycenaean palace further confirmed for Dörpfeld and others that the setting of Homeric poetry was the Mycenaean world. Poetry's effect on the interpretation of the site can be seen in Dörpfeld's analysis, which labels rooms and features with Homeric terms and explains them with Homeric references, and in a plan, reproduced in Jebb's article, which is labelled as if it could indeed be the palace of Odysseus (Figure 1.1).[25]

The competing theory was the so-called conventional or Hellenic type, promoted by Gardner and Jebb, which followed a Hellenic plan, that is, it was modelled on later classical houses (Figure 1.2). Gardner and Jebb both rejected the idea that the Mycenaean palaces were the type of house occupied by Odysseus.[26] Gardner made his case for the Hellenic plan before the publication of Schliemann's *Tiryns*; Jebb, however, made his by studying the action in Odysseus' house and comparing it with Dörpfeld's description of Tiryns. He concluded, 'If the Tiryns type is assumed as that which the Homeric poet intended, the *Odyssey* ceases to

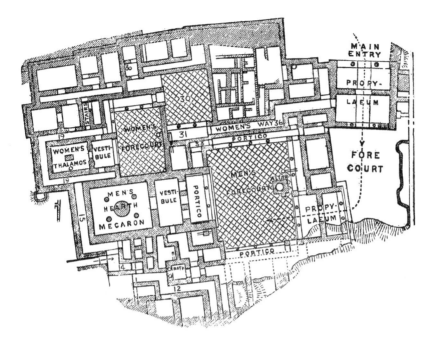

Figure 1.1 Jebb's plan of Tiryns with Homeric labels, following Dörpfeld (Jebb 1886: 172).

be intelligible.'[27] The Homeric house was, therefore, according to Jebb, a precursor to later Greek houses, something entirely different in type and in 'Greekness' from the earlier supposedly Oriental-style Mycenaean palaces. Jebb clearly understood the stakes: 'This is a very important issue, not only for Homeric archaeology, but for all study of Homer.'[28] Since Dörpfeld and Schliemann initially held that the palace at Tiryns was of prehistoric Phoenician origin,[29] the implications of finding the Homeric palace in its ruins would have been very interesting indeed and 'troubling' for the origins of Greek and European literature and culture. Jebb conceived of a division between an earlier Oriental prehistory and a later purely Hellenic history (a division that coincided neatly with the idea of a Dorian invasion). So, in rejecting a Mycenaean origin for the Homeric house, he put Homer clearly on the Greek side of history.

Despite Jebb's concerns, however, the Mycenaean plan for the Homeric house won the day. Schliemann and Dörpfeld's initial conjecture that the Bronze Age palaces were Phoenician in origin did not gain wide acceptance, rooted as it was in the idea of early Phoenician colonizers in Greece, which was contemporarily fashionable but ultimately insupportable.[30] Instead, in the early 20th century, the Bronze Age palaces suggested a

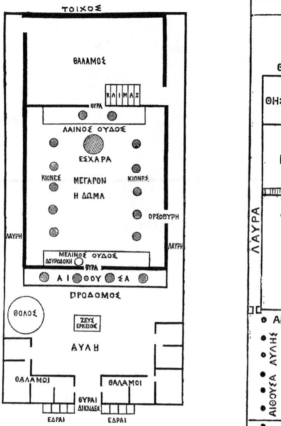

Figure 1.2 Two plans of Odysseus' house following the conventional Hellenic type. Left: Gardner's version (1882: 266). Right: the plan supported by Jebb (1886: 173).

deeper European antiquity, if not a specifically Greek one. The potential to illuminate the world of the heroes with the new archaeological finds, which on the surface seemed to coincide so well with the poetry, was alluring. This allure is evident in the gushing enthusiasm of Gladstone's introduction to Schliemann's *Mycenae*.[31] As part of this passion for a European Bronze Age antiquity, Mycenaean palaces became the dominant model for the Homeric house. It continued to be well into the 1960s.

An Homeric Society Illuminated by Archaeology

The early debates about the Mycenaean setting of Homeric poetry also set the positivist tone for the study of the Homeric house, which used

archaeology to illuminate the poetry, as if the poetry had a direct relationship with a historical reality able to be fixed in time. Myres, like those
before him, was particularly interested in the palace of Odysseus, and his
questions about the Homeric house were inspired by his reading of the
poetry: Where were the women's quarters? Where did Penelope do her
sobbing? Was it behind the *megaron*? Where were the two *oudoi* in relation
to the entrance of the *megaron*? Did the *megaron* have one door or two?
Where and what were the various parts of the palace (the *prodomos*,
aithousa, *orsothurē*, *laurē*, and *rhōges*)?[32] Myres answered these questions
by carefully studying the poetry. Since there is no one description of the
palace of Odysseus in the *Odyssey*, he traced the poetic action, especially
the movements of the characters into, around and out of rooms. For
example, in his investigation on whether the *megaron* had one or two
doors, Myres tracks the movements of Eumaios: 'Eumaios enters the
μεγάρον from the αὐλή, ἐρχόμενον κατὰ δῶμα; – going *into* the house –
and takes, as he passes, a chair from near the carver, who is serving the
guests in order δόμον κάτα, from a station near the door.'[33] Myres then
compares such movements to Middleton's (based on Dörpfeld's) plan and
elevation of the hall at Tiryns (Figure 1.3) and finds that the poetry fits well
with the archaeology. Something of Myres' method can be seen in his own
elevation of the hall at Tiryns (also based on Middleton's), which he labels
with the very Homeric terms he was discussing (Figure 1.4). Although

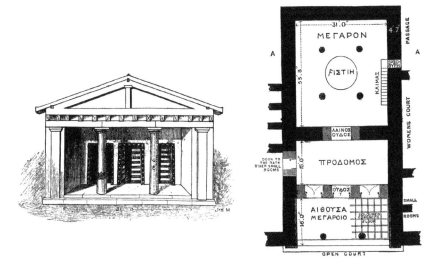

Figure 1.3 Reconstruction of the hall at Tiryns by Middleton. Left: elevation of the
front of the hall (Middleton 1886: 162). Right: ground plan (Middleton 1886: 164).

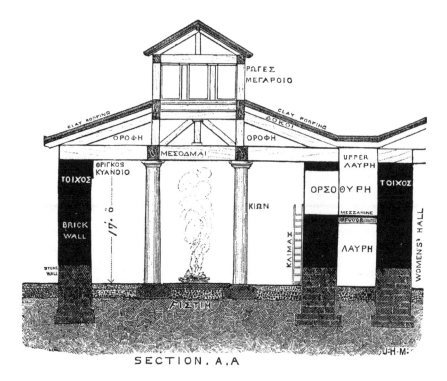

Figure 1.4 Elevation of Odysseus' palace by Myres (1900: 147), following Middleton's elevation.

critics had suggested that there were too many inconsistencies in the poetry to be able to reconstruct an accurate picture of Homeric palaces, Myres asserted that the poet had a clear and consistent vision of the houses which the heroes inhabited, and that the Homeric house could therefore be reconstructed through careful study of the poetic material and by analogy to the Mycenaean palaces.[34] This positivism established the method for studying the Homeric house that would remain dominant in the scholarship up to the 1950s and beyond.

Scholarship operated on the premise that Odysseus' palace was consistent and fully realized, each room imagined in detail by the poet.[35] An analogous palace should be able to be found in the archaeological record, which would reveal information about the poems and the poet. A corollary held that the poet either had real houses or remembrances of real houses as models. The debates were about which structures were the best match for the poetry. For example, shortly after Myres, Noack contended that the Minoan and Mycenaean palaces were not simple enough in style for the palaces of the poetry. The Bronze Age palace at Arne (Gla) was a more suitable analogy.[36] He did not dwell long, however, on the archaeology.

Instead, like Myres, he sought to identify the features, rooms and layout of Homeric palaces from the poetry, as if certain terms referred to specific, discrete rooms in a larger structure: the *megaron* was a living room (with a few exceptions) where members of the household also slept, the *thalamos* was a room where children slept (again with a few exceptions), and guests slept in the *aithousa*.[37] He was particularly concerned with locating exactly where everybody slept in the Homeric house, as if some custom, read out of the poetry, dictated that each household member had to consistently sleep in a specific room. In doing so, Noack was retrojecting contemporary patterns of domestic use of space, both into the poetry and into the historical world the poetry supposedly depicted.[38]

Such positivism was tempered slightly by the idea that the poet never fully described houses, because they were meant to be background and because the poet's audience would have known the setting so well.[39] It was therefore thought helpful to turn to the archaeology to fill in the gaps in the plan of the Homeric house. To this end, the material record was matched carefully with what was determined about the house from the poetry. For example, Rider wrote in a section on the Homeric palaces in her book on the Greek house:

> In the evening [the *megaron*] was lighted by means of λαμπτῆρες or braziers, around which logs were laid and kindled (*Od.* XVIII.307), and which must have given additional heat as well as light. The lampstand found in the Royal Villa at Knossos, and those of the palace at Hagia Triada, provide an analogy.[40]

The impulse behind this kind of fleshing-out was to make the Homeric world richer in detail. The interest was partly poetic and partly historical. Even though Rider's book was on the historical Greek house, when she got to the chronological point of the Mycenaean palaces she turned almost exclusively to Homeric poetry, describing each palace that appears in it. Rider cast the archaeology into the role of providing analogies and filling in holes in the reconstruction of the Homeric house. The historical house was Homer's, and the archaeological structures of the Bronze Age were an aid to understanding that historical house. This is a history filled in by poetry and illuminated by archaeology.

The scholarship continued to be concerned with figuring out which archaeological period Homeric society belonged to and which to draw analogies from: Minoan, Mycenaean or post-Mycenaean.[41] The search was on, therefore, for the Homeric house, not the archaeological house. Some even looked beyond the Aegean for archaeological models that matched their poetic visions. Lang, in 1906, rejecting Myres and Noack's Mycenaean models and Jebb's Hellenic model, turned to the houses of the rich landowners of Icelandic sagas.[42] He was adamant that the dwellings of Homeric heroes could not have been the Hellenic house of the classical period, but rather would have reflected the society inhabited by the heroes. Since, he surmised, the heroic society described in the Icelandic sagas was analogous to that described in Homeric poetry, by ethnographic analogy the heroic house in Homer must look something like the heroic house of medieval Iceland. Palmer, in 1948, also rejected the Mycenaean palace as 'the mise-en-scène for Homer's story' and looked instead to find analogies for the Homeric house in a widespread type of Indo-European house.[43] In *The Homeric and the Indo-European House*, he takes the reader on a descriptive tour room-by-room through Odysseus' palace. He reconstructed the Homeric house primarily, as Myres and Rider had, through analysis of the movements of the characters in the poetry, bringing in archaeology and ethnographic evidence as corroborated his interpretations of the text. Palmer's plan of Odysseus' house, therefore, was less influenced by archaeology than by the text (Figure 1.5). The use of archaeology and ethnography to locate examples or models for the house reconstructed from poetry thus remained dominant in the scholarship, whether or not the archaeology was of the Bronze Age or the ethnography Greek.

The positivism of reconstructing the Homeric house prevailed, as scholarship continued in the mid-20th century to illuminate Homeric society through the archaeology. A prime exemplar of this impulse is Lorimer, who wrote in her preface to *Homer and the Monuments*,

> The primary object of this book is to review the archaeological record of the Late Bronze and Early Iron Ages in the Aegean area, to give as full an account as possible of those elements in it which find a place in the Homeric poems, and to relate this survey to that other record, shadowy, fragmentary, often enigmatic, which is preserved in the poems themselves.[44]

In her chapter on the Homeric house, Lorimer followed up a quotation of Odysseus' description of his palace with 'and no better succinct description could be given of the restored palace of Tiryns'.[45] Thus, Lorimer presented the palace as a close model for Odysseus' house, as Myres had done in 1900, and continued the tradition of the Mycenaean model of Odysseus' house.[46] The influence can be seen in her reconstruction of Odysseus' palace (Figure 1.6), which bears a striking likeness to the plan of the palace at Tiryns presented on the following page in her book. The continuing

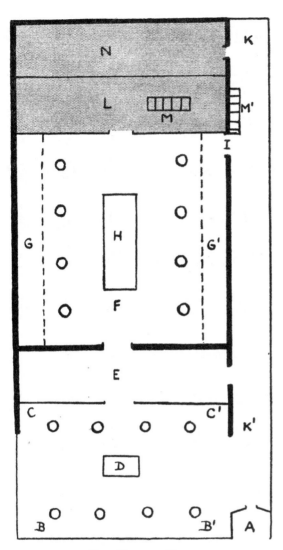

THE HOMERIC HOUSE

A πρόθυρον with θύραι αὔλειαι   H ἐσχάρα
B–B', C–C' αἴθουσαι   I ὀρσοθύρη
D βωμός of Ζεὺς ἔρκειος   K–K' λαύρη
E πρόδομος   L μυχός
F μέγαρον   M–M' κλῖμαξ
G–G' ῥῶγες   N θάλαμος

   A second storey lies above the shaded part.

Figure 1.5 Palmer's (1948: 95) reconstruction of the
Homeric house of Odysseus. By kind permission of John
Wiley and Sons

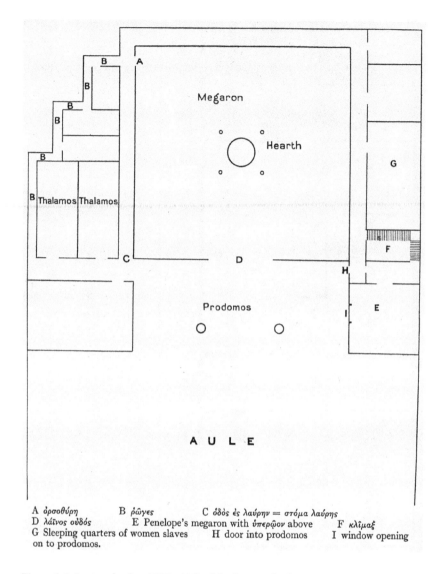

A ὀρσοθύρη   B ῥῶγες   C ὁδὸς ἐς λαύρην = στόμα λαύρης
D λάϊνος οὐδός   E Penelope's megaron with ὑπερῷον above   F κλῖμαξ
G Sleeping quarters of women slaves   H door into prodomos   I window opening
on to prodomos.

Figure 1.6 Lorimer's plan (1950: 408) of the house of Odysseus. By kind permission Somerville College, Oxford

effect of Mycenaean archaeology on envisioning the palace of Odysseus and the *megaron* in general is clear here. Despite appearing only two years before the news of the translation of Linear B was announced in 1952, Lorimer's book set the tone for the continuing debate about the nature of Homeric society in two key ways. First, Lorimer found that, although Homeric society was largely Mycenaean, there were significant elements from the early Iron Age in the poetry.[47] Second, Lorimer used the archaeological record for making connections between historical periods and Homeric poetry, through which one could tease out the nature of Homeric society and of the epics themselves. Her final conclusions, after all, were about the composition of the *Iliad* and the *Odyssey*.[48] As more archaeological evidence on the Bronze and early Iron Ages became available toward the middle of the 20th century, the scholarship on Homeric society accepted that there were Iron Age elements in the poetry. It did not, however, change tack in its approach to text and archaeology; it simply made more and different connections between material culture and Homeric society.

Although this approach persisted, it did meet with some criticism. In 1955, Gray anticipated later scholarship on the relationship between Homer and history, by rejecting the premise that the archaeology of houses provided direct models for the poetry. Astutely, she writes that late Bronze Age and early Iron Age houses, such as had been so far discovered, were similar to those in Homeric poetry but were not 'sufficiently like to have been the historical prototypes.'[49] Instead she suggests that the house of Homeric poetry is an ideal type transmitted by the tradition of heroic poetry: 'knowledge of the proper sort of house for the heroes of legend to live in was preserved [from late the Bronze Age] in the vocabulary of oral poetry and in the stories which were continuously retold by poets.'[50] Perhaps, therefore, the Homeric house was not to be found so directly and precisely in the archaeology after all.

The Mycenaean Question Resurgent and Homeric Society Revisited

The debate over the Mycenaean basis of Homeric poetry was renewed following the translation of the Linear B documents in the 1950s. Was the Mycenaean world revealed by the Linear B documents really the best fit for the setting of Homeric poetry? Was it the correct background for the actions of the heroes? Or did Homeric society more accurately reflect or belong to the Dark Age? Lorimer's *Homer and the Monuments* laid down some of the groundwork, by recognizing both Iron Age and Mycenaean elements in the epics. It was Finley, however, who most prominently led the salvo against the Mycenaean position in the *World of Odysseus*, in which he advocated for a historical background for Homeric poetry in the 9th and 10th centuries.[51] To Finley and others, the world of complex palace economies and bureaucracies revealed by the documents seemed quite foreign to the world of honour, warrior leaders, personal obligations, and simpler agrarian economies inhabited by the Homeric heroes.[52] The epics and the Linear B documents suggested two very different social and economic realities. Those advocating for a Mycenaean background, however, saw in the Linear B documents details that further confirmed and elucidated a Bronze Age Homeric world.[53] The historicity of that world (in which period it was rooted and how it related to history) again became one of the great debates of classical scholarship.[54] Just as earlier debates about the Mycenaean background of Homeric poetry were inspired by Schliemann's discoveries, this debate was not contained to simply understanding the epics better: it directly affected what one concluded about continuity (or discontinuity) from the Bronze to the early Iron Age and, therefore, about the origins of Greek civilization.[55]

Exploring the historicity of the epics and their historical background was primarily a matter of comparing the poetry with the Linear B documents and Bronze Age archaeology. Did the world in the epics match Mycenaean evidence or not? Among those who maintained that Homeric poetry had a Mycenaean background, there was a trend to try to understand elements of the Homeric world through Bronze Age archaeology.[56] This can be seen in the continuing scholarship on the Homeric house, which remained anchored in the Mycenaean world. In Wace and Stubbings' companion to Homer, Wace uses Mycenaean palaces to illustrate the houses in the poetry: 'The references to the various parts of the house given in the Odyssey can be illustrated reasonably by the plans of the Mycenaean palaces.'[57] Rather than the palace at Tiryns, however, Wace turns to the House of the Columns at Mycenae, which he describes room by room with Homeric terms (*aithousa* for porch, *prodomos* for vestibule and *megaron* for main room).[58] Wace, like Lorimer before him and like Myres and Rider before her, studies the terms from Homeric poetry, determining what area of the house they referred to and how the room was used, matching them with whatever they could in the remains of Mycenaean and Minoan structures.[59] The desire was to understand the Homeric house, pressing the archaeology into service.

The debate about the historicity of Homeric poetry was less concerned with the archaeology of the early Iron Age, especially the structures. That was partly because it was much harder to compare, point by point, the heroic world of the epics with the small settlements of small houses attested archaeologically in the early Iron Age. Finley also struggled with finding confirmatory archaeological evidence that would place the world of Homer in the early Iron Age.[60] The lack of correlations between Homeric poetry and the archaeology of the early Iron Age, especially the relative poverty of the early Iron Age, formed a significant part of Snodgrass' argument in

1974 that Homeric society had no clear historical basis.[61] Those proposing a Dark Age or later historical background, however, had a different conception of the relationship between poetry and historical realities, which led them to expect few direct parallels between material culture and poetry. Carpenter, who argued against a fundamentally Mycenaean background, cautioned that one must recognize the division between a poem's cultural reference (an earlier heroic age) and its immediate cultural context (in the 8th century) and that this division can result in the presence of different cultural strata.[62] Others similarly recognized the complexity of the cultural reference points in Homeric poetry as the product of a long oral tradition which drew on elements from different centuries and conflated them into an heroic age (which seemed Mycenaean to varying degrees).[63] Finley, possibly the strongest voice on the Iron Age side of the debate, responded to his critics in an appendix in the second edition of the *World of Odysseus*, in which he denounced the correlation of elements of Mycenaean archaeology with the poems as proving little beyond the existence of a long oral tradition.[64] He envisioned a more complex relationship between poetry and historical reality than both those who wanted to find it in the Mycenaean archaeology and documents as well as those who rejected any historical basis for the Homeric world. According to Finley, Homeric society was indeed a poetic world, but that did not preclude the presence of consistent historical social realities that were not poetic inventions, like gift-giving.[65] Homeric poetry, therefore, had a historical basis of a kind, which he placed in the 10th and 9th centuries (before the poetry's composition and performance context in the 8th century). One should not, however, expect the Homeric world to appear exactly as depicted in a specific time or place.[66] Thus the debates generated by Bronze Age archaeology and the translation of Linear B inspired less positivist approaches to the historicity of Homer and how material culture relates to text.

Whither the Homeric House?

The influence of these modified approaches can be seen in the distance Drerup created between the material culture of the early Iron Age and the poetic world of Homer, in his study of geometric houses published in 1969. On the surface, Drerup shared a common purpose with Wace and Lorimer: studying the archaeology would help in understanding the architecture of the Homeric world.[67] In his volume, he followed the editors' conviction 'daß das homerische Weltbild ... seine archäologische Beglaubigung ausschließlich in der geometrischen Architektur findet' (that the Homeric worldview ... finds its archaeological attestation exclusively in geometric architecture).[68] For Drerup, the Homeric world was appropriately placed in the protogeometric and geometric periods and could therefore be better understood by studying protogeometric and geometric houses.

In his study, however, Drerup made little use of Homeric poetry. Instead of referring to the features of the house of Odysseus, Drerup described the archaeological remains of houses by shape and number of rooms, thereby developing a typology of houses for the geometric period. He concluded from this study that the poetic depiction of the house of Odysseus was untouched by developments in the geometric period house.[69] The 8th-century house simply did not match the Homeric house. Drerup was criticized for this absence of the texts by at least one contemporary reviewer, who lamented, 'There is little discussion of the numerous problems of architectural detail found in Homer, and an index of such Homeric terms as might be wanted, is lacking.'[70] The reviewer also found fault with Drerup for focusing on the geometric period alone, instead of including Minoan and Mycenaean evidence.[71] In these two respects, however, Drerup's volume was an important development for the study of early Greek housing. It separated geometric period houses from being studied alongside and as a development from Bronze Age palace structures, and it distanced the archaeological study of early Greek houses from the poetry. The absence of the text and terms that the reviewer lamented set Greek houses free of the match-game that scholars had been playing between the archaeology and the poetry. Drerup's classification system, moreover, with its typologies of geometric Greek houses, provided a means to talk coherently about the limited and yet varied archaeological remains of early Greek housing. This meant it could be studied, categorized and described apart from Homer. And it was.

Following Drerup, the archaeology of early Greek houses became significantly detached from the Homeric house and free of doing service to it. Recent approaches to early Greek housing have moved beyond Drerup's typologies, to recognize and analyse access patterns, use of space, and settlement practices.[72] Homeric poetry sometimes makes an appearance in studies of the early house (for example, Mazarakis-Ainian uses it to flesh out the social and political background of Dark Age settlements and structures, and Morris to explain early divisions of gendered space),[73] but the house from Homer does not appear. Despite advocating for using textual sources to access ancient perceptions of domestic spaces, Nevett chooses not to draw on Homeric poetry in her recent study of the early Iron Age house. This is a fair decision; the estrangement of the Homeric house from the archaeological house was necessary for scholarship to move beyond old positivist premises and projects. One can quite fruitfully study early Greek housing without reference to the poetry, but one does not have to.

The challenge now, in keeping with the theme of this volume, is how to recombine the poetic and the archaeological house. How, in so doing, can we avoid the pitfalls and politics of previous approaches and embrace current ideas about Homeric society and its complex relationship with history? Ulf suggests that one could compare the literary world of the epics with the world depicted by archaeology to determine historicity.[74] The suggestion seems to be that if one proceeds carefully enough, assessing text and archaeology independently, such a project would give us some answers.[75] But over a century of such work, in studies of significant degrees of depth and diligence, as outlined above, has yielded quite contradictory results. Direct comparisons between text and archaeology have been done, and yet the epics still defy attempts to pin them down in a time or place, or to define clearly how they relate to one or many times and places.[76] The amount of ink spilled trying to do this suggests that Morris is correct in stating that we cannot use archaeology to fix a Homeric world in a time and a place, but should instead use poetry and archaeology together as sources for cultural history.[77] That recent approaches to early Greek housing seek to understand domestic structures as they were used and experienced in three dimensions by living people means there is a place to build poetry in as the cultural output of those people. Again, the poetry gives us access to ways of seeing the world.[78] If we can combine such ways of seeing the world in early Greek poetry, particularly ideas about the house and home, with the archaeology of housing, we might learn something about the people in the houses.

How can we bring Homer and the house back together without recreating the mistakes of the past? It begins with 1) not being driven by philological imperatives to use archaeology to illuminate the world of the poetry or to use poetry to interpret the archaeology; and 2) a nuanced approach to the relationship between Homer and history. Accordingly, I begin here by reviewing the use of the stock phrase *en megaroisi* as a metonym in early Greek poetry, to expose an early Greek perception that kinship and prosperity were expressed by the physical house. I then turn to the archaeology of domestic architecture, which likewise suggests that kinship and prosperity have their expression in the house. Although the approach followed here presents a sort of return to the study of terminology, it is crucially attuned to the idea and the metonymy behind the phrase, rather than geared towards locating actual halls.[79] The approach is also based on a different understanding of the relationship between poetry and history. Inspired by current debates on Homeric society and its relationship to history, I do not assume a historical Homeric society, placed either in the Bronze or early Iron Age, but instead a poetic world with a complex relationship to history.[80] I accept that the Homeric world has much of its social background in the early Iron Age.[81] The poetry does not describe the world of 8th-century Greece, but rather a world of 8th-century Greek *imagining*. Yet we should not call Homeric society a fiction; fiction and non-fiction are anachronistic for describing ancient ideas about the past, especially a heroic past so central to Greek identity and thought.

The old idea, addressed above, that the Homeric house had historical parallels or models to be found in the archaeological record rested upon the premise that the terms in the poetry refer consistently to specific rooms in a structure that would have been familiar to the audience. This idea of audience familiarity and recognition, however, has given way to the understanding that the Homeric world needed to be *comprehensible* by its audience, not necessarily recognisable.[82] I accept that the world would probably have been intelligible enough to an 8th-century audience for the events and ideas to make sense and have meaning without extensive ethnographic interpretation (as we often have to do to make parts of it intelligible for a 21st-century audience). Again, it is a world of imagining, rooted in the contemporary but about an earlier age, at some distance from the contemporary world in time and heroic character. It contains anachronisms (perhaps imprecisely understood elements held over from a long oral tradition and re-visualized) as well as deliberate archaisms and creative, heroic exaggerations that gave the heroes and their actions a glorious epic distance and ideological usefulness for an emerging elite.[83] Despite elements from multiple centuries that are sometimes befuddled, I also approach the world of the epics as internally consistent, at least enough to be able to be subject to social analysis.[84] The poetry may have the appearance of an amalgam, but I do not think it is possible to dissect it into elemental parts or for titbits of this place and that time. The narrative is too cohesive: that is where meaning is embedded and the power of the epics is to be found.[85] Homer cannot be excavated, but must be read as poetry, that is, as art.

Kinship 'in the Halls'

In translations of Homer, the stock phrase *en megaroisi* is usually translated into English as 'in the palace', 'in the halls', 'in the household', 'at home' or 'in the house', and often translated with a possessive pronoun proceeding the noun ('in his palace' or 'in her halls'). It is found in the *Iliad* and *Odyssey, Theogony, Works and Days, Catalogue of Women* and *Homeric Hymns*, as well as in a fragment of Stesichorus.[86] It appears very sparingly in the poetry and prose of the 5th and 4th centuries. In the 3rd century BCE, the phrase was picked up again by Apollonius of Rhodes as part of his affected epic style in the *Argonautica*, where its usage not surprisingly mirrors that in Homeric poetry.[87] The Homeric Greek–English lexicons and *Liddell–Scott–Jones* present the *megaron* in early Greek poetry as the main room or hall of a palace or a house, and sometimes a bedchamber or women's apartment; in the plural (and sometimes in the singular too) they present it as the halls collectively, house, or palace.[88] Autenrieth added men's dining hall to his definition of the *megaron* as the chief room of the house, drawing on a common late 19th-century interpretation of the *megaron* of Homer (and of the Mycenaean palaces) as the men's hall, juxtaposed with the women's *thalamos*. This gendered interpretation broke down in early and mid-20th-century scholarship, which mostly identified the *megaron* as the main living room of the house.[89] Autenrieth, envisioning the *megaron* as the main room of a Homeric palace, with a hearth and posts supporting the roof, also provided a drawing of the *megaron* in Odysseus' palace (Figure 1.7).[90] Like the reconstructions of the Homeric house from a tour of the rooms discussed above, these definitions are philologically derived, that is, they were arrived at through interpreting the poetic use of *megaron*.

Although the phrase *en megaroisi* references a physical structure, it should not be read as if it reveals a reality that could be sought in the

Figure 1.7 Drawing of a *megaron* in Autenrieth's *Homeric Dictionary* (1880: 202).

archaeological record or reconstructed as the Homeric house. It can, however, be considered abstractly as an indicator of the importance of physical space in the conception of the household. A useful parallel may be made with the hearth. Even though the lack of a hearth is the norm for ancient Greek houses, the concept of the hearth is so dominant in the ancient literature that it once led scholars to anticipate the hearth archaeologically in domestic architecture.[91] 'In the halls' may point to a similarly important cultural idea that is not directly reflected in the material record. As Rougier-Blanc shows, the housing and construction terms in Homer and Hesiod carry poetic and social significance within the world of the epics.[92] This particular phrase appears in early Greek poetry in the context of ritual action, the bearing and raising of children, and the possession of property, as I will outline below. In these contexts, *en megaroisi* is an expression of the importance of the physical space of kinship – the location, the house, the home. What follows is a review of the use of *en megaroisi* in early Greek poetry, from Homer and Hesiod up to the end of the Archaic period (when its usage drops off). The contexts that emerge from sorting the appearances of the phrase in the poetry are: being or becoming family, giving birth, inheriting, possessing, mourning, growing old, dying, making sacrifices, reading omens, giving or receiving hospitality, and committing a transgression against a man and/or his family. In these contexts, *en megaroisi* is sometimes an indicator of physical location, but more often a metonym for the household. The physical structure or location implied by 'halls' stands in metonymically for the conceptual locus of family relationships, the activities of home life, the ongoing formation of the household, and the achievement, maintenance and expression of its success.

The Metonymy of 'In the Halls'

In early Greek poetry, *en megaroisi* at its most basic indicates the current physical location of someone or something, for example: οὐδ' εὖρ' Ἀνδρομάχην λευκώλενον ἐν μεγάροισιν (But he did not find white-armed Andromache in the halls); οἱ δὲ δὴ ἄλλοι / Ζηνὸς ἐνὶ μεγάροισιν Ὀλυμπίου ἀθρόοι ἦσαν (Meanwhile the rest of the gods were gathered in the halls of Olympian Zeus); and καί μοι ἐείσατο καπνὸς ἀπὸ χθονὸς εὐρυοδείης / Κίρκης ἐν μεγάροισι διὰ δρυμὰ πυκνὰ καὶ ὕλην (Smoke appeared to me through the brush and forest from the wide-stretching earth in the halls of Circe).[93] Frequently, however, *en megaroisi* is figurative, expressing that something or someone belongs to a man or is connected to a household. For example, it expresses the location of a man's possessions – the things that make him wealthy and respected – suggesting that the things within the walls of a man's house belong to him.[94] The halls are also the location in which the hospitality of the household is extended to guests and in which the quality of the hospitality and behaviour of the guests is judged.[95] These are more than literal references to where receiving, feasting and entertaining occur (this is how early scholarship on the Homeric house tended to take such references, identifying certain activities with certain rooms).[96] When guests are invited into this domestic sphere, how they are treated *en megaroisi* is a matter of honour and reputation, a reflection on the man and the family. While such activities in the poetry are sometimes said to occur specifically and literally in a *megaron, en megaroisi* in the plural indicates something more abstract: the sphere in which domestic life and kinship were centred and into which the guest is invited.[97]

The metonymic use of *en megaroisi* signifies the halls as the location of the activities and states of being of the household and its domestic life: being at home or away, kindling a fire, setting up a loom, preparing a meal, entertaining guests, making a sacrifice, bearing and raising children, and living, dying and mourning. When Stesichorus writes that five sons remained *en megaroisi* instead of going to war as their elder brother had, the sense is that they remained 'at home' as opposed to being away at war, not that they stayed confined within a specific room or even the house.[98] Similarly, Acamas, a Trojan warrior, proclaims that a man going to war wishes to leave someone close to him behind *en megaroisi*, at home, in order to avenge his death in battle.[99] In *Iliad* 6, Andromache pleads for Hector not to return to battle, speaking of her 'seven brothers in the halls' (οἳ δέ μοι ἑπτὰ κασίγνητοι ἔσαν ἐν μεγάροισιν) who were killed by Achilles while tending their livestock.[100] Again *en megaroisi* here does not express physical location, but the location of kinship bonds; her relationship to them was conceptually situated in the halls. When Penelope sets up a loom *en megaroisi*, the sense conveyed is not that she sets it up in a specific location or inside the halls as opposed to outside of them, but that she sets it up in *her* halls, the halls that belong to her husband and family.[101] In the context of the *Odyssey*, setting the loom up in the halls is a defiant act of delaying, through which she asserts that she and the halls remain Odysseus' as long as she is weaving the shroud for Laertes. The phrase is a metonym for the more abstract idea of Odysseus' home, the family sphere into which the suitors have intruded and which they are attempting to appropriate as their own. *En megaroisi* in these instances signifies the locus of kinship, as a metonym for the household sphere to which people, their relationships and things belong.

The Life Cycle 'In the Halls'

The life cycle of the family also plays out conceptually 'in the halls', that is, metonymically 'at home' as opposed to inside a physical structure. The phrase indicates the conceptual domestic sphere where women are brought in marriage, children are born and raised, daughters live until their own marriages, sons remain or return to, elders live out their final years, and family members die and are mourned. In early Greek poetry, *en megaroisi* is frequently used in the context of begetting and bearing children.[102] Even animals are bred *en megaroisi*.[103] In the fragments of the *Catalogue of Women*, in which women are the links between male lineages and generations, *en megaroisi* is a metonym for the household in which women performed their maternal and maidenly roles. In the fragments, the phrase almost always occurs in a childbearing context, especially when a woman bears children *for* her husband, for example, ἣ δέ οἱ ἐν μ]εγάροισιν ἐγείνατο φαίδιμα τέκ[να (she bore him splendid children in the halls) or ἣ οἱ παῖδας ἐγείνα[τ' ἀμύ]μονας ἐν μεγάροισιν (she bore him excellent sons in the halls).[104] Of the fourteen times the phrase appears in the *Catalogue of Women*, only in three of these is the phrase not directly related to the birth of children. One time, the text is so fragmented that the context is obscured, but it appears to be the story of Ino leaving the baby Dionysus in the care of the daughters of Leucon.[105] The other two times, *en megaroisi* situates maidens in the halls of their fathers.[106] Both contexts are also situations in which women fulfil maternal and maidenly roles in the life cycle of the household.

The life-cycle contexts for *en megaroisi* are more extensive in Homeric poetry.[107] Some people considered family are received, not born, into the halls. Upon the Greek warrior Lycophron's death in battle, Ajax says, ἶσα φίλοισι τοκεῦσιν ἐτίομεν ἐν μεγάροισι (We honoured him in the halls just as we did our parents).[108] Although the man had come from elsewhere, he was welcomed and treated as family in the halls. Some men not killed in battle grow old in their halls, for example, Lycurgus and Nestor, but not Eurytos, who was denied that fate 'in the halls' by Apollo.[109] When family members die outside of battle, they often die *en megaroisi*. Andromache's mother died in the halls of her father.[110] Laertes prays to Zeus that his spirit will leave his body 'in the halls'; Odysseus' mother died of grief, not because sickness or the Lady of Arrows set upon her with painless arrows 'in the halls'.[111] There is an important juxtaposition in the epics between a hero's glorious death away at war and inglorious death at home that signals that the meaning of *en megaroisi* is metonymic, rather than specific (that is, referring to location in a physical structure). The phrase indicates a death at home, as opposed to a death abroad while travelling or at war. The Achaean hero Euchenor, for example, after being given a prophecy, was faced with a choice between being killed at Troy or dying of painful sickness *en megaroisi*.[112] Euchenor's choice between dying 'in the halls' or in battle at Troy mirrors the opposition that echoes Achilles' famous choice of fates: to die young and glorious in battle winning undying fame, or to live a long mortal life quietly and without glory. It is a fundamental opposition in the Homeric world, and it suggests that 'the halls' represent more than a physical location; they represent home and home life. They are the locus of the life cycle of the family, so that individuals die not *specifically* and *physically* inside structures called *megarons*, but rather *figuratively* and *metonymically* at home in the household just as children are born into it.

Mourning also occurs *en megaroisi*, where the dead are laid out[113] and the bereaved lament and prepare the funerary rituals.[114] Family members fear and lament being left widows and orphans *en megaroisi*.[115] Possessions are spoken of as left behind in the halls as inheritance. When Odysseus pleads in the court of the Phaeacians to be sent home swiftly, he wishes the present company that particular good fortune: τοῖσιν θεοὶ ὄλβια δοῖεν, / ζωέμεναι, καὶ παισὶν ἐπιτρέψειεν ἕκαστος / κτήματ᾽ ἐνὶ μεγάροισι γέρας θ᾽, ὅ τι δῆμος ἔδωκεν (May the gods grant that they live prosperously and may each leave to his children his possessions in the halls and whatever prize the people have given him).[116] Achilles laments that no generation of strong sons was born to his father in the halls, only one short-lived son: ἀλλ᾽ ἐπὶ καὶ τῷ θῆκε οἱ οὔ τι / παίδων ἐν μεγάροισι γονὴ γένετο κρειόντων / ἀλλ᾽ ἕνα παῖδα τέκεν παναώριον.[117] Nestor gives Telemachus hospitality with an offer that will last as long as he lives and his sons are left behind him in the halls to entertain guests: ὄφρ᾽ ἂν ἐγώ γε / ζώω, ἔπειτα δὲ παῖδες ἐνὶ μεγάροισι λίπωνται / ξείνους ξεινίζειν.[118] Longevity of the household (and the offer of *xenia*) is expressed through the continuity of the family in their familial home. Similarly, for helping Odysseus, the suitors threaten Mentor (Athena in disguise) with death, confiscation of his property and especially destruction of his family: οὐδέ τοι υἷας / ζώειν ἐν μεγάροισιν ἐάσομεν, οὐδὲ θύγατρας / οὐδ᾽ ἄλοχον κεδνὴν Ἰθάκης κατὰ ἄστυ πολεύειν (Nor will we allow your sons to live in the halls, nor your daughters and devoted wife to go out about the town of Ithaca).[119] No sons left in the halls would destroy the line of Mentor. The family thrives or withers *en megaroisi*.

Domestic Prosperity 'In the Halls'

The uses of the phrase *en megaroisi* identified and discussed above are concerned both with the household and with its fortunes: its membership, continuation and propagation, wealth, and reputation. They concern whether it is well regarded or not, whether it can be considered blessed or unlucky and whether it will continue or be destroyed. Many of the uses of *en megaroisi* belong to situations where some transgression has occurred or may occur against the household and threaten it. Sometimes a man's possessions and wealth are threatened,[120] as when the suitors are eating Odysseus' family out of house and home, abusing hospitality; other times, there is a betrayal or more general harm against the man and his house.[121] Sometimes the members are in danger 'in the halls'[122] or their relationships are, like Agamemnon's or Odysseus' marriages.[123] The denial of hospitality similarly endangers a household.[124] Ill-treatment of guests in a man's home diminishes his honour and reputation; it should not be done 'in the halls'.

If danger and ruin can come to the halls for the family, so too can prosperity. A successful and blessed Homeric household sees children born into it and inherit the possessions of their father; an unlucky or cursed household sees sons killed or dispossessed and wives, mothers, and daughters cast out or taken as slaves. All of this is centred *en megaroisi*, metonymically in the home or household. Heroes sacrifice *en megaroisi* for good outcomes for their ventures.[125] As we saw above, women bear children for their husbands *en megaroisi*, ensuring the continuity of the family. In Homeric genealogies, such domestic bliss (a good wife and sons) is spoken of alongside having a fine house and agricultural wealth. It is seemingly the whole domestic package, as expressed, for example, in Diomedes' heroic genealogy in the *Iliad*. It is dominated by his father's story: he moved to Argos, received a well-born wife, set up a house and held lands rich in produce.[126] Besides prowess in war and in words, Homeric heroes are also associated with economic and domestic status, that is, having a good wife, a house and agricultural wealth. Rougier-Blanc, who takes a similar approach to housing in early Greek poetry, also detects a link between elitism and the language and descriptions of housing in the Homeric epics. The architectural language in Homer, she argues, reproduces status distinctions within the epics. The descriptions, including those that allude to the materials and techniques of construction, point to the importance of domestic architecture in the epics not just as settings for poetic action, but as indicators of social identities.[127] Just as the stories of monster killings, great battles, and foundations of cities and peoples fill the genealogical stories of heroes and distinguish them as extraordinary and worthy to lead, so too do stories of economic and domestic success. The halls are not only the locus of family bonds, but also the locus of a family's prosperity or ruin.

Prosperity in the Early Greek House

This conceptual link between the prosperity of the family and the physical house is also seen in early Greek domestic architecture. As we will see below, at sites like Zagora and Eretria, the locus of the success of the family is the house, as it is modified to accommodate and express changes in size, economic activity, wealth, and status. Small one-room houses were the standard in early Greek communities, whether free-standing or in conglomerations. However, multi-room houses with more complex access patterns begin to appear in the late 8th century with more regularity. Then there is a spike in the, albeit limited, pool of evidence in their numbers in the 7th century, when they come close to equalling the number of one-room houses.[128] At some sites houses with either one or two rooms and relatively simple access patterns appear to be renovated into multiroom houses with complex access patterns. A good example is at Zagora on Andros in the late geometric period. From phase 1 to phase 2 at the site, some house complexes with one- and two-room houses (so-called *megaron* houses)[129] were modified to complexes of multiple-room houses. At Eretria too, there is a progression in the 8th century from small one-room oval houses to larger one-room curvilinear structures to rectilinear two-room houses with serial access patterns (*megaron* houses) at the end of the century and beginning of the 7th century.[130] At Megara Hyblaea, remarkably uniform one-room houses in the 8th century develop over the 7th and 6th centuries into more diverse multi-room houses with more complex access patterns.[131] At the site, throughout the 7th century, some one-room houses were modified into multiple-room houses, some with courtyards, while others remained as they were. Some new one-room houses were built as well as some multi-room houses. In the 6th century multi-room houses became more standard at the site.[132]

While there was a movement toward more complex access patterns at a number of sites, most early Greek houses, even in the 7th and 6th centuries, were relatively modest one-room houses.[133] And at individual sites, old and new designs often existed side by side at the same site, as Morris points out citing as examples the existence of oval and rectilinear houses at Miletus in the mid-8th century, the gradual conversion of houses at Megara Hyblaea in the seventh century, and the combination of rectilinear and curvilinear architecture at Lathouresa in the 7th century.[134] Moreover, although there does seem to be a trend toward more rooms and more complex access patterns in houses at those sites where we can track changes in domestic architecture, not all sites parallel the changes that took place at Zagora, Megara Hyblaea and Eretria.[135] The development of Greek domestic architecture was far from uniform and the similarities and differences in the development of domestic architecture between sites may be linked to differing participation and success in local and wider economies.

Some houses in some early Greek communities were, therefore, modified to create larger spaces and/or more complex access patterns. The motivation for these renovations seems to be to provide a modest level of functional specialization for and as a result of economic participation: to increase storage, to include space for receiving visitors, and possibly to match the family's growth in size and status. From the 8th century BCE on, households in early Greek communities were participating in wider economic systems, that is, participating in networks of storage, production and trade in their communities and beyond. This is suggested by an increase in areas in houses used partly for storage, and by the presence of *pithoi* and *amphorae*, as well as evidence of processing materials.[136] There was a murex-dyeing workshop discovered in a house with multiple rooms and a courtyard at the site of Euesperides in Cyrenaica.[137] Loom-weights and spindle-whorls found in domestic contexts across many early Greek sites suggest processing activity, turning wool into cloth.

Features connected to storage are the most prominent evidence we have of early Greek domestic architecture besides foundation walls, and therefore it appears to be a significant concern for domestic structures in this period. Fagerström's overview of the benches from the early Iron Age suggests that most by far were used for this reason, particularly in domestic contexts.[138] Benches vary so greatly in height, width, shape and construction that it seems reasonable that they could be as multifunctional as the rooms in which they were located.[139] On the basis of the finds and features associated with several benches in domestic contexts in Fagerström's overview (for example, holes for *pithoi* and sherds of *pithoi* and other pottery shapes), storage would seem to have been one of the functions. Benches in a number of rooms at Zagora (for example, H18, H19, H26–27 phases 1 and 2) were used by households to hold large *pithoi* for storage.[140] Benches elsewhere in domestic contexts were also used for storage, at, for example, Xobourgo (unit V), Thorikos (room G) and Vathys Limenaris (House X7).[141] Other types of storage include cisterns (for example, at Telos), bins for water or possibly grain storage if inside the house (for example, at Zagora, Nichoria, Vathys Limenaris and Tsikkalario), and indoor pits (for example, at Asine, Smyrna, Xobourgo and Nichoria).[142] It has been suggested that the silos found in 8th-century houses in Megara Hyblaea on Sicily were used for the storage of grain, and surplus grain in particular.[143] This could indicate a role for households in the trade in surplus agricultural produce.

Parisinou suggests the triangular windows in rooms at Zagora in which there is evidence of storage, seem to be placed and shaped not so much to provide good light to work in, but rather ventilation for better storage conditions.[144] Rooms with the most amount of privacy (that is, the least amount of through-traffic according to access patterns) may also have had a very limited amount of natural light, making them ideal places for storage of light- or heat-sensitive items, such as foodstuffs or oils. This would be especially true in houses with serial access patterns, in which the final room in the series was set far back from the entrance, but also in houses with more complex access patterns, such as House A at Onythe and Building IV at Xobourgo, in which evidence of storage has been found in rooms which would have received little or no natural light.[145] The storage rooms from phase one at Zagora, as they become divided in phase two, provide even less light and more segregation of storage space.

The modifications in 8th-century houses at Zagora toward more complex access patterns seem to have been motivated in part to increase storage space and separate it from areas where guests may have been received.[146] Sherds of *pithoi* found in several of the back rooms of the modified houses suggest that at least one purpose for the rooms was storage.[147] The renovations also seem to have created reception or dining space, a place in the household to receive and possibly entertain visitors, as suggested by finds of drinking vessels in the larger rooms.[148] Thus the renovations provided more functional specialization for the rooms in the house, although not complete specialization. Rooms were still multifunctional.

These kinds of renovations to the house suggest that the inhabitants were experiencing some degree of success, economically, but possibly socially and politically as well, to require or desire such changes. The increased complexity of access patterns and the increased functional specialization of rooms may have changed in tandem with economic growth at certain sites at certain times, as they seem to do at Zagora through the 8th century.[149] The expansion and increased functional specialization of domestic space at Zagora represent what can happen to the physical house when the economic situation of the household and community is on the rise. More storage may need to be incorporated into the home, places not only for the keeping of surplus, but also for the conspicuous display of surplus. The resources to expand the house may become available and the desire to display one's success may arise. The material assemblages, however, at Zagora and elsewhere are not those of a very wealthy, extremely prosperous community, and the increase must be seen in relative terms. The expansion of houses may also be related to population growth, as Green argues, which could also be linked to economic prosperity and an increased 'quality of life'.[150] The evidence of storage, however, seems a primary consideration, although an increase in household members and a need for more dedicated storage space could certainly be two sides to the same coin. The abandonment of the site after only a few generations may likewise indicate changes in the economic situation in the Cyclades at the end of the 8th century and into the 7th.

That only some houses are modified at each of these sites suggests that there were winners and losers. Not every household was successful enough to have the means, need or desire to either expand or modify their domestic space. The degree of differentiation in early Greek settlements is, however, fairly low. There is some differentiation discernible between houses, in shape, size and finds, but overall the picture is of modest houses within modest settlements with a modest amount of wealth not vastly disproportionately divided.[151] That there were some members of the community who were more successful economically and socially than others, but only relatively so, and perhaps held higher status in the community, seems to be a fair description of early Greek economic and social differentiation and a reasonable interpretation of the archaeological evidence of housing and settlements of early Greece. There are no vast disparities, but rather subtle hints that stratification is occurring or beginning to occur. In these small changes are, perhaps, the kernels of later social, economic and political stratification attested in the Archaic poetry of Solon and Theognis. This is not to say that these particular households (for example, from Zagora) later became the elites of the Archaic period, but rather that the beginnings of later stratification probably lie in these sorts of differences in prosperity between households within communities.

Kinship and Prosperity in Poetic Words and Material Walls

By combining the archaeology of early Greek houses with the ways of seeing the world in early Greek poetry, we arrive at an idea of the family and its ongoing formation and prosperity that is expressed 'in the halls'. Early Greek poetry uses the 'halls' to represent metonymically the abstract relationships that a structure might contain, as one might now use 'home' to indicate not the physical structure itself, but the abstract things that the physical structure is thought to contain (family, warmth, familiarity, safety, sense of belonging, etc.). In the poetic world, *en megaroisi* indicates where the bonds of kinship are conceptually located, regardless of a person's physical presence within the halls. The small activities of domestic life are lived out *en megaroisi*, as well as the major moments of the household's life-cycle. Children are born into it to continue the family line and ensure its future. Men grow old, die and are mourned in it. In the halls was where a hero was rich and prosperous in livestock, produce, possessions, but also in family, as opposed to glorious in battle or deeds. The metonymy of *en megaroisi* shows the centrality of the physical inhabited space in how kinship and prosperity were perceived.

This metonymy draws upon physical space to stand in for the abstract idea of household, home and a family's success in early Greek poetry. Perhaps, it is therefore not surprising to find prosperity similarly manifested in the archaeological house. The house, like the halls of *en megaroisi*, was tied to the family's fortunes, economic and otherwise. The evidence of domestic architecture tells us that economic and social success was something experienced by some households in early Greek communities. In the houses, people were participating in a broader economic system, processing materials and storing surplus. Some made modifications to houses seemingly to increase or adapt storage areas, to make areas better suited to receiving and entertaining guests, and perhaps to provide more living space for the family. Many others did not. The prosperity of the household came to affect and be reflected in the physical house, just as in early Greek poetry the prosperity of a household was connected to the physical house by the metonymy of *en megaroisi*. The prosperity of the household, both economic and domestic, was thought to be 'in the halls'.

Poetry, Homeric or otherwise, should not be excavated for fragments of historical reality. To do so is to strip the epics of the meaning and, therefore, neglect the power they held in their historical context. What would an ancient listener have heard? It was probably not that various elements sounded like a pot, brazier, lamp or house one might have (an Iron Age equivalent of 'I can see my house from here'). It was more likely the great deeds, events, ideas and themes that run through the epics, like Achilles' rage and its consequences, the heroism, honour and power that sit at the root of his conflict with Agamemnon, the heroism and gore of battle, the tragedy of Hector defending home and family, the extraordinary cunning of Odysseus, the wide world travelled by the hero, and the struggle of the warrior returning home. The embedded themes, questions, and ideals are the importance that the poetry carries for the history and archaeology of early Greece. Given the paucity of sources for this period, this is a gift. But the combination of poetry and archaeology need not be constrained to where we have limited sources. All poetry gives us access to ideas and ways of seeing the world that can be combined fruitfully with material culture. Through poetry we gain access to ancient perceptions not only of domestic space, but about any number of things and topics, which can be used in conjunction with material culture to pursue the complex questions – questions about, for example, social relationships and organization, kinship and community, and elitism and power – we have of the ancient world.

Notes

1 Finley 1978: 148.
2 Finley 1978: 148. Finley notoriously placed a historical background for the Homeric world in the earlier part of the early Iron Age.
3 Cf. Hall 2014: 11.
4 As Muhly writes about the history of Bronze Age scholarship, 'Behind all of this, past and present, looms the figure of Homer' (2012: 4).
5 Drerup 1969.
6 For a significant move towards studying the Homeric house poetically before approaching the historical and archaeological house, see Rougier-Blanc 2002; 2005; 2009.
7 The bibliography on this is vast; significant contributions toward these theories include (but are not limited to) Finley 1954; Snodgrass 1974; Morris 1986; 1997; 2000; Van Wees 1992; Crielaard 1995; Raaflaub 1997; 1998; 2011; Osborne 2009: 140–52; Rose 2012: 108–14.
8 For example, Morris 2000: 171–72; Hall 2007: 26; Osborne 2009: 149–52.
9 Snodgrass 1974; Cartledge 2001: 157.
10 For example, Crielaard 1995; Raaflaub 1998; 2011.
11 For example, Morris 1998; Mazarakis-Ainian 2001; 2006; 2007; Nevett 2003; 2007; 2010: 22–42; Lang 2005; 2007. On the desirability, even necessity, for more such approaches, see Nevett 1999: 21, 29–33; 2010: 4–5.

12 Nevett 2010: 23.

13 For example, Morris 1986; 1997: 539, 557–58; 2000: 171–76; Van Wees
   1992: 5, 262; Crielaard 1995; Raaflaub 1998: 186–87; 2011: 10; Cartledge
   2001: 157.

14 Similarly, Redfield 1975: x–xi; Van Wees 1992: 10, 262–63; Raaflaub 2011: 5.

15 Osborne 2009: 149.

16 Morris 1997: 539; 2000: 171–72.

17 Nevett 1999: 36–39.

18 Myres drew particularly on the reconstructions of Tiryns by Middleton 1886.

19 For example, Gardner 1882; Jebb 1886; Helbig 1887: 96–125.

20 Gladstone 1878.

21 Schuchhardt summarizes the early criticisms of Schliemann's conclusions,
   including the fundamental criticism that the finds did not appear to match the
   Homeric epics as well as many would have liked (1891: 310–22). In contrast to
   Gladstone's exuberance, Schuchhardt provides a welcome note of sober
   caution: 'We must not forget that for all the resemblances there are numerous
   differences between Homer and Mycenae, and that the people whom he calls
   Achaeans may have been quite unlike what we have hitherto imagined from his
   poems' (Schuchhardt 1891: 314).

22 This philological imperative to ask questions of material remains determined
   by the text was typical of most 19th- and early 20th-century classical
   archaeological pursuits (see Hall 2014: 8–13). As noted above and reviewed
   below, the guiding interest of Homeric poetry, a clear philological imperative,
   continued to shape Bronze Age scholarship well beyond Schliemann's time (see
   Muhly 2012: 4; cf. Hall 2014: 11).

23 Myres 1900: 129–32.

24 Dörpfeld 1885; also Middleton 1886, among others.

25 Dörpfeld 1885.

26 Gardner 1882; Jebb 1886.

27 Jebb 1886: 188.

28 Jebb 1886: 170.

29 Schliemann 1885: 28.

30 Schliemann 1885: 20–28. See McDonald and Thomas 1990: 71–72; Traill
   1995: 246.

31 Gladstone 1878.

32 Myres 1900: 132–48.

33 Myres 1900: 141, referencing *Od.* 17.329.

34 Myres 1900: 128–29.

35 Gray 1955 finally provided a strong critique of the assumption that houses in
   the archaeology could have served as direct models for Homer, without,
   however, fully rejecting the possibility.

36 Noack 1903: 69–73.

37 Noack 1903: 42–54.

38 Such projections about the use of domestic spaces in antiquity have been a problem in scholarship on houses, as Nevett has noted (2010: 16–19). Interpretative frameworks are necessary for understanding the use of domestic space, but too often those frameworks have been rooted in implicit assumptions based on modern Western domestic patterns and activities.

39 For example, Rider 1916: 179.

40 Rider 1916: 179.

41 Evans had recently promoted the idea that Homeric poetry had its origins in Minoan culture (1912: 288), but the idea does not seem to have had traction in scholarship on the Homeric house.

42 Lang 1906: 209–28.

43 Palmer 1948: 111.

44 Lorimer 1950: vii.

45 Lorimer 1950: 407.

46 Lorimer 1950: 407–10.

47 McDonald and Thomas 1990, 309–11.

48 Lorimer 1950, 452–528

49 Gray 1955, 12.

50 Gray 1955: 11.

51 Finley 1954; also, Finley 1957.

52 Finley 1954; 1957; Thomas 1966.

53 Page 1959; Webster 1964: 91–135; Palmer 1965, 96–142; Luce 1975: 71–99, esp. 76–77.

54 In 1970, Thomas labelled the question of the historicity of Homeric society as one of four major aspects of the Homeric Question among questions about the existence of Homer, dual authorship of the *Iliad* and *Odyssey*, and the nature of epic language (Thomas 1970: 4).

55 Again, the issue emerged of the Aegean Bronze Age's connection with the Near East: were the Mycenaean palace societies more like that of Homeric poetry or more like the 'contemporary temple economies of the orient'? (Palmer 1965: 97).

56 Page 1959; Webster 1964: 91–135; Palmer 1965: 97–142; Luce 1975.

57 Wace 1962: 490–91. Similarly, Wace 1951.

58 That the terminology still used for Bronze Age and early Iron Age structures was taken from Homeric poetry is a direct result of using the poetry to identify archaeological remains. It points clearly to the match-game played between archaeological discoveries and textual sources. This is problematic because the language drawn from the poetry has not functioned as a simple label, but as a means to identification and interpretation. So, is it possible to interpret the material evidence with any degree of independence, if the language we use begins with the texts? On this problem in Greek household contexts, see Nevett 1999: 25–26, 41. On this problem in Roman household contexts, Leach 1997; Allison 1999.

59 The terms Lorimer and Wace study are: *thalamos, tholos, klimax, laurē, megaron, mesodmai, muchos, orsothurē, oudos* and *rhōges*.

60 Finley 1978: 157.

61 Snodgrass 1974. This lack of direct parallels can also be seen in Drerup's study of geometric period houses discussed below (Drerup 1969).

62 Carpenter 1946: 27.

63 Bowra 1961: 84–86; Thomas 1970: 4–5. Those who advocated for a dominantly Mycenaean basis for an Homeric society also recognized that there were later elements in the epics, too, attributable to oral tradition (for example, Webster 1964: 208–23).

64 Finley 1978: 150–51. Critics, for example, like Luce (1975: 74–77).

65 Finley 1978: 49–50, 144–46.

66 Finley 1978: 48–50.

67 The work was, after all, published in *Archaeologia Homerica*.

68 Drerup 1969: 1.

69 Drerup 1969: 133.

70 Hemelrijk 1972: 110.

71 Hemelrijk 1972: 110 ultimately suggests that the reader must 'fall back' on the work of Lorimer and of Wace and Stubbings.

72 For example, Nevett 1999; 2003; Lang 2007.

73 Morris 2000; Mazarakis-Ainian 2001; 2006; 2007.

74 Ulf 2009: 83.

75 Crielaard's attempt at assessing the archaeological material and poetry independently perhaps comes the closest to achieving this end (1995).

76 See Raaflaub 1998: 169–70; 2011: 3–4 on this 'historian's headache', about which careful, thoughtful and methodologically sound studies can come to quite different conclusions.

77 Morris 1997: 539; 2000: 171–72.

78 Osborne 2009: 149.

79 A complementary approach can be found in the work of Rougier-Blanc (2002; 2005; 2009). Rougier-Blanc examines the language of housing in Homer and Hesiod within its poetic context, before linking poetry and 'reality' (e.g., 2009: 57–60).

80 The full debate in recent scholarship is far too extensive to be covered in detail here. See Raaflaub 1998 and 2011 for usefully measured introductions to current opinions.

81 For example, Morris 2000: 171–72; Hall 2007: 26; Osborne 2009: 149–52.

82 Similarly, Redfield 1975: xi; Raaflaub 2011: 5.

83 Morris 1986; 2000: 171–76; Crielaard 1995; Raaflaub 1998: 175–76, 187; 2011.

84 Similarly, Finley 1978: 145–46; Van Wees 1992: 28–58; Raaflaub 1998: 173–74. Contra Snodgrass 1974; Cartledge 2001: 157.

85 Similarly, Osborne 2009: 149–50; Rose 2012: 108–12.

86 A search of the *Thesaurus Linguae Graecae* reveals that the phrase in variations of ἐν(ὶ) μεγάροισι(ν) appears 145 times in Homeric poetry, fifteen times in the fragments of the pseudo-Hesiodic *Catalogue of Women*, five times in the Homeric Hymns, once in a fragment of Stesichorus, and once each in the *Theogony* and *Works and Days*.

87 For example, Ap. Rhod. *Argon* 3.305. On Apollonius' use of Homeric vocabulary, see Acosta-Hughes 2014: xi–xii.

88 LSJ, s.v. μέγαρον; Autenrieth 1880, s.v. μέγαρον; Cunliffe 1924, s.v. μέγαρον.

89 For example, Rider rejected the late-19th-century idea that women were secluded in either the *thalamos* or their own *megarons* as 'altogether foreign to the Homeric poems' (1916: 196). See also, Noack 1903: 48–49; Lorimer 1950: 427; Wace 1962: 494.

90 Autenrieth 1880, s.v. μέγαρον. The image bears no trace of the influence of Mycenaean palaces that would later give the poetic *megaron* its standard look and layout (for example, in Myres 1900 and Lorimer 1950). The other lexica do not provide such a detailed description or an image.

91 On this problem, see Jameson 1990a, 192–95; 1990b, 105–106; Foxhall 2007; Tsakirgis 2007.

92 Rougier-Blanc 2002, 107–11; 2009, 52–57.

93 *Iliad* 6.371; *Odyssey* 1.26–27; *Od.* 10.150–51. All translations by the author; *Iliad* and *Odyssey* hereafter abbreviated *Il.* and *Od.*

94 For example, *Il.* 5.193, *Od.* 11.341, 23.355.

95 *Il.* 3.207, 6.217, 5.805; *Od.* 8.42, 10.452, 13.8, 17.358, 18.221, 19.217, 19.327, 21.424, 22.56, 23.60.

96 For example, Noack 1903.

97 This is analogous, perhaps, to welcoming someone into your *home*, rather than simply into your house, hallway or dining room.

98 πέντε γ]ὰρ ὀψίγονοι τε καὶ ἀσπασί- / οι μένο]ν ἐν μεγάρ[ο]ισιν (five late-born and welcomed sons remained in the halls) (Stes. frag. 45, cited from Page 1968). Campbell translates the phrase as 'at home' in his Loeb edition (1991: 135).

99 *Il.* 14.484–85.

100 *Il.* 6.421.

101 ἡ δὲ δόλον τόνδ' ἄλλον ἐνὶ φρεσὶ μερμήριξε· / στησαμένη μέγαν ἱστὸν ἐνὶ μεγάροισιν ὕφαινε, / λεπτὸν καὶ περίμετρον (She contrived this other scheme in her mind; setting up in the halls a great loom with long and fine threads, she was weaving) (*Od.* 2.93–94). Similarly, *Od.* 19.138–39 and 24.129–30.

102 For example, *Il.* 1.418; 24.497; *Od.* 7.12; Hesiod, *Theogony* 384; *Homeric Hymn to Pan* 35.

103 Mares at *Il.* 5.270 and dogs at *Il.* 22.69.

104 *Cat.* frag. 31.8; *Cat.* frag. 10.51. References and quotations from the *Catalogue of Women* are from Most 2007.

105 *Cat.* frag. 41.2.

106 *Cat.* frag. 2 and 69.57.

107 The phrase appears most often in the *Odyssey*. Perhaps, this should not be surprising since the epic is the story of a return home and the troubles *en megaroisi* (in the hero's house and home) during his absence.

108 *Il.* 15.439.

109 Lycurgus: *Il.* 7.148; Nestor: *Od.* 4.210; Eurytos: *Od.* 8.227.

110 *Il.* 6.428.

111 *Od.* 15.354. *Od.* 11.198.

112 *Il.* 13.667.

113 *Il.* 24.757.

114 *Il.* 14.502, 18.325, 22.510; *Od.* 4.101.

115 *Il.* 22.484, 24.726; *Od.* 20.68.

116 *Od.* 7.148–50.

117 *Il.* 24.539–40.

118 *Od.* 3.353–55.

119 *Od.* 22.221–23.

120 *Od.* 1.295, 2.299, 16.314.

121 *Od.* 19.497, 22.47, 22.151.

122 Od. 16.411, 20.274, 24.162.

123 Od. 3.256, 16.77.

124 *Od.* 18.221, 19.254, 23.28.

125 *Il.* 24.427, *Od.* 4.763, 10.523, 11.31, 22.322.

126 *Il.* 14.121–24.

127 Rougier-Blanc 2002; 2005. Rougier-Blanc also sees a difference in the language and significance of housing between Homer and Hesiod. She notes that the language of housing, prevalent and significant to the poetic narrative in the Homeric epics (2009), is less prevalent in the *Works and Days* and the *Theogony*. Where it does appear, it either seems to emphasize the might of Zeus or, in an inversion of Homeric usage, a homogeneous modesty in domestic architecture.

128 Lang 1996: 106; Nevett 2003: 17, fig. 3; 2010, 39. Such houses can be found throughout the Greek world, for example at Aegina, Corinth, Koukounaries on Paros, Kalabektepe at Miletos, Vroulia on Rhodes, Syracuse and Megara Hyblaea on Sicily, and Dreros, Kavousi Kastro and Onythe on Crete. For a thorough account of multi-room houses known from published excavations, see the houses listed under *Mehrraumhäuser: Hof- und Korridorhaus* (Lang 1996: 95–97) and *Pastas- und Prostashaus* (Lang 1996: 98–101).

129 This term is, of course, a sign of the continuing use of Homeric vocabulary in archaeological labels and typologies of houses.

130 Morris 1998: 16, 18, fig. 5.

131 Morris 1998:23; De Angelis 2003: 17–32.

132 De Angelis 2003: 17–32, figs. 7, 9–13, 16–18.

133 Nevett 2003: 17–18, fig. 3.

134 Morris 1998: 22–23. For Megara Hyblaea, see also Vallet *et al.* 1976: 337–39.

135 For example, Kastanas in Macedonia underwent what seems to be the opposite changes: an 8th-century multi-room house with single units accessed from the outside was remodelled in the 7th century into attached smaller two-room units (Lang 1996: 108; 2005: 22–23; Morris 1998: 46). Later in the 6th century the whole complex was levelled and replaced by two-room detached houses. The houses at the site of Tragilos, also in Macedonia, underwent a similar transformation (Lang 2005: 22–23).

136 See also Lang 2005: 27, on the 'Economic Sphere.'

137 Gill and Flecks 2007.

138 Fagerström 1988: 133–37.

139 See also Christophilopoulou 2007: 30.

140 Cambitoglou *et al.* 1971: 25–26; 1988: 154.

141 Fagerström 1988: 136.

142 Cisterns: Hoepfner 1999: 182–83, although the cisterns may be of a date in the 6th century. Bins: Fagerström 1988: 131–32. Pits: Fagerström 1988: 137. The structure at Xobourgo, however, may not be domestic, but religious (Kourou 2002: 62–66 contra Kontoleon 1953).

143 De Angelis 2002.

144 Cambitoglou *et al.* 1971: 25; Parisinou 2007: 215.

145 Parisinou 2007: 217. Onythe: Platon 1955: 300–301; Lang 1996: 88;. Xobourgo: Fagerström 1988: 83–84, 136; Hoepfner 1999: 191.

146 Cambitoglou *et al.* 1988: 154; Morris 2000: 285; Ault 2007: 260.

147 Rooms H25, H40, H27, H19, H22, H23, H28 and D1. While some of the *pithoi* fragments found at the site may represent the use of *pithoi* for collection of rainwater, they likely only make up a fraction of the fragments, since many of the fragments are found indoors. Cambitoglou *et al.* suggest this usage as a possibility, since there are no natural springs or evidence of wells at the site (Cambitoglou *et al.* 1971: 9).

148 Cambitoglou *et al.* 1971: 13–16; 1988: 71–73, 79–106, 107–17, 118–28

149 See also Lang 2005: 19.

150 Green 1990.

151 Similarly, Rose 2009: 472.

References

Acosta-Hughes, B. (2014). Introduction to *Jason and the Argonauts*, trans. Aaron Poochigian. New York: Penguin, vii–xix.

Allison, P. M. (1999). Labels for ladles: interpreting the material culture of Roman households. In P. M. Allison, ed., *The Archaeology of Household Activities*. London and New York: Routledge, 57–77.

Ault, B. (2007). *Oikos* and *oikonomia*: Greek houses, households and the domestic economy. In R. Westgate, N. Fisher and J. Whitley, eds., *Building*

Communities: House, Settlement and Society in the Aegean and Beyond: Proceedings of a Conference Held at Cardiff University 17–21 April 2001. London: British School at Athens, 259–65.

Autenrieth, G. (1880). *Homeric Dictionary*, trans. Robert Keep. New York: Harper and Brothers.

Bowra, C. M. (1961). Homer's age of heroes. *Horizon* 3(3), 73–99.

Cambitoglou, A., Birchall, A., Coulton, J. J. and Green, J. R. (1988). *Zagora 2.* Athens: Athens Archaeological Society.

Cambitoglou, A., Coulton, J. J., Birmingham, J. and Green, J. R. (1971). *Zagora 1.* Sydney: Sydney University Press.

Campbell, David A., ed. (1991). *Greek Lyric III: Stesichorus, Ibycus, Simonides, and Others.* Loeb Classical Library. Cambridge, MA: Harvard University Press.

Carpenter, R. 1946 (1962). *Folk Tale, Fiction and Saga in the Homeric Epics.* Berkeley: University of California.

Cartledge, P. (2001). *Spartan Reflections.* Berkeley: University of California Press.

Christophilopoulou, A. (2007). Domestic space in the geometric Cyclades: a study of spatial arrangements, function and household activities in Zagora on Andros and Kastro on Siphnos. *Proceedings of the Danish Institute at Athens* 5, 23–33.

Crielaard, J. P. (1995). Homer, history and archaeology: some remarks on the date of the Homeric world. In J. P. Crielaard, ed., *Homeric Questions: Essays in Philology, Ancient History, and Archaeology.* Amsterdam: J.C. Gieben, 201–88.

Cunliffe, R. J. (1963) [1924]. *A Lexicon of the Homeric Dialect.* Norman, OK: University of Oklahoma Press.

De Angelis, F. (2002). Trade and agriculture at Megara Hyblaia. *Oxford Journal of Archaeology* 21, 299–310.

(2003). *Megara Hyblaia and Selinous: The Development of Two Greek City-States in Archaic Sicily.* Oxford: Oxford University School of Archaeology.

Dörpfeld, W. (1885). The buildings of Tiryns. In H. Schliemann, ed., *Tiryns: The Prehistoric Palace of the Kings of Tiryns.* London: J. Murray, 177–308.

Drerup, H. (1969). Griechische Baukunst in geometrischer Zeit. *Archaeologia Homerica* 2, 1–136.

Evans, A. (1912). The Minoan and Mycenaean element in Hellenic life. *Journal of Hellenic Studies* 32, 277–97.

Fagerström, K. (1988). *Greek Iron Age Architecture: Developments through Changing Times.* Stockholm: Paul Åströms Förlag.

Finley, M. I. (1954). *The World of Odysseus.* New York: Viking Press.

(1957). 'Homer and Mycenae: property and tenure.' *Historia: Zeitschrift für Alte Geschichte* 6(2), 133–59.

(1978). *The World of Odysseus*, 2nd rev. ed. London: Penguin.

Foxhall, L. (2007). House clearance: unpacking the 'kitchen' in Classical Greece. In R. Westgate, N. Fisher and J. Whitley, eds., *Building Communities: House, Settlement and Society in the Aegean and Beyond: Proceedings of a*

Conference Held at Cardiff University 17–21 April 2001. London: British School at Athens, 233–42.

Gardner, P. (1882). The palaces of Homer. *Journal of Hellenic Studies* 3: 264–82.

Gill, D. and Flecks, P. (2007). Defining domestic space at Euesperides, Cyrenaica: archaic structures on the Sidi Abeid. In R. Westgate, N. Fisher and J. Whitley, eds., *Building Communities: House, Settlement and Society in the Aegean and Beyond: Proceedings of a Conference Held at Cardiff University 17–21 April 2001*. London: British School at Athens, 205–11

Gladstone, W. E. (1878). Preface. In H. Schliemann, *Mycenae; A Narrative of Researches and Discoveries at Mycenae and Tiryns*. London: John Murray, vi–xxvi.

Gray, D. (1955). Houses in the *Odyssey*. *Classical Quarterly* 5,1–12.

Green, J. R. (1990). Zagora population increase and society in the later eighth century BC. In J.-P. Descoeudres, ed., *Eumousia: Ceramic and Iconographic Studies in Honour of Alexander Cambitoglou*. MeditArch Suppl. no. 1, 41–46.

Hall, J. (2007). *A History of the Archaic Greek World*. Oxford: Blackwell.

(2014). *Artifact and Artifice: Classical Archaeology and the Ancient Historian*. Chicago: University of Chicago Press.

Helbig, W. (1887). *Das homerische Epos aus den Denkmälern erläutert, archäologische Untersuchungen*, 2nd ed. Leipzig: Teubner.

Hemelrijk, J. M. (1972). Review of *Griechische Baukunst in geometrischer Zeit*, by H. Drerup. *Mnemosyne* 25, 110.

Hoepfner, W. (1999). 'Die Epoche dei Griechen.' In W. Hoepfner, ed., *5000 v. chr.– 500 n. chr. Vorgeschichte – Frühgeschichte – Antike*. Stuttgart: Deutsche Verlags-Anstalt, 129–607.

Jameson, M. (1990a). Domestic space in the Greek city-state. In S. Kent, ed., *Domestic Architecture and the Use of Space: An Interdisciplinary Cross Cultural Study*. Cambridge: Cambridge University Press, 92–113.

(1990b). Private space and the Greek city. In O. Murray and S. R. F. Price, eds., *The Greek City: From Homer to Alexander*. Oxford: Clarendon Press, 171–95.

Jebb, R. C. (1886). The Homeric house, in relation to the remains at Tiryns. *Journal of Hellenic Studies* 7, 170–88.

Kontoleon, N. (1953). Ἀνασκαφὴ εν Τήνῳ. *Praktika Tes En Athenais Archaiologikes Etaireias* 1953, 258–67.

Kourou, N. (2002). Tenos – Xobourgo: from a refuge place to an extensive fortified settlement. In M. Stamatopoulou and M. Yeroulanou, eds., *Excavating Classical Culture: Recent Archaeological Discoveries in Greece*. Oxford: Archaeopress, 255–68.

Lang, A. (1906). *Homer and His Age*. London: Longmans, Green, and Company.

Lang, F. (1996). *Archaische Siedlungen in Griechenland: Struktur und Entwicklung*. Berlin: Akademie Verlag.

(2005). Structural change in Archaic Greek housing. In B. A. Ault and L. Nevett, eds., *Ancient Greek Houses and Households*. Philadelphia: University of Pennsylvania Press, 12–35.

(2007). House – community – settlement: the new concept of living in Archaic Greece. In R. Westgate, N. Fisher and J. Whitley, eds., *Building Communities: House, Settlement and Society in the Aegean and Beyond: Proceedings of a Conference Held at Cardiff University 17–21 April 2001*. London: British School at Athens, 183–93.

Leach, E. W. (1997). Oecus on Ibycus: investigating the vocabulary of the Roman house. In S. E. Bon and R. Jones, eds., *Sequence and Space in Pompeii*. Oxford: Oxbow, 50–72.

Lorimer, H. L. (1950). *Homer and the Monuments*. London: Macmillan.

Luce, J. V. (1975). *Homer and the Heroic Age*. London: Thames and Hudson.

Mazarakis-Ainian, A. (2001). From huts to houses in Early Iron Age Greece. In R. Brandt and L. Karlsson, eds., *From Huts to Houses: Transformation of Ancient Societies*. Jonsered: Paul Åströms Förlag, 139–61.

(2006). The archaeology of *Basileus*. In S. Deger-Jalkotzy and I. S. Lemos, eds., *Ancient Greece: From the Mycenaean Palaces to the Age of Homer*. Edinburgh: Edinburgh University Press, 181–211.

(2007). Architecture and social structure in Early Iron Age Greece. In R. Westgate, N. Fisher and J. Whitley, eds., *Building Communities: House, Settlement and Society in the Aegean and Beyond: Proceedings of a Conference Held at Cardiff University 17–21 April 2001*. London: British School at Athens, 157–68.

McDonald, W. A. and Thomas, C. G. (1990). *Progress into the Past: The Rediscovery of Homeric Greece*. Bloomington: Indiana University Press.

Middleton, J. H. (1886). A suggested restoration of the Great Hall in the Palace of Tiryns. *Journal of Hellenic Studies* 7, 161–69.

Morris, I. (1986). The use and abuse of Homer. *Classical Antiquity* 5, 81–138.

(1997). Homer and the Iron Age. In I. Morris and B. Powell, eds., *A New Companion to Homer*. Leiden: Brill, 535–59.

(1998). Archaeology and Archaic Greek history. In N. R. E. Fisher, H. van Wees and D. Dickmann Boedeker, eds., *Archaic Greece: New Approaches and New Evidence*. London: Duckworth, 1–92.

(2000). *Archaeology As Cultural History: Words and Things in Iron Age Greece*. Oxford: Blackwell. Most, G. W., ed. (2007). *Hesiod: The Shield, Catalogue of Women, and Other Fragments*. Loeb Classical Library. Cambridge, MA: Harvard University Press.

Muhly, J. D. (2012). History of research. In E. H. Cline, ed., *The Oxford Handbook of the Bronze Age Aegean (ca. 3000–1000 BC)*. Oxford: Oxford University Press, 3–10.

Myres, J. L. (1900). On the plan of the Homeric House, with special reference to Mykenaian analogies. *Journal of Hellenic Studies* 20, 128–50.

Nevett, L. (1999). *House and Society in the Ancient Greek World*. Cambridge: Cambridge University Press.

(2003). Domestic space as a means of exploring social change: household organisation and the formation of the classical Greek polis. In M. Droste and A. Hoffmann, eds., *Wohnformen und Lebenswelten im interkulturellen Vergleich*. Frankfurt am ain: Peter Lang, 11–20.

(2007). Greek houses as a source of evidence for social relations. In R. Westgate, N. Fisher and J. Whitley, eds., *Building Communities: House, Settlement and Society in the Aegean and Beyond: Proceedings of a Conference Held at Cardiff University 17–21 April 2001*. London: British School at Athens, 5–10.

(2010). *Domestic Space in Classical Antiquity*. Cambridge: Cambridge University Press.

Noack, F. (1903). *Homerische Paläste; eine Studie zu den Denkmälern und zum Epos*. Leipzig: Teubner.

Osborne, R. (2009). *Greece in the Making: 1200–479 BC*, 2nd ed. London: Routledge.

Page, D. L. (1959). *History and the Homeric Iliad*. Berkeley: University of California Press.

(1968). *Lyrica Graeca Selecta*. Oxford: Oxford University Press.

Palmer, L. R. (1948). The Homeric and the Indo-European house. *Transactions of the Philological Society* 47, 92–120.

(1965). *Mycenaeans and Minoans: Aegean Prehistory in the Light of the Linear B Tablets*, 2nd ed. London: Faber and Faber.

Parisinou, E. (2007). Lighting dark rooms: some thoughts about the use of space in early Greek domestic architecture. In R. Westgate, N. Fisher and J. Whitley, eds., *Building Communities: House, Settlement and Society in the Aegean and Beyond: Proceedings of a Conference Held at Cardiff University 17–21 April 2001*. London: British School at Athens, 213–23.

Platon, N. (1955). Ἀνασκαφὴ Ονυθὲ γουλεδιανῶν ρεθύμνης. *Praktika Tes En Athenais Archaiologikes Etaireias* 1955, 298–305.

Raaflaub, K. (1997). Homeric society. In I. Morris and B. Powell, eds., *A New Companion to Homer*. Leiden: Brill, 624–48.

(1998). A historian's headache: how to read 'Homeric Society'? In N. R. E. Fisher, H. van Wees and D. Dickmann Boedeker, eds., *Archaic Greece: New Approaches and New Evidence*. London: Duckworth, 169–94.

(2011). Riding on Homer's chariot: the search for a historical 'epic society'. *Antichthon* 45, 1–34.

Redfield, J. M. (1975). *Nature and Culture in the* Iliad: *The Tragedy of Hector*. Chicago: University of Chicago Press.

Rider, B. C. (1916). *The Greek House*. Cambridge: Cambridge University Press.

Rose, P. W. (2009). Class. In K. A. Raaflaub and H. van Wees eds., *A Companion to Archaic Greece*. Oxford: Blackwell, 468–82.

(2012). *Class in Archaic Greece.* Cambridge: Cambridge University Press.

Rougier-Blanc, S. (2002). Maisons modestes et maisons de héros chez Homère. *Matériaux et techniques. Pallas* 58, 101–15.

(2005). *Les maisons homériques: Vocabulaire architectural et sémantique du bâti.* Etudes d'archéologie classique 13. Paris: Association pour la diffusion de la recherche sur l'Antiquité.

(2009). Remarques sur le vocabulaire architectural chez Hésiode. *Pallas* 81, 43–62.

Schliemann, H. (1885). *Tiryns: The Prehistoric Palace of the Kings of Tiryns.* London: J. Murray.

Schuchhardt, C. (1891). *Schliemann's Excavations: An Archaeological and Historical Study.*,trans. E. Sellers. London: Macmillan.

Snodgrass, A. M. (1974). An historical Homeric society? *Journal of Hellenic Studies* 94, 114–25.

Thomas, C. G. (1966). The roots of Homeric kingship. *Historia: Zeitschrift für Alte Geschichte* 15(4), 387–407.

(1977 [1970]). *Homer's History: Mycenaean or Dark Age?* Huntington, IN: Robert E. Krieger.

Traill, D. A. (1995). *Schliemann of Troy: Treasure and Deceit.* New York: John Murray.

Tsakirgis, B. (2007). Fire and smoke: hearths, braziers and chimneys in the Greek house. In R. Westgate, N. Fisher and J. Whitley, eds., *Building Communities: House, Settlement and Society in the Aegean and Beyond: Proceedings of a Conference Held at Cardiff University 17–21 April 2001.* London: British School at Athens, 225–31.

Ulf, C. (2009). The world of Homer and Hesiod. In Kurt A. Raaflaub and Hans Van Wees, eds., *A Companion to Archaic Greece.* Oxford: Blackwell, 81–99.

Vallet, G., Villard, F. and Auberson, P. (1976). *Mégara Hyblaea I.* Rome: École française de Rome.

Van Wees, H. (1992). *Status Warriors: War, Violence and Society in Homer and History.* Amsterdam: J.C. Gieben.

Wace, A. J. B. (1951). Notes on the Homeric House. *Journal of Hellenic Studies* 71, 203–11.

(1962). Houses and palaces. In A. J. B. Wace and F. H. Stubbings, eds., *A Companion to Homer.* London: Macmillan, 489–97.

Webster, T. B. L. (1964). *From Mycenae to Homer,* 2nd ed. London: Methuen.

2 | Domesticating the Ancient House

The Archaeology of a False Analogy

CASPAR MEYER

Understanding the past is always as much about facing our preconceptions as it is about the surviving evidence and its interpretation.* While such an aphorism would seem misplaced in many other contexts of debate, the study of ancient housing offers plenty of reminders of how deep the preconceptions of historical retrospection run. As I hope to show, modern ideas about what constitutes a home not only affect how we interpret evidence of ancient houses; they determine the very notion of what counts as significant evidence and what kind of story about the past constitutes a competent historical account.

In this chapter, I approach the role of preconception in the study of houses through their evolving representation as sites of domesticity in museums. I have chosen to focus on museums because they present a primary site for articulating interpretations of the past that draw on material and textual sources. Furthermore, they play an important, if understudied, role in relaying such interpretations among a diverse public and in forming an idea of the past as an origin and justification for our own society. Owing to their importance in education, museums impart knowledge about the past – a shared awareness of where we come from and who we are – long before their youngest visitors are able to read about history. For many older visitors, museums provide one of few points of direct contact with the outcomes of specialist academic research based on the integration of textual and material evidence. However, since much of this historical knowledge is conveyed implicitly, through the selection and organization of the exhibits rather than explicit statements, its content is not easily recognized as an outcome of interpretation open to scrutiny and criticism.

A survey of three representative museum displays, ranging from 18th-century Italy to contemporary California, indicates a shift in the nature of the ideal type to which the archaeological finds were assimilated. Over the years, they substituted the models provided by the grandiose estates of monarchs and aristocrats with the home of the Victorian citizen, characterized by its gendered distinctions between private and public. The changing patrons, audiences and objectives of the institutions provide only part of an explanation for that shift, as I hope to demonstrate. Just as important is the appearance in the mid-19th century of a new class of archaeological object – Athenian painted pottery with scenes of 'domestic life' – that allowed ancient homes to be envisioned in the mould of modern domesticity. A closer look at this class reveals its uncertain value as a record of lived reality. The very notion that vase images should depict everyday life depends on distinctions between myth and reality which are extrinsic to the material under consideration and privilege the constructed authenticity of the scenes over the historically situated contexts of pottery consumption. Museum displays which are structured around 'domestic scenes' accordingly turn out to be dependent on definitions of significant action that are aesthetic and, as I aim to show, gendered. On the same grounds, displays based on the distinction between domestic and public promote gender-specific ideas of historical progress and inertia. Such displays draw on false analogical reasoning since a single perceived similarity between past and present is represented as a constant feature of ancient society.

In recent years, archaeologists and historians have grown increasingly sensitive to the contemporary perceptual filters affecting our interpretations of the ancient world. The burgeoning field of household studies in classical scholarship has been pivotal in fostering self-reflexive approaches to archaeological project design, fieldwork and publication, not least because the subject poses particular risks of overdetermined explanation. In most historical settings, 'home' has been too familiar an experience to occasion recognition, let alone critical analysis, of the social and ideological forces that underpin its culture as a contingent formation. The centrality of the home in one's own social cosmos has all too often nurtured the presumption that its foundational values are profoundly human, if not universal. It would be disingenuous to claim that current scholarship is unaware of the risks of prejudgement based on personal experience. A number of studies have demonstrated how modern notions of the home as a highly privatized site of consumption and social reproduction have conditioned earlier interpretations of Greek and Roman household remains to focus on formal criteria of house types and correlate their distinctive features inappropriately with distinct functions and gender divisions.[1] In fact, the dangers of anachronism have been raised so often that a separate contribution devoted to the problem may be felt to require special pleading.

In the conventional definition of historical insight as positive knowledge about the past, nothing is to be gained from contemplating a false analogy. But just as any false analogy is rooted in contemplation of perceived similarities, so the problem of equating ancient houses with domesticity as it is known in the modern West is also related to the broader methodological problem of analogical inference in archaeology and ancient history. However naïve any given instance of analogical thinking may seem, it should never obscure that the past only ever acquires meaning through its relations of similarity and difference to the present.[2] By the same token, any interpretation of past phenomena, be it mediated in texts or artefacts, rests on implicit referential ties to present phenomena. Any interpretation of historical texts or artefacts involves a more or less explicit process of formulating and eliminating hypotheses on the basis of analogy to other artefacts and situations.

To date, Graeco-Roman antiquity has not featured prominently in methodological considerations of analogical inference, in spite (or precisely because) of the manifold opportunities its textual and archaeological sources hold out for comparative study. The goal of this chapter is to highlight some of the benefits which such consideration can bring to the subject. In particular, I intend to show that comparative approaches to artefacts and historical or ethnographic sources pose the same theoretical challenges in so far as the properties that are being compared (1) constitute one observer-determined selection of data out of an infinite number of possible selections, and (2) have either spatial or temporal dimensions, depending on whether the data consist of archaeological assemblages or textual descriptions of processes or practices. A comparative procedure that tests the validity of spatially or temporally distributed analogies equally against a scale of relational complexity is favourable because (1) it makes explicit the observer-centred bias inherent in historical reasoning, and (2) it allows us to compare and contrast the interpretations posited by different disciplinary specialists, working from material assemblages or written sources. A scale of comparison common to historians and archaeologists alike also encourages us to think in a more organized way about the implications of using evidence of household activities from different registers of ideological awareness and intentionality, such as artefactual deposits and visual or textual representations of home life.

For the purpose of this chapter, the analogical deductions that allowed ancient houses to be represented through the lens of modern domesticity are investigated through museum displays concerned with private life in ancient Greece and Rome. Such displays seem to me better suited to reveal the normative assumptions of their time than do contemporaneous scholarly publications. One of the case studies to be considered, the Museo Ercolanese at Naples, was arranged to convey ideas of domesticity at a time when antiquarian folios ordered their material not thematically, but by material, type and, increasingly, on a scale of formal evolution.

The focus on museums also presents advantages for the historiography of modern domesticity, by enabling us to view antiquities as agents of modernization. As a site of non-verbal communication, the museum display endowed modern ideas of the domestic with a quasi-objective dimension and, in so doing, reified its underlying assumptions as historical knowledge. As a result, the interpretations which museums gave rise to also shed light on the 19th-century social transformations associated with industrialization, including the rise of middle-class consciousness and the oppositional definitions of public to private, male to female, and sacred to profane. A museum-centred approach promises to enrich the orthodox accounts of Victorian domestication of households, as exemplified in the scholarship on the 'Separate Sphere' ideology, which has long been criticized for its rigid prioritizing of productive relations over the interdependent connections between materials, consumption and systems of understanding.[3]

Representing Domesticity in Museums

The three displays we will look at come from very different periods and types of institution. The oldest example is the Museo Ercolanese in the Palazzo Reale at Portici, King Charles VII's personal treasure house for the finds excavated at Herculaneum and Pompeii. Opened in 1758, the museum soon became one of Italy's foremost attractions for northern European travellers. The history of the collection and its presentation is plagued by a dearth of contemporary records. Access was strictly regulated, and visitors were forbidden to take any notes or draw the exhibits. The Bourbons reserved the right to publish the finds from the Vesuvian sites in the lavishly illustrated *Antichità di Ercolano Esposte* (eight volumes, 1757–92). Furthermore, the display was constantly enlarged and updated to reflect the progress of the excavations. Agnes Allroggen-Bedel and Helke Kammerer-Grothaus were able to piece together a fairly detailed history of the exhibits' arrangement from unauthorized accounts, especially those of the art historian Johann Joachim Winckelmann and the mathematician Johann Bernoulli. Important information derives also from the inventory lists drawn up when the collection was evacuated during the Revolution of 1789 and eventually, from 1808, transferred to the Museo dei Vecchi Studi in Naples (later Museo Borbonico, now Nazionale).[4]

The second case study is the original incarnation of the Greek and Roman Life Room at the British Museum. Inaugurated in 1908, the 'Life Room', as it came to be known, existed relatively unchanged until its evacuation at the outbreak of World War II and the destruction of the gallery by German bombs.[5] The exhibition was the brainchild of the then Keeper, Cecil Smith, and is well documented thanks to the guidebooks authored by him.[6] Drawing together pieces that had previously lingered in disparate sections of the Department of Greece and Rome, the room was conceived, as the preface to the 1908 guide explains, to 'illustrate the purpose for which the objects were intended, rather than their artistic quality or their place in the evolution of craft or design'. It was a highly successful innovation, as press reviewers noted; the throngs of visitors who flocked to the gallery seemed to value the contrast it offered to the formal display of monuments on the ground floor. As Ian Jenkins pointed out, the interest in everyday life and custom resonated with the recent anthropological trends pioneered by James Frazer, Jane Harrison and the French sociological school of Émile Durkheim.

A third example is the galleries relating to 'Men in Antiquity' and 'Women and Children' that greeted visitors at the Getty Villa in Malibu upon its reopening in January 2006. The story of the villa is too well known to warrant detailed description.[7] A modern-day replica of the *Villa dei Papiri* at Herculaneum, the structure had been commissioned in the late 1960s by the reclusive oil magnate Jean Paul Getty, to accommodate in a suitable setting his expanding art collection and the growing number of visitors who had come to see it at his previous residence at the site. When the collection was moved to the new Getty Center in Brentwood in 1997, the Villa was closed for extensive renovations and transformed into a state-of-the-art museum for Greek and Roman antiquities with purpose-designed galleries, conservation laboratories, research facilities, cafes, a shop, and an amphitheatre.[8] In the process, it became one of a growing number of museums to organize its displays thematically rather than chronologically.[9]

The three institutions may seem too dissimilar to permit comparison. As a site museum of sorts, the Museo Ercolanese derived its character not only from the extraordinary formation processes of Vesuvian archaeology; the comprehensive (if destructive) sampling policies set down by the Bourbon administration also could not have been more different from the art retrieval operations which the British Museum and the Getty Museum encouraged through either third-part prospecting or commercial agents. As private collections, both the Museo Ercolanese and the Getty Villa articulated and legitimated the aspirations of their owners by associating them with a genealogy of enlightened patronage originating with the Roman emperors. In its avowed mission of civilizing its visitors through aesthetic experience, on the other hand, the Getty collection, as conceived by its founder, shares closer affinities with the British Museum. Getty himself discerned the elevating power of art through his highly personal experience of beauty – the connoisseur's love of art that justifies the art of collecting.[10] In the British Museum, the didactic goals favoured by the curators and trustees transpire from the institution's efforts to offer its visitors a comprehensive chronological survey. Such a panoramic presentation remained a long-standing but unfulfilled ambition. Even where the collection would have permitted a strictly chronological survey, its realization was quickly sacrificed if its principles threatened to conflict with the illustration of art's 'perfection' in Classical Greece.[11] The clash between the museum's missions in aesthetic and historical education also comes to the fore in the debates of the 1850s, surrounding the proposed break-up of its collection into separate institutions, with items classed as 'art' (most notably the Parthenon sculptures) being earmarked for transfer to a new national gallery in South Kensington that was under consideration at the time.[12] The British Museum was by no means alone in its struggle for a coherent disciplinary identity. The uneasy combination of historicist and aesthetic principles of display is characteristic of most 'encyclopaedic' museums established in the 19th century. It descends from the equally uneasy, if rhetorically compelling, compromise which Winckelmann struck between historical explanation of the Greeks' privileged conditions and his uninhibited idealization of their art.[13]

Regardless of these divergent aims and modes of acquisition, however, the three institutions operate on the basis of a shared comprehension of objects that is pivotal for understanding the function of museum space. Besides their general historical background and provenance, the objects exhibited in the three collections by and large lack the specific contextual information that would allow us to interpret excavated remains, without relying on contemporary testimonia, in terms of social practices. In the absence of contextual data, the objects were arranged according to a scheme that did not *reproduce* their archaeology but *represented* their presumed meaning. The museum as a space of representation was born in early modern Europe, as a result of the epistemic rift between things and concepts. As Michel Foucault famously argued, following this rupture the meaning of things was no longer understood to be in the objects themselves but in the system of understanding that related visible things to invisible concepts.[14] As systems of understanding were now thought to depend on human rationality rather than divine creation, a gap between things and concepts opened up in which one never quite adequately succeeded in representing the other. The museum came to provide the foremost space for contemplating and trying to resolve this inconsistency between material signifiers and immaterial signifieds. The subject of museum display is consequently less a preferred domain of natural history or antiquity than the dominant system of representation that renders objects meaningful.

In the three case studies I deal with, it was, as a result, not enough to order objects according to formal criteria or presumed function; the displays were also required to explain and control the objects' significatory potential in relation to contemporary values. In the Museo Ercolanese, the intention of conveying ideas of 'home' comes to the fore in the separation between finds considered art and decorative or utilitarian objects. Artworks included the monumental sculpture, reliefs and architectural elements exhibited in the courtyard and the stairway of the palace, and the wall-paintings which were sawn from their original context and set in frames for display in a 'picture' gallery on the ground floor of the Portici Palace.[15] The museum proper, containing the rest of the antiquities, by 1762 occupied almost the entire first floor of the annexe overlooking the Bay of Naples, the Palazzo Caramanico (Figure 2.1).[16] Programmatic features were the triclinium in Room 6 and the reconstructed Pompeian kitchen in the vaulted Room 7, complete with a hearth and cooking utensils suspended from the walls. This dining area appears to have provided a focal point for the exhibits' overall organization and theme. Together with the museum director Camillo Paderni, Winckelmann enjoyed a Roman-style banquet on the stepped, marble-lined construction, using vessels and candelabra from the collection. Without this 'immersive' attraction, it would be difficult to discern whether the museum was meant to offer anything more than a taxonomical and decorative array of finds. Most of the other rooms ordered 'like with like' according to use-shape and material, such as the separate cupboards for lamps and surgical and musical instruments in Room 1, market weights and scales in Room 4, writing equipment and bronze portrait busts in Room 5 and the most prized possessions in Room 10 – jewellery, metal plate and foodstuffs, including bread loaves, flour, grain, beans, figs and dates.[17] From the perspective of later display strategies, the most striking aspect of the museum is the seamless blending of utilitarian instruments and luxury decoration – with ancient floors, candelabra and vessels adorning most of the rooms – and the lack of

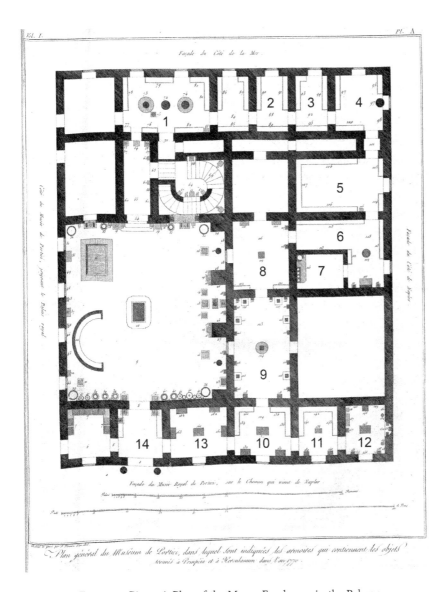

Figure 2.1 Francesco Piranesi. Plan of the Museo Ercolanese in the Palazzo Caramanico at Portici, depicting the cupboards that contain the objects found at Pompeii and Herculaneum, 1803. After *Antiquités de la Grande Grèce, Aujourd'hui Royaume de Naples*, Vol. 1 (Paris, 1807). Etching, 55.5 × 80.5 cm. Universitätsbibliothek Heidelberg.

differentiation between objects relating to production and consumption. In Room 4, the performance of work was even part of the display, as visitors were able to witness Father Antonio Piaggio operating his ingenious apparatus for unrolling papyri.[18]

This blurring between ancient and modern prefigures to some degree the arrangement in the Getty Villa. As at Portici, visitors are cued by the building's architecture to understand the contents as expressions of personal wealth. The proximity of the research facilities, located nearby in Getty's Ranch House, strongly suggests to museumgoers that the specialists who can be seen working there have been enabled to do so by the patron's largesse. The new interior in some respects maintains this personal tenor through the sumptuous marble floors and walls and the Roman-style gallery furniture, but also undercuts it with the sleek museological equipment – display cases, spotlights and didactic signage and labels. The exhibits' thematic organization reveals a similar contrast, with some galleries trying to instruct about everyday life in antiquity, while others are more palpably indebted to the collector's predilections for fine art and consummate craftsmanship.

The clash between the museum's origins in the collector's aesthetic outlook, and the current stewards' ambition to educate, is probably nowhere clearer than in the two large rooms above the Villa's inner peristyle, displaying respectively 'Women and Children' and 'Men in Antiquity' (Figures 2.2 and 2.3).[19] The world of men is presented through objects depicting men the way they wanted to be seen – mostly portraits of various media and formats and figure-decorated pottery, categorized into sub-themes relating to war, work and leisure. Quite the opposite is the case with women, who are frequently represented through figured monuments made for men to look at, among them symposium pottery showing entertainers or stereotyping supposed womanly vices for comic effect (Figure 2.4).[20] The association of women with children is particularly incongruous in the portraits of elite women displayed in the room – such women in antiquity had little to do with the practicalities of childrearing. The odd implications for our understanding of Greek antiquity, of associating women intrinsically with children and childcare, comes to the fore in the red-figure kylix, included in the gallery's display case 'Children in Art', with a paederastic courting scene in its tondo.[21] All in all, the Getty Villa accomplished in these galleries a bourgeois domestication of ancient society by stressing boundaries of gender and age at the expense of the class differences to which the objects speak and isolating explicitly religious antiquities (i.e. statues of gods and goddesses) in separate rooms on the ground floor.

If the modernizing effect of the Getty Villa is implicit yet persistent, its displays transpose into a fine art museum the historicizing principles that had been established earlier on in the Greek and Roman Life Room of the British Museum. The scholarly trends to which the didactic intentions behind the original Life Room of 1908 responded have been remarked

Figure 2.2 Women and Children in Antiquity. Interior of gallery 207 in the Getty Villa refurbished by Rodolpho Machado and Jorge Silvetti (1993–2005). The J. Paul Getty Museum, Villa Collection, Malibu, California, 2007

upon by Jenkins.[22] Its innovative documentary purpose is especially clear from the inclusion in the display of photographs, casts and other reproductions of objects held elsewhere in the museum or in other institutions, as well as from the strict organization of the exhibits into sections (Figure 2.5). Although the individual artefact groups may be seen to fall quite 'naturally' into classes of purpose, as the guidebook states,[23] the same claim does not hold for the binary division of the gallery space into public and domestic. Why should ancient religion and industry be classified into either of these divisions? What was 'public' about the arms and armour of the many citizen militias of antiquity? And most perplexingly, how did women become prisoners of the domestic sphere?

'Where Stories Have No Plot': Domesticity as a Problem of Narration

The three museum displays we have looked at demonstrate that the boundary between public and private in the reception of Greek and

Figure 2.3 Men in Antiquity. Interior of gallery 209 in the refurbished Getty Villa. The J. Paul Getty Museum, Villa Collection, Malibu, California, 2007

Roman antiquities acquired its central importance fairly recently. In the Museo Ercolanese, it was of no concern; by the time the first Life Room at the British Museum was inaugurated, the dichotomy between public and private had become the explicit organizing principle. It supported the presentation of homes as a secular sphere, the domain of women, children, semi-durable consumables (furniture, dress, etc.), as well as home industry, agricultural production, crafts and exchange. The particular alignment this division took, both at the British Museum and the Getty Villa, cannot be termed historically accurate in relation to either Greece or Rome, let alone the whole of antiquity. To understand its origins we need to recognize not

Figure 2.4 Elderly woman guzzling wine from a large skyphos while her maid is looking on in embarrassment. The reverse of the vessel shows the interior of a household storeroom. Athenian red-figure skyphos, 460s BCE. H 15.3 cm, D 18.8 cm. Malibu, Getty Villa Inv. 86.AE.265. Digital image courtesy of the Getty's Open Content program

PUBLIC LIFE.		**PRIVATE LIFE.**	
I.	Politics and Slavery.	X.	House and Furniture.
II.	Coins.	XI.	Dress and Toilet.
III.	Marriage.	XII.	Weights and Measures.
IV.	Religion and Superstition.	XIII.	Tools and Building.
V.	Drama.	XIV.	Domestic Arts.
VI.	Athletics.	XV.	Industrial Arts.
VII.	Chariot-racing and the Circus.	XVI.	Medicine and Surgery.
VIII.	Gladiators and the Arena.	XVII.	Painting.
IX.	Arms and Armour.	XVIII.	Education, Toys and Games.
		XIX.	Horses and Chariots.
		XX.	Agriculture.
		XXI.	Shipping.
		XXII.	Music and Dancing.
		XXIII.	Methods of Burial.

Figure 2.5 List of sections comprised in the exhibition of antiquities in the Greek and Roman Life Room at the British Museum. After Smith 1908: 1–2

only how industrialization and the concomitant changes in class consciousness affected attitudes to the home (e.g. the rise of Separate Sphere ideology
mentioned above), but also how the archaeology available at the time
allowed the past to be drawn upon as a resource to corroborate the present.

If the 19th century was the period of archaeological discovery par
excellence, no discovery has arguably had such a profound impact on
modern accounts of ancient domesticity as the multitude of Athenian
painted pottery showing so-called scenes of life. To be sure, 18th-century
antiquarians had already been widely familiar with Greek finewares; but it
was only with the excavations in the Etruscan cemeteries from 1828, when
the later red-figure pottery found in South Italy and Sicily was supple-
mented with Athenian black-figure and early red-figure, that the relevant
material attained a critical mass and the scenes of life entered scholarly
awareness as a separate class.[24] The significance of pottery with 'illustrations of ancient life' is also stressed in the arrangement of exhibits in the
current Life Room at the British Museum, as its author emphasizes: 'Topics
of anthropological nature – "Children", "Women", "Marriage", "Burial
Customs" – have a strong Greek bias, because of the light shed upon them
by vase-painting.'[25] The staggering range of scenes that seem to show the
specifics of the quotidian has often been commented on: eating, drinking,
sex, sacrifice, weddings, funerals, men leaving for war, women going about
household chores, athletics, education, agricultural labour, game hunting,
workshop activities and so on. Taken together, the corpus develops a
discourse of the real from which notions of domesticity emerge through
recurrent associations between gender and space and, as we shall see, the
temporal characterization of the depicted occurrences as episodic and
unremarkable rather than unrepeatable.

The scenes that are most commonly cited to illustrate ancient domesticity show women in interior spaces occupied with various tasks. In early
(Archaic) red-figure painting, women are engaged in wool-working, food-
production and childcare. In later red-figure, from the 430s BCE, the range
of depicted activities is increasingly narrow, with most scenes focusing on
body care, self-adornment and wedding preparations. The interior setting
is evoked by indexical signs – implements painted on the plain background, as if suspended from a wall, as well as furniture, doors, columns
and the different states of casual dress or undress.[26] It is easy to see how
such depictions of domestic bliss appealed to Victorian sensibilities. They
seem to bridge the chasm of time in an unproblematic way, intimating that
things back then were how they were supposed to be – in good order. It is
also easy to see why they came to be viewed as straightforward historical

documents, given that so many of these pictures bring to mind the kind of gendered segregation we hear about in the discourse of the *gynaikōnitis* ('women's quarters') in classical sources.[27] On the basis of this correspondence between texts and images, it is all too tempting to conclude that the metonymic relation between women and homes in visual representation signified domesticity in ancient life.

Household archaeology has demonstrated beyond doubt that the spatial organization of classical homes could not have been as rigid as some sources have led scholars to believe.[28] Concurrently, studies of vase-painting have shown that the visual definition of homes as the site of female privacy was a convention propagated on specific pot shapes, for specific audiences and limited periods. Other pots seem to challenge this convention with images of men indoors and women (not necessarily prostitutes or slaves) engaging in a range of occupational, leisurely and religious tasks, sometimes outside the house and alongside men.[29] In view of the full pictorial diversity of image types, the category of the 'domestic scene' reveals considerable bias. It amounts to a subjective selection out of an infinite number of possible selections, the consequence of classification on the basis of implicit criteria conditioned by modern expectations.

The problem of domestic scenes in Athenian vase-painting is a sub-species of the larger problem of everyday scenes in classical representation. The status of such representations between ideology and practice mostly remains an unacknowledged issue. On the one hand, scholars introduce discussions of such material habitually by pointing out that vase images do not provide 'snapshots' of ancient life; but when they set about writing history from these images they tend, despite all caution, to indulge in the impossible pursuit of extracting lived reality from ideological representation. The resulting situation is contradictory, with different scholars invoking an expedient selection of images to support competing models of ancient behaviour. Debates converge on those manifestations of gender and sexuality (same-sex courting and consummation, in addition to gender segregation) where there is most at stake, morally or legally, in having the ancient Greeks as a precedent for modern-day aspirations. In some cases, opposing historical propositions are built on the very same set of images, as is the case with the scenes of women fetching water at a fountain house. Almost eighty examples of the subject are known from Athenian black-figure painting, chiefly on hydriae (vessels for carrying water) dating between 520 and 480 BCE.[30] Most recently, Lisa Nevett has argued that these scenes, in combination with the archaeological and textual evidence for the construction of fountain houses in Archaic Athens, confirm that even freeborn women enjoyed significantly more freedom of movement than the norm of gender segregation familiar from textual accounts would have us expect.[31] Previously, Gloria Ferrari had argued that the fantastical elements that appear on many of the vases – such as the fawns, the luscious vegetation, the inscribed 'speaking names', and the figures of Dionysus and Hermes included in a fountain house scene on a hydria in London – are more easily explained as an imaginative depiction of Athens' mythical past, at the prehistoric Callirhoe fountain.[32] In this explanation, the scenes are understood to reflect Athenian beliefs about the ancestral past. It appears that at the time these pots were painted at least some Athenians had come to believe that the primitive social differentiation that had supposedly prevailed in early Athens had permitted practices opposed to those of the present, in particular in relation to women. By implication, Ferrari's interpretation maintains the norm of relative female seclusion in Archaic and Classical Greece.

Nevett's matter-of-fact approach shows little regard for consistency. She isolates, in accordance with a predetermined argument, pictorial traits that may be compatible with lived reality from a general combination that could not have drawn on visible reality. Images cannot be idealizing and somehow realistic at the same time. If we submit to this illusion and dissect images selectively into pictorial elements that support our arguments, while disregarding others that contradict our favoured explanation, we risk assimilating the data to the explanatory model rather than vice versa. In other words, we risk misconstruing ancient behaviour on the basis of a false analogy, for the purpose of countering a specific historiographical consensus.

Far from rejecting the intention of 'reading against the grain', however, I would hold that household archaeology has not yet gone far enough in realizing its destabilizing potential. The assumption that Athenian depictions of women fetching water allow us to catch a glimpse of actual Athenian women deviating from the norms of society exemplifies the broader assumption that archaeology can reveal everyday practice in pristine form, beyond the distortions inflicted by norms. Where archaeology fails to achieve this goal, the reasons are according to this view to be sought in the failure of properly investigating the stratigraphy, spatial organization, assemblages and formation processes of ancient houses. Yet on reflection, it is undeniable that every activity, however mundane its task, is dependent on situational factors. Different activities may differ in their degree of intentionality and performativity, which in turn depend on such criteria as visibility, duration and ritual necessity, but never take place outside the constraints of social conditioning, regardless of whether the given norms are being maintained or subverted in a particular instance. Even if archaeology could substantiate that women in ancient Greece regularly ventured outside their homes (as they certainly did) we cannot be sure whether they perceived themselves, in their subjective awareness, to have entered the same public space as the men around them going about their civic duties.[33]

If archaeology does not have privileged access to ancient reality, the different convergences between ideology and practice that are embodied in material remains nevertheless provide new opportunities for understanding how everyday experiences were shaped and maintained. These opportunities can be explored either from synchronic or diachronic perspectives. In synchronic approaches, the material is examined with a focus on the discrepancies it reveals internally and in relation to other registers of representation, such as texts, whereas diachronic perspectives concentrate on the possibilities which antiquity provides for self-identification in the present. To remain with our example of 'domesticity' in Greek art, synchronous examination of household scenes in different media and contexts demonstrates that in the collective representation of some Athenians (and presumably other Greek communities) the symbolic articulation of the public–private opposition was indeed aligned with the gender opposition between male and female. At the same time, a closer look at the inconsistencies in surviving images reveals that the opposition originated in ideals that could not have corresponded to visible reality.

To illustrate such discrepancies, we may turn to the example of Athenian white *lekythoi* showing a couple bidding farewell (Figure 2.6).[34] In scenes of this type, normally thought to have been produced for graves commemorating a deceased spouse, the man is depicted in various states of outdoor dress or nudity, while the woman is shown as being indoors, as is indicated by the furniture and the household equipment in the background. The man is already out of the house where he belongs, whereas the woman is right next to him but symbolically enclosed in ideal domesticity. Although the figures may look lifelike to us, the images portray conventional types and settings, not particular individuals in a particular moment of time. Temporal consistency was disregarded so as to highlight the gendered dichotomy, or 'matrimonial harmony', between public and private. The same strategy of representation can be found on 4th-century BCE sculpted grave reliefs with men shown as being outdoors, sporting military or gymnastic equipment, but standing next to their wives, who are portrayed barefoot and clothed as quintessential denizens of the house.[35]

Figure 2.6 a, b (a) Arming and departure for war. The scene shows a woman seated on a *klismos* before a man holding a Corinthian helmet in his right hand and a shield and spear in his left. (b) Athenian white *lekythos* attributed to the Achilles Painter. From Eretria. 430s BCE. H. of vessel 42.6 cm. Athens, National Museum Inv. 1818

Figure 2.7 Circe offers her skyphos with potion to Odysseus. The effects of her magic are exemplified by the boar-headed companion to the left, fleeing the scene in dismay. Athenian black-figure *lekythos*, 480s BCE. H. of vessel 29 cm. After Sellers 1893: pl. 2. Athens, National Museum Inv. 1133

In scenes representing traditional stories, the contrast between indoors and outdoors could assume a narrative function, characterizing the moral status of the actions and the figures depicted. On a black-figure *lekythos* of the early 5th century BCE, for instance, the sorceress Circe rises from her *diphros* to offer her enchanted potion to Odysseus, who is seated on a rock, holding his spears and wearing the shoes and cap of a travelling hero (Figure 2.7).[36] While spatially incoherent, the juxtaposition of indoors and outdoors explains the episode by way of an ethical contrast, playing on male anxieties about female secrecy, seduction and subterfuge.

A diachronic approach to the same scenes entails a shift in focus away from their past existence to their presence as a materialized order of meaning. To put it differently, in adopting a diachronic perspective the aim is less to understand the historical changes that households experienced in antiquity than to change the way we evaluate the home as a sphere of meaningful human interaction. To adopt such an approach, we need to realize that the 'everyday scenes' in modern accounts of Classical Greece are a default category originally devised to rationalize the vase-paintings from Etruscan cemeteries whose pictorial content was more easily identified by reference to general ideas about contemporary life rather than specific stories familiar from texts. The category therefore is a function of the division of ancient representations as being either mythical or generic, a division which Ferrari has shown to be anachronistic.[37] In trying to resolve this fallacy, however, she introduced a classification according to 'narrative capacity', which is by now commonplace among historians of Greek art, but no less problematic. To evaluate a scene's narrative capacity more often than not means to apply a binary categorization into either narrative or non-narrative. The criteria of this classification are derived from the key authors of modern structuralist analysis, such as Roland Barthes and Tzvetan Todorov. They require us to determine whether the episode depicted could serve as a hinge-point in a narrative – whether the event asserts a teleological tension or the capacity to bring about structural change in the social conditions that define the portrayed event as a crisis.[38]

The criteria at first sight appear to be neutral but in actual fact go back (or are at least analogous to) Aristotle's aesthetic analysis of dramatic plots. Aristotle presents his basic definition of tragic plot in the opening of chapter 7 of his *Poetics*, stressing that it must be (1) complete (*teleia*), (2) whole (*olē*) and (3) of 'a certain magnitude' (*echousē ti megethos*).[39] None of his criteria can be said to be independent of cultural norms. His stress on the unity of the represented action is later on (1451a11–15) more closely specified as a course of action experienced by a protagonist in a fairly limited timespan, during which the agent's condition is reversed either from prosperity to adversity or vice versa. The stress on the teleological consequences of narrated actions is the critical overlap between Aristotelian and structuralist plot analysis. Yet, it is still not clear why this criterion of emplotted life-reversal should in principle valorize acts committed by heroic men but devalue as non-narrative or episodic such familiar events as a communal meal or the birth of a child. The key comes from Aristotle's definition of action (*praxis*) outlined in his *Ethics* (iii, 2, 111b8–10, 1139a31) as a self-directed movement requiring the agent's choice or deliberation about ends (*prohairesis*). As Cynthia Freeland has demonstrated, this stress on choice explains why Aristotle's theory prefers as best plots those structured around agent-centred 'moral-luck' (i.e. a noble protagonist with freedom of choice, erring due to some failure or ignorance of fact) rather than those in which characters suffer due to actions and circumstances beyond their control.[40] The criterion of wholeness and completeness in representations of action turns out to be about ethical perceptions of human volition. The stress on volition in most historical circumstances has meant (at least until Bertolt Brecht's conception of epic theatre) that representations of male agency were judged as being a priori different and better than those focusing on characters (usually female) who have little choice or are the victims of more powerful agents.

Aristotle's insistence on dramatic unity provided the grounding not only for modern poetological theory but also for Western academic painting from the 16th century.[41] In the realm of pictorial representation, the stress on unity of action resulted in the aesthetic and pedagogical canons that prioritized agent-centred dynamism, monochronic consistency and perspectival effects, as familiar from the grand tradition of history painting. Until the demise of academic art in the 20th century, history painting was ranked as the most accomplished genre, requiring the master to select and fashion key moments from history to create the illusion of sublime presence. The relation in art between history painting and lesser genres is analogous to that between textual representations that recount the past in a narrative form and those that openly adopt a perspective in reporting the past. As Hayden White has emphasized, the difference between historical representations that narrativize the past by leading it to a dramatic resolution and those that resist imposing the structures of stories on past events has less to do with the modes of objective perception which historical narrative presupposes than with the refusal of non-narrative modes 'to represent the *moral* under the aspect of the *aesthetic*'.[42] For the same reason of implicit moral judgement, the concept of narrative capacity in modern studies of vase-painting is dependent on the ethical criteria set out by Aristotle, or the bodily attributes and dynamics of the depicted figures that manifest freedom of choice aesthetically.[43]

These criteria may well be historically correct, in the sense that many ancient viewers interpreted the significance of actions represented on pots against norms of narrative closure similar to Aristotle's. But this historical consistency should not be taken to imply that all ancient viewers understood images through such criteria or that those criteria should be transubstantiated in modern scholarship and museum displays as a seemingly neutral presentation of historical reality. That presentation, as we have seen, depends to a considerable extent on visual representations in Athenian vase-painting and the classification of those images according to clear-cut distinctions as being either narrative or non-narrative in nature. Narrativity, after all, is the taxonomical principle which guided the allocation of objects in the British Museum and the Getty Villa into galleries exhibiting significant public action or the 'inconsequential' processes germane to the private sphere. If Greek vase images were as critical as my sample survey of museum displays suggests in defining the ancient house as a domestic domain in the modern sense (as a privatized and secular sphere, populated by women and subordinate to the public sphere), then the domestication of the ancient household may originate not just in false analogical inferences from modern conditions; the very category of the domestic that emerged in the modern West in the course of the 19th century in fact perpetuates androcentric conceptions of dramatic plot transmitted in ostensibly gender-neutral forms in classical art and narratological theory.

In flagging the modern-day ramifications of our categories of interpretation, scholarship does not renounce its academic commitment to historical truth. On the contrary, to acknowledge the bias inherent in any explanation of antiquity is tantamount to acknowledging the historical fact that already in antiquity different audiences looked at ancient vases and appraised the scenes depicted on them in ways not necessarily intended by the artists or their patrons. The interpretative habits of the dominant group of commissioners and purveyors are not the whole historical truth. Museums of course cannot avoid adopting a particular classificatory scheme in ordering their displays but, rather than presenting its classes as self-evident and natural, we would do better – for the sake of academic integrity – to make explicit the subjective nature of its criteria. With regard to the vase images of everyday activities, the decision whether a given example belongs to the default category of non-narrative scenes should not be presented as a foregone conclusion but as an open-ended question – one that requires the viewer to compare different forms of representation and question their ethical direction and context of use, and allows her or him to recognize the multiple projections of reality that constitute social awareness at any one point in time. The goal of such a presentation of history is not to falsify one or the other source of evidence, but to communicate the diversity of past experiences and clarify the links between them. For the same reason, our histories of antiquity are poorly served if the realm of the house is treated as a disconnected strand, juxtaposing the 'subaltern' to conventional accounts instead of highlighting the intricate web of connections between less accessible voices and the dominant voice of ancient historiography.

In this chapter, I have tied together different forms of representation from museums and vase-painting to elucidate their decisive role at the juncture between present and past by allowing the material and textual legacies of ancient housing to be re-scripted through the prism of modern domesticity. The work which ancient and modern representations are made to perform in the production of knowledge draws on the mutual conjunctions between visual and verbal orders of meaning – between the apparent truths of naturalistic images and the unspoken assumptions of morality and habituation. Its effects are as subtle as they are pervasive, establishing which aspect of the past is assigned significance and what kind of occurrence warrants inclusion into an authoritative historical narrative. In a framework that values aesthetic integrity above experiential variety, the routines of home life will always appear less interesting than the spectacle of high-risk outdoor pursuits. The textual and material sources of classical antiquity offer abundant possibilities to show that in real-life situations one aspect of society cannot do without the other. Accounts that pretend otherwise are built on false analogies which enlist a segmental view of the past to fortify an equally partisan view of the present.

Notes

* I thank Alexandra Villing (British Museum) and David Saunders (Getty Villa) for providing information on the history of the displays in their institutions. David Saunders and Abi Baker have read and commented on draft versions of this chapter. All remaining errors and misrepresentations are my own. During the gestation of this volume the display of Greek and Roman art in the Getty Villa was reorganized, and the thematic arrangement discussed in this chapter abandoned for a chronological one (see Potts 2018 for discussion).

1 See especially Allison 1999, 2004, Cahill 2002. The most extensive historiographical critique is Spencer-Wood 1999: 162–89.

2 Wylie 1985 remains fundamental for any discussion of the problems and possibilities of analogy in archaeological interpretation.

3 Wolff 1988: 117–34; cf. Vickery 1993.

4 Allroggen-Bedel and Kammerer-Grothaus 1980, cf. Bernoulli 1778. More recently on the museum, see Represa Fernández 1988; Mattusch 2005: 55–61; D'Alconzo 2009: 351–58.

5 For further discussion of the first and two later versions, see Jenkins 1982, 1986a, 1986b.

6 Smith 1908, revised editions 1920 and 1923.

7 On the Villa's history, see Lapatin 2005: 9–27, 2010: 129–38, 2011: 270–85. For a review of the reopened museum, see Moltesen 2007: 155–59.

8 True and Silvetti 2005.

9 The director of the Getty Museum announced plans to reinstall the villa's collection along cultural-historical lines shortly after this chapter had been submitted for publication (see Potts 2015). The new display opened to the public in April 2018 (see Potts 2018).

10 See Getty 1976: 277: 'Twentieth-century barbarians cannot be transformed into cultured, civilized human beings until they acquire an appreciation and love for art. The transformation cannot take place until they have had the opportunity

to be exposed to fine art – to see, begin to understand and finally to savor and marvel.' Also cited in Lapatin 2010: 129.

11 Jenkins 1992: 56–74; cf. Elsner 1996.

12 Jenkins 1992: 198–205; Whitehead 2009.

13 Wyss 1999: 104–10; Siapkas and Sjögren 2013: 18–111.

14 Foucault 2002, with discussion in Lord 2006.

15 Mattusch 2005: 57–58.

16 Winckelmann (1952: 362) counted some sixteen rooms on his second visit to the museum in 1762, and Bernoulli (1775, cf. 1778: 153–270) describes eighteen rooms in his report first published in 1775.

17 Bernoulli 1778: 235–37, 239.

18 Fackelmann 1970, cf. Harris 2007: 44–61.

19 The displays described here have recently been disbanded: see note 10.

20 E.g. Inv. 82.AE.14 (red-figure kylix attributed to Onesimos, showing naked female banqueter), Inv. 90.AE.122 (black-figure *mastos* cup showing a 'flute-girl'), Inv. 86.AE.265 (red-figure skyphos depicting a double-chinned, overweight woman raiding the domestic storeroom for wine). All these examples are admittedly confined to a single display case.

21 Inv. 86.AE.290: red-figure cup attributed to Douris.

22 Jenkins 1982, 1986a.

23 Smith 1908: preface.

24 On the discovery of Vulci, see Nørskov 2009: 63–76. The category of everyday scenes received its first extended study in Panofka 1843. For critical examination, see Bažant 1980, 1981: 13–22; Ferrari 2002: 1–10, 2003.

25 Jenkins 1986a: 69.

26 For an overview, see Lewis 2002: 130–71.

27 E.g. Xenophon, *Oec.* 9. 5, *Symp.* 1. 4; Lysias 1. 9–10, with recent discussion in Davidson 2011: 599–601. The gendered division of Greek houses is stated as fact in the guide to the Life Room, without further reference; see Smith 1908: 106–107.

28 Nevett 1995, 1999: 12–20, 68–74, 154–55; Foxhall 2013: 24–44.

29 Lewis 2002: 83–129, 172–209; cf. Dillon 2002, Connelly 2007, Eaverly 2013.

30 For a collection of examples, see Manakidou 1992.

31 Nevett 2011: 582.

32 Ferrari 2003: 45–50, with Thucydides 2. 15. 3–6. The hypothesis that some Athenian vase images derive from intentional anachronism is further developed by Topper 2009, 2012. For other interpretations treating the scenes either as emblematic projections or as cult-related, see Manfrini-Aragno 1992: 127–48; Pfisterer-Haas 2002; Schmidt 2005: 232–46; Sabetai 2009: 103–14.

33 See Davidson 2011: 607–11, with reference to the practice and meaning of veiling, as studied by Llewellyn-Jones 2003.

34 Surveyed in Oakley 2004: 57–68.

35 See for instance the large *naiskos* from the peribolos of Hierokles from Rhamnous, juxtaposing an indoor and an outdoor scene within the same architectural frame. The original publication surmised that the apparent incongruity must result from a workshop error rather than contemporary pictorial conventions; see Petrakos 1999: I, 396. Another relevant case is the stele in Budapest, Museum of Fine Arts (Inv. 6259), placing alongside each other a nude mature man with athletic equipment and a chlamys, and his fully clothed wife; cf. Hallett 2005: 29, pl. 15.

36 Athens, National Museum Inv. 1133, Carpenter 1989: 260; Giuliani 2013: 160, fig. 37.

37 Ferrari 2003: 38–39.

38 E.g. Barthes 1975, Todorov 1990: 27–38.

39 Aristotle, *Poet.* 1450b24–27: 'We have stipulated that tragedy is mimesis of an action that is complete, whole, and of magnitude (for one can have a whole which lacks magnitude). A whole is that which has a beginning, middle and end' (tr. Halliwell),

40 Freeland 1992: 114–17, 126–27, with Curran 1998: 289–326.

41 Tomasi Velli 2007, cf. Giuliani 2013: 10–15.

42 White 1980: 27.

43 For visual narrative defined explicitly in Aristotelian terms, see Giuliani 2013 15–17. One of few classical archaeologists who explore the narrative potential of descriptive scenes on vases is Stansbury-O'Donnell 1999: 44–53; cf. Kannicht 1982 for methodological considerations.

References

Allison, P. M. (ed.) (1999). *The Archaeology of Household Activities*. London: Routledge.

(2004). *Pompeian Households: An Analysis of the Material Culture*. Los Angeles: Cotsen Institute of Archaeology, University of California.

Allroggen-Bedel, A. and Kammerer-Grothaus, H. (1980). Das Museum Ercolanese in Portici. *Cronache Ercolanesi* 10, 175–217.

Barthes, R. (1975). An introduction to the structural analysis of narrative. *New Literary History* 6(2), 237–72.

Bažant, J. (1980). Classical archaeology and French nineteenth-century realists. *Listy filologické* 103(4), 193–201.

(1981). *Studies on the Use and Decoration of Athenian Vases*. Prague: Academia.

Bernoulli, J. (1775). *Beschreibung des Herkulan. Musäums nach den Zimmern. Neue Bibliothek der schönen Wissenschaften und der freyen Künste* 17.1, 77–87.

(1778). *Zusätze zu der neuesten Reisebeschreibungen von Italien nach der in Herrn D. J. J. Volkmanns historisch-kritischen Nachrichten angenommenen Ordnung zusammengetragen* Vol. II, Leipzig.

Cahill, N. (2002). *Household and City Organization at Olynthus*. New Haven and London: Yale University Press.

Carpenter, T. H. (1989). *Beazley Addenda: Additional References to ABV, ARV2 & Paralipomena*. Oxford: Oxford University Press.

Connelly, J. (2007). *Portrait of a Priestess: Women and Ritual in Ancient Greece*. Princeton: Princeton University Press.

Curran, A. (1998). Feminism and the narrative structures of the poetics. In C. Freeland, ed., *Feminist Interpretations of Aristotle*. University Park, PA: Pennsylvania State University Press, 289–326.

D'Alconzo, P. (2009). Das Herculanense Museum in Portici. In S. Pisani and K. Siebenmorgen Reimer, eds., *Neapel: Sechs Jahrhunderte Kulturgeschichte*. Berlin: Reimer, 351–58.

Davidson, J. (2011). Bodymaps: sexing space and zoning gender in ancient Athens. *Gender & History* 23(3), 597–614.

Dillon, M. (2002). *Girls and Women in Classical Greek Religion*. London: Routledge.

Eaverly, M. A. (2013). *Tan Men/Pale Women: Color and Gender in Archaic Greece and Egypt. A Comparative Approach*. Ann Arbor: University of Michigan Press.

Elsner, J. (1996). The 'new museology' and classical art. *American Journal of Archaeology* 100, 769–73.

Fackelmann, A. (1970). The restoration of the Herculaneum Papyri and other recent finds. *Bulletin of the Institute of Classical Studies* 17, 144–47.

Ferrari, G. (2002). *Figures of Speech: Men and Maidens in Ancient Greece*. Chicago: University of Chicago Press.

(2003). Myth and genre on Athenian vases. *Classical Antiquity* 22(1), 37–54.

Foucault, M. (2002). *The Order of Things: An Archaeology of the Human Sciences*. London: Routledge.

Foxhall, L. (2013). *Studying Gender in Classical Antiquity*. Cambridge: Cambridge University Press.

Freeland, C. (1992). Plot imitates action: aesthetic evaluation and moral realism in Aristotle's *Poetics*. In A. Rorty, ed., *Essays on Aristotle's Poetics*. Princeton: Princeton University Press, 111–32.

Getty, J. P. (1976). *As I See It: The Autobiography of J. Paul Getty*. London: W. H. Allen.

Giuliani, L. (2013). *Image and Myth: A History of Pictorial Narration in Greek Art*. Chicago: University of Chicago Press.

Hallett, C. H. (2005). *The Roman Nude: Heroic Portrait Statuary, 200 BC–AD 300*. Oxford: Oxford University Press.

Harris, J. (2007). *Pompeii Awakened: A Story of Rediscovery*. London: I.B. Tauris.

Jenkins, I. (1982). The British Museum and its Life Rooms: a postscript. Hesperiam. *Journal of the Joint Association of Classical Teachers* 5, 33–48.

(1986a). Greek and Roman life at the BM. *Museums Journal* 86(2), 67–69.

(1986b). *Greek and Roman Life*. London: British Museum Publications for the Trustees of the British Museum.

(1992). *Archaeologists & Aesthetes in the Sculpture Galleries of the British Museum, 1800–1939*. London: Trustees of the British Museum.

Kannicht, R. (1982). Poetry and art: Homer and the monuments afresh. *Classical Antiquity* 1, 70–86.

Lapatin, K. (2005). *Guide to the Getty Villa*. Malibu, CA: J. Paul Getty Museum.

(2010). The Getty Villa: recreating the Villa of the Papyri in Malibu. In M. Zarmakoupi, ed., *The Villa of the Papyri at Herculaneum: Archaeology, Reception and Digital Reconstruction*. Berlin: De Gruyter, 129–38.

(2011). The Getty Villa: art, architecture, and aristocratic self-fashioning in the mid-twentieth century. In S. Hales and J. Paul, eds., *Pompeii in the Public Imagination from Its Rediscovery to Today*. Oxford: Oxford University Press, 270–85.

Lewis, S. (2002). *The Athenian Woman: An Iconographic Handbook*. London: Routledge.

Llewellyn-Jones, L. (2003). *Aphrodite's Tortoise: The Veiled Woman of Ancient Greece*. Swansea: Classical Press of Wales.

Lord, B. (2006). Foucault's museum: difference, representation, and genealogy. *Museum and Society* 4, 1–14.

Manakidou, E. (1992). Athenerinnen in schwarzfigurigen Brunnenhausszenen. *Hephaistos* 11, 51–91.

Manfrini-Aragno, I. (1992). Femmes à la fontaine: réalité et imaginaire. In Ch. Bron and E. Kassapoglou, eds., *L'Image en jeu: De l'Antiquité à Paul Klee*. Lausanne: Institut d'archéologie et d'histoire ancienne, Université de Lausanne, 127–48.

Mattusch, C. (2005). *The Villa dei Papiri at Herculaneum: Life and Afterlife of a Sculpture Collection*. Los Angeles: J. Paul Getty Museum.

Moltesen, M. (2007). The reopened Getty Villa. *American Journal of Archaeology* 111, 155–59.

Nevett, L. (1995). Gender relations in the classical Greek household: the archaeological evidence. *Annual of the British School at Athens* 90, 363–81.

(1999). *House and Society in the Ancient Greek World*. Cambridge: Cambridge University Press.

(2011). Towards a female topography of the ancient Greek city: case studies from late archaic and early classical Athens (c.520–400 BCE). *Gender & History* 23(3), 576–96.

Nørskov, V. (2009). The affairs of Lucien Bonaparte and the impact on the study of Greek vases. In V. Nørskov, L. Hannestad, C. Isler-Kerényi and S. Lewis, eds., *The World of Greek Vases*. Rome: Edizioni Quasar, 63–76.

Oakley, J. H. (2004). *Picturing Death in Classical Athens: The Evidence of the White Lekythoi*. Cambridge: Cambridge University Press.

Panofka, T. (1843). *Bilder antiken Lebens*. Berlin.

Petrakos, V. Ch. (1999). *Ho dēmos tou Ramnountos: synopsē tōn anaskaphōn kai tōn ereunōn (1813–1998)*. Athens: Hē en Athēnais Archaiologikē Hetaireia.

Pfisterer-Haas, S. (2002). Mädchen und Frauen am Wasser. Brunnenhaus und Louterion als Orte der Frauengemeinschaft und der möglichen Begegnung mit einem Mann. *Jahrbuch des Deutschen Archäologischen Instituts* 117, 1–79.

Potts, T. (2015). Letter from Los Angeles. *Apollo*, February issue: www.apollo-magazine.com/letter-february-apollo-los-angeles.

(2018). A new vision for the collection of the Getty Villa. *Iris*, 2 April: https://blogs.getty.edu/iris/a-new-vision-for-the-collection-at-the-getty-villa.

Represa Fernández, M. F. (1988). *El Real Museo de Portici (Nàpoles) 1750–1825: aproximación al conocimiento de la restauración, organización y presentación de sus fondos. Studi Archaeologica* 79. Valladolid: Universidad de Valladolid.

Sabetai, V. (2009). The poetics of maidenhood: visual constructs of womanhood in vase-painting, In S. Schmidt and J. H. Oakley, eds., *Hermeneutik der Bilder: Beiträge zur Ikonographie und Interpretation griechischer Vasenmalerei, CVA Deutschland Beiheft 4*. Munich: C.H. Beck, 103–14.

Schmidt, S. (2005). *Rhetorische Bilder auf attischen Vasen: Visuelle Kommunikation im 5. Jahrhundert v. Chr.* Berlin: Reimer.

Sellers, E. (1893). Three Attic lekythoi from Eretria. *Journal of Hellenic Studies* 13, 1–12.

Siapkas, J. and Sjögren, L. (2013). *Displaying the Ideals of Antiquity: The Petrified Gaze*. London: Routledge.

Smith, Cecil (1908). *A Guide to the Exhibition Illustrating Greek and Roman Life*. London: Routledge.

Spencer-Wood, S. M. (1999). The world their household: changing meanings of the domestic sphere in the nineteenth century. In P. M. Allison, ed., *The Archaeology of Household Activities*. London: Routledge, 162–89.

Stansbury-O'Donnell, M. (1999). *Pictorial Narrative in Ancient Greek Art*. Cambridge: Cambridge University Press.

Todorov, T. (1990). *Genres in Discourse*. Cambridge: Cambridge University Press.

Tomasi Velli, S. (2007). *Le immagini e il tempo. Narrazione visiva, storia e allegoria tra Cinque e Seicento*. Pisa: Edizioni della Normale.

Topper, K. (2009). Primitive life and the construction of the sympotic past in Athenian vase painting. *American Journal of Archaeology* 113(1), 3–26.

(2012), *The Imagery of the Athenian Symposium*. Cambridge: Cambridge University Press.

True, M. and Silvetti, J. (2005). *The Getty Villa*. Malibu, CA: J. Paul Getty Museum.

Vickery, A. (1993). Golden Age to separate spheres? A review of the categories and chronology of English women's history. *Historical Journal* 36(2), 383–414.

White, H. (1980). The value of narrativity in the representation of reality. *Critical Inquiry* 7(1), 5–27.

Whitehead, C. (2009). *Museums and the Construction of Disciplines: Art and Archaeology in Nineteenth-Century Britain*. London: Duckworth.

Winckelmann, J. J. (1951–57). *Briefe*, Vols. I–IV, ed. Walter Rehm. Berlin: W. de Gruyter.

Wolff, J. (1988). The culture of separate spheres: the role of culture in nineteenth-century public and private life. In J. Wolff and J. Seed, eds., *The Culture of Capital: Art, Power and the Nineteenth-Century Middle Class*. Manchester: Manchester University Press, 117–34.

Wylie, A. (1985). The reaction against analogy. *Advances in Archaeological Method and Theory* 8, 63–111.

Wyss, B. (1999). *Hegel's Art History and the Critique of Modernity*, trans. Caroline Dobson Saltzwedel. Cambridge: Cambridge University Press.

3 | Mind the Gap

Reuniting Words and Walls in the Study of the Classical
Greek House

JANETT MORGAN

In 1990, the renowned American scholar Michael Jameson observed that
ideas drawn from ancient textual sources

> continue to prevail in discussions of the Greek house and have been
> imposed upon the interpretation of the physical remains without giving
> the latter their due as independent evidence.[1]

Jameson's criticism was stimulated by first-hand experience. While excavating residential areas in Classical Greek towns, he had noticed a gap between
the descriptions of Greek houses presented in ancient texts and what was
revealed by archaeology. Features that were clear in texts, such as the
household hearth, could not be seen in the remains of houses.[2] Words and
walls did not appear to fit and this discrepancy led some archaeologists to
assert that descriptions in ancient Greek texts were 'literary ideals', which
contrasted with the 'social and archaeological reality' of excavated evidence.[3]
Archaeologists began to criticize scholars who sought to approach the
Classical Greek house through words, for example with Jameson saying that
Pesando's *Oikos e Ktesis. La Casa greca in Età Classica*, was 'very much a
product of the library rather than of first-hand acquaintance with Greek
houses and towns',[4] while Lisa Nevett in *House and Society in the Ancient
Greek World* was similarly critical of 'using archaeology to illustrate hypotheses derived from readings of the textual evidence'.[5] The gap between sources
became a gap between scholars.

In this chapter I will look more closely at the history of words and walls
in the Classical Greek house. By investigating the historiography of Greek
house plans and the use of 'domestic' terminology, I will show that the gap
between texts and archaeology is artificial. It reflects the different
approaches of Classical scholars and Classical archaeologists rather than
revealing significant problems with the evidence. I will suggest that it is
time to put aside the 'battle of the sources' and to look at how using our
two sources in parallel rather than in combination can help us to close the
gap between words and walls in the Classical Greek house.

Planning the Classical Greek House

Studies of ancient Greek domesticity began with words rather than walls. In the 1st century BCE, Marcus Vitruvius Pollio, a Roman author, architect and engineer, wrote a treatise on architecture for Augustus, *princeps senatus* (first citizen) of the new Roman Empire.[6] *De architectura* was a study of Roman buildings, which also contained discussions of Greek architecture, including a chapter on the Greek house.[7] Vitruvius' Greek house was a lavish building with dining rooms, colonnades, coffered wooden ceilings, a library and a picture gallery.[8] Vitruvius labelled most of the spaces in his Greek house with contemporary Latin words, such as *triclinium* (dining room), but for some spaces he used transliterated versions of what appeared to be Greek domestic terms, such as *thalamos* (inner room) and *gynaeconitis* (women's space).[9] He offered no information about the precise date or location of his Greek house and did not set out the sources of his transliterated terms. As a result, we have no way of knowing whether Vitruvius derived his information from Classical texts, or from Greek houses at the time he was writing, *c*. 30–15 BCE. His Greek house is an isolated construct, difficult to ground in any historical context.[10]

When *De architectura* was 'rediscovered' in the 15th century, Italian humanist scholars sought to use Vitruvius' descriptions of Classical buildings and his architectural theories to inspire new designs. They began to develop critical editions of the text to assist with this.[11] Kruft notes that the first reliable version of the text was compiled by Giovanni Giocondo in 1511.[12] Giocondo was a fascinating man. He was a Classical scholar who made transcriptions of ancient manuscripts but he was also an archaeologist, draughtsman and architect and he used those skills to embellish his edition by including plans of Vitruvius' buildings.[13] Giocondo's edition of *De architectura* had 136 woodcut pictures and building plans, including a plan of the Greek house, as shown in Figure 3.1.[14]

The plan is simple; drawn from the words of Vitruvius and enhanced by Giocondo's knowledge of surviving Roman architecture. Giocondo gave the rooms of his Greek house names taken from *De architectura*, such as the *prostas* or *thalamos*. Giocondo's edition played an important role in the development of Renaissance architecture, as Vitruvian ideas and Vitruvian style, filtered through the plans and drawings of Giocondo, became integrated into contemporary art and architectural forms.

In 1556 Cardinal Daniele Barbaro published an Italian translation of *De architectura*.[15] His aim was to allow the text to be used more widely as an

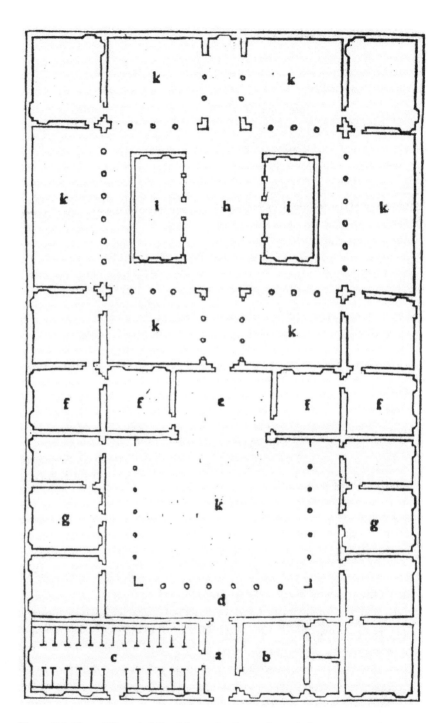

Figure 3.1 Plan of Vitruvius' Greek house by Giocondo, including peristyle (d), *prostas* (e), *thalamos/amphithalamos* (f) and *oecus* (k). The *gynaikonitis* is unmarked as Giocondo viewed it as the rooms around the front court, rather than a single room. From Giocondo 1511: 67

architectural treatise by Italian designers and planners. In order to encourage this, Barbaro asked Andrea Palladio, a young man under his patronage, to create his own plans for the buildings. Palladio built onto Giocondo's plans, adding cross-sections and other embellishments.[16] Palladio's building career was already well under way at this stage and the drawings are undoubtedly influenced by his own interpretation of Classical forms and styles.

Like Giocondo, Palladio drew a building with two courtyards, rooms for male and female use, a library, a picture gallery and guest apartments, as shown in Figure 3.2.[17] Although he labelled it using the same mix of Latin and transliterated Greek terms as found in Vitruvius' text, there are significant variations between the two buildings. While Giocondo's plan is simple, with eleven different types of space, Palladio's is far more complex, using twenty-six different types of space. Both men read the same words, yet they both produced very different plans. Their designs represent their unique responses to Vitruvius' text. Both Giocondo and Palladio had built walls from words because, in the absence of any excavated Greek houses, Renaissance scholars had no idea what a Greek house looked like. Despite this, models of the Greek house by Giocondo and Palladio continued to be reproduced by scholars discussing Vitruvius and the Greek house until well into the 20th century BCE.[18]

Renaissance scholars were looking to the past for inspiration. They wanted walls and were using words to create plans for them. In doing this, they chose to ignore the purpose of Vitruvius's text. *De architectura* was not a technical manual designed for planners and builders, but a complex philosophical treatise on the subject of order.[19] It was written to please and flatter Augustus, by describing a world of order and balance, brought about by his reign. *De architectura* is a cultural document.[20] It explores a wide range of topics such as beauty, civic society and astrology.[21] It integrates discussions from Greek philosophy alongside its studies of domestic buildings.[22] Vitruvius' Greek house is a philosophical construct rather than a specific historical building: it links words and walls in the service of knowledge, not town planning.

In 1840 Wilhelm Becker took a different approach to studying the Greek house. He sought to use ancient texts as evidence of cultural behaviour. Becker published a novella *Charikles: Bilder altgriechischer Sitte, zur genauren Kenntnis des griechischen Privatslebens*, which was an exploration of life in Classical Athens.[23] The book was an adventure story, written for schoolboys, about a young man named Charicles, who returned to Athens after military service overseas.[24] As well as tales of his hero's exploits, Becker included several essays detailing the sources he had used to create

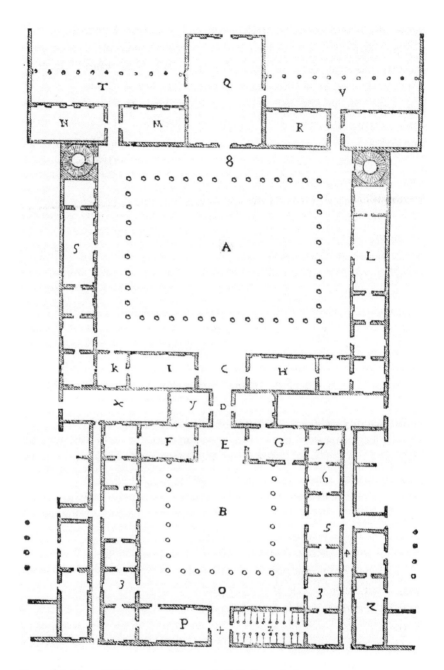

Figure 3.2 Plan of Vitrivius' Greek house by Palladio, including peristyle (A, B), *prostas* (E), *thalamos* (7), *amphithalamos* (F, G), *gynaikonitis* (H, I) and *oecus* (L, S, Y). From Barbaro 1567: 227

his picture of 'everyday life'. In the first of these essays, Becker included a plan of a house from Charicles' time, as shown in Figure 3.3.[25] Like his predecessors, Becker created his plan using descriptions from texts, as no Classical Greek houses had yet been excavated.

Becker was highly critical of scholars who relied on Vitruvius to understand Classical Greek houses, and rejected evidence from *De architectura*, pointing out that Vitruvius was not a Classical author and may have been writing about Greek houses from a different time.[26] Instead, Becker used ancient Greek texts to explore ancient Greek households and construct his picture of domestic life.[27] Becker's discussion uses the terms 'Greek' and 'Athenian' interchangeably, although the texts he read for his reconstruction were predominantly from Classical Athens, making his reconstruction more historically contextualized.[28] His aim was not to produce an authoritative model house plan, but to understand how residents used their domestic spaces and to incorporate this information into his design.

Becker retained the two-court model, in recognition of the division of male and female spaces in Classical texts, but his plan is much simpler than the earlier Vitruvian examples. There is no library or picture gallery. Instead, Becker used his study of Classical texts to expand, 'elucidate and correct' the description of Vitruvius.[29] He noted that 'Athenian residences at the time of the Peloponnesian War were certainly neither large nor stately structures.'[30] He also observed that women and men lived together, with women retiring into their separate quarters only when strangers visited the house.[31] In Becker's Classical Athenian house, altars were portable, roofs were flat and could be used as a household space, and the building was heated by small portable braziers.[32]

Becker also acknowledged that his plan was a fiction. He wanted to explore the Greek house as a functional space, where occupants manipulated their environment to utilize spaces to their best advantage. Becker's plan was a tool to enable discussion about the meaning of words and their relationship to domestic life. His study used words as a source for understanding domestic behaviour and he shows a prescient awareness of source problems, noting that, 'In the absence of any remains of a Grecian house, in the scarcity of trustworthy descriptions, and the great confusion of the terms used for its various parts, to reconstruct it in a satisfactory manner is no easy task.'[33] Becker's reconstruction filtered into discussions of Greek houses by 19th- and early 20th-century scholars.[34]

When Classical Greek houses were finally excavated at Athens and Piraeus, scholars sought to add walls to their words but the results were disappointing. Gardner and Jevons note that most of the houses found at

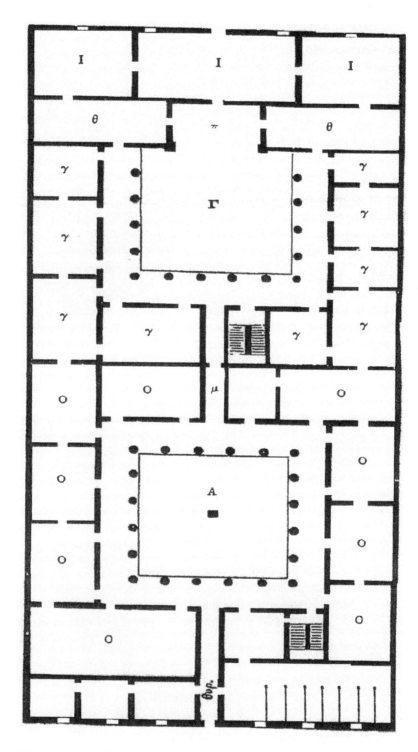

Figure 3.3 Plan of Vitruvius' Greek house by Becker. The house is divided into male and female rooms set around the two courts, with women's spaces towards the rear of the building. From Becker 1911: 262–63

Athens, 'consisted of a single cell' where 'extensive rooms and extended series were rare' and, whilst houses at the Piraeus were larger, these were less well preserved, so that their internal arrangements could not be satisfactorily reconstructed.[35] The houses at Athens and the Piraeus bore little resemblance to the Greek house of Vitruvius. But this was not unexpected, as Becker's work on Classical domesticity had already shown that the Vitruvian house was likely to be exceptional; the fragmentary houses paralleled fragmentary passages in Classical texts.

It was not until excavations began at Delos and Priene that greater quantities of house plans could be more clearly accessed, reconstructed and studied.[36] The houses at Delos contained mosaics and decoration but varied in size and organization.[37] At Priene, the houses had few areas of correspondence with the Vitruvian model.[38] Some Classical scholars, such as Winckler, Gardner and Jevons, continued to follow the two-court plan, while others, such as Gardner and Rider, redrew their plans to show only one court, taking into account evidence from the newly excavated houses, as shown in Figure 3.4. Even then, scholars recognized that their reconstructions were not definitive. Gardner and Jevons call their plan 'speculative', while Rider labels her plan as 'imaginary'.[39] Words and walls were not expected to make a perfect match.

It is at this point where I believe we see a gap begin to emerge between the needs of Classical scholars and archaeologists. For Classical scholars, plans were a tool to stimulate discussions about ancient culture, not an attempt to reconstruct a definitive vision of ancient buildings. In their plans, words were not presented as fixed labels, as their meaning could change with context or with a new translator and frequently did. Rooms could move around the Greek house, following the author's interpretation of text and remains.[40] While Classical scholars were happy to use fragmentary texts and material remains to discuss domesticity as a cultural phenomenon, archaeologists needed to take a more scientific and determined approach. They needed to find a way to define and discuss their discoveries. They needed words to become labels that described walls.

We can see an early example of this in Wiegand and Schrader's discussion of the houses at Priene.[41] Although certain spaces could be recognized, such as the court by its rough floor and open aspect, or the porch by its narrow roof and pillars, other rooms could not be so clearly identified. Wiegand and Schrader began to look for repeated patterns in the arrangement of rooms which they could use to create a typology of spaces and houses. They found one such pattern in the repeated presence of a small suite of rooms, consisting of a porch area opening onto the court with one

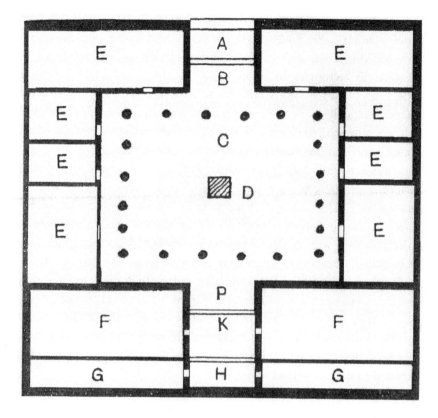

Figure 3.4 Rider's 'imaginary' Greek house, including *pastas* (P), *andronitis* (F) and *gynaikonitis* (G). Other spaces are more generally identified as rooms (E) and types of entrances (A, B, H, K). From Rider 1916: 237, fig. 40

or two rooms at the rear: an example of this suite can be seen in Figure 3.5.[42] Wiegand and Schrader decided to name this suite the *oecus*,[43] a word lifted from the text of Vitruvius, who described how

> In his locis introrsus constituuntur oeci magni, in quibus matres famil-
> iarum cum lanificis habent sessionem

> In the inner space here are situated large rooms, in which matrons of
> households sit working wool (Vitruvius, *De architectura* 6.7.2)

This passage highlights the flaw at the heart of Wiegand and Schrader's decision. It is not the rooms that matter to Vitruvius, but the presence of the mother of the house and her activity in working wool. She is an illustration of ideal behaviour in the Roman household. Vitruvius is not using the word *oecus* as an architectural term, only as a general description. Indeed, Vitruvius also uses the word *oecus* to refer to the male dining

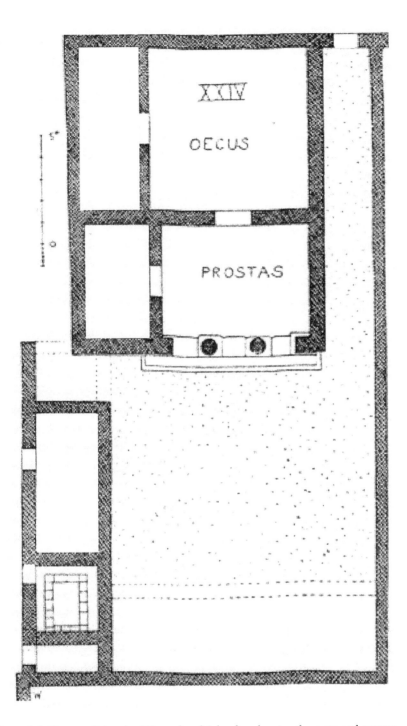

Figure 3.5 House at Priene by Wiegand and Schrader, showing the *oecus* and *prostas*. From Wiegand and Schrader 1904: 287

rooms in his Greek house.[44] In isolating the word *oecus* from its text, Wiegand and Schrader removed it from its wider cultural context and fixed it with a new meaning, designed to suit their need for a spatial terminology.

The process of identifying and labelling Classical Greek domestic spaces crystallized into a full terminology as a result of excavations at the site of Olynthus in northern Greece. Work took place there from 1928 to 1938 under the management of David Robinson, and produced and published more than 100 houses.[45] Robinson's doctoral student J. Walter Graham instituted a careful system of recording, which linked artefacts to their find-spots, enabling the excavators to undertake a detailed reconstruction of the domestic environment.[46] In order to analyse the reconstructed spaces, a clear terminology was essential. Robinson and Graham examined ancient texts and selected a mixture of ancient and modern words to describe the internal arrangements of the buildings.[47]

Some spaces were named from areas described in ancient sources. A long corridor usually situated to the north of the court and recognizable by its size and the presence of column bases or footings was labelled the *pastas*, following Vitruvius and Classical texts.[48] The *andron* was identified by its off-centre door, border for couches and mosaic.[49] Other areas were identified by their architecture or features but given modern names. The open area of the house could be recognized by its size, location, type of flooring and the presence of installations such as wells and cesspits. This area was not named the *aule*, as in Classical texts, but the courtyard.[50] Similarly, the bathroom was identified by its bath.[51]

A third category of spaces was identified by observing patterns in the material record and then choosing names from ancient texts, following the pattern of Wiegand and Schrader. The names were highly subjective. Graham renamed Wiegand and Schrader's *oecus* the 'kitchen-complex'.[52] In 1946, Mylonas renamed Graham's 'kitchen-complex' the '*oecus* unit'.[53] Where patterns of spatial use were not as easy to recognize, Robinson and Graham guessed at function on the basis of size or similarity to other rooms and labelled the spaces accordingly. In House B vi 3 Robinson notes that Room (d) was probably an *andron* on the grounds that it seemed to be accessed via an anteroom and was large and in the right place, even though it lacked the architectural features they had established to identify *androns*.[54] Despite their careful efforts to identify spaces, some rooms defied definition, leaving Robinson and Graham to note that 'we are frequently at a complete loss to know what a particular room may have been used for'.[55]

Robinson and Graham wanted words to describe their walls. Their chosen names wove ancient and modern words together to create a terminology without any consideration for the cultural aspect of houses. The words that different groups use to describe their dwelling places offer a unique source of cultural information. When we write modern words onto ancient contexts, we interpret remains through an external filter. We embed our own ideas of domesticity into the walls of ancient architecture.

The domestic terminology and practices from Olynthus became a model for other excavations. At Athens, excavators looked for the same rooms and features as at Olynthus, even though the buildings at Athens did not conform to any standard pattern.[56] Shear identified a *pastas* in one of his Athenian houses.[57] Jones, Sackett and Graham searched the Dema House for the *andron* that they expected to find, while Young suggested that Room 3 in House C at Athens was an *andron* on the basis that it was the largest room in the house and occupied the best position.[58] The Olynthus excavation had established a toolkit of domestic spaces, which excavators now expected to find in Classical Greek houses. Ancient and modern words were nailed to the walls of the Classical Greek house and to traditions of scholarship.

In an effort to move away from the problems of using architecture to identify spatial use, Bradley Ault's investigations at Halieis and Nicholas Cahill's re-examination of buildings at Olynthus looked at the presence of artefacts as a means to understand how spaces were used.[59] They found it was still not possible to identify room function with certainty. From the vantage point of Classical archaeologists, this is unsurprising. Given the fragmentary state of many of the buildings we study, we have to acknowledge that we cannot tell whether we are looking at primary contexts of use or places of storage, and whether the processes of deposition and erosion have moved an artefact to its find-spot.[60] For scholars of Classical texts, this is equally unsurprising. Ancient words do not make good labels.

As Becker observed in 1840, ancient words can have many meanings which differ according to their contexts of use.[61] This linguistic flexibility is not confined to architectural terms. Vase names can shift and change, resulting in a situation where many names can be used for one item.[62] Artefacts used in domestic rituals can change their names at the moment of use.[63] If we try to give ancient artefacts precise and specific names and then use those names to identify domestic spaces, we create an imprecise tangle of words, artefacts and walls, ending up with a set of fixed labels for domestic spaces which do not truly reflect their spatial use or meaning.[64]

It is interesting to consider why we do not change this; are we caught in an inescapable tradition, where we cannot change a terminology that has become too embedded in scholarly narratives, or are we simply unwilling to acknowledge our mistakes and look at the evidence afresh?[65] We would be wise to heed the advice given by Kurtz and Boardman who noted in their study of dress terminology that:

> The more we learn about the Greek use of 'technical' words for dress, utensils or implements, the less precise that use proves to have been and it would be a pity to exclude associations of words and representations through insisting on over-precise identifications.[66]

For the remainder of this chapter I will to look again at how we use texts as a source for understanding ancient domesticity. I will move back towards the approach of earlier Classical scholars in viewing houses as social and cultural constructs that receive meaning from the acts and actions of their residents, as well as social and political influence from the community.[67] Without people, a house does not exist; it is just an empty set of walls. It is not walls or words that make a house but human needs, action and perception.[68] Rather than measure walls and isolate words by removing them to use as labels, I will re-place words into their literary contexts and will explore the evidence for patterns of domestic behaviour in the texts of 4th-century BCE Athens. I will offer a more human-centred approach to 'reading' textual evidence and I will show how an approach that begins with texts can enhance our understanding of domestic archaeology.

A Tale of Two Houses

I will begin my study with an overview of the representation of two 4th-century BCE Athenian houses, setting out details of their residents, their physical structure, and their patterns of use in the text. I will then move on to discuss the implications of their representation. The two houses that I have selected come from either side of the 4th century BCE and both are located in the urban centre of Athens. Our first house appears in the law court speech *On the Murder of Eratosthenes*.[69] The date of the speech is uncertain but the career of Lysias is generally held to have begun after 403 BCE and the speech was composed for delivery to a jury of Athenian citizens in the Delphinion.[70] In the case, an Athenian citizen, Euphiletos, stands accused of murdering another citizen in his home, where the victim, Eratosthenes, had been conducting an affair with Euphiletos' wife.

Euphiletos lives with his wife, child and servant girl.[71] It is a small household and the description of the house is basic. Euphiletos tells the jury that his home (οἰκίδιον) is on two levels (διπλοῦν).[72] These are equal in area, with a women's area (γυναικωνῖτις) upstairs and a male area (ἀνδρωνῖτις) downstairs.[73] The house has a court (αὐλή), which has an external door from the street into the building (αὔλειος) and an internal door from here into the court (μέταυλος).[74] The only other significant features or furniture mentioned in the speech are the stairs (κλῖμαξ), the hearth (ἑστία) and a couch (κλίνη).[75]

When reading Euphiletos' description, it is important to remember that he is on trial for murder and seeking to persuade the jury that his action in murdering Eratosthenes was fully justified.[76] Euphiletos uses his house as a metaphor for his life. His description is designed to show the jury he is a model citizen. His house is an οἰκίδιον (little house); it is a modest home, rather than a large, wealthy dwelling.[77] Although the house is small, it is organized appropriately with separate spaces for men and women. Euphiletos may live modestly, but his domestic arrangements are unimpeachable. He respects the importance of reputation, separating his household by gender for certain times and occasions.[78]

Euphiletos' οἰκίδιον is separated from the street by double doors and these are an important part of the case. When he heard his wife leaving the house in the night, Euphiletos questioned her and was content with her response that the lamp had gone out. He is a careful but trusting spouse.[79] He denies dragging Eratosthenes into the house to kill him, and the double doors are mitigating evidence as it is much harder to drag someone through two sets of doors without being seen or heard. Euphiletos presents himself as a modest man who reacted without premeditation to the horror of catching Eratosthenes and his wife having sex in his own home.

Todd disputes Euphiletos' assertions of modesty and domestic simplicity, noting that he is 'evidently a farmer' with land in the *chora* as well as the town.[80] Yet evidence in the passage supports Euphiletos' claims. The only rooms in his property with given names are the γυναικωνῖτις ('woman's room', situated upstairs) and ἀνδρωνῖτις ('men's room', situated downstairs).[81] While these indicate the practice of gender division, it is not a permanent arrangement. After the birth of his child, Euphiletos' wife relocates to the ground floor. It is a matter of safety, allowing her to avoid carrying the baby downstairs during the night (κινδυνεύῃ κατὰ τῆς κλίμακος καταβαίνουσα).[82] Euphiletos moves to the upper floor. If this was a house with many rooms on each level, his move would not be necessary. Euphiletos' wife could move into one of the downstairs rooms and

Euphiletos could take another. Euphiletos is seeking to present himself as a considerate spouse, but his wholesale relocation seems rather extreme. It is possible that he had no other option.

When Euphiletos' friend comes for dinner, both men eat upstairs.[83] There is no alternative location. Euphiletos' wife also dines upstairs with him, but goes back downstairs when the baby cries.[84] This is a small residence and it may well consist of only two rooms. When Euphiletos dines with his wife on the upper storey, he does not call the space the γυναικῶνιτις, as it is not being used this way at that time. He calls it a δωμάτιον, which is a general term meaning a built space.[85] When he catches his wife and her lover in the downstairs room, he does not call it an ἀνδρῶνιτις; he uses the term δωμάτιον again.[86]

As part of his defence, Euphiletos claimed that Eratosthenes did not make contact with the hearth in his house.[87] Hearths, whether public or domestic, were sacred to the goddess Hestia and could provide a place of refuge. Contact with the hearth ensured that the suppliant was protected by the gods and should not be harmed.[88] In his study of the speech, Gareth Morgan assumes that this hearth was a fixed feature, located in the house kitchen.[89] There is no evidence for this in the text. The hearth is in the room where Euphiletos catches Eratosthenes. This is the downstairs room he referred to earlier as the ἀνδρωνῖτις and then the δωμάτιον.[90] The hearth may be a small brazier, being used as a light source in the room. If Eratosthenes made a grab for this, it would explain why Euphiletos found it easy to restrain him and prevent him claiming sanctuary.

Room names in Euphiletos' house are temporal, reflecting use and users at a particular moment in time. It is a pattern that is suited to a small property where rooms need to play many roles. In order to facilitate spatial flexibility, artefacts must be small and portable. Euphiletos is able to move upstairs with ease. A brazier can be used for cooking in the open space of the courtyard, allowing smoke to float away.[91] The same brazier can be used for heating, lighting or household cult. Euphiletos's house is a canvas for the activities of the household and the role of its spaces and artefacts shifts accordingly.

Our second house appears in the Menander play *Samia*, written at the end of the 4th century BCE.[92] The house of Demeas is on a street in Athens. The play was written for an audience of mixed festival-goers and, although it is a comedy, it is still a play about 'real' life. The portrayal of spatial use must have been recognizable to the audience as a reflection of their own households and homes in Athens.[93] In this play, most of the action takes place in the street, and the houses, their internal workings and their use by residents are described for the audience by the characters. It is a larger household than the household of Euphiletos. Demeas shares his property with his adopted son, Moschion, his companion Chrysis and a number of slaves, including Parmenion and the old nurse of Moschion.[94] Moschion tells us in the prologue that Demeas is a rich man.[95]

The house is referred to as a dwelling-place (οἰκία), as our dwelling-place (τὴν οἰκίαν τὴν ἡμετέραν) or, more frequently by gesturing to the frontage on stage and noting that events or individuals are within.[96] We know there are at least two floors, as women are described as coming down from an upper to a lower storey (κατέβαιν' ἀφ' ὑπερῴου). We are also told that the women carry gardens up to the roof for the festival of the Adonia. These offerings could be placed at the edges of the roof, but an interesting conversation between Demeas and his neighbour Nikeratos about the rape of Plangon notes that the roof was where this act took place.[97] This suggests that the building has an area of flat roof space, capable of being used by the household.[98]

Some of the rooms in the house are labelled with specific terms. Demeas has a ταμιεῖον, an ὀπτάνιον and a ἱστεών in his house. Arnott translates these as 'pantry', 'kitchen' and 'weaving room' respectively.[99] The appearance of these names may reflect the needs of the play and the importance of explaining the contexts of action to the audience. It might also be designed to reflect the wealth of the house owner and reinforce the idea that his property is a suitably large size. The only furniture referred to in the play is a couch.[100] There may be an altar present, as there are references to sacrifices and incense burning, but there is no clear evidence for this.[101]

Where room names are given, they all come from artefacts. Arnott translates ὀπτάνιον as 'kitchen', yet the cook in the play queries whether the ὀπτάνιον has a roof above it.[102] His question implies that not all ὀπτάνιον do. Liddell and Scott translate ὀπτάνιον as 'a place for roasting'.[103] Like Euphiletos' hearth, the ὀπτάνιον could be a temporary structure, rather than a specific room permanently devoted to the act of food preparation and cooking.[104] Indeed, the cook who asks about the structure of the ὀπτάνιον is named as a *mageiros*, a specialist who has been brought into the house to perform the sacrifice and roast for the wedding.[105] The ὀπτάνιον may be a fire, set up and sanctified for this one, special occasion.

Access to the upper level and to the storeroom in Demeas' house comes through the space called the ἱστεών, a word translated by both Arnott and Robinson as 'weaving room'.[106] The ἱστεών is not a common description of Classical domestic spaces; this is its only appearance in a Classical text.[107] The same space is also referred to as an οἴκημα (room).[108] Again, this may reflect a temporally specific use of space. Cahill notes that looms required spaces with sufficient light, area and comfort for the weavers and were often packed away when not in use.[109] No one is using this loom and its appearance in what appears to be an access space reinforces the idea that the ἱστεών is the place where the loom is stored rather than permanently set up.

Demeas' house is a collection of intertwined rooms: some lead into other spaces and others contain stairs. It would be difficult to turn this into a house plan. Again, this arrangement may be part of the needs of the play. The intimacy of the rooms with their internal access routes and accessible roof may reflect the conjoined lives of the domestic residents.[110] However, it must have made sense to the audience too. The haphazard relationships between the rooms hint that spatial arrangements in 4th-century Athenian houses were not always as clear or as ordered as our reconstructions of house plans tend to suggest.

The house of Demeas is a setting for the activities associated with domestic life, including eating and sleeping. There is no indication of any permanent architectural separation of genders in the domestic space, and characters appear to move freely within the house. The households in the play also join together to celebrate two key ritual occasions, the festival of the Adonia and the wedding of Moschion.[111] At the Adonia the women of the house of Demeas and the household of Nikeratos celebrate together on the roof of Demeas' house.[112] Moschion is also able to join in with the women, as he tells the audience this is where he raped Plangon. Demeas further informs us that Chrysis, his companion, is not only present but well-behaved and self-controlled in the presence of men from outside the family.[113] This freedom of movement may reflect her more insecure position in the household, as a companion.[114] It is interesting that she is the only woman to appear on the street and to speak before the audience. Nikeratos' wife and daughter remain inside their house until the moment of the wedding and when Plangon is brought into the street for the wedding ceremony, she does not walk alone. A piper and torchlit procession lead the new bride to her new home in the house of Demeas.[115] As Becker noted in 1840, divisions between men and women are created as needed. They are social and temporal, rather than built into architecture.

The View From Texts

Using our two houses as case studies, we can now turn to look at what we can learn from them about houses in 4th-century BCE Athens. The first issue to consider is how are they understood by their users: what is a house? Characters most commonly offer us the words οἰκία, οἶκος or οἰκίδιον. These are neutral words that do not carry the exclusive meaning of 'house'. They come from the verb οἰκέω, meaning to dwell or inhabit, and are used to differentiate a place that is occupied from a place that is not. In light of this, it is not surprising to find that words derived from οἰκέω can have a range of uses in wider texts. They can mean an occupied room in a building, or a place occupied by a god; they can be a single space or a multiple of spaces; they can mean those within the spaces or a building and the land around it.[116] 'House' is our translation of this word and it is important to remember that translations are not perfect. They may not always reflect the meaning of the word as intended in the text. Indeed, Athenian texts use a range of words to identify places of habitation, such as δόμος, θάλαμος or occasionally a μέλαθρον.[117] None of these terms is specific to houses; the words δόμος, θάλαμος and οἶκος can be applied to built environments with a wide range of different uses in both public and private contexts.[118]

The 'house' words that our two passages use are generic references to a built environment. It is the act of residence or activities of residents that give a building domestic meaning. We can see this in the use of a possessive pronoun to add meaning to the generic word. Euphiletos refers to 'my building' (τῆς οἰκίας τῆς ἐμῆς) and Moschion to 'our building' (τὴν οἰκίαν τὴν ἡμετέραν).[119] The houses of friends are similarly identified by the genitive case.[120] In other Classical texts, the meaning of 'home' is given by reference to the presence of a father or a hearth in the building. It is the place where the head of the family or the site of family worship is situated.[121]

At Athens, the meaning of 'house' and 'home' is temporal. If people are living there, it is a house but this does not imply that a building is always a house. Meaning can change as users change, as we see in the following passage by Aeschines:

> οὐ γὰρ τὰ οἰκήματα οὐδ' αἱ οἰκήσεις τὰς ἐπωνυμίας τοῖς ἐνοικήσασι παρέχουσιν, ἀλλ' οἱ ἐνοικήσαντες τὰς τῶν ἰδίων ἐπιτηδευμάτων ἐπωνυμίας τοῖς τόποις παρασκευάζουσιν

> For it is neither the building nor the act of dwelling there which gives name to those living in them, but it is the inhabitants who give to places the names of their own practices.[122]

In this law court speech from 346 BCE, the orator Aeschines is trying to refute charges of treason by establishing that his prosecutor, Timarchus, was a prostitute.[123] On the basis that mud sticks, Aeschines wants to show that Timarchus reveals his profession by his action. In order to illustrate how a man can perform many roles, Aeschines offers the jury examples of how the same space can change from doctor's practice, to smithy, to laundry, to carpenter's shop to brothel, simply as a result of different occupiers.[124] The names of spaces are defined by the actions of users.[125] The house of Euphiletos and the house of Demeas are buildings that they inhabit. If they both moved out, the buildings might be used for other non-domestic purposes and they would be houses no more.

The words used to name internal spaces are reflections of use and users at a moment in time. The use of these spaces can change easily. The δωμάτιον in the house of Euphiletos can become a male space or a female space and can move or dissolve as the needs of the family require.[126] Although there appears to be a differentiation between the simple space of Euphiletos' house and the more complex arrangements of Demeas, this could be an illusion created by overly technical translation.[127] In the house of Demeas, the 'names' given to rooms reflect the places where particular objects are kept; there is a room for storing food and a room for storing the loom, but the names are not permanently fixed to the domestic spaces. The ἱστεών (loom place) is the place where the loom is at that moment.[128] The ὀπτάνιον is an artefact for cooking at a special occasion, rather than a room set aside permanently for cooking in.

In his 4th-century BCE study of household management, the *Oeconomicus*, Xenophon tells us that rooms in the house of Ischomachus were organized according to their best use. There was an inner space, the θάλαμος, to keep the most valuable coverings (στρώματα) and vessels (σκεύη).[129] There was a dry, roofed place for the corn (τὰ δὲ ξηρὰ τῶν στεγνῶν τὸν σῖτον), a cool place for wine (τὰ δὲ ψυχεινὰ τὸν οἶνον), light rooms for work and vessels needing light (τὰ δὲ φανὰ ὅσα φάους δεόμενα ἔργα τε καὶ σκεύη ἐστι), and decorated rooms for living (διαιτητήρια), as well as separate female quarters (γυναικωνῖτις) and male quarters (ἀνδρωνῖτις) for the slaves, to stop them from forming family groups.[130]

Most of Xenophon's descriptions relate to the perceived qualities of the rooms. These qualities have influenced Ischomachus' decisions about how to organize his domestic space. Like Vitruvius, Xenophon's study is a philosophical treatise comparing the order of a state to a well-ordered house. The link between place and organizinion is an essential part of his thesis, not a blueprint for the presentation of Athenian domestic space. Like the houses of Euphiletos and Demeas, Ischomachus' dwelling is a blank canvas that can be utilized as he wishes. If Ischomachus moved out, his possessions would move with him and the new occupant could change the use of the spaces as he saw fit, whether for domestic, industrial or religious activities. This flexibility suggests that efforts to create a toolkit of artefacts and spaces are doomed to failure. We should not try to build rigid models when the material evidence, at best, can only show us the last moments of spatial use.[131]

Ancient houses are not constrained by the need to install sewage pipes, or to fit domestic kitchens. Users were free to dictate use as they saw fit. Objects could be moved and the use of rooms altered as a result. In Plato's *Protagoras*, Callias converts his father's θάλαμος into a room for sophists to sleep when hosting a philosophical gathering.[132] In Aristophanes' *Wasps*, Bdelycleon tries to teach his father how to behave at a symposium.[133] It is interesting that no specific name is given to the room; there is no ἀνδρών (male place). The space is created by the bodies of participants and the artefacts put out for the occasion, such as bronzes and tapestries.[134] When the occasion is over, the items are put away and the meaning of the space can be altered.[135]

We can see this process at work in the creation of domestic religious spaces. In his satirical study of an overly superstitious man, the writer Theophrastus describes how this man creates a shrine to a hero in his house:

> καὶ ἐὰν ἴδη ὄφιν ἐν τῆ οἰκίᾳ,
> ἐὰν παρείαν, Σαβάζιον καλεῖν,
> ἐὰν δὲ ἱερόν ἐνταῦθα ἡρῷον
> εὐθὺς ἱδρύσασθαι

> ...and if he sees a snake in the house, if a cheek-snake, he calls Sabazios, but if it is a godly snake, he sets up straightaway a herōon there...[136]

The shrine is not created at a particular place within a house but in the place where the snake appeared. The immediacy of the act shows that the shrine can be set up with speed and without the need for specialized objects. The Superstitious Man can utilize whatever artefacts, images or foliage is instantly available to him.[137] The shrine offers an area for communication between hero and householder. Its space is differentiated by the actions performed as it is set up, while it exists and also by the intentions of its creator. While the meaning of the shrine area is changed, the wider space in which it is located can continue to be used as it was formerly.[138]

Ritual occasions require interaction between human and deity and offer an excellent example of the interplay between presence, action and artefact in defining and articulating domestic space.[139] At childbirth, the baby was delivered by the goddess Artemis, who needed to be summoned directly into the house.[140] Texts tell us that the house was marked and divided from the space of the city.[141] The body of the expectant mother was then marked by purification, charms or protective symbols.[142] The area around the birthing mother was further demarcated by a separation of genders, with a group made up exclusively of other women coming to assist the woman in labour.[143]

Praxagora explains her absence in the house at night as a result of helping at a birth.[144] In *Thesmophoria*, the husband is sent out from the room when the baby is about to be born.[145] The women are there for practical reasons but their presence heightens the sense of occasion and identifies the birth area as special. They play an active role in encouraging the goddess to come into the house. Plato describes midwives giving drugs and singing incantations.[146] The sound may serve an apotropaic function, but it also sends a message to the goddess that a space and mother are ready for her.[147] In Euripides' *Hippolytus* the nurse states:

τὰν δ' εὔλοχον οὐρανίναν
τόξων μεδέουσαν αὔτευν
Ἄρτεμιν . . .

And I called out to the one who cares for and helps in childbirth, heavenly Artemis of arrows.[148]

Vase paintings of births show us the birth of gods, yet the position of female participants at the event is interesting. They stand around the 'mother' with their arms raised, like a chorus.[149] While in ancient choral dances the centre was filled by the director or by a cult object such as an altar, at birth the focal point is the mother-to-be. She is placed at the centre of an all-female protective circle, which is designed to protect her, as well as the goddess.[150] The actions and song of the women imbue the process of birth with the air of a festival such as the Thesmophoria. As the baby arrives, the goddess leaves and the sanctity of the space dissolves. It can revert to its previous state. Birth is a ritual moment taking place in a space created and sanctified by the acts of those present. Despite its domestic location, it is no less valid a religious space than the area of a sanctuary, it differs only by virtue of its temporal nature.

Understanding the Archaeology of 4th-Century BCE Houses Through Texts

Our case studies raise interesting questions about how we investigate ancient houses. If a house is simply a built space that becomes occupied by an individual or group, then it need not be a whole, discrete building, it might be a portion of one. In her investigation of the domestic hearth Foxhall noted evidence for many small fires distributed throughout Classical buildings.[151] Although the focus of her article is on the absence of a 'kitchen' or single cooking place in houses, evidence for more than one fire within a building could also suggest that more than one family group was present, cooking at different places within the house.[152] Descriptions of the households involved in the two law court speeches *Against Boeotus* show that second or even third marriages could produce complex arrangements of close and distant family members sharing property.[153] Patterns of residence may have been similar to those of contemporary Iranian houses, in which the married couple can leave to set up their own home but may also stay in the family building, differentiating their designated space from those of the wider family by symbolic marking and separate fires.[154]

It is possible that larger buildings were inhabited by a number of different groups. In Antiphon's speech *On the Prosecution of the Stepmother for Poisoning*, we are told that the mother, stepfather and son lived in a building where their friend Philoneus and his mistress also lived.[155] In his appraisal of the use of Athenian buildings Aeschines notes that 'if there are many living there, we call it a *sunoikia*'.[156] It is possible that houses in 4th-century Athens consisted of only one or two rooms, whether separate or as part of a larger building.[157] Euphiletos' two-room house may also be part of a larger, shared building. If we approach material remains with clear plans of discrete buildings in mind, we will fail to appreciate the unique nature of what lies before us. We will be searching for our expectations, rather than seeing what is there.

When homes consist of one or two rooms, efficiency becomes a key determinant of spatial meaning within the house. Rooms need to host different household activities simultaneously and there is evidence in Athenian texts for the use of screens to separate spaces or change the meaning of spaces as required. In Aristophanes' *Wasps*, Philocleon is instructed to admire the hangings in the court (κρεκάδι αὐλῆς θαύμασον).[158] These may have formed part of the construction of the dining room and its separation from the household.[159] Hangings or tapestries also appear as a means to create a dining space in a fragment by the orator Hyperides:

οἱ δὲ ἐννέα ἄρχοντες εἰστιῶντο ἐν τῇ στοᾷ, περιφραξάμενοί τι μέρος αὐτῆς αὐλαίᾳ.

And the nine archons were honouring the gods in the stoa, having screened off some part of it with a curtain.[160]

Brigger and Giovannini have suggested that a temporary tent was used to contain the corpse after a death in the household.[161] Darkness can also be used as a screen: Deianeira hides her 'love' potion for Heracles in an area called the *muchos*; it is in the *muchos* of the campaign tent that the Trojan women are placed by their Greek captors and in the *muchos* of the room where baby Heracles sleeps.[162] The *muchos* is a space in shadow; its division is made by the contrast between darkness and light rather than being defined by walls.[163] It is a protected space within a room, created by the perception that dark places are safe places and differentiated from the remaining space of the room. In a crowded city such as Athens, space was at a premium and these patterns of spatial flexibility would certainly allow for the most efficient use of urban buildings.

Ethnography and Spatial Use

We can gain a deeper understanding of how this type of 'condensed' living worked from a study of ethnographic analogy. In his thesis on vernacular buildings in the village of Eressos on Lesbos, Pavlides noted that the names given to domestic spaces were very general, tending to differentiate only between indoors and outdoors, or private and formal. As in our 4th-century BCE Athenian texts, domestic terminology did not indicate fixed spatial meanings based on the presence of specific artefacts.[164] Instead, spatial meaning was linked to temporal needs and 'zoned' according to the activities performed at a given time. These zones occurred in each house, irrespective of size, and could exist as discrete spaces or as a part of a single space, depending on the needs of the household. The 'Formal' Zone was the locus for significant life-cycle events such as the celebrations of births, marriages and festivals. It was also the place where visitors were received and could sleep and where members of the family who required separation, whether for illness or childbirth, could be placed. The 'Everyday' Zone was the area where the activities of spinning, knitting, embroidery, food prep-aration and informal socializing took place. The 'Utility' Zone was a space for the storage of tools and the performance of messy work, such as the killing and plucking of chickens.[165]

Pavlides was able to access information from a period stretching back 130 years, to a time before plumbing and central heating were introduced. For the period 1850–89, he identified seven distinct house types, varying from Type I, with a single internal space, to Type VII with three floors and a number of internal spaces.[166] Each house maintained the division between zoned areas irrespective of how many rooms they had. The divisions were indicated by the use of a symbolic system of furnishings and cupboards, which signalled to the visitor the meaning of the space at any given time. In houses with a single room, the meaning of space could move from 'Utility' to 'Formal' through the use of decorated carpets and more formal dining ware. The rooms of these houses were thus capable of accommodating a wide range of functions. Space was defined by the character of an activity or by the individuals participating and was multifunctional, with an ability to change its meaning as required. This pattern fits well with the spatial flexibility shown by texts and reinforces my belief that our desire to fix static labels to spaces in Classical Greek houses is harming our ability to understand the cultural role of domestic space.

Closing the Gap

Words and walls work best as parallel studies. If we treat texts solely as a source of terminology and ignore their cultural value, we end up with a strange hybrid of modern expectations and ancient words painted onto plans of ancient remains. It is clear why we do this; it is certainly much easier to compare evidence within a site or between sites if we approach the material believing that all ancient houses have the same features and that all ancient residents behaved consistently. We have produced a domestic terminology that suggests this. Indeed, this may be the reason why we have not changed our approach. Adherence to a doctrine of consistency helps us to bring order to chaos but it also creates a homogenized past that ignores difference and the unique insights that a study of difference might reveal. If we ignore texts, we lose a valuable source of comparative ethnographic material.

In Classical Athens, words and walls tell us a tale of human behaviour, human need and adaptation to available space. In 4th-century BCE Athens, a house was a place where people lived; if they moved out, it was a house no longer. Domesticity could be a temporary condition, allowing 'houses' to be shaped by wealth, family structure, temporal needs and available space. If we descend on the buildings of Athens holding a toolkit of set architectural shapes, set rooms and set features in Athenian buildings, we will find a gap. Words and walls will not match. Ancient texts are complex, multifaceted artefacts whose words must be considered in context and not in isolation.

On the other hand, if we prioritize texts at the expense of material remains, we lose our ability to see the bigger picture of how communities are built and work, and we lose out on the checks and balances that an integrated approach can ensure. We also lose the chance to explore regional diversity. Athens dominates our view of the Classical house, but it does not follow that all Greek communities represented or used their domestic space in the same way.

Ancient houses are cultural artefacts as much as they are mudbrick ones. If we seek to push words and walls together, we will find gaps. It is only when we separate words and walls, and view them in their own, unique historical, social and political contexts, that we can truly bring them together and learn from them.

Notes

1 Jameson 1990: 92.
2 Jameson 1990: 98–99, 105–106.
3 Whitley 2001: 322. On relationships between texts and archaeology in studies of the Classical era, see Morris 1994; Shanks 1995; Schnapp 1996; Hall 2014: 1–16.
4 Jameson 1989: 478–79; Pesando 1987.
5 Nevett 1999: 26–27.
6 Morgan 1914 [1960].
7 Vitruvius, *De architectura* 6.7.
8 Vitruvius, *De architectura* 6.7.3.
9 Vitruvius, *De architectura* 6.7.2, 5.
10 On Vitruvius' own context, see Romano 2016.
11 Kruft 1994: 66–72.
12 Giocondo 1511; Kruft 1994: 66–67.
13 Ciaponni 1984.
14 Giocondo 1511: 67.
15 Barbaro 1556.
16 Cellauro 2004.
17 Barbaro 1556: 227.
18 Winckler offers a list of scholars whose work included discussions of Vitruvius and Greek houses from 1615 to 1867 (Winckler 1868: 10–12). Morgan's translation of Vitruvius in 1914 sets a two-court plan alongside a single court plan from Delos (Morgan 1914 [1960]: 186–87).
19 McEwen 2003.
20 On the cultural role of information in Roman technical treatises, see the essays in Whitmarsh and König 2008.
21 Fisher 2015.
22 McIntosh 2014.
23 Becker 1840. The novella was translated into English in 1911.
24 Garland 2009: xi; Brown 2013.

25 Becker 1911: 251–71, esp. 262–63.

26 Becker 1911: 251.

27 These included works such as Plutarch's *Life of Alcibiades*, a biography of the Classical general but written at a later period (Becker 1911: 268).

28 For examples, see Becker 1911: 251, 259.

29 Becker 1911: 252, 258.

30 Becker 1911: 259.

31 Becker 1911: 254.

32 Becker 1911: 258, 267, 271.

33 Becker 1911: 251.

34 Examples of Becker's influence can be found in Petersen 1851: 9; Winckler 1868: 11; Gardner and Jevons 1895: 35; Morgan 1914 [1960]: 186; Rider 1916: 216.

35 Gardner and Jevons 1895: 32, 33. See also Rider 1916: 218–20.

36 The houses at Delos and Priene were also dated to the Hellenistic rather than the Classical period, making it difficult to use them as a guide to Classical houses (Gardner, 1901: 298).

37 Paris 1884; Chamonard 1906, 1922.

38 Wiegand and Schrader 1904: 285–328.

39 Gardner and Jevons 1895: 35; Rider 1916: 237, fig. 40.

40 See the alterations in plans from Figure 3.1 to Figure 3.4.

41 Wiegand and Schrader 1904: 285–99.

42 Wiegand and Schrader 1904: 288–89.

43 Wiegand and Schrader 1904: 289.

44 Vitruvius. *De architectura* 6.7.4.

45 Cahill 2002: 74; Kaiser 2015: xii.

46 Kaiser 2015: 48–50.

47 The reasons for their choice of spatial labels are given in Robinson and Graham, 1938: 167–212.

48 The connection between the *pastas* and the domestic context is made in Xenophon *Memorabilia* 3.8.9. For a description of the Olynthian *pastas*, see Robinson and Graham 1938: 161–66.

49 For a description of the features of an Olynthian *andron*, see Robinson and Graham 1938: 171–85.

50 For the courtyard, see Robinson and Graham 1938: 157–59.

51 For the use of bathtubs to identify bathrooms at Olynthus, see Robinson and Graham 1938: 199–204.

52 For the kitchen, see Robinson and Graham 1938: 185–98. See also Graham 1954: 328–46.

53 Wiegand and Schrader 1904: 285–99; Holland 1944: 123–62; Mylonas 1946: 369–96, esp. 386.

54 Robinson 1946: 117.

55 Robinson and Graham 1938: 167.

56 Graham 1966; Thompson and Wycherley 1972: 180. The same point is also made in Jones 1975: 66.

57 Shear 1973: 153.

58 Young 1951: 206; Jones, Sackett and Graham 1962: 109–11.

59 For Halieis, see Ault 2005. For Olynthus, see Cahill 2002.

60 A description of depositional processes is offered in Ault and Nevett 1999: 47–49. Similarly La Motta and Schiffer note that the process of abandonment and choice of artefacts left behind can skew attempts to reconstruct household activities (1999: 22). There are also further dangers in the inherent assumption that each area of a house is mono-functional with a set of related finds, see Berry 1997: 185; Allison 1999.

61 Becker 1911: 251.

62 Sparkes and Talcott 1958: 3. This is especially true of religious artefacts, such as the *hiera* and *heroon*, see Morgan 2007a, 2011a. For a recent examination of the role and use of the *lekythos*, see Volioti, Chapter 4 of this volume.

63 On the *hiera* and *heroon*, see Morgan 2007a, 2011a.

64 Cahill calls the names 'arbitrary' (2002: 154). He further points out that in modern houses, although a name might reveal the primary function of space, it does not necessarily indicate an exclusive use (2002: 78).

65 For studies of the problem of cultural baggage and the distance it creates, see Nevett 1997: 283–84; Goldberg 1999: 43; and Meyer, Chapter 2, this volume.

66 Kurtz and Boardman 1986: 35–70. Nevett has made a similar point when discussing the appearance of gendered terms in texts relating to the Athenian house (1995; 1999: 18). For further examples of the problems in using ancient texts to reconstruct ancient houses and domestic life, see Uytterhoeven, Chapter 8, Pudsey, Chapter 9, and Speksnijder, Chapter 10, this volume.

67 Points convincingly made about Roman and late antique Egyptian houses in Allison 1993 and Alston 1997, 2007. See also Alston, Chapter 14, this volume.

68 Morgan 2007a, 2010. On the role of human perception and action in constructing meaning, see Brown 2001; Hodder 2012.

69 Lysias 1. Edwards and Usher 1985.

70 Carey 1989: 2–3; Todd 2007: 12–13. For debates on whether the speech was delivered, see Nývlt 2013.

71 Gareth Morgan gives Euphiletos two female servants, suggesting that (θεράπαινα) and (παιδίσκη) indicate different women (1982: 115). In my view there is only one, since (θεράπαινα) is used by Euphiletos (§8, 11, 18) and the more intimate term (παιδίσκη) by the wife (§12), whose maidservant it is. Todd also reconstructs the household with one female slave (2000: 14). The mother dies early in the speech (§8), which Euphiletos sees as a causal factor in his wife's behaviour.

72 Lysias 1.9.

73 Lysias 1.9.

74 Lysias 1.13, 17, 23, 24.

75 Stairs (§9, see also references to going up and down at §§10, 22, 23), hearth (§27), couch (§25).

76 For wider studies of important social issues raised by the case, see Cohen 1989, 1991; Carey 1995, 1997; Porter 2007; McHardy 2008.

77 Lysias 1.9.

78 Lysias 1.22.5–23.5.

79 Lysias 1.13.

80 Todd 2000: 14.

81 Lysias 1.9.

82 Lysias 1.9–10.

83 Lysias 1.23.

84 Lysias 1.11–12.

85 Lysias 1.17. 'Δωμάτιον' is constructed from the verb δέμω, meaning 'to build'.

86 Lysias 1.17, 24.

87 Lysias 1.27.

88 A public example of supplication at the hearth can be seen in Thucydides 1.136.

89 Morgan 1982: 120.

90 Lysias 1.9, 27.

91 Sparkes 1962; Foxhall 2007; Tsakirgis 2007; Morgan 2010: 150–52.

92 For details of dating elements in the play, see Arnott 2000: 7–12.

93 Patterson, 1998: 195–205, 215–19.

94 Arnott notes that there is a "large cast of characters in the play" (2000: 13).

95 Lines 1–18.

96 For οἰκία, see lines 133, 352, 382; for τὴν οἰκίαν τὴν ἡμετέραν, see 649–50; for 'within', see lines 39–41, 135. Patterson notes that Menander often uses οἰκία (household) to emphasize the connections brought about through the patterns of household life (1998: 196).

97 On the gardens of Adonis, see line 45; for the conversation between Demeas and Nikeratos, see 588–99. In Aristophanes *Lysistrata*, the festival of the Adonia also takes place on the roof (387–96).

98 On women and roofs, see Morgan, 2007a: 300–301.

99 See Arnott 2000 lines 229 (ταμιεῖον), 234 (ἱστεών), 291 (ὀπτάνιον).

100 Lines 225–26.

101 Lines 157–59. Arnott includes an altar in his translation of the lines (2000: 48).

102 At lines 291–92.

103 Liddell–Scott, *s.v.* ὀπτάνιον.

104 For the ὀπτάνιον as a moveable cooking support, see Morris 1985: 398–99.

105 See also Menander, *Dyscolus* 398–401; Ar. *Aves* 1637. On the *mageiros*, see Dalby 1996: 9; Wilkins 2000: 369–414.

106 At lines 232–36; Robinson 1946: 460. See also Cahill 2002: 171.

107 Our main references to weaving are Homeric, yet even in the Homeric palace there is no specific space for weaving (Homer, *Iliad* 22.440; *Odyssey* 1.361, 15.517). On reading Homeric domestic space, see Varto, Chapter 1, this volume.

108 Line 234.

109 Cahill 2002: 170–71.

110 On the complex sexual and social relationships in the play, see Salmenkivi 1997; Lape 2004: 137–70.

111 Adonia, see lines 35–46; preparations for the wedding of Moschion 219–31, 287–92. On the Adonia, see Burkert 1985: 196–97. On weddings, see Oakley and Sinos 1993.

112 Lines 25–46.

113 At lines 343–45.

114 See Lape 2004: 147–50, 159–167.

115 Lines 725–31. For houses and weddings, see Morgan 2010: 26–31.

116 See Morgan, 2007b; 2010: 52–54.

117 Thus, in a single play, the paternal home of Heracles is referred to as a δόμος (Euripides, *Hercules Furens* 138–39), an οἶκος (327–31) and a μέλαθρον (336–38). On the *melathron* of Homer, see Varto, Chapter 1, this volume.

118 A μέλαθρον can be a cave (Euripides, *Cyclops* 491) as well as a palace (Euripides *Heracleidae* 107); a δόμος can refer to a temple (Aeschylus, *Eumenides* 205) but as δωμάτιον can refer to a room in a building (Aristophanes, *Ecclesiazusae* 8). The term μέλαθρον is mostly used to describe domestic space in tragedy and epic poetry; it may reflect a poetic use rather than a contemporary practice.

119 Lysias, 1. 4, 15, 25, 38; Menander, *Samia* 649–50.

120 Lysias, 1.18.

121 Euripides, *Medea* 681; Lycurgus, *Against Leocrates* 131.5.7; Dinarchus, *Demosthenes* 66.4–5.

122 Aeschines, *Against Timarchus* 123–24.

123 Fisher 2001.

124 For further links between Athenian rhetoric and domestic architecture, see Nevett, Chapter 6, this volume.

125 For a study of temporality and archaeology, see Foxhall 2000.

126 Lysias 1.9.6–10.1. Another occasion requiring female separation was the entry of non-familial males into the house (Nevett 1994). For an example, see Lysias, 3.6. Again, this is a temporal need.

127 For a comprehensive list of names for domestic rooms based on readings from Athenian texts, see Robinson 1946: 453–71.

128 For the ἱστεών, see Menander, *Samia* 234.

129 The word θάλαμος indicates a more private room rather than a room with a particular function. See Morgan 2007b.

130 Xenophon, *Oeconomicus* 9.2–9.5.

131 For discussions on temporality and domestic archaeology, see Foxhall 2000, and Baird, Chapter 13, this volume.

132 Plato, *Protagoras* 315D–E.

133 Aristophanes, *Vespae* 1212–17.

134 For a study of problems in our use of the word ἀνδρών, see Morgan 2011b.

135 Ischomachus places great importance on the care of the household artefacts; they are listed as the things used for sacrificing, things used often and things used for festivals (Xenophon, *Oeconomicus* 9.6–7). These artefacts are not described, neither are they kept permanently on display. They are brought out and used when needed.

136 Theophrastus, *Characters* 16.4.

137 Morgan 2007b.

138 For a similar description of the setting-up of an altar, see Aristophanes, *Pax.* 923–73. Morgan 2007b, 2010: 143–53.

139 See Morgan 2007a, 2007b.

140 For a discussion of the spatial elements of rites of transition, see Morgan 2010: 26–31.

141 We do not know how this was achieved but it must have been visible, as the Superstitious Man can identify and avoid places where a child has been born (Theophrastus, *Characters* 16.9). A later commentary by Photius asserts that pitch was used to mark the house (Photius *s.v.* rhamnos).

142 On the river Kephisos as 'birth-giving', see Soph. *OC* 685–93. For birth charms, see Ar. *Eccl.* 504; Theophrastus *HP.* 9.9.3 (Cyclamen). The use of amulets to protect and speed delivery is also recommended in Diosc. 5.154; Plutarch, *Moralia* 964C. The birth charms may have been to protect the baby; they frequently appear as a means to identify unknown relations in the plays of Menander, such as *Epitrepontes*.

143 Garland 1990: 61. This appears to be contradicted by the image on the *lekythos* of Theophante, which shows the woman in labour being supported by a male figure. However, vase images cannot be relied on as a representation of reality. Demand suggests that the birth memorials may be for midwives and show them with their patrons (1994: 130–34).

144 Aristophanes, *Ecclesiazusae* 530.

145 Aristophanes, *Thesmophoriazusae* 507–509.

146 Pl. *Theat.* 149d.

147 Noise as an apotropaic tool is referred to by Plato (*Phaedo* 77E3–9, *Theaetetus* 149C–D) and Soranus (*Gynaeceia* 1.4.4). It is discussed by Johnston 1999: 167 and Oakley and Sinos 1993: 26.

148 Euripides, *Hippolytus* 166–68; see also Callimachus' *Hymn III – To Artemis* 20–23.

149 See the birth of Athena, *LIMC* Athena 339.

150 Calame 1997: 36.

151 Foxhall 2007.

152 There are two fires in House A iv 9: at Olynthus (Morgan 2010: 79–81) and also in the Dema House (Jones *et al*, 1962).

153 Demosthenes 39 and 40. For an analysis of the family members see Gallant 1991: 24–25.

154 Kramer 1982.

155 Antiphon 1.

156 Aeschines. *Against Timarchus* 123–24.

157 Possible examples of free-standing small 'houses' include M18 and O18 in the Athenian Agora (Thompson 1959: 101; Jordan and Rotroff 1999: 147–54).

158 Aristophanes *Vespae* 1215.

159 In Euripides' *Ion*, a dining rooms is created at the sanctuary by using a frame hung with textiles (lines 1128–66).

160 Hyperides (fr. 139; Pollux iv.122).

161 Brigger and Giovannini 2004.

162 Deinaeira (Sophocles, *Trachiniae* 685–86); Trojan Women (Euripides, *Trojan Women* 298–99, see also Euripides *Hecuba* 1040); Heracles (Pindar, *Nemean Odes* I, 41–42).

163 For a discussion on the *muchos*, see Morgan, 2007b.

164 Room names can be related to location, such as the *axaito* (outside), a room controlling access to other upstairs rooms, and the *katoi* (down), a storage space or room. They can also be related to the individuals using the space, such as the *nonta*, a word derived from the Turkish phrase '*musafir nonta*' (room for guests) or the *yereve*, possibly derived the word *yeros* (old man), indicating the room used by older relatives. For a full glossary see Pavlides 1985: 425–28.

165 A fuller description of the Zones and domestic activities associated with them can be found in Pavlides 1985: 118–28. For details of the *avli*, see Pavlides 1985: 100–114.

166 For further details, see Pavlides 1985: 158–95.

References

Allison, P. M. (1993). How do we identify the use of space in Roman housing? In E. M. Moorman, ed., *Functional and Spatial Analysis of Wall Painting. Proceedings of the Fifth International Congress on Ancient Wall Painting, Amsterdam 8–12 Sept 1992*. Bulletin antieke beschaving. Annual Papers on Classical Archaeology. Leiden: Stichting BABESCH, 1–8.

   (1999). Labels for ladles: interpreting the material culture of Roman households. In P. M. Allison, ed., *The Archaeology of Household Activities*. London and New York: Routledge, 57–77.

Alston, R. (1997). Houses and households in Roman Egypt. In R. Laurence and A. Wallace-Hadrill, eds., *Domestic Space in the Roman World: Pompeii and Beyond*. Portsmouth, RI: Journal of Roman Archaeology, 25–39.

    (2007). Some theoretical considerations and a Late Antique house from Roman Egypt. In R. C. Westgate, N. R. E. Fisher and A. J. M. Whitley, eds., *Building Communities: House, Settlement and Society in the Aegean and Beyond*. London: British School at Athens, 373–78.

Arnott, W. G. (2000). *Menander. Volume III*. Cambridge, MA, and London: Loeb.

Ault, B. A. (2005). *Halieis: Excavations at Porto Cheli, Greece. Vol. 2. The Houses: the Organisation and Use of Domestic Space*. Bloomington and Indianapolis: Indiana University Press.

Ault, B. A. and Nevett, L. C. (1999). Digging houses: archaeologies of Classical and Hellenistic Greek domestic assemblages. In P. M. Allison, ed., *The Archaeology of Household Activities*. London and New York: Routledge, 43–56.

Barbaro, D. (1556). *I Dieci libri dell'Architettura: di M. Vitruvio, tradotti & commentati da Mons. Daniel Barbaro eletto Patriarca d'Aquileia*. Venice.

Becker, W. A. (1840). *Charikles: Bilder altgriechischer Sitte, zur genauren Kenntnis des griechischen Privatlebens*. Leipzig: Friedrich Fleischer.

    (1911). *Charicles, or Illustrations of the Private Life of the Ancient Greeks*, trans. F. Metcalfe. London: Longmans, Green, and Co.

Berry, J. (1997). Household artefacts: towards a re-interpretation of Roman domestic space. In. R. Laurence and A. Wallace-Hadrill, eds., *Domestic Space in the Roman World: Pompeii and Beyond*. Portsmouth, RI: Journal of Roman Archaeology, 183–96.

Brigger, E. and Giovannini, A. (2004). *Prothésis*: Étude sur les rites funéraires chez les grecs et chez les étrusques, *Mélanges de l'École française de Rome* 116, 179–248.

Brown, B. (2001). Thing theory. *Critical Inquiry* 28(1), 1–22.

Brown, J. (2013) The ephebe and the schoolboy: the Classical narrative of Becker's *Charikles or Illustrations of the Private Life of the Ancient Greeks*. *Journal of Classics Teaching* 28, 1–14.

Burkert, W. (1985) [1996 reprint]. *Greek Religion*, trans. J. Raffan. Oxford: Blackwell.

Cahill, N. (2002). *Household and City Organisation at Olynthus*. New Haven and London: Yale University Press.

Calame, C. (1997). *Choruses of Young Women in Ancient Greece: Their Morphology, Religious Role and Social Functions*, trans. D. Collins and J. Orion. Lanham, MD: Rowman & Littlefield.

Carey, C. (1989). *Lysias. Selected Speeches*. Cambridge: Cambridge University Press.

    (1995). Rape and adultery in Athenian law. *Classical Quarterly* 45, 407–17.

    (1997). *Trials from Classical Athens*. London and New York: Routledge.

Cellauro, L. (2004). Daniele Barbaro and Vitruvius: the architectural theory of a Renaissance humanist and patron. *Papers of the British School at Rome* 72, 293–329.

Chamonard, J. (1906). Fouilles de Délos 1904: fouilles dans le quartier du théâtre. *Bulletin de Correspondence Hellénique* 30, 485–606.

(1922–24). *Le quartier du Théâtre: étude sur l'habitation délienne à l'époque hellénistique*, 3 vols. Exploration archéologique de Délos VIII. Paris: Editions de Boccard.

Ciapponi, L. A. (1984). Fra. Giocondo da Verona and his edition of Vitruvius. *Journal of the Warburg and Courtauld Institutes* 47, 72–90.

Cohen, D. (1989). Seclusion, separation, and the status of women in Classical Athens. *Greece and Rome* 36, 3–15.

(1991). *Law, Sexuality and Society: The Enforcement of Morals in Classical Athens*. Cambridge: Cambridge University Press.

Dalby, A. (1996). *Siren Feasts: A History of Food and Gastronomy in Greece*. London: Routledge.

Demand, N. (1994). *Birth, Death and Motherhood in Classical Athens*. Baltimore and London: Johns Hopkins University Press.

Edwards, M. and Usher, S. (1985). *Greek Orators 1: Antiphon and Lysias*. Warminster: Aris and Phillips.

Fisher N. (2001). *Aeschines, Against Timarchos. Translated, with Introduction and Commentary*. Oxford: Oxford University Press.

Fisher, S. (2015). Philosophy of architecture. In E. N. Zalta, ed., *The Stanford Encyclopedia of Philosophy* (Winter 2016 Edition). https://plato.stanford .edu/archives/win2016/entries/architecture, accessed 11 August 2020.

Foxhall, L. (2000). The running sands of time: archaeology and the short term. *World Archaeology* 31, 484–98.

(2007) House clearance: unpacking the 'kitchen' in Classical Greece. In R. C. Westgate, N. R. E. Fisher and A. J. M. Whitley, eds., *Building Communities: House, Settlement and Society in the Aegean and Beyond*. London: British School at Athens, 234–42.

Gallant, T. W. (1991). *Risk and Survival in Ancient Greece: Reconstructing the Domestic Economy*. Cambridge: Polity.

Gardner, E. (1901). The Greek house. *Journal of Hellenic Studies* 21, 293–305.

Gardner, P. and Jevons, F. B. (1895). *A Manual of Greek Antiquities*. New York: Charles Scribner's Sons.

Garland, R. (1990). *The Greek Way of Life*. London: Duckworth.

(2009). *Daily Life of the Ancient Greeks*, 2nd ed. London: Greenwood Press.

Giocondo, G. (1511). *M. Vitruvius per Jocundum solito castigatior factus cum figuris et tabula ut iam legi et intelligi pos sit*. Venice: G. da Tridentino.

Goldberg, M. (1999). Spatial and behavioural negotiation in Classical Athenian houses. In P. M. Allison, ed., *The Archaeology of Household Activities*. London and New York: Routledge, 142–61.

Graham, J. W. (1954). Olynthiaka 6. The kitchen-complex. *Hesperia* 23, 328–46.

   (1966). Origins and interrelations of the Greek house and the Roman house. *Phoenix* 20, 3–31.

Hall, J. M. (2014). *Artifact and Artifice: Classical Archaeology and the Ancient Historian*. Chicago and London: University of Chicago Press.

Hodder, I. (2012). *Entangled: An Archaeology of the Relationships between Humans and Things*. Chichester: John Wiley.

Holland, L. B. (1944). Colophon. *Hesperia* 13, 91–171.

Jameson, M. H. (1989). Review of F. Pesando *Oikos e ktisis. American Journal of Archaeology* 93, 478–79.

   (1990). Domestic space in the Greek city-state. In S. Kent, ed., *Domestic Architecture and the Use of Space*. Cambridge: Cambridge University Press, 92–113.

Johnston, S. I. (1999). *Restless Dead*. Berkeley: University of California Press.

Jones, J. E. (1975). Town and country houses of Attica in Classical times. In H. Mussche, P. Spitaels and F. Goemaere-De Poerk, eds., *Thorikos and the Laurion in Archaic and Classical Times: Papers and Contributions of the Colloquim held in March 1973 at the State University of Ghent*. Misc Graeca 1. Ghent: Belgian Archaeological Mission in Greece, 63–133.

Jones, J. E., Sackett, L. H. and Graham, A. J. (1962). The Dema house in Attica. *Annual of the British School at Athens* 57, 75–114.

Jordan, D. R. and Rotroff, S. I. (1999). A curse in a chytridion: a contribution to the study of Athenian pyres. *Hesperia* 68, 147–54.

Kaiser, A. (2015). *Archaeology, Sexism and Scandal: The Long Suppressed Story of One Woman's Discoveries and the Man Who Stole Credit for Them*. London and New York: Rowman & Littlefield.

Kramer, C. (1982). *Village Ethnoarchaeology: Rural Iran in Perspective*. New York: Academic Press.

Kruft, H.-W. (1994). *A History of Architectural Theory: From Vitruvius to the Present*. London: Zwemmer.

Kurtz, D. C. and Boardman, J. (1986). Booners. In *Greek Vases in the John Paul Getty Museum. Occasional Papers on Antiquities 2*. Malibu: The John Paul Getty Museum, 35–70.

La Motta, V. M. and Schiffer, M. B. (1999). Formation processes of house floor assemblages. In P. M. Allison, ed., *The Archaeology of Household Activities*. London and New York: Routledge, 19–29.

Lape, S. (2004). *Reproducing Athens. Menander's Comedy, Democratic Culture and the Hellenistic City*. Princeton and Oxford: Princeton University Press.

McEwen, I. K. (2003). *Vitruvius: Writing the Body of Architecture*. Cambridge, MA: MIT Press.

McHardy, F. (2008). *Revenge in Athenian Culture*. London: Duckworth.

McIntosh, G. (2014). *Amor* and *Roma*: Understanding Vitruvius through Eryximachus' erotic *logos* in Plato's *Symposium. L'Antiquité Classique* 83, 15–30.

Morgan, G. (1982). Euphiletos' house: Lysias I. *Transactions of the American Philological Association* 112, 115–23.

Morgan, J. (2007a). Women, Religion and the Home. In D. Ogden, ed., *The Blackwell Companion to Greek Religion*. Oxford: Blackwell, 297–310.

(2007b). Space and the notion of a final frontier: searching for cult boundaries in the Classical Athenian home. *Kernos* 20, 113–29.

(2010). *The Classical Greek House*. Bristol and Exeter: Bristol Phoenix Press.

(2011a). Families and religion in Classical Greece. In B. Rawson, ed., *Family and Household in Greece and Rome: A Companion*. Oxford: Wiley-Blackwell, 447–64.

(2011b). Drunken men and modern myths: searching for the *andron* in Classical Greece. In S. D. Lambert, ed., *Sociable Man. Essays in Greek Social Behaviour in Honour of Nick Fisher*. Swansea: Classical Press of Wales, 267–90.

Morgan, M. H. (1914) [1960]. *Vitruvius. The Ten Books on Architecture*. New York: Dover.

Morris, I. (1994). Archaeologies of Greece. In I. Morris, ed., *Classical Greece: Ancient Histories and Modern Archaeologies*. Cambridge: Cambridge University Press, 8–47.

Morris, S. P. (1985). ΛΑΣΑΝΑ: a contribution to the ancient Greek kitchen. *Hesperia* 54, 393–409.

Mylonas, G. E. (1946). Excursus II: the oecus unit of the Olynthian house. In D. M. Robinson, ed., *Excavations at Olynthus XII. Domestic and Public Architecture*. Baltimore: Johns Hopkins University Press, 369–98.

Nevett, L. C. (1994). Separation or seclusion? Towards an archaeological approach to investigating women in the Greek household in the third to fifth centuries BC. In M. Parker-Pearson and C. Richards, eds., *Architecture and Order: Approaches to Social Space*. London: Routledge, 98–112.

(1995). Gender relations in the Classical Greek household: the archaeological evidence. *Annual of the British School at Athens* 90, 363–81.

(1997). Perceptions of domestic space in Roman Italy. In B. Rawson and P. Weaver, eds., *The Roman Family in Italy: Status, Sentiment, Space*. Oxford: Oxford University Press, 281–98.

(1999). *House and Society in the Ancient Greek World*. Cambridge: Cambridge University Press.

Nývlt, P. (2013). Killing of Eratosthenes between reality and mime (or was Lysias 1 really pronounced?). *Graeco-Latina Brunensia* 18(1), 159–70.

Oakley, J. H. and Sinos, R. H. (1993). *The Wedding in Ancient Athens*. Madison: University of Wisconsin Press.

Paris, P. (1884). Fouilles de Délos: maisons du second siècle av. J.-C. *Bulletin de Correspondence Hellénique* 8, 473–96.

Patterson, C. B. (1998). *The Family in Greek History*. Cambridge, MA, and London: Harvard University Press.

Pavlides, E. (1985). *Vernacular architecture in its social context: a case study of Eressos, Greece.* (PhD thesis, University of Pennsylvania; Ann Arbor, MI: University Microfilms.)

Pesando, F. (1987). *Oikos e Ktesis. La Casa Greca in Età Classica.* Perugia: Quasar.

Petersen, C. (1851). *Der Hausgottesdienst der alten Griechen.* Cassel: Theodor Fischer.

Porter, J. (2007). Adultery by the book: Lysias 1 and comic diēgēsis. In E. Carawan, ed., *Oxford Readings in the Attic Orators.* Oxford: Oxford University Press, 60–88.

Rider, B. C. (1916). *The Greek House: Its History and Development from the Neolithic Period to the Hellenistic Age.* Cambridge: Cambridge University Press.

Robinson, D. M. (1932). The residential districts and the cemeteries at Olynthus. *American Journal of Archaeology* 36, 118–38.

(1946). *Excavations at Olynthus XII: Domestic and Public Architecture.* Baltimore: Johns Hopkins University Press.

Robinson, D. M. and Graham, A. J. W. (1938). *Excavations at Olynthus VIII: The Hellenic House.* Baltimore: Johns Hopkins University Press.

Romano, E. (2016). Between republic and principate: Vitruvius and the culture of transition. *Arethusa* 49(2), 335–51.

Salmenkivi, E. (1997). Family life in the comedies of Menander. In J. Frösén, ed., *Early Hellenistic Athens: Symptoms of a Change.* Papers and Monographs of the Finnish Institute at Athens. Vol. VI. Helsinki: Finnish Institute at Athens, 183–94.

Schnapp, A. (1996). *The Discovery of the Past: The Origins of Archaeology.* London: Abrams.

Shanks, M. (1995). *Classical Archaeology of Greece: Experiences of the Discipline.* London: Routledge.

Shear, T. L. Jr (1973). The Athenian Agora: excavations of 1971. *Hesperia* 42, 123–79.

Sparkes, B. (1962). The Greek kitchen. *Journal of Hellenic Studies* 82, 121–37.

Sparkes, B. and Talcott, L. (1958). *Pots and Pans of Classical Athens.* Princeton: American School of Classical Studies at Athens.

Thompson, H. A. (1959). Activities in the Athenian Agora: 1958. *Hesperia* 28, 91–108.

Thompson, H. A. and Wycherley, R. E. (1972). *The Athenian Agora XIV: The Agora of Athens. The History, Shape and Uses of an Ancient City Centre.* Princeton: The American School of Classical Studies at Athens.

Todd, S. C. (2000). *Lysias.* Austin: University of Texas Press.

(2007). *A Commentary on Lysias (Speeches 1–11.)* Oxford: Oxford University Press.

Tsakirgis, B. (2007). Fire and smoke: hearths, braziers and chimneys in the Greek house. In R. C. Westgate, N. R. E. Fisher and A. J. M. Whitley, eds., *Building Communities: House, Settlement and Society in the Aegean and Beyond.* London: British School at Athens, 425–31.

Whitley, J. (2001). *The Archaeology of Ancient Greece.* Cambridge: Cambridge University Press.

Whitmarsh, T. and König, J., eds. (2008). *Ordering Knowledge in the Roman Empire.* Cambridge: Cambridge University Press.

Wiegand, T. and Schrader, H. (1904). *Priene: Ergebnisse der Ausgrabungen und Untersuchungen in den Jahren 1895–1898.* Berlin: G. Reime.

Wilkins, J. (2000). *The Boastful Chef: The Discourse of Food in Ancient Greek Comedy.* Oxford: Oxford University Press.

Winckler, A. (1868). *Die Wohnhäuser der Hellenen.* Berlin: Calvary.

Young, R.S. (1951). An industrial district of ancient Athens. *Hesperia* 20, 135–250.

4 | A Family Affair

The Household Use of Attic lekythoi*

KATERINA VOLIOTI

In this chapter, I examine a particular item of material culture as one way in which to explore textual and, mostly, material relationships within (and beyond) the house. As also emphasized in other contributions to this volume, the Greek house was not just a building with facility areas.[1] Through the actions, preferences and movements of its inhabitants and visitors the house was also a physical and temporal space for acquiring, storing, using and parting with portable objects.

Lekythoi and the *Oikos*: Ambiguous Walls and Words

An early 5th-century bce white *lekythos*, an Attic funerary vessel shape par excellence, shows a pair of standing and seated women (Figures 4.1 and 4.2).[2] Above the seated woman appear an *oinochoe* at the far left, with its distinctive bulbous body, high handle and trefoil mouth, and a *lekythos* further to the right, identified by its tapering lower body, flat shoulder, long narrow neck, short vertical handle, and cup mouth.[3] Both shapes tilt to the right at a considerable angle, which presumably denotes that they are empty. The two vessels here seem to hang on the wall, invisible and ambiguous as it may be, of a domestic interior, probably in women's quarters deep inside the Classical house. The *oinochoe*, a wine-serving jug, fits in well with the affairs of the household, with formal and informal drinking parties, when family and guests filled their cups from an *oinochoe*. By contrast, a *lekythos*, an oil-carrying bottle that was customarily offered in graves, seems out of place in a domestic setting. The scene on the *lekythos* here could imply the women's imminent visit to a tomb monument, as known from other white *lekythoi*.[4] Indeed, scholars' quasi-obsession with the funerary iconography of white *lekythoi* would favour such an interpretation.[5]

My aim in this chapter is to investigate whether *lekythoi* could also have been household items, used actively in daily life, including in the *symposion*, rather than simply being stored in the house with the

Figure 4.1 Fifth-century *lekythos*, Athens, National Museum, 1826. Left side.
Photographer: Eleftherios A. Galanopoulos. © Hellenic Ministry of Culture and Sports /
Archaeological Receipts Fund. Published with permission

Figure 4.2 Fifth-century *lekythos*, Athens, National Museum, 1826. Right side. Photographer: Eleftherios A. Galanopoulos. © Hellenic Ministry of Culture and Sports / Archaeological Receipts Fund. Published with permission

intention of being used only when somebody in the family, a relative or a friend died. The depicted *lekythos*, just like the *oinochoe*, may have been part and parcel of a house's inventory and a family's preferences for particular material objects. Drawing from theories of object biographies in social anthropology, my working hypothesis is that a *lekythos*, as a portable and functional piece of pottery, acquired familial, cultural and social salience within the household and beyond it.[6] The timeframe under discussion is from approximately 500 to 450 BCE, covering both the late Archaic and the early Classical periods and the time before and after the Persian Wars.

My investigation is especially indebted to the work of two scholars. John H. Oakley, in his analysis of the iconography of white *lekythoi*, argues convincingly that depictions of *lekythoi*, even when shown suspended on ambiguous (non-existent) walls on or near the stelae of tomb monuments, allude to the *oikos*.[7] Kathleen Lynch on the other hand, having studied the full ceramic assemblage from a private house in the Athenian Agora, proposes that plain black and black-figured *lekythoi* served portions of table oil to spice food in household *symposia*.[8] Both the discussion of fine *lekythoi* by Oakley and that of less finely decorated ones by Lynch stress the meaningful presence of *lekythoi* in the house, strengthening sporadic statements in scholarship that early 5th-century *lekythoi* did not have an exclusively funerary function.[9] My objective is to elaborate on this premise.

The word '*lekythos*' – the etymology of which remains contested – was used flexibly in antiquity to describe oil bottles of various shapes.[10] A pre-firing incised ownership inscription on a commissioned red-figured *aryballos* from 490 to 480 BCE describes it as a *lekythos*: 'ΑΣΟΠΟΔΟΡΩ ΗΕ ΛΕΓΥΘΟΣ' (Asopodorō he legythos).[11] There were, moreover, regional variations in the use of words. The term '*aryballos*' was the Doric word for the Athenians' '*lekythos*'.[12] Textual references to *lekythoi* include Homer's mention of a golden *lekythos* prepared for Nausicaa that contained liquid oil (Hom. *Od.* VI.79) and a scholiast to Plato (*Hippias Minor* 368c) who cites a *lekythos* in passing alongside other objects for everyday use.[13]

In Aristophanes, there are multiple references to *lekythoi* of an unspecified shape and material, and the pots are associated with both the living and the dead.[14] Particularly puzzling has been the meaning of the word '*lekythion*' (small *lekythos*) in a scene about a competition between Aeschylos and Euripides in Aristophanes' *Frogs* (1200–1248).[15] Some scholars have associated '*lekythion*' with other words starting with the syllable 'lek-', such as 'ληκώ' and 'λαικάζω', and argued for a lekythion's sexual connotations. As Jeffrey Henderson has convincingly shown, however, 'lekythion' here denotes a small oil flask that has performative and acoustic value. Aristophanes plays with words and sounds, and a small lekythos matches other bathing items appearing in the same verse (1203): a small towel and a small purse. More recently, David Sansone has elaborated further on the hidden meaning of words. According to Sansone, 'lekythion' describes a personal oil bottle that was stolen, and the theft parodies Euripides' characters. The late 5th-century/early 4th-century date of Aristophanes' plays, nonetheless, would imply squat lekythoi, for which their iconography and find-spots point to the domestic domain, and white or marble lekythoi that were used as grave markers.[16] Words alone appear to be ambiguous, and they can be of limited use in examining the presence of lekythoi in households during 500–450 BCE.

This chapter concerns lekythoi as containers, their depiction on vases and their occurrence in the archaeological record.[17] My investigation consists of three sections. First, I discuss how lekythoi have been studied in scholarship, and how the shapes and surfaces of lekythoi of a common type can inform us about contents and repeated use. Second, I consider vase scenes that include depictions of lekythoi to appreciate the social occasions, within and beyond the house, in which lekythoi and their contents mattered. Third, I examine archaeological evidence for the use of lekythoi in houses and provide an overview of find-spots and find contexts in Athens, in Greece and across the Mediterranean. I argue against an exclusive link between lekythoi and perfumes for the dead. Rather, lekythoi were functional oil jars within easy reach in the house, and their use on various social occasions, as suggested by iconography and archaeology, could have made a statement about the household possession of olive oil. I supplement Oakley's and Lynch's approaches by discussing lekythoi other than white ones and find-spots beyond the Athenian Agora.

Lekythoi in Scholarship: Perfumes and Graves

Between 500 and 450 BCE, the dominant lekythos shape was the shoulder lekythos, while globular and squat lekythoi were rare.[18] The shoulder lekythos is characterized by a cylindrical body resting on a foot, a strong carination at the body/shoulder junction, a flat or almost flat shoulder (the area that joins the neck with the body) and a long narrow neck

(Figures 4.1 and 4.2).[19] Regardless of how shoulder *lekythoi* were held when tipped to pour out their contents – either by the handle or by resting one's thumb(s) on the shoulder and fingers against the body – the long neck would have controlled the flow of liquid, which was apparently a valuable feature. Notwithstanding the possible eastern origins of the shape, the large-scale Attic production of shoulder *lekythoi* (especially black-figured ones) and their export to markets across the Greek world would have established these pots as quintessentially Attic shapes in the minds of ancient people.[20] As a result, the contents of shoulder *lekythoi*, whether real or imaginary, may also have correlated with – or at least recalled – that for which the Attic countryside was famous: its superlative olive oil.[21]

Scholars have hesitated to associate shoulder *lekythoi* with olive oil, especially with its domestic uses in cooking, bathing and lighting.[22] Two primary factors may account for this hesitation. First, as mentioned, the funerary scenes on white *lekythoi* have received considerable scholarly attention, and this has resulted in generalizations regarding the burial use of all early 5th-century *lekythoi*. Second, there is a tendency to construct diachronic narratives about the use of perfume flasks in cemeteries, from Archaic *aryballoi* to Classical *lekythoi*, to Hellenistic *unguentaria* and to Pagenstecher *lekythoi*.[23] It is worth discussing these two factors in greater detail.

White *lekythoi* – perhaps more so than other Greek vases – have been praised for the beauty and realism of their freestyle drawings, as if these pots were only *objets d'art* to be seen but not touched.[24] The faint drawings, multiple colours and chalky white background all suggest the fragile surface of pottery that was not destined for repeated use.[25] The proliferation of funerary scenes on white *lekythoi*, including scenes that show the offering of *lekythoi* at tombs, would further corroborate the one-off use of white *lekythoi*, either as burial gifts or for libations. Potters fitted some white *lekythoi* with a small clay container inside them, below the neck, minimizing the amount of liquid held, which is presumed, but not confirmed scientifically, to have been scented oil.[26]

Still, white *lekythoi* were neither the most abundant nor the most widespread shoulder *lekythoi* between 500 and 450 BCE. The most prolifically produced and widely distributed shoulder *lekythoi* were small pots, used by one or a few individuals at a time.[27] Such *lekythoi* could be plain black, hastily decorated pieces in black figure, commonly showing a mythological scene or upright palmettes, or white ground *lekythoi* featuring ivy leaves in the silhouette technique (without any incisions).[28] By contrast, red-figured shoulder *lekythoi*, and red-figured pots in general, are scarce in most parts of the Greek world in the early 5th century.[29] The prolifically produced types have received little systematic study, owing to their low aesthetic merit and large numbers, surviving as they do in their thousands.[30] In this chapter, I shall refer to them collectively as 'common-type *lekythoi*'. These abundant ceramics, which were implicated in the lives of different individuals owing to their wide circulation, could, I believe, be indicative of ancient patterns of use, including the role of *lekythoi* within the house.

The emphasis on perfumes and on the sepulchral domain could be discussed separately. Scholars have long been preoccupied with perfumes, since ancient authors, such as Theophrastos and Pliny, mention varieties of scented oil rather than olive oil.[31] Many parts of the Greek world, however, produced different varieties of olive oil, which depended on regionally diverse species of olive tree, altitude, microclimate, soil, time of harvesting and pressing technology.[32] A painted inscription reading '*hirinon*', iris perfume, on the mouth of a *lekythos* decorated with palmettes in silhouette need not lead to generalizations about all *lekythoi*.[33] The inscription here may have arisen from this painter's (the Diosphos Painter) general interest in writing.[34] As a pre-firing painted inscription, rather than a post-firing incised one, it could have marked the potential, and not necessarily the actual, contents of the *lekythos* after it left the workshop.[35]

A chemical analysis of organic residues from the inside of common-type *lekythoi* is currently missing in scholarship. Such analyses are few even for dedicated perfume containers of the Archaic period, rendering the results inapplicable to large numbers of vases.[36] *Lekythoi*, and specifically black-figured *lekythoi*, are thought to have claimed a share of the international perfume market across the Mediterranean, since their abundance in the early 5th century coincided with an eclipse of all other perfume flasks, including those from the Peloponnese, Crete and Etruria.[37] As I discuss below, however, it remains questionable whether *lekythoi* were traded for their contents. This eclipse could reflect wider shifts in trade patterns, since other Attic shapes, such as cups, and not just *lekythoi* flood the Mediterranean markets during this time.[38] In fact, the transition from Corinthian *aryballoi* to Attic *lekythoi* is not well understood in scholarship, and any continuity regarding contents and functions remains to be proven.[39] Far more *aryballoi* than *lekythoi* have been found in Greek graves and sanctuaries. The capacity of *lekythoi*, moreover, is generally greater than that of *aryballoi*. In the early 5th century, perfumes were held, in all likelihood, in *alabastra* and glass vases, rather than in *lekythoi*.[40] Expensive perfumes in particular could be packaged in flasks of luxurious materials, such as alabaster, faience and metal, from which *lekythoi* are not known to have been made.[41] It is unlikely that common-type *lekythoi* emulated the appearance of perfume containers made from metal and other expensive materials.[42]

The scholarly preoccupation with burial evidence stems, at least to some degree, from the nature of the archaeological record for the early 5th century. The vagaries of preservation and excavation have favoured large cemeteries, such as the Athenian Kerameikos, rather than settlements. Early 5th-century houses were small and unpretentious, unlike their 4th-century counterparts.[43] The considerable reuse of space at Athens has meant that only small parts of house floors survive.[44] For our timeframe, there is no equivalent to the later Classical town of Olynthus.[45] The focus of traditional archaeology has been on house plans and architecture, while fills that could contain potsherds from a house's inventory have been disregarded.[46] Deposits from habitation layers, moreover, usually fail to provide a synchronic view of pottery use and tend to reflect the accumulation of refuse over time.[47] At Lerna, in the Argolid, late Archaic and early Classical wells were filled when their associated buildings, probably houses, were destroyed, and not during periods of house use.[48] People in antiquity packed figured wares when they left a house, as suggested by the small numbers of decorated ceramics found in the late 5th-century farmsteads at Dema and Vari, in the countryside of Attica.[49] Evidently, the use of Attic pottery inside the house, let alone that of *lekythoi*, does not appear to be archaeologically visible for the early 5th century, a point to which I shall return when discussing settlements below.

Taken together, the almost exclusive focus on perfumes and the burial record have restricted our understanding of the wide range of uses of *lekythoi*. Perfumes were highly esteemed and had connotations of a wealthy and exotic lifestyle.[50] Herodotos (3.107.1 and 3.113) points out that exotic spices from Arabia – frankincense, myrrh, cassia, cinnamon and gummastic – produced a divinely sweet fragrance. Such textual references can be misleading when studying the material relationships of common-type *lekythoi* and their contents. Ancient people also used perfumes in cooking and to flavour wine and medicines, but these everyday uses have not been linked with *lekythoi*.[51] Olive oil, likewise, had multiple uses within the house. An aristocrat's annual demand for oil for food, bathing and lighting could have been approximately fifty to eighty-two litres, suggesting bulk storage of oil in the Classical house inside large vessels, such as *pithoi* and trade *amphorae*.[52] Small pitchers would have been needed to dispense oil and *lekythoi* could have performed this function. The amount of oil needed for lighting at a *symposion* is estimated at half a litre, which is the capacity of some large, black-figured *lekythoi*.[53] The use of *lekythoi* as pitchers that were filled from large containers, and then used to fill small vessels, such as cups and lamps, remains underexplored. For common-type *lekythoi*, a study of their materiality, including details of shape and surface, could further support their use as pitchers.[54]

First, potters endowed common-type *lekythoi* with functional attributes. The *lekythoi* are hard-fired and durable. For those with a white background, the white slip has adhered to the pot's surface and does not disintegrate upon touch.[55] The walls of the body and neck are thick, ensuring the pot's stability and robustness. Standardized dimensions for height and diameter probably denoted containers of small, medium and large capacities.[56] Apparently, these ceramic bottles were made to hold liquids, and were not fragile, ephemeral imitations of functional pottery. The presence of contents is also implied by the recent excavation of a large, black-figured *lekythos*, lidded with a clay stopper, *c.* 510–500 BCE, that was found in a grave on the outskirts of Athens.[57]

Second, common-type *lekythoi* do not consistently exhibit a sharp ridge on the inside of the lip, which aimed to dispense oil in small quantities and minimize spillage by drawing the oil back into the *lekythos*.[58] When tipped, such *lekythoi* would be fast-pouring pots, as befitted oil pitchers. The presence of black glaze on the inside of the mouths of differently shaped structures, such as cups and chimneys, seems to have facilitated the smooth and fast flow of oil. Rapid pouring could mean that the *lekythoi* held cheap varieties of oil, rather than perfumes whose every drop mattered. Corinthian *aryballoi*, by contrast, were suited to holding perfume, as indicated by a small neck aperture and a broad mouthplate with a slightly concave top.[59]

Third, there is some evidence of repeated use in the form of wear and tear, repairs and ownership graffiti. Striations at the edge of the underfoot, as observed on a black-figured *lekythos* found in Thessaly, could have arisen from dragging *lekythoi* along a hard surface, such as a table.[60] Repairs include two black-figured *lekythoi* with mended bases from graves in the Athenian Agora and in Rhitsona, and another black-figured *lekythos* with a restored neck from Taranto, Italy.[61] At least five black-figured *lekythoi* have markings that seem to be ownership graffiti. One reads 'Salama', which is an otherwise unknown name,[62] another 'Lykas'[63] and yet another 'Mikion'.[64] Two letters, 'EY', could have denoted ownership.[65]

A more elaborate statement reads 'I belong to Nyno, daughter of Aineso'.[66] Such evidence of repeated use is significant, given how little close attention the surfaces of such *lekythoi* have received.

The shapes and surfaces of *lekythoi* show that these ceramics were not always meant to be used only once, that is, when somebody died. A strong symbolic and functional correlation with the sepulchral domain, over and above potential use in daily life, does not necessarily hold true. *Lekythoi* may have been offered empty, as indicated by their customary sideways deposition inside and outside graves.[67] Contemporary mortuary practices entailed the burial of upturned and thus emptied cups. This need not suggest that *lekythoi* were always empty during their life cycles. The absence of any lining from the inside of oil-carrying *lekythoi* would surely have increased the porosity of their clay,[68] but *lekythoi* could nonetheless have held oil for short periods of time, especially as pitchers that poured oil into open containers. Oil contributed to an object's biography, and linked *lekythoi* with other vessels. What additional evidence is there to support the use of *lekythoi* as oil jars within the house? To address this, I turn to an examination of vase iconography.

Early 5th-Century Vase Scenes

In this section, I investigate the extent to which representations of *lekythoi* denote household items and whether or not an association with olive oil can be made. Any study of *lekythoi* in vase iconography is biased by scenes on white *lekythoi* that feature *lekythoi* at the steps of monumental tombs, as exemplified by the Bosanquet Painter's *oeuvre* of the 440s BCE.[69] Such scenes have become iconic, showing images of *lekythoi* as burial offerings, and as synonymous with the ideology of death.[70] My assumption, however, is that, depending on the subject of the scene, the *lekythoi* depicted indicate material objects, and not just symbolic entities.

I have identified seventy-seven vase scenes, appearing mostly on white *lekythoi*, which date to approximately 500–450 BCE (Table 4.1).[71] *Lekythoi*, in contrast to drinking shapes, are seldom present in vase iconography.[72] Hence, the dataset of seventy-seven vases is considerable and, to some extent, indicative of ancient patterns surrounding the use of *lekythoi*. The depicted *lekythoi* are shoulder *lekythoi*, except for three footless pieces.[73] They are rendered in outline or painted black, so that their exact type remains unclear and does not necessarily coincide with that of the *lekythos* on which they appear.[74]

Table 4.1. *Early 5th-century vase scenes that include representations of lekythoi*

#	Collection	BAPD number	Technique and shape
1	Malibu (CA), The J. Paul Getty Museum: 86.AE.199	195	red-figured pelike
2	Madison (WI), Elvehjem Museum of Art: 70.2	1433	white *lekythos*
3	Athens, National Museum, Unknown No.	2155	white *lekythos*
4	Athens, National Museum, Unknown No.	2156	white *lekythos*
5	Boston (MA), Museum of Fine Arts: 1970.428	2752	white *lekythos*
6	Paris, Musée du Louvre: CA1640	2753	white *lekythos*
7	Athens, National Museum: 12801	2755	black-figured / semi-outline *lekythos*
8	Paris, Musée du Louvre: G109	2851	red-figured cup
9	Boston (MA), Museum of Fine Arts: 99.526	2930	black-figured *lekythos*
10	Paris, Louvre: CA3758	3032	white *lekythos*
11	Tarquinia, Museo Nazionale Tarquiniese: RC1063	8235	black-figured pelike
12	Paris, Cabinet des Médailles: 312	11342	black-figured alabastron
13	Cambridge, Fitzwilliam Museum: GR60.1864	12762	black-figured *lekythos*
14	New York (NY), Metropolitan Museum: Unknown No.	15057	white *lekythos*
15	Florence, Museo Archeologico Etrusco: Unknown No.	15585	black-figured pelike
16	Ticino, Private: K315	21581	white *lekythos*
17	Athens, Dinopoulos: 8	21582	white *lekythos*
18	Vatican City, Museo Gregoriano Etrusco Vaticano: 413	31764	black-figured pelike
19	Malibu (CA), The J. Paul Getty Museum: 96.AE.99	44095	white *lekythos*
20	Athens, National Museum, Acropolis Coll.: F49	46731	red-figured *pyxis*
21	St Petersburg, State Hermitage Museum: 2662	46957	white *lekythos*
22	Bari, Museo Archeologico Provinciale: 8693	202270	red-figured column *krater*
23	Bonn, Akademisches Kunstmuseum: 349	203347	red-figured cup
24	Cambridge, Fitzwilliam Museum: GR12.1927	204826	red-figured cup
25	Berlin, lost: F2254	206367	red-figured alabastron
26	Vatican City, Museo Gregoriano Etrusco Vaticano: 17851	206697	red-figured pelike
27	Berne, Historisches Museum: 12227	206905	red-figured pelike

Table 4.1. (*cont.*)

#	Collection	BAPD number	Technique and shape
28	Cambridge (MA), Harvard Univ., Arthur M. Sackler Mus: 60.341	207134	red-figured hydria
29	Laon, Musée Archéologique Municipal: 37.969	207502	red-figured *lekythos*
30	Athens, National Museum: 1645	207601	red-figured *lekythos*
31	Brussels, Musées Royaux: A1019	207607	white *lekythos*
32	Edinburgh, National Museums of Scotland: 1956.460	207739	red-figured alabastron
33	Gela, Museo Archeologico: 139	207815	red-figured neck amphora
34	Taranto, Museo Archeologico Nazionale: 20309	208170	white *lekythos*
35	Cambridge (MA), Harvard Univ., Arthur M. Sackler Museum: 60.335	209185	white *lekythos*
36	Athens, National Museum: 1929	209186	white *lekythos*
37	Athens, National Museum: 1826	209201	white *lekythos*
38	London, British Museum: D26	209203	white *lekythos*
39	Paris, Cabinet des Médailles: 476	209231	white squat *lekythos*
40	Athens, National Museum: 17287	209237	white *lekythos*
41	Madrid, Museo Arqueologico Nacional: L299	209238	white *lekythos*
42	Athens, National Museum: 1958	209239	white *lekythos*
43	Athens, National Museum: 1959	209240	white *lekythos*
44	Berlin, Antikensammlung: 3245	209243	white *lekythos*
45	Tampa (FL), Museum of Art: 86.79	209247	white *lekythos*
46	London, British Museum: 1905.11-1.1	209253	white *lekythos*
47	Athens, National Museum: 1982	209259	white *lekythos*
48	London, British Museum: D65	209272	white *lekythos*
49	Providence (RI), Rhode Island School of Design: Q6.050	209388	white *lekythos*
50	Havana, Museo Nacional de Bellas Artes: 163	211643	red-figured cup
51	St Petersburg, State Hermitage Museum: 4224	211729	red-figured skyphos
52	Florence, Museo Archeologico Etrusco: PD266	211763	red-figured cup
53	Ancona, Museo Archeologico Nazionale: 3130	211902	white *pyxis*
54	Philadelphia (PA), University of Pennsylvania: 5670	212216	red-figured cup

55	Brussels, Musées Royaux: A1380	212253	red-figured *lebes*
56	Athens, National Museum: 12747	212314	white *lekythos*
57	Athens, National Museum: 12739	212315	white *lekythos*
58	Berlin, Schloss Charlottenburg: 3262	212316	white *lekythos*
59	Athens, M. Vlasto: Unknown No.	212350	white *lekythos*
60	New York (NY), Metropolitan Museum: 51.11.4	212352	white *lekythos*
61	Athens, National Museum: 2018	212364	white *lekythos*
62	Athens, National Museum: 2019	212365	white *lekythos*
63	Switzerland, Private	212371	white *lekythos*
64	Basel, Market	212392	white *lekythos*
65	Lausanne, Private	212393	white *lekythos*
66	Basel, Market	212402	white *lekythos*
67	Toronto, Royal Ontario Museum: 929.22.7	212453	white *lekythos*
68	Paris, Musée du Louvre: CP2692	213223	red-figured *pyxis*
69	Oxford, Ashmolean Museum: 1942.2	213521	red-figured hydria
70	London, British Museum: 1892.7-18.10	275017	red-figured alabastron
71	Basel, Market	351529	black-figured alabastron
72	Philadelphia (PA), Market	351530	black-figured alabastron
73	Lausanne, Private	361401	black-figured bail vase
74	Paris, Market	390187	black-figured *lekythos*
75	Munich, Arndt: 8278	9024936	red-figured *lekythos*
76	Berlin, Antikensammlung F 2445; Zimmermann-Elseify, 2011: 30-32, pl. 14.1-5.	Not in BAPD	white *lekythos*
77	Once Basel; Fritzilas, 2006: 212, pl. 122.396.	Not in BAPD	black-figured alabastron

Table 4.2. *Classification of* lekythoi *scenes on the seventy-seven vases in Table 4.1*

Iconographic subject	Number of vases	BAPD number
Funerary / Visit to the tomb	33	1433; 2155; 2156; 2752; 2753; 2755; 3032; 15057; 21581; 21582; 209238; 209239; 209240; 209243; 209247; 209253; 209259; 209272; 209388; 212314; 212315; 212316 212350; 212352; 212364; 212365; 212371 212392; 212393; 212402; 212453; 361401; and not in BAPD
Domestic, possibly preparing for visiting the tomb	4	195; 207134; 207607; 209185
Domestic setting, women, or women and men interacting	22	11342; 46731; 46957; 206367; 207502; 207601; 207739; 207815; 208170; 209186; 209201; 209203; 209231; 211643; 212216; 212253; 213223; 213521; 275017; 44095; 203347; 202270
Sale of liquids outdoors, in shop, and in palaistra	9	8235; 15585; 31764; 206905; 351529; 351530; 390187; 2930; and not in BAPD
Courtship between men and women	3	204826; 211729; 211763
Mythological	4	2851; 206697; 211902; 12762
Other	2	209237; 9024936
TOTAL	77	

Based on the classification of iconographic subjects in Table 4.2, it is possible to make the following observations. A large number of scenes show funerary subjects (thirty-three of seventy-seven), especially a visit to the tomb. Domestic scenes, too, could relate to a likely tomb visit, and I have identified four such scenes showing explicit preparations for a visit. Yet another twenty-two scenes show women or women and men interacting in a domestic setting, and any funereal connotations are subtle. Of these twenty-two scenes, seventeen show *lekythoi* hanging in the background, four show *lekythoi* being held at the base by women and one shows a *lekythos* standing on a chest. The hanging *lekythoi* could be a drawing convention for walls, or perhaps for shelves, and the *lekythoi* could represent objects within easy reach in the Classical house.[75] Indeed, the *lekythoi* appear together with, or instead of, other household items hanging on the wall, such as mirrors and baskets.[76] The hanging *lekythoi* appear to have been in constant view inside the house, ready to be used when the need arose. Holding *lekythoi* at the base seems to follow a general rule for ceramics in vase iconography and need not imply that a *lekythos'* surface was fragile and not to be touched.

Lekythoi are not as absent from sympotic scenes as one may assume at first sight. Amongst the twenty-two domestic scenes, a fine fragmentary cup

Table 4.3. *Shapes of pottery in Table 4.1*

#	Shape	No. of pieces
1	Shoulder *lekythos*	47
2	Alabastron	7
3	Cup	6
4	Pelike	6
5	*Pyxis*	3
6	Hydria	2
7	Bail vase	1
8	Column *krater*	1
9	*Lebes*	1
10	Neck amphora	1
11	Skyphos	1
12	Squat *lekythos*	1
	TOTAL	**77**

by Onesimos shows a male lyre player before a seated female and a hanging *lekythos* between them.[77] The setting here could relate to, or at least take cues from, a *symposion*. In addition, a psychter from *c.* 500 BCE showing a *symposion* features a hybrid between a *lekythos* and an *oinochoe* in the frieze below the scene.[78] Depictions of hydriae and amphorae are also rare in sympotic scenes, although these shapes were essential to actual *symposia* for carrying water and wine.[79] By comparison, *lekythoi* would have been connected visually, and in real life, with dining and drinking, as implied also by their presence on eight drinking shapes (six kylikes, one skyphos and one *krater*) amongst the seventy-seven pieces of my dataset (Table 4.3).

Concerning the contents of *lekythoi*, vase scenes are far from explicit. As I mentioned in the introduction, *lekythoi* are customarily displayed at a slanting angle and are thus empty. The active use of *lekythoi*, upturning them to release liquids, is never shown. Only two images exist, both from after 450 BCE, that feature *lekythoi* held at the neck and the handle, perhaps signifying that a libation is about to happen.[80] *Lekythoi* appear in nine sales scenes, and the transactions take place inside a building, probably a shop and a palaistra, and outdoors near trees, which could imply open markets and itinerant merchants.[81] In these scenes, *lekythoi* are intended to be filled from larger vessels, from amphorae and pelikai, which are thought to have carried olive oil and perfume respectively.[82] The depiction of a funnel in one scene suggests that the liquid contents were valuable, but their specific type remains unclear.[83]

Any strong association between *lekythoi* and perfumes becomes especially problematic, since rods for stirring scented oil to release its fragrance are shown in alabastra rather than *lekythoi*.[84] An exception is a scene on an alabastron, where a woman holds a rod in one hand, a *lekythos* in the other, and a large *lekythos* stands on the ground.[85] This scene, however, is almost identical to two other scenes on alabastra by this painter (the Theseus Painter), in which the woman holds an alabastron and not a *lekythos*.[86] Clearly, the painter here drew the alabastra and *lekythoi* interchangeably, and the *lekythos*' connection with a stirring rod is weak. The presence of *lekythoi* in three courtship scenes need not imply that the *lekythoi* held perfume, which is known to have been used in seduction.[87] Artificial light also played a role in intimacy, and the *lekythoi* here may have alluded to oil for lighting.[88] In a similar fashion, the *lekythos* depicted in a mythological scene, which shows maenads with torches and a satyr, may have held oil for lighting the torches.[89] Overall, vase iconography testifies to the presence of *lekythoi* in houses, but the role and contents of *lekythoi* cannot be determined with certainty. To further investigate the domestic use of *lekythoi*, I now examine archaeological evidence from settlements.

Lekythoi from Settlements

When considering the find-spots and find contexts of *lekythoi*, a quantitative assessment falls beyond my scope. Even in the Athenian Agora, only a selection of excavated pottery has been published.[90] In brief excavation reports, *lekythoi* are mentioned or illustrated only as evidence for the presence of Attic pottery, rendering any statistical analysis impossible. Another limitation is that early 5th-century *lekythos* fragments have hardly ever been found in surface surveys of habitation patterns. Surface finds, when they do occur, are likely to originate from damaged graves, rather than settlements.[91] Hence, an investigation of *lekythoi* from houses necessitates an examination of excavated material. My objective is to provide an overview of some relevant evidence. First, I discuss finds from the Athenian Agora and second, from areas beyond Athens.

The Athenian Agora

In the Athenian Agora, evidence for the household use of early 5th-century *lekythoi* comes from secondary deposits, from wells and pits filled with dumped refuse. Relevant to our timeframe of 500–450 BCE are twenty-two deposits that were sealed after the Persian attacks on Athens in 480/479

BCE, and at least two non-Persian deposits, with pottery that dates to
c. 450 BCE.

The Persian deposits, with the exception of J 2:4 published by Lynch,
cannot be associated with any surviving walls: contemporary late Archaic
houses were completely destroyed and abandoned, and later houses built
over these deposits had new plans and orientations.[92] There has been
hesitation over the association of the deposits, either exclusively or in part,
with household activity. Rather, two of the largest deposits, the Rectangular
Rock Cut Shaft (RRCS) and the Stoa Gutter Well (SGW), have been
considered dumps of pottery workshops. In both deposits, the large
amounts of black-figured lekythoi from few and related stylistic workshops
would appear to substantiate this claim.[93] Pottery-making and industrial
activity in general, however, declined in the Agora during this period and
evidence for wasters in the RRCS and the SGW is weak.[94] Misfired pots
were not necessarily workshop refuse, as they were used and traded
widely.[95] Even fine pieces, such as two red-figured column-kraters by the
Pan Painter from c. 470 BCE, can display misfired areas, owing to the
uneven flow of hot gases during firing in the kiln.[96]

Another interpretation has been that multiples of lekythoi made by the
same hand indicate sales shops; this interpretation, which has become
accepted, may apply to the SGW and the upper fill of the RRCS.[97] As with
the pottery workshop scenario, a reluctance to associate multiples of
lekythoi with the domestic sphere also holds true here. The occurrence of
batches of lekythoi produced by the same hand in graves is thought to
imply workshops and sales shops, where people could buy wholesale lots
when somebody died. The possibility that multiples of lekythoi, and of
other shapes as shown by Lynch's study of drinking cups, were stored (and
used) inside the house has received little attention.[98] In fact, all Persian
deposits have yielded tiles and mud bricks, presumably from houses, as
well as plain household ceramic wares.[99] The majority of lekythoi from
these deposits, therefore, must originate from the cupboards of Athenian
houses, as scholars have begun to admit in recent years.[100]

The non-Persian deposits include a pit with pottery from the second and
third quarters of the 5th century, which was used by state officials for
public dining, and a well with mid-5th century pottery from private
dwellings.[101] In both deposits, the lekythoi are small, of a common type,
and few when compared to drinking shapes. Two explanations may
account for the difference in numbers. First, as they were small, closed
shapes with rounded bodies, lekythoi were less prone to breakage and thus
less likely to be discarded. Second, lekythoi could serve more than one diner

at a time. 'A single *lekythos* can pour oil onto many salads,' as Susan Rotroff and John H. Oakley noted.[102]

Beyond Athens

The overview of evidence, provided below, is not exhaustive; rather, my aim is to highlight problems regarding the interpretation of find-spots from settlements, and to this end, I discuss locations at an increasing distance from Athens.[103] Two houses at Thorikos, Attica, have yielded a *lekythos* each, although one could be a later intrusion.[104] At Kolonna, Aegina, fragments from small *lekythoi* have come from a building of unconfirmed function and from an adjacent road, in addition to well fills.[105] At Eretria, the find-spots of black-figured *lekythoi* can be difficult to interpret.[106] According to its excavator, Petros Themelis, a household deposit with Attic pottery, architectural debris, clay busts and animal bones, resulted from the Persian destruction of Eretrian houses in 490 BCE.[107] Busts, however, are known from both houses and sanctuaries, and the black-figured *lekythos* here, if not a later intrusion, as suggested by the dating of its shape, could have originated from domestic or votive activity, or a combination of the two.[108] An assemblage of broken ceramics, which includes 123 small *lekythoi* from the very late 6th and very early 5th century (up to 490 BCE), seems to derive from sales stores in the Archaic agora.[109] It remains unclear from short excavation reports whether additional black-figured *lekythoi* come from a house, road or damaged grave.[110]

In Thessaly, there are three find-spots of *lekythoi* from settlements. At Soros, south of the Demetrias peninsula, a trial excavation of a large building inside the acropolis of the ancient town recovered a small plain black *lekythos*, said to be from the late 6th century, together with numerous drinking shapes.[111] At Argissa Magoula, west of Larissa, stray finds from the Archaic/Classical settlement on this prehistoric mound included two black-figured *lekythoi*.[112] At Neochori Ayias, east of Larissa, small-scale excavations on a hilltop gave habitation debris, such as roof tiles, and a black-figured *lekythos*.[113]

Further to the north, a small, plain black *lekythos* from a building at Palaiochora, Corfu, seems to testify to the use of *lekythoi* in house shrines.[114] Preliminary publication of the Attic pottery from the settlement at Karabournaki, Thessaloniki, has included a black-figured *lekythos*, which could come from a household or a commercial storage facility.[115] The published specimens from the town of Argilos, eastern Macedonia, include a black-figured *lekythos* of globular shape, which was rare in the early 5th century.[116] At the acropolis of Mytilene, a few fragmentary *lekythoi* come from habitation debris.[117] On the Black Sea, small *lekythoi*, mostly plain black and black-figured ones, have been found in the settlements at Olbia and Phanagoria.[118]

To the south and south-east of Athens, the kitchen area of a house at Azoria, Crete, has given a few black-figured *lekythoi*, excavated together with cooking and household coarse wares.[119] This evidence suggests the use of *lekythoi* in food preparation (perhaps as containers of condiments), and not just in dining. The town on Karantina Island at Klazomenai has yielded some black-figured *lekythoi*.[120] At Old Smyrna, fragmentary *lekythoi* have been excavated from the trenches of 6th- and 5th-century houses.[121] Two *lekythoi*, surprisingly almost complete, are said to have come from habitation layers in the small port-town of Bat Yam, south of Jaffa.[122] A number of *lekythoi* have been excavated in the large town at Tel Dor, Israel.[123]

To the west of Athens, at Feia, the main port of Elis, fragments of black-figured *lekythoi* were recovered beside a wall, the purpose of which remains undetermined in the small-scale excavation.[124] These pots might have been ritual offerings placed at the foundations of buildings.[125] The settlement at Adria, northern Italy, has reportedly given some black-figured *lekythoi*, but the nature of their find context remains unclear because of excavation in the 18th and 19th centuries.[126] At Monte Maranfusa, Palermo, Sicily, a black-figured *lekythos* was found in an abandoned house.[127]

At the Sicilian Archaic settlement of Monte Iato, a few fragmentary *lekythoi* have come from the West Quarter, Area of Trench 480.[128] Specifically, one *lekythos* was recovered from the fill of the floor of a Hellenistic house (*Peristylhaus* 1) and another two *lekythoi* come from a wall to the north-east of this house.[129] The excavator, Hans Peter Isler, was puzzled about the function of the late Archaic buildings that yielded the *lekythoi* and originally suggested that they were houses.[130] In 2009, Isler revised this view and interpreted the Archaic structural remains near *Peristylhouse* 1, again with reservation, as a group of temples.[131] Another late Archaic building at Monte Iato, however, with no sacral function has produced early 5th-century *lekythoi*, indicating that the domestic use of *lekythoi* in this town was likely.[132]

Lekythoi from Houses: Question Mark

On the whole, the occurrence of *lekythoi* in settlements is low. Even patterned *lekythoi*, which may have been more versatile in their non-burial uses than other *lekythoi*, have been found in small quantities, as shown by the detailed publication of material from Old Smyrna, Al Mina in Syria and Tel Dor.[133] To my knowledge, no domestic deposit has yielded a high number of *lekythoi*, compared with those evidenced in graves. On the one hand, a low number of *lekythoi* in settlements seems to support the assumption that *lekythoi* played no role in the house and were bought only in time for a funeral from potteries and sales shops. On the other hand, even a low occurrence of *lekythoi* is indicative of their domestic function for two main reasons. First, the burial use of *lekythoi* could affect their occurrence in settlements. Irrespective of where people kept *lekythoi*, in houses, shops or other buildings, they took *lekythoi* out of circulation by placing them in graves. Cups, as observed in the Athenian Agora, outnumber *lekythoi* in all settlements,[134] but their presence in contemporary graves is minimal. Second, the vagaries of excavation and preservation may mean that we have yet to excavate, or to identify, a domestic depot of early 5th-century *lekythoi* similar, for example, to the hoard of late 5th-century/early 4th-century BCE oil flasks of local manufacture found inside a storage bin in a burnt house at Al Mina.[135]

Obviously, we are faced with difficult data, and much of the evidence is tentative. The surviving *lekythos* fragments are usually small and/or stray finds that cannot be associated with architectural remains.[136] The purpose of buildings can be perplexing, even to excavators, as exemplified by Monte Iato. It can be hard to distinguish household activity from other practices, especially from religious rites within or beyond a domestic setting.

What is clear, however, is that *lekythoi* are usually of a common type, and from stylistic workshops, such as those of the Class of Athens 581ii, the Haimon Group and the Beldam Painter, that engaged in large-scale production and distant trade. This does not necessarily mean that other types of *lekythoi* were not used in the house. Rather, the prolifically produced and common types are more likely to occur. The question arises as to whether we find *lekythoi* in settlements because of the overall wide distribution of these types, within and across different sites. It becomes necessary to also examine archaeological evidence from burial and other non-burial find-spots, as these may preserve what was stored inside the house.

Linking Houses with Other Places

The abundance of common-type *lekythoi* in burials is well noted.[137] Traditionally, the *lekythoi* have been taken to signify women's possessions and offerings for the poor in Athens and for those with a conservative taste abroad.[138] Such *lekythoi* have been excavated in their dozens, in pairs and as single finds in burials of diverse types, ranging from simple pits, to cist graves, to expensive sarcophagi.[139] Further funerary accoutrements vary, and, usually, include other Attic and non-Attic ceramics as well as, less commonly, elaborate objects of metal (jewellery, weapons, mirrors) and of exotic materials (glass, alabaster, ivory).[140] Within and across different regions, people did not bury *lekythoi* with a specific set of other items, as if *lekythoi* were cult objects. There is no typical burial assemblage that includes *lekythoi*.

The versatile use of *lekythoi* is evident also from their presence in graves of individuals who differed in age, gender and social standing, judging from the size and expenditure of the burial and the full inventory and, where analysis exists, from osteological data.[141] The absence of clear patterns implies that these ceramics, as possessions and/or offerings, were relevant to the lives and/or the personae of diverse groups of people. The broad social acceptance of *lekythoi* must have been sustained by their wide circulation, which was in turn facilitated by trade, production and social networks in Attica and beyond.

Wide circulation is also informed by finds in sanctuaries and workshops. At sacred sites, people may have used *lekythoi* as votives, for bathing and for libations.[142] In workshops, *lekythoi* may have held oil for polishing metal plate.[143] Stray finds, such as those from roads, resulted from use contexts that cannot be ascertained, but the possibility of ritual and industrial activity may deserve more scholarly attention.[144]

Trade in *lekythoi*, regardless of whether or not they were made in Attica, appears to have been ongoing and far-reaching. The use of *lekythoi* by different individuals and on diverse social occasions depended on the good availability of these pots, placing demands on traders and, through them, on potters and painters. In envisaging a model of intensive production to meet consumer demand, the presence of *lekythoi* in houses must have been much higher in antiquity than we can detect from the problematic archaeological record that survives. We may need to look beyond settlements to appreciate household use of *lekythoi*.

Archaeologists may have been too eager to derive meaning from one type of archaeological context alone. In a positivist fashion, the preponderance of *lekythoi* in cemeteries and their low occurrence in settlements would reflect the occasional use of burial shapes within households. Such an interpretative framework leaves little room for exploring the physical, emotional and cognitive connections between different domains.[145] For widely used and widely travelled ceramics such as *lekythoi*, different social

activities may have overlapped. As Lynch has argued for the Athenian
Agora, the use of *lekythoi* in the house accounted for their offering
in graves.[146]

Lynch's argument would also apply to areas beyond Athens. Burial find-
spots are far too numerous and too widely distributed to assume that sales
shops existed near each and every cemetery, and specifically that these
shops were well stocked with *lekythoi* throughout the year to serve a
family's needs for funerary offerings when somebody died. Instead, people
living far away from Athens must have bought *lekythoi* during the sailing
season, when consignments of traded entities arrived, and stored these pots
in the house for use as required. The material qualities of a *lekythos* were
neither prescriptive of its social function, nor its (final) deposition in a
grave. People engaged actively with the materiality of these pots and their
contents. Settlement data ought to be studied alongside and even integrated
with other archaeological contexts, including burial evidence. Conversely,
the burial record can potentially inform us about household inventories.
An assemblage of *lekythoi* and terracotta figurines in a child's grave could
have derived from the house.[147] I turn now to examine whether we can also
associate *lekythoi* with the family.

Lekythoi in the Family

The family as a kinship group of related individuals of different ages and
genders, and of different social standings, if we consider house slaves and/
or relatives in an extended family, inhabited one or more, possibly neighbouring, dwellings. And yet, the family existed also as a set of relationships
dispersed in time and space, beyond the physical confines of a house or
group of houses.[148] The non-patterned use of *lekythoi* in the burial record
makes it unlikely that these ceramics structured interpersonal relationships
within the extended family in the form of binary oppositions, such as
young–old, male–female and poor–wealthy. The material attributes of
these flasks, nonetheless, were suited to storing and serving personal
portions of oil, and this may have reinforced ideas about well-being, caring
for the body and identity differentiation. In addition, the *lekythoi* may have
played a role in familial interactions in terms of learning and exchanging
information about material objects.[149] Individuals' acculturation with
lekythoi, as popular, abundant and versatile ceramics, must have taken
place within the household, since all individuals in the family were potential users of *lekythoi* and the oil in them. In exploring family preferences

vis-à-vis *lekythoi*, firstly I consider some putative evidence from the burial record and secondly I discuss the salience of olive oil.

For the period 500–450 BCE, it appears that there is little convincing evidence for designated family burial plots, since periboloi date from the late 5th century onwards.[150] It is possible, nonetheless, to make inferences from topography. Cemeteries are usually situated alongside major and minor roads leading away from settlements. Even small towns had more than one cemetery, running along roads in different directions (north, south, east and west). These cemeteries could have served the needs of different parts of the town. For logistical reasons people may have chosen the closest cemetery for transporting the body of the deceased. Neighbouring houses, presumably belonging to the same family or kinship group, may have used one section of a cemetery and hence had graves near one another. The placement of *lekythoi* in nearby graves, which is attested archaeologically, could reflect a family's preference for these ceramics. Multiple burials in the same grave and in the same spot, containing *lekythoi* of different stylistic workshops and dates, could suggest that families persistently favoured *lekythoi* over the years.[151] Family members may have passed knowledge about *lekythoi* from one generation to the next.

The abundance of *lekythoi* in single burials, where we see dozens of *lekythoi* from the same or a few workshops, need not indicate wholesale buying at the time of the funeral.[152] This purchasing model has been applied even to the Marathon Tumulus, not least because of Thucydides' (II.34.5) implicit reference to a rushed burial at Marathon.[153] Instead, multiples of *lekythoi*, regardless of whether they were full when offered, could have alluded to the storage of oil in the household of the deceased. Whether a particular house possessed large quantities of oil may have been of little relevance here. Using large numbers of *lekythoi* offered an excuse for the friends and family of the deceased, as well as others who gathered at the funeral, to also appreciate a household as a fictitious entity with claims to status.[154] As a commodity, olive oil related both to accumulated wealth and to social storage that could be exchanged in times of need, and it involved a family's connections and social networks.[155] During a period when legislation prohibited ostentatious displays in funerary rites, *lekythoi* as transient oil containers made a subtle, yet powerful, statement about the real or imaginary social status of the deceased and their family.[156]

The popularity of *lekythoi* at different levels, within a family, town, region and across different cultures in the Mediterranean, pertained also to ideas about the multiple uses of and high esteem for olive oil. *Lekythoi* were probably traded as empty flasks, since the bulk transport of olive oil would have taken place in large storage vessels, the thick walls of which made them less prone to breaking during sea and overland journeys and prevented evaporation of the oil in them.[157] People could fill *lekythoi* with local varieties of olive oil, perhaps family-produced and/or from farmsteads that belonged to the (extended) family.[158] The geographical distribution of *lekythoi* need not only be linked with mortuary customs, but also with regional commodities, culinary habits, ideas about well-being and perceptions of wealth, all of which pertained to the affairs of the household.[159]

For the most abundant black-figured *lekythoi*, the shapes of those bearing figural scenes and patterned decoration (upright palmettes) are different.[160] Potters catered for the production of specialized packages, which made a visual statement about different types of liquids, and possibly varieties of olive oil. For figural pieces, the iconography, especially drawings of chariot processions, imitates that of quintessential oil containers, the Panathenaic and other black-figured amphorae,[161] which mattered as special display and sympotic pieces within the house. *Lekythoi*, given their ubiquity and smaller size, brought the kudos of amphorae and their contents closer to individual family members, influencing people's understandings of material relationships.

Conclusion: *Lekythoi* Inside and Outside the House

In this chapter, I have brought together different classes of evidence so as to overcome typically held assumptions, largely inspired by ancient texts, about the use of *lekythoi* as perfume-carrying pots for the dead. Specifically, I have emphasized the material attributes of early 5th-century common-type *lekythoi*, the variety of settings in which *lekythoi* appear in vase iconography and the archaeology of settlements alongside that of graves and other find-spots. The prolific presence and wide distribution of *lekythoi* in 500–450 BCE suggest the increased salience of olive oil that was stored, valued and consumed within the house during this period.

When re-examining the white *lekythos* of Figures 4.1 and 4.2, it is now possible to understand that the hanging *lekythos* shown in the scene is not necessarily symbolic of death and a visit to the tomb. There is also realism in this scene. The smelling gesture by the standing woman who holds flowers in her hands need not imply that the hanging *lekythos* would be filled with scented oil (perfume).[162] Rather, the *lekythos* here, just like the *oinochoe*, was an item from the household inventory to be filled and emptied again as required, most likely with olive oil. The object biographies of these pots and their contents, therefore, were constructed and grafted inside the *oikos*. As such, all members of the family were potential users of these versatile ceramics, and the importance of the *lekythos* was a family affair within and beyond the house.

Notes

* I am indebted to Jen Baird and April Pudsey for their patience, support and invaluable edits, and to Hannah Platts and Amy C. Smith for reading and commenting on earlier versions of this chapter. For useful discussion and bibliographic references, I would like to thank Athina Chatzidimitriou, Marco Fantuzzi, Richard N. Fletcher, Georg Gerleigner, Stefanos Gimatzidis, Kathleen Lynch, Stratos Nanoglou, Cornelis Neeft, Victoria Sabetai, Amy C. Smith and Michalis Tiverios. For permission to study pottery in their care, I am grateful to the directors of the 1st, 2nd, 3rd, 9th, 10th, 13th, 17th and 18th Ephorates, the Ephorates of Speleology and of Private Collections in Athens, the National Archaeological Museum in Athens, the Archaeological Museum of Thessaloniki, and to Jean-Jacques Maffre (Archaeological Museum of Thasos), Jutta Stroszeck (Kerameikos excavations), Amy C. Smith (Ure Museum, Reading), Alexandra Villing (British Museum, London) and Lucilla Burn (Fitzwilliam Museum, Cambridge).

1 See, in particular, Chapter 6 by Lisa Nevett, Chapter 3 by Janett Morgan and Chapter 1 by Emily Varto.

2 Athens, National Archaeological Museum, 1826; *BAPD* 209201. Name piece of the Painter of Athens 1826, *c.* 460 BCE, found in a grave at Eretria (Oakley 2004: 43; Schmidt 2005: 49, with references). *BAPD* = Vase number in the Beazley Archive Pottery Database, https://www.beazley.ox.ac.uk/carc/pottery.

3 For *oinochoai* and *lekythoi* of various shapes, see Sparkes and Talcott 1970: 58–69, 150–55.

4 A tomb monument appears on another white *lekythos* by the same painter from this grave: Athens, National Archaeological Museum, 1825; BAPD 209212. Schmidt 2005: 49–50.

5 See, for example, Bosanquet 1896; 1899; Beazley 1938; Trinkl 2014. For the reception of white *lekythoi*, see Van De Put 2006b: 61–62; Kunze-Götte 2010: 7–10. For the lack of physical touch between the living and the dead on white *lekythoi*, see Arrington 2018: 17.

6 For object biographies, see Kopytoff 1986; Hoskins 2006; Bundrick 2016: 15, with references. For the movement of white *lekythoi* between the private and public spheres, see Arrington 2015: 250–53.

7 Oakley 2004: 187, 191.

8 Lynch 2011: 135–40.

9 For plain black and pattern *lekythoi*, see Kurtz 1975: 131, 143. For black-figured *lekythoi*, see De Vries 1977: 544; Stansbury-O'Donnell 2006: 41; Algrain *et al.* 2008: 151; Hatzivassiliou 2010: 97. For red-figured *lekythoi*, see Zimmermann-Elseify 2013: 17.

10 On etymology, see Bender 1934. For textual references, see Richter and Milne 1935: 14–15; Săndulescu 1962: 42; Oakley 2004: 4–5, 37–38. The word '*lekythos*' can also denote the Adam's apple (*LSJ* s.v. *lekythos*).

11 Athens, National Archaeological Museum, 15375; *BAPD* 205321; *AVI* 906. *AVI* = Vase number in the database of Attic Vase Inscriptions, https://avi .unibas.ch. The *aryballos* was found with black-figured *lekythoi* (Papaspyride and Kyparissis 1927–28: 93, 108). For discussion, see Williams 2013: 41–43.

12 Johnston 1979: 33.

13 See Pinjuh 2014: 175.

14 Aristophanes, *Frogs* 1200–1248; *Assembly Women* 538, 744, 996, 1032, 1101, 1111; *Birds* 1589; *Wealth* 810–11; *Women at the Thesmophoria* 139. See, for example, Walters 1905: 132, 195; Quincey 1949; Kurtz 1975: 73–74.

15 Henderson 1972; Sansone 2016: 319–21, with references.

16 For squat *lekythoi*, see Van De Put 2006b: 37–38; Zimmermann-Elseify 2015: 60–63. At Olynthus, squat *lekythoi* have been found together with tableware and loom weights in *pastas*, women's quarters, kitchens and shops integrated in houses (Cahill 2002: 89, 92, 105–107, 126, 139). For marble *lekythoi* and their putative familial associations, see Margariti 2018: 98, with references.

17 On the intertwined relationship between containers and contents, see Robb 2018: 32–33.

18 Sparkes and Talcott 1970: 151–53.

19 *ABL* 7 (Haspels 1936: 7, hereafter *ABL*); Moore and Philippides 1986: 44.

20 For eastern origins, see De La Genière 1984: 94; Houby-Nielsen 1995: 166–68; Fletcher 2011: 29–32. A comprehensive study of trade patterns is lagging behind in the literature. Small black-figured *lekythoi* were probably also produced outside Athens. The brown clay fabric of unpublished palmette *lekythoi* from the Artemision in Thasos is suggestive of local workshops (Archaeological Museum of Thasos, *vidi* April 2008). Future research could ascertain whether imitations of Attic *lekythoi* were traded widely.

21 Boardman 1977: 190; Bentz 1998: 117, in passing. For the cultivation of olive trees in Attica, see *PW* (Pauly *et al.* 1937, hereafter *PW*), s.v. *Ölbaum*, 2001–2002 [A. S. Pease], with references to ancient sources. Olive oil from Attica was not exported, except for the oil in Panathenaic amphorae (see Bresson and Rendall 2016: 406). It is likely, however, that transport amphorae rather than prize Panathenaics held the oil (see Eschbach 2020: 88–95). The harvest of olive trees is shown on two black-figured amphorae from *c.* 520 BCE, and the inscription on one of them could imply that

people aspired to become wealthy from the sale of oil (see Lewis 2018: 38; Oakley 2020: 85).

22 Olive oil has been studied in conjunction with large containers, such as Panathenaic amphorae (see Tiverios 1974; Shear 2003; Shapiro 2014: 227). *Lekythoi* are not mentioned in discussions of oil in: Amouretti 1986; Parisinou 2000a; 2000b; Foxhall 2007. Only lately has it been argued that *lekythoi* held small portions of edible oil (see Steinhart 1996: 77; Frère 2006b: 196, in passing; Lynch 2011: 140, 146, 149; Klebinder-Gauss 2019: 119).

23 See, for example, Wright 1886: 386; Kurtz and Boardman 1971: 100–101; Parko 2001; De La Genière 2004: 149; Turner 2005: 67–68; Massar 2009; Lambrugo 2015: 286.

24 See, for example, Mertens 1975: 27; Robertson 1992: 210; Garyfallopoulos 2019: 127, with references.

25 See, for example, Beazley 1938: 6; Bundrick 2020: 121, in passing.

26 See Oakley 2004: 8.

27 The average heights of black-figured *lekythoi* of the Haimon Group (*c.* 500–450 BCE) range from 13 to 20 cm (Volioti 2014: 162) and those of red-figured *lekythoi* of a secondary type are between 15 and 18 cm (Cook 1991: 210).

28 I am unaware of undecorated shoulder *lekythoi* with unglazed surfaces. For a plain globular *lekythos* from the Southeast Fountain House in the Agora, Athens, see Paga 2015: 372, no. 10.

29 See Plassart 1928: 173–74; Knigge 1976: 15; De Vries 1977: 449, with references; Boardman 1979: 37; Tuna-Nörling 1996: 16; 1999: 19; Goette and Weber 2004: 81; Stewart and Martin 2005: 80; Hatzivassiliou 2010: 8; Klebinder-Gauss 2012: 57. For the large numbers of red-figured *lekythoi* in southern Italy and Sicily, see Gex-Morgenthaler 1988: 170; Cook 1991: 222; Gex 1993: 21–22; Torelli 2004: 28.

30 Many *lekythoi* remain unpublished in museum storage. The Beazley Archive Pottery Database lists 1758 *lekythoi* by the Haimon Painter and of the Haimon Group (Full Database figures, www.beazley.ox.ac.uk/pottery, accessed 28 September 2020), which is an underestimate of extant *lekythoi* from this workshop.

31 See, for example, Noble 1988: 66; Massar and Verbanck-Piérard 2013: 278; Jubier-Galinier 2014. For textual references, including Theophrastos' *On Odours* and Pliny's *Natural History*, see Touzé 2008: 54–57.

32 For crushing techniques, see Livarda 2014: 112, with references. For olive tree cultivation, see Bresson and Rendall 2016: 127–29.

33 Athens, National Archaeological Museum, 12271; *ABL*: 12–15, 124–25, 235.66, pl. 37.2; Algrain *et al.* 2008: 149; *BAPD* 6038; *AVI* 870.

34 Immerwahr 2006: 150–55; Hatzivassiliou 2010: 79; Jubier-Galinier 2016: 65–68.

35 Note, for example, incised Greek inscriptions of spices on Babylonian alabaster alabastra: Finkel and Reade 2002: 40–45.

36 For Archaic flasks: Biers *et al.* 1988; 1994; 1995; Frère 2008: 211–12; Garnier and Frère 2008: 61. Payne (1931: 288, no. 486) reports scent coming out of a Corinthian *aryballos*.

37 Frère 2006a: 108; 2008: 210.

38 See, for example, Smith and Volioti 2019: 176, with references.

39 For a comprehensive discussion of *aryballoi*, which may have been deposited empty, see Neeft 2006: 77 fn. 5. Arguments about a competition between the Corinthian and Attic perfume industry rest on tenuous ground (see Plassart 1928: 173). Archaeological evidence for perfumeries prior to the Hellenistic period is missing, and the alleged operation of a Hellenistic perfume factory on Delos (Brun 2000; 2008) has relied largely on reconstructions from Roman frescoes (Foxhall 2007: 164–65).

40 Cf. the replacement of ceramic perfume flasks with faience and glass containers on the island of Rhodes in the 6th century BCE (Villing and Mommsen 2017: 144). Glass was an exotic material, as indicated by an extensive supply network. Scientific analyses point to a Syro-Palestinian origin of raw glass for perfume vases that date from the 6th to the 4th centuries BCE from Pieria, northern Greece (Blomme *et al.* 2017: 135, 145).

41 A small bronze *lekythos* found near an early 5th-century pottery workshop (Zachariadou *et al.* 1985: 48) probably originates from adjacent Hellenistic/ Roman graves and is not of the shoulder type. The shape of the aforementioned golden *lekythos* in Homer's *Odyssey* remains unclear.

42 Wooden dedications from the Sanctuary of Artemis at Brauron, Attica, include a fragmentary *lekythos*, which seems to imitate a small, early 5th-century shoulder *lekythos* (Pologiorgi 2015: 170, fig. 58, no. 49, 177). Imitations in wood further strengthen the idea that clay *lekythoi* were cheap containers.

43 See Westgate 2015: 67–68 and Nevett's chapter (Chapter 6) in this volume.

44 See Tsakirgis 2005: 67–69.

45 See Nevett 2010: 54–55.

46 Tsakirgis 1996: 777; Ault and Nevett 1999: 43–44; Rotroff 1999: 65; Bentz 2003: 45; Morgan 2010: 4–5.

47 Ault and Nevett 1999: 47–48, 51; Sgourou 2002: 4.

48 Erickson 2018: 115, 378.

49 Jones *et al*, 1962. 88; 1973: 396; Rotroff 1999: 65.

50 See Shelmerdine 1995: 103; Bodiou and Mehl 2008: 142–48; Lallemand 2008: 37–38, 42–43.

51 See Foxhall 2007: 88–89.

52 See Amouretti 1986: 195; Foxhall 2007: 86.

53 Foxhall 2007: 86, table 4.1. Erlangen Antikensammlung, I 171 and I 237, measuring 23 and 27 cm in height and holding 50 and 59 cl. respectively; Dräger 2007: 54–56, pl. 20.3–4, 6–10. Smaller black-figured *lekythoi* with capacities ranging from 8.5 to 41 cl.: Massar and Verbanck-Piérard 2013: 297, with references.

54 On materiality and the multiple ways in which people negotiate with the affordances of things, see Robb 2020: 124, with references.

55 For example: Athens, Ephorate of Speleology K2931. Unpublished *lekythos* by the Beldam Painter (*vidi* September 2010).

56 For 600 *lekythoi* of the Haimon Group, their heights form clusters at around 13 cm, 16–17 cm and 19–20 cm. For 210 of them, for which the diameter is recorded, the height is directly proportional to the diameter at a ratio of 3–1 (Volioti 2014: 153–56, 162).

57 Of the Phanyllis Group (Pologiorgi 2003–2009: 176–78, figs. 48–50). The stopper fits perfectly the neck and mouth (M. Pologiorgi, pers. comm.). The large size (height 28 cm) could mean that this *lekythos* was a storage jar. Cook (1991: 222) argues that small red-figured *lekythoi* were perhaps plugged with beeswax or another organic material. I am unaware of lidded *lekythoi* in vase iconography.

58 For the function of the ridge, see Sparkes and Talcott 1970: 151; Moore and Philippides 1986: 43; Noble 1988: 65. I have observed the absence of a ridge and variation in its sharpness by running my fingers on the inside of the mouth of over 100 *lekythoi*, mostly small black-figured specimens, in museums in Greece (Abdera, Amphipolis, Athens, Delphi, Thebes, Thessaloniki and Volos) and in the UK (the British Museum, the Fitzwilliam Museum and the Ure Museum). The ridge varies even for *lekythoi* of the same potter/painter. Two unpublished *lekythoi* by the Diosphos Painter feature a sharp and a non-existent ridge (Volos, K1273 and K1276). Scans by computer tomography also reveal a variation in the ridge (compare, for example, Amsterdam, 8873 with 3341; Van De Put 2006a: 44–47).

59 For a 6th-century *aryballos* (Athens, Ephorate of Private Archaeological Collections, ΕΑΙΑΣ 72) the diameter of the neck and the mouthplate measures 0.9 cm and 3.9 cm respectively (Volioti and Papageorgiou 2014–15: 108).

60 See Volioti 2007: 97. For Greek vases, only few studies exist on wear patterns (see Villing 2020: 104, with references).

61 Agora: Athens, Agora P 15654; Young 1951: 92–93, grave no. 11. Rhitsona: Thebes, 6151(R.26.84); Sabetai 2001: 69–70, pl. 62, fig. 33. Taranto: Taranto, Museo Archeologico Nazionale, unknown inventory number; Neutsch 1956: 232–33, 235 fig. 28; Beazley 1971: 274.

62 Not attested in the *LGPN*. Oslo University, 36276; Beazley 1971: 282; Marstrander and Seeberg 1964: pl. 29.5–6; *BAPD* 351977.

63 Simon 1989: 73, no. 132.

64 Athens, Agora, P15867; *BAPD* 28619; Dinsmoor 1941: 142, fig. 70.38.

65 Naples, SA 118; Fritzilas 2006: 230, no. 4.

66 Manganaro 1998: 268; *BAPD* 45454.

67 Knigge 1976: 15.

68 See *ABL*: 103; Tiverios 1974: 152.

69 See Kurtz 1975: 38, with references; Oakley 1997; Arrington 2014.

70 According to Pipili (2009: 243), both domestic and funerary scenes communicate the family's devotion to the deceased.

71 Gericke (1970: 145–46) gathered twenty-one scenes, including vases that date after 450.

72 Gericke 1970: 77–82; Halm-Tisserant 2004: 35.

73 The first piece (Table 4.1, no. 25) probably resulted from the Pan Painter's efforts to avoid superimposition with the human figure (A. C. Smith, pers. comm.). The second is a hybrid between a *lekythos* and an *oinochoe* (Table 4.1, no. 26). The third could represent an *aryballos* of a rare shape (Table 4.1, no. 76), perhaps comparable to Athens, 3rd Ephorate, A 15535; Baziotopoulou-Valavani 2000: 309–10, no. 311.

74 See Oenbrink 1996: 82.

75 For shelves, see Heinemann 2009: 173 n. 18.

76 One *lekythos* shows a mirror, *lekythos*, basket and an alabastron, all hanging.

77 Table 4.1, no. 23.

78 Princeton, Art Museum, unknown inventory number; Lissarrague 2001: 28, fig. 17.

79 Steiner 2007: 237–38.

80 Neck: Oka Collection, 17; Mizuta 1991: 39, pl. 34.5; *BAPD* 217647. Handle: Tubingen, Antikensammlung der Universität S./27 5368; Burow 1986: 68, fig. 29, pl. 30.7; *BAPD* 16829.

81 Shop: Table 4.1, no. 9; Kei 2008: 198, fig. 2. Palaistra: Table 4.1, nos. 71, 72, 77. Outdoors: Table 4.1, no. 18; Chatzidimitriou 2008: 237, fig. 1a–b.

82 Webster 1972: 101, with references.

83 Table 4.1, no. 18. Frère 2006b: 200; Osborne 2011: 134–35, in passing.

84 For alabastra, see Varoucha 1925–26: 117–19, with references. Athens, National Archaeological Museum, 1199; Kei 2008: 197, fig. 1; *BAPD* 207715.

85 Table 4.1, no. 72.

86 Table 4.1, nos. 71 and 77.

87 See Badinou 2003: 65.

88 On artificial light, see Parisinou 2000a; 2000b. Olive oil was the most common lamp fuel in antiquity, and experiments have confirmed its suitability for use as a light source because it is brighter and produces less odour and smoke than other oils or solid fuels (Velenis and Zachariadis 2019: 184–85).

89 Table 4.1, no. 13 (*vidi* August 2013).

90 For unpublished pottery from two major deposits in the Agora, the Rectangular Rock Cut Shaft and the Stoa Gutter Well, see Thompson 1955: 63; Shear 1993: 387–88.

91 For a black-figured *lekythos* from a disturbed grave at Psachna, central Euboea, see Sackett *et al.* 1966: 56, no. 33, fig. 9, pl. 12c.

92 Shear 1993: 405–406; Camp 1996: 245.

93 Shear 1993: 390, table 2.

94 See Lawall *et al.* 2002: 418; Jubier-Galinier *et al.* 2003: 38.

95 Contra Vanderpool 1946: 266; Roberts 1986: 4.

96 Malibu, The J. Paul Getty Museum, 83.AE.252; *BAPD* 13373; Tsiafakis 2019: 15. Basel, Antikenmuseum und Sammlung Ludwig, BS 1453; *BADP* 31853; Blome 1999: 67. I am grateful to Professor Amy C. Smith for informing me about misfiring on the Basel *krater*.

97 Lynch 2011: 45, 139.

98 Lynch 2011: 79, 105, 110, 125.

99 Shear 1993: 401–402. Wells, being sources of water, are also likely to be associated with nearby houses, as indicated by broken water-drawing vessels found in bottom layers (Miles 1998: 29).

100 Shear 1993: 393. See, for example, Papadopoulos 2003: 278; Schmidt 2005: 31; Lynch 2009: 73–74.

101 Public dining facility: Rotroff and Oakley 1992. Private houses: Boulter 1953: 62.

102 Rotroff and Oakley 1992: 24.

103 Reports do not always give details of exact find-spots, and it is necessary to cross-check references and/or contact excavators.

104 Spitaels 1978: 86(TC76.7); *BAPD* 7667. Van De Put and Docter 2012; W. Van De Put, pers. comm.

105 Felten *et al.* 2003: 46, fig. 7.4; 2007: 98, fig. 15; 2010: 57, fig. 15. Klebinder-Gauss 2012: 35, no. 11, pl. 72; 66, nos. 287, 288, 289, pl. 95; 76, no. 439, pl. 103. For a *lekythos* with upright palmettes from an area potentially used for ritual dining and ancestor worship, see Klebinder-Gauss 2019: 119, fig. 6.

106 For a ritual function of *lekythoi* from the settlement, see Gex 1993: 60.

107 Themelis 1981: 151–53.

108 For busts, see Chrysanthaki-Nagle 2009. Serbeti (1997: 497) argues for later intrusions. The *lekythos* (Themelis 1981: pl. 113) is of Knigge's shape IV/1 or IV/2 and dates from 480 BCE onwards (Knigge 1976: table 77).

109 T. Saggini, pers. comm. Saggini 2019: 369–72.

110 Kahil 1965: 286–87, no. 13, pl. 337g; 1967: 285, pl. 184d–e; Descoeurdes 1967: 281. Vlavianou-Tsaliki 1981: 79, pl. 42e. Sapouna-Sakellaraki 1987: 213, pl. 123a left; *BAPD* 43497.

111 Batziou-Efstathiou and Triantafyllopoulou 2009: 258–60.

112 Hanschmann 1981b: 86, nos. 5, 8, pl. 131.5, 131.8; 1981a: 120.

113 Gallis 1973; 1975: 193.

114 Corfu, 3782; Spetsiéri-Chorémi 1991: 198–99, no. 35, fig. 46.

115 Tiverios 2009: 390, fig. 7.

116 Amphipolis, C4085; Perreault and Bonias 2006: 53, pl. VIII.4. Common-type *lekythoi* have also been found at Argilos (*vidi* April 2008), J. Y. Perreault pers. comm.

117 Schaus 1992: 370–71, nos. 60, 61, 74.

118 Olbia: Nazarčuk 2010: 150; Phanagoria: Morgan 2004: 188–92.

119 Haggis *et al.* 2007: 249–51, 260, 262, 283, 312. For a further black-figured *lekythos* from a storage facility of another building, see Haggis and Mook 2011: 376.

120 Tuna-Nörling 1996: 16, 18–20, 22–23, 28, 51.

121 Boardman 1958–59: 169–70.

122 Yeivin 1952: 142, pl. 27A. The find-spot is described as 'habitation debris'.

123 Stewart and Martin 2005: 82, table 2.

124 Yialouris 1957: 40–41, pl. 9d.

125 Cf. the careful deposition of miniature closed shapes under Archaic and Classical houses in Leukas, western Greece (Stavropoulou-Gatsi 2010: 89–90, 96, fig. c).

126 Vallicelli 2004: 9–10, 12. No illustration. M. Cristina Vallicelli, pers. comm.

127 Wilson 1996: 114. No illustration.

128 Isler 1984: 31, pl. 7.5 (K 6750); *BAPD* 41233; 1995: 30, pl. 10.6 (K15305); *BAPD* 19730; 1996: 58, pl. 11.4 (K 16833); *BAPD* 19717; 1997: 51, pl. 10.6 (K15303); *BAPD* 19723. The fourth fragment actually joins with the fragment published in 1995 (Isler 1995: 30, pl. 10.6).

129 Isler 1984: 31, pl. 7.5 (K 6750); *BAPD* 41233; 1997: 51.

130 Isler 1996: 52.

131 Isler 2009: 169–76.

132 For the building, see Isler 2000: pl. 21.5 (K 18964); 2009: 191–93, figs 54–57.

133 Old Smyrna: Boardman 1958–59: 170, nos. 108–109, 113–14. Al Mina: Woolley 1938b: 139; Tel Dor: Stewart and Martin 2005: 82, table 2.

134 Lynch 2011: 69. Also note the few *lekythoi*, including fine and secondary red-figured specimens, from the dining debris of deposit H 4:5, *c.* 475–425 BCE, at the Agora (Rotroff and Oakley 1992: 12, 15, 131–34). Further, see Nazarčuk 2010: 145, 169.

135 Woolley 1938a: 12, 24, pl. IV; 1938b: 139.

136 Non-diagnostic fragments are neither recorded nor published.

137 *Lekythoi* were offered both inside and outside graves. See, for example, Kallipolitis 1965: 116, grave no. 50, pl. 84–85.

138 See Boardman 1974: 146.

139 See Volioti 2011: 142, with references.

140 See, for example, Boulter 1963: 115–20; Smith and Volioti 2019: 178–83.

141 See Volioti 2014: 152, with references.

142 See, for example, discussion of the Sacred Spring, Corinth (Steiner 1992; Pemberton 2020: 314) and of Athenian roadside shrines (Best 2015: 105).

143 For a *lekythos* found near Phidias' workshop at Olympia, see Burow 2000: 256. A grave at Toumba, Thessaloniki, contained an iron sword and two iron knives, one of which had been placed carefully under a *lekythos* (Soueref 1999: 184). Such burial contexts could imply that oil was used on metal.

144 For a fragment from a road at Halieis, Porto Cheli, see Rudolph 1984: 126–28, 153.A40.

145 Volioti 2021, 2022.

146 Lynch 2011: 135–40.

147 See, for example, Knigge and Willemsen 1964: 45, pl. 40a.

148 Cf. Emily Varto's understanding of kinship in this volume (Chapter 1).

149 Cf. Bourdieu's concept of *habitus* (Bourdieu 1992).

150 Closterman 2007: 633; Paillard 2014: 81–83; Galiatsatou 2020: 57, with references.

151 For multiple burials in *pithoi* at Naupaktos, western Greece, see Dekoulakou 1973. For black-figured and red-figured *lekythoi* from sarcophagi in an earth mound at Krannon, Thessaly, see Chourmouziades 1970; Zaouri 1989; Adrimi-Sismani *et al.* 2004: 114, no. 16; 135, no. 40.

152 Contra *ABL*: 77.

153 Burial at the battlefield, rather than in the *demosion sema*, was common, and Thucydides' account may target non-Athenians (Toher 1999). Judging from drawings and photographs, not all *lekythoi* from the Marathon Tumulus date to 490 BCE. I note a *lekythos* of the Phanyllis Group from *c.* 500 BCE and another of the Haimon Group from 480 to 470 BCE (Athens, National Archaeological Museum, 1894; 1549; Stais 1893: 51.3–4). A further *lekythos* of the Haimon Group dates to 470–450 BCE (Athens, National Archaeological Museum, 1033; Rhomaios 1932: pl. 10.12; *ABL*: 166; Knigge 1976: 36; Steinhauer 2009: 139).

154 Cf. Nevett's argument in this volume about the domestic space's rhetorical claims to status.

155 For social storage and other food storage strategies at household level, albeit for prehistoric and not Classical Greece, see Christakis 1999: 2–3, with references.

156 For prohibiting legislation, see Kurtz and Boardman 1971: 97, 100; Kurtz 1984: 323; Salskov-Roberts 2002: 28. For late black figure expressing social equality, see Brendle 2018: 135.

157 Cf. Jones 1993: 294 on the Phoenicians' perfume trade.

158 For farmsteads, and people's mobility in and out of cities on a daily basis, see Maeve McHugh's chapter in this volume (Chapter 7).

159 Note, for example, the difference between an olive-oil versus an animal-fat diet in coastal and mountainous areas in recent times (see Kyriakopoulos 2015: 253).

160 Knigge 1976: 33–37 and table 77.

161 See Kunze-Götte 1992: 109.

162 On smelling, see Algrain 2015.

References

Adrimi-Sismani, V. *et al.* (2004). *Αγώνες και Αθλήματα στην Αρχαία Θεσσαλία.* Athens.

Algrain, I. (2015). "A l'ombre des jeunes filles en fleur" – Women and flowers on Attic pottery. In C. Lang-Auinger and E. Trinkl, eds., *Corpus Vasorum Antiquorum, Österreich, Beiheft 2: ΦΥΤΑ ΚΑΙ ΖΩΙΑ. Pflanzen und Tiere auf griechischen Vasen*. Vienna: Verlag der österreichischen Akademie der Wissenschaften, 47–54.

Algrain, I., Brisart, T. and Jubier-Galinier, C. (2008). Les vases à parfum à Athènes aux époques archaïque et Classique. In A. Verbanck-Piérard, N. Massar and D. Frére, eds., *Parfums de l'Antiquité. La rose et l'encens en Méditerranée*. Mariemont: Musée royal de Mariemont, 145–64.

Amouretti, M.-C. (1986). *Le pain et l'huile de la Grèce antique. De l'araire au moulin*. Paris: Besançon.

Arrington, N. T. (2014). Fallen vessels and risen spirits: conveying the presence of the dead on white-ground lekythoi. In J. H. Oakley, ed., *Athenian Potters and Painters III*. Oxford and Philadelphia: Oxbow, 1–10.

(2015). *Ashes, Images, and Memories: The Presence of the War Dead in Fifth-Century Athens*. Oxford: Oxford University Press.

(2018). Touch and remembrance in Greek funerary art. *The Art Bulletin* 100, 7–27.

Ault, B. A. and Nevett, L. C. (1999). Digging houses: archaeologies of Classical and Hellenistic Greek domestic assemblages. In P. M. Allison, ed., *The Archaeology of Household Activities*. London and New York: Routledge, 43–56.

Badinou, P. (2003). *La laine et le parfum. Épinetra et alabastres, forme, iconographie et fonction. Recherche de céramique attique féminine*. Leuven and Dudley, MA: Peeters.

Batziou-Efstathiou, A. and Triantafyllopoulou, P. (2009). Επιφανειακές Έρευνες στο «Σωρό», *Αρχαιολογικό Έργο Θεσσαλίας και Στερεάς Ελλάδας* 2, 257–67.

Baziotopoulou-Valavani, E. (2000). From tomb 1099. In L. Palarma and N. C. Stampolidis, eds., *Athens: The City beneath the City: Antiquities from the Metropolitan Railway Excavations*. New York and London: Harry N. Abrams, 304–12.

Beazley, J. D. (1938). *Attic White Lekythoi*. Oxford: Oxford University Press.

(1971). *Paralipomena: Additions to Attic Black-Figure Vase-Painters and to Attic Red-Figure Vase-Painters*. Oxford: Clarendon.

Bender, H. H. (1934). Lekythos: *Archäologische, sprachliche und religionsgeschichtliche Untersuchungen* by L. J. Elferink. *American Journal of Archaeology* 38, 614–15.

Bentz, M. (1998). *Panathenäische Preisamphoren. Eine athenische Vasengattung und ihre Funktion vom 6.–4. Jahrhundert v. Chr.* Basel: Vereinigung der Freunde antiker Kunst.

(2003). Objet d'usage ou objet de prestige? Les vases dans l'habitat. In P. Rouillard and A. Verbanck-Piérand, eds., *Le vase grec et ses destins*. Munich: Biering & Brinkmann, 45–48.

Best, J. (2015). Roadside assistance: religious spaces and personal experience in Athens. In M. Miles, ed., *Autopsy in Athens: Recent Archaeological Research on Athens and Attica*. Oxford: Oxbow, 100–107.

Biers, W. R., Gerhardt, K. O. and Braniff, R. A. (1994). *Lost Scents: Investigations of Corinthian 'Plastic' Vases by Gas Chromatography–Mass Spectrometry*. MASCA Research Papers in Science and Archaeology 11. Philadelphia: University of Pennsylvania Museum of Archaeology and Anthropology.

(1995). Scientific investigations of Corinthian 'plastic' vases. *American Journal of Archaeology* 99, 320.

Biers, W. R., Searles, S. and Gerhardt, K. O. (1988). Non-destructive extraction studies of Corinthian plastic vases: methods and problems. A preliminary report. In J. Christiansen and T. Melander, eds., *Proceedings of the 3rd Symposium on Ancient Greek and Related Pottery. Copenhagen August 31– September 4 1987*. Copenhagen: Ny Carlsberg Glyptotek, 33–50.

Blome, P. (1999). *Antikenmuseum Basel und Sammlung Ludwig. Basel Museum of Ancient Art and Ludwig Collection*. Geneva and Zurich: Schweizerisches Institut für Kunstwissenschaft.

Blomme, A., Degryse, P., Dotsika, E., Ignatiadou, D., Longinelli, A. and Silvestri, A. (2017). Provenance of polychrome and colourless 8th–4th century BC glass from Pieria, Greece: a chemical and isotopic approach. *Journal of Archaeological Science* 78, 134–46.

Boardman, J. (1958–59). Old Smyrna: the Attic pottery. *Annual of the British School at Athens* 53–54, 152–81.

(1974). *Athenian Black Figure Vases: A Handbook*. London: Thames and Hudson.

(1977). The olive in the Mediterranean: its culture and use. In J. B. Hutchinson, G. Clark, E. M. Jope and R. Riley, eds., *The Early History of Agriculture: A Joint Symposium of the Royal Society and the British Academy*. Oxford: Oxford University Press, 187–96.

(1979). The Athenian pottery trade. *Expedition* 21, 33–39.

Bodiou, L. and Mehl, V. (2008) Sociologie des odeurs en pays grec. In L. Bodiou, D. Frère and V. Mehl, eds., *Parfums et odeurs dans l'Antiquité*. Rennes: Presses universitaires de Rennes, 141–63.

Bosanquet, R. C. (1896). On a group of early Attic lekythoi. *Journal of Hellenic Studies* 16, 164–77.

(1899). Some early funeral lekythoi. *Journal of Hellenic Studies* 19, 169–84.

Boulter, C. (1953). Pottery of the mid-fifth century from a well in the Athenian Agora. *Hesperia* 22, 59–115.

(1963) Graves in Lenormant Street, Athens. *Hesperia* 32, 113–37.

Bourdieu, P. (1992). *The Logic of Practice*, 2nd ed. Cambridge: Polity.

Brendle, R. (2018). Athenian use of black-figure lekythoi in fifth-century burials. *Archäologischer Anzeiger* 2018(1), 121–38.

Bresson, A. and Rendall, S. (2016). *The Making of the Ancient Greek Economy: Institutions, Markets, and Growth in the City-States*, trans. S. Rendall. Princeton and Oxford: Princeton University Press.

Brun, J.-P. (2000). The production of perfumes in antiquity: the cases of Delos and Paestum. *American Journal of Archaeology* 104, 277–308.

(2008). Une parfumerie à Délos à la fin de l'époque hellénistique. In A. Verbanck-Piérard, N. Massar and D. Frére, eds., *Parfums de l'Antiquité. La rose et l'encens en Méditerranée*. Mariemont: Musée royal de Mariemont, 245–50.

Bundrick, S. D. (2016). Athens, Etruria, Rome, Baltimore: reconstructing the biography of an ancient Greek vase. *Memoirs of the American Academy in Rome* 61, 1–21.

(2020). Visualizing music. In T. A. Lynch and E. Rocconi, eds., *A Companion to Ancient Greek and Roman Music*. New York: Wiley-Blackwell, 117–30.

Burow, J. (1986). *Corpus Vasorum Antiquorum Germany 54, Tübingen 5*. Munich: C.H. Beck.

(2000). Attisch schwarzfigurige Keramik. In E. Kunze-Götte, J. Heiden and J. Burow, eds., *Archaische Keramik aus Olympia. Olympische Forschungen; Bd. 28*. Berlin and New York: W. de Gruyter, 203–316.

Cahill, N. (2002). *Household and City Organization at Olynthus*. New Haven and London: Yale University Press.

Camp, J. McK. (1996). Excavations in the Athenian Agora: 1994 and 1995. *Hesperia* 65, 231–61.

Chatzidimitriou, A. (2008). Représentations de vente et d'achat d'huile sur les vases attiques à l'époque archaïque et Classique. In L. Bodiou, D. Frère and V. Mehl, eds., *Parfums et odeurs dans l'Antiquité*. Rennes: Presses universitaires de Rennes, 237–44.

Chourmouziades, G. (1970). Ανασκαφή εν Κραννώνι. *Archaiologikon deltion* 25, 279–82.

Christakis, K. S. (1999). Pithoi and food storage in Neopalatial Crete: a domestic perspective. *World Archaeology* 31, 1–20.

Chrysanthaki-Nagle, K. (2009). Πήλινες γυναικείες προτομές και λατρείες στις οικίες της Μακεδονίας και της Θράκης. *Archaiologia & Technes* 113, 57–63.

Closterman, W. E. (2007). Family ideology and family history: the function of funerary markers in Classical Attic Peribolos tombs. *American Journal of Archaeology* 111, 633–52.

Cook, B. F. (1991). Attic red-figured lekythoi, secondary types: Class 6L. *Oxford Journal of Archaeology* 10, 209–30.

De La Genière, J. (1984). «Parfumés comme Crésus». De l'origine du lécythe attique. *Bulletin de Correspondence Hellenique* 108, 91–98.

(2004). Vasi attici dalle necropolis di Gela. In R. Panvini and F. Giudice, eds., *Ta Attika. Veder Greco a Gela. Ceramiche attiche figurate dall'antica colonia*. Rome: "L'Erma" di Bretschneider, 149–55.

De Vries, K. (1977). Attic pottery in the Achaemenid Empire. *American Journal of Archaeology* 81, 544–48.

Dekoulakou, I. (1973). Αλωνάκι Ναυπάκτου. *Archaiologikon deltion* 28, 391–93.

Descoeurdes, J.-P. (1967). Terrain F/5. *Archaiologikon deltion* 22, 278–83.

Dinsmoor, W. B. (1941). Observations on the Hephaisteion. *Hesperia Supplements* 5.

Dräger, O. (2007). *Corpus Vasorum and Antiquorum Germany 84, Erlangen 2.* Munich: C.H. Beck.

Erickson, B. (2018). *Lerna VIII. The Historical Greek Village.* Princeton: American School of Classical Studies at Athens.

Eschbach, N. (2020). Kein Öl in Panathenäischen Preisamphoren? Zu Funktion und Bedeutung einer repräsentativen Gefäßgattung der attischen Vasenmalerei. In M. Langner and S. Schmidt, eds., *Die Materialität griechischer Vasen. Mikrohistorische Perspektiven in der Vasenforschung. Corpus Vasorum Antiquorum. Deutschland. Beihefte; Band 9.* Munich: München Bayerische Akademie der Wissenschaften, 87–99.

Felten, F., Hiller, S., Reinholdt, C., Gauss, W. and Smetana, R. (2003). Ägina-Kolonna 2002. Vorbericht über die Grabungen des Instituts für Klassische Archäologie der Universität Salzburg. *Jahreshefte des Österreichischen Archäologischen Instituts* 72, 41–65.

Felten, F., Reinholdt, C., Pollhammer, E., Gauss, W. and Smetana, R. (2007). Ägina-Kolonna 2006. Vorbericht über die Grabungen des Fachbereichs Altertumswissenschaften/Klassische und Frühägäische Archäologie der Universität Salzburg. *Jahrshefte des Osterreichischen Archaologischen Instituts* 76, 89–119.

(2010). Ägina-Kolonna 2009. Vorbericht über die Grabungen des Fachbereichs Altertumswissenschaften/Klassische und Frühägäische Archäologie der Universität Salzburg. *Jahrshefte des Osterreichischen Archaologischen Instituts* 79, 43–66.

Finkel, I. L. and Reade, J. E. (2002). On some inscribed Babylonian alabastra. *Journal of the Royal Asiatic Society* 12, 31–46.

Fletcher, R. N. (2011). Greek–Levantine cultural exchange in Orientalising and Archaic pottery shapes. *Ancient West & East* 10, 11–42.

Foxhall, L. (2007). *Olive Cultivation in Ancient Greece: Seeking the Ancient Economy.* Oxford: Oxford University Press.

Frère, D. (2006a). Parfums, huiles et crèmes parfumées en Etrurie orientalisante. *Mediterranea* 3, 87–119.

(2006b). Gestes quotidiens pour un parfum d'immortalité. In L. Bodiou, D. Frère and V. Mehl, eds., *L'expression des corps. Gestes, attitudes, regards dans l'iconographie antique.* Rennes: Presses universitaires de Rennes, 195–212.

(2008). Un programme de recherches archéologiques et archéométriques sur des huiles et crèmes parfumées dans l'Antiquité. In L. Bodiou, D. Frère and

V. Mehl, eds., *Parfums et odeurs dans l'Antiquité*. Rennes: Presses universitaires de Rennes, 205–14.

Fritzilas, S. (2006). *Ο Ζωγράφος του Θησέα. Η Αττική αγγειογραφία στην εποχή της νεοσύστατης Αθηναϊκής δημοκρατίας*. Athens.

Galiatsatou, P. (2020). Mortuary practices in the ancient rural demoi of southeastern Attica under the light of recent evidence from five cemeteries in Mesogaia. In N. Dimakis and T. Dijkstra, eds., *Mortuary Variability and Social Diversity in Ancient Greece: Studies on Ancient Greek Death and Burial*. Oxford: Archaeopress, 50–62.

Gallis, K. G. (1973). Νομός Λαρίσης. Παλαιόκαστρον Νεοχωρίου Αγιάς (Λακέρεια). *Archaiologikon deltion* 28, 327–29.

——— (1975). Παλαιόκαστρο Νεοχωρίου Αγιάς (Λακέρεια). *Archaiologikon deltion* 30, 193–94.

Garnier, N. and Frère, D. (2008). Une archéologie de l'évanescent. In A. Verbanck-Piérard, N. Massar and D. Frére, eds., *Parfums de l'Antiquité. La rose et l'encens en Méditerranée*. Mariemont: Musée royal de Mariemont, 61–71.

Garyfallopoulos, A. (2019). Αττικές λευκές λήκυθοι «κυρίου» τύπου στο Βόρειο Αιγαίο και την περιφέρειά του: διασπορά και χρονολόγηση, χρήση, εικονογραφία. In E. Manakidou and A. Avramidou, eds., *Classical Pottery of the Northern Aegean and Its Periphery (480–323/300 BC)*. Thessaloniki: Thessalonikē University Studio Press, 127–38.

Gericke, H. (1970). *Gefässdarstellungen auf griechischen Vasen*. Berlin: Hessling.

Gex, K. (1993). *Rotfigurige und weissgrundige Keramik. Eretria. Ausgrabungen und Forschungen IX*. Lausanne: Payot.

Gex-Morgenthaler, C. (1988). Red-figure lekythoi from Eretria. In J. Christiansen and T. Melander, eds., *Proceedings of the 3rd Symposium on Ancient Greek and Related Pottery. Copenhagen August 31 – September 4 1987*. Copenhagen: Ny Carlsberg Glyptotek, 170–74.

Goette, H. R. and Weber, T. M. (2004). *Marathon. Siedlungskammer und Schlachtfeld. Sommerfrische und Olympische Wettkampfstätte*. Mainz am Rhein: P. von Zabern.

Haggis, D. C. and Mook, M. S. (2011). The Archaic houses at Azoria. *Hesperia Supplements* 44, 367–80.

Haggis, D. C. *et al.* (2007). Excavations at Azoria, 2003–2004, Part 1. The Archaic Civic Complex. *Hesperia* 76, 243–321.

Halm-Tisserant, M. (2004). *"Keimenon"*: de l'objet réifié à l'objet "sujet" dans la peinture de vases grecque. *Pallas* 65, 33–48.

Hanschmann, E. (1981a). *Die deutschen Ausgrabungen auf der Argissa-Magula in Thessalien IV. Die Mittlere Bronzezeit*. Vol. I. Bonn: Rudolf Habelt.

——— (1981b). *Die deutschen Ausgrabungen auf der Argissa-Magula in Thessalien IV. Die Mittlere Bronzezeit*. Vol. II. Bonn: Rudolf Habelt.

Haspels, C. H. E. (1936). *Attic Black-Figured Lekythoi*. Paris.

Hatzivassiliou, E. (2010). *Athenian Black Figure Iconography between 510 and 475 B.C.* Rahden: Verlag Marie Leidorf.

Heinemann, A. (2009). Bild, Gefäß, Praxis: Überlegungen zu attischen Salbgefäßen. In S. Schmidt and J. H. Oakley, eds., *Hermeneutik der Bilder*. Beiträge zur Ikonographie und Interpretation griechischer Vasenmalerei. Beihefte zum Corpus Vasorum Antiquorum, Deutschland, 4. Munich, 161–75.

Henderson, J. (1972). The lekythos and *Frogs* 1200–1248. *Harvard Studies in Classical Philology* 76, 133–43.

Hoskins, J. (2006). Agency, biography and objects. In C. Tilley, W. Keane, S. Kuechler, M. Rowlands and P. Spyer, eds., *Handbook of Material Culture*. London: Sage, 74–84.

Houby-Nielsen, S. H. (1995). 'Burial language' in Archaic and Classical Kerameikos. *Proceedings of the Danish Institute at Athens* 1, 129–91.

Immerwahr, H. R. (2006). Nonsense inscriptions and literacy. *Kadmos* 45, 136–72.

Isler, H. P. (1984). Grabungen auf dem Monte Iato 1983. *Antike Kunst* 27, 25–32.

(1995). Grabungen auf dem Monte Iato 1994. *Antike Kunst* 38, 26–37.

(1996). Grabungen auf dem Monte Iato 1995. *Antike Kunst* 39, 52–64.

(1997). Grabungen auf dem Monte Iato 1996. *Antike Kunst* 40, 48–60.

(2000). Grabungen auf dem Monte Iato 1999. *Antike Kunst* 43, 110–20.

(2009). Die Siedlung auf dem Monte Iato in archaischer Zeit. *Jahrbuch des [kaiserlich] deutschen archäologischen Instituts* 124, 135–222.

Jones, D. W. (1993). Phoenician unguent factories in Dark Age Greece: social approaches to evaluating the archaeological evidence. *Oxford Journal of Archaeology* 12, 293–303.

Jones, J. E., Sackett, L. H. and Graham, A. J. (1962). The Dema house in Attica. *Annual of the British School at Athens* 57, 75–114.

(1973). An Attic country house below the cave of Pan at Vari. *Annual of the British School at Athens* 68, 355–452.

Johnston, A. W. (1979). *Trademarks on Greek Vases*. Warminster: Aris & Philips.

Jubier-Galinier, C. (2014). "Τοῖς νεκροῖσι. . .τάς ληκύθους": l'évolution des usages du lécythe dans le rituel funéraire athénien aux époques archaïque et Classique. *Pallas* 94, 39–59.

(2016). Des inscriptions et des peintres: l'utilisation de l'écriture chez les peintres à figures noires tardives. In R. Wachter, ed., *Töpfer – Maler – Schreiber: Inschriften auf attischen Vasen. Akten des Kolloquiums vom 20. bis 23. September 2012 an den Universitäten Lausanne und Basel*. Zurich: Akanthus Verlag für Archäologie, 55–78.

Jubier-Galinier, C., Laurens, A.-F. and Tsingarida, A. (2003). Les ateliers de potiers en Attique. De l'idée à l'objet. In P. Rouillard and A. Verbanck-Piérand, eds., *Le vase grec et ses destins*. Munich: Biering & Brinkmann, 27–43.

Kahil, L. (1965). Rapport de céramique géometrique archaïque. *Archaiologikon deltion* 20, 285–87.

(1967). Céramique de l'époque géométrique, subgéométique et archaïque. *Archaiologikon deltion* 22, 283–85.

Kallipolitis, V. (1965). Αρχαιότητες και Μνημεία Αττικής και Νήσων. *Archaiologikon deltion* 20, 110–17.

Kei, N. (2008). La fleur. Signe de parfum dans la céramique attique. In L. Bodiou, D. Frère and V. Mehl, eds., *Parfums et odeurs dans l'Antiquité*. Rennes: Presses universitaires de Rennes, 197–203.

Klebinder-Gauss, G. (2012). *Keramik aus klassischen Kontexten im Apollon-Heiligtum von Ägina-Kolonna: Lokale Produktion und Importe*. Vienna: Austrian Academy of Sciences Press.

(2019). Dining with the ancestors: the Late Archaic–Classical *Westkomplex* in Aegina-Kolonna. In I. S. Lemos and A. Tsingarida, eds., *Beyond the Polis. Rituals, Rites and Cults in Early and Archaic Greece (12th–6th centuries BC)*. Brussels: CREA Patrimoine, 115–32.

Knigge, U. (1976). *Kerameikos 9. Der Südhügel*. Berlin: De Gruyter.

Knigge, U. and Willemsen F. (1964). Die Höhe östlich des Querweges. *Archaiologikon deltion* 19, 42–46.

Kopytoff, I. (1986). The cultural biography of things: commoditization as process. In A. Appadurai, ed., *The Social Life of Things. Commodities in Cultural Perspective*. Cambridge: Cambridge University Press, 64–91.

Kunze-Götte, E. (1992). *Der Kleophrades-Maler unter Malern schwarzfiguriger Amphoren. Eine Werkstattstudie*. Mainz am Rhein: Philipp von Zabern.

(2010). *CVA Germany 87, Munich 15, Attisch weissgrundige Lekythen*. Munich: C.H. Beck.

Kurtz, D. C. (1975). *Athenian White Lekythoi. Patterns and Painters*. Oxford: Clarendon Press.

(1984). Vases for the dead, an Attic selection, 750–400 B.C. In H. A. G. Brijder, ed., *Ancient Greek and Related Pottery. Proceedings of the International Vase Symposium in Amsterdam 12–15 April 1984*. Amsterdam: Allard Pierson Museum, 314–28.

Kurtz, D. C. and Boardman, J. (1971). *Greek Burial Customs*. London: Thames and Hudson.

Kyriakopoulos, Y. (2015). Aegean cooking-pots in the modern era (1700–1950). In M. Spataro and A. Villing, eds., *Ceramics, Cuisine and Culture: The Archaeology and Science of Kitchen Pottery in the Ancient Mediterranean World*. Oxford and Philadelphia: Oxbow, 252–68.

Lallemand, A. (2008). L'imaginaire des parfums dans la littérature antique d'Homère à Ovide. In A. Verbanck-Piérard, N. Massar and D. Frère, eds., *Parfums de l'Antiquité. La rose et l'encens en Méditerranée*. Mariemont: Musée royal de Mariemont, 37–44.

Lambrugo, C. (2015). Dying young in Archaic Gela (Sicily): from the analysis of the cemeteries to the reconstruction of early colonial identity. In M. Romero

Sánchez, G. E. Alarcón and J. G. Aranda, eds., *Children, Spaces and Identity.* Philadelphia: Oxbow, 282–93.

Lawall, M. L. *et al.* (2002). Notes from the Tins 2: research in the Stoa of Attalos. *Hesperia* 71, 415–33.

Lewis, D. (2018). Behavioural economics and economic behaviour in Classical Athens. In M. Canevaro, A. Erskine, B. Gray and J. Ober, eds., *Ancient Greek History and Contemporary Social Science.* Edinburgh: Edinburgh University Press, 15–46.

Lissarrague, F. (2001). *Greek Vases: The Athenians and Their images.* New York: Riverside.

Livarda, A. (2014). Archaeobotany in Greece. *Archaeological Reports* 60, 106–16.

Lynch, K. M. (2009). The Persian destruction deposits and the development of pottery research at the Agora excavations. In J. McK. Camp II and C. A. Mauzy, eds., *The Athenian Agora: New Perspectives on an Ancient Site.* Mainz: Von Zabern, 69–76.

(2011). The Symposium in context: pottery from a Late Archaic house near the Athenian Agora. *Hesperia Supplements* 46.

Manganaro, G. (1998). Modi dell'alfabetizzazione in Sicilia (dall'Arcaismo all'Ellenismo). *Mediterraneo Antico Economie Società Culture* 1, 247–70.

Margariti, K. (2018). Lament and death instead of marriage: the iconography of deceased maidens on Attic grave reliefs of the Classical Period. *Hesperia* 87, 91–176.

Marstrander, S. and Seeberg, A. (1964). *CVA Norway Public and Private Collections 1.* Oslo: Norske videnskaps-akademi i Oslo.

Massar, N. (2009). Parfumer les morts. Usage et contenu des balsamaires hellénistiques en contexte funéraire. In A. Tsingarida, ed., *Shapes and Uses of Greek Vases (7th–4th centuries B.C.). Proceedings of the Symposium held at the Université Libre de Bruxelles 27–29 April 2006.* Brussels: CReA-Patrimoine, 307–18.

Massar, N. and Verbanck-Piérard, A. (2013). Follow the scent... marketing perfume vases in the Greek world. In A. Tsingarida and D. Viviers, eds., *Pottery Markets in the Ancient Greek World (8th–1st centuries B.C.). Proceedings of the International Symposium held at the Université libre de Bruxelles 19–21 June 2008.* Brussels: CReA-Patrimoine, 273–98.

Mertens, J. R. (1975). A white lekythos in the Getty Museum. *The J. Paul Getty Museum Journal* 2, 27–36.

Miles, M. M. (1998). *The City Eleusinion. The Athenian Agora 31.* Princeton: American School of Classical Studies.

Mizuta, A. (1991). *CVA Japan 2. Schwarz- und Rotfigurige Vasen in Japanischen Sammlungen.* Tokyo: Japan Society for the Promotion of Science.

Moore, M. B. and Philippides, M. Z. P. (1986). *Attic Black-Figured Pottery. The Athenian Agora 23.* Princeton: American School of Classical Studies at Athens.

Morgan, C. (2004). *Attic Fine Pottery of the Archaic to Hellenistic Periods in Phanagoria.* Leiden and Boston: Brill.

Morgan, J. (2010). *The Classical Greek House*. Bristol: Bristol Phoenix Press.

Nazarčuk, V. I. (2010). Black-figured pottery. In N. A. Lejpunskaja, P. Guldager Bilde, J. Munk Højte, V. V. Krapivina and S. D. Kryžickij, eds., *The Lower City of Olbia (Sector NGS) in the 6th Century BC to the 4th Century AD*. Aarhus: Aarhus University Press, 143–69.

Neeft, C. W. (2006). Camarina e la sua ceramica corinzia. In P. Pelagatti, G. Di Stefano and L. de Lachenal, eds., *Camarina. 2600 anni dopo la fondazione. Nuovi studi sulla città e sul territorio. Atti del Convegno Internazionale. Ragusa, 7 dicembre 2002/7–9 aprile 2003*. Ragusa: Centro studi Feliciano Rossitto, 77–107.

Neutsch, B. (1956). Archäologische Grabungen und Funde im Bereich der unteritalischen Soprintendenzen von Tarent, Reggio di Calabria und Salerno (1949–1955). *Archäologischer Anzeiger* 1956, 192–450.

Nevett, L. (2010). *Domestic Space in Classical Antiquity*. Cambridge: Cambridge University Press.

Noble, J. V. (1988). *The Techniques of Painted Attic Pottery*, rev. ed. London: Thames and Hudson.

Oakley, J. H. (1997). The Bosanquet Painter. In J. H. Oakley, W. D. R. Coulson and O. Palagia eds., *Athenian Potters and Painters I. The Conference Proceedings*. Oxford: Oxbow, 241–48.

(2004). *Picturing Death in Classical Athens: The Evidence of White Lekythoi*. Cambridge: Cambridge University Press.

(2020). *A Guide to Scenes of Daily Life on Athenian Vases*. Madison: University of Wisconsin Press.

Oenbrink, W. (1996). Ein 'Bild im Bild'-Phänomen – Zur Darstellung figürlich verzierter Vasen auf bemalten attischen Tongefäßen. *Hephaistos* 14, 81–134.

Osborne, R. (2011). *The History Written on the Classical Greek Body*. Cambridge: Cambridge University Press.

Paga, J. (2015). The Southeast Fountain House in the Athenian Agora: a reappraisal of its date and historical context. *Hesperia* 84, 355–87.

Paillard, E. (2014). The structural evolution of fifth-century Athenian society: archaeological evidence and literary sources. *Mediterranean Archaeology* 27, 77–84.

Papadopoulos, J. K. (2003). Ceramicus redivivus: the Early Iron Age Potters' Field in the area of the Classical Athenian Agora. *Hesperia Supplements* 31.

Papaspyride, S. and Kyparissis, N. (1927–28). Νέα Λήκυθος του Δούριδος. *Archaiologikon deltion* 11, 91–110.

Parisinou, E. (2000a). *The Light of the Gods: The Role of Light in Archaic and Classical Greek Cult*. London: Duckworth.

(2000b). 'Lighting' the world of women: lamps and torches in the hands of women in the Late Archaic and Classical Periods. *Greece & Rome* 47, 19–43.

Parko, H. (2001). Small Corinthian oil-containers: evidence of the Archaic perfume trade? In C. Scheffer, ed., *Ceramics in Context. Proceedings of the Internordic Colloquium on Ancient Pottery, held at Stockholm, 13–15 June 1997*. Stockholm: Almqvist & Wiksell, 55–60.

Pauly, A. F., Wissowa, G. and Kroll, W. (1937). *Paulys Real-Encyclopädie der classischen Altertumswissenschaft*, vol. 17. Stuttgart: J. B. Metzlerscher Verlag.

Payne, H. (1931). *Necrocorinthia: A Study of Corinthian Art in the Archaic Period*. Oxford: Clarendon Press.

Pemberton, E. (2020). Small and miniature vases at Ancient Corinth. *Hesperia* 89, 281–338.

Perreault, J. Y. and Bonias, Z. (2006). L'habitat d'Argilos: les céramiques archaïques, un aperçu. In J. De La Genière, ed., *Les clients de la céramique grecque. Actes du Colloque de l'Académie des Inscriptions et Belles-Lettres. Paris, 30–31 janvier 2004. Cahiers du Corpus Vasorum Antiquorum*. Paris: Académie des inscriptions et belles-lettres, 49–54.

Pinjuh, J.-M. (2014). *Platons Hippias Minor. Übersetzung und Kommentar*. Tübingen: Narr.

Pipili, M. (2009). White-ground lekythoi in athenian private collections: some iconographic observations. In J. Oakley and O. Palagia, eds., *Athenian Potters and Painters, Volume II*. Oxford and Oakville: Oxbow, 241–49.

Plassart, A. (1928). *Delos 11. Les sanctuaires et les cultes du Mont Cynthe*. Paris: De Boccard.

Pologiorgi, M. (2003–2009). Ανασκαφή Νεκροταφείου στο Χαλάνδρι. *Archaiologikon deltion* 58–64, 143–210.

(2015). Ιερό Αρτέμιδος Βραυρωνίας: τα ξύλινα ευρήματα των ανασκαφών 1961–1963. *ΑΡΧΑΙΟΛΟΓΙΚΗ ΕΦΗΜΕΡΙΣ* 154, 123–216.

Quincey, J. H. (1949). The metaphorical sense of Ληκυθος and Ampulla. *Classical Quarterly* 43, 32–44.

Rhomaios, K. A. (1932). *CVA Greece 1, Athens, National Museum 1*. Paris: H. Champion.

Richter, G. M. A. and Milne, M. J. (1935). *Shapes and Names of Athenian Vases*. New York: Metropolitan Museum of Art.

Robb, J. (2018). Contained within history. *History and Anthropology* 29, 32–36.

(2020). Material time. In I. Gaskell and S. A. Carter, eds., *The Oxford Handbook of History and Material Culture*. Oxford: Oxford University Press, 123–39.

Roberts, S. (1986). The Stoa Gutter Well: a Late Archaic deposit in the Athenian Agora. *Hesperia* 55, 1–72.

Robertson, M. (1992). *The Art of Vase-Painting in Classical Athens*. Cambridge: Cambridge University Press.

Rotroff, S. I. (1999). How did pots function within the landscape of the daily living?. In E. Villanueva Puig *et al.*, eds., *Céramique et peinture grecques. Modes d'emploi*. Paris: La Documentation Française, 63–74.

Rotroff, S. I. and Oakley, J. H. (1992). Debris from a public dining place in the Athenian Agora. *Hesperia Supplements* 25.

Rudolph, W. W. (1984). Excavations at Porto Cheli and vicinity, preliminary report VI: Halieis, the stratigraphy of the streets in the northeast quarter of the lower town. *Hesperia* 53, 123–70.

Sabetai, V. (2001). *CVA Greece 6, Thebes, Archaeological Museum 1.* Athens: Académie d'Athènes.

Sackett, L. H., Hankey, V., Howell, R. J., Jacobsen, T. W. and Popham, M. R. (1966). Prehistoric Euboea: contributions toward a survey. *Annual of the British School at Athens* 61, 33–112.

Saggini, T. (2019). Perserschutt in Eretria?: pottery from a pit in the Agora. In R. Morais, D. Leão, D. Pérez and D. Ferreira, eds., *Greek Art in Motion: Studies in honour of Sir John Boardman on the occasion of his 90th Birthday.* Oxford: Archaeopress, 366–74.

Salskov-Roberts, H. (2002). Were pots purpose-made for the funeral or reused? Can inscriptions throw light on the problem? In A. Rathje, M. Nielsen and B. Bundgaard Rasmussen, eds., *Pots for the Living, Pots for the Dead.* Copenhagen: University of Copenhagen, 9–31.

Săndulescu, C. (1962). Studiu asupra onomatologiei ceramice grecești. *Studii Clasice* 4, 35–48.

Sansone, D. (2016). Whatever happened to Euripides' Lekythion (*Frogs* 1198–1247)? In P. Kyriakou and A. Rengakos, eds., *Wisdom and Folly in Euripides.* Berlin and Boston: De Gruyter, 319–34.

Sapouna-Sakellaraki, E. (1987). Αμάρυνθος, θέση Γεράνι ή Αγία Κυριακή. *Archaiologikon deltion* 42, 200–214.

Schaus, G. P. (1992). Archaic imported fine wares from the Acropolis, Mytilene. *Hesperia* 61, 356–74.

Schmidt, S. (2005). *Rhetorische Bilder auf attischen Vasen. Visuelle Kommunikation im 5. Jahrhundert v. Chr.* Berlin: Reimer.

Serbeti, E. (1997). Attic pottery from a deposit in Eretria. In J. H. Oakley, W. D. R. Coulson and O. Palagia, eds., *Athenian Potters and Painters I. The Conference Proceedings.* Oxford: Oxbow, 491–99.

Sgourou, M. (2002). Excavating houses and graves: exploring aspects of everyday life and afterlife in ancient Thasos. In M. Stamatopoulou and M. Yeroulanou, eds., *Excavating Classical Culture.* Oxford: Beazley Archive, 1–12.

Shapiro, H. (2014). The Robinson Group of Panathenaic Amphorae. In J. Oakley ed., *Athenian Potters and Painters III,* Oxford and Philadelphia: Oxbow, 221–30.

Shear, J. L. (2003). Prizes from Athens: the list of Panathenaic prizes and the sacred oil. *Zeitschrift für Papyrologie und Epigraphik* 142, 87–108.

Shear, L. (1993). The Persian destruction of Athens: evidence from agora deposits. *Hesperia* 62, 383–482.

Shelmerdine, C. W. (1995). Shining and fragrant cloth in Homeric epic. In J. B. Carter and S. P. Morris, eds., *The Ages of Homer. A Tribute to Emily Townsend Vermeule.* Austin: University of Texas Press, 99–107.

Simon, E. (1989). *Die Sammlung Kiseleff im Martin-von-Wagner-Museum der Universität Würzburg. Minoische und griechische Antiken.* Mainz am Rhein: P. Von Zabern.

Smith, A. C. and Volioti, K. (2019). Lesser pots go places: the Attic "brand" in Macedonia and Thrace. In E. Manakidou and A. Avramidou, eds., *Classical Pottery of the Northern Aegean and Its Periphery (480–323/300 BC).* Thessaloniki: Thessalonikē University Studio Press, 175–87.

Soueref, K. (1999). Τούμπα Θεσσαλονίκης 1999. Ανασκάπτοντας στην Τράπεζα και στο αρχαίο νεκροταφείο. *Αρχαιολογικό Έργο Μακεδονίας και Θράκης* 13, 177–90.

Sparkes, B. A. and Talcott, L. (1970). *Black and plain pottery of the 6th, 5th and 4th centuries B.C. The Athenian Agora 12.* Princeton: American School of Classical Studies at Athens.

Spetsiéri-Chorémi, A. (1991). Un dépôt de sanctuaire domestique de la fin de l'époque archaïque à Corfou. *Bulletin de Correspondence Hellenique* 115, 183–211.

Spitaels, P. (1978). Insula 3. Tower Compound 1. *Thorikos VII*, 39–110.

Stais, V. (1893). Ο εν Μαραθώνι Τύμβος. *Mitteilungen des deutschen archäologischen Instituts (Athenische Abteilung)* 18, 46–63.

Stansbury-O'Donnell, M. (2006). *Vase Painting, Gender and Social Identity in Archaic Athens.* Cambridge: Cambridge University Press.

Stavropoulou-Gatsi, M. (2010). New archaeological researches in Aitolia, Akarnania, and Leukas. In C. Antonetti, ed., *Lo spazio ionico e le comunità della Grecia nord-occidentale. Territorio, società, istituzioni. Atti del Convegno Internazionale Venezia, 7–9 gennaio 2010.* Pisa: ETS, 79–96.

Steiner, A. (1992). Pottery and cult in Corinth: oil and water at the Sacred Spring. *Hesperia* 61, 385–408.

(2007). *Reading Greek Vases.* Cambridge: Cambridge University Press.

Steinhart, M. (1996). *Töpferkunst und Meisterzeichnung. Attische Wein- und Ölgefäße aus der Sammlung Zimmermann.* Mainz: Von Zabern.

Steinhauer, G. (2009). *Marathon and the Archaeological Museum.* Athens: John S. Latsis Public Benefit Foundation.

Stewart, A. and Martin, R. (2005). Attic imported pottery at Tel Dor, Israel: an overview. *Bulletin of the American Schools of Oriental Research* 337, 79–94.

Themelis, P. (1981). Ανασκαφή Ερέτριας. *Πρακτικὰ τῆς ἐν Ἀθήναις Ἀρχαιολογικῆς Ἑταιρείας* 137, 141–53.

Thompson, H. A. (1955). Activities in the Athenian Agora: 1954. *Hesperia* 24, 50–71.

Tiverios, M. (1974). Παναθηναϊκά. *Archaiologikon deltion* 29, 1 42–53.

(2009). Η Πανεπιστημιακή ανασκαφή στο Καραμπουρνάκι Θεσσαλονίκης. In P. Adam-Veleni and K. Tzanavari, eds., *20 χρόνια. Το Αρχαιολογικό Έργο στη Μακεδονία και στη Θράκη*. Thessaloniki, 385–96.

Toher, M. (1999). On 'Thucydides' blunder': 2.34.5. *Hermes* 127, 497–501.

Torelli, M. (2004). The red-figured ceramics from Gela: a contribution to the reconstruction of the cultural profile of a city. In R. Panvini and F. Giudice, eds., *Ta Attika. Veder Greco a Gela. Ceramiche attiche figurate dall'antica colonia*. Rome: "L'Erma" di Bretschneider, 27–32.

Touzé, R. (2008). Les matières premières employées dans la confection des huiles, onguents et poudres parfumés en Grèce ancienne. Les aromates à l'épreuve de l'expression. In L. Bodiou, D. Frère and V. Mehl., eds., *Parfums et odeurs dans l'Antiquité*. Rennes: Presses universitaires de Rennes, 45–59.

Trinkl, E. (2014). Grabkult in klassischer Zeit – weißgrundige Lekythen in ihrem Kontext. In G. Thür, ed., *Grabrituale Tod und Jenseits in Frühgeschichte und Altertum: Akten der 3. Tagung des Zentrums Archäologie und Altertumswissenschaften an der Österreichischen Akademie der Wissenschaften*. Vienna: Verlag der österreichischen Akademie der Wissenschaften, 77–94.

Tsakirgis, B. (1996). Houses and households. *American Journal of Archaeology* 100, 777–81.

(2005). Living and working around the Athenian Agora: a preliminary case study of three houses. In B. A. Ault and L. C. Nevett, eds., *Ancient Greek Houses and Households: Chronological, Regional, and Social Diversity*. Philadelphia: University of Pennsylvania Press, 67–82.

Tsiafakis, D. (2019). *CVA USA 40, Malibu 10. Athenian Red-Figure Column and Volute Kraters*. Los Angeles: The J. Paul Getty Museum.

Tuna-Nörling, Y. (1996). *Attische Keramik aus Klazomenai*. Saarbrücken: Saarbrücker Druckerei und Verlag.

(1999). *Daskyleion I. Die attische Keramik*. Izmir: Ege Üniversitesi Edebiyat Fakültesi.

Turner, M. (2005). Aphrodite and her birds: the iconology of Pagenstecher Lekythoi. *Bulletin of the Institute of Classical Studies* 48, 57–96.

Vallicelli, M. C. (2004). La ceramica a figure nere di Adria: i rinvenimenti da abitato. In C. Reusser and M. Bentz, eds., *Attische Vasen in etruskischem Kontext – Funde aus Häusern und Heiligtümern. Corpus Vasorum Antiquorum. Deutschland. Beihefte; Band 2*. Munich: C. H. Beck, 9–16.

Van De Put, W. D. J. (2006a). *CVA The Netherlands 9, Amsterdam 3. Black-Figure, Pattern and Six Technique Lekythoi*. Amsterdam: Allard Pierson Museum.

(2006b). *CVA The Netherlands 10, Amsterdam 4. Red-Figure and White-Ground Lekythoi*. Amsterdam: Allard Pierson Museum.

Van De Put, W. D. J. and Docter, R. (2012). A lekythos found in house 1 at Thorikos (2007 Campaign). In R. Docter, ed., *Thorikos 10 Reports & Studies*. Ghent: Department of Archaeology, Ghent University, 51–56.

Vanderpool, E. (1946). The Rectangular Rock-Cut Shaft. *Hesperia* 15, 265–336.

Varoucha, E. A. (1925–26). Κυκλαδικοί Τάφοι της Πάρου. *ΑΡΧΑΙΟΛΟΓΙΚΗ ΕΦΗΜΕΡΙΣ* 1925–26, 98–114.

Velenis, G. and Zachariadis, S. (2019). Considerations on the function and usage of pottery lamps, inspired by finds from the Forum of Thessaloniki. In I. Motsianos and K. Garnett, eds., *Glass, Wax and Metal: Lighting Technologies in Late Antique, Byzantine and Medieval Times.* Oxford: Archaeopress, 184–94.

Villing, A. (2020). Using Greek vases: developing use-wear analysis as an archaeology of practice. In M. Langner and S. Schmidt, eds., *Die Materialität griechischer Vasen. Mikrohistorische Perspektiven in der Vasenforschung. Corpus Vasorum Antiquorum. Deutschland. Beihefte; Band 9.* Munich, 101–15.

Villing, A. and Mommsen, H. (2017). Rhodes and Kos: East Dorian pottery production of the Archaic period. *Annual of the British School at Athens* 112, 99–154.

Vlavianou-Tsaliki, A. (1981). Ανασκαφή Τάφων στην Ερέτρια. *Archaiologikon deltion* 36, 58–81.

Volioti, K. (2007). Visual ambiguity in the *oeuvre* of the Gela Painter: a new lekythos from Thessaly. *Rivista di Archeologia* 31, 91–101.

(2011). The materiality of graffiti: socialising a lekythos in Pherai. In J. A. Baird and C. Taylor, eds., *Ancient Graffiti in Context.* New York: Routledge, 134–52.

(2014). Dimensional standardization and the use of Haimonian lekythoi. *BABesch Suppl.* 25, 149–68.

(2021, 2022). Leafless cups: towards a relational understanding. In D. Palaiothodoros and W. Van De Put, eds., *Oikos, Taphos, Temenos. Attic Pottery and Iconography in Greek Contexts.*

Volioti, K. and Papageorgiou, M. (2014–15). A new signed Corinthian *aryballos.* *Talanta* 46–47, 107–20.

Walters, H. B. (1905). *History of Ancient Pottery. Greek, Etruscan and Roman*, vol. I. London: J. Murray.

Webster, T. B. L. (1972). *Potter and Patron in Classical Athens.* London: Methuen.

Westgate, R. (2015). Space and social complexity in Greece from the Early Iron Age to the Classical Period. *Hesperia* 84, 47–95.

Williams, D. (2013). Greek potters and painters: marketing and movings. In A. Tsingarida and D. Viviers, eds., *Pottery Markets in the Ancient Greek World (8th–1st Centuries B.C.). Proceedings of the International Symposium held at the Université Libre de Bruxelles, 19–21 June 2008.* Brussels: CReA-Patrimoine, 39–60.

Wilson, R. J. A. (1996). Archaeology in Sicily, 1988–1995. *Archaeological Reports* 42, 59–123.

Woolley, L. (1938a). The excavations at Al Mina, Sueidia. I. *Journal of Hellenic Studies* 58, 1–30.

(1938b). The excavations at Al Mina, Sueidia. II. *Journal of Hellenic Studies* 58, 133–70.

Wright, J. H. (1886). Unpublished white lekythoi from Attika. *American Journal of Archaeology and of the History of the Fine Arts* 2, 385–407.

Yeivin, S. (1952). Archaeological news. Near East (Supplement). Israel. September 1950–October 1951. *American Journal of Archaeology* 56, 141–43.

Yialouris, N. (1957). Δοκιμαστικαί έρευναι εις τον κόλπον της Φειάς Ηλείας. *ΑΡΧΑΙΟΛΟΓΙΚΗ ΕΦΗΜΕΡΙΣ* 96, 31–43.

Young, R. S. (1951). Sepulturae intra urbem. *Hesperia* 20, 67–134.

Zachariadou, O., Kyriakou, D. and Baziotopoulou, E. (1985). Σωστική Ανασκαφή στον Ανισόπεδο Κόμβο Λένορμαν-Κωνσταντινουπόλεως. *Athens Annals of Archaeology* 18, 39–50.

Zaouri, A. (1989). "Κραννών. Αγρός Κ. Ρετζέπη", *Archaiologikon deltion* 44, 231–33.

Zimmermann-Elseify, N. (2011). *CVA Germany 89, Berlin 12. Attisch weissgrundige Lekythen.* Munich: C. H. Beck.

(2013). *CVA Germany 93, Berlin 13. Attisch Rotfigurige Lekythen.* Munich: C. H. Beck.

(2015). *CVA Germany 99, Berlin 16. Attische Salbgefässe.* Munich: C. H. Beck.

5 | Textiles in Alkestis' *thalamos*

AMY C. SMITH

In Greece, as elsewhere, marriage is or has traditionally been the key to maintaining the family unit that occupies the house in which it resides. Despite the resulting importance of marriage to the household and to the preservation of its inhabitants – that is, family – scholars have hardly tried to understand the role of the house and its furnishings in Greek marriage rituals. By furnishings I refer particularly to bedding and other textiles that cover furniture, drape house interiors and thus endow a home not only with warmth and comfort but also visible wealth.[1] Part of William Shakespeare's will – 'I gyve unto my wife my second best bed with the furnishings' – famously emphasizes the value of the textiles in relation to the bed itself.[2] In early modern times, as in pre-modern times, furniture was kept for a lifetime or more: Shakespeare's 'second best' bed and its furnishings therefore may have been the marriage bed that he shared with his wife, Anne. Textiles have therefore predominated as dowry or other wedding gifts, also because they bring comfort and visible wealth, thus luxury, to the bride's new home.[3] While this volume more broadly seeks to clarify evidence for houses in antiquity, this chapter addresses those elements that, at least in Greece, have traditionally made a house into a home, namely the marriage on which was built the *oikos* or family unit and the furnishings that were provided for that unit, initially through the wedding rituals. In this chapter I bring together marriage and textiles in the *thalamos* or private chamber that housed the bed on which the marriage was consummated. I suggest moreover that bed furnishings played a larger part in the ancient marriage festivals than hitherto recognized. The marriage festivals and textiles are those of any Greek woman, but I use the unlikely heroine Alkestis as 'every woman' because the bedchamber and furnishings are highlighted in her story.[4] As evidence of the bedchamber, its furniture and furnishings, like marriage ritual, is scant in the philological and archaeological records, I also employ ethnographic analogies and consider more recent Greek folklore studies in my reading of the visual and textual sources.

Thalamos

Scholarly interpretations of ancient Greek marriage and its constituent parts, especially the *gamos* or three-day wedding, have long relied on selective interpretation of the evidence, whether textual, material, or both, as in Oakley and Sinos' *The Wedding at Ancient Athens* (1993). From these sources we understand that the culminating moment of an ancient Greek wedding was the transfer of the newly wedded couple and particularly the bride from her own *oikos* or family home to that of her groom.[5] The event was accompanied by an elaborate procession conducted by family, attendants and onlookers, with music, song and perhaps a few gifts. While the visual evidence, mostly on vases given as wedding gifts or otherwise used in wedding processions,[6] amply documents the preparations and processions, there is less evidence of the actual transferral of the bride, seemingly at the door of the groom's house, and no evidence of the union itself in the *thalamos*, or chamber that housed the marriage bed.[7]

The modest reluctance of the artists to show the most intimate of private moments of the wedding, within the *thalamos*, is understandable. The best we can hope for is a glimpse into the *thalamos*, through an opened door. The door is, in fact, the most potent symbol of the bride's transition in the visual arts of ancient Greece. On a black-figure *dinos* in the British Museum, Sophilos, Athens' first named painter, shows King Peleus at the door to his palace, where he receives the divine guests to celebrate his wedding to the sea nymph Thetis (Figure 5.1).[8] The door is opened just far enough to reveal from behind it an elegantly presented bed.[9] The bed identifies the room into which the door opens as the *thalamos*. The bed and *thalamos* in turn symbolize the nuptial nature of the scene of which they are a part. Likewise, the Amasis Painter's *lekythos* in New York (Figure 5.2) shows the marriage procession approaching a double door, presumably the outside door (because of its size), on the other side of which we see the *thalamos*, symbolized by the bed within. Rarely is the nature of the door clarified.[10] Just as the door shown in Figures 5.1 and 5.2 symbolizes the home,[11] the bed – barely visible – serves a symbolic function to indicate the wedding. In juxtaposition with the bed, therefore, any single door is metaphorically the *thalamos* door.

The room known as *thalamos* is hard to identify in archaeological contexts because it might be any room used for the purpose of conjugal activity (on one or more occasions) with the imposition of a bed. Beds might be made of perishable materials, so are archaeologically elusive, as is

Figure 5.1 Attic black-figure *dinos* signed by Sophilos, *c.* 570 BCE, showing King Peleus receiving guests at the door to his palace. London, British Museum 1971.11-1.1. BAPD 350099. © Trustees of the British Museum

Figure 5.2 Rolled-out view of the frieze decorating an Attic black-figure *lekythos* attributed to the Amasis Painter, *c.* 540 BCE, showing a marriage procession approaching an external door, with a view of the *thalamos* within. New York, Metropolitan Museum of Art 56.11.1. BAPD 350748. © The Metropolitan Museum of Art

discussed below. Beds were used for other purposes, moreover, so the presence of a bed does not necessarily identify a *thalamos*. That is, a bed distinguishes the *thalamos* as a bed chamber primarily on the occasion of a marriage. Ancient artists present a sumptuously covered bed behind a door as a symbol of the *thalamos*, therefore of the culmination of the *gamos* and, in turn, the wedded relationship, as noted above (and shown in Figures 5.1 and 5.2). The *thalamos* is important as a symbol of marriage also in ancient literature. It is central to the aetiology for pre-nuptial sacrifices to Artemis, for example, in the story of Admetos of Pherai's efforts to win the hand of Alkestis, daughter of Pelias, for which he was required to yoke a lion and a boar to a chariot.[12] An Attic black-figure *lekythos* in the Yale University Art Gallery (Figure 5.3) illustrates this yoking of wild animals, an allusion to the (equally challenging) yoking of a woman in marriage.[13] Frontisi-Ducroux and Lissarrague (2009) suggest Artemis' presence recalls Admetos' failure to make a pre-nuptial sacrifice to Artemis, the punishment for which (again, according to Apollodoros) was that his *thalamos* or marriage chamber was filled with coiled snakes.[14]

In tragedy as elsewhere in Greek thought, however, this *thalamos* is symbolized by and perhaps synonymous with the marriage bed. Some time later, Alkestis died in the place of her husband, Admetos, because Apollo had persuaded the Moirai to release Admetos from death should someone die for him. This story, as poignantly told by Euripides in *Alkestis*, unfortunately encourages us to concentrate on the deathbed rather than the marriage bed. Even in this tragicomedy, however, the bed serves both for marriage and death, because Alkestis is returned to life by Persephone/Kore or Herakles.[15] *Kline*, the Greek word for a banqueting couch, might also be used of the funerary bed or bier. For a marriage bed the usual word is *lektron* or (Homeric) *lechos*,[16] as a result of which *alochos* is wife or bed companion. As Sanders notes, however, these and other bed words – *eunê* and *koitê* – are commonly used in Greek tragedies to denote sex as well as marriage, no less than thirty-six times in Euripides' *Medea*, with reference to both Jason's old marriage to Medea and his new marriage to Glauke.[17] Pindar makes a verbal allusion to the marriage bed in his seventh *Olympian Ode*:

> As when a man takes from his rich hand a bowl foaming inside with dew of the vine and presents it to his young son-in-law with a toast from one home to another – an all-golden bowl, crown of possessions – as he honors the joy of the symposium and his own alliance, and thereby with his friends present makes him envied for his harmonious marriage. (Pindar, *Olympian Odes* 7.1–6: trans. Race 1997: 121)

Figure 5.3 Attic black-figure *lekythos* attributed to the Edinburgh Painter, *c.* 500 BCE, showing Apollo mounting a chariot drawn by a lion, a lioness, a boar and a wolf, with Leto, Hermes and Artemis in attendance. Yale University Art Gallery 1913.111. BAPD 3200. © Yale University Art Gallery

This translation gets the point right, despite having reconfigured the verb *eunao* (εὐνάω, for εὐνάζω), 'to lay', into the marriage itself.

Beds

As with the *thalamos*, however, the marriage bed is more of a concept than an archaeologically attestable entity, yet without a single noun.[18] Both Greeks and Romans had words for bed that were used interchangeably for dining, sleeping and sex. The Latin *grabātus* and its Greek equivalent *kravatos* may have emerged simultaneously and were widely used in the Common Era,[19] but Pollux (10.35) informs us that the Greek term was used in new comedies – Rhinthon's *Telephos* (late 4th–early 3rd centuries BCE) and Kriton's *Messenia* (early 2nd century BCE) – while a scholiast on Aristophanes' *Clouds* 254 also uses it. Eusthathius *ad. Il.* 16.608, writing in the 4th century CE, calls it an Attic word referring to a 'cheap and low bed which is near the ground', while Phynichos (frag. 44), writing in the 2nd century CE, emphasizes that the Attic equivalent was *skimpous*, which is more broadly understood as a small couch or hammock on which, for example, Sokrates sits in Plato's *Protagoras* (310c). As it turns out, whether because of its Latin equivalent or itself, *kravatos* is the bed word that has been in continuous use ever since, not only in (modern) Greek (*krebáti*), but also Turkish (*kerevet*), Albanian (*krevat*), Portuguese (*gravato*), Russian (*krovát*) and even French (*grabat*). Whatever might have been the form or composition of these later beds, the term *kravatos* may have derived from a Macedonian-Illyrian word for 'oak' through use of oak for wooden bed frames.[20] The literary sources suggest wood, such as maple and olive – was most commonly used for frames and legs.[21] Wooden bed parts are archaeologically attested, moreover, both in houses and in tombs. The Macedonian evidence emerges more strongly from tombs and there is as much evidence of metal parts.[22] Later literary references are awash with gold and silver couches[23] and elegant 'Chian' and 'Milesian' beds with incisions and inlays.[24]

Beds made of yet more perishable materials such as straw (e.g. mattresses, baskets, or cribs) either haven't survived in the archaeological record or have been overlooked in excavations.[25] Yet no intact bed has survived in a domestic complex, so we must rely on the funerary evidence, namely bed-shaped structures and bed bases made of both stone (for inhumations) and wood (for cremations) primarily found in Macedonian tombs.[26] It remains unclear, however, whether even movable funerary beds (whose use and decoration are suggestive of real life) replicate the beds ancient Greeks used for sleep or other daily activities.

Beds were clearly used and reused for other activities after the marriage, until and including death, as amply illustrated by the story of Alkestis, mentioned above. The iconographic evidence also gives us a picture of multitasking beds. Beds that seem to have appeared on stage, as in a purported dramatic scene on the upper frieze of an Apulian *krater* in the British Museum (Figure 5.4), might have been stage props that served alternatively as altars, benches or even tombs.[27] Sympotic images suggest that *klinai*, beds or couches on which heroes or symposiasts recline, were bedecked with similar cushions and covers, yet preceded by tables that indicate some sort of ritual dining (Figure 5.5).

Although metal and ivory parts and inlay might add luxury to a bed frame, the literary evidence overwhelmingly suggests that textiles mattered to the ancient Greeks more than bed frames or bases.[28] Philokleon in Aristophanes' *Wasps* 1215, for example, is told to admire the woven hangings in the court. The furnishings, however, are also lost from the archaeological record, although a few Macedonian funerary beds were found with leather or cloth coverings, at Veroia and Foinikas, in Thessaloniki.[29] There is no archaeological evidence of covers or pillows, however, from any domestic complex.[30] The elegant 'Milesian' beds noted above might have earned this name because they were bedecked with luxurious Milesian bed covers, which garnered admiration in Aristophanes' *Frogs* 544.[31] Other exotic textile centres noted in ancient literature include Akragas (mattresses),[32] Sardis (carpets)[33] and Phoenicia (curtains).[34] Lydia had an ancient gold-weaving tradition, although Pliny places the invention of embroidery (decorative stitching with a needle) to King Attalos in Phrygia, and damask (fabric woven with many threads) to Alexandria.[35] The bedcover shown on the bed in the top scene on the Apulian krater (figure 5.4) boasts a complex diamond twill pattern.[36] The best 5th-century BCE source for furnishings, as indeed furniture, is the so-called Attic Stelai, which list the property confiscated from Alcibiades and his followers, in 415/14.[37] Alcibiades' own property included two of the many words for pillow (*proskephalaion* and *knephallon*),[38] while Pollux later mentions that pillows made of wool, leather[39] and linen were sold from this property.[40] *Pleroma*, woollen flock for stuffing pillows, is also noted in these stelai.[41] By the 2nd century CE, Pollux amasses a long list of diverse adjectives for bed covers, describing colours, including gold, their shining effect, border decoration, thread quality, fineness and of course crafts(wo)manship.[42] Hesychios and Suidas, lexicographers writing in the

Figure 5.4 Apulian red-figure calyx *krater* attributed to the Laodamia Painter, *c.* 340 BCE, showing a love scene perhaps from a tragedy (above) and a centaur carrying off Laodamia, the bride of Peirithoos (below). London, British Museum 1870,0710.2. *RVAp* 18/14. © Trustees of the British Museum

5th and 10th centuries CE, respectively, are similarly effusive. Together Pollux and Athenaios have furnished us with a bewildering array of words for bedclothes,[43] including carpets and curtains that might serve multiple purposes, as in Berber tents. Aristophanes tells of a *sisyran*, a goat-hair cloak used as a coverlet by night.[44] Likewise the same mattress might serve for sleeping or sitting and the *kline* or couch on which it

Figure 5.5 Attic red-figure bell *krater* attributed to the Meleager Painter, *c.* 380 BCE, showing two pairs of symposiasts. Reading, Ure Museum of Greek Archaeology 45.8.1. BAPD 217955. © University of Reading

lay might be used in life and death, as discussed above. This is completely in line with Nevett's observation that Greek rooms themselves were multifunctional.[45]

Neither does iconographic evidence for beds and other furnishings help us to distinguish marriage beds or their textiles, except in the context of wedding stories. The partial and even fragmentary nature of our corpus of Greek art means that many other images of beds might be lost. It is a challenge for even the experienced iconographer to reconstruct a bed from the image of lion's paw leg of furniture or a tasselled cushion. Of course some vase painters were more precise (or know their textiles or woodworking) better than others.[46] The painter of an image on the side of an *epinetron* or knee thimble conveniently labelled the woman at far right, who leans on the bed end, as Alkestis (Figure 5.6). Our recollection of Alkestis' sad tale helps us to understand the furniture on which she leans as a bed. This artist, the so-called Eretria Painter, however, has remembered that beds are made most easily recognizable through the frame of a door and has therefore also shown the door to the *thalamos*. Alkestis' bed has been decorated in preparation for the wedding, yet she is shown already there, for which reason this scene is normally and rightly interpreted as the *epaulia* or aftermath (day after) of the *gamos*, meaning that the marriage has already been consummated. When was the bed

Figure 5.6 Attic red-figure *epinetron*, name vase of the Eretria Painter, *c.* 430 BCE. Side C, showing the *epaulia* of Alkestis. Athens, National Museum 1629 (CC 1588). BAPD 216971. Photo: Giannis Patrikianos © Hellenic Ministry of Culture and Sports/ Archaeological Receipts Fund

decorated and was it ever put on display in the ancient Greek ritual? A diachronic consideration of Greek marriage rituals reveals a long-standing emphasis on the decoration of the marriage bed, particularly through the *krevatia* or ritual through which the bed is decorated up until modern times.[47] A synthesis of Greek folklore[48] and ancient sources might then aid in building a more thorough understanding of the importance of the marriage bed and its room, the *thalamos*, in the ancient Greek home and through wedding rituals. The *thalamos* and its bed provide an opportunity for us to unite the modern *krevatia*, literally the festival of the bed, with the ancient *anakalypteria*, an unveiling festival. Before we can understand the unveiling rituals, however, it is necessary to seek a better understanding of the relevance of textiles to the ancient Greek wedding.

Sumptuous textiles were present throughout the three days of the wedding and many would decorate the marriage bed. The marriage bed was not merely a symbol of the physical union of the couple, but embodied the importance of the textile tradition in marriage. In marrying a woman skilled in textiles, a man added textile production to his household assets. 'Textile production was among those skills that were thought to have enabled man to create civilization; thus, a wife who spun or wove not only conformed to society's expectations, but helped to sustain that civilised society.'[49] According to Hesiod *Works and Days* 63–64, Athena had taught women the art of weaving, so it was both a divine gift and a fundamentally feminine activity.[50] The latter point was emphasized in Classical Athens by the suspension of a tuft of wool over the entrance door to mark the birth of a girl.[51] Plato speaks of male textile workers, such as sail makers (*histiorrhaphoi*) and rope makers (*styppeio-plokoi*, later called *kalostrophoi*), in Athens' Agora or marketplace, although some scholars have suggested he is referring to women weavers.[52] Yet most ancient Greek textile manufacture was accomplished in the home, sometimes in a special space inside the *gynaikeion* or women's quarters. An *histeon*, meaning 'space dedicated to the loom'[53] can be attested archaeologically from post-holes indicating uprights of a warp-weighted loom, together with grouped loom-weights, as in houses at Olynthos.[54] Weaving paraphernalia, however, does not necessarily identify a domestic or industrial space in which weaving was done, but might represent votive dedications in ritual contexts. Dedications of loom-weights and spindle whorls have been found throughout the Mediterranean from all periods. Both because weaving and – by associ-ation – textile production were divine gifts, as noted above, and because of the important role women played in religion, there is a large overlap between domestic and ritual contexts that provide evidence of both textile production and the textiles themselves. The best iconographic evidence of the ritual use of textiles comes from a group of votive terracottas found at Lokroi Epizephyroi in south Italy, which seem to indicate textile dedica-tions to a goddess.[55] Which goddess? Aphrodite and Persephone were the primary deities here, while Demeter was also worshipped at a nearby Thesmophorion. Persephone is the best candidate because here she was relevant to maturation, marriage and childbirth, as were Artemis and Hera on the mainland, and thus received *proteleia* or pre-marriage dedications, perhaps textiles.[56] Gaifman rightly cautions us, however, that votive reliefs like all religious art are visual constructs related to cultic realities, not direct reflections of actual realities.[57] Yet written sources also inform us of textile offerings to deities in connection with the wedding.

Gamos

The *Proaulia*, meaning literally the day before the *gamos*, comprised the bride's time among female relatives, friends and servants, who were all involved with preparations, as well as the dedication of *proteleia* or

Figure 5.7 Attic red-figure *pyxis* attributed to the Oppenheimer Group, *c.* 450 BCE. Mainz, University of Mainz 118. BAPD 220643. Photo used with permission

offerings, as expressed, for example, by Euripides in *Iphigenia in Aulis* 433–39.[58] Textile offerings would be childhood garments[59] and new garments, manufactured for this votive purpose, and even dolls' dresses.[60] The belt used in maidenhood was supposed to have been dedicated to Artemis before marriage,[61] as was the veil that a woman had begun to use at *menarche*, the onset of menstruation.[62] A *pyxis* in Mainz shows a bride, with her mother, bringing offerings to the temple of Artemis (within which Artemis herself is shown) (Figure 5.7). Pollux calls this first day of the wedding (or day before) the *apaulia*, when he discusses it in the context of sleeping arrangements.[63] He reports that, on the *apaulia*, the bride would sleep with the *pais amphithales*, a small boy with parents on both sides, while the groom would sleep with a little girl, also with both parents living.[64] He informs us that the bride on this occasion gave an *apaulisteria chlanis*, or luxurious garment, probably woven by herself, to the groom, thus recalling the literary *topos* of the weaving bride, especially Homeric paradigms of Penelope and Helen at their looms[65] and the role of Athena Ergane dressing Hera and Pandora, the first brides, for their weddings.[66] Neither Pollux nor any other sources, however, divulge the purpose for this cloth, the only gift from the bride. The relative absence of textiles in the archaeological record, let alone names for textiles in particular contexts, hinders our ability to identify the format of the *apaulasteria chalnis*. Was it necessarily a garment to be worn? Or could it have been a textile with another function?

Figure 5.8 Rolled-out view of the frieze decorating an Attic red-figure *pyxis*, *c.* 430 BCE, showing bridal preparations. New York, Metropolitan Museum of Art 1972.118.148. BAPD 44750. Drawing by author

Textiles may have been used in connection with the ritual bathing that accompanied perhaps every religious event but was conducted by both bride and groom in anticipation of the wedding. For the marriage bath at Athens the water was fetched, usually in a *loutrophoros* (bath carrier) from the Enneakrounos spring.[67] Like the *proteleia*, or marriage sacrifice, this procession took place in the outdoors, accompanied by ritual songs, and was thus a conspicuous sign of the approach of the wedding.[68] A *pyxis* in New York shows a bathing scene but also the next stage after the bath, that is, the adornment of the bride (Figure 5.8). Particularly with such images of the ritual procedures, it becomes unclear to us whether successive events or a single moment are depicted. There are ample inclusions of textiles in images of these and other preparations so it is clear that a variety of textiles were prepared, used and displayed throughout the three-day festival.

Perhaps the most important wedding textile – for which there is alas mostly post-classical evidence – was the *pastos* or *aulaeum* (as it was called in Latin), a broad rectangular piece of woven fabric that covered the bed on which the marriage would be consummated, but by association symbolized the union.[69] In a textile sense the *pastos* is the cover, yet the same word came to refer to the bridal bed, chamber, and even hymn (LSJ[9] s.v. *pastos*). In the procession it might also serve as a canopy – forming a sort of shrine – and as such would symbolize the couple's care for each other. In the Roman wedding it was the backdrop for the *dextrarum iunctio* (joining of right hands).

The *gamelia* refers to the second day, the wedding feast,[70] and the torchlit procession from the bride's home to the groom's[71] – perhaps also known as the *nymphagogia* – to the sound of proclamations, such as 'Get up! Make way! Carry the torch!'[72] This most public and elaborate event of the three-day wedding, with dances, music and vases, as well as torches, was the most popularly represented scene on Athenian vases, such as a

Figure 5.9 Rolled-out view of the frieze decorating an Attic red-figure *pyxis* attributed to the Marlay Painter, *c.* 440 BCE, showing a bridal procession. London, British Museum 1920.12-12.1. BAPD 216210. © Trustees of the British Museum

scene that wraps around a *pyxis* attributed to the Marlay Painter, now in London (Figure 5.9). The procession, led by the *proegetes*, or usher, approaches the groom's house, indicated by the door on the far right. The *parochos* or best man, entrusted with the bride's safety during this journey, is followed by several women carrying containers. The bride herself might carry household vessels to symbolize or advertise her domestic skills; textiles might have been enclosed in some of the boxy containers. Behind the procession is the opened door of the bride's family's house, which they have left. On the far right, at the house of the groom, Eros and the mother-in-law wait to welcome the new couple. A glimpse of the *thalamos*, with the bridal bed revealed within, is visible through the partially opened door. This latter door was guarded fiercely by another of the groomsmen, a *thororos*.[73]

The *ekdosis* or transfer of the bride from the *kyrios* or guardian to another man, i.e. the groom, took place on arrival at the groom's home, where the marriage was consummated. Again, it is a challenge to identify the handover of the bride. In what manner, by whom, and with what accoutrements might the bride have been handed over? Perhaps with a handshake, as shown on a few vases, e.g. a *loutrophoros-amphora* in Boston (Figure 5.10). Both the red wreath that hangs above the bearded father-in-law and clean-shaven groom in this image and the wedding scenes on the other side of the same vase allude to the wedding and thus confirm its nuptial context.[74] But the handshake was the hallmark of the *engye* or pledge of marriage, i.e. betrothal, which may have happened years before

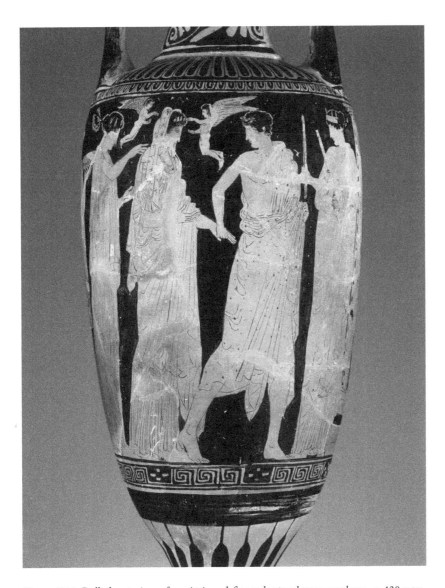

Figure 5.10 Rolled-out view of an Attic red-figure *loutrophoros-amphora*, *c.* 430 BCE, showing an *engye* or betrothal. Boston, Museum of Fine Arts 03.802. BAPD 15815. Photograph © 2018 Museum of Fine Arts, Boston

the wedding and had nothing to do with the women, but was rather an oral agreement, sealed with a handshake, between the men.[75] Herodotos also describes the significance of the handshake at the engagement of Megakles of Athens to Agariste, daughter of Kleisthenes, the tyrant of Sikyon.[76]

Neither is the crowning of the bride with her *stephane* a symbol of the *ekdosis*.[77] This moment, shown on the name vase of the Painter of Athens

Figure 5.11 Attic red-figure *lebes gamikos* (wedding bowl), name vase of the Painter of Athens 1454, *c.* 420 BCE, showing a procession of women with containers and the crowning of the bride. Athens, National Museum 1454. BAPD 215616. Photo: Stephanos Stournaras © Hellenic Ministry of Culture and Sports/Archaeological Receipts Fund

1454, a *lebes gamikos* (wedding bowl), shows another procession of women with containers, jewellery and garments approaching the bride, as she is crowned (Figure 5.11).[78] The illustration of bridal crowns, in adornment or even procession scenes, however, is quite inconsistent. Such scenes frequently decorate ointment and perfume containers – alabastra, *lekythoi* and *plemochoai* – and jewellery boxes – *pyxides* and *lekanides* – used for the prenuptial preparations. These scenes almost never include men and so it is clear that the crowning occurs as part of the preparations, thus *proteleia*, and not as part of the *gamos* or second day. And there is no evidence for a bridal crown in the primary written sources on the topic.[79]

The symbol of *ekdosis* to which scholars have most readily acquiesced is an unveiling of the bride, perhaps the best evidence for which is found on side A of the Boston *loutrophoros-amphora*, which shows the *nympheutria*, or bridesmaid, assisted by Erotes, adjusting the bride's veil (Figure 5.10).[80] Again, however, this symbol is not evidenced in the ancient texts, let alone other vase images.[81] Scholars have searched in vain for some indication, from the visual evidence, of the timing and importance of a veil ceremony, but aside from a little nip and tuck from Eros and his brothers, little is done with it. It is unclear whether the veil is being put on or taken off, and most of the images of the taking of the bride, with the *xeir epi karpo* wrist-grabbing gesture, would suggest a veil is not even needed. The (un)veiling of the bride has persisted in scholarship, however, since Deubner connected it with the *anakalypteria* festival in his pioneering article on the *epaulia*.[82] Yet there is no evidence that the veil has ever been necessary at a Greek wedding.[83] Since Deubner, moreover, scholars have struggled to understand the timing, role and even meaning of the *anakalypteria*, whose name indicates some sort of veiling. After a brief discussion of the *epaulia* or third day of the wedding, I will disentangle the *katachysmata* and *anakalypteria*, festivals that – according to primary sources – occurred on the third day but which scholars have preferred to understand as happening on the second day, after the *gamelia*.

The newlyweds were awakened for another day of festivities, at dawn on the third day, known as the *epaulia*, with more food, songs and dances. Most descriptions and images (e.g. Figure 5.6) indicate that the foci of attention were the bride and the gifts that she received. Eustathius gives a full description of the *epaulia*, which suggests that it was an even more elaborate procession than that which had taken place the night before:[84]

> ... the day of *epaulia* is that after the bride is first quartered [*epaulistai*] in the groom's house, and *epaulia* are also the gifts brought by the bride's father to the bride and groom in the form of a parade, on the day following the wedding. He [Pausanias] says that a child led it, wearing a white cloak and carrying a flaming torch, and then came another child, a girl, carrying a basket [*kanephoros*], and then the rest, bringing *lekanides*, unguents, clothing, combs, chests, bottles, sandals, boxes, murrh, soap and sometimes, he says, the dowry.[85]

Gifts are held by female companions and are similar if not identical to those used in preparations. In more recent, but traditional Greek weddings, the big feast occurs also after three days of preparations, particularly involving preparing the bridal chamber.

Anakalypteria and *Krevatia*

An ancient ritual that occurred at the groom's home involved *tragemata* or *katachysmata*,[86] a medley of dried fruit and nuts seemingly poured

Figure 5.12 Fragment of an Attic red-figure *loutrophoros* attributed to the Phiale Painter, *c.* 440 BCE, showing the *katachysmata*. Boston, Museum of Fine Arts 10.223. BAPD 214222. Drawing by author

over the couple, as illustrated on a fragment of the Phiale Painter's *loutrophoros* in Boston (Figure 5.12), showing a basket containing the *katachysmata* held above the groom.[87] The bride, who is barely visible here, seems to be hiding under a veil held by the *nympheutria* or brides- maid. Oakley and subsequent scholars have used this 'evidence' of the (un)veiling of the bride to conflate the *katachysmata* with the *anakalyp- teria*, and prefer to see both as occurring on the second day of the wedding, after the *gamelia*, on arrival at the groom's home. Deschodt rightly warns that these images aren't photographs and that the artist may have intentionally combined three separate 'pictures' of the wedding in one: unveiling, *katachysmata* and adornment.[88] I might add that any (un)veiling might be easily confused or conflated with adornment. This necessitates a thorough analysis of the *anakalypteria* that steps beyond overinterpretation of the fact of a bride wearing a veil.

Our earliest source on the subject, Pherekydes of Syros (*c.* 6 c. BCE), specifies that the *anakalypteria* occurred on the day of the *epaulia* or third day of the wedding and thus in connection with the presentation of gifts.[89] Confusingly, however, Pherekydes also cites it as the occasion of the *ekdosis*, which has been assumed to have occurred on the second day, at the end of the *gamelia*, as noted above. So Deubner and subsequent scholars have preferred to push the *anakalypteria* back to the second day, before or after the procession, to align the timing with that noted by Bekker.[90] Yet Pherekydes is the only ancient source that connects the *anakalypteria* with the *gamelia*. In any case, the *anakalypteria* is connected with and seems synonymous with gifts.[91] Those given through the *gamos* are alternatively called *opteria*, *theoretra* or *anakalypteria dora*.[92] The first two words for the gifts, i.e. *opteria* and *theoretra*, both derive from words for seeing,[93] stressing perhaps the importance of the entire community serving witness to the scene and the gifts. Yet there are no ancient sources to back up this supposition. The assumption that gifts might have only been given on one occasion, and that therefore the *anakalypteria dora* would necessarily be the same as the *opteria* and *theoretra*, is unwarranted. So textile gifts are given also on the first day, moreover, in the form of the *apaulasteria chlanis*, as noted above.

The assumption that *anakalypteria dora* were synonymous with *opteria* and *theoretra* has, however, encouraged scholars to understand a visual aspect as essential to the *anakalypteria*.[94] An (un)veiling of the bride would satisfy this visual emphasis, insofar as underlining the importance of the groom finally seeing the bride's face. The best and perhaps only reason to connect the *anakalypteria* with an (un)veiling (of the bride), however, is the meaning of the word *anakalypteria* and a lexically related word, *anakalypsis*, now commonly used in transliteration by iconographers with regard to every veiling or unveiling of a female figure. There remains a disagreement about its meaning: while some interpret it as an unveiling of a bride,[95] others see it rather as a veiling, a gesture to hide the face.[96] In any case, I would agree with those who see the veil as a status symbol.[97] Quite simply put, a married woman wears a himation, with which she can veil herself, and thus the fact of veiling or having a veil simply indicates that a woman is or is about to be married. Deschodt rightly notes that holding a veil is not identical to unveiling[98] and that there is a great variety of nuptial images showing veils in different contexts.[99] She thus removes the presence of the *anakalypsis* gesture from any possible interpretation of the *anakalypteria*. Another reason to see it as a veiling rather than unveiling is understanding of the prefix *ana*, which normally conveys a sense of 'up', 'on' or 'upon'.

As it turns out from an investigation of the textual material, *anakalypsis* is never used to refer to the (un)veiling of a woman in Greek literature. If we look to the literature for uses of the verb, *kalypto*, moreover, we find that it is not used for bridal veils but rather for poetic unveilings, which range from the exposure of a sand bar or island by receding seas[100] to the covering or uncovering of furniture, even beds, with cloths.[101] So it turns out that Deubner's *anakalypteria* and the *anakalypsis* that was supposedly central to it are, in fact, modern constructs.

If not an (un)veiling of the bride, what then was this *anakalyptria* that was the focus or at least culmination of the ancient Greek wedding, particularly during the *epaulia* (or third day), but also the destination of the festival procession on the *gamelia* (or second day), and reason for such preparations on the *proteleia* (or first day)? If indeed the *anakalypteria* was a veiling or unveiling, was the bride (un)veiled once, after the *gamelia* (day two)[102] or in the *thalamos*[103]; or was it a series of (un)veilings, as ingeniously suggested by Lloyd Llewellyn-Jones,[104] or was something else (un)veiled? While Ferrari has exhorted us to overcome the idea that there was a ceremonial unveiling at all, scholars have hitherto failed to offer an alternative.[105] A solution that suits the evidence, would have occurred over three days and finds a parallel with the post-Classical Greek nuptial traditions, however, is that the *anakalypteria* concerned the decoration, redecoration and unveiling of the marriage bed, with richly decorated fabrics, perhaps even the *apaulasteria chlanis*, discussed above.

The dominant three-day wedding festival in Greek weddings through to the present is the *krevatia*, which comprises dressing – and in some variations successive undressing and redressing – of the bridal bed with the elaborate and precious bed coverings that made up the dowry.[106] Women from both sides and nowadays men too would gather in the bridal chamber. Fruit and nuts, other fertility symbols like rose petals, cash, even children might be thrown on the bed, with good wishes, often sung, for the bridal couple. An emphasis on seeing the bride at this ritual is suggested in this modern *krevatia* song:

> Open up the windows so the doves can come in and see the bride and the dowry, the white sheets. With all my heart Anthea the man you picked for you to live with until you get old . . .[107]

Might the *krevatia* derive from the ancient *anakalypteria*? Both entail covering and uncovering, involve presence of friends and family in this most 'private' of spaces, incorporate a *katachysmata*, or medley of dried fruits and nuts, and concern the revelation of the dowry and/or other gifts. The presence of the child on the bed – the so-called 'flipping of the baby' ritual[108] – might also correspond to the ancient ritual of the *pais amphithales* noted above. Pollux had confusingly included this sleeping with a child as happening on the first day, which he also called *apaulia*. Could that be a lexical mistake for *epaulia*? Pollux would then be vindicated in placing the *pais amphithales* tradition on the *epaulia* (third day) or eve thereof, in connection with the *katachysmata*, *anakalypteria* and associated *dora* or gifts.

This suggested interpretation of the *anakalypteria* as a festival of (un) veiling of the bed, inside the *thalamos* of the groom's house, either on or after the arrival of the wedded couple at their new home, brings together our scraps of ancient textual and material evidence for rituals that may have accompanied the *ekdosis* or transfer of the bride, from one man to another, from one home to another. These rituals involved not just (un)veiling of the bed – *anakalypteria* – but also symbols of fertility – *katachysmata* – associated gifts – *dora* – and community (both women and men) witnessing the joining of the newly married couple. It is certain that it occurred after the *gamelia*, both feast and procession. It is to some degree irrelevant whether it occurred late on the second day or more likely on the third day, as suggested by the majority of ancient sources. It does not help us determine when exactly the marriage was consummated yet that would have been a matter only of concern to the married persons. While my connection of the *anakalypteria* with the *krevatia* on present evidence cannot be proven, perhaps subsequent scholars will seek and find evidence to support this suggestion. And perhaps philologists will demonstrate more conclusively that the veiling at the heart of the *anakalypteria* festival, and therefore the ancient Greek wedding, was the decoration, redecoration and unveiling of the marriage bed, with richly decorated fabrics, in ancient as in subsequent times.

Notes

1 As noted by Andrianou 2009: 90, the 1601 inventory from Hardwick Hall, Derbyshire, demonstrates that beddings and other fabrics could hold a greater pecuniary value than wooden furniture in pre-modern times. For that inventory see Boynton and Thornton 1971. For the evaluation of domestic material evidence as wealth indicators (in a modern Kurdish village) see Kramer 1979: 149–56.

2 25 March 1616. UK National Archives PROB 1/4A.

3 Herzfeld 1980. On chests that held the textiles used for dowry see Brümmer 1988.

4 Schmidt 1981a: 533–44.

5 Smith 2011: 83–84, 91–92.

6 Smith 2011 and 2005.

7 Xenophon, Economics 9, 3; Nevett 1999: 37.

8 Homer, *Iliad* 18, 432–36; 24, 58–63; Hesiod, *Theogony* 1006–1007; Pindar, *Isthmian Odes* 8, 25–48; Pindar, *Nemean Odes* 4, 62–68.

9 Oakley and Sinos 1993: 35–37.

10 Smith 2016.

11 Sourvinou-Inwood 1991: 71.

12 According to Apollodoros, *Library* 1.9.15, followed by Hyginus, *Fables* 50–51, Apollodoros, Library 1, 9.15 and Pausanias 3, 18.10–12, 18.15–16 tells us of Bathykles of Magnesia's sculptured representation of this story on the throne of Apollo at Amyklai, showing that Admetos yoked the animals himself.

13 Frontisi-Ducroux and Lissarrague 2009; Matheson 2016: 33–35.

14 The coiled snakes are not known, however, in ancient imagery. See Schmidt 1981b: 218–21.

15 Halleran 1988; see also Buxton 1987 and Rehm 1984.

16 *IG* I^3 423, l. 8, 425 l. 11; Pollux 10.35.

17 Sanders 2013: 45.

18 Further to this brief discussion see the mention of bed words above and Andrianou 2009: 31–33.

19 Kramer 1995; Mols 1999: 127.

20 Beekes 2009: 766.

21 Homer, *Odyssey* 23.195 and Pollux 10.35.

22 Tubular legs made of hollow bronze (Déonna 1938, 2–3) or wood (Siebert 1976: 799–821 esp. 813, figs. 24–25; 2001: 91, pl. 42.4); arm- or headrests (Andrianou 2009: 34); and fulcra made of wood or metal (Kyrieleis 1969 compares the visual evidence on 5th-century BCE Athenian vases and, because of the paucity of references to metal furniture in contemporary literary sources, suggests wood was used for the rails at the back of fulcra exclusively until the middle of the 4th century).

23 See e.g. Arrian, *Anabasis* 6.29.5–6; Demosthenes 24.129; Athenaios 5.197a–b and 6.255e. For a synthesis see, more recently, Faust 1989.

24 Chian and Milesian beds are often cited in temple accounts as well as the Attic stelai. See Ransom 1905: 54.

25 Athenaios 4.138f. uses *stibas* to refer to rough couches (of wood) used at a festival, while Menander, *Dyskolos* 420 uses the same term to refers to straw mattresses outside a cave during a ritual celebration.

26 Andrianou 2009: 39–41 updates Simanidis 1997.

27 Taplin 2007: 131–32.

28 Emerging literature on textiles includes Walter-Karydi 1994 (from High
    Classical); Andrianou 2009: *passim* and 2006 (from Late Classical); and Sanidas
    2011 (Hellenistic). Richter 1966: 118 pioneered in collecting the visual sources
    for textiles in connection with her study of ancient furniture. See also Carroll
    1965: 37–64 and, more recently, Vickers 1999.

29 Drougou and Touratsoglou 1980: 93 (Veroia, tomb A); Tsimbidou-Avloniti
    2005: 81 (Foinikas).

30 See Moraitou and Margariti 2008.

31 Aristophanes, Frogs 544.

32 *FGrH* 3B, 566, F26a, 607.

33 Noted by Klearchos of Soloi according to Athenaios 6.255e.

34 *Exodus* 26, 31 and 36, 35; cf. Homer, *Odyssey* 15, 417–18.

35 Greenewalt and Majewski 1980: 136–37; Pliny, *Natural History* 8.196. For more
    on the history of damask (a modern term) see Galliker 2017: 368. Ten
    fragments of silk (?) cloth, enriched with silver and gold threads, from Koropi,
    in Attica (now in the Victoria and Albert Museum, London), however, are said
    to have been found with bones in a bronze *kalpis* (now lost), dated to the late
    5th–early 4th centuries BCE. See Beckwith 1954: 114–15; Carroll 1965: 7–8;
    Gleba 2008; Andrianou 2009: 92–93 cat. 90.

36 Spantidaki 2017: 207.

37 Pritchett 1953: 225–99; 1956: 178–317; Amyx 1958: 163–310; Lalonde *et al.*
    1991: 70.

38 *IG* I^3 422, 257, 259–60; *IG* I^3 421, 190–914: see Pritchett 1956: 253–54.
    Cushions are attested also in Aristophanes, *Wealth* 542; Plato, *Republic* 328c;
    and Plutarch, *Moralia* 59c.

39 See also *IG* I^3 422, 257–58.

40 Linen pillows are also included in the Delian accounts: *IDélos* 104 (26bisc)
    11–12.

41 *IG* I^3 421, 108; 422, 261.

42 Pollux 10.42; see Andrianou 2009: 90.

43 Pollux 10.42, Athenaios 2.48b–3, 6.255e. These are listed and translated by
    Andrianou 2009: 97, following Richter 1966: 118.

44 Aristophanes, *Birds* 122; *Clouds* 10; *Frogs* 1459.

45 Nevett 1999.

46 Simpson 2002.

47 Foster 2003: 128–29.

48 See, e.g., Friedl 1963; Campbell 1964; Sant Cassia and Bada 1992.

49 Sebesta 2002: 127. See more recently Berg 2016.

50 Lewis 2002: 62; Spantidaki 2016: 9.

51 Hesychios 1791.2. For discussion see Kissel 1918: 236 and Loraux 1981: 169
    n. 46.

52 Plato, Statesman 308d6–308d11; Reuthner 2006: 256–60.

53 Menander, *Samia* 234.

54 Wilson 1930: 118–28; see also Spantidaki 2016: 10.

55 Brøns 2017: 25–26. See also Boloti 2017.

56 Maclachlan 1995; Larson 2007: 83.

57 Gaifman 2008: 99.

58 Cf. Euripides, *Iphigenia in Aulis* 718–19; Pollux 3.38; Xenophon of Ephesus 1.8.1; Plutarch, *Aristides* 20, 7–80; *SEG* 9, 72, 84–85.

59 E.g. *Palatine Anthology* 6.200.

60 *Palatine Anthology* 6.280.

61 Cf. *Palatine Anthology* 6.201. Athena also received belts, at least at Troizen (Pausanias 2.33.1). See also Suda s.v. *lysiziones gyne*; Dillon 2002: 210f.

62 *Anthologia Palatina* 6.133. For a collection of further examples see Losfeld 1991: 322–23. See also Llewellyn-Jones 2003: 215–18.

63 See Deubner 1913 on differentiating *apaulia* from *epaulia*.

64 Pollux 3.39–40.

65 Homer, *Odyssey* 2, 94; *Iliad* 3.125–28.

66 Hesiod, *Works and Days* 72; Homer, *Iliad* 14.178.

67 Weiß 1988; Winkler 1999; Mösch-Klingele 2006.

68 Smith 2005.

69 Scheid and Svenbro 2001: 88.

70 Homer, *Odyssey* 1.275–78.

71 Homer, *Iliad* 18.490–96.

72 Aristophanes, *Wasps* 1326 and *Birds* 1720.

73 Pollux 3.41, Hesychios, s.v. *thyroros*; Theokritos, *Idylls* 15.77; Apollonios of Rhodes, *Argonautica* 4.1141–64.

74 Sutton 1989.

75 *N.B.* Pindar. *Olympian Odes* 7, quoted above.

76 Herodotus 6.130.

77 Although crowning both parties is an essential element of the modern Greek wedding: Foster 2003: 123–24; see also Antzoulatou-Retsila 1999.

78 Cf. Sgorou 1994.

79 The *pais amphithales* might wear a crown of thistles mixed with acorns (Zenobios 3, 98).

80 See especially Oakley 1982.

81 See, however, the discussion of another Boston *loutrophoros*, Figure 5.12.

82 Deubner 1900; see also Deubner 1913.

83 Foster 2003: 125.

84 In quoting the 2nd-century lexicographer Pausanias.

85 Eustathius, *Ad Iliadem* 24.29.

86 Schol. Aristophanes, *Plutus* 798; Theopompos *PCG* VII *fr.* 15; Harpokration *s.v. katachysmata*; Demosthenes, 45.74; Hesychios *s.v. katachysmata*.

87 Following Sutton 1989: 353–54.

88 Deschodt 2011: 3.

89 As do two of the lexica, by Harpokration and the *Suda*; see also Deschodt 2011: 2, following Gherchanoc 2009.

90 In *Anecdota graeca* Bekker 1: 200, 6–8.

91 Gherchanoc 2009.

92 The latter meaning literally 'gifts on the occasion of the *anakalypteria*'; cf. Lysias, *apud Theon, Progymnasmata* 2, p. 69 Spengel.

93 See Pollux 2.59.

94 As emphasized particularly by Gherchanoc 2006.

95 Deubner 1900: 149; Neumann 1965: 66; Oakley 1982: 114.

96 Tartaglia 1983: 264.

97 Mayo 1973: 200; Pemberton 2007: 116.

98 Deschodt 2011: 6, following Llewellyn-Jones 2003: 102.

99 Deschodt 2011: 7.

100 E.g. Strabo, *Geography* 1.2.31.

101 E.g. Josephus, *Jewish Antiquities* 6.218.

102 Following Deubner 1900: 149; Erdman 1934: 256; Sutton 1981: 192; Redfield 1982: 109; Brulé 1987: 141–42; Halleran 1988: 127; Paterson 1991: 68 n. 40; Oakley and Sinos 1993: 25; Cairns 1996: 80; Brulé 2001: 187; Ferrari 2002: 187.

103 Following Toutain 1940: 349; Rehm 1984: 141–44; Buxton 1987: 167; Sissa 1987: 119; Hague 1988: 35; Garland 1990: 221; Vérilhac and Vial 1998: 312.

104 Llewellyn-Jones 2003: 230–38, following Rehm's suggestion that private and public unveilings might have occurred separately: Rehm 1984: 142.

105 Ferrari 2003; cf. Ferrari 2004.

106 For the wealth of furnishings and furniture in Greek dowry documents in modern and pre-modern times see Imellos 1990: 124–28 and Fillipidis 1998: 132–34.

107 https://greekweddings.wordpress.com/2010/05/02/a-song-to-sing-at-the-krevatia, accessed 15 September 2014.

108 Mordecai 1999: 184.

References

Amyx, D. A. (1958). The Attic Stelai, Part III. *Hesperia* 27, 163–310.

Andrianou, D. (2006). Late Classical and Hellenistic furniture and furnishings in the epigraphical record. *Hesperia* 75, 561–84.

(2009). *The Furniture and Furnishings of Ancient Greek Houses and Tombs.* Cambridge: Cambridge University Press.

Antzoulatou-Retsila, E. (1999). *Wedding Crowns in Modern Greece.* Athens: Ekdoseis Alexandros.

Beckwith, J. (1954). Textile fragments from Classical Antiquity: an important find at Koropi, near Athens. *Illustrated London News* 224 (3 January), 114–15.

Beekes, R. (2009). *Etymological Dictionary of Greek I.* Leiden: Brill.

Berg, R., ed. (2016). *The Material Sides of Marriage: Women and Domestic Economies in Antiquity.* Acta Instituti Romani Finlandiae 43. Rome.

Boloti, T. (2017). Offering of cloth and/or clothing to the sanctuaries: a case of ritual continuity from the 2nd to the 1st millennium B.C. in the Aegean? In C. Brøns and M.-L. Nosch, eds., *Textiles and Cult in the Ancient Mediterranean. Ancient Textiles 31.* Oxford: Oxbow, 3–16.

Boynton, L. and Thornton, P. (1971). The Hardwick Hall Inventory of 1601. *Furniture History 7,* 1–14.

Brøns, C. (2017). *Gods and Garments: Textiles in Greek Sanctuaries in the 7th to the 1st Centuries BC. Ancient Textiles 28.* Oxford: Oxbow.

Brulé, P. (1987). *La fille d'Athènes. La religion des filles à Athènes à l'époque classique.* Mythes, cultes et société. Paris: Les Belles Lettres.

(2001). *Les femmes grecques à l'époque classique.* Paris: Hachette littératures.

Brümmer, E. (1988). Griechische Truhenbehälter. *Jahrbuch des Deutschen Archäologischen Instituts* 100, 1–168.

Buxton, R. (1987). Le voile et le silence dans Alceste. *Cahiers du Gita* 3, 167–78.

Cairns, D. L. (1996). 'Off with her ΑΙΔΩΣ': Herodotus 1.8.3–4. *Classical Quarterly* 46, 78–83.

Campbell, J. K. (1964). *Honour, Family and Patronage.* Oxford: Oxford University Press.

Carroll, D. L., (1965). *Patterned textiles in Greek art* (PhD thesis, UCLA, Los Angeles.)

Déonna, W. (1938). *Exploration archéologique de Délos, 18. Le Mobilier Délien.* Paris: Fontemoing.

Deschodt, G. (2011). Images et marriage, une question de méthode: le geste d'anakalypsis. *Cahiers Mondes anciens* 2, 2–14.

Deubner, L. (1900). Epaulia. *Jahrbuch des Deutschen Archäologischen Instituts* 15, 148–50.

(1913). APAYLIA. *Archiv für Religionswissenschaft* 16, 631–32.

Dillon, M. P. J. (2002). *Girls and Women in Classical Greek Religion.* London: Routledge.

Drougou, S. and Touratsoglou, I. (1980). *Ellenistikoi Lazeytoi Taphoi Beroias.* Athens: Athenai.

Erdman, W. (1934). *Die Ehe im alten Griechenland.* Munich: C. H. Beck.

Faust, S. (1989). *Fulcra: Figürlicher und ornamentaler Schmuck an antiken Betten.* Mainz: von Zabern.

Ferrari, G. (2002). *Figures of Speech: Men and Maiden in Ancient Greece.* Chicago: University of Chicago Press.

(2003). What kind of rite of passage was the ancient Greek wedding? In D. B. Dodd and C. A. Faraone, eds., *Initiation in Ancient Greek Rituals and Narratives: New Critical Perspectives.* London: Routledge, 27–42.

(2004). The 'anodos' of the bride. In D. Yatromanolakis and P. Roilos, eds., *Greek Ritual Poetics.* Cambridge, MA: Harvard University Press, 245–60.

Fillipidis, D. (1998). Διακοσμητικές τέχνες. Athens.

Foster, H. B. (2003). An Athenian wedding, year 2000. In H. B. Foster and D. C. Johnson, eds., *Wedding Dress across Cultures*. Oxford: Berg, 123–39.

Friedl, E. (1963). *Vasilika: A Village in Modern Greece*. New York: Holt, Rinehart and Winston.

Frontisi-Ducroux, F. and Lissarrague, F. (2009). Char, marriage et mixité: Une métaphore visuelle. In D. Yatromanolakis, ed., *An Archaeology of Representations: Ancient Greek Vase Painting and Contemporary Methodologies*. Athens: Institut du Livre, A. Kardamitsa, 91–92.

Gaifman, M. (2008). Visualized rituals and dedicatory inscriptions on votive offerings to the nymphs. *Opuscula* 1, 85–108.

Galliker, J. (2017). Terminology associated with silk in the Middle Byzantine Period (AD 843–1204). In S. Gaspa, C. Michel and M.-L. Nosch, eds., *Textile Terminologies from the Orient to the Mediterranean and Europe, 1000 BC to 1000 AD*. Zea E-Books 56, 346–73.

Garland, R. (1990). *The Greek Way of Life from Conception to Old Age*. London: Duckworth.

Gherchanoc, F. (2006). Le(s) voile(s) de marriage. Le cas particulier des anakaluptêria. *Métis* 4, 239–67.

   (2009). Des cadeaux pour nymphai: dôra, anakalyptêria et épaulia. In L. Bodiou and V. Mehl, eds., *La religion des femmes en Grèce ancienne*. Rennes: Presses universitaires de Rennes, 207–23.

Gleba, M. (2008). *Auratae vestes*: gold textiles in the ancient Mediterranean. In C. Alfaro and L. Karali, eds., *Purpureae Vestes* II. *Vestidos, Textiles y Tintes. Estudios sobre la Producción de Bienes de Consumo en la Antigüedad (Actas del II Symposium Internacional sobre Textiles y Tintes del Mediterráneo en el Mundo Antiguo [Atenas, 24 al 26 de Noviembre, 2005])*. Valencia: Universitat de València, 61–78.

Greenewalt, C. H. and Majewski, L. J. (1980). IX. Lydian Textiles. In K. DeVries, ed., *From Athens to Gordion: The Papers of a Memorial Symposium for Rodney S. Young*. Philadelphia: University Museum Papers, 133–47.

Hague, R. (1988). Marriage Athenian style. *Archaeology* 41, 32–36.

Halleran, M. F. (1988). Text and ceremony at the close of Euripides' *Alkestis*. *Eranos* 86, 123–29.

Herzfeld, M. (1980). Dowry in Greece: terminological usage and historical reconstruction. *Ethnohistory* 27, 225–41.

Imellos, S. (1990). Paradosiakas epipla kai skeue sto Elleniko spiti (Endeitikes episemaneis). *Laographia* 35, 104–28.

Kissel, M. L. (1918). Greek yarn-making. *Metropolitan Museum of Art Bulletin* 13, 235–37.

Kramer, C. (1979). An archaeological view of a contemporary Kurdish village: domestic architecture, household size, and wealth. In C. Kramer, ed.,

Ethnoarchaeology: Implications of Ethnography for Archaeology. New York: Columbia University Press, 139–63.

Kramer, J. (1995). Κράβατος, κραβάτιον und Verwandtes in den Papyri. *Archiv für Papyrusforschung und verwandte Gebiete* 42, 205–16.

Kyrieleis, H. (1969). *Throne und Klinen: Studien zur Formgeschichte altorientalischer und griechischer Sitz- und Liegemöbel vorhellenistischer Zeit.* Jahrbuch des Deutschen Archäologischen Instituts – Ergänzungshefte 24. Berlin: De Gruyter.

Lalonde, G. V., Langdon, M. K. and Walbank, M. B. (1991). *Athenian Agora 19. Inscriptions: Horai, Poleitai Records, Leases of Public Lands.* Princeton: The American School of Classical Studies at Athens.

Larson, J. (2007). *Ancient Greek Cults. A Guide.* New York: Routledge.

Lewis, S. (2002). *The Athenian Woman: An Iconographic Handbook.* London: Routledge.

Llewellyn-Jones, L. (2003). *Aphrodite's Tortoise: The Veiled Woman of Ancient Greece.* Swansea: Classical Press of Wales.

Loraux, N. (1981). *Les enfants d'Athèna : Idées anciennes sur la citoyenneté et la division des sexes.* Paris: François Maspero.

Losfeld, G. (1991). *Essai sur le costume grec.* Paris: De Boccard.

Maclachlan, B. (1995). Love, war, and the goddess in fifth-century Locri. *Ancient World* 25–26, 205–23

Matheson, S. B. (2016). *Corpus vasorum antiquorum. Yale University Art Gallery* 2 [USA 29]. Darmstadt: Philipp von Zabern.

Mayo, M. E. (1973). The gesture of Anakalupteria. *American Journal of Archaeology* 77, 220.

Mols, S. T. A. M. (1999). *Wooden Furniture in Herculaneum: Form, Technique and Function.* Amsterdam: Gieben.

Moraitou, G. and Margariti, C. (2008). Excavated archaeological textiles in Greece: past, present and future. In C. Alfaro and L. Karali, eds., *Purpureae Vestes* II. *Vestidos, Textiles y Tintes. Estudios sobre la Producción de Bienes de Consumo en la Antigüedad (Actas del II Symposium Internacional sobre Textiles y Tintes del Mediterráneo en el Mundo Antiguo [Atenas, 24 al 26 de Noviembre, 2005]).* Valencia : Universitat de València, 165–70.

Mordecai, C. (1999). Greece. In *Weddings: Dating and Love Customs of Cultures Worldwide Including Royalty.* State College, Pennsylvania: Nittany, 184–85.

Mösch-Klingele, R. (2006). *Die 'loutrophóros' im Hochzeits- und Begräbnisritual des 5. Jhs. v. Chr. in Athen.* Bern: P. Lang.

Neumann, G. (1965). *Gesten und Gebärden in der griechischen Kunst.* Berlin: De Gruyter.

Nevett, L. C. (1999). *House and Society in the Ancient Greek World.* Cambridge: Cambridge University Press.

Oakley, J. (1982). The Anakalypteria. *Archäologischer Anzeiger* 97, 113–18.

Oakley, J. and Sinos, R. (1993). *The Wedding at Ancient Athens.* Madison: University of Wisconsin Press.

Paterson, C. (1991). Marriage and the married woman in Athenian law. In S. Pomeroy, ed., *Women's History and Ancient History.* Chapel Hill: North Carolina University Press, 48–72.

Pemberton, E. G. (2007). The gods of the east frieze of the Parthenon. *American Journal of Archaeology* 80, 113–24.

Pritchett, W. K. (1953). The Attic Stelai, Part I. *Hesperia* 22, 225–99.

(1956). The Attic Stelai, Part II. *Hesperia* 25, 187–317.

Race, W. H. (1997). *Pindar* I. Cambridge, MA: Harvard University Press.

Ransom, C. L. (1905). *Studies in Ancient Furniture: Couches and Beds of the Greeks, Etruscan and Romans.* Chicago: University of Chicago Press.

Redfield, J. (1982). Notes on the Greek wedding. *Arethusa* 15, 181–201.

Rehm, R. (1984). *Marriage to Death: The Conflation of Wedding and Funeral Rituals in Greek Tragedy.* Princeton: Princeton University Press.

Reuthner, R. (2006). *Wer webte Athenes Gewänder? Die Arbeit von Frauen im antiken Griechenland.* Frankfurt: Campus.

Richter, G. M. A. (1966). *The Furniture of the Greeks, Etruscans and Romans.* London: Phaidon Press.

Sanders, E. (2013). Sexual jealousy and Eros in Euripides' *Medea.* In E. Sanders, C. Thumiger, C. Carey and N. J. Lowe, eds., *Eros in Ancient Greece.* Oxford: Oxford University Press, 41–57.

Sanidas, G. M. (2011). Les activités textiles dans les villes grecques aux époques hellénistique et romaine; questions d'espace et d'économie. In C. Alfaro, J.-P. Brun, P. Borgard and R. Pierobon Benoit, eds., *Purpureae Vestes* III. *Textiles y Tintes en la Ciudad Antigua. Actas del III Symposium Internacional sobre Textiles y Tintes del Mediterráneo en el Mundo Antiguo (Nápoles, 13 al 15 de Noviembre, 2008).* Valencia: Universitat de València, 31–40.

Sant Cassia, P. and Bada, C. (1992). *The Making of the Modern Greek Family: Marriage and Exchange in Nineteenth-Century Athens.* Cambridge: Cambridge University Press.

Scheid, J. and Svenbro, J. (2001). *The Craft of Zeus: Myths of Weaving and Fabric,* trans. C. Volk. Cambridge, MA: Harvard University Press.

Schmidt, M. (1981a). Alkestis. In *Lexicon Iconographicum Mythologiae Classicae* I. Zurich: Artemis, 533–44.

(1981b). Admetos I. In *Lexicon Iconographicum Mythologiae Classicae* I. Zurich: Artemis, 217–73.

Sebesta, J. L. (2002). Visions of gleaming textiles and a clay core: textiles, Greek women, and Pandora. In L. Llewellyn-Jones, ed., *Women's Dress in the Ancient Greek World.* London: Duckworth, 125–42.

Sgorou, M. (1994). *Attic lebetes gamikoi* (PhD thesis, University of Cincinnati.)

Siebert, G. (1976). Délos, le quartier de Skardhana. *Bulletin de Correspondance Hellénique* 100, 799–821.

(2001). *Exploration archéologique de Délos* 38. *L'Îlot des bijoux, l'Îlot des bronzes, la Maison des sceaux.* Paris: de Boccard.

Simanidis, K. (1997). Κλίνες και κλινοειδείς κατασκευές των Μακεδονικών τάφων. Athens: Ταμείο Αρχαιολογικών Πόρων και Απαλλοτριώσεων.

Simpson, E. (2002). The Andokides painter and Greek carpentry. In A. J. Clark and J. Gaunt, eds., *Essays in Honor of Dietrich von Bothmer.* Amsterdam: Allard Pierson Museum, 303–16.

Sissa, G. (1987). *Le corps virginal: Le virginité feminine en Grèce ancienne.* Paris: J. Vrin.

Smith, A. C. (2005). The politics of weddings at Athens: an iconographic assessment. *Leeds International Classics Studies* 4, 1–32.

(2011). Marriage in the Greek world. In *Thesaurus Cultus et Rituum Antiquorum* 6, 83–94.

(2016). Looking inside on the outside of a Greek pot. In A. Glazebook and B. Tsakirgis, eds., *Houses of Ill-Repute: The Archaeology of Houses, Taverns and Brothels.* Philadelphia: University of Pennsylvania Press, 143–68.

Sourvinou-Inwood, C. (1991). *'Reading' Greek Culture: Texts and Images, Rituals and Myths.* Oxford: Clarendon.

Spantidaki, S. (2016). Textile production in Classical Athens. In J. Ortiz, C. Alfaro, L. Turell and M. J. Martínez, eds., *Textiles, Basketry and Dyes in the Ancient Mediterranean World. Ancient Textiles* 27. Valencia: Universitat de València, 125–38.

(2017). Remarks on the interpretation of some ambiguous Greek textile terms. In S. Gaspa, C. Michel and M.-L. Nosch, eds., *Textile Terminologies from the Orient to the Mediterranean and Europe, 1000 BC to 1000 AD.* Zea E-Books 56, 202–209.

Sutton, R. F. (1981). *The interaction between men and women portrayed on Attic red-figure pottery.* (PhD thesis, University of North Carolina, Chapel Hill.)

(1989). On the classical Athenian wedding: two red-figure loutrophoroi in Boston. In R. F. Sutton, ed., *Daidalikon. Studies in Memory of R. V. Schoder.* Wauconda, IL: Bolchazy-Carducci Publishing, 331–59.

Taplin, O. (2007). *Pots & Plays. Interactions between Tragedy and Greek Vase-Painting of the Fourth Century B.C.* Los Angeles: J. Paul Getty Museum.

Tartaglia, L. C. (1983). A depiction of veiling in black figure art. *American Journal of Archaeology* 87, 264.

Toutain, J. (1940). Le rite nuptial de l'anakalypterion. *Revue des Études Anciennes* 42, 345–53.

Tsimbidou-Avloniti, M. (2005). Μακεδονικοί Τάφοι στον φοίνικα και στον Αγιο Αθανάσιο Θεσσαλονίκης. Athens.

Vérilhac, A.-M. and Vial, C. (1998). *Le marriage grec du VIe s. a. C. jusque'à l'époque d'Auguste.* Athens: École Française d' Athènes.

Vickers, M. (1999). *Images on Textiles: The Weave of 5th-century Athenian Art and Society*. Konstanz: Universitätsverlag Konstanz.

Walter-Karydi, E. (1994). *Die Nobilitierung des Wohnhauses. Lebensform und Architektur im spätklassischen Griechenland*. Konstanz: Universitätsverlag.

Weiß, C. (1988). Ein bislang unbekanntes Detail auf dem Hochzeitsbild der Karlsruher Lutrophoros 69/78. In J. Christiansen and T. Melander, eds., *Proceedings of the 3rd Symposium on Ancient Greek and Related Pottery*. Copenhagen: Carlsberg Glyptotek, 652–64.

Wilson, L. (1930). Loomweights. In D. Robinson, ed., *Excavations at Olynthus*, part II: *Architecture and Sculpture, Houses and Other Buildings*. London: Humphrey Milford, 118–28.

Winkler, H. (1999). *Lutrophorie. Ein Hochzeitskult auf attischen Vasenbildern*, Freiburg (Breisgau): HochschulVerlag.

Architectural Rhetoric and the Rhetoric of Architecture

Athens and Macedon in the Mid-4th Century BCE

LISA NEVETT

Introduction*

Research on the archaeological evidence for Greek housing has developed almost completely within the framework of the ancient texts, which have shaped both the research questions being posed and the interpretations which have been made of the material remains.[1] In this chapter, I suggest that we can also reverse the process and use archaeological evidence to provide a contextual framework which can illuminate texts, offering new and valuable perspectives on both archaeology and literature. As an example, I focus on a specific historical context, the relationship between Athens and Macedon during the mid-4th century BCE.

I begin with words, rather than walls: a set of three separate, well-known, passages of Demosthenes all touch on a common theme, although the speeches themselves are on different topics (and indeed one is judicial while the other two are political):

> In those times the public affairs of the polis were great and glorious, but in private life no one surpassed the majority. As evidence, if any of you knows the sort of house that Themistocles or Miltiades or any of the glorious men of those times lived in, see how it is no more pretentious than the houses of the majority. On the other hand, the architecture and the furnishing of the civic buildings were on such a scale and of such quality that the generations who followed were left no opportunity to surpass them: such monumental gate-ways, ship-sheds, stoas, Peiraeus, and the other buildings you see equipping the city. (*Against Aristocrates*, 206–207, 353/352 BCE)

> The private houses of those coming to power were so modest and so in keeping with the style of our constitution that the houses of Themistokles, Kimon, Aristides and others who were famous at that time, as you can see if any of you knows them, are no more ostentatious than those of their neighbours. But today, men of Athens, while our city likes to provide roads and fountains for the public ... private individuals in charge of public

affairs ... have some of them constructed private houses, not only more pretentious than the homes of most of the population, but more ostentatious than our civic buildings. (*On Organisation*, 29–30[2]; *c.* 350 BCE)

With public money [our ancestors] made such things and of such a kind for us, temples and offerings to the gods, so that no-one in subsequent generations could surpass them; but in private they were so modest and so very much in keeping with the spirit of the constitution, that the houses of ... Aristides, Miltiades, and the famous men of that time as any of you who knows them can see, were no more pretentious than those of their neighbours ... (*Olynthiacs* III.25–26, 349/348 BCE)

Taking these three passages together, it seems clear that Demosthenes is drawing two different contrasts: first, between what we might call 'the good old days' – a time of relative personal modesty – and his own time, in which the politicians are living extravagant lifestyles; second, he is also contrasting two different architectural styles, those which he considers fitting for public buildings and those which are appropriate for domestic ones. Significantly, the same set of ideas is repeated in these different passages: Demosthenes does not waste his good material by using it only once. This repetition suggests that the references were successful in getting the point across, and they must therefore have found some resonance with the audience's views.

It is relatively unimportant whether the houses, or the contrasts, which Demosthenes is invoking here are (or were) in any sense 'real'. His point is to criticize the behaviour of contemporary politicians.[3] But what I think is interesting is why he chooses to spatialize this criticism, invoking housing, in particular. One reason may be simply that it is part of a duality, lying at the other end of the spectrum from the splendid civic and religious buildings he also mentions. Nonetheless, just as those monumental structures evoke the admirable achievements of past generations, so housing also stands for something – a man's level of modesty. Demosthenes is therefore drawing attention here to an important role played by architecture: just like the 'words', which are the tools of his own trade, buildings – or 'walls' (in the terms of this volume) – could act as a medium through which messages could be conveyed – the 'rhetoric of architecture' of my title. In his eyes, this is as true of private houses as it is of the civic and religious buildings which modern scholars more commonly think of in this connection (for example, the column drums of the pre-Parthenon left as a memorial to the Persian sack).

We can reasonably connect Demosthenes' references with a larger discourse about conspicuous consumption and excess (*tryphe* which was particularly debated in Hellenistic times) and about the extent to which high levels of wealth and luxury were acceptable for individuals. In this chapter, however, I suggest that the archaeological evidence for housing offers a physical context which adds another dimension to our understanding of the texts, demonstrating that these passages are not simply a rhetorical trope. Rather, they are pointing to changes not – or not only – in the way in which domestic architecture was regarded, but also in that architecture itself. I argue that these are changes which can be detected at Athens, in Macedon and across the Greek world as a whole.

Variability in the Scale and Elaboration of Greek Domestic Buildings

Scale and elaboration are two dimensions which not only crystallize the points Demosthenes seems to have in mind, but are also relatively easily explored using archaeological evidence. Some years ago, Moritz Kiderlen raised the possibility that continuously between the Early Iron Age through to Hellenistic times, a minority of the population of Greece lived in extremely large houses.[4] Nevertheless the archaeological evidence he cited was less than compelling: before the later 5th century he offered only two examples, both involving quite radical departures from the excavators' interpretations of their own material.[5] I would agree with him that there was a concept of monumental domestic architecture (perceptible, for example, in the palace of Alkinöos conjured up in the *Odyssey*)[6] but it is difficult to argue that this concept went beyond poetic invention, memory (or experience of the remains) of the Late Bronze Age, or an awareness of the architectural practices of the Near East (or indeed a combination of all three of these elements). There was certainly some inequality in house size, but with the exception of Cyprus, actual palaces (defined here as structures on a completely different scale from domestic accommodation which seem to include official or ceremonial spaces as well as residential ones) are a phenomenon appearing in Greece only in the 4th century BCE. I argue that when they do appear, those palaces should be seen against the backdrop of changes in the economic and political landscape of this particular period.

Ian Morris has suggested that through the Archaic and Classical periods there was a sustained increase in economic productivity and that, as a consequence, there was a steady rise in standards of living, particularly after 425 BCE.[7] Housing is one of the sources of evidence Morris points to, but as he himself admits, this change is difficult to document in detail. To me it seems most evident in the increasing manipulation of domestic buildings as ostentatious symbols of personal status. There is no individual site for which we have both an adequate sample size and a sufficient chronological spread of houses, to enable us to be certain whether the erstwhile inhabitants became more prosperous through time. Nevertheless, Morris is right that if we take Greek communities in aggregate, the evidence does broadly support his model: Archaic houses were relatively small, but by the earlier 4th century a significant minority of houses (we cannot quantify the proportion) were both relatively large and ornately decorated compared with their peers, and the pace of change in both dimensions seems to have been particularly rapid between the late 5th and the late 4th centuries BCE.

At Athens, the rock-cut foundations which offer the most plentiful evidence of the city's residential suburbs suggest that most houses were relatively small with few rooms. Although they are difficult to date and to interpret, I think Emile Burnouf's suggestion is quite reasonable, that many of those in the Koile Valley, at least, may date to the era of the Peloponnesian War, since the area between the Long Walls may have provided space for refugees from the countryside.[8] For the same reason, however, they may not be representative of the Athenian housing stock of this period more generally. Currently, our most detailed evidence for Athenian housing comes from the area around the Agora. Although the sample of houses excavated here is small, it suggests quite significant diversity in size (Figure 6.1). While many of the structures we know of from this area seem to lack significant decorative features such as mosaic floors, there are a few examples which do possess them.[9] There are also a few examples of houses with mosaic decoration found during rescue excavations elsewhere in Athens.[10] Evidence for the existence of a peristyle court at Athens during this period is lacking if we exclude the central house from the north-west shoulder of the Areopagos which, as Barbara Tsakirgis has pointed out, was reconstructed by the original excavators with a peristyle solely on the basis that the poorly preserved courtyard was large enough to have had one.[11]

House size, mosaic floors and architectural elaboration all provide evidence of expenditure on housing, and of a desire to create a pleasing and perhaps impressive environment. We know that portable items would have been used to supplement and embellish them. These are impossible to quantify in the case of any single house, let alone compare between structures. We must, nevertheless, imagine a variety of such furnishings: a limited range is preserved or imitated in funerary contexts (especially in the interiors of Macedonian tombs), while images on vases show rich

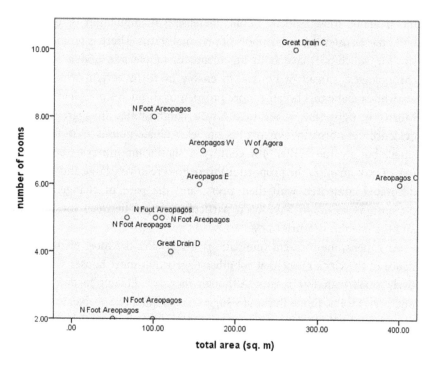

Figure 6.1 Diversity of size in Athenian housing.

textiles, wooden furniture, and utensils.[12] We should not assume a priori that funerary items are accurate replicas of domestic counterparts, that Macedonian funerary practices necessarily bear a close similarity to Athenian living practices, or that painted images represent a photographic record. Nevertheless, the impression this material creates overall is supported by textual sources. For example, the lists of domestic equipment confiscated from the Hermocopidae and documented on the Attic stelai offer a broad array of household equipment.[13] These lists give a sense of some of the objects which do not generally survive in excavated houses, even if we cannot always be sure of the exact meaning of each word or know whether the lists represent complete or only partial inventories.

At a general level, then, differences in scale, and the presence and absence of decorative features, serve as indicators which suggest a trend through time towards increasingly large, elaborate houses. The pattern is clearer if we look at a larger sample of structures which has to be taken from across the Greek mainland as a whole. Particularly noticeable is the appearance of a handful of houses, from the early 4th century BCE onwards, which are abnormally large, comprising two different courtyards and a variety of decorated rooms. A prominent example is the House of Mosaics at Eretria in Euboea

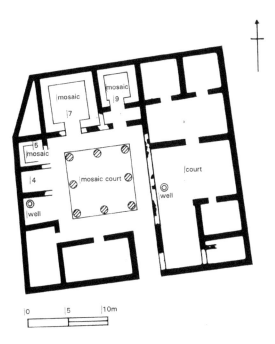

Figure 6.2 House of Mosaics at Eretria in Euboea.
Author, originally published in Nevett 1999: fig. 32

(Figure 6.2), built in the early 4th century BCE, which covered an area of about 625 m^2 and had three different mosaic-paved rooms.[14] Additional features were used here to enhance the monumentality of the building, such as a peristyle in the outer, western, courtyard, which gave access to the mosaic rooms. The decorative features also included terracotta figurines and appliqués, and a single, sculpted male figure. Comparison with other, less well-preserved, houses from Maroneia (Thrace) and Erythrai (a Greek city on the coast of present-day Turkey) shows that they share some of these features.[15] Buildings such as these are in no sense 'typical' – in fact it is difficult to find other examples of this date. They do, nevertheless, seem to represent an extreme version of a trend in which the house had come to be used in symbolic fashion to convey wealth and status.[16]

The Symbolic Manipulation of Domestic Space: Examples From Northern Greece

One of the regions in which I would suggest that this kind of manipulation is clearest is the northern area of the modern Greek state, in the Halkidiki peninsula and ancient Macedon. The housing quarter on the North Hill at Olynthos (in Halkdiki) offers extensive insight because of the large number of houses excavated there. This part of the city is generally assumed to have been laid out during the late 5th century BCE.[17] About fifty houses there have been excavated in their entirety and although there was some limited variation in their size and amenities, most were relatively large, covering about 290 m^2, which in many cases was probably augmented by further space in an upper storey[18]. A few also had colonnades around more than one side of the court, even occasionally forming a complete peristyle, as with the Villa of Good Fortune.[19] About thirty percent of the excavated houses had a room which the excavators termed an *andron*. This was characterized by its decoration (which could include coloured wall plaster together with some of earliest known floor mosaics in the Greek world) and by the organization of space (an off-centre doorway and raised borders may have accommodated couches or cushions, suggesting the occupants of the room would have reclined, as depicted on painted pottery and in literary descriptions of the *symposium* or male drinking party). Some of these houses also had bathing facilities consisting of terracotta hip-baths, which are relatively uncommon elsewhere in Greece at this time.[20] In one or two instances, cut ashlar blocks replace the usual river cobbles as the basis for the wall socles on the house façade (for instance, in house D v 6). A number of *ounai*, inscriptions recording the use of the house as collateral in financial transactions, show the value of some individual houses and incidentally reveal the importance of location as an element of that value which is more difficult to detect archaeologically.[21]

In some of my work I have used the detailed information about Olynthos as an aid to understanding the organization of housing and the use of space in other, less extensively documented, settlements, including Athens.[22] This was done not only because of the large sample of excavated houses but also because Olynthos provides detailed published information on the distribution of artefacts through space – which is lacking for most other settlements, including Athens. While the houses at Olynthos exemplify many features found elsewhere, their spaciousness and the frequency with which the group as a whole incorporates facilities such as bathing areas and decorated *andrones* are unusual. If the Olynthian houses are compared with (for example) the five excavated houses from Halieis in the Argolid, a city which was also laid out on a grid,[23] the unusual uniformity of the Olynthos houses also becomes apparent. Here I return to my point about the rhetorical value of domestic space. An individual house was not only a functional area; it was also a claim to a certain status and/or lifestyle. Ownership of a particular type of house, or of specific rooms or features, may therefore have been symbolic or aspirational as much as, or more than, strictly functional. Interestingly, as Nicholas Cahill noted in his re-analysis of the Olynthos material, there are relatively few *kraters* or drinking cups from the site.[24] This raises the possibility that the numerous rooms identified by the excavators as *andrones* were not, or not only, used strictly for *symposia*, but may have been included in many of these houses for other reasons.[25]

The frequent presence of decorated *andrones* at Olynthos, and also the elaboration of the court, may have announced the wealth and status of the owners of these houses,[26] but there may also be further nuances which can be added. Given that the city was located both on the fringes of the Greek world and also within the sphere of Macedonian influence, how might features like these be interpreted from these different perspectives? And how might their meaning(s) have changed through time as political alliances shifted?[27] In the absence of precise stratigraphic information from Robinson's excavations it is difficult to be certain whether the *andrones* are contemporary with the initial construction of the houses in which they were installed, but in some instances the role of the room is signalled in the design of the walls through the selective use of ashlars and an off-centre doorway. At the same time some of the mosaic floors, such as the one in house AVI 3, do show signs of wear and ancient repairs. It therefore seems possible that these rooms were incorporated into the houses at the time they were built. If the houses themselves date to a phase of expansion of the city in the late 5th century BCE, then they may originate in a context in which the community was looking towards Perdikas, king of Macedon, for support against Athens. According to Thucydides, it was Perdikas himself who encouraged the *anoikismos*, the abandonment by neighbouring cities of their coastal settlements in favour of joining a consolidated community at Olynthos (Thucydides I.58). The generous scale and facilities of each house might perhaps have helped to persuade the households of these communities to abandon their homes and move. Regional politics were volatile, however, and by the time of Demosthenes' speeches, quoted above, Olynthos had turned to Athens for support against the growing power of another Macedonian monarch, Philip II, who eventually besieged and conquered the city in 348 BCE. At the time of its destruction, most of the features such as mosaic floors and painted wall-plaster seem still to have been in use. Some alterations had, nevertheless, been made to certain of the houses. For example, the owners of A v 6 seem to have purchased part of the neighbouring house, A v 8, enlarging their own property at the expense of their neighbours' in order to provide a large cobbled courtyard.[28]

How might the large houses with their generous amenities at Olynthos have been interpreted and reinterpreted during their use lives, and what might they have implied to observers with different perspectives? Here I want to introduce the evidence of the Macedonian royal palaces – particularly the palace at Vergina – in order to consider the possible cultural associations of scale and decoration. Based on her recent work at the site, Angeliki Kotaridi has redated the Vergina building to the mid-4th century BCE on both stylistic and stratigraphic grounds.[29] A monumental precursor to the surviving building has also been suggested.[30] The Vergina structure attests to the aggressive symbolic use of monumentality and decoration, at least by the mid-4th century BCE. It covers a massive area in comparison with any of those discussed here so far: 15,000 m^2 (Figure 6.3). Although stone was only used for the socle, while the super-structure was mud brick, the labour involved in construction was still enormous – for example, Kottaridi estimates that 20,000 m^3 of stone were used from quarries 15 km away, to make the foundation and stone architectural elements. The decorative features included mosaics laid in red-dyed pozzolana mortar, and some 1450 m^2 of floor covered in mosaic or marble.[31]

The main part of the Vergina building was organized around a central courtyard with a full peristyle. On the ground floor, space was almost exclusively occupied by decorated rooms of different sizes, laid out like domestic *andrones* but on a much bigger scale: the largest were able to accommodate about thirty couches lined up along their walls. The sheer size of most of these rooms would have meant that the experience of using them was very different from that of a domestic *andron*, and indeed it has been suggested that they were intended primarily to provide spectacle: an opportunity to view the monarch.[32] The second, western court, which is much less elaborately constructed, is now considered by Kottaridi to have been contemporary with the original building because she identified a continuous foundation underlying both sections.[33] Finds from here have not been reported in detail but this is generally assumed to have been a service area,[34] and the more ephemeral construction supports this suggestion.

In many ways the Vergina building seems like a monumental version of a private house of double courtyard type, such as the House of the Mosaics at Eretria, with reception and service quarters focused around different courtyards. (In the palace, residential space may, however, have been included in the main peristyle: Inge Nielsen has suggested that the north wing may have housed apartments for the monarch and his family,

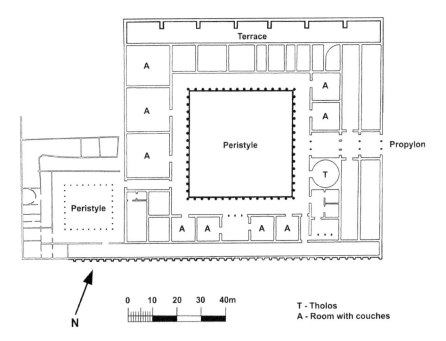

Figure 6.3 Palace at Vergina. Drawn by Laurel Fricker based on Saatsoglou Paliadeli 2001: fig. 1 and Kottaridi 2011: fig. 3

pointing out a close spatial relationship between the official and residential functions.[35] The western wing of the main peristyle may also have had an upper storey which could potentially have included residential quarters, although we have no definite evidence of how those spaces were used.) Despite some organizational differences, it is perhaps worth pursuing the analogy with a house a little further: if the palace really was conceived as simply a large domestic complex – as the architecture seems to suggest – then it would make sense that the most dominant distinction may have been between areas used for entertaining and those used for service, rather than the more straightforward 'public/private' contrast seen in modern, Western culture. This is the division seen between the two courtyards, and the configuration would actually suit Nielsen's interpretation of the style of Macedonian king as something of a 'first among equals' (in her terms, an 'ethnic, national monarch'), rather than an absolute and remote ruler (a 'personal monarch').[36] It might also suggest that the physical material-ization of a monumental palatial structure was a relatively recent phenom-enon and that there were perhaps no close architectural models for such a building in the Greek world during this period, so that the palace was conceived simply as a house writ large. At the very least, it seems that the organization of the Vergina building was intimately linked with the development of domestic architecture during the 4th century BCE.

This argument can be taken a step further by looking at contemporary private housing from another site, the nearby city of Pella. There, the monumental late 4th-century BCE houses south of the Agora offer a striking example of an intermediate step between the residential and palatial scales.[37] It is not always clear where the boundaries between different properties would have lain, but we can see that some of these structures featured multiple courtyards. The House of Dionysos, for example, had at least two peristyles, and if it covered the whole city block, it would have had an area of over 5,000 m².[38] It provided multiple decorated rooms featuring mosaic floors with geometric and figured scenes. In some rooms the walls were also embellished with painted panels and architectural elements. This house, and three neighbours which were built on a similar scale and with comparable decoration, can also be connected with the earlier double courtyard houses mentioned above. All of these structures, including the palace at Vergina, used the same architectural vocabulary to convey the status aspirations of their occupants, although on different scales.

Through the 4th century BCE, then, Macedon seems to have witnessed a process of interaction between domestic and palatial architecture, in which both used the same visual and spatial language, a language which is also seen in Greek communities to the south by the early 4th century BCE, albeit on a more modest scale. This close relationship between palace and house does not seem to have been sustained, however. The new palace at Pella shared some similar features, but on an even more massive scale[39] and – importantly – with a seemingly different conception of the role of a palace and its relationship with other types of architecture, from that seen at Vergina. With this building, begun during the late 4th century BCE, the Macedonian monarchs seem to move away from the domestic sphere as a model. The complex grew over time to comprise at least six different courtyards and cover an area of more than 70,000m². Not only was the scale much larger, but the range of facilities was much broader, than those provided at Vergina, encompassing a combination of ceremonial areas, service courtyards, workshops, storerooms, a palaistra and a manufacturing area. The development of this structure suggests that the concept of a palatial building moved away from that of an enlarged domestic complex, towards more of a self-contained community dominated by an absolute ruler, like those of the Near East and Egypt.

Conclusion: Contextualizing Demosthenes

Having highlighted the manipulation of housing as a status symbol from the mid- to late 4th century BCE, I want finally to return to my starting place, the passages of Demosthenes quoted in my introduction. It is clearly difficult to date the archaeology as precisely as philologists have dated the texts of some of Demosthenes' speeches. But while it might be tempting to dismiss Demosthenes' references to the increasing elaboration of the housing of the elite as simply a rhetorical trope, I would argue that the evidence points to the use of housing as a symbol of wealth and to the emergence of a group of houses which were becoming more and more ostentatiously monumental. This trend seems to be very noticeable in northern Greece, particularly in the kingdom of Macedon, during the mid- to late 4th century BCE. The use of some of the basic architectural elements at Olynthos, as early as the late 5th century BCE, suggests that they were already part of the architectural vocabulary in this region. Nevertheless, the palace visible today at Vergina – which may have been constructed around the time Demosthenes was writing – took them to a whole new level.

The archaeological evidence of housing thus provides a broader context within which Demosthenes' references can be situated. I think he is picking up on a general pattern of increased expenditure on housing and on a growing tendency to view a house as a symbol of its owner's status and prosperity, both of which can be inferred from the archaeological record. Furthermore, it is possible that there was sufficient knowledge of Macedonian structures, such as the palace at Vergina and perhaps other northern Greek buildings including the houses at Olynthos, to give expenditure on such relatively large, lavishly decorated houses (or palaces) a distinctively northern, if not specifically Macedonian, flavour. This could therefore lend an additional implication of buildings that were in some sense 'un-Athenian'. I would speculate, then, that in conjuring up the simple dwellings of past Athenian statesmen, Demosthenes may also be evoking a symbol of the democratic spirit which he is trying to defend against the power of the Macedonian monarchy, and implicitly accusing contemporary politicians of behaving like Macedonians.

While we can never be absolutely certain about the way in which these different political and cultural influences actually played out, I have tried to suggest that by combining the information from 'words' with that to be gained from 'walls' (in the terms of this volume), we can reach a more nuanced understanding of some of the undercurrents of the literary texts, as well as illuminating the potential significance material evidence. Finally, I would suggest that reversing the usual relationship between texts and archaeology in this way is a particularly appropriate move, given that our written evidence is very specific. Our relatively sparse references each voice the view of a single author at a particular place and moment in time. In contrast, archaeological material consists of multiple buildings and sites, supporting the creation of an aggregate picture which is nuanced across space and time and is therefore well suited to providing a context within which to situate the individual voices of the texts.

Notes

* I would like to thank Jen Baird and April Pudsey for their invitation to speak at the 'Words and Walls' conference, and to contribute my paper to this volume. I am grateful to the other conference participants and to David Stone for their comments and suggestions on this chapter, and to David Potter for helpful conversations and books. The responsibility for all errors of omission and commission is, of course, my own.

1 Both Greek and Latin texts have been used, primarily Lysias I and Ps.-Xenophon's *Oikonomikos* – together with the description of 'the Greek house' by Vitruvius (VI.7.1–6)

2 All translations in this chapter are my own. The dates given here for Demosthenes' works are taken from MacDowell 2009, summarized at p. 12.

3 Compare MacDowell 2009: 237.

4 Kiderlen 1995: *passim*.

5 For further detail see the reviews in Nevett 1997; Ault 1998.

6 See also Braund 2001.

7 Morris 2005.

8 Burnouf 1878: 30.

9 For example, the central house from the north shoulder of the Areopagus, dating to the late 4th century BCE (Thompson 1968), and the so-called House of the Greek Mosaic dating to *c.* 300 BCE, Thompson 1966 and Thompson and Wycherley 1972: 180–82.

10 For example the house excavated beneath the New Acropolis Museum which dates to the late 5th century BCE: Eleutheratou 2010: 148.

11 Tsakirgis 2005: 80 n. 2.

12 Andrianou 2009.

13 Pritchett 1953; 1956; 1958.

14 Ducrey *et al.* 1993.

15 Respectively, Karadedos 1990 and Hoepfner 1999: 450–51.

16 See Walter-Karydi 1998; a similar argument has been made widely for the Roman world; see, most famously, Wallace-Hadrill 1994.

17 Cahill 2002: 38–39.
18 Robinson and Graham 1938; Robinson 1946: fig. 2.
19 Robinson and Graham 1938: 56.
20 Trümper 2011.
21 Nevett 2000.
22 For example Nevett 1999.
23 Ault 2005.
24 Cahill 2002: 181–89.
25 There are, of course, other potential explanations as well, such as Cahill's suggestion that metal, rather than ceramic, vessels were used, and were removed at the time of the city's destruction. It also seems possible that different practices attended wine consumption here from those described in the, largely Athenian, textual sources. It is also possible that this pattern results from the excavators' publication and discard practices, rather than being a feature of the original assemblage, since more recent work at the site has recovered *krater* fragments in significant numbers, albeit they are from a single house: see Ault *et al.* 2019.
26 Housing has been observed to operate in this way in traditional societies observed ethnographically, for example, Blanton's 'indexical' mode of communication: Blanton 1994.
27 For a summary of the historical information about these shifts, see, for example, Cawkwell 2011: 390–91.
28 Robinson and Graham 1938: 92.
29 Kottaridi 2011: 301–304.
30 For example Nielsen 1994: 81; 1997: 141.
31 Respectively, Kottaridi 2011: 310 and 298.
32 Nielsen 1998: 124–25.
33 Kottaridi 2011: 304.
34 For example, Kottaridi 2011: 328.
35 Nielsen 1994: 84.
36 Nielsen 1997.
37 Indeed, they have sometimes been considered to have been 'palatial' themselves: for example Etienne 2006: 106.
38 Makaronas and Giouri 1989: *passim*.
39 Chrysostomou 1996; 2008.

References

Andrianou, D. (2009). *The Furniture and Furnishings of Ancient Greek Houses and Tombs*. Cambridge: Cambridge University Press.

Ault, B. (1998). (M.) Kiderlen Megale Oikia. Untersuchungen zur Entwicklung aufwendiger griechischer Stadthausarchitektur von der Fruharchaik bis ins 3 Jh. v. Chr. *Journal of Hellenic Studies* 118, 244–45.

Ault, B. A. (2005). *The Excavations at Ancient Halieis 2. The Houses: The Organization and Use of Domestic Space*. Bloomington: Indiana University Press.

Ault, B. A., Lynch, K. M., Panti, A., Archibald, Z. H., Nevett, L. C. and Tsigarida, E. B. (2019). The Olynthos Project: Classical pottery in an urban and domestic context. In E. Manakidou and A. Avramidou, eds., *Classical Pottery of the Northern Aegean and Its Periphery*. Thessaloniki: University Studio Press, 423–30.

Blanton, R. (1994). *Houses and Households: A Comparative Study*. New York and London: Plenum.

Braund, D. (2001). Palace and polis: Dionysus, Scythia and Plutarch's Alexander. In I. Nielsen, ed., *The Royal Palace Institution in the First Millennium*. Aarhus: Aarhus University Press, 15–31.

Burnouf, E. (1878). Maisons privées de l'ancienne Athènes. *Revue Générale de l'Architecture et des Travaux Publics* 35, 129–34.

Cahill, N. D. (2002). *Household and City Organization at Olynthus*. New Haven: Yale University Press.

Cawkwell, G. (2011). The defence of Olynthus. In *Cyrene to Chaeronea: Selected Essays on Ancient Greek History*. Oxford, Oxford University Press: 369–91.

Chrysostomou, P. (1996). Το Ανάκτορο της Πέλλας. *Αρχαιολογικό Έργο στη Μακεδονία και στη Θράκη* 10(A), 105–42.

(2008). Πέλλης βασίλειον. *Αρχαιολογικό Έργο στη Μακεδονία και στη Θράκη* 22, 129–40.

Ducrey, P., Metzger, I. R. and Reber, K. (1993). *Le Quartier de la maison aux mosaïques*. Lausanne: Editions Payot.

Eleutheratou, S. (2010). Ανασκαφή οικοπέδου Μακρυγιάννη για την ανέγερση του Νέου Μουσείου Ακροπόλεως. *Αρχαιολογικον Δελτιον* 56–59, Χρονικά Β'1, 147–52.

Etienne, R. 2006. Architecture palatiale et architecture privée en Macédoine, IVe–IIe s. av. J.-C. In A.-M. Guimier-Sorbets, M. B. Hatzopoulos and Y. Morizot, eds. (2006) *Rois, cités et nécropoles: Institutions, rites et monuments en Macédoine, Actes des colloques de Nanterre, décembre 2002 et d'Athènes, janvier 2004, Meletimata 45*. Athens, 105–16.

Hoepfner, W. (1999). Die Epoche der Griechen. In W. Hoepfner, ed., *Geschichte des Wohnens*, vol. 1. Ludwigsburg: Wüstenrot Stiftung, 123–608.

Karadedos, G. (1990). Υστεροκλασικό Σπίτι στη Μαρώνεια Θράκης. *Εγνατία* 2, 265–97.

Kiderlen, M. (1995). *Megale Oikia. Untersuchungen zur Entwicklung aufwendiger griechischer Stadthausarchitecktur*. Hürth: Lange.

Kottaridi, A. (2011). The Palace of Aegae. In R. Lane-Fox, ed., *Brill's Companion to Ancient Macedon: Studies in the Archaeology and History of Macedon, 650 BC–300 AD*. Leiden: Brill, 297–334.

MacDowell, D. M. (2009). *Demosthenes the Orator*. Oxford: Oxford University Press.

Makaronas, C. and Giouri, E. (1989). *Οι Οικίες Αρπαγής της Ελένης και Διονύσου, της Πέλλας*. Athens: Athens Archaeological Society.

Morris, I. (2005). Archaeology, standards of living, and Greek economic history. In J. G. Manning and I. Morris, eds., *The Ancient Economy: Evidence and Models*. Stanford: Stanford University Press, 91–126.

Nevett, L. C. (1997). Review of *Megale Oikia* by Moritz Kiderlen. *American Journal of Archaeology* 101, 602–603.

(1999). *House and Society in the Ancient Greek World*. Cambridge: Cambridge University Press.

(2000). A 'real estate market' in Classical Greece?: the example of town housing. *Annual of the British School at Athens* 95, 329–43.

Nielsen, I. (1994). *Hellenistic Palaces*. Aarhus: Aarhus University Press.

(1997). Royal palaces and type of monarchy: do the Hellenistic palaces reflect the status of the king? *Hephaistos* 15, 137–61.

(1998). Royal banquets: the development of royal banquets and banqueting halls from Alexander to the Tetrarchs. In I. Nielsen and H. Sigismund Nielsen, eds., *Meals in a Social Context*. Aarhus: Aarhus University Press, 102–33.

Pritchett, W. K. (1953). The Attic Stelai: Part I. *Hesperia* 22, 225–99.

(1956). The Attic Stelai: Part II. *Hesperia* 25, 178–328.

(1958). The Attic Stelai: Part III. *Hesperia* 27, 255–310.

Robinson, D. M. (1946). *Excavations at Olynthus XII: Domestic and Public Architecture*. Baltimore: Johns Hopkins University Press.

Robinson, D. M. and Graham, J. W. (1938). *Excavations at Olynthus VIII: The Hellenic House*. Baltimore: Johns Hopkins University Press.

Saatsoglou-Paliadeli, C. (2001). 'The palace at Vergina-Aegae and its surroundings'. In I. Nielson, ed., *The Royal Palace Institution in the First Millennium BC: Regional Development and Cultural Interchange between East and West*. Monographs of the Danish Institute at Athens. Athens: The Danish Institute at Athens, 201–13.

Thompson, H. A. (1966). Activities in the Athenian Agora: 1960–65. *Hesperia* 35, 37–5?.

(1968). Excavations in the Athenian Agora: 1966–67. *Hesperia* 37, 36–72.

Thompson, H. A. and Wycherley, R. E. (1972). *Excavations in the Athenian Agora Volume XIV: The History, Shape and Uses of an Ancient City Centre*. Princeton: American School of Classical Studies at Athens.

Trümper, M. (2011). Bathing culture in Hellenistic domestic architecture. In *Städtisches Wohnen im Mittelmeerraum 4 Jh. v. Chr. 1 Jh. n. Chr.: Akten des internationalen Kolloquiums vom 24-27 Oktober 2007*. Vienna: Österreichischen Akademie der Wissenschaften, 529–68.

Tsakirgis, B. (2005). Living and working around the Athenian Agora: a preliminary case study of three houses. In B. A. Ault and L. C. Nevett, eds., *Ancient Greek Houses and Households*. Philadelphia: University of Pennsylvania Press, 67–82.

Wallace-Hadrill, A. (1994). *Houses and Society in Pompeii and Herculaneum*. Princeton: Princeton University Press.

Walter-Karydi, E. (1998). *The Greek House: The Rise of Noble Houses in Late Classical Times*. Athens: Athens Archaeological Society.

7 | The Reconstruction of an Agricultural Landscape

Seeking the Farmstead

MAEVE MCHUGH[*]

The intersection between texts and archaeology is a valuable tool in building narratives of the ancient past. When this relationship works well, archaeology provides insight into past practices at a site that the textual evidence supports or vice versa. It is not the case, however, that texts and archaeology are always synchronous, and we have to bear in mind that textual sources relate events specific to the purpose of the text and intention of the author; our sources are not intentionally misleading, but it is best to consider the nature of the source before we stretch our conclusions too far. Archaeological evidence too is not without its obstacles, obscure as they often are from ancient ways of conceptualizing and experiencing the world. The potential for inconsistency in our sources speaks to one of the core issues that has plagued the study of ancient farming practices, especially the identification of farmsteads and their role in agricultural industry.[1]

'Farmsteads' as a descriptive term and a concept are problematic because the word was born from a need to categorize a type of site which was visible in ceramic data generated by extensive archaeological surveys. Farmsteads, then, were not based on structures testified by ancient textual sources but on a specific form of archaeological evidence. Indeed, the term 'farmstead' has evolved from a shorthand description of pottery scatters in pedestrian landscape surveys to an archaeological site type which is used to reconstruct socio-economic practices. The repeated use of the term by numerous archaeological field surveys throughout Greece has reinforced and codified the label as a descriptive term for rural sites that supported agriculture by providing a space for occupation and industry. Despite issues raised in scholarship regarding how we identify such sites and interpret their agricultural role,[2] the use of farmstead has taken hold in archaeological reports. The variation of such sites identified in the archaeological record, however, reveals differences in the nature of activities at these so-called farmsteads in comparison to textual accounts of farming practices. Such inconsistencies have resulted in much analysis concerning how best to interpret the archaeological data in conjunction with the textual accounts.[3] The results of such studies have broader implications for the practices of farming, the complexity of agricultural industry and, more generally, how individuals and groups lived in the Classical Greek landscape.

Following the aims of this volume, this chapter will interrogate the intersection between the textual and archaeological evidence for Greek farmsteads and suggest new methods of reconstructing how people moved and worked in the countryside using computational modelling. To address this aim, I provide a synthesis of two of the central issues concerning the use of the term 'farmstead' in scholarship and consider the terminology associated with farming in texts. I then set out a methodology to identify farmsteads from the results of pedestrian landscape survey, and categorize the variations evident in each site type using a role-based typology. This provides a framework for the identification and classification of farmsteads which also utilizes the textual record. Once I have set out a model for identifying and understanding the roles of farmsteads in the agricultural landscape, I will reconstruct the temporal and physical experience of movement through the countryside using computational modelling. The conclusions from this chapter will illustrate the great potential in combining archaeological and textual data with new methodologies to give a fresh perspective on how farmers moved and worked in the countryside.

Defining Farmsteads

A detailed account of the various aspects and concerns around the identification and use of the ancient farmstead would stretch the ability of a single chapter.[4] Therefore, I restrict my synthesis to questions concerning the terminology and role of such sites. With the advent of pedestrian landscape survey from the 1960s onwards,[5] the term 'farmstead' was used to describe a small feature in the landscape.[6] The adoption of the term by numerous surveys throughout Greece[7] reinforced the application of 'farmstead' as a descriptive term for sites characterized by their small size and with a predominately coarse-ware ceramic signature.[8] The signature of sites identified as farmsteads is not consistent within and across surveys, however. On one end of the spectrum of sites labelled as farmsteads are ephemeral low-resolution pottery scatters[9] and on the other extreme are large sites with well-built structures, ancillary buildings, sometimes a tower,[10] and pressing equipment.[11] The variations in site types lead surveyors to conclude that the observed differences were indicative of the wealth and economic objectives of farmers in the territory. At Atene, for example, Lohmann catalogued several types and variations of rural structures broadly identified as farmsteads.[12] Similar patterns of differences in structure type, distribution, and variations within them are present in the results of multiple surveys across the Greek world.[13] These differences are one of the major stumbling blocks in categorizing and determining the role of farmsteads in the archaeological record.

It was not the case, however, that the application of the term 'farmstead' and its socio-economic implications were widely accepted. Scholars took the term itself to task and argued that a farmstead in a modern sense was not an applicable model for the Classical Greek world;[14] indeed, there is no ancient Greek equivalent for the English term 'farmstead'. However, that does not necessarily mean that rural sites which supported a variety of domestic and industrial activities did not exist in the countryside. Descriptions of what an ancient farm might look like are variable across texts, but we can take for example Demosthenes 47, which recalls the raid carried out by Euergos and Mnesiboulos, which offers us a critical description of the plaintiff's farm:

> They [the plaintiff's family] were lunching in the court (αὐλῇ) when these men burst in and found them there and began to seize the furniture. The rest of the female slaves (they were in a tower room where they live), when they heard the tumult, closed the door leading to the tower (πύργῳ), so the men did not get in there; but they carried off the furniture from the rest of the house (οἰκίας) [...] (47.56).

The 'οἰκία, πὺργος and αὐλή' formed a site in this case which clearly provided occupation for the plaintiff's extended family. The excavation of other sites[15] that match this type of farm has indicated that they too could support a wide range of agricultural activity.[16] It is not the case, however, that there is consistency in the description of farms in the Classical record. The lease of the demesman of Peiraieus *IG* II₂ 2498 l.22–24 (321/0 BCE), for example, states that the tenant receives a watertight house (οἰκία), but the text makes no mention of the nature of the structure.[17] Equally, in the lease of the *orgeones* of Egretes *IG* II₂ 2499 l.5–7 (306/365 BCE) it is stipulated that the tenant will whitewash and decorate the house (οἰκία).[18] Another lease states that the tenant may build on the land (χωρίον), and when he leaves at the end of his lease, he may take the tiles, doors and woodwork (*SEG* 24.203) (333/332 BCE). In these instances, the structures are simply described as οἰκία, but it is not necessarily clear that these are domestic spaces similar to urban structures with the same name.[19] Researchers debated the types of activity facilitated by these sites based on these variations, offering suggestions ranging from full-scale year-round domestic occupation – similar to their urban counterparts – to single-use storage huts.[20] The evidence, however, was poorly supported by the textual sources; for example, Osborne writes, 'only in rare circumstances can we be confident that a structure referred to [in epigraphy] was a primary or permanent residence'.[21]

The archaeology of farms illustrates that there was considerable variation in the type of sites, and I shall discuss this further in the following section. The lack of detailed descriptions of such sites in textual sources means that it is not possible to directly map textual and archaeological data onto each other. It does not mean, however, that farms did not exist in the countryside, and we have to rely on textual and archaeological evidence that is fragmentary by nature: on scatters of sherds and passing descriptions, such as the plaintiff whose farm is described because it explains the actions and movements of the household during a raid. Farmsteads, I argue, were implicitly present in the textual rural landscape rather than explicitly described.

It is essential to bear in mind that the Greeks classified real property differently from the modern way of doing so.[22] Thus it is unlikely that the term 'farmstead' would have much meaning to an ancient Greek farmer. It is even conceivable, based on the epigraphic data, that it was not necessary to provide a detailed description of structures on farmed land. For example, in the case of the Delian inscriptions, the use of χωρίον may refer to all components of the farm, including land, structures and portable items.[23] Property was made up of separate components, so an οἰκία (house) could be found in the city as well as the countryside. It was then further defined by including information about the type of land or structures associated with the οἰκία, such as 'οἰκία, πύργος and αὐλή', as above, along with 'χωρίον καί οἰκία' (land and house) or 'οἰκία καί ἀγρός' (house and field) both of which may describe a farm.[24] Thus, the textual record carries as much variation and ambiguity as the archaeological record, and farms were described in comparatively vague terms, because an understanding of the implications was taken for granted. Consequently, these sources provide little information about what farms looked like, or how their role facilitated agriculture. Despite this, textual evidence does hint at a variety of different site types that supported agricultural activity in particular landscapes, and I argue that the incorporation of textual and archaeological data in tandem gives us a better picture of how farms and farmed land[25] functioned in different landscapes. Therefore, an approach to the data that incorporates texts, the archaeology of farmsteads, plus the archaeology identified from 'off-site' scatters creates an opportunity to reconstruct the spaces for planting and sowing, areas for harvesting and storage, and production and sale. In doing so we gain a much better sense of how agriculture functioned within a joined-up physical and social landscape in any one territory.

With the above in mind, I define farmsteads as rural sites that supported either year-round or temporary occupation by a free or enslaved labour force engaged in agricultural activity either for subsistence or economic gain.[26] My definition is deliberately broad in order to encompass the variety of farmstead types that existed across the Greek world. As I shall argue further below, there is no one type of farmstead precisely because these sites reflect the range of needs and intentions of individuals and groups within a specific landscape working within unique socio-economic frameworks. Farmsteads, therefore, are variable and flexible site types in terms of their function within a territory. Instead of this being a hindrance to their identification and classification, I argue that such sites are a valuable source of information for how households and the wider community enacted their agricultural endeavours through the activities carried out at these sites. Thus, the term 'farmstead' serves as a shorthand term for sites that were an integral part of agricultural activity, which grant us a unique perspective on agriculture from the position of those working the land.

The difficulty in comparisons between texts and archaeology, and finding equivalences between these types of data, is symptomatic of the challenging nature of research into ancient Greek farming. The debate surrounding farmsteads is a complex one, and, as Pečírka noted, there need not be one single explanation for all farms and their systems.[27] For me, it is vital to move away from issues concerning the interpretation of the terminology used to describe farmsteads and fixating on one type of farm versus another. The variety of words used to describe these sites is associated with their lack of uniformity across the Greek world, rather than their non-existence; when comparing textual and archaeological data we must remain aware that it is not possible to assess the evidence on the principle of one size fits all.

The Identification and Classification of Farmsteads in the Archaeological Record

The sites uncovered from rescue excavations, often connected to modern road-building, have shed much light on the nature of rural farmsteads in their complete and near-complete state.[28] Excavation results have illustrated that some of these sites were similar in form to urban houses and hosted a range of activities one would expect within a domestic setting at the same time as providing spaces for agricultural production.[29] However, farmsteads documented in pedestrian landscape survey are not as easy to identify and interpret as their excavated counterparts. In this section, I present criteria based on site location, site size and ceramic signature for farmstead identification along with a typology of farmstead types, which will further elucidate their role.

The question of where households lived and the nature of settlements are interrelated with both regional and local factors.[30] Research on the social and economic changes in territories along with changes in inheritance and leases have illustrated that farmed land was inextricably linked with these matters.[31] As a result, farmers may have lived in the nearest town or village and commuted to their arable land and worked plots closer to a larger settlement. In Attica, for example, the settlement data[32] illustrates a landscape of different settlement types ranging from nucleated demes to more widely distributed hamlets and individual households.[33] Not only were farmers limited to fragmented plots of land that they had the authority to farm, but they were also further limited by the type of crop and the nature of the soil available to them.[34] Ancient, non-mechanized farming[35] meant that farmers were restricted to the land below 15 degrees of slope,[36] and had rudimentary means (terracing) to improve their farmland.[37] Thus, arable land was a precious resource, and it may not have been the case that farmsteads were located directly on farmed land.[38] When we consider all the human and environmental factors that affected where a farmer may have farmed, we begin to understand how fragmented, small and scattered plots of land belonging to one farm may be. Therefore, accessibility was a critical factor in site location.

Many analyses have gone into measuring the amount of land needed to support the Classical household both for subsistence and also for market engagement.[39] These results have created benchmarks for a range of sizes of farm dependent upon the economic objectives of the farmer.[40] It is difficult, however, in the archaeology to draw comparisons with these benchmarks because the economic analyses hypothesize the amount of farmable land needed to achieve their economic goal. In contrast, the archaeology, especially from pedestrian landscape survey, often yields information about the main areas of human occupation rather than the extent of farmed land.[41] Most frequently, farmsteads in surveys are measured by the extent of the ceramic density indicative of human activity, which are often small and discrete entities,[42] with a size range of 2,000 square metres at Methana,[43] 5,000 square metres in the Nemea Valley[44] and up 10,000 square metres in the southern Argolid.[45] The size of these densities varies widely, and, critically, there is clearly no fixed size of 'farmstead',[46] probably because these sites conformed to the resources and needs of individual farmers. Therefore, their size, shape and variations thereof were indicative of the resources available to their farmers when they went into use.[47] While the variation in site size may cause problems for cross-territory comparison between various farmstead types, within a specific landscape the scale of farmsteads can inform us more, about the practices of agriculture for individual households and landscapes. The epigraphic examples cited above shed more light on this issue, as farmers could add to and renovate existing structures depending on the nature of the lease. Significantly, the size and nature of these sites reveal the economic capabilities of the household, and in that sense we have an opportunity to reconstruct how they made use of the land available to them. The size and the nature of the site thus grants us insight into the economic endeavours of individual households and allows us to understand more about the practicalities of farming from the perspective of those who were carrying it out.

In terms of their ceramic composition, Kristina Winther-Jacobson's analyses of farmsteads from Methana, the Laconia Rural Sites Project and the Troodos Archaeological and Environmental Survey Project illustrated that 'approximate pottery index range of 20% cooking ware, 25% heavy utility/pithoi, 40% plain ware, <5% transport ware, and 10% table ware' was sufficient to mark a 'farmstead signature'.[48] This signature mostly consists of coarse wares for the preparation and cooking of food, along with large storage vessels for the storage of agricultural produce. Such a signature is consistent with the ceramic material recovered from the Vari house and broadly fits the parameters of what we would find within a domestic urban setting.[49] Lin Foxhall's analysis of the material culture from the Methana survey, and its comparison with excavated domestic sites within urban and rural settings, led to the conclusion that farmsteads sit on a continuum of human activity where the fullest range of activity is present in domestic urban settings, which gradually decreases in farmsteads.[50] Based on recent excavations of farmsteads in Attica and elsewhere in the Greek world, as discussed above, it is clearly the case that some farmsteads were comparable to urban domestic houses in the types of activities that they supported, whereas others lack comparable evidence, and clearly had different roles in the landscape. The ceramic characteristics of farmsteads, in general terms, indicate that these sites hosted the preparation and consumption of food-stuffs along with the long-term storage of supplies, and with close examination of the vessel ranges along with site size we can reconstruct different forms of activity at farmsteads along a rural sites continuum that is illustrative of sites for intermittent use and storage to sites that supported activity equal to urban houses.[51] In order to categorize these sites further we can apply the evidence of site size and ceramic repertoire to reconstruct the activity that they supported. For example, analyses of the sherd densities and weight from the Nemea Valley survey that had been classed as 'off-site' scatters revealed that they were indeed ephemeral places for rural storage.[52] The nature of ceramic types recorded at farmsteads coupled with the size of the ceramic density allows us to make more informed reconstructions of past agricultural practices. This in conjunction with the variation within the ceramic repertoire for farmsteads is compelling evidence of the differences in farming practices and household objectives within a landscape, and if analysed sympathetically offers us a new and vital insight into the lives and experiences of rural communities.

The application of the criteria of location, size and ceramic signature narrows down what we might identify as a farmstead in the archaeological record. These site types are not consistent in form or character; rather, the criteria help us to specify the types of sites we can associate with farming, and we can categorize the sites further to add greater nuance into the nature of farmsteads. The most prominent reminder of farmsteads in the landscape are towers and tower-houses, which are found in several contexts and probably served several functions depending on the nature and setting of the structure.[53] In using this role-based typology we can distinguish agricultural towers and tower-houses from other towers connected to civic or economic roles. Perhaps the most apparent function for towers in an agricultural context is for the storage of goods and chattel, and as we have seen above, towers provided a space to retreat to in case of attack.[54] The phrase 'οἰκία, πὐργος and αὐλή' clearly relates to a farm with a tower, and equally, ἔπαυλις[55] may describe fortified farms or farms that may have a tower connected to them.

The most ubiquitous type of farmstead recorded in surveys are discrete dense pottery scatters, which may have some evidence of a small structure associated.[56] The function and identification of these sites are the most contentious in scholarship because, as discussed above, the term 'farm-stead' implies types of activity, which these sites sometimes lack evidence for. The wholesale application of 'farmstead' to these sites obscures the nuances inherent within them. As I have argued above, not all people in the landscape were farming in the same manner. Therefore, it is better to create a site type that allows for the variations of farming practices. I use the term 'simple rural site' based on the differences evident in their ceramic signatures. To explain the differences evident in farmsteads, Foxhall proposes an urban–rural continuum, with domestic activity present in urban sites which gradually diminishes in rural sites.[57] I have modified this model to measure rural sites on a continuum ranging from activity comparable to urban domestic contexts to seasonal activity and occupation. Within this typology, sites which demonstrate evidence of year-round activity and occupation, indicated by the presence of all the components of the ceramic classes and other objects such as loomweights, lamps and grinders for food preparation, could be considered farmsteads. In contrast, sites that have a less regular activity or a more specialized role, such as processing centres, could be considered seasonal farmsteads, *spitakia* or single-use sites. By applying the criteria of site size and vessel type at each of these sites and categorizing sites based on their form, we can add depth to our analyses of the agricultural activities taking place in the landscape.

The presence of agricultural installations or tools at a site is a more definite indicator of agricultural activity. These were immobile, fixed spaces used in the processing of agricultural goods: e.g. for olive and vine crops they most often took the form of lever-presses and *trapeta* and for grain crops, threshing floors. Installations can be found in urban and rural structures such as lever-presses and *trapeta* found within houses of Halieis and Olynthus.[58] In these instances, the installations were likely used primarily by that household or family group. Equally, there is evidence of installations located in the landscape, often near roads, that were likely to have serviced a wider community.[59] For example, during the survey of the Methana peninsula, archaeologists recorded site MS123, located in the centre of the peninsula along a potential ancient route. The site included an ancient tower along with six press beds, two press-beam blocks, and eight *patitiria* that date to the Classical–Hellenistic periods.[60] The number of installations here exceeds what we may expect of a household's production requirements, and this site offers us a unique opportunity to understand more about the spaces that supported the narratives that took place between the individual and the community as they negotiated the harvesting, movement and processing of crops.[61]

For the ancient Greek farmer (whatever status and gender they were), it was unnecessary to provide detailed descriptions of their farms. Each farm was different, perhaps not drastically so, but their variations in structure type and repertoire of ceramic types are a significant indicator of the economic objectives of the household. When trying to compare the textual and archaeological data, we can equate some similarities, but also differences. As with the nature of ancient Greek agriculture, we can recognize a variety of rural sites accommodating various activities (storage, occupation, processing) across a spectrum of society. Therefore, the concept of a farmstead, defined solely as a place for habitation and agriculture, may not have been recognizable to all Greeks. Instead, the evidence indicates that the agricultural landscape was full and busy, with a variety of farmsteads and also with roads and travellers, animals and workers that created a dynamic and ever-changing space.

Space–Time Anchors and Travel

Travel was a necessity of ancient daily life, and we can envisage multiple scales of travel, ranging from short to long distance with multiple purposes in mind.[62] With regard to the present analysis, the nature of farmed land, the distribution of farmsteads, the location of markets (both fixed and temporary), along with other social and civic factors, necessitated travel. Therefore, accessibility was a key factor in agricultural production. The land a farmer needed to work, the sites for habitation and storage, the sites for the processing of agricultural produce, and the markets they engaged with needed to be reachable for the household to survive. In order to gain greater insight into the experiences of travel concerning agricultural production, the application of the concept of time geography[63] grants us the opportunity to measure travel from the perspective of the traveller.[64] The concept of time geography measures the urgency and necessity of travel by recognizing the point of origin for the traveller and their destination as two fixed points in the landscape known as space–time anchors.[65]

Understanding how travel could be achieved, based solely on textual sources, is challenging because they often lack detailed descriptions of routes and the experience of travel. There are several instances in texts where characters travel, of course, but not much attention is paid to the means of doing so. For example, the dramatic raid carried out by Euergos and Mnesiboulos (Demosthenes 47.60–65), quoted in earlier in this chapter, paints a vivid picture of passers-by, workers, neighbours and slaves witnessing the raid on the house and reporting the encounter to the defendant who was in Athens at the time. The space–time anchors here are the defendant's house and his location in Athens, both of which the protagonists of the story need to get to quickly. We can easily imagine the commotion of the raid, the movement and rushing about of neighbours and travellers, who are witnessing the events unfold before them. In that moment, the roads are the facilitator of movement and interaction between the witnesses and neighbours of the assault. We must be careful with such limited detail in our sources that we do not underestimate the significance and importance of roads in the ancient landscape. Roads, paths, tracks and lanes[66] facilitated travel, and the road network across any of the territories and landscapes of the Greek world would have some consistency in the form of their construction, especially across mountainous terrain with the use of switchbacks, terracing and rock-cut grooves to support travel.[67] The more ephemeral tracks, paths and trails, which are attested in ancient Greek nomenclature, but which are mostly impossible to identify in the archaeological record, illustrate the potential for an extensive network of routes that connected space–time anchors in the landscape

Travel could be conceived of in terms of the time it took to get to a destination. For example, the route between Athens and Oropos via the deme of Aphidna is described as 'about a day's journey for a pedestrian without baggage, uphill all the way'.[68] Similarly the need to travel before dark impacts the decision-making processes in Demosthenes' *Against Eubulides*.[69] In this case, the demesmen travel to and from Halimous to Athens (roughly 6.5 kilometres one way) to hear testimony concerning the disenfranchisement of deme members. What is of particular interest to us is that the demesmen travelled to Athens for the assembly, and more importantly, they travelled back to Halimous intending to return to Athens the following day.[70] In this case, it seems that the physical and temporal cost of travel, imposed by the space–time anchor of the deme assembly, was less than that required to source lodgings within Athens.

These events and other more mundane encounters that do not survive in our sources give us some insight into the fullness of the landscape, not only in terms of settlement and spaces for social, civic and economic practices but also the infrastructure created and used to support it. Movement and travel in the landscape was a constant dialogue between the individual and the landscape, consisting of multiple decisions aimed at achieving the intended outcome of the journey. In my estimation, the landscape was a vibrant space full of multiple types of human interactions and sites used for multiple purposes at various times of the year. Concerning agriculture, time geography is particularly useful in this analysis because, at several points in the agricultural calendar, there are periods of high time-stress where the labourer must plant, plough, harvest and process crops within a specific time frame.[71] Therefore the need to complete agricultural chores and the spaces where the farmer may complete them formed an interconnected framework of actions and reactions across the agricultural landscape.[72] The stress on the farmer to complete allocated tasks within a given time frame meant that they needed to be in dialogue with their fellow labourers, the landscape and the surrounding human and physical environment. As a result, the application of such a concept very much allows us to gain insight into the mentalities of travel, especially related to agriculture in this scenario, and this is particularly helpful when we consider the urgency of travel associated with the harvesting and production of crops.

A Reconstruction of the Agricultural Landscape

We have seen already that the nature of farmed land and the variety of farms used for agricultural production necessitated travel and movement across the landscape. To explore the concept of a connected landscape further, we can investigate the temporal and physical experience of farmers moving through the countryside between farmstead types. A farmer may have several reasons for regular travel between sites of habitation and farmed land to check on crops and livestock, and travel to settlements, markets and cult sites to engage in fixed and temporary markets for trade and barter along with other civic and social participation. In terms of the agricultural year, a point of considerable time-stress occurred when the farmer came under pressure to collect, process and store crops before the end of the harvesting season.[73] Thanks to the application of computer modelling, we can reconstruct the movement of these individuals as they experience the landscape both physically and temporally as they move across it for the storage and processing of crops during the harvest.

During the survey of the southern Argolid (Figure 7.1), the team recorded the three large settlements (first-order sites) of Halieis, Mases and Hermione, along with second-order sites (hamlets and villages), cult sites and Classical–Hellenistic farmsteads.[74] To model the agricultural landscape of the Akte peninsula, I divided the archaeological data of

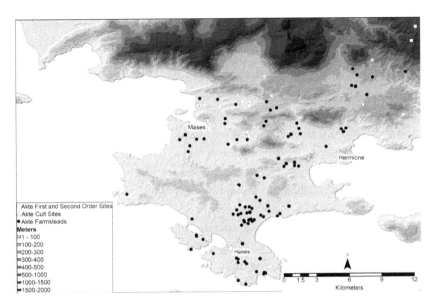

Figure 7.1 The Akte peninsula, southern Argolid. The map illustrates the location of first-order sites (Halieis, Hermione and Mases), second-order sites (villages/hamlets), cult sites and farmsteads used in this analysis. Author.

farmsteads into the classes of towers/tower-houses, installations and simple rural sites. I also digitized the modern roads between the three first-order sites, which the surveyors believe follow the routes of the ancient roads.[75] A path-distance model and least-cost path model were then created based upon these data. The path-distance model generates an estimate of the temporal cost of a journey in time by taking into account the slope and elevation of the terrain[76] from a set starting point. For example, the model can illustrate travel time between Athens and Sparta in hours and minutes. The temporal model depends on the nature of the landscape; therefore, the steeper the terrain, the longer it takes to move across it. The path-distance model allows us to visualize how an ancient farmer may have perceived the landscape, in its physical form, and its temporal form. To explain further, a farmer, when planning whether to travel, would have considered several factors including the time the journey took, to measure against whether they needed to source accommodation and their means of travel, as in the similar situation described in *Against Eubulides* above. Thus, by creating a path-distance model of the landscape, we can measure physical distances in tandem with temporal distances.[77] The results of this combination grant us a more holistic view of the experience of travel from the farmer's perspective.

The least-cost path model complements the path-distance model by generating the most physically cost-effective[78] route across the landscape. Like the path-distance model, the least-cost path model shares the same base data of slope, elevation and cost-distance rasters. Unlike the path-distance model, however, the least-cost path model calculates a path between two points following the path of least resistance, based on the accumulated data from the elevation, slope and cost-distance rasters. In conceiving of the landscape as made up of space–time anchors and modelling the landscape in its temporal form, along with illustrating routes across it, we can gain a much better sense of what it was like to work in and move through the agricultural landscape. It is important to note, however, that the models proposed are period-specific, and the sites mapped are those with ceramic evidence of a use range within the Classical period; of course that does not mean all sites were in use at any one time, and some may have fallen out of use and abandoned before others came into use. Thus, the model illustrates all farmsteads from the Classical period, without any further chronological refinement. Nor do the models take into account the effect of season, weather and environmental factors, which may impede travel. With these caveats in mind, this analysis is still useful because it illustrates in real terms the time and effort it took to cross a landscape, which we can then measure against archaeological and textual evidence as described further below.

To illustrate the usefulness of this methodology, Figure 7.2 illustrates the path-distance model from Halieis, where each halo equals thirty minutes of travel time measured at a walking pace of 5 kilometres per hour. Thanks to the gentle topography of the peninsula, a traveller can reach Hermione and Mases in the space of two and a half to three hours at a walking pace. In addition to illustrating the temporal landscape, I have mapped the space–time anchors of first and second-order sites along with the known ancient routes (solid black line). The majority of urbanized settlements can be reached via these ancient routes, and in several areas the least-cost path (broken black lines) maps neatly onto the ancient road. In some instances, especially to the north, however, the major known ancient routes do not reach these second-order sites, and in these occasions the least-cost paths can help complete the circuit of ancient routes across the peninsula.[79] By envisaging the landscape as a physical and temporal space we gain much better insight into how a traveller may have approached and made sense of the countryside around them.

To apply more specificity in relation to agricultural production we can apply estimates using the parameters for the kinds of load, speed and

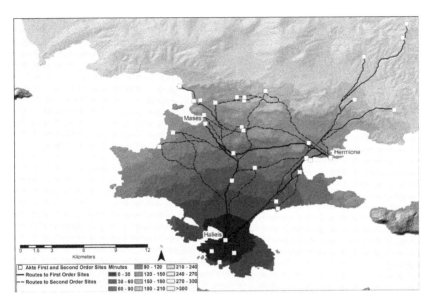

Figure 7.2 Path-distance model from Halieis, ancient roads between Halieis, Hermione and Mases, and least-cost paths to second-order sites. Author.

transport for ancient Greek and Roman contexts to the model (Table 7.1).[80] Based upon the evidence of installations in the peninsula associated with olive oil production, both within domestic contexts and in the countryside, researchers argued that households were involved in different economic agendas along a spectrum from market involvement to long-term storage for subsistence purposes.[81] Figure 7.3 illustrates the same base data as Figure 7.2, with the inclusion of farmsteads categorized as installations, towers, and simple rural sites. It is striking to note that, with a few exceptions, the majority of farmsteads are located close to a route through the peninsula; again due to the nature of farming and the parameters within which the farmer worked, accessibility was a key factor in site location, a point which this map helps to illustrate. On the whole, by examining the least-cost paths in relation to site distribution, it is apparent that there is a correlation between the location of farm sites and these routes. This may imply that the position of rural agricultural sites was relative to the position of ancient roads, particularly along the very fertile Flamboura plain (eastern Akte). This would have obvious, significant implications for the accessibility of farm sites, particularly installations, for the agricultural economy, especially if pressing installations were being shared amongst multiple farms. The positioning of farmsteads, especially

Table 7.1. *Ancient performance estimates for transport, speed and load*

Type of transport	Speed (km/h)	Load (kg)
Human pedestrian	4–5	n/a
Human porter	2.5–3	30–60
Pack donkey	2.5	60–100

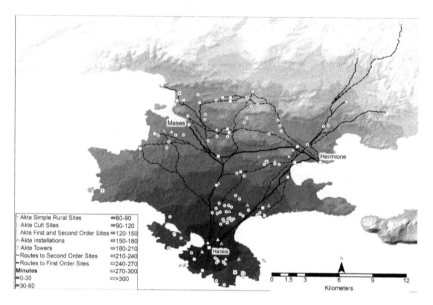

Figure 7.3 Location of farmsteads categorized as installations, towers and simple rural sites on the Akte peninsula. Author.

along the east and north, suggests that there was a road network facilitating access to these sites that the least-cost paths can help reconstruct.

To illustrate further the potential of this type of modelling, we can envisage a scenario in which goods were transported from the south of the peninsula to Hermione.[82] Table 7.1 supplies figures for a human porter carrying a load of 30 kg and averaging a speed of 2.5–3 kilometres per hour.[83] A traveller will walk the 11.5 kilometres to Hermione in approximately three to four hours. A donkey carrying a load between 60 and 100 kg and based on a speed of 2.5 kilometres per hour would reach the city in five to six hours. These results indicate that the countryside and agricultural sites could be accessed from urban centres, and vice versa, within a day's journey. While this example shows the efficacy of such an analysis, it is important to emphasize that it is not the case that travel was only directed to urban settlements, neither were urban settlements the nexus for all socio-economic movement, and the final destination for all agricultural produce. The example considered here serves to highlight the feasibility of travel and its temporal cost, and it is entirely conceivable that a traveller may move between their farms and other types of settlements (hamlets and villages) and cult sites in the landscape that provided temporary markets in tandem with other activities.[84]

Travel in any landscape was multidirectional and multipurpose, and my intention here is to illustrate the fluidity between a series of space–time anchors, and the role that roads had in supporting the function of travel. The example from Lysias' *On the Murder of Eratosthenes* illustrates this point well. During the speech, Euphiletus describes how he discovered his wife's affair when 'I came home unexpectedly from the country'.[85] He explains further that his wife met Eratosthenes, her lover, at the Thesmophoria, while Euphiletus was in the countryside.[86] Upon discovering the affair, Euphiletus planned to confront the lovers and travelled to his friend's house to gather a witness. It was then that he came upon his friend Sostratus, who was returning home from the countryside.[87] After dining with Sostratus and going to bed, Euphiletus was awoken by the servant who informed him that Eratosthenes and his wife were in the house. Euphiletus then went out again to seek witnesses amongst his neighbours 'and found some of them at home, while others were out of town'.[88]

It is significant to note in Euphiletus' account that time and movement play critical roles in his narrative. Euphiletus, Sostratus and his neighbours all appear to move seamlessly between urban and rural spaces for different lengths of time, potentially for farming purposes, but this is not explicitly stated. Euphiletus was gone long enough for his wife to meet Eratosthenes and to begin their affair, while Sostratus seems to have travelled more frequently between his urban home and the countryside, since Euphiletus intentionally plans to come upon Sostratus at sunset 'as I knew that, arriving at the hour, he would find none of his circle at home'.[89] In the case of the two men, and if they are farmers – and there is nothing in the text to suggest otherwise – perhaps Euphiletus was someone who made use of a longer-term domestic setting in the countryside, while Sostratus may be better classed as a commuter-farmer who moved back and forth between the town and his fields daily. The practices of the two men may also be extended to his neighbours since some were at home while others were not when Euphiletus called them to witness the affair.

Of importance for this analysis is the depiction of the continual movement of people as evidenced in *The Murder of Erotosthenes*.[90]

We understand, in principle, that travel and the movement of people, animals and produce were constant across the agricultural year, and the example from Lysias 1 helps illuminate the interconnection between travel and time for the ancient individual. Additionally, it illustrates the differences in the types and lengths of journey, and the ability for individuals to relocate to other parts of the landscape for parts of the year. The archaeological evidence for farmsteads combined with the computational modelling of time and distances allows us to visualize the nature of journeys such as Euphiletus' and Sotratus' and by extension moves us one step closer to reconstructing the experience of farming 'from the ground up'.

Finally, I wish to bring together a number of points I have made through this chapter and model them using this methodology. Farmsteads reflect the economic resources, needs and objectives of the household and wider community. Their variation and location can tell us a great deal about how agriculture functioned for the farmer. To highlight how this model helps illuminate this further, I have measured the distances between installations and other farmstead types. Lest we forget, the harvest was a crucial moment in the agricultural calendar, which required the farmer and the community to engage in near-continuous labour to achieve the successful harvesting, transportation and processing of crops. Studies of pre-mechanized farming in modern Greece have illustrated how, at these moments of time-stress, the community may have shared resources in the form of human labour, beasts of burden and equipment to ensure the successful completion of the harvest.[91] If we conceive of installations as space–time anchors that were shared by the community during intense periods of work, the completion of which had significant implications for the economic survival of the household, we create a more well-rounded understanding of what ancient agriculture was like for those carrying it out, which can then be further nuanced by adding greater depth to the chronological narrative of site use and abandonment in a landscape.

Figure 7.4 shows the same sites and least-cost paths as the two previous maps, and illustrates the cost in time measured from installations. Strikingly, the map highlights that the majority of installations within the peninsula are located less than thirty minutes away from sites that have evidence of occupation and storage. It shows too that there are clusters of farmsteads in close association with each other at various points in the landscape, around the three larger settlements, and also between the settlements along roads that connected the landscape. In these instances the space–time anchors of installations are within easy reach of farmsteads within the landscape. By modelling the agricultural landscape both from

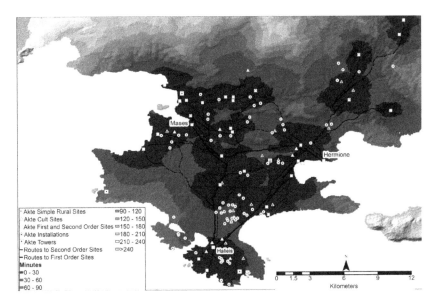

Figure 7.4 Path-distance model from installations. Author.

the perspective of the city and from the countryside we begin to break down old binaries of urban and rural, and instead perceive one space made up of different settlement types. In populating the landscape in this way, it is clear that the landscape is not fragmented, nor are the majority of its sites isolated: instead it comprises a series of space–time anchors that inform and influence the practices of the farmers.

Conclusion

The characteristics of ancient Greek farmsteads were intrinsically linked to the motivations of the individual household and also the human and physical environment of the territory. There was no one type of farm, nor one type of farming strategy, that was suitable for the entirety of the Greek world. The variation in topography, socio-economic factors and civic organization quickly dashes any hopes of finding uniformity in the archaeological record; similarly, the textual record too reflects these differences, where each farm mentioned is different from the others. So, how to move forward? Crucially, there are advantages to the diversity of farmsteads in our sources. Each farmstead site type offers us a glimpse into the household's experience of agriculture and their interactions with their community, which in turn tell us more about their economic objectives.

In utilizing a methodology that applies both the archaeological and the textual record, we learn more about the interconnected nature of site placement, farmable land and site type. We can reconstruct the activities at these sites through realizing that the farmstead signature describes how people cooked, ate and stored food, and this analysis serves to illustrate the potential of communal interaction more than simple economic processing of agricultural produce. The assessment of the relationship between various farmstead types, too, especially installations, illustrates the social complexity of the agricultural landscape. On this basis, we can ask questions about how installations were used and shared by farmers and how the farming community made sense of periods of time-stress where the demand for installations and spaces to process produce was high. The application of computer modelling to the agricultural landscape and the measurement of temporal and physical distances between site types provide a means to measure the connectivity of the physical landscape along with the social landscape. The physical environment that influenced site placement, farmed land and the roads through the countryside created a network of points that the farmer could work from. By measuring the temporal distance, we gain better insight into the perception of the farmer through a method that made sense to them, where it was likely that distance between sites for various purposes was measured in time, more so perhaps than physical distance. To conclude, the term 'farmstead' which was born from a need to describe sites uncovered in pedestrian landscape survey helps identify a broad range of sites used in agricultural production. Each farmstead is unique because it reflects the needs of the household that was using it. Thus, farmsteads were used, modified, added to and abandoned depending on the fluctuations of the household's economic success.

Notes

* This chapter stems from research conducted related to my monograph on the ancient Greek farmstead (McHugh 2017). My thanks to the editors for giving me the opportunity to contribute to this volume, Catherine Steidl for her insight and advice, and the reviewers for their helpful comments. All errors are my own.

1 See, for example, the conflicting views in Lohmann 1992 and Osborne 1992.

2 For an overview of issues relating to farmstead identification in pedestrian landscape survey see the following: Lohmann 1992; Foxhall 2001; Osborne 2001; Pettegrew 2001; 2003; Bintliff et al. 2002; Winther-Jacobsen 2010a; Winther-Jacobsen 2010b; concerning Roman agricultural sites in Greece see Stewart 2013; 2014.

3 For example, these small rural sites have sometimes been correlated with the presence of middling farmers; see Morris 2000: 155–57; 2007: 238; cf. Van Wees 2013: 222–24. There is an excellent discussion of the textual evidence for the statuses of farmers in Zurbach 2017: 355–97.

4 See McHugh 2017 for a comprehensive account of the ancient Greek farmstead, with accompanying bibliography.

5 For example, the Minnesota Messenia Expedition (1959–69) (MacDonald and Rapp 1972; as discussed in Cherry 2003: 141–42).

6 A feature that did not have an immediately defensive, cultic, civic or industrial (excluding agriculture) role (see Pettegrew 2001: 190–92; Bintliff *et al.* 2007: 39; Stewart 2014 who synthesizes the use of the term in survey).

7 For example, the Laconia Survey Project (Cavanagh *et al.* 1996; *et al.* 2002); Laconia Rural Sites Project (Cavanagh *et al.* 2005); the southern Argolid (Jameson *et al.* 1994); Methana Survey (Mee and Forbes 1997); Asea (Forsén and Forsén 2003); Thespiai (Bintliff *et al.* 2007); Sikyon (Lolos 2011); Karystos, southern Euboea (Keller 1985; Keller and Schneider 2009); Kea (Mendoni 1994).

8 See analysis of the ceramic repertoire in several pedestrian landscape surveys in Winther-Jacobsen (2010a and 2010b).

9 The manuring hypothesis encapsulates some of the issues relating to interpreting off-site scatters in relation to past agricultural practices; see Forbes (2013) for a synthesis of the topic.

10 See Morris and Papadopoulos (2005) for the use of towers and slave labour.

11 The large farmstead at Komboloi, which consists of a tower-house with several domestic and storage spaces, and evidence of large-scale processing of olive oil and grapes. For the archaeological report on this farm and others along the via Egnatia see Adam-Veleni *et al.* 2003. For an analysis of the grape remains at Komboloi see Margaritis and Jones 2006.

12 Lohmann 1993: 136–39. The types included: turmgehöfte, gehöfte, anwesen, and unsicher.

13 See survey reports *supra* no. 7.

14 Foxhall 2001: 216; see also Osborne 1992.

15 Perhaps the most well-known of which is the Vari house, Attica (Jones *et al.* 1973). Similar sites have been recorded at Sounion (Young 1956) and elsewhere in the Greek world (Morris 2001; Morris and Papadopoulos 2005; Caraher *et al.* 2010).

16 For example, the Komboloi farmstead discussed in note 12 above.

17 Jones 2004: 30.

18 Jones 2004: 30.

19 Osborne 1985: 120–25; cf. Jones 2000: 83.

20 Osborne 1987: 55–74; Foxhall 2004: 259–65.

21 Osborne 1985: 126.

22 Finley 1951: 53–55 and 60–61. Property in Classical Greece, according to Aristotle, can consist of land, structures, slaves and chattel (*Politics* 2.1267b).

23 χωρίον meaning a landed estate (Pritchett and Pippin 1956: 269; Hellman 1992: 209–10). See Pritchett and Pippin 1956: 269 for a list of terms associated with property on the *Horoi* inscriptions.

24 In relation to the *Rationes Centesimarum* Lambert (1993: 226) discusses a range of terminology relating to farms in the countryside. In Theophrastus' character of the boorish country bumpkin his dog guards the 'property and household' (τὸ χωρίον καὶ τὴν οἰκίαν) (Langdon 1990–91: 211); For the terminology used to describe land and property on leases see Pernin 2014.

25 See McHugh 2019b for a discussion on how agricultural fields provide an opportunity for agricultural workers to come together in taskscapes.

26 McHugh 2017: 1.

27 Pečírka 1973: 114.

28 A search of the database of *Archaeology in Greece* (https://chronique.efa.gr) with the parameters 'Rescue Excavation' and 'Agricultural Facility' yielded 167 results; this number increases to 213 with the inclusion of research excavations and survey.

29 For example, the site at Delpriza, Kranidi (Kossyva 2011), had an olive press within a domestic space (similar combinations were also found in the settlement of Halieis (Ault 2005: 39–45)). At Metaponto the excavation of the farm at Ponte Fabrizio (Lanza *et al.* 2014) is an essential publication that shows the potential information one can draw from the study of such sites.

30 Osborne 1987: 54; Cavanagh *et al.* 2005: 4–5; McHugh 2017: 27–33.

31 For a synthesis of how Boeotian territory and its city-states change over time, which has an impact on the nature of available land, see Bintliff 2019. For the impact of inheritance on landownership, in terms of Sparta, see Hodkinson 2000: 100–101 and 400–404.

32 Andreou 1994; Steinhauer 1994; Korres 2009; Vassilopoulou and Katsarou-Tzeveleki 2009.

33 Patterns of settlement and residence are complex within and throughout different territories: in southern Attica, for example, the pattern of settlement in the rural landscape coincides with the farming system employed and the status of those who were working on or owned the farm (Lohmann 1992: 39–51). But in other areas of the Greek world (e.g. islands) residence is not wholly reliant on the social and agricultural regimes (Osborne 1987: 68–69).

34 Zangger 1992: 15; Theophrastus' section on soils (*De causis plantarum* II.4.1–12) refers to the different types of soil found in various geographical regions, and farmers' soil type preferences.

35 Non-mechanized farming can be characterized by small-scale farming, inconsistent outputs, with a high level of human labour, and organic fertilizers (Bogaard *et al.* 2000, 129).

36 For example, on Keos (Whitelaw 2000: 234–35) and Kythera (Bevan and Conolly 2002–2004: 126) analyses of site location and arable land illustrated that 15 degrees of slope was the extent of farmed land.

37 See Foxhall (1996) for a discussion on the strategies an ancient farmer could employ to farm steeper slopes.

38 At Atene, farmsteads were not located on cultivated land; instead they were located on rocky soil (Lohmann 1993: 188)

39 See, for example, Gallant 1991; Moreno 2007.

40 Gallant 1991: 82–92.

41 For a synthesis of the debates concerning the identification of off-site scatters see Forbes 2013: 552–53 and 555–59, with accompanying references.

42 The Southern Argolid Survey (Jameson *et al.* 1994: 420) recorded 'small isolated' sites between 0 and 3,000 m^2. In the Laconia Survey, 'simple farmsteads' (Catling 2002: 162) averaged 7,000 m^3; and farmsteads in the Methana Survey (Mee and Forbes 1997: 67) ranged between 616 and 1,380 m^4.

43 Mee and Forbes 1997: 37.

44 Alcock *et al.* 1994: 160–64.

45 Jameson *et al.* 1994: 420. See discussion in Pettegrew 2001: 203; Winther-Jacobsen 2010a: 271.

46 There is evidence of field walls associated with rural structures. For example, farm C-54 at Karystos, Euboea, may have had a wall that enclosed approximately 9 hectares (Keller and Wallace 1988: 154). These enclosed spaces may have been used as 'gardens' (*kepos*) for intensive cultivation that required irrigation (Krasilnikoff 2010: 109–10).

47 See Winther-Jacobsen 2010a: 270–93 for the impact of formation processes (site abandonment, reuse, modern ploughing) on sites recovered in landscape survey. See discussion and references to surveys that have considered these processes in Winther-Jacobsen 2010a: 271–73.

48 Winter-Jacobsen 2010b: 108–109, table 45 table 45 and fig. 33.

49 Whitelaw's (1998 and 2000) ceramic use typology categorized ceramics based on their function and found overlap with the material from urban domestic spaces and rural farms.

50 Foxhall 2004: 260–65.

51 Foxhall 2004: 266; see McHugh 2017: 57–60 and 85–87.

52 Cloke 2016: 235.

53 As lighthouses Kozelj and Wurch-Kozelj 1989; Morris 2001: 340. For mining, Osborne 1987: 63–69. For defence, Ober 1985. For agriculture, Young 1956: 133ff.; Munn 1983: 30–42. Multipurpose function for towers in the Corinthia see Caraher *et al.* 2010.

54 Osborne 1987: 67.

55 From Diodorus Siculus' account of the Athenian army plundering and terrorizing the Peloponnese in 430 BCE: '... laid waste the part of the coast which is called Acte [the Akte peninsula] and sent up the farm-buildings (ἐπαύλεις) in flames' (12.43).

56 Roof tiles are often the only indicator of a structure in pedestrian landscape survey (Cavanagh *et al.* 2005: 292).

57 Foxhall 2004: 266; see McHugh 2017: 85–87.

58 For example, House D at Halieis (Ault 1994: 560–61) and Olynthos House A6 (Cahill 2002: 242).

59 For example, the 4th-century BCE fortified trading post at Vrasna had comparable evidence of agricultural production, located within a public space along the via Egnatia (Adam-Veleni *et al.* 2003: 95–99). Several installations were found in the southern Argolid survey (Jameson *et al.* 1994; see list of sites in McHugh 2017: 189). These installations will be used in the analysis below. An early 20th-century photograph taken at Kambia on Chios illustrates several threshing floors close together being used by the whole community simultaneously. Pericles Papachatzidakis (ΦΑ_2_546), Benaki Museum.

60 Foxhall 1997: 266.

61 McHugh 2019b: 212.

62 McHugh 2019a: 207–208.

63 Miller 2007: 512; Mlekuž 2010: 2.

64 Charleux 2015: 262–63.

65 Miller 2007: 512.

66 See Lolos 2003 for the terminology concerning road types in ancient Greek.

67 For evidence of ancient routes in Attica see Lohmann 2002; Kakavogianni 2009; and their role Fachard and Pirisino 2015. Roads in Laconia: Armstrong *et al.* 1992; Pikoulas 2012. A discussion of the major road between Boeotia and the Peloponnese: Hammond 1954. The Argolid: (Wells 1990; 2002.

68 Ober 1985: 115–20.

69 Demosthenes 57.9–16.

70 For further instances of groups travelling back and forth between Athens and the countryside to attend the law courts and assemblies: Lysias 17.8; Demosthenes 53.4; Isaeus 9.21. For the role of the witness in law-court speeches see Mirhady 2002: 261–63.

71 Foxhall 2007: 127.

72 See McHugh 2019b for a discussion on how communities can express shared labour through song during the harvest.

73 Halstead and Jones 1989: 47; McHugh 2019b.

74 The data used in this analysis was compiled from Jameson *et al.* 1994: 415–538. The map illustrates all Classical–Hellenistic farmsteads (black dots) identified as part of the survey. In the following maps they will be divided into the farmstead types discussed above.

75 Jameson *et al.* 1994: 48; Pausanias, *Description of Greece* 2.36.1.

76 Topographic data were imported in the form of a 30 m ASTER DEM from the online earth explorer portal for the United States Geological Survey (USGS) at https://earthexplorer.usgs.gov.

77 As discussed in relation to travel across Attica in McHugh 2019a.

78 In this instance cost-effective describes the relation between the physical expenditure of travel and the nature of the route.

79 Fachard and Pirisino 2015: 141.

80 Adapted from Bevan 2013: 6.

81 See Acheson who argues that the evidence of olive presses in the peninsula was not wholly indicative of cash crops as the surveyors had initially concluded (Jameson *et al.* 1994: 394). Instead the differences in the distribution and pattern of presses in settlements and the countryside indicated a variety of economic priorities in the landscape (Acheson 1997: 181).

82 Hermione was an important port in the peninsula Jameson *et al.* 1994: 593; Bresson 2015: 360–62. For transport over land see Raepsaet 2008, 581; Pikoulas 2007.

83 A red-figure *pelike* (*c.* 470 BCE) illustrates two men, possibly farmers, one of whom is carrying a yoke with two baskets on his shoulders. The other man has a bag over his shoulder; they also have a pig and piglet with them (Fitzwilliam Museum, Cambridge, GR.9.1917).

84 See Paga's discussion of how deme theatres in Attica provided spaces for socio-economic activity for the surrounding rural inhabitants to travel to and participate in (2010: 367, 380–81).

85 Lysias 1.11. '... ἦκον μὲν ἀπροσδοκήτως ἐξ ἀγροῦ ...'

86 Lysias 1.20.

87 Lysias 1.22.

88 Lysias 1.23. '... καὶ τοὺς μὲν ἔνδον κατέλαβον, τοὺς δὲ οὐκ ἐπιδημοῦντας ηὗρον.'

89 Consequently, Euphiletus invites him to dinner (Lysias 1.22).

90 See McHugh 2019a for a discussion on the frequency of travel in Attica.

91 Petropoulos 1994: 20; Halstead 2014: 309–10.

References

Acheson, P. (1997). Does the 'economic explanation' work? Settlement, agriculture and erosion in the territory of Halieis in the Late Classical–Early Hellenistic Period. *Journal of Mediterranean Archaeology* 10(2), 165–90.

Adam-Veleni, P., Poulaki, E. and Tzanavari, K. (2003). *Ancient Country Houses on Modern Roads: Central Macedonia.* Athens: Archaeological Receipts Fund.

Alcock, S., Cherry, J. F. and Davis, J. L. (1994). Intensive survey, agricultural practice, and the classical landscape in Greece. In I. Morris, ed., *Classical Greece: Ancient Histories and Modern Archaeologies.* Cambridge: Cambridge University Press, 137–70.

Andreou, I. (1994). Ο δῆμος των Αξονίδων Αλών. In W. Coulson, O. Palagia, T. Shear, H. Shapiro and F. Frost, eds., *The Archaeology of Athens and Attica under the Democracy: Proceedings of an International Conference Celebrating 2500 Years since the Birth of Democracy in Greece, Held at the American School of Classical Studies, Athens, December 4–6 1992.* Oxford: Oxbow, 191–209.

Armstrong, P., Cavanagh, W., and Shipley, G. (1992). Crossing the river: observations on routes and bridges in Laconia from the Archaic to Byzantine periods. *Annual of the British School at Athens* 87, 293–310.

Ault, B. (1994). *Classical houses and households: an architectural and artefactual case study from Halieis, Greece.* (PhD thesis, Indiana University, Bloomington.)

(2005). *The Excavations at Ancient Halieis Volume 2: The Organisation and Use of Domestic Space.* Bloomington and Indianapolis: Indiana University Press.

Bevan, A. (2013). Travel and interaction in the Greek and Roman world: a review of some computational modelling approaches. In S. Dunn and S. Mahoney, eds., *Digital Classicist.* London: Institute of Classical Studies/Wiley-Blackwell, 3–24.

Bevan, A. and Conolly, J. (2002–2004). GIS, archaeological survey, and landscape archaeology on the Island of Kythera, Greece. *Journal of Field Archaeology* 29, 123–38.

Bintliff, J. (2019). City-archaeology in Boeotia: continuity, discontinuity, localism and globalisation. In T. Lucas, C. Müller and A-C. Oddon-Panissié, eds., *La Béotie de l'archaïsme à l'époque romaine. Frontières, territoires, paysages.* Paris: Éditions de Boccard.

Bintliff, J., Farinetti, E., Howard, P., Sarri, K. and Sbonias, K. (2002). Classical farms, hidden prehistoric landscapes and Greek rural survey: a response and an update. *Journal of Mediterranean Archaeology* 15(2), 259–65.

Bintliff, J., Howard, P. and Snodgrass, A. (2007). *Testing the Hinterland: The Work of the Boeotia Survey (1989–1991) in the Southern Approaches to the City of Thespiai.* Cambridge: McDonald Institute Monographs.

Bogaard, A., Charles, M., Halstead, P. and Jones, G. (2000). The scale and intensity of cultivation: evidence from weed ecology. In P. Halstead and C. Frederick, eds., *Landscape and Land Use in Postglacial Greece.* Sheffield: Sheffield Academic Press, 129–35.

Bresson, A. (2015). *The Making of the Ancient Greek Economy: Institutions, Markets, and Growth in the City-States,* trans. S. Rendall. Princeton: Princeton University Press.

Cahill, N. (2002). *Household and City Organisation at Olynthus.* New Haven: Yale University Press.

Caraher, W. R., Pettegrew, D. and James, S. (2010). Towers and fortifications at Vayia in the southeast Corinthia. *Hesperia* 79, 385–415.

Catling, R. (2002). The survey area from the Early Iron Age to the Classical Period 1050–300 BC. In W. Cavanagh, J. Crouwel, R. Catling and G. Shipley, eds., *The Laconia Survey, Volume I: Methodology and Interpretation.* London: British School at Athens, 151–257.

Cavanagh, W., J. Crouwel, R. Catling and G. Shipley, eds. (1996). *Continuity and Change in a Greek Rural Landscape. The Laconia Survey Volume II. Archaeological Data.* London: British School at Athens.

(2002). *Continuity and Change in a Greek Rural Landscape. The Laconia Survey Volume I. Methodology and Interpretation*. London: British School at Athens.

Cavanagh, W., Mee, C. and James, P. (2005). *The Laconia Rural Sites Project*. London: British School at Athens.

Charleux, L. (2015). A GIS toolbox for measuring and mapping person-based space-time accessibility. *Transactions in GIS* 19, 262–78.

Cherry, J. F. (2003). Archaeology beyond the site: regional survey and its future. In J. Papadopoulos and R. Leventhal, eds., *Theory and Practice in Mediterranean Archaeology: Old World and New World Perspectives*. Los Angeles: Cotsen Institute of Archaeology, 137–60.

Cloke, C. (2016). *The Landscape of the Lion: Economies of Religion and Politics in the Nemean Countryside (800 B.C. to A.D. 700)*. (Unpublished dissertation, University of Cincinnati.)

Fachard, S. and D. Pirisino. (2015). Routes out of Attica. In M. Miles, ed., *Autopsy in Athens: Recent Archaeological Research on Athens and Attica*. Oxford: Oxbow, 139–53.

Finley, M. (1951). *Studies in Land and Credit in Ancient Athens 500–200 BC: The Horos Inscriptions*. New Brunswick: Rutgers University Press.

Forbes, H. (2013). Off–site scatters and the manuring hypothesis in Greek survey archaeology: an ethnographic approach. *Hesperia* 84, 551–94.

Forsén J. and Forsén, B., eds. (2003). *The Asea Valley Survey: An Arcadian Mountain Valley from the Palaeolithic until Modern Times*. Stockholm: Åström.

Foxhall, L. (1996). Feeling the earth move: cultivation techniques on steep slopes in classical antiquity. In G. Shipley and J. Salmon, eds., *Human Landscapes in Classical Antiquity*. London: Routledge, 44–67.

(1997). Appendix 1: Ancient farmsteads, other farmsteads, and equipment. In C. Mee and H. Forbes, eds., *A Rough and Rocky Place: The Landscape and Settlement History of the Methana Peninsula, Greece*. Liverpool: Liverpool University Press, 257–69.

(2001). Colouring in the countryside. Response to David K. Pettegrew 'Chasing the Classical Farmstead'. *Journal of Mediterranean Archaeology* 14(2), 216–22.

(2004). Small, rural farmstead sites in ancient Greece: a material cultural analysis. In F. Kolb, ed., *Chora und Polis*. Munich: De Gruyter, 249–70.

(2007). *Olive Culture in Ancient Greece: Seeking the Ancient Economy*. Oxford: Oxford University Press.

Gallant, T. (1991). *Risk and Survival in Ancient Greece: Reconstructing the Ancient Economy*. Oxford: Polity.

Halstead, P. (2014). *Two Oxen Ahead: Pre-mechanised Farming in the Mediterranean*. Oxford: Wiley Blackwell.

Halstead, P. and Jones, G. (1989). Agrarian ecology in the Greek islands: time, stress, scale, and risk. *Journal of Hellenic Studies* 109, 41–55.

Hammond, N.G.L. (1954). The main road from Boeotia to the Peloponnese through the Northern Megarid. *Annual of the British School at Athens* 49, 102–22.

Hellman, M.-C. (1992). *Recherches sur le vocabulaire de l'architecture grecque d'après les inscriptions de Délos*. Paris: Bibliothèques de l'Ecole française d'Athènes et de Rome – Série Athènes.

Hodkinson, S. (2000). *Property and Wealth in Classical Sparta*. Swansea: The Classical Press of Wales.

Jameson, M., Runnels, C., VanAndel, T. and Munn, M. (1994). *A Greek Countryside: The Southern Argolid from Prehistory to the Present Day*. Stanford: Stanford University Press.

Jones, J. E., Graham, A. J., Sackett, L. H. and Geroulanos, M. I. (1973). An Attic country house below the Cave of Pan at Vari. *Annual of the British School at Athens* 68, 355–452.

Jones, N. (2000). Epigraphic evidence for farmstead residence in Attica. *Zeitschrift für Papyrologie und Epigraphik* 133, 75–90.

   (2004). *Rural Athens under the Democracy*. Philadelphia: University of Philadelphia Press.

Kakavogianni, O. (2009). Ἀρχαῖες οδοί στα νότια και δυτικά Μωσόγεια και τη Λαυρεωτική. In M. Korres, ed., *Αττικής οδοί. Αρχαίοι δρόμοι της Αττικής*. Athens: Melissa, 182–96.

Keller, D. (1985). *Archaeological survey in southern Euboea, Greece: a reconstruction of human activity from Neolithic times through the Byzantine period*. (PhD thesis, Indiana University, Bloomington.)

Keller, D. and Schneider, R. (2009). The Classical–Hellenistic period at the Palio Pithari farm site and the Cape Mnima Emborio site in the context of contemporary sites and findspots on the Paximadi Peninsula. In D. Rupp and J. Tomlinson, eds., *Euboea and Athens: Proceedings of a Colloquium in Memory of Malcolm B. Wallace: Athens 26–27 June 2009*. Toronto: Canadian Institute in Greece, 95–113.

Keller, D. and Wallace, M. (1988). The Canadian Karystia project: two classical farmsteads. *Echoes du Monde* 7(2), 151–57.

Korres, M., ed. (2009). *Αττικής οδοί. Αρχαίοι δρόμοι της Αττικής*. Athens: Melissa.

Kossyva, A. (2011). The invisible dead of Delpriza, Kranidi. In H. Cavanagh, W. Cavanagh and R. Roy, eds., *Honouring the Dead in the Peloponnese*. Nottingham: Centre for Spartan and Peloponnesian Studies, 329–70.

Kozelj, T. and Wurch-Kozelj, M. (1989). Phares de Thasos. *Bulletin de Correspondance Hellénique* 113, 161–81.

Krasilnikoff, J. (2010). Irrigation as innovation in ancient Greek agriculture. *World Archaeology* 42, 108–21.

Lambert, S. (1993). *Rationes Centesimarum: Sale of Public Land in Lykourgan Athens*. Amsterdam: Brill.

Langdon, M. (1990–1991). On the farm in Classical Attica. *Classical Journal* 86, 209–13.

Lanza, E., Swift, K. and Coleman Carter, J. (2014). *A Greek Farmhouse at Ponte Fabrizio. The Chora of Metaponto 5.* Austin: University of Texas Press.

Lohmann, H. (1992). Agriculture and country life in Classical Athens. In B. Wells, ed., *Agriculture in Ancient Greece: Proceedings of the Seventh International Symposium at the Swedish Institute at Athens, 16–17 May, 1990.* Stockholm: Swedish Institute at Athens, 29–58.

　(1993). *Atene: Forschungen zu Siedlungs – und Wirtschaftsstruktur des klassischen Attika.* Köln: Böhlau.

　(2002). Ancient roads in Attica and the Megaris. In H. Goette, ed., *Ancient Roads in Greece, Proceedings of a Symposium Organised by the Cultural Association Aigeas (Athens) and the German Archaeological Institute (Athens) with the Supportof the German School at Athens, November 1998.* Athens: German School at Athens, 73–91.

Lolos, Y. (2003). Greek roads: a commentary on the ancient terms. *Glotta* 79, 137–74.

　ed. (2011). *Land of Sikyon, Archaeology and History of a Greek City-State.* Princeton: American School of Classical Studies.

MacDonald, W.A. and Rapp, G. (1972). *The Minnesota Messenia Expedition: Reconstructing a Bronze Age Regional Environment.* Minneapolis: University of Minnesota Press.

Margaritis, E. and Jones, M. (2006). Beyond cereals: crop processing and *Vitis vinifera* L. Ethnography, experiment and charred grape remains from Hellenistic Greece. *Journal of Archaeological Science* 33(6), 784–805.

Mee, C. and Forbes, H., eds. (1997). *A Rough and Rocky Place: The Landscape and Settlement History of the Methana Peninsula, Greece.* Liverpool: University of Liverpool Press.

McHugh, M. (2017). *The Ancient Greek Farmstead.* Oxford: Oxbow.

　(2019a). Going the extra mile: travel, time and distances in Classical Attica. *Annual of the British School at Athens* 114, 207–40.

　(2019b). To reap a rich harvest: experiencing agricultural labour in ancient Greece. *World Archaeology* 51, 208–25.

Mendoni, G. (1994). The organisation of the countryside in Kea. In P. Doukelles and G. Mendoni, eds., *Structures rurales et sociétés antiques: actes du colloque de Corfou, 14–16 mai 1992.* Paris: Les Belles Lettres, 147–62.

Miller, H. (2007). Place-based versus people-based geographic information science. *Geography Compass* 1, 503–35.

Mirhady, D. (2002). Athens' democratic witnesses. *Phoenix* 56, 255–74.

Mlekuž, D. (2010). Time geography, GIS, and archaeology. In F. Contreras, M. Forjas and F. C. Melero, eds., *Fusion of Cultures. Proceedings of the 38th Annual Conference on Computer Applications and Quantitative Methods in Archaeology, Granada, Spain, April 2010.* Oxford: British Archaeological Reports, 443–45.

Moreno, A. (2007). *Feeding the Democracy: Athenian Grain Supply in the Fifth and Fourth Centuries B.C.* Oxford: Oxford University Press.

Morris, I. (2000). *Archaeology As Cultural History: Words and Things in Iron Age Greece.* Oxford: Wiley.

(2007). Early Iron Age Greece. In W. Scheidel, I. Morris and R. Saller. eds., *The Cambridge Economic History of the Greco-Roman World.* Cambridge: Cambridge University Press, 211–41.

Morris, S. (2001). The towers of ancient Leukas: results of a topographic survey, 1991–1992. *Hesperia* 70, 285–347.

Morris, S. and Papadopoulos, J. (2005). Greek towers and slaves: an archaeology of exploitation. *American Journal of Archaeology* 109, 155–225.

Munn, M. (1983). *Studies on the territorial defences of fourth-century Athens.* (PhD thesis, University of Pennsylvania, Philadelphia.)

Ober, J. (1985). *Fortress Attica: Defence of the Athenian Land Frontier 404–322 BC.* Leiden: Brill.

Osborne, R. (1985). Buildings and residence on the land in Classical and Hellenistic Greece: the contribution of epigraphy. *Annual of the British School at Athens* 80, 119–28.

(1987). *Classical Landscape with Figures: The Ancient Greek City and Its Countryside.* London: George Philip.

(1992). Is it a farm? The definition of agricultural sites and settlements in ancient Greece. In B. Wells, ed., *Agriculture in Ancient Greece. Proceedings of the Seventh International Symposium at the Swedish Institute at Athens.* Stockholm: Swedish Institute at Athens, 21–28.

(2001). Counting the cost. Comments on David K. Pettegrew, 'Chasing the Classical Farmstead'. *Journal of Mediterranean Archaeology* 14(2), 212–16.

Paga, J. (2010). Deme theatres in Attica and the trittys system, *Hesperia* 79, 351–84.

Pečírka, J. (1973). Homestead farms in Classical and Hellenistic Hellas. In M. Finley, ed., *Problèmes de la terre en Grèce.* Paris: Mouton, 113–47.

Pernin, I. (2014). *Les baux ruraux en Grèce ancienne : Corpus épigraphique et étude.* Travaux de la Maison de l'Orient, 66. Lyon: Maison de l'Orient et de la Méditerranée.

Petropoulos, J. C. B. (1994). *Heat and Lust: Hesiod's Midsummer Festival Scene Revisited.* Lanham, MD: Rowman & Littlefield Publishers.

Pettegrew, D. (2001). Chasing the classical farmstead: assessing the formation and signature of rural settlement in Greek landscape archaeology. *Journal of Mediterranean Archaeology* 14(2), 189–209.

(2003). Counting and colouring Classical farms: a response to Osborne, Foxhall and Bintliff et al. *Journal of Mediterranean Archaeology* 15(2), 267–73.

Pikoulas, G. (2007). Travelling by land in Ancient Greece. In C. Adams and J. Roy. eds., *Travel, Geography, and Culture in Ancient Greece, Egypt and the Near East.* Oxford: Oxbow, 78–87.

(2012). *Το Οδικό Δίκτυο της Λακωνικής*. Athens: Horos.

Pritchett, W. and Pippin, A. (1956). The Attica Stelai: Part II. *Hesperia* 22, 178–328.

Raepsaet, G. (2008). Land transport, part 2: riding, harnesses, and vehicles. In J. Oleson, ed., *The Oxford Handbook of Engineering and Technology in the Classical World*. Oxford: Oxford University Press, 580–606.

Steinhauer, G. (1994). Παρατηρήσεις στην οικιστική μορφή των αττικών δήμων. In W. Coulson, O. Palagia, T. Shear, H. Shapiro and F. Frost, eds., *The Archaeology of Athens and Attica under the Democracy: Proceedings of an International Conference Celebrating 2500 years since the Birth of Democracy in Greece, Held at the American School of Classical Studies, Athens, December 4–6 1992*. Oxford: Oxbow, 175–89.

Stewart, D. (2013). *Reading the Landscape of the Rural Peloponnese: Landscape Change and Regional Variation in an Early 'Provincial' Setting*. Oxford: British Archaeological Reports.

(2014). Rural sites in Roman Greece. *Archaeological Reports for 2013–2014*: 117–32.

Van Wees, H. (2013). Farmers and hoplites: models of historical development. In D. Kagan and G. F. Viggiano, eds., *Men of Bronze: Hoplite Warefare in Ancient Greece*. Princeton: Princeton University Press.

Vassilopoulou, V. and Katsarou-Tzeveleki, S. (2009). *Απο τα Μεσογεια στον Αργοσαρωνικο: Β' Εφορεια Προιστορικων και Κλασικων Αρχαιοτητων: το εργο μιας δεκαετιας, 1994–2003: πρακτικα συνεδριου, Αθηνα, 18–20 Δεκεμβριου 2003*. Municipality of Markopoulo of Mesogeia.

Wells, B. (1990). Trade routes in north-east Argolid. *Hydra Working Papers in Middle Bronze Age Studies* 7, 87–91.

(2002). The kontoporeia – a route from Argos to Korinth. In K. Ascani, V. Gabrielsen, K. Kvist and A. Rasmussen, eds., *Ancient History Matters: Studies Presented to Jens Erik Skydsgaard on his Seventieth Birthday*. Rome: L'Erma di Bretschneider, 69–77.

Whitelaw, T. (1998). Colonisation and competition in the polis of Koressos: the development of settlements in North-West Keos from the Archaic to the late Roman periods. In L. Mendoni and A. Mazarakis-Ainian, eds., *Kea-Kythnos: History and Archaeology: Proceedings of an International Symposium, Kea-Kynthos, 22–25 June 1994*. Athens: Kentron Hellēnikes kai Rōmaikēs Archaiotētos, 227–57.

(2000). Reconstructing a classical landscape with figures: some interpretive explorations in northwest Keos. In R. Francovich, H. Patterson and G. Narke, eds., *Extracting Meaning from Ploughsoil Assemblages*. Oxford: Oxbow, 227–43.

Winther-Jacobsen, K. (2010a). The classical farmstead revisited: activity differentiations based on a 'ceramic use typology'. *Annual of the British School at Athens* 105, 269–90.

(2010b). *From Pots to People: A Ceramic Approach to the Archaeological Interpretation of Ploughsoil Assemblages in Late Roman Cyprus*. Leuven: Peeters.

Young, J. (1956). Studies in south Attica: country estates at Sounion. *Hesperia* 25, 122–46.

Zangger, E. (1992). Prehistoric and historic soils in Greece: assessing the natural resources for agriculture. In B. Wells, ed., *Agriculture in Ancient Greece: Proceedings of the Seventh International Symposium at the Swedish Institute at Athens, 16–17 May, 1990*. Stockholm: Swedish Institute at Athens, pp. 13–21.

Zurbach, J. (2017). *Les hommes, la terre et la dette en Grèce, c. 1400 – c. 500 a.c.* Bordeaux: Ausonius.

8 | Mudbricks and Papyri from the Desert Sand

Housing in the Ptolemaic and Roman Fayum

INGE UYTTERHOEVEN[*]

Thanks to the rich textual and material evidence of Graeco-Roman dwellings in the Egyptian Fayum, rarely found in the same quantity elsewhere in the Mediterranean, the area presents us with an ideal test case for studying ancient housing through the combination of archaeology, papyrology and history. The material remains of houses with their particular layout and ornamentation can, complemented with their contents (e.g. pottery and other artefacts, bone and plant remains), give us information upon the nature of the houses and their chronology, as well as upon the use of space and the role houses played as sociocultural markers in the society. However, a much more detailed picture of the physical appearance of houses and their socio-economic and cultural implications can be obtained when texts are combined with archaeological data. For instance, written documents can help to explain archaeologically attested differences in size, configuration and decoration of spaces as defined by particular factors, such as the social and cultural background of the house owner. Moreover, texts are indispensable for understanding the composition of the household and the relations between family members and outsiders, while also revealing the history of houses, including practices of passing property rights between generations. A combined textual–archaeological approach thus leads to a detailed understanding of the different people who lived and used the houses of Hellenistic–Roman Egypt and greatly helps in reconstructing the use of space and daily activities that took place behind the house facades. However, the integration of papyri and material data also has challenges, as information from the texts cannot always be easily identified in the field data, and the two source categories, each with its own research methods, frequently highlight different elements of private life. It is exactly this partly overlapping, partly complementary, character of the two types of evidence for housing in the Fayum that makes a combined study of 'words' and 'walls' extremely valuable, since only the integrated study of texts and material remains, surpassing a one-sided viewpoint, can give us a comprehensive insight into the private living practices of this area of the Mediterranean.

The Fayum

The Fayum is a semi-oasis located approximately 80 kilometres to the south of Cairo (Figure 8.1). The area receives its water supplies via the Bahr Yussuf, a natural branch of the River Nile, and is occupied by Lake Qarun at its north-western end. By means of an extensive land reclamation project the inhabitable area of the Fayum was greatly extended in the 20th–19th centuries BCE (Twelfth Dynasty). Centuries later, Ptolemy I (323–283 BCE) and Ptolemy II (283–246 BCE) carried out a second land reclamation programme. A large number of Greeks, as well as Egyptians from other *nomes*, were settled in the region. Administratively, the area was known as the Arsinoite *Nome* and subdivided into three *merides* (Herakleides, Polemon and Themistos). Together with the already existing Pharaonic settlements, the newly founded Ptolemaic living centres continued flourishing into the Roman period. The Fayum reached its zenith between the 3rd century BCE and the 3rd century CE, characterized by high population density and agricultural productivity. After this period, villages along the lakeshore were overtaken by the rising water level due to poor maintenance of the water-controlling channels, while some settlements at the edges of the Fayum

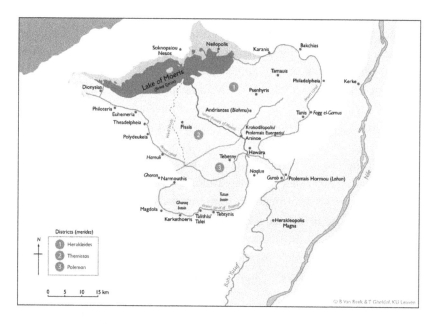

Figure 8.1 Map of the Fayum. Courtesy Fayum Project of Leuven University.

were abandoned. The settlements that continued to exist became gradually Christianized and by the 5th century CE churches and monasteries
were built all over the area. Finally, with the Arab conquest in the 640s,
the region became part of the Arab world.[1] The development of the
Fayum region as a flourishing agricultural area densely settled by people
from different backgrounds is reflected in its well-preserved material
remains and exceptional number of texts on papyrus.

The first travellers and scholars who visited the Fayum in the late 18th
and early 19th century mainly aimed to identify the monuments
described by ancient authors, such as Herodotus.[2] However, by the late
19th century the ancient settlements themselves became a focus of
attention. Digs carried out in this time, both with and without the
permission of the Supreme Council of Antiquities, developed into
real 'papyrus hunts' that hardly paid attention to the context of the finds
and led to the complete pillaging of archaeological sites and their
cemeteries.[3] Thus, the fieldwork carried out by papyrologists B. P.
Grenfell and A. S. Hunt (1895–1900) resulted in the publication of many
papyri, but the houses in which texts and objects were found were only
considered peripherally.[4] In contrast, when O. Rubensohn investigated
Theadelpheia and Tebtynis in 1902, he did record the houses from which
the papyri originated.[5] Between 1908 and 1910 P. Viereck excavated
further houses, for instance at Philadelpheia, but unfortunately these
received only superficial attention in his publications.[6] Meanwhile,
F. Luckard gathered evidence for the first comprehensive study of
Ptolemaic–Roman houses in Egypt.[7]

The distorted picture of the Ptolemaic–Roman Fayum, caused by the
late 19th- to early 20th-century focus on textual evidence, only began to be
remedied from the 1920s onwards. The excavations at Karanis (1924–34)
and Soknopaiou Nesos (1931–32) were a milestone in the archaeology and
papyrology of the region.[8] For the first time, detailed attention was devoted
to houses, while papyri and archaeological objects, as well as botanical and
archaeozoological remains, were recorded in detail.[9] However, frequently
only a selection of texts belonging to the same archive were published,
separately from their archaeological contexts,[10] and at Soknopaiou Nesos
parts of the Roman houses were destroyed in order to reach older,
Ptolemaic levels.[11]

Around the same time, the investigations of A. Vogliano and
G. Bagnani at Narmouthis (1924–39), as well as those of E. Breccia and
C. Anti at Tebtynis (1929–35), paid great attention to papyrus finds, but

also included a topographical and architectural study of the sites.[12] After some important expeditions initiated after the Second World War at Dionysias (1948–50), Karanis (1967–75) and Narmouthis (1966–present),[13] during which several houses were excavated, it was only in the 1980s and especially the 1990s that the need for a combined research of archaeological remains and texts was expressed. The first initiatives were taken by papyrologists and historians, including P. Van Minnen.[14] Similarly, the first systematic surveys in the Fayum in 1995 were initiated by an historian, D. Rathbone, who aimed at an integrated study of material and written sources for the reconstruction of the Graeco-Roman settlement history.[15]

Since then new and renewed interdisciplinary field projects and collaborations, involving archaeologists, philologists, historians, as well as archaeozoologists and palaeobotanists, have significantly increased the available evidence for the Graeco-Roman Fayum and ancient housing in particular. These include excavations and surveys at Narmouthis, Bakchias (Figure 8.2), Soknopaiou Nesos, Tebtynis, Karanis and Hawara,[16] and conferences gathering different researchers.[17] Additionally, site management and long-term planning focusing on the preservation of the cultural heritage of the Fayum has become increasingly important.[18] The recent

Figure 8.2 View on one of the well-preserved large houses at Bakchias. Courtesy Bakchias Project of the Università di Bologna

research on the Fayum sites has produced extensive new material data, as well as large numbers of papyri and ostraca in Greek, Demotic, Hieratic and Coptic,[19] whose find-spots have been meticulously recorded. This has resulted in several new publications, although many texts are still awaiting publication.[20] Older, legacy archaeological and textual data are also being restudied with interesting results.[21]

'Walls' and 'Words' in Housing Studies of the Graeco-Roman Fayum

The availability of well-preserved house remains and abundant textual sources makes the Fayum an interesting locus for ancient housing research. However, the old and new archaeological remains are only a small sample of what originally existed. The destruction of houses already began in antiquity, for instance due to overbuilding by new houses.[22] Moreover, in the 4th century CE a dam breach of an extended irrigation basin in the south-west of the Fayum may have caused the desiccation of the zones supplied by the basin, whereas settlements located around Lake Qarun were flooded as a result of the rise of the lake level.[23] In later times both natural and human processes played a devastating role. The Graeco-Roman settlements at the edges of the Fayum have generally been preserved the best, since they disappeared under the sand quickly after their abandonment and were for a long time located far from zones of intense human activity.[24] However, these well-preserved sites were heavily threatened by the re-extension of the agricultural area and *sebakh* extraction in the 19th century.[25] *Sebakh*, consisting of decayed organic material and mudbrick, was very much sought after to use as a fertilizer.[26] On some of the major Fayum sites, such as Karanis, large sections of the ancient living quarters were entirely destroyed by *sebakh* farmers.[27] Other sites, including Medinet el-Fayum, Theadelpheia and Philadelpheia, were even erased entirely. Many objects and texts produced during *sebakh* digging reached the antiquities market.[28] Archaeological excavations, both legal and illegal, have damaged many housing areas, since they were excavated out of a solely papyrological interest. Some houses that were in the time of their investigation still preserved up to several metres high have now almost entirely disappeared as a result of wind and water erosion, having been left exposed.[29]

The expansion of agricultural lands and industrial areas, underground water-level issues, 'desert tourism' and illegal excavations are all disastrous for the ancient Fayum settlements.[30] Similar natural and human processes pose a danger to the texts which supply information about Graeco-Roman Fayum houses. Particularly, wet and acid conditions caused by a rising water table and the extension of agricultural and industrial areas near the sites are pernicious. Indeed, one of the stimuli to begin or resume excavations in the Fayum in the 1990s was to safeguard papyri and ostraca before they disappeared.[31]

The content of the texts from the Fayum allows us insight into the daily life of 'normal' people, which is generally not available for other areas of the Graeco-Roman world.[32] Papyri frequently include housing data, such as architectural descriptions, geographical indications, dimensions, prices and descriptions of activities that took place in domestic contexts. Moreover, certain texts list the people living together in particular houses. In order to avoid missing valuable information, textual material in all languages and material categories should be taken into account.[33] Several of the aspects of housing mentioned in the papyri, especially those related to architecture, ornamentation, dimensions and use of space, can be directly correlated to the archaeological data and aid in the reconstruction of the appearance, layout and functional arrangement of houses. However, other elements are less easy to match. For instance, a central problem is the correlation between the terminology of rooms used in the papyri and architectural spaces of archaeologically preserved dwellings.[34] With this problem, the houses of the Graeco-Roman Fayum are in line with those of other regions of the Mediterranean, where an exact functional identification of spaces often remains equally tentative.[35] Therefore, the material housing evidence and papyri should be considered complementary source categories that, besides the common information they offer, each reveal additional data about different aspects of the Graeco-Roman dwelling and the related daily life.

As objects themselves, papyri can – to a certain extent – also function as a chronological indicator within their stratigraphic context.[36] However, papyri, especially those belonging to archives, are often found in contexts later than the text suggests, since documents were often kept for generations to prove ownership of properties.[37] Identifications of house owners based on texts found within the houses should equally be approached with caution.[38] In the mid-1990s P. Van Minnen gathered all available archaeological and textual data for one particular house at Karanis, the 'House of Sokrates'.[39] However, rather than precisely informing us about the life and family of one particular house owner, Sokrates, this investigation reflected a range of activities carried out in the house at certain, possibly different, moments of its occupation.[40] A similar study, conducted by A. Verhoogt and R. P. Stephan for the 'Archive of Tiberianus' at Karanis, equally shows that the link between papyri from a domestic context and the house occupants is not always clear.[41] In spite of these limitations and issues the integration of 'walls' and 'words' can largely extend, refine and adjust our picture of various aspects of Graeco-Roman housing, given the supplementary character of the two source categories.

The Broader Picture: Houses and Residential Quarters

Excavations and surveys give us an idea of the general layout of the villages and smaller towns, as well as of the ways residential areas were inserted in the larger settlement fabric.[42] The sites of the Graeco-Roman Fayum were generally characterized by a basic regularity in their layout, combining rigid elements of Greek city planning, introduced by the Ptolemies, with more loosely mapped orthogonal features typical of traditional Egyptian towns. Since different officials seem to have been in charge of the foundation of the early Ptolemaic settlements and pre-existing Egyptian settlements were frequently adapted and enlarged, different schemes were applied, adapting to the local topographical situation. This resulted in unique plans for each settlement,[43] ranging from sites with a strict orthogonality (e.g. Philadelpheia, Narmouthis, Hawara and Bakchias (Figure 8.3))[44] and those whose individual quarters had a differently oriented regular street network (e.g. Tebytnis)[45] to even less regular sites typified by quarters showing various degrees of regularity and housing blocks of different dimensions (e.g. Soknopaiou Nesos (Figure 8.4) Karanis)[46]. In the Roman period the settlements generally became larger and more densely built than before because of population growth.[47]

Although field data give us an idea of the housing blocks, our understanding of their organization within the broader settlement context is often hampered by the damage caused to the settlements. Frequently, the visible surface remains represent different occupation phases. We thus have to focus on smaller sub-areas that have been stratigraphically excavated and offer insight into the development of a particular part of a settlement,[48] including possible sociocultural implications related to, for instance, differences in house dimensions during various occupation phases.

The location of houses in the settlements is also recorded in the papyri, especially in those dealing with real estate, such as sales and marriage contracts. In these documents (parts of) houses and/or building plots are

Figure 8.3 General view on the northern residential quarter of Bakchias. Courtesy Bakchias Project of the Università di Bologna

described in a rather uniform way. Reoccurring elements are the location of the building (village/town and specific quarter), dimensions, the names of the owners and/or inhabitants of houses and plots bordering the property in the north, south, east and west, and the description of adjacent landmarks, such as public buildings and streets.[49] In addition to the archaeological evidence, these data thus give an idea of the way living areas were organized with their different types of buildings/plots and open areas (*psiloi topoi*),[50] how they were defined by the street network and how private houses related to public buildings.[51] Interestingly, in some bilingual documents the information provided in the Greek and Demotic sections differs. For example, in the sales contracts of houses at Soknopaiou Nesos only the Demotic part names the village quarter in which the dwelling was located.[52]

The names of the neighbours of houses/plots make it possible to link different papyri composed at various dates with each other, allowing the reconstruction of larger parts of a site quarter over several generations. Documents mentioning possessions located near easily recognizable urban features, such as temples, are especially helpful for placing a particular house in its settlement context and thus localizing it within a site. The development of a domestic quarter can, for instance, be followed in the

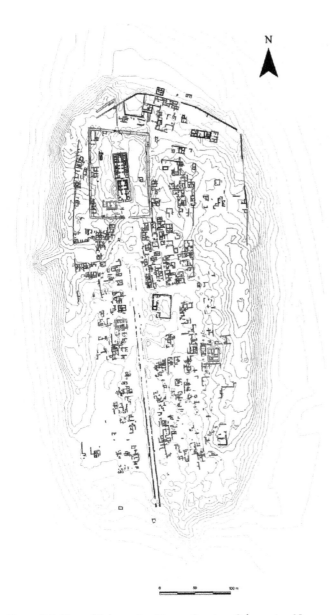

Figure 8.4 Plan of Soknopaiou Nesos. Courtesy Soknopaiou Nesos
Project of the Università del Salento.

papyri of the 'Hawara Undertakers Archives' that deal with 'House A'
(Figure 8.5): in the course of the 3rd century BCE it was surrounded by
different plots and constructions belonging to undertakers' families. The
papyri thus also inform us about the social organization of this living area,
as it was inhabited by members of the same professional group.[53]

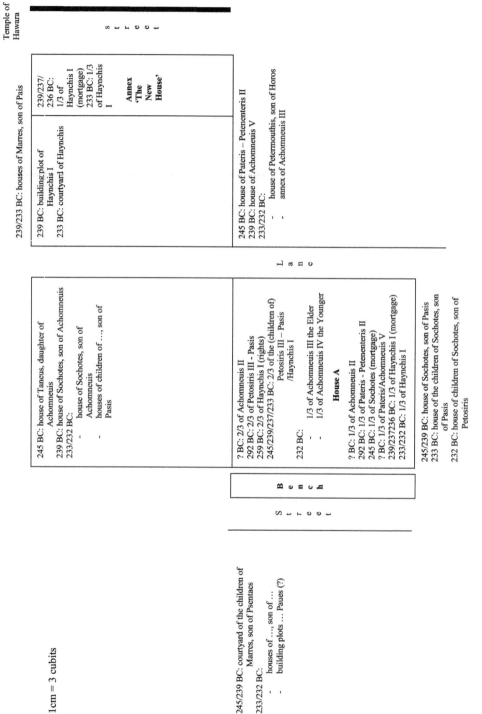

Figure 8.5 Reconstruction of 'House A' and its neighbours at Ptolemaic Hawara (292–232 BCE). Author.

Architectural Features of Graeco-Roman Fayum Houses

In general, Fayum houses seem to have remained rather uniform between the early Hellenistic and late Roman periods regarding their ground plans, construction materials and elevations, although variations existed, for instance, when houses were rebuilt throughout their occupation history to meet the needs of their inhabitants.[54] This makes dating house remains extremely difficult, if not impossible, without a well-dated stratigraphic context.

Davoli has distinguished three main categories of Ptolemaic–Roman houses. Alongside houses with a square or almost square plans, of which 'tower-houses' formed a separate sub-category, rectangular houses (proportion 1:3 or 1:4) occurred, as well as L-shaped or irregular ones. The last, less frequently attested, group enclosed the most lavish and complex houses[55]. Davoli's general typology is complemented with the more specific classification composed by Hadji-Minaglou for Tebtynis, who considers 'tower-houses' and peristyle dwellings separately, while classifying all other houses on the basis of the number of rooms, which ranged from two to four. Houses with three rooms were most common and normally had a courtyard at the back, as well as a long corridor with a staircase.[56] A closer look at the types and features of the houses shows that the variations in their elaboratation may reflect socio-economic and cultural differences between their occupants.

Both archaeological and textual evidence attest to a broad range of house dimensions,[57] which may, at least sometimes, have been defined by the status and wealth of the house owner. The limited number of spaces in most of the houses suggests that these could be the scene of a range of activities carried out by different groups of occupants in the course of the day,[58] and that outdoor activities may have played an important role in the daily life of the Fayum inhabitants.[59] In addition to the ground floor, many Fayum houses had an underground level and one or more storeys.[60] Especially during the Roman period this 'vertical' construction may have been the result of increasing habitation density,[61] bringing members of different households together under one roof. Houses of square or rectangular plan were provided with cellars at the underground level.[62] Upper floors are still recognizable in houses that are (or were at the time of their excavation) still standing up to their flat-roofed upper floor levels, or can sometimes be deduced from the presence of staircases. The most common access to the upper floors and the roof was a staircase built around a central pillar, placed either in the corner of a room or in the centre.[63]

The example of the 'tower-houses', known as *pyrgoi* in the papyri, illustrates how texts can help in interpreting field remains. At Soknopaiou Nesos, Bakchias and Tebtynis, houses provided with exceptionally thick walls and partly preserved upper floors have been identified as *pyrgoi*, since the thickness of the walls suggests that they could carry a large number of floors.[64] The frequent papyrological attestation of *pyrgoi* indicates that they were a regularly occurring house type, thus adjusting our picture based on the limited archaeological data; some houses were even provided with two towers (*oikiai dipurgiai*).[65] Furthermore, in the upper storeys of the houses dovecotes could be built, which, alternatively, could also take a tower-like shape on top of the roof. Since the upper part of the houses has exceptionally been preserved, only a limited number of examples are known (e.g. at Karanis), but pigeon breeding in Egypt is attested by several ancient authors, while dovecotes and taxes paid for them are also frequently mentioned in the papyri. Typically, these 'pigeon houses' consisted of pots placed horizontally in the mudbrick walls. The body part of the pot functioned as nesting place, which could be accessed via the opening. Under the pots two or three rows of niches, possibly for young birds, were inserted in the walls.[66] Given the dimensions of these constructions, with up to at least 1,000 pots, the pigeons must have been raised for commercial reasons and their dung used as manure on the fields, thus playing an economic role for the house.[67] Here again, the material evidence gains an extra dimension and clearer meaning when combined with the papyrological data.

Internal circulation within the houses was rather limited, especially in houses composed of few rooms, and controlled via a single entrance door, which was located above street level and accessed by a stone staircase.[68] Sometimes the entrance door was located on the first floor,[69] a common type of access in tower-houses.[70] The occurrence of higher-located entrance stairs may have been related to the quickly rising floor level in the Fayum settlements, due to wind-blown sand accumulation.[71] As well as doors,[72] the exterior walls had windows, generally located just underneath the roof. These windows typically had small dimensions in order to protect the house against desert sand and heat, but allow enough sunlight and air.[73] In entirely excavated houses the location of the internal doors allows us to understand which spaces were communicating with each other and how people could move from one space (room or courtyard) to another. However, who exactly had access to which spaces is less easily deduced from the available evidence.

The open courtyard, frequently accessed via secondary exits,[74] was well adapted to the Egyptian climate and seems to have been a fixed element of all types of Graeco-Roman Fayum houses.[75] Houses could have one or two open courtyards, which were sometimes bordered by an enclosure wall and frequently shared by neighbours.[76] Presses, mortar stones and ovens attest that the courtyards were used for food processing, while also playing a role for small animal husbandry.[77]

The peristyle house, the typical elite house type in the eastern Mediterranean, characterized by a courtyard enclosed with porticoes,[78] is thus far archaeologically known only through one 1st-century BCE house at Tebtynis.[79] Although this exceptional example reflects a certain influence of the widespread Graeco-Roman peristyle house, most Fayum houses, even those of the well-to-do, seem to have followed the Egyptian tradition of the courtyard house, developed in relation to outdoor household activities, in spite of the presence of many upper-class Greeks and Romans in the region.[80] This is in contrast to other Egyptian areas, including the region of Alexandria and even more remote regions, such as the Dakhla Oasis, where the strong Graeco-Roman influence was reflected in elite peristyle houses with Graeco-Roman decoration types.[81]

Upper-class members apparently chose other typical Graeco-Roman elite features than the peristyle to distinguish their houses from those of lower-ranked people, as attested by large houses with a complex room configuration. One such house is mentioned in a letter belonging to the 3rd-century BCE 'Archive of Zenon', thus attesting correspondence in Ptolemaic elite circles. The house of the sub-manager Diotimos at Philadelpheia was provided with a vestibule and two dining rooms, a seven-couch room and a five-couch one.[82] These rooms are in line with examples of luxurious reception spaces in Hellenistic private contexts elsewhere that were at some moments of the day used to receive male guests at the domestic *symposium*.[83] Large decorated spaces, presumably reception rooms similar to Diotimos' dining halls, in which an elite house owner could receive guests and impress them, are also archaeologically attested, particularly in L-shaped or irregular Fayum houses. These large rooms typically had one open side with two supportive pillars carrying limestone capitals, while the wall curtains were provided with niches, decorated with stone and stucco elements, giving them a more luxurious character than the rest of the house.[84] The entrance area of the houses seems to have been used to display the status of the occupants. Some house

Figure 8.6 Mudbrick wall in the late Roman living quarter of Hawara. Photo by author

owners monumentalized the entrances by means of an elaborate facade and door, often reached via a frontal staircase.[85] The entrance could also acquire a more private character by adding a separate area bordered by a wall in front of the house.[86]

As for building materials, the most used material in Graeco-Roman Fayum houses was unbaked mudbrick, still a widespread construction material in Egypt and the Middle East (Figure 8.6).[87] Fired bricks or stone were only occasionally used, mostly as consolidating elements at the corners of buildings, for stairs or the foundation of mudbrick elevations.[88] On the basis of their dimensions, colour and bonding patterns, mudbricks can be chronologically grouped, since these parameters changed throughout time.[89] Combined with timbering to reinforce the weaker points in the construction,[90] mudbrick was a low-cost, quickly produced, and long-living building material, as long as it was regularly maintained, for instance, by renewing the protective mortar coating. Wood was also used for door and window frames, cupboard niches and stair treads.[91] In addition, for the roofs of houses palm wood beams were used, combined with reed matting and mudbrick.[92]

The floors of the Fayum houses often consisted of stamped soil or a mixture of mud and straw. Fired bricks of clay and covered with plaster, as well as limestone slabs seem to have been more 'luxurious' pavement types.[93] Walls were generally simply plastered and painted. However, sometimes extra decorative elements were added, which increased the lavishness of a room and apparently enhanced the wealth and social prestige of the owner. The L-shaped or irregular houses were particularly characterized by rich stone and painted plaster decoration in the 'Classical Style'.[94] The application of imitation marble plates in the so-called 'Masonry Style', which was very much in vogue in upper-class houses in the Eastern Mediterranean between the 4th and 2nd centuries BCE,[95] had a similar effect. Moreover, as with the elaborate reception spaces, this ornamentation type attests a certain cultural interaction with elites in the rest of the Mediterranean. This is evidenced in houses at Narmouthis[96] and in Diotimos' house at Philadelpheia, which was decorated by Theophilos, a painter from Alexandria.[97] Moreover, these imitation stone panels were sometimes combined with figurative paintings in niches,[98] while entirely figurative paintings with mainly mythological or religious content also appeared.[99] Sometimes movable decorative elements were added, such as framed paintings.[100] A framed portrait of a woman found in the Roman Hawara necropolis may first have hung in a house before being buried with the mummy of the represented dead.[101] Finally, ceilings could also be decorated, as in the dining room of Diotimos' house, which increased the luxurious character of the room.[102] The combination of papyri and archaeological remains thus gives us a clear picture of the way architectural features and the associated decoration were used as tools to express the message of status and power the house owner wanted to communicate to outsiders.

The Inhabitants of the Fayum Houses

Solely on the basis of the material house remains it is difficult to be definitive concerning the number of their inhabitants, their kin or non-kin interrelationship, socio-economic situation and ethnic background.[103] Here the papyri are of a great help, although identifying direct connections between a particular archaeologically preserved house and specific descriptions in the texts is often challenging.[104] Scholars have proposed a range of numbers for house occupancy in Graeco-Roman Egypt, with averages varying between seven and ten people.[105] Important evidence for ancient household compositions is provided by Ptolemaic tax registers, mentioning adult taxpayers,[106] and Roman census returns.[107] However, children, who often remain invisible in the texts, were also part of the household.[108] The textual evidence suggests that a household in ancient Egypt comprised people living together in a housing unit (a house or part of it) and included both kin and non-kin co-residents, being free or slave dependants of the family.[109] Non-kin dependants included people working inside the house (such as slaves and wet nurses), as well as outside (pastoral/agricultural dependants).[110] Some situations may have been rather complex, for instance when a household included fatherless children.[111] Other complicated situations existed when a man lived together with more than one wife and their children or when multiple households shared a single house as a result of sons bringing their wives into the family house after marriage.[112]

The tentative number of people inhabiting a house apparently differed according to the ethnic background of the households. For the 3rd century BCE the difference between Greek (average: 5.0) and Egyptian households (average: 4.0) may express the position in the society of these different ethnic groups. The Greek military settlers, army and veteran families, forming the economically privileged elite of the Egyptian countryside, were living in significantly larger households, composed of more household slaves and dependants.[113] Some of the larger archaeologically preserved Ptolemaic houses may indeed reflect the living patterns of this privileged Greek group that are attested in the written sources.

The papyri suggest that during the Ptolemaic period smaller houses, inhabited by smaller units, were the main house category, while houses and households became larger in the Roman period. This has been interpreted as a result of possible intrinsic population growth and immigration in the Fayum.[114] As mentioned above, this difference is not clearly visible in the material remains, which point instead to a continuity in house plans and types throughout the Hellenistic–Roman period. The papyrological evidence suggests that the number of households sharing a single house in the Fayum villages increased in the Roman period, perhaps indicating an increased density of occupation.[115] However, our understanding is impeded by the fact that houses were often divided among several persons and we do not know whether all owners were also actually all living with their households under the roof of that property. Moreover, since no architectural elements dividing the houses physically into separate units have been archaeologically retraced thus far, sharing houses may have had rather an economic/conceptual than a practical meaning.[116] Owners of part of a building sometimes tried to obtain a larger share.[117] This is, for instance, attested at Ptolemaic Hawara, where Haynchis, a female member of one of the undertaker families, gradually became sole owner of the above-mentioned 'House A' and a related bench.[118] The issue of the inhabitants of the houses and the composition of households is thus an example of how a full integration of textual and material evidence is sometimes not a sinecure and still leaves open several questions concerning Graeco-Roman housing in the Fayum.

Conclusion

Thanks to a growing scientific approach to both archaeological remains and texts in the Fayum during the last century, two exceptionally rich datasets are available for the study of Graeco-Roman housing in the region. Although each source category individually offers important information about house-related topics, the research of different aspects, ranging from the layout, building materials and decoration of the house, to the use of space by its inhabitants and the role of the house as social and cultural marker, has to be based on the combination of archaeological and textual evidence. Even if the textual and material sources sometimes supply rather supplementary than integrative information concerning certain housing aspects, such as the development of households inhabiting the Fayum houses through time, the combination of all available data leads to valuable insights into Graeco-Roman housing that go beyond a picture based on a single source type. One of the aspects that become clear from such a combined study is that, in spite of what might seem, at first sight, rather limited attestations of 'Graeco-Roman' house types in the Fayum, the architecture and decoration of the elite houses and the role lavish representative spaces seem to have played in these houses may have been more in line with 'Graeco-Roman' vogues in the Mediterranean world and ideas of elite self-representation than currently assumed. Together with less elaborate houses following local Egyptian traditions, these upper-class houses clearly reflect the variety and multicultural character of the Graeco-Roman Fayum population and their way of living in the broader context of the Mediterranean.

Notes

* I would like to thank the editors for their comments and additions and Aimee Miles for editing the English.
1 For the topography and general development of the Fayum, cf. Davoli 2001; 2010b; 2011: 70–71; 2012, 152–55; Bagnall and Rathbone 2004: 127–29. The reclamation and resettlement programme of the Ptolemies in the Fayum is

discussed in Müller 2006: 149–51. For the population of the Fayum, see Rathbone 1990; Müller 2011. For the monasteries of the region, see the contributions in Gabra 2005.

2 E.g. the 'Egyptian Labyrinth'; cf. Uytterhoeven and Blom-Böer 2002; Uytterhoeven 2009: 238–40.

3 Particularly W. M. F. Petrie's discovery of mummy masks, portraits and papyri at Hawara and of mummy cartonnages at Ghurob stimulated researchers to explore Fayum sites. For the first exploration of the Fayum, cf. Davoli 2012: 155–61. For an overview of the history of papyrology in Egypt, cf. Hanson 2001; Cuvigny 2009 (esp. 32–38). For the development of papyrology, archaeology and Egyptology; see also Davoli 2008b; 2015b; Bagnall and Davoli 2019. For the archaeological research on Roman Egypt in general; see Davoli 2014.

4 Grenfell and Hunt 1901: 4, 25; Montserrat 1996; Davoli 2001; 2011: 69; Van Minnen 2010: 439–40;. For an overview of the discovery of the 'Fayum Papyri', see Grenfell et al. 1900: 17–26, with a brief discussion of the architecture and urbanistic features of the Fayum settlements (22–24).

5 Rubensohn 1905. See also Davoli 2012: 158.

6 Viereck and Zucker 1926: 2–7; Viereck 1928: 7–16. See also Davoli 2012: 157–58.

7 Luckhard 1914.

8 Karanis: Boak and Peterson 1931; Boak 1933; Husselman 1979. Soknopaiou Nesos: Boak 1935. See further Van Minnen 1994: 227–29; Cuvigny 2009: 38–39; Davoli 2012: 158; Wilfong 2012.

9 Boak 1933: 87.

10 E.g. the 'Archive of Tiberianus'; see Stephan and Verhoogt 2005. See also Cuvigny 2009: 48; Van Minnen 2010: 463, 465; Nevett 2011: 18–20.

11 Especially in the north-western quarter of the site; see De Maria et al. 2006: 28. For the excavations at Soknopaiou Nesos, see further Boak 1935; De Maria et al. 2006: 34–36.

12 Medinet Madi: Vogliano 1936; 1937; 1938; Begg 2008. Tebtynis: Gallazzi and Hadji-Minaglou 2000: 11–12.

13 Dionysias: Schwartz and Wild 1948: 10–38 ; Bagnall and Rathbone 2004: 139. Karanis: Davoli 2012: 161. Narmouthis: Bresciani et al. 2006; Giammarusti 2006; Bresciani et al. 2010.

14 See also Van Minnen 2010: 443–44; Verhoogt 2012. For Van Minnen's 'house-to-house' enquiries at Karanis, see below. Earlier and contemporaneous initiatives combining textual and material evidence for the study of Ptolemaic–Roman houses in the Fayum include Nowicka 1969; Husson 1983; Maehler 1983; Alston 1997. See also Nevett 2011: 11, 16; Malouta 2012: 295.

15 Kirby and Rathbone 1996: 29; Rathbone 1996; 1997; 2001: 1109. The 'Fayum Survey Project' was first directed by D. Rathbone (1995–98), afterwards by D. Obbink and C. Römer (1999 and 2001) and between 2002 and 2013 solely by

C. Römer. See further Bagnall 2001: 234; Römer *et al.* 2004; Römer 2015. For the survey results from the *Themistou Meris*; see Römer 2019.

16 For an overview of recent archaeological work in the Fayum; see Bagnall and Davoli 2011; Davoli 2012: 161–62. Narmouthis: Bagnall 2001: 234; Bresciani *et al.* 2006; 2010; www.egittologia.unipi.it/pisaegypt. Bakchias: Pernigotti and Capasso 1994; Pernigotti 1999; 2005; 2006; 2007; 2010; Davoli 2003; 2005a; Bagnall 2001: 234; Buzi 2007; 2020a; 2020b. Soknopaiou Nesos: Davoli 2005a ; 2005b ; 2005c ; 2008a; 2010a; De Maria *et al.* 2006; Davoli *et al.* 2010. See also Spencer 2007: 26; 2009: 28–29; 2010: 31; 2012: 26; www.museopapirologico.eu/. Tebtynis: Gallazzi and Hadji-Minaglou 1989; 2000; Bagnall 2001: 234; www .ifao.egnet.net/archeologie/tebtynis. Karanis: Wendrich *et al.* 2006; www .archbase.com/fayum; Wilburn *et al.* 2014. 'Hawara 2000 Survey', carried out as part of the Leuven 'Fayum Project' of W. Clarysse (cf. www.trismegistos.org/fayum): Uytterhoeven 2001; 2007; 2009; Uytterhoeven and Blom-Boër 2002.

17 E.g. Lippert and Schentuleit 2005; 2008; Capasso and Davoli 2006; Barrett 2018. For the relationship between archaeology and papyrology, see further Gagos *et al.* 2005; Manning 2005; Moreland 2006; Davoli 2015b. For Pharaonic Egypt; see Smith 2010.

18 E.g. Karanis: Wendrich *et al.* 2006; Wilburn 2010; www.archbase.com/fayum/project_2008.htm; Barnard *et al.* 2016. Narmouthis: Spencer 2009: 29; 2012: 25; www.egittologia.unipi.it/pisaegypt. Soknopaiou Nesos: Wilburn 2001.

19 For recent papyrus finds, see also Cuvigny 2009: 40. E.g. Tebtynis: Gallazzi 1990; 2000; Di Cerbo 2004; Quenouille 2004; Reiter 2005; Andorlini 2008; Guermeur 2008; Litinas 2008; Van Minnen 2010: 460; Verhoogt 2012: 509–10. Bakchias: Davoli 1997: 211; Capasso 1999. Narmouthis: Bagnall and Davoli 2011: 121. Soknopaiou Nesos: Capasso 2005; 2010; Jördens 2005; Schentuleit and Liedtke 2008; Lippert 2010; Bagnall and Davoli 2011: 117.

20 See also Gallazzi 2012.

21 For instance, the restudy of the pottery excavated at Karanis in the 1930s has made clear that the site was not abandoned in the early 5th century CE, as previously assumed, but in the 7th century CE; see Pollard 1998. For the re-evaluation of papyri at Tebtybis, see Begg 1998.

22 E.g. at Narmouthis: Bagnall and Rathbone 2004: 145; Bresciani *et al.* 2006. Tebtynis: Bagnall and Davoli 2011: 120.

23 See Römer 2013; Barnard *et al.* 2015.

24 Davoli 2012: 155; 2015b: 93.

25 See Davoli 2010b: 354; 2011: 69; 2012: 155; 2015b: 94–105.

26 The destructive interventions of the *sebakhin* on archaeological sites were already a major concern for the late 19th-century scholars. See Davoli 2003: 147; 2005a, 217–18; 224–25; 2008: 107–11; 2010a: 59; 2012: 155–56; Cuvigny 2009: 32–33. Bakchias: Pernigotti 2010: 299–300; Giorgi 2020a: 36. Tebtynis: Gallazzi and Hadji-Minaglou 2000: 9–13. Karanis: Barnard *et al.* 2016: 86.

27 Wilfong 2012: 225.

28 See also Van Minnen 2010: 456; Davoli 2011: 71–72. Kiman Fares: Davoli and Mohammed Ahmed 2006; Davoli 2015b: 91, 93.

29 E.g. at Karanis: www.archbase.com/fayum/project_2009.htm. For issues related to the conservation of mudbrick architecture at Karanis; see Barnard *et al.* 2016. For mudbrick deterioration; see Friesem *et al.* 2011.

30 See also Gallazzi 2012: 276–78; Bagnall and Davoli 2019: 717–18. For issues with the water level at Hawara; see Keatings *et al.* 2007. For desert tourism at Soknopaiou Nesos; see Davoli 2005b, 29; www.museopapirologico.eu/?page_id=1804. For the development of new tourism plans respecting the archaeological sites; see Khalifa and El-Khateeb 2011.

31 Gallazzi 1994: 2000, 106; 2012.

32 See Pudsey, Chapter 9 in this volume, for a study of particular aspects of housing and daily life, viewed from the papyri and archaeology.

33 For the need to involve written evidence in different languages in the research; see Lippert 2010; Vandorpe 2010: 159.

34 Housing terms attested in the papyri have been brought together in Husson 1983.

35 On this issue, see also Speksnijder, Chapter 10 in this volume.

36 See also Van Minnen 1994: 230; Wilfong 2012: 231.

37 E.g. Demotic family archives; see Uytterhoeven 2009. For the formation of papyrus archives; see Vandorpe 1994.

38 For illustrations of this issue taken from Karanis and Kellis, see also Nevett 2011.

39 For these 'house-to-house' enquiries, see Van Minnen 1994; Cuvigny 2009: 48; Van Minnen 2009: 647; 2010.

40 For a critical discussion of Van Minnen's approach Nevett 2011: 18–19.

41 Stephan and Verhoogt 2005; Nevett 2011: 19.

42 As pointed out by Davoli 2011: 70; 88, several Fayum settlements (e.g. Dionysias, Soknopaiou Nesos, Karanis, Philadelpheia) can, based on their complex plan, the presence of a temple, *dromos*, *temenos* and well-developed public and private buildings, rather be considered small towns than villages ('third-rank urban settlements' after *poleis* and *metropoleis* [nome capitals]). For the size and hierarchy of Fayum settlements Müller and Lee 2005; Müller 2006: 96–104 and 187–91. For settlement communities Broux 2016.

43 See also Davoli 1998: 350–51; 2010b, 359; 361; 2011: 81; 89; Müller 2006: 121.

44 The 1:2 proportion of the blocks of 100 m × 50 m forming the basic units of Philadelpheia is in line with other Hellenistic foundations. See also Davoli 1998: 350; 105–106; 2010b, 359–60; 2011: 73; 2012: 163–64; Müller 2006: 116–19; 149. Narmouthis: Giammarusti 2006: 257–58; Van Minnen 2010: 457–58; Davoli 2011: 75; 2012: 165. Hawara: Uytterhoeven 2009: 311–14. Bakchias: Bagnall and Rathbone 2004: 135; Giorgi 2011. For the urban developments of Bakchias; see also Rossetti 2013 and 2017; Giorgi 2020a and 2020b (Northern District with several investigated houses).

45 Gallazzi 1995: 114; Davoli 2011: 75. For the reconstruction of a housing quarter at Tebtynis, see Van Minnen 2010: 458–59.

46 Soknopaiou Nesos: Boak 1935: 14–18; Maehler 1983: 122–23; Davoli 2005b, 32; 2010a : 58; 2011: 74; Davoli *et al.* 2010: 150. For the general urban development of this site; see De Maria *et al.* 2006: 62–73; 80–89. The layout of Karanis was entirely different from all other known plans: in the Roman Period (late 1st to mid-2nd centuries CE) the settlement plan consisted of irregular building plots defined by orthogonal streets, which generally ended in T-junctions. See Husselman 1979: 29–31, 33–48; Alston 1997: 53; Davoli 2010b, 361; 2011: 75; 2012: 165. For the extension of Karanis in the 4th century CE with regularly planned eastern and western sections; see Barnard *et al.* 2015.

47 For instance, at Soknopaiou Nesos Roman houses were inserted in the areas that had previously been left open. For the general evolution during the Roman Period and the example of Soknopaious Nesos, see Davoli 2010b, 363; 2011: 74; 89; 2012: 164–65.

48 See also Davoli 2010b, 358; 2011: 73; 2012. Apart from the older 'large-scale' excavations of well-defined living zones at Karanis and Soknopaiou Nesos, the best-studied residential area is known from Tebtynis. The eighteen houses on the south side of the so-called *dromos* of Tefresudj(ty?) offer a picture of the organization and evolution that the houses of an entire quarter underwent during three stratigraphic phases, between the second half of the 1st century BCE and the mid-1st century CE. See Hadji-Minaglou 2007 and 2008. For preliminary discussions of the houses of Tebtynis; see Hadji-Minaglou 1995; Gallazzi and Hadji-Minaglou 2000: 21, 26, 97. The *dromos* is named after a deity, whose name has been reconstructed on the basis of a Demotic papyrus text.

49 E.g. at Hawara, Talei and Soknopaiou Nesos; see below.

50 See also Husson 1983. For instance, at Soknopaiou Nesos three large empty zones enclosed by rough stone walls, probably related to animal keeping, are visible in the field; see Davoli 2005b: 32; 2010a: 52.

51 See also Alston and Alston 2007: 203; Schentuleit and Liedtke 2008: 220.

52 Therefore, it is extremely important to include also the Demotic sections of this type of document in the study of settlement history. See also Lippert 2010: 434.

53 Uytterhoeven 2009: 326–27. Other examples of reconstructed domestic areas include quarters at Ptolemaic Talei and Roman Soknopaiou Nesos. Talei: Malouta 2010. Soknopaiou Nesos (1st century CE of the settlement's western quarter): Schentuleit and Liedtke 2008: 220–21. For the survey results in the western quarter of Soknopaiou Nesos; see De Maria *et al.* 2006: 73–80.

54 See also Davoli 1998: 354; 2015a: 176.

55 Davoli 1998: 354–55, 358 fig. 163; 2012: 166; 2015a: 176–77. In addition to Davoli's fieldwork, the houses at Bakchias have been studied by Paolucci 2009.

56 Houses with two rooms generally had a staircase in the corner of the building, while houses with four rooms had a staircase in the central south; see Hadji-Minaglou 2007; 2008: 125–26.

57 For instance, at Karanis the house dimensions, based on the ground floors, ranged between less than 40 m² and 200 m², with an average of 70 m²; see Alston 1997: 27–28; Malouta 2012: 295. For a comparison between archaeological and papyrological figures; see Nowicka 1969. See also Hobson 1995: 215.

58 This was, for instance, also the case in Late Classical–Hellenistic houses in Greece and Asia Minor and in Roman houses in Italy; see Nevett 2010: 49; 97–113.

59 For Roman Egypt; see also Boozer 2017: 177–78. Apart from household activities (e.g. cooking), less retraceable activities took place in the house, for instance, of a religious kind. For the house as a place of religious actions; see e.g. Lesko 2008; Abdelwahed 2016; Frankfurter 2016.

60 Alston 1997: 28; Alston and Alston 1997: 208–209; Davoli 1998: 355.

61 See also Marouard 2008: 118.

62 These could either be small barrel-vaulted spaces, accessible via narrow trapdoors, or larger intercommunicating cellar rooms with flat ceilings, entered via larger staircases; see Davoli 1998: 355; 2012: 166.

63 Husson 1983; Davoli 1998: 355; 2012: 166. Karanis: Husselman 1979: 38–39. Philadelpheia: Viereck and Zucker 1926: 6. Archaeological attestations of staircases are complemented with papyrological evidence. For instance, at Hawara stairs are attested for the 3rd century BCE through Demotic (e.g. P.Chic.Haw. 5, 7A and 9; P.Hawara Lüdd. III; P.Chic.Haw. Appendix) and Greek papyri (e.g. SB XVIII 133).

64 Alston 1997: 29–31; Alston and Alston 1997: 209; Davoli 2012: 166; 2015a: 177–79. House II 201 at Soknopaiou Nesos: Boak 1935. The Tebtynis examples (House 2800 and House 2400-III), dating to the second half of the 1st century BCE and Augustan period, seem to have had at least six rooms per floor and were additionally provided with cellars, see Gallazzi 1999: 17; Hadji-Minaglou 2007; 2008: 124–25, 127–28, where she mentions a possible third example for Tebtynis.

65 As is, for instance, attested at Tebtynis: PSI X 1159. For the *pyrgos* and *oikia dipurgia*; see Husson 1983: 248–52.

66 Husselman 1953: 82–84.

67 Husselman 1953; Wilfong 2012: 234–36.

68 Davoli 1998: 355. For instance, entrance doors are attested in Demotic texts from 3rd-century BCE Hawara (e.g. P.Chic.Haw. 5, 7A and 9; P.Hawara Lüdd. III; P.Chic.Haw. Appendix).

69 E.g. at Philadelpheia: Viereck 1928: 9. Narmouthis: Bresciani *et al.* 2006; 2010. Tebtynis: Hadji-Minaglou 2007.

70 Alston 1997: 29–31; Alston and Alston 1997: 209.

71 Marouard 2008: 120.

72 Several examples of well-preserved wooden doors, sometimes including the intact lock system, have been preserved. E.g. at Narmouthis; see Bresciani 2006: 228, 240. For the different known types of doors; see Nowicka 1969: 80–96.

73 Marouard 2008: 122–23; Davoli 2012: 166. E.g. Karanis: Husselman 1979: 44. Philadelpheia: Viereck 1928: 15; Viereck and Zucker 1926: 5. For the various known types of windows; see Nowicka 1969.

74 These exits are known archaeologically and are, for instance, also known from 3rd-century BCE Hawara papyri (P.Chic.Haw. 7A and 9; P.Hawara Lüdd. III; P.Chic.Haw. Appendix).

75 For papyrological attestations of courtyards; see Husson 1983: 45–54.

76 This can be deduced from the house plans, as well as from descriptions in the papyri. E.g. at Karanis; see Husselman 1979: 49.

77 Ovens have, for instance, been excavated at Soknopaiou Nesos in the 1930s, while more examples have recently been detected during survey activities on the same site. See Boak 1933: 8–9; Husselman 1979: 49; De Maria *et al.* 2006: 35; Davoli 2010a, 58, 64, 73. Finds, such as animal bones, plant and seed remains, household utensils and basketry fit within the same framework. See Husselman 1979: 8 for Karanis. For House MM003/I at Narmouthis, whose courtyard was equally provided with facilities for cooking and food processing; see Bresciani *et al.* 2006; 2010. For ovens in Graeco-Roman Egypt; see Depraetere 2002.

78 For the development of the peristyle courtyard as element of palaces and other elite houses in the Hellenistic Greek World, see Nielsen 1999: 81–94; Rumscheid 2010: 122.

79 The Tebtynis house had a courtyard with porticoes at four sides, see Hadji-Minaglou 2007; 2008: 124–26; Davoli 2012: 167.

80 See also Davoli 1998: 355–56; 2011: 82; Uytterhoeven 2006: 89; Marouard, 2008: 118. For Egyptian houses, see further Arnold 2001. For the 'Egyptian identity' of the houses of Graeco-Roman Egypt; see Abdelwahed 2016: 75–101. For the elites of the Ptolemaic and Roman Fayum; see Monson 2013.

81 See also Davoli *et al.* 2010: 359. Alexandria: Rodziewicz 1976; 1984; Majcherek 1995; 2010; 471; Kołataj *et al.* 2007; Pensabene and Gasparini 2019. Marina el-Alamein: Bąkowska-Czerner and Czerner 2019; Daszewski 2019: 3–6. Dakhla Oasis: Kellis and Ismant el-Kharab: Hope 2009; Davoli 2011: 87, 90; Trimithis – Amheida: McFadden 2010; Davoli 2011: 84–85; Boozer 2012; 2014; 2015. For examples of Roman-style mosaics and paintings in Egypt, see Whitehouse 2010. For housing as expression of 'cultural identity', see Boozer 2019: 363–69.

82 P. Cairo Zenon III 59445. See also Vanderborght 1942; Davoli 2015a: 182–83.

83 Reception spaces consisting of multiple rooms are, for instance, known at Hellenistic Priene and Pergamon in Asia Minor, where they took the shape of three-room suites. Priene: Rumscheid 2010: 122, 127. Pergamon: Wulf-Rheidt 2014: 343–44. For the *symposium*; see also Nevett 2010: 43–62.

84 Roman and late Roman examples of this kind of room have been preserved at Theadelpheia, Dionysias and Narmouthis; see Davoli 1998: 221 fig. 136; 233 fig. 112; 2012: 167; 2015a: 179–80; Bresciani 2006: 245–46.

85　Marouard, 2008: 120. E.g. Karanis: Boak 1933; Husselman 1979: plan 12-3, pl. 40-2. Narmouthis: Bresciani 2006: 231; Bresciani *et al.* 2010. Tebtynis: Hadji-Minaglou 2007. The only peristyle dwelling known thus far, at Tebtynis, was also accessed by means of a frontal staircase; see Hadji-Minaglou 2007; 2008: 126.

86　E.g. at Karanis, Street CS52 (3rd century CE); see Marouard, 2008: 119.

87　Davoli 1998: 356; 2011: 81; Uytterhoeven 2009: 158–71, 321. For mudbrick in ancient Egypt and the way individual bricks were combined in various types of bonding patterns (e.g. herringbone pattern), see Spencer 1994; Morgenstein and Redmount 1998. For Mesopotamia, see Oates 1990.

88　Spencer 1979: 133; Davoli 1998: 356. E.g. Karanis: Husselman 1979: 35, 38. Dionysias: Schwartz and Wild 1948: 15, 18. An exceptional house of stone is papyrologically attested at 3rd-century BCE Hawara (SB XVIII 13314); see Uytterhoeven 2009: 321.

89　For instance, differences in the dimensions of mudbricks that can with certainty be dated to the Ptolemaic, Roman and late antique periods based on the stratigraphic context of the buildings or pottery data have been studied at various sites. E.g Tebtynis: Anti 1933. Karanis: Husselman 1979: 9–10, 33. Soknopaiou Nesos: De Maria *et al.* 2006: 38–39. Hawara: Uytterhoeven 2009: 164–68.

90　E.g. Soknopaiou Nesos: Boak 1933: 12. Karanis: cf. Husselman 1979: 34, 37, 40–45. Philadelpheia: cf. Viereck and Zucker 1926: 4. Besides, this construction technique is also mentioned in the papyri. E.g. Hawara: P.Hawara Lüdd. III (233 BCE); P.Hawara Lüdd. IXa (118 BCE).

91　Spencer 1979: 98–100, 130–33; Davoli 2011: 81. For the use of wood in Egypt, see Gale *et al.* 2000.

92　See Davoli 2012: 166. E.g. Karanis: Husselman 1979: 37–38. Soknopaiou Nesos : Boak 1933: 12. Philadelpheia: Spencer 1979: 99. Narmouthis: Bresciani *et al.* 2006: 231; 2010; Bagnall and Davoli 2011: 121.

93　E.g. at Philadelpheia: Viereck 1928, 10; Viereck and Zucker 1926: 4.

94　Davoli 2012: 166–67. For the 'Classical Style', see Bailey 1990.

95　The 'Masonry Style' was also adopted in the West, where it was known as the 'First Pompeian Style'. See Andreou 1989; Mielsch 2001: 21–25.

96　Bresciani 1976: 25ff.; 2001; 2002; Bagnall and Davoli 2011: 121. See further Whitehouse 2010; Davoli 2011: 82.

97　P. Cairo Zenon III 59445. The vestibule and the two dining rooms of Diotimos' house were decorated with imitation marble panels and decorative top mouldings. See also Whitehouse 2010: 1023. For this painter; see Nowicka 1984.

98　E.g. Philadelpheia: Viereck 1928: 15. Theadelpheia: Rubensohn 1905: 5–15; Davoli 2015a: 180–82. See further Whitehouse 2010: 1025–26.

99　As attested at Karanis; see Boak and Peterson 1931 figs. 47–48, 49, 71; Whitehouse 2010: 1026. One *in situ* painting shows a group of standing and seated gods in a mixed 'Egyptian' and 'Graeco-Roman' style. Other paintings include images of Heron, Harpocrates and a sphinx, Isis and Harpocrates and possibly a Mithraic offering scene; see Wilfong 2012: 233–34. For religious paintings, see further Abdelwahed 2016: 47–50.

100 Framed paintings are known from Tebtynis. One painting represents Isis with Harpokrates, and Souchos. From the same house originates a similar but unframed painting of Athena with lance and *aegis* next to a military figure or deity; see Rubensohn 1905; Whitehouse 2010: 1029–30.

101 Uytterhoeven 2009: 196.

102 P. Cairo Zenon III 59445. Whitehouse 2010: 1026 suggests that the ceiling decoration in the house of Diotimos may have consisted of coffering.

103 For houses as a source for 'social history'; see Alston 2007: 373–74.

104 See also Nevett 2011. For houses and contractual arrangements in 1st c. CE Tebtynis, see Langellotti 2020.

105 Bowman 2011: 346–48.

106 For the issues related to the use of these lists for the reconstruction of households, see Clarysse and Thompson 2006: 227–29.

107 See Bagnall and Frier 1994, who have, however, been critiqued by several scholars, including Parkin 2005; Pudsey 2011. For a reconstruction of household structures based on census returns, see Huebner 2013: 38–39.

108 For parents and children in Roman Egypt; see Huebner 2013: 65–91.

109 Clarysse and Thompson 2006: 230, 246–54; Malouta 2012: 296.

110 Clarysse and Thompson 2006: 241, 260–85.

111 Nowak 2016.

112 For marriage and households, see Clarysse and Thompson 2006: 295–300; Huebner 2013: 48–50. For families in Roman Egypt and their 'evolution' at various life stages, see Pudsey 2011.

113 Clarysse and Thompson 2006: 241–46.

114 Clarysse and Thompson 2006: 291–92; Bowman 2011, 335.

115 For the relation between houses and households; see Clarysse and Thompson 2006: 285–93. See also Pudsey, Chapter 9, this volume.

116 Muhs 2008; Nevett 2011: 27–29; Davoli 2012: 167; Huebner 2013: 40; Boozer 2017: 177. For female owners of (parts of) houses; see Hobson 1983 (esp. 314).

117 Hobson 1995: 224.

118 For shared properties at Hawara; see Uytterhoeven 2009: 322–23, 388–90, Muhs 2010.

References

Abdelwahed, Y. E. H. (2016). *Houses in Graeco-Roman Egypt: Arenas for Ritual Activity*. Oxford: Archaeopress Publishing.

Alston, R. (1997). Houses and households in Roman Egypt. In R. Laurence and A. Wallace-Hadrill, eds., *Domestic Space in the Roman World: Pompeii and Beyond*. Portsmouth, RI: Journal of Roman Archaeology, 25–39.

(2007). Some theoretical considerations and a Late Antique house from Roman Egypt. In R. Westgate, N. Fisher and J. Whitley, eds., *Building Communities: House, Settlement and Society in the Aegean and Beyond.* London: British School at Athens Studies 15, 373–78.

Alston, R. and Alston, R. D. (1997). Urbanism and the urban community in Roman Egypt. *Journal of Egyptian Archaeology* 83, 199–216.

Andorlini, I. (2008). Old and new Greek papyri from Tebtunis in the Bancroft Library of Berkeley: work in progress. In S. Lippert and M. Schentuleit, eds., *Graeco-Roman Fayum: Texts and Archaeology. Proceedings of the Third International Fayum Symposion, Freudenstadt, May 29 – June 1, 2007.* Wiesbaden: Harrassowitz, 1–13.

Andreou, A. (1989). *Griechische Wanddekorationen.* (Dissertation, Mainz University, Michelstadt).

Anti, C. (1933). Primi elementi per la cronologia delle costruzioni egiziane in mattoni (Scavi di Tebtunis). *Atti della Societa Italiana per il Progresso delle Scienze* 21(4), 69–73.

Arnold, F. (2001). Houses. In D. B. Redford, ed., *The Oxford Encyclopedia of Ancient Egypt.* New York and Oxford: Oxford University Press, 122–27.

Bagnall, R. (2001). Archaeological work on Hellenistic and Roman Egypt, 1995–2000. *American Journal of Archaeology* 105(2), 227–43.

Bagnall, R. S. and Davoli, P. (2011). Archaeological work on Hellenistic and Roman Egypt, 2000–2009. *American Journal of Archaeology* 115(1), 103–57.

(2019). Papyrology, stratigraphy, and excavation methods. In A. Nodar and S. Torallas Tovar, eds., *Proceedings of the 28th International Congress of Papyrology, Barcelona 2016. Universitat Pompeu Fabra.* Barcelona: Scripta Orientalia 3, 717–24.

Bagnall, R. S. and Frier, B. W. (1994). *The Demography of Roman Egypt.* Cambridge: Cambridge University Press.

Bagnall, R. S. and Rathbone, D. W., eds. (2004). *Egypt from Alexander to the Copts: An Archaeological and Historical Guide.* London: The British Museum Press.

Bailey, D. M. (1990). Classical architecture in Roman Egypt. In M. Henig, ed., *Architecture and Architectural Sculpture in the Roman Empire.* Oxford: Oxford University Committee for Archaeology (Monograph 29), 121–37.

Bąkowska-Czerner, G. and Czerner, R. (2019). Marina el-Alamein, Greco-Roman town in Egypt. In G. Grażyna Bąkowska-Czerner and R. Czerner, eds., *Greco-Roman Cities at the Crossroads of Cultures: The 20th Anniversary of Polish–Egyptian Conservation Mission Marina el-Alamein.* Oxford: Archaeopress, 19–39.

Barnard, H., Wendrich, W. Z., Nigra, B. T., Simpson, B. L. and Cappers, R. T. J. (2015). The fourth-century AD expansion of the Graeco-Roman settlement of Karanis (Kom Aushim) in the Northern Fayum. *Journal of Egyptian Archaeology* 101, 51–67.

Barnard, H., Wendrich, W. Z., Winkels, A., Bos, J. E. M. F., Simpson, B. L. and Cappers, R. T. J. (2016). The preservation of exposed mudbrick architecture in Karanis (Kom Aushim). *Egypt. Journal of Field Archaeology* 41(1), 84–100.

Barrett, C. (2018). *'Better to Dwell in Your Own Small House': Households of Ptolemaic and Roman Egypt in Context. Conference Schedule and Abstracts A.D. White House, Cornell University Friday April 27 – Saturday April 28, 2018.* Ithaca, NY. https://blogs.cornell.edu/householdsincontext.

Begg, D. J. I. (1998). It was wonderful, our return in the darkness with … the baskets of papyri! Papyrus finds at Tebtunis from the Bagnani Archives, 1931–1936. *Bulletin of the American Society of Papyrologists* 35, 185–210.

(2008). Gilbert Bagnani's role in discovering and excavating Medinet Madi. *The 59th Annual Meeting of the American Research Center in Egypt, Grand Hyatt Seattle, Seattle, WA*, April 25, 2008.

Boak, A. E. R. (1933). *Karanis. The Temples, Coin Hoards, Botanical and Zoological Reports. Seasons 1924–31.* Ann Arbor: University of Michigan Press.

(1935). *Soknopaiou Nesos. The University of Michigan Excavations at Dimê in 1931–32.* Ann Arbor: University of Michigan Press.

Boak, A. E. R. and Peterson, E. E. (1931). *Karanis. Topographical and Architectural Report of Excavations during the Seasons 1924–1928.* Ann Arbor: University of Michigan Press.

Boozer, A. L. (2012). Globalizing Mediterranean identities: the overlapping spheres of Egyptian, Greek and Roman worlds at Trimithis. *Journal of Mediterranean Archaeology* 25(2), 219–42.

(2014). Urban change at Late Roman Trimithis (Dakhleh Oasis, Egypt). In E. O'Connell, ed., *Egypt in the First Millennium AD: Perspectives from New Fieldwork.* Leuven: Peeters, 23–42.

(2015). *A Late Romano-Egyptian House in the Dakhla Oasis: Amheida House B2.* Amheida, 2. New York: New York University Press.

(2017). Towards an archaeology of household relationships in Roman Egypt. In S. R Huebner and G. S. Nathan, eds., *Mediterranean Families in Antiquity: Households, Extended Families, and Domestic Space.* Malden, MA: Wiley Blackwell, 174–203.

(2019). Cultural identity: housing and burial practices. In K. Vandorpe, ed., *A Companion to Greco-Roman and Late Antique Egypt.* Oxford: Wiley-Blackwell, 361–79.

Bowman, A. (2011). Ptolemaic and Roman Egypt: Population and settlement. In A. Bowman and A. Wilson, eds., *Settlement, Urbanization, and Population.* Oxford: Oxford University Press, 317–58.

Bresciani, E. (1976). *Rapporto preliminare delle campagne di scavo 1968 e 1969.* Milan: Istituto editoriale Cisalpino-La goliardica.

(2001). Rapporto di scavo sulla missione archeologica a Medinet Madi nel Fayum nell'autunno 2000. Le case della collina. *Egitto e Vicino Oriente* 24, 65–70.

(2002). Preliminary report of the archeological mission at Medinet Madi (Faiyum) and at Khelwa in Autumn 2001, Pisa University, with Messina and Trieste Universities. *Egitto e Vicino Oriente* 25, 155–62.

Bresciani, E., Giammarusti, A., Pintaudi, R. and Silvano, F., eds., (2006). *Medinet Madi: venti anni di esplorazione archeologica 1984–2005*. Pisa.

Bresciani, E., Radwan, A., Giammarusti, A., el-Leithy, H. and Siliotti, A., eds. (2010). *Medinet Madi: Archaeological Guide*. Verona.

Broux, Y. (2016). Detecting settlement communities in Graeco-Roman Egypt. *Bulletin of the American Society of Papyrologists* 53, 295–313.

Buzi, P. (2007). Bakchias tardo-antica: la chiesa del kom sud. *Aegyptus* 87, 377–91.

(2020a). Bakchias in Late Antiquity and the Early Middle Ages. In P. Buzi and E. Giorgi, eds., *The Urban Landscape of Bakchias: A Town of the Fayyūm from the Ptolemaic–Roman Period to Late Antiquity*. Oxford: Archaeopress, 81–96.

(2020b). Bakchias: its rediscovery, its cults. In P. Buzi and E. Giorgi, eds., *The Urban Landscape of Bakchias: A Town of the Fayyūm from the Ptolemaic–Roman Period to Late Antiquity*. Oxford: Archaeopress, 5–17.

Capasso, M. (1999). Sei anni di scavo a Bakchias (1993–1998): Bilancio papirologico. *Papyrologica Lupiensia* 8, 11–26.

(2005). Alcuni papiri figurati magici recentemente trovati a Soknopaiou Nesos. In M. Capasso and P. Davoli, eds., *New Archaeological and Papyrological Researches on the Fayyum. Proceedings of the International Meeting of Egyptology and Papyrology* = Papyrologica Lupiensia 14, 49–66.

(2010). Soknopaiou Nesos 2004–2006. In T. Gagos and. A. Hyatt, eds., *Proceedings of the Twenty-Fifth International Congress of Papyrology, Ann Arbor 2007*. Ann Arbor: American Studies in Papyrology, 105–108.

Capasso, M. and Davoli, P., eds. (2006). *New Archaeological and Papyrological Researches on the Fayum. Papyrologica Lupiensia14*. Lecce.

Clarysse, W. and D. Thompson (2006). *Counting the People in Hellenistic Egypt. Volume II. Historical Studies*. Cambridge: Cambridge University Press.

Cuvigny, H. (2009). The finds of papyri: the archaeology of papyrology. In R. S. Bagnall ed., *The Oxford Handbook of Papyrology*. Oxford: Oxford University Press, 30–58.

Daszewski, W. A. (2019). Greco-Roman cities at the crossroads of cultures – Marina el-Alamein in Egypt. In G. Grażyna Bąkowska-Czerner and R. Czerner, eds., *Greco-Roman Cities at the Crossroads of Cultures: The 20th Anniversary of Polish–Egyptian Conservation Mission Marina el-Alamein*. Oxford: Archaeopress, 1–6.

Davoli, P. (1997). Problemi dell'archeologia dell'Herakleides. *Akten des 21. Internationales Papyrologenkongress, Berlin 1995. Archiv für Papyrusforschung, Beiheft 3*. Leipzig: Schwabe & Co., 204–16.

(1998). *L'archeologia urbana nel Fayum di eta ellenistica e romana*. Napoli: Missioni congiunta delle Università di Bologna e di Lecce in Egitto Monograph 1. Bologna: Generoso Procaccini.

(2001). Aspetti della topografia del Fayum in epoca ellenistica e romana. *Atti del XXII Congresso Internazionale di Papirologia, Firenze 1998 Istituto Papirologico 'G. Vitelli'*. Florence: Istituto Papirologico 'G. Vitelli', 353–59.

(2003). New archaeological evidence from Bakchias (Kom Umm al-Atl, Fayum). In Z. Hawass and L. Pinch Brock, eds., *Egyptology at the Dawn of the Twenty-First Century. Proceedings of the Eighth International Congress of Egyptologists, Cairo, 2000. Volume 1. Archaeology*. Cairo: American University in Cairo Press, 147–53.

(2005a). Examples of town planning in the Fayyum. *Bulletin of the American Society of Papyrologists* 42, 213–34.

(2005b). New excavations at Soknopaiou Nesos: the 2003 season. In S. Lippert and M. Schentuleit, eds., *Tebtynis und Soknopaiu Nesos – Leben im römerzeitlichen Fajum, Akten des Internationalen Symposions vom 11. bis 13. Dezember 2003 in Sommerhausen bei Würzburg*. Wiesbaden: Harrassowitz, 29–39.

(2005c). Soknopaiou Nesos: i nuovi scavi dell'Università di Lecce, risultati e prospettive. In F. Crevatin and G. Tedeschi, eds., *Scrive Leggere Interpretare. Studi di Antichità in onore di Sergio Daris*. Trieste: Università degli Studi di Trieste, 180–97.

(2008a). Nuove risultati delle campagne di scavo 2004–2006 a Soknopaiou Nesos (Egitto). In S. Lippert and M. Schentuleit, eds., *Graeco-Roman Fayum: Texts and Archaeology. Proceedings of the Third International Fayum Symposion, Freudenstadt, May 29 – June 1, 2007*. Wiesbaden: Harrassowitz, 75–92.

(2008b). Papiri, archeologia e storia moderna. *Atene e Roma NS Seconda* 1–2, 100–124.

(2010a). Archaeological research in Roman Soknopaiou Nesos: results and perspectives. In K. Lembke, M. Minas-Nerpel and S. Pfeiffer, eds., *Tradition and Transformation: Egypt under Roman Rule. Proceedings of the International Conference, Hildesheim, Roemer- and Pelizaeus-Museum, 3–6 July 2008*. Culture and History of the Ancient Near East 41. Leiden and Boston: Brill, 53–77.

(2010b). Settlements – distribution, structure, architecture: Graeco-Roman. In A. B. Lloyd, ed., *A Companion to Ancient Egypt*. Malden, MA, Oxford and Chichester: Wiley-Blackwell, 350–69.

(2011). Reflections on urbanism in Graeco-Roman Egypt: a historical and regional perspective. In E. Subías, P. Azara, J. Carruesco, I. Fiz and R. Cuesta, eds., *The Space of the City in Graeco-Roman Egypt. Image and Reality*. Tarragona: Institut Catalá d'Arqueologia Clàssica, 69–92.

(2012). The archaeology of the Fayum. In C. Riggs, ed., *The Oxford Handbook of Roman Egypt*. Oxford: Oxford University Press, 152–70.

(2014). Hellenistic and Roman Egypt, archaeology of. In *Encyclopedia of Global Archaeology* (http://link.springer.com/referenceworkentry/10.1007/978-1-4419-0465-2_1105/fulltext.html).

(2015a). Classical influences on the domestic architecture of the Graeco-Roman Fayyum sites. In A. A. Di Castro, C. A. Hope and B. E. Parr, eds., *Housing and Habitat in the Mediterranean World: Responses to Different Environments. International Archaeology Conference Organised by the Centre for Archaeology and Ancient History, Monash University and the Soprintendenza Archeologica per la Toscana Monash Prato Centre 29th June to 1st July 2011*. Leuven: Bulletin Antieke Beschaving. Supplement 26, 173–84.

(2015b). Papyri, archaeology, and modern history: a contextual study of the beginnings of papyrology and Egyptology. *Bulletin of the American Society of Papyrologists* 52, 87–112.

Davoli, P. and Mohammed Ahmed, N. (2006). On some monuments from Kiman Fares (Medinet el-Fayyum). *Studi di Egittologia e di Papirologia* 3, 81–109.

Davoli, P., Chiesi, I., Occhi, S. and Raimondi, N. (2010). Soknopaiou Nesos Project: the resumption of the archaeological investigation. The settlement and its territory. In T. Gagos and A. Hyatt, eds., *Proceedings of the Twenty-Fifth International Congress of Papyrology, Ann Arbor 2007*: American Studies in Papyrology, 149–64.

De Maria, S., Campagnoli, P., Giorgi, E. and Lepore, G. (2006). Topografia e urbanistica di Soknopaiou Nesos. *Fayyum Studies* 2, 23–90.

Depraetere, D. (2002). A comparative study on the construction and the use of the domestic bread oven in Egypt during the Graeco-Roman and late antique/ early Byzantine period. *MDAI Kairo* 58, 119–56.

Di Cerbo, C. (2004). Neue demotische Texte aus Tebtynis. In F. Hoffmann and A. J. Thiessen, eds., *Res severa verum gaudium. Festschrift für Karl-Theodor Zauzich zum 65. Geburtstag am 8. Juni 2004*. Leuven: Peeters, 109–19.

Frankfurter, D. (2016). The spaces of domestic religion in Late Antique Egypt. *Archiv für Religionsgeschichte* 18–19, 1. (https://doi.org/10.1515/arege-2016-0002.)

Friesem, D., Boaretto, E., Eliyahu-Behar, A. and Shahack-Gross, R. (2011). Degradation of mud brick houses in an arid environment: a geoarchaeological model. *Journal of Archaeological Science* 38, 1135–47.

Gabra, G., ed. (2005). *Christianity and Monasticism in the Fayoum Oasis. Essays from the 2004 International Symposium of the Saint Mark Foundation and the Saint Shenouda the Archimandrite Coptic Society in Honor of Martin Krause*. Cairo: American University in Cairo Press.

Gagos, T., Gates, J. E. and Wilburn, A. T. (2005). Material culture and texts of Graeco-Roman Egypt: creating context, debating meaning. *Bulletin of the American Society of Papyrologists* 42, 171–88.

Gale, R., Gasson, P., Hepper, N. and Killen, G. (2000). Wood. In P. T. Nicholson and I. Shaw, eds., *Ancient Egyptian Materials and Techniques*. Cambridge: Cambridge University Press, 334–71.

Gallazzi, C. (1990). La 'Cantina dei Papiri' di Tebtynis e ciò che essa conteneva. *Zeitschrift für Papyrologie und Epigraphik* 80, 283–8.

   (1994). Trouvera-t-on encore des papyrus en 2042? In A. Bulow-Jacobsen, ed., *Proceedings of the 20th International Congress of Papyrologists*. Copenhagen: Museum Tusculanum Press, 131–35.

   (1995). La ripresa degli scavi a Umm-el-Breigât (Tebtynis) *Acme* 48, 3–24.

   (1999). Further surprises from Tebtynis. *Egyptian Archaeology* 14, 16–17.

   (2000). Nuovi ritrovamenti di papiri ed ostraka: il caso di Tebtynis. In W. Clarysse and H. Verreth, eds., *Papyrus Collections World Wide*. Brussels: Vlaams Kennis-en Cultuurforum, 101–106.

   (2012). Trouvera-t-on encore des papyrus en 2042? In P. Schubert, ed., *Actes du 26e congrès international de papyrologie. Genève, 16–21 août 2010, Recherches et rencontres*. Geneva: Publications de la Faculté des Lettres de l'Université de Genève 30, 275–82.

Gallazzi, C. and Hadji-Minaglou, G.(1989). Fouilles anciennes et nouvelles sur le site de Tebtynis. *Bulletin de l'Institut Française d'Archéologie Orientale* 89, 179–91.

Gallazzi, C. and Hadji-Minaglou, (2000). *Tebtynius I. La reprise des fouilles et le quartier de la chapelle d'Isis-Thermouthis*. Cairo: Institut française d'archéologie orientale.Giammarusti, A. (2006). La citta. In E. Bresciani, A. Giammarusti, R. Pintaudi and F. Silvano, eds., *Medinet Madi. Venti anni di esplorazione archeologica. 1984– 2005*. Pisa: Universita di Pisa, 252– 61.

Giorgi, E. (2011). Riflessioni sull'urbanistica di Bakchias. In P. Buzi, D. Picchi and M. Zecchi, eds., *Aegyptiaca et Coptica. Studi in onore di Sergio Pernigotti*. Oxford: British Archaeological Reports International Series, 183–94.

   (2020a). The genesis and urban development of Bakchias. In P. Buzi and E. Giorgi, eds., *The Urban Landscape of Bakchias: A Town of the Fayyūm from the Ptolemaic–Roman Period to Late Antiquity*. Oxford: Archaeopress, 21–37.

   (2020b). The Northern District. In P. Buzi and E. Giorgi, eds., *The Urban Landscape of Bakchias: A Town of the Fayyūm from the Ptolemaic–Roman Period to Late Antiquity*. Oxford: Archaeopress, 55–64.

Grenfell, B. P. and Hunt, A. S. (1901). C. Graeco-Roman branch. Excavations in the Fayûm. *Egypt Exploration Fund. Archaeological Report 1900–1901*, 4–7.

Grenfell, B. P., Hunt, A. S. and Hogarth, D. G. (1900). *Fayûm Towns and Their Papyri*. London: Egypt Exploration Society, 17–26.

Guermeur, I. (2008). Les nouveaux papyrus hiératiques exhumés sur le site de Tebtynis: un aperçu. In S. Lippert and M. Schentuleit, eds., *Graeco-Roman Fayum: Texts and Archaeology. Proceedings of the Third International Fayum Symposion, Freudenstadt, May 29 – June 1, 2007*. Wiesbaden: Harrassowitz, 113–22.

Hadji-Minaglou, G. (1995). Tebtynis et l'urbanisme gréco-romain dans le Fayoum. *Topoi* 5, 111–18.

(2007). *Les habitations à l'est du temple de Soknebtynis*. Cairo : Fouilles de l'Institut Français d'Archéologie Orientale du Caire 56 – Fouilles franco-italiennes Tebtynis 4.

(2008). L'habitat à Tebtynis à la lumière des fouilles récentes: Ier s. av. –Ier s. apr. J.-C.. In S. Lippert and M. Schentuleit, eds. *Graeco-Roman Fayum: Texts and Archaeology. Proceedings of the Third International Fayum Symposion, Freudenstadt, May 29 – June 1, 2007*. Wiesbaden: Harrassowitz, 123–33.

Hanson, A. E. (2001). Papyrology: minding other people's business. *Transactions of the American Philological Association* 131, 297–313.

Hobson, D. W. (1983). Women as property owners in Roman Egypt. *Transactions of the American Philological Association* 113, 311–21

(1995). House and Household in Roman Egypt. *Yale Classical Studies* 28, 211–29.

Hope, C. (2009). Ismant el-Kharab: an elite Roman Period residence. *Egyptian Archaeology* 34, 20–24.

Huebner, S. R. (2013). *The Family in Roman Egypt: A Comparative Approach to Intergenerational Solidarity and Conflict*. Cambridge: Cambridge University Press.

Husselman, E. M. (1953). The dovecotes of Karanis. *Transactions and Proceedings of the American Philological Association* 84, 81–91.

(1979). *Karanis. Excavations of the University of Michigan in Egypt 1928–1935. Topography and Architecture. A Summary of the Reports of the Director, Enoch E. Peterson*. Kelsey Museum of Archaeology Studies Vol. 5. Ann Arbor : University of Michigan Press.

Husson, G. (1983). *Oikia: le vocabulaire de la maison privée en Egypte d'après les papyrus grecs*. Paris : Université de Paris IV – Paris/Sorbonne – Série 'Papyrologie' 2.

Jördens, A. (2005). Griechische Papyri in Soknopaiu Nesos. In S. Lippert and M. Schentuleit, eds., *Tebtynis und Soknopaiu Nesos – Leben im römerzeitlichen Fajum, Akten des Internationalen Symposions vom 11. bis 13. Dezember 2003 in Sommerhausen bei Würzburg*. Wiesbaden: Harrassowitz, 41–56.

Keatings, K., Tassie, G. J., Flower, R. J., Hassan, F. A., Hamdan, M. A. R., Hughes, M. and Arrowsmith, C. (2007). An examination of groundwater within the Hawara Pyramid, Egypt. *Georchaeology: An International Journal* 22(5), 533–54.

Khalifa, M. A. and El-Khateeb, S. M. (2011). Fayoum Oasis between problems and potentials: towards enhancing ecotourism in Egypt. *URBENVIRON CAIRO 2011. 4th International Congress on Environmental Planning and Management. Green Cities: A Path to Sustainability. December 10–13, 2011*. Cairo: Cairo and El-Gouna, Egypt, 1–16.

Kirby, C. and Rathbone, D. (1996). Kom Talit: the rise and fall of a Greek town in the Faiyum. *Egyptian Archaeology* 8, 29–31.

Kołątaj, W., Majcherek, G. and Parandowska, E. (2007). *Villa of the Birds: The Excavation and Preservation of the Kom al-Dikka Mosaics*. American

Research Center in Egypt Conservation Series 3. Cairo: American University in Cairo Press.

Langellotti, M. (2020). *Village Life in Roman Egypt: Tebtunis in the First Century AD*. Oxford: Oxford University Press.

Lesko, B. S. (2008). Household and domestic religion in ancient Egypt. In J. Bodel and S. M. Olyan, eds., *Household and Family Religion in Antiquity*. Malden, MA, Oxford and Victoria: Wiley-Blackwell, 197–209.

Lippert, S. L. (2010). Seeing the whole picture: why reading Greek texts from Soknopaiou Nesos is not enough. In T. Gagos and A. Hyatt, eds., *Proceedings of the Twenty-Fifth International Congress of Papyrology, Ann Arbor 2007*. American Studies in Papyrology. Ann Arbor: University of Michigan Press, 427–34.

Lippert, S. and Schentuleit, M., eds. (2005). *Tebtynis und Soknopaiu Nesos – Leben im römerzeitlichen Fajum, Akten des Internationalen Symposions vom 11. bis 13. Dezember 2003 in Sommerhausen bei Würzburg*. Wiesbaden: Harrassowitz.

Lippert, S. and Schentuleit, M., (2008). *Graeco-Roman Fayum: Texts and Archaeology. Proceedings of the Third International Fayum Symposion, Freudenstadt, May 29 – June 1, 2007*. Wiesbaden: Harrassowitz.

Litinas, N. (2008). *Tebtynis III. Vessels' Annotations from Tebtynis*. Cairo: Fouilles Franco Italiennes.

Luckhard, F. (1914). *Das Privathaus im ptolemäischen und römischen Ägypten* (PhD dissertation, Giessen).

McFadden, S. (2010). Art on the edge: the Late Roman wall paintings of Amheida, Egypt. In N. Zimmermann, ed., *Antike Malerei zwischen Lokalstil und Zeitstil. Akten des XI. Internationalen Kolloquiums der AIPMA (Association Internationale pour la Peinture Murale Antique) – 13.–17. September 2010 in Ephesos*. Österreichische Akademie der Wissenschaften. Philosophisch-Historische Klasse. Denkschriften 468 / Archäologische Forschungen 23. Vienna, 359–70.

Maehler, H. (1983). Häuser und ihre Bewohner im Fayum in der Kaiserzeit. *Das römisch-byzantinische Ägypten: Akten des internationalen Symposions 26.–30. September 1978 in Trier*. Mainz am Rhein: Aegyptiaca Treverensia 2, 119–37.

Majcherek, G. (1995). Notes on the Alexandrian habitat: Roman and Byzantine houses from Kom el-Dikka. *Topoi* 5, 133–50.

(2010). The Auditoria on Kom el-Dikka: a glimpse of Late Antique education in Alexandria. In G. Traianos, ed., *Proceedings of the Twenty-Fifth International Congress of Papyrology, Ann Arbor 2007*. American Studies in Papyrology. Ann Arbor: University of Michigan Press, 471–84.

Malouta, M. (2010). Texts in context: a methodological case study in the topography of Talei. In G. Traianos, ed., *Proceedings of the Twenty-Fifth International Congress of Papyrology, Ann Arbor 2007*. American Studies in Papyrology. Ann Arbor: University of Michigan Press, 485–92.

(2012). Families, households and children. In C. Riggs ed., *The Oxford Handbook of Roman Egypt*. Oxford: Oxford University Press, 288–304.

Manning, J. G. (2005). Texts, contexts, subtexts and interpretative frameworks: beyond the parochial and toward (dynamic) modelling of the Ptolemaic economy. *Bulletin of the American Society of Papyrologists* 42, 235–56.

Marouard, G. (2008). Rues et habitats dans les villages de la chôra égyptienne à la période gréco-romaine (IIIe s. av.–IVe s. apr. J.-C.): quelques exemples du fayoum (nome arsinoïte). In P. Ballet, N. Dieudonné-Glad and C. Saliou, eds., *La rue dans l'Antiquité. Définition, aménagement et devenir de l'Orient méditerranéen à la Gaule. Actes du Colloque de Poitiers, 7–9 septembre 2006 organisé par l'équipe d'accueil EA 3811 (HeRMA), Université de Poitiers*. Rennes: Presses universitaires de Rennes, 117–28.

Mielsch, H. (2001). *Römische Wandmalerei*. Darmstadt: Wissenschaftliche Buchgesellschaft.

Monson, A. (2013). Greeks in an Egyptian landscape: the Faiyum under Ptolemaic and Roman rule. In H. Beinlich, R. Schulz and A. Wieczorek, eds., *Egypt's Mysterious Book of the Faiyum*. Dettelbach: J.H. Röll Verlag, 89–103.

Montserrat, D. (1996). 'No papyri and no portraits': Hogarth, Grenfell and the first season in the Fayum 1895–6. *Bulletin of the American Society of Papyrologists* 33, 133–76.

Moreland, J. (2006). Archaeology and texts: subservience or enlightenment? *Annual Review of Anthropology* 35, 135–51.

Morgenstein, M. E. and Redmount, C. A. (1998). Mudbrick typology, sources, and sedimentological composition: a case study from Tell el-Muqdam, Egyptian Delta. *Journal of the American Research Centre in Egypt* 35, 129–46.

Muhs, B. (2008). Fraction of houses in Ptolemaic Hawara. In S. Lippert and M. Schentuleit, eds., *Graeco-Roman Fayum: Texts and Archaeology. Proceedings of the Third International Fayum Symposion, Freudenstadt, May 29–June 1, 2007*. Wiesbaden: Harrassowitz, 187–97.

(2010). A Late Ptolemaic grapheion archive in Berkeley. In T. Gagos, ed., *Proceedings of the Twenty-Fifth International Congress of Papyrology*. Ann Arbor, 581–88.

Müller, K. (2006). *Settlements of the Ptolemies: City Foundations and New Settlement in the Hellenistic World*. Studia Hellenistica 43. Leuven, Paris and Dudley, MA: Peeters.

(2011). Past and present population trends in the Fayyum region. in E. Subías, P. Azara, J. Carruesco, I. Fiz and R. Cuesta, eds., *The Space of the City in Graeco-Roman Egypt: Image and Reality*. Tarragona: Institut Catalá d'Arqueologia Clássica, 129–43.

Müller, K. and Lee, W. (2005). From mess to matrix and beyond: estimating the size of settlements in the Ptolemaic Fayum/Egypt. *Journal of Archaeological Science* 32, 59–67.

(2010). *Domestic Space in Classical Antiquity: Key Themes in Ancient History.* Cambridge: Cambridge University Press.

(2011). Family and household, ancient history and archaeology: a case study from Roman Egypt. In B. Rawson, ed., *A Companion to Families in the Greek and Roman World.* Chichester: Wiley-Blackwell, 15–31.

Nielsen, I. (1999). *Hellenistic Palaces: Tradition and Renewal.* Aarhus: Aarhus University Press.

(2016). The fatherless and family structure in Roman Egypt. In D. F. Leão and G. Thür, eds., *Symposion 2015: Vorträge zur griechischen und hellenistischen Rechtsgeschichte (Coimbra, 1.-4. September 2015)*, Österreichische Akademie der Wissenschaften Philosophisch-Historische Klasse Documenta Antiqua – Antike Rechtsgeschichte 25. Vienna: Austrian Academy of Sciences Press, 99–114.

Nowicka, M. (1969). *La maison privee dans l'Egypte ptolémaïque.* Bibliotheca Antiqua 9. Wrocław, Warsaw and Kraków: Zakład Narodowy im Ossolińskich.

(1984). Théophilos, peintre alexandrin, et son activité. In N. Bonacasa and A. di Vita, eds., *Alessandria e il mondo ellenisticoromano: Studi in onore di Achille Adriani*, vol. 2. Rome: Bretschneider, 256–59.

Oates, D. (1990). Innovations in mud-brick: decorative and structural techniques in ancient Mesopotamia. *World Archaeology* 21(3), 388–406.

Paolucci, G. (2009). Edifici privati di Bakchias: studio preliminare. *Fayyum Studies* 3, 35–62.

Parkin, T. G. (2005). The ancient Greek and Roman worlds. In P. Thane, ed., *The Long History of Old Age.* London: Thames and Hudson, 31–69.

Pensabene, P. and E. Gasparini (2019). Houses, architectural orders and *opera sectilia*: some reflections on the society of Cyrenaica and Egypt during the Imperial Period. In G. Grażyna Bąkowska-Czerner and R. Czerner, eds., *Greco-Roman Cities at the Crossroads of Cultures: The 20th Anniversary of Polish–Egyptian Conservation Mission Marina el-Alamein.* Oxford: Archaeopress, 174–93.

Pernigotti, S. (1999). Five seasons at Bakchias. *Egyptian Archaeology* 14, 26–27.

(2005). *Villaggi dell'Egitto antico I: Bakchias.* Piccola Biblioteca di Egittologia 8. Imola: Edizioni La Mandragora.

(2006). *Villaggi dell'Egitto antico II: Soknopaiou Nesos.* Piccola Biblioteca di Egittologia 9. Imola: Edizioni La Mandragora.

(2007). Bakchias 2006: la quindicesima campagna di scavi. *Aegyptus* 87, 369–75.

(2010). Archaeological research in Roman Bakchias: results and perspectives. In K. Lembke, M. Minas-Nerpel and S. Pfeiffer, eds., *Tradition and Transformation: Egypt under Roman Rule. Proceedings of the International Conference, Hildesheim, Roemer- and Pelizaeus-Museum, 3-6 July 2008.* Culture and History of the Ancient Near East 41. Leiden and Boston: Brill, 299–311.

Pernigotti, S. and Capasso, M. (1994). *Bakchias. Una città del deserto egiziano che torna a vivere. La prima campagna di scavo della Missione archeologica delle Università degli Studi di Bologna e di Lecce nel Fayyum*. Naples: Procaccini.

Pollard, N. (1998). The chronology and economic condition of Late Roman Karanis: an archaeological reassessment. *Journal of the American Research Centre in Egypt* 35, 147–62.

Pudsey, A. (2011). Nuptiality and the demographic life cycle of families in Roman Egypt. In C. Holleran and A. Pudsey, eds. *Demography and the Graeco-Roman World: New Insights and Approaches*. Cambridge: Cambridge University Press, 60–98.

Quenouille, N. (2004). Tebtynis im Spiegel neuer griechischer Papyri. In S. Lippert and M. Schentuleit, eds., *Tebtynis und Soknopaiu Nesos – Leben im römerzeitlichen Fajum, Akten des Internationalen Symposions vom 11. bis 13. Dezember 2003 in Sommerhausen bei Würzburg*. Wiesbaden: Harrassowitz, 117–30.

Rathbone, D. (1990). Villages, land and population in Graeco-Roman Egypt. *Proceedings of the Cambridge Philological Society* 36, 103–42.

(1996). Towards a historical topography of the Fayum. In D. M. Bailey, ed., *Archaeological Research in Roman Egypt*. Journal of Roman Archaeology Supplement, Ann Arbor: Journal of Roman Archaeology, 50–56.

(1997). Surface survey and the settlement history of the ancient Fayum. In *Archeologia e papiri nel Fayum. Storia della ricerca, problemi e prospettivi. Atti del convegno internazionale. Siracusa, 24–25 maggio 1996*. Quaderni del Museo del Papiro – Siracusa 8. Syracuse, 7–19.

(2001). Mapping the south-west Fayyum: sites and texts. In *Atti del XXII Congresso Internazionale di Papirologia, Firenze 1998 Istituto Papirologico 'G. Vitelli'*. Florence: Istituto Papirologico 'G. Vitelli', 1109–17.

Reiter, F. (2005). Symposia in Tebtynis. Zu den griechischen Ostraka aus den neuen Grabungen. In S. Lippert and M. Schentuleit, eds., *Tebtynis und Soknopaiu Nesos – Leben im römerzeitlichen Fajum, Akten des Internationalen Symposions vom 11. bis 13. Dezember 2003 in Sommerhausen bei Würzburg*. Wiesbaden: Harrassowitz, 131–40.

Rodziewicz, M. (1976). *La céramique romaine tardive d'Alexandrie*. Alexandrie 1. Varsovie: Éditions scientifiques de Pologne.

(1984). *Les habitations romaines tardives d'Alexandrie: à la lumière des fouilles polonaises à Kôm el-Dikka*. Alexandrie 3. Varsovie: Éditions Scientifiques de Pologne.

Römer, C. (2013). Why did the villages in the Themistou Meris die in the 4th century AD? In C. Arlt and A. Stadler, eds., *Das Fayyum in Hellenismus und Kaiserzeit*. Wiesbaden: Harrassowitz, 169–79.

(2015). Fayum, Ägypten: Das Fayum Survey Projekt. *DAI e-Forschungsberichte* 1, 22–23. (https://publications.dainst.org/journals/index.php/efb/article/view/1686/4595.)

(2019). *The Fayoum Survey Project: The Themistou Meris. Volume A, The Archaeological and Papyrological Survey.* Collectanea hellenistica - KVAB, 8. Leuven and Bristol: Peeters.

Römer, C. E., Brosch, P., el-Muhammad, S., Bailey, D. M. Kirby, C. and Obbink, D. (2004). Philoteris in the Themistou Meris: Report on the archaeological survey carried out as part of the Fayum Survey Project. *Zeitschrift für Papyrologie und Epigraphik* 147, 281–305.

Rossetti, I. (2013). Bakchias alla luce delle ultime scoperte: topografia e urbanistica. *Aegyptus* 93, 189–200.

(2017). Reshaping the urban space: Bakchias in Ptolemaic and Roman times. In S. Garagnani and A. Gaucci, eds. *Knowledge, Analysis and Innovative Methods for the Study and the Dissemination of Ancient Urban Areas – Proceedings of the KAINUA 2017 International Conference in Honour of Professor Giuseppe Sassatelli's 70th Birthday (Bologna, 18–21 April 2017).* Archeologia e Calcolatori 28:2. Bologna, 291–300.

Rubensohn, O. (1905). Aus *griechisch-römischen Häusern* des *Fayum. Jahrbuch des Deutschen Archäologischen Instituts* 20, 1–25.

Rumscheid, F. (2010). Fragen zur bürgerlich-hellenistischen Wohnkultur in Kleinasien. In S. Ladstätter and V. Scheibelreiter, eds., *Städtisches Wohnen im östlichen Mittelmeerraum 4. Jh. v. Chr.–1. Jh. n. Chr. Akten des internationalen Kolloquiums vom 24.–27. Oktober 2007 an der Österreichischen Akademie der Wissenschaften.* Vienna: Verlag der Österreichischen Akademie der Wissenschaften, 119–43.

Schentuleit, M. (2009). Nicht ohne Vormund? Frauen in römerzeitlichen bilinguen Urkunden aus Soknopaiu Nesos. In Eberhard, R., Kockelmann, H., Pfeiffer, S. and Schentuleit, M., eds., *'...vor dem Papyrus sind alle gleich!' Papyrologische Beiträge zu Ehren von Bärbel Kramer (P. Kramer).* Archiv für Papyrusforschung Beiheft 27. Berlin and New York: Walter de Gruyter, 192–212.

Schentuleit, M. and Liedtke, C. (2008). Dime online: eine prosopographische und topographische Datenbank zu Soknopaiu Nesos. In S. Lippert and M. Schentuleit, eds., *Graeco-Roman Fayum: Texts and Archaeology. Proceedings of the Third International Fayum Symposion, Freudenstadt, May 29 – June 1, 2007.* Wiesbaden: Harrassowitz, 217–22.

Schwartz, J. and H. Wild (1948). *Fouilles franco-suisses. Rapports, 1. Qasr-Qarun/Dionysias 1948.* Cairo: Institut Français d'Archéologie Orientale.

Smith, S. T. (2010). A portion of life solidified: understanding Ancient Egypt through the integration of Archaeology and History. *Journal of Egyptian History* 3(1), 159–89.

Spencer, A. J. (1979). *Brick Architecture in Ancient Egypt.* Warminster: Aris and Phillips.

(1994). Mud brick: its decay and detection in Upper and Lower Egypt. In C. Eyre, A. Leahy and L. Montagno Leahy, eds., *The Unbroken Reed. Studies in* the Culture and Heritage of Ancient Egypt in Honour of A.F. Shore. London: The Egypt Exploration Society Occasional Publications 11, 315–20.

Spencer, P. (2007). Digging diary 2006–2007. Egyptian Archaeology 31, 25–29.

(2009). Digging diary 2008. Egyptian Archaeology 34, 27–30.

(2010). Digging diary 2009. Egyptian Archaeology 36, 29–32.

(2012). Digging diary 2011. Egyptian Archaeology 40, 25–28.

Stephan, R. P. and Verhoogt, A. (2005). Text and context in the Archive of Tiberianus (Karanis, Egypt; 2nd century AD). Bulletin of the American Society of Papyrologists 42, 189–201.

Uytterhoeven, I. (2001). Hawara (Fayum): tombs and houses on the surface. A preliminary report of the K. U. Leuven Site Survey. Ricerche di egittologia e di antichità copte 3, 45–83.

(2006). Housing in Late Antiquity: regional perspectives. In L. Lavan, L. Özgenel and A. Sarantis, eds., Housing in Late Antiquity: From Palaces to Shops. LAA Supplementary Series 1. Leiden: Brill, 67–96.

(2007). Hawara in the Graeco-Roman period. In M. Capasso and P. Davoli, eds., New Archaeological and Papyrological Researches on the Fayum. Papyrologica Lupiensia 14. Lecce: Congedo, 314–44.

(2009). Hawara in the Graeco-Roman Period: Life and Death in a Fayum Village. OLA 174. Leuven, Paris and Walpole, MA: Peeters.

Uytterhoeven, I. and Blom-Böer, I. (2002). New light on the Egyptian labyrinth: evidence from a survey at Hawara. Journal of Egyptian Archaeology 88, 111–20.

Vanderborght, E. (1942). La maison de Diotimos, à Philadelphie. Chronique d'Égypte 33, 117–26.

Vandorpe, K. (1994). Museum archaeology or how to reconstruct Pathyris' Archives. In Proceedings of the Vth Congress of Demotists. Pisa, 4th–8th September 1993. Pisa: Egitto e Vicino Oriente 17, 289–300.

(2010). The Ptolemaic Period. In A. B. Lloyd ed., A Companion to Ancient Egypt. Oxford and Chichester: Wiley-Blackwell, 159–79.

Van Minnen, P. (1994). House-to-house enquiries: an interdisciplinary approach to Roman Karanis. Zeitschrift für Papyrologie und Epigraphik 100, 227–51.

(2009). The future of papyrology. In R. S. Bagnall, ed., The Oxford Handbook of Papyrology. Oxford: Oxford University Press, 644–60.

(2010). Archaeology and papyrology: digging and filling holes? In Lembke, K., Minas-Nerpel, M. and Pfeiffer, S., eds., Tradition and Transformation: Egypt under Roman Rule. Proceedings of the International Conference, Hildesheim, Roemer- and Pelizaeus-Museum, 3–6 July 2008. Culture and History of the Ancient Near East 41. Leiden and Boston: Brill, 437–74.

Verhoogt, A. (2012). Papyri in the archaeological record. In C. Riggs, ed., The Oxford Handbook of Roman Egypt. Oxford: Oxford University Press, 507–15.

(2019). Unique sources in an unusual setting. In K. Vandorpe, ed., A Companion to Greco-Roman and Late Antique Egypt. Oxford: Wiley-Blackwell, 1–13.

Viereck, P. (1928). *Philadelphia: die Gründung einer hellenistischen Militärkolonie in Ägypten*. Leipzig: J.C. Hinrichs.

Viereck, P. and Zucker, F. (1926). *Papyri Ostraka und Wachstafeln aus Philadelphia im Fayûm*. Berlin: Weidmannsche Buchhandlung.

Vogliano, A. (1936). *Primo Rapporto degli scavi condotti dalla Missione archeologica d'Egitto della R. Università di Milano nella zona di Madinet Madi. (campagna inverno e primavera 1935 – XIII)*. Milan: Impr. de l'Institut français d'archéologie orientale.

   (1937). *Secondo rapporto degli scavi condotti dalla Missione archeologica d'Egitto della R. Università di Milano nella zona di Madinet Madi (campagna inverno e primavera 1936 – XIV)*. Milan: Impr. de l'Institut français d'archéologie orientale.

   (1938). Rapporto preliminare della IV° campagna di scavo a Medinet Madi. *Annales du Service des Antiquité de l'Egypte* 38, 533–49.

Wendrich, W. Z., Bos, J. E. M. F. and Pansire, K. M. (2006). VR modeling in research, instruction, presentation and cultural heritage management: the case of Karanis (Egypt). In M. Ioannides, D. Arnold, F. Niccolucci and K. Mania, eds., *The 7th International Symposium on Virtual Reality, Archaeology and Cultural Heritage VAST*. Nicosia, 1–6.

Whitehouse, H. (2010). Mosaics and painting in Graeco-Roman Egypt. In A. B. Lloyd, ed., *A Companion to Ancient Egypt*. Oxford: Wiley-Blackwell, 1008–31.

Wilburn, D. (2001). The Spatial Analysis/Geographic Information Systems Initiative. *Kelsey Museum Newsletter*. (http://www.umich.edu/~kelseydb/Publications/fall2001/GIS.html.)

   (2010). Re-mapping Karanis: Geographic Information Systems (GIS) and site analysis. In T. Gagos and A. Hyatt, eds., *Proceedings of the Twenty-Fifth International Congress of Papyrology, Ann Arbor 2007*. American Studies in Papyrology. Ann Arbor: University of Michigan Press, 777–88.

Wilburn, D., Gates-Foster, J. and Cook, R. J. (2014). The Karanis Housing Project: a new approach to an old excavation. In T. G. Wilfong, ed., *Karanis Revealed: Discovering the Past and Present of a Michigan Excavation in Egypt*. Ann Arbor: University of Michigan Press, 157–60.

Wilfong, T.G. (2012). The University of Michigan excavation of Karanis (1924–1935). Images from the Kelsey Museum Photographic Archives. In C. Riggs, ed., *The Oxford Handbook of Roman Egypt*. Oxford: Oxford University Press, 223–43.

Wulf-Rheidt, U. (2014). The Ancient Residential Buildings of Pergamon. In F. Pirson and A. Scholl, eds., *Pergamon. Anadolu'da Hellenistik Bir Başkent – A Hellenistic Capital in Anatolia*. Istanbul: Yapi Kredi Yayilari, 336–51.

9 | Housing and Community

Structures in Houses and Kinship in Roman Tebtynis

APRIL PUDSEY

Familial and social structures across Roman Egypt from the 1st to the 3rd centuries CE were varied and fluid, reflecting a diversity in socio-economic circumstances for Egypt's inhabitants.* Egypt's particular phys-ical and ecological environment played an important role in its inhabitants' living conditions and their social organization; from the fertile villages and towns of the Fayum region around Lake Moeris, to the Hellenized metro-poleis of Oxyrhynchos and Hermopolis Magna and the desert regions of the Thebaid, family and community life operated to some degree in response to ecological, agricultural and economic and cultural change. Greek and Macedonian immigration into the Fayum region in the Hellenistic period had been responsible for large-scale development of land for agriculture and settlement, and by the Roman period the region had become home to a broad mix of populations, with particular villages retaining Egyptian and/or Greek population groups and social structures.[1] It is possible to observe economic, social and cultural change through their influence on architectural elements of housing in Fayum villages over a long period, and to open up avenues to exploring elements of familial and communal life for their inhabitants. A balance of family and community dynamics pivoted around how individuals and families were able to utilize their house or parts of it, through occupation, leasing, sale and inheritance; this is particularly crucial for families in the Fayum villages, for whom their house was a focal point of their standing in their relatively small commu-nity. We observe in the material some crucial considerations of the house in terms of its function, both as a physical place for the family to live and work in within a small community, and in terms of its symbolic function for both the immediate family and that family's ability to engage with members of the local community over generations. Documentary papyri from these villages present a wealth of information in relation to aspects of the house, and archaeological material from the village of Tebtynis introduces an opportunity for us to explore the relationships between considerations of housing which were documented on papyrus, and how they manifested in the architecture of houses, albeit over a more extended life cycle. This chapter will explore relationships between these two types of evidence in relation to physical, cultural, familial, social, economic and symbolic functions of the house.

Archaeological and textual material from the best-documented villages of Karanis, Tebtynis and Soknopaiou Nesos offers us a glimpse into how these considerations played out for specific individuals, families and houses; it reveals the outcomes of practices in which houses morphed in shape and structure along with changing family and household structures, and of social bonds and communal ties being forged, fractured, broken or mended through house ownership, leasing and use.[2] For the inhabitants of Tebtynis, among other Fayum villages, the house featured prominently in concerns about one's familial obligations and privileges, but it also functioned as a primary focus for adjusting the dynamics of one's position within the local community. Sales of house shares are among the most common of objects of sale in the documentary record for these villages, and are integrally connected with the traditional Egyptian system of inheritance and marriage through which women could inherit property and bequeath it. This allowed for continuity in the joint ownership of a house, the focal point for day-to-day life of numerous people living together under the same roof. Together, these documents detail a range of transactions between kin and between non-kin through which we might trace some of the ways in which communal ties could be forged, whether between individuals, families or, for instance, priests, gymnasiarchs and other potentially influential people and groups.

The particularly fluid nature of kinship structures and obligations within the Romano-Egyptian family warrants some attention here, and is nowhere more evident than in the wealth of documentary papyri surviving from the first three centuries CE of the province.[3] Marriage, divorce and inheritance documents detail domestic and other arrangements, and can hint at the range of expectations placed on various family members in respect of their duties towards one another throughout the life cycles of those families; a sizeable proportion of surviving documentation concerns itself with houses and housing, its use, division and transmission between family and household members. As such it is indicative of the ways in which kinship obligations and structures pivoted around considerations of house and home. Such papyrological material reflects a multiplicity of arrangements regarding buying and selling, loans, mortgages and the sharing and bequeathing of not just houses, but sections and shares of them, either to other family members or to non-kin, such as neighbours or socially prominent families.

In Roman Egypt three predominant cultural practices lay at the heart of the relationships between housing and kinship: virilocal marriage (in which a woman would join her new husband's natal home); endogamy (most notably brother–sister marriages, but also connecting branches of families); and partible inheritance allowing women to own, inherit, bequeath and sell property in their own names.[4] It is evident that considerations of house use, ownership and division were a crucial part of kinship to the extent that they influenced marriage and family strategies, and worked to strengthen women's social position, at the same time as valuing the patrilineal line. Previous studies of the papyrological material for families and households, and kinship, in Roman Egypt have explored the division of houses through the recorded sales and leases of house shares, but there is some debate as to whether these shares manifest themselves physically in housing structures; if not, what does that say about familial and non-kin use of domestic space, in both legal divisions and day-to-day practice?[5]

As with other chapters in this volume, the difficulty in reconstructing these historical patterns lies in addressing both the archaeological and documentary material, often contradictory and rarely representative of the same individuals or families, and almost always representing a lifespan of timescales of different orders of magnitude. Whilst architectural remains indicate the changing nature of village house use over time for unspecified individuals, families and neighbours, the documentary papyri record specific events relating to known persons and their houses over much shorter time periods (often fewer than the fourteen years of a census cycle, and typically offering little more than a 'snapshot' in time). This chapter will examine material from the Fayum villages, in particular Tebtynis, to establish the nature of housing's importance in kinship as can be as inferred from behaviours seen in the papyri and on the ground.[6] How did considerations of the ownership and use of space reflect and shape kinship ties and obligations? Is it possible to observe aspects of these interrelations from structures in houses themselves, as well as in papyri?

The Fayum Villages

The Fayum is the primary source of most of our documentary papyri, in particular the Romano-Egyptian household census material which has revealed a great deal about household and family formation and life cycles over the first three centuries CE in the Fayum region.[7] Much of the demographic profile relating to marriage strategies and familial obligations is drawn from this material, but can also be supported by the information contained within marriage and divorce contracts, sale and lease agreements and contracts, and receipts.[8] Using the house as the focal point of family relationships, particularly generational relationships, these papyri can be explored with a view to examining the role of domestic property within kin networks. But how can we make use of archaeological study of houses in Tebtynis and surrounding villages? As is demonstrated by Uytterhoeven,[9] the focus of initial archaeological excavations in the early 20th century was on the papyrological documents rather than on the housing itself, but also we must consider the documents as archaeological artefacts themselves, found in particular contexts.[10]

Archaeological work on the Fayum villages has been ongoing since initial excavations in the early 20th century and has highlighted some interesting aspects of the housing in which families lived, particularly in the well-known village of Karanis.[11] Husselman's original excavations at Karanis presented an important feature of village housing: the practice of house-sharing in which we observe the repeated occurrence of the court-yard shared between two houses.[12] These excavations revealed that houses, though typically relatively small (30 square metres), were multi-storeyed and compact, usually comprising two ground-floor rooms with additional rooms in a second storey, a basement and a courtyard. In a simple comparison with documentary evidence from the site, some aspects of the family's arrangement of the living space in the Karanis houses are reflected in documents that were found there.[13] One example in the well-known Taesion/Taesis archive details a widow sharing one of the multi-roomed houses with her sons and their children, and other houses show shared use of courtyards or passageways between extended families. In the domestic properties at Tebtynis and Soknopaiou Nesos we find similar patterns in these layouts and clear usage patterns, particularly of courtyard spaces.[14]

One of the methodological difficulties here lies in matching the archaeo-logical remnants of individual houses with known families whose archives survive. The scale of analysis of textual material on the one hand, and archaeological on the other, creates problems in establishing change over the life cycles of houses and the families who inhabit them, and while attempts have been made to explore this through detailed examination of individual houses, the sporadically preserved material does not fully allow a systematic approach to the function of the house in this way.[15] At the macro level, systematic studies of the houses across the Fayum have proved fruitful in contextualizing the papyrological material within its archaeological and topographical contexts.[16] Somewhere between these broad macro surveys and micro house-by-house inquiries lies a study of houses in the Fayum towns and villages which takes into account the continued occupation of the house over the family's changing life cycle, and the associated documentary material relating to specific houses and particular social groups and/or large well-documented families. This approach must not fall into the trap of trying, unrealistically, to match up specific houses with specific texts, nor must it take too broad an overview, neglecting elements of change over an individual house's life cycle; where we must aim to look, rather, is through a more abstract approach in our examination of the processes of changes in house use in both social and material terms. As Nevett has argued, it is possible to discern a degree of continuity in house use in which extra walls and rooms were added at various phases of occupation throughout the first three centuries CE.[17] The documentary material indicates that houses changed hands frequently, but in general the archaeology reflects a pattern of change that saw the development of larger rooms and boundary changes as households shared fewer, but larger, spaces. The household census documents from the Fayum region are broadly supportive of this picture. They show that a common stage of the family life cycle involved young adults living in households with a considerable number of other people; this is a direct consequence of the phenomenon of a *frérèche*-type familial arrangement resulting from a marriage pattern in which one or more brother brought his new wife into the household. This typically virilocal marriage pattern of Roman Egypt, combined with ancient sex-specific mortality and fertility regimes, led to these *frérèche* arrangements becoming a common stage of many families' life cycles where married sons and their wives and children lived together in the parental home.[18]

Houses excavated at Tebtynis reflect quite a steady change, relatively speaking, in the nature of occupation from the Ptolemaic period across the first three centuries of Roman rule. Throughout the Ptolemaic period the houses, built on different levels, featured entrances on the north side and the courtyard to the south side, with an entrance to each room being accessible through another; this made for a highly interconnected space within the house in terms of movement of its inhabitants throughout it.[19] Throughout the Roman period, space became more compact, as is evidenced by House 6300 of the Ptolemaic/ Roman period, with its entrance on the north-east side, an open courtyard to the south and entrance patterns for its rooms only through each other. Davoli initially divided the houses at Tebtynis according to a typology of rectangular and L-shaped houses, tower-houses and peristyle houses, each with two, three or four separate spaces along with a courtyard and a connecting staircase. Tower-houses at Soknopaiou Nesos had at least six spaces per floor.[20] More significant is the organization of rooms in the house, hinting perhaps at the rationale behind their arrangement: continuing through the Roman period the main entrance to each house was through a vestibule and a further space, usually on the north side of the house, and a courtyard lay at the south of each house, not at its centre, and had porticoes at four sides.[21] In some houses we see an open courtyard that would have been shared with occupants of adjoining and neighbouring houses in some of its functions.[22]

House 3200 at Tebtynis (Figure 9.1) has a north-east entrance: the main room (to the north-east) serves also as a room and an entrance point and is in fact the single point of entry to the house, with an open courtyard (F) to the south (potentially leading, at some point in the house's history, to direct entry into the house from the street on the south?). Evidence of walls between the main room (to the north-east) and its adjacent room (to the north-west) partially survives and the entrance to each room is, again, through another room. The organization of space and rooms around such separation of the courtyard from the main rooms is of interest in the occupants' use of space; there is a tendency towards shared use of space in the house, but with entrance to the house, and between certain rooms, restricted. This type of access is highly suggestive of a pattern which would suit *frérèche*-type arrangements we see in the household census, with multiple conjugal units living under the same roof.[23]

Many documents on papyrus from the region of Tebtynis reveal the negotiations of the use of space in houses, given that rooms and access to them were not apparently distinct and clear-cut. House and land lease documents from across the Fayum region reflect a pattern of the subdivision of houses as the family life cycle develops and new members enter or leave the household, but with the physical extent of shares being described in detail in the documents.[24] As Nevett has argued in the case of Karanis, the practical aspects of running a household took precedence. Houses were clearly divided up at least nominally through inheritance, but even in the contracts and legal disputes and petitions the actual shares of the house were 'virtual'.[25] More important, from the perspective of those appealing through such documents and procedures, was the day-to-day use of space within the house.

In one document from Tebtynis we see one such interesting aspect of the housing division within a family in which Marepsemis and his sister Tamerres (who acts with her guardian/husband), both in their early

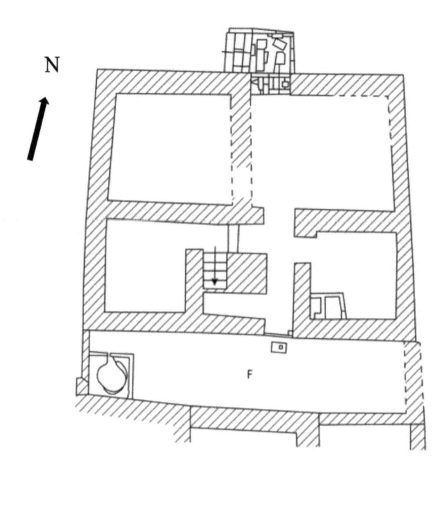

N

0   5m

Figure 9.1 House plan of Tebtynis 3200-III. Redrawn by Lloyd Bosworth after Hadji-Minaglou 2007: fig. 56

thirties, agree to divide up ownership and use of their inherited portions of a house in Tebtynis.[26] The siblings have formally and legally agreed a division which incorporates the house and the vacant space around its walls (all of which they own jointly) and the vacant space in a separate area, and a third-share of a priest's lodgings and its surroundings which they own (it is not stated who owns the other two-thirds). The outlining of the various restrictions and obligations of the ownerships here reflect two important family dynamics: first, that siblings (both male and female) were equally entitled to, and in practice did, inherit, own and trade in house property and house shares; second, that the distribution of, and subjection and access to, these restrictions and obligations can tell us something about sibling relationships and their place within the family and household dynamic. Part way through this agreement we see conditions imposed in an elaborate description of access to the properties, favouring Marepsemis, but which also includes the (current and future) assigns and heirs of each sibling.[27] The priest's lodgings are described as having two storeys which are common and remain undivided physically, but in which Marepsemis only now owns a third-share, while his sister Tamarres is now the owner of the vacant area. The contract details some further specific areas in relation to the roads and entrances and exits of this house and other lodgings close by. Tamarres and her assigns and heirs are explicitly entitled by the terms of this contract to use the entrance and exit on the west of the public road (on the east of the other priests' lodgings). There is a clause imposing a fine of 200 drachmas for any party in violation of the provisions of this contract.[28] Not only has this document made formal the transmission of the family property to these two siblings (in consideration of each of them as individuals), it has also laid explicit claim to the house's function as a means of furthering Tamarres' and her brother's means of acquiring rent, and of maintaining good relations with the priest who is lodging with them; the specifics of the deal take great care in ensuring the arrangement suits all parties and does not inconvenience those wishing to continue living in the property or part of it.

Day-to-day sharing of space and access to various rooms, entrances and courtyard space was a particular concern of this and similar other documents from Tebtynis and Karanis, amongst other villages of the Fayum region; these houses would have been designed and adapted with these considerations in mind. But it is not just day-to-day use of space that is the main concern of the documents. The particular legal position of women in Roman Egypt led to nuanced patterns of house usage, division and transmission; women were entitled to own and inherit property in their own names and so there was a real risk of fragmentation of family property, especially houses.[29] The implication here is that the physical structure and operation of the house, along with negotiation of its ownership and transmission through the family, impacted directly on various aspects of kinship.

Endogamy and Other Marriage Strategies

As noted above, partible inheritance in Roman Egypt was a tradition continued into the Roman period and this had an impact on women's social, legal and financial positions, adding further nuance to ancient marriage and family strategies. In elite families we see, as is often historically the case, the practice of endogamy with the outcome of preserving family property and wealth. But we also see such practices further along the social spectrum within the social groups represented in the Fayum villages; the 'elite' of Tebtynis comprises a set of particular interests which are not necessarily homogeneous.[30]

The prevalence of close-kin, particularly brother–sister, marriage in Roman Egypt has attracted a degree of academic interest in recent years.[31] The focus of this debate is the overwhelming evidence of the practice of the close-kin marriages as a conscious family strategy, in the form of census documents, marriage and divorce agreements, other documentary papyrological material, and in literary references to the practice in Egypt.[32] Both the culture of marriage and family strategies across most sections of the population of Roman Egypt, and the economic benefits of keeping wealth and domestic property within the family, can be shown to support the argument for the widespread and continued phenomenon. Women in Roman Egypt were legally entitled to inherit and own property in their own right, and frequently did so, which meant that marriage posed the very real risk of leading to dotal and inherited property becoming fragmented between families, or down generations of a family, in the absence of strategies to deal with this.[33]

Particular marriage strategies were a common feature of family dynamics in the Graeco-Roman world and we see a number of them play out in Egypt across the periods. We see the betrothal of young women or girls into a new household at certain ages far ahead of their actual marriage age. We also see, at a widespread level, the practice of endogamous marriage arrangements in which close family members are married to one another (notably brothers and sisters), or two branches of a large family being connected by marriage and sharing ownership and habitation of a divided house. Many of these marriage strategies had a wealth of cultural backing behind them and continued through generations of the same family. But often there was an economic logic behind strategies that worked to keep property and money within one family: in Egypt, women were entitled to inherit and own land and property and so it was in the family's interest to keep a daughter connected by marriage to the extended parts of the family into which she was born. These practices can be observed in the demographic census data and inferred from family archives of documentary material and private letters across the social spectrum of families in Roman Egypt. In one family from Tebtynis we see a very clear and incontrovertible description of a half-brother–sister marriage that has preserved the unity of the family house and property.[34]

But it is among the urban milieu of Roman Egypt in the first three centuries CE that we see further concerns come into play in families' marriage strategies. Family dynamics were an integral part of civic life and administration at the local level in the Hellenized metropoleis and the larger towns of Egypt, and families who were part of the urban and often governing elite attached a great deal of significance to preserving, and often improving, their collective social status. Documents from the family archives are helpful in illuminating a variety of considerations taken by women upon marriage, such as whether to marry into a family, or branches of a family, with little actual wealth, but with access to important administrative functions in the cities, or with links to local *gymnasia*. Considerations of the family house and other property often lay at the centre of marital strategies.

These are families whose members have been at various times, according to the documentation, in post with various roles in local government, and owned land. The archive of the descendants of Patron, also from Tebtynis, spans a century and details the activities of a family further up the social scale, and some of the family members were in high office in the administration of the Ptolemais Euergetes – gymnasiarchs, exegetes, *kosmetes* and so on – and owned land across the Fayum. The family is recorded over three generations: Kronion I, his children and his grandchildren (106–153 CE). The house was here a key player in shaping and strengthening both broader kinship patterns and social structures beyond kin. Kronion the Younger, son of Pakebkis, gave rent in kind and in cash for *katoikic* land near Theogonis to former gymnasiarchs.[35] Kronion the elder, son of Pakebkis, leased a parcel of land in 133 CE and extended the lease in 138 CE and 143 CE from Didymos alias Lourios, son of Lysiumachos, grandson of Herakleides alias Lourios. He paid in advance for lease of land and property. One of his five children, Kronion II, and his wife Taorsenouphis divorced after twenty-five years and three children in 138 CE and Kronion I wrote his will a couple of months before this, appointing two sons, Harphaesis and Harmiusis, and a granddaughter, Thephorsais, as heirs. His daughters were to be given a certain amount of cash to complement their share which they already had got as dowry.

Land and money leases show that there were complex relationships between leaser and lessees amongst this gymnasial class. For example Lurius/Apollonius had leases with metropolitan elites (such as Dioskorus) and with villagers (such as Kronion). Endogamous marriages were key to protection of wealth, and status – often status at the expense of some of the family's wealth. Tebtynis was an important and very large village, where administrative roles in local government – and the various privileges that went along with them – were the preserve of elite families who had held office as local scribes for generations, and in which wealthy elite families sought to increase their social standing through connection with those office-holders.[36]

The equal division of property through inheritances (even in intestate cases) between both sons and daughters in Egypt meant that sons' and daughters' right and roles in the transmission of wealth and status through descent were equally important, and more so than those of other members of the extended family. Prevailing virilocal marriage patterns meant that women would enter a new household on marriage, placing elite women in a particularly strong position when it came to their marriage decisions, particularly within the social elite of Tebtynis. For most families in Roman Egypt, marriage alliances were crucial for maintaining the family's wealth – a concern which is met with a preference for endogamous marriages of one sort or another, and house-sharing between branches of the family. For the elite families of large villages like Tebtynis, the crucial element worth protecting through marriage was social status, for which some families would sacrifice a not insignificant amount of their wealth. Social mobility for elite families was an important aspect of maintaining the family's high social standing in the long term, and in the urban elite groups the importance of status within the gymnasial class led more to the sort of endogamous marriages we see in ordinary families elsewhere. Concerns for social status and financial security often lay behind a range of marital strategies; women's rights to own and inherit land equally gave them a lot more say in their marriage decisions, and a great deal of agency in the family's social position. Against this background of maintaining family security and status, the use of property as a means of strengthening kin ties and communal bonds becomes very clear.

Leasing of Houses and House-Sharing

The sharing and leasing of houses, and parts of houses, is common throughout the Fayum region; often these arrangements are between neighbours and non-kin, but the practice of leasing and sharing is also frequently adopted to preserve the property of elite (and often struggling) families and to forge links between branches of families.[37] One contract concerns the two-year lease of a house in the large village of Tebtynis to a metropolite, the son of Phibis, by Heron, of the well-known Patron family, for 80 drachmas per year, which is not an immodest amount in comparison with other house leases in the area.[38] In another agreement we observe the leasing of a dining room from the Philosarapis family to Deios that indicates a long-term agreement, in which back-rent is paid.[39] In this document, Herakleides and his nephew had rented the room to Deios for a period of twenty-eight years, according to various terms contained within the contract; however they require no actual payment until the end of the lease, a very long lease at that. It is clear from this agreement that financial concerns were not the most immediate or pressing. Deios is noted as a member of the local gymnasial class, one of the Hellenized elite group with connections to local government and authority in the town, and so the nature of this arrangement must most likely have been born of concerns to connect the family with individuals in local powerful positions or groups. Whether or not this was a successful pay-off for Herakleides and his family we cannot know from the text, but the trust associated with a twenty-eight-year lease on credit (or, alternatively, a lack of financial necessity) indicates that there was a much more useful outcome anticipated to this agreement than one of a straightforward rental arrangement.

Houses and shares of them were an important aspect of the links between families of the gymnasial class, such as the Patron family, and metropolites and villagers such as the Kronion family. For instance, Kronion's lease on the house costs him twenty-eight drachmas annually and was paid to an ex-gymnasiarch Apollonios, one of the wealthy metropolitan elite well-connected with the Kronion family.[40] The links between metropolitan elite families are complex, and many metropolites appear to have been keen to take leases on houses or shares of them in Tebtynis (not just houses, but also functioning economic concerns such as dining rooms).

In another agreement, likely between brothers, we see Heron requesting of Taarmiusis the lease of half a house along with a yard and a courtyard, for four years at twenty drachmas per year, not a very substantial amount at all.[41] It appears to have been very common in the Fayum region to lease out yards separately or to share them with other houses and households.[42] In another contract it is stated that the owners will not be permitted to use the house themselves, or to lease part of it to other parties, while it is being leased under such an agreement.[43] Areios leased a house from Geminus, Pasis and one other person, and a sum of 152 drachmas was paid in advance for six years, for the house and its courtyard. We know little of these individuals beyond their names (which may indicate their social or ethnic status), but again it is very clear that the property is being rented to members of the Hellenized social groups of the town, who would undoubtedly therefore have been connected with the dominant socio-political orders and institutions, to varying degrees. In cases where we see property divisions (*homologia eksteseos* and *homologia aperispastor*),[44] we frequently find that the lease of shares of the house does not restrict the creditor from use of other parts of the house, and it is far from evident that the rented portion is intended to be used more regularly than for one-off functions or purposes.[45]

Conclusion

As Muhs has argued in the case of Ptolemaic Hawara,[46] many of the documents dealing with division of houses here do not discuss *physically* divided houses, nor does the extant archaeology suggest that the physical structures were divided up in such a way as to separate shares of houses, despite their division between heirs as detailed in the documents. In fact in many of the cases discussed above, the documents, particularly contracts, go to great lengths to specify which areas of the house and which entrances and exits are available to those owning particular shares, and the ways in which access may or may not be restricted to each party to the agreement, suggesting that physical barriers were not in place. It is therefore unsurprising that we do not see such divisions play out in the archaeological remains of houses, irrespective of timescale. Yet we do of course see the gradual shifts, discussed earlier in this chapter, from distinct and small individual houses, to clusters of houses in which courtyards and other sections appear to have been added, adjusted and extended in relation to one another; the trend in a rather fluid and often communal nature of some of these aspects of houses is in keeping with the fluid and communal instances of leasing, sharing and transmission of property that we see in the documentary material on a smaller timescale.

Shared use of some spaces, particularly courtyards, and the leasing of whole houses or shares of houses was a common means of creating or cementing kinship ties and/or other social relationships. One further way of dealing with the subdivision of houses necessitated by partible inheritance was to limit the degree to which such properties were actually fragmented, and one means of accomplishing this was the widespread practice of brother–sister marriage across social groups, and various endogamous arrangements amongst the elite. By arranging inheritance of shares of property between married siblings, fragmentation was avoided.[47] Nevett's argument that the avoidance of fragmentation of houses was key to the household is observable in both the archaeology and the papyri from Tebtynis.[48] One other means, also suggested by Muhs,[49] is by giving daughters a dowry as their inheritance in place of a share in the house.

The house, both as physical entity on the ground and a conceptual and symbolic entity in documentation, was in fact the focal point of many of the family and marriage strategies for families in Roman Egypt, and considerations of its continued ownership within the family was one of the key forces behind already culturally accepted practices, such as endogamous marriage, virilocal marriage and women's ownership of property. The practical and day-to-day aspects of the use of domestic space were evident in the papyri detailing access to parts of the domestic space, something which the archaeological record hints at in the development of houses with additional space in accordance with the developmental life cycles of families; physical divisions or figurative 'white lines' dividing living space between the various conjugal units living in a house were not necessary, as access and shared use was not only negotiated in legal documents, but permitted by the layout and movement through the house.

The material and discussion presented above has raised a number of issues about regionally and socially specific patterns of familial and household structures; practices perhaps peculiar to Egypt, more so even to particular groups within Egypt, impacted on the economic, social and symbolic value of the house. But further questions arise: the village patterns discussed relate to one particular well-documented group of inhabitants of the town of Tebtynis, but how 'elite' and actively connected to local or regional power was this urban elite? Can we consider their patterns of household and kinship behaviours to have been broadly reflective of those of the Hellenized, literary urban elite of, say, Oxyrhynchos? No archaeological material survives for housing in such metropolitan centres, but one cannot escape the fact that the inhabitants of the villages of Roman Egypt, however well-heeled and well-connected, would have faced different circumstances and challenges than those in urban contexts: the practice of, say, endogamy might have been a response to a different set of problems there. Moreover, there is the question of what alternative house and family strategies were available and why particular groups chose endogamy over those alternatives. The answer must surely lie in the desire to privilege household interaction and social interaction over the legality of house use, ownership and division. The archaeological material is here useful in that it demonstrates micro-divisions of space, spatial complexity and overlapping attributions of spaces to architectural units, all of which are also reflected in papyrological documentation of independent letting of sub-spaces within houses. Occupation and use of space was flexible and the use of shared spaces between family members, families and neighbours allowed individuals to move between and share the house and their experience of living in it. These types of studies offer us ways of thinking about and beginning to map the spatial values of particular segments of Romano-Egyptian society, not just within domestic space, but also in relation to community, neighbourhood, and village or city.

Notes

* The author would like to thank Richard Alston, Jen Baird and Micaela Langelotti for their comments on earlier drafts of this chapter, and the participants in the 'Between Words and Walls' conference, Birkbeck (London), for their comments and suggestions.

1 See Monson 2012; Fischer-Bovet 2014. See also Uytterhoeven, Chapter 8 in this volume, for an overview of the Fayum region and its archaeology, with bibliography. For more on the ecological setting of the Nile Delta, see Blouin 2014.

2 For detailed mapping, bibliography and documents lists relating to the Fayum villages, see the digital resources and database of the Trismegistos Fayum Project: www.trismegistos.org/fayum.

3 Pudsey 2011, cf. Huebner 2013. See also Bagnall and Frier 2006.

4 For example, *P. Mich.* VI 370 (189 CE), a census registration document from the village of Karanis in which we see documented a collection of courtyards and shares in houses owned by the women of the family, and transmitted (by sale or inheritance) between them. For discussion of nuptiality and family life cycles in Roman Egypt, see Pudsey 2011. See also Yiftach-Firanko 2003; Huebner 2013; Takahashi, 2021.

5 Cf. Baird, Chapter 13 in this volume, who shows that house divisions do manifest themselves in the walls of houses at Dura. See also Baird 2014. See Alston 1997; Nevett 2011.

6 On Tebtynis' domestic housing, see Gallazzi and Hadji-Minaglou 2000; Hadji-Minaglou 2007; Bagnall and Davoli 2011. See also Uytterhoeven, Chapter 8 in this volume.

7 In particular, the census documentation collated in Bagnall *et al.* 1997 and Bagnall and Frier 2006, and discussed in Pudsey 2011.

8   In particular, see Yiftach-Firanko 2009; Takahashi forthcoming.

9   Uytterhoeven, Chapter 8 in this volume.

10 See especially Vandorpe 2009: 216–55; Bagnall 2011. See also Langellotti 2020 and Langellotti and Rathbone 2020 for more detailed discussion of papyri and village institutions in Tebtynis.

11 Hobson 1985; Rowlandson 1988: 133–39; Nevett 2011.

12 Husselman 1979. See also Boak and Peterson 1931; Alston 1997: esp. 26–32.

13 Rowlandson 1988: 133–39.

14 Boak 1935; De Maria et al. 2006: 34–36; Cuvigny 2009: 38–39; Bagnall and Davoli 2011. Reports and illustrations in Van Minnen 1994; Gallazzi and Hadji-Minaglou 2000; Hadji-Minaglou 2007.

15 Van Minnen 1994. See also Nevett's criticisms, Nevett 2011. See also Baird, Chapter 13 in this volume.

16 Rathbone 1996, 2001. See also Alston 2007: 203; Lippert and Schentuleit 2008: 220.

17 Nevett 2011.

18 See Pudsey 2011, in which the census material is examined with a view to elucidating life cycles through marriage. See also Pudsey 2012; 2013; 2015.

19 Gallazzi and Hadji-Minaglou 2000; Hadji-Minaglou 2007. In house 6300, papyri found in the building itself detail these patterns in usage. See, for example, *P.Cairo. dem.* CG 30612 (97/6 BCE).

20 See Utterhoevern, Chapter 8 in this volume; Alston 1997: 29–31; Davoli 2012: 166. House II 201 in Boak 1935. House 2800 and House 2400-III in Gallazzi 1999: 17; Hadji-Minaglou 2007; 2008: 124–25, 127–28. See also Davoli 1998; 2005; 2008; 2010; 2011.

21 Gallazzi and Hadji-Minaglou 2000; Hadji-Minaglou 2007.

22 See below, discussion of use of such courtyard space in papyrus contract.

23 See Pudsey 2011.

24 Muhs 2008; Nevett 2011: 29, who argues that, in the Fayum village of Karanis, the practical aspects of running a household were more significant than considerations of family.

25 For instance in *P.Tebt.* II 319 (248 CE) in which Marcus Aurelius Herodes and Marcus Aurelius Sarapammon had inherited jointly a house in Kerkeosiris very close to Tebtynis, and here approach the *archdikastes* for division of the land and property. The house is mentioned towards the end of the contract, in which we see that Herodes has already sold his half-share of the house.

26 *P.Tebt.* II 383 (46 CE).

27 ' . . . on the conditions that Marepsemis has obtained for his share the aforesaid third-share of the aforesaid two-storeyed priest's lodging called of which the adjacent areas are on the south another priest's lodging belonging to Marsisouchos son of Marepsemis, on the north and open space and the entrance and exit of the temple, on the west the priest's lodging of son of

Marsisouchos, on the east the priest's lodging of Marres and his partners, while Tamarres has on her side obtained for her share the aforesaid vacant area enclosed with walls, of which the measurements are from south to north 11 cubits, from west to east 5½ cubits, the measurements of the aforesaid vacant area called Achenes' in another parcel being from south to north cubits two palms, from west to east 5½ cubits, and the adjacent areas are for the area surrounded by walls on the south and east the entrance and exit of Marsisouchos son of N.N. and his partners, on the north a royal road, on the west the areas owned by Lusimachos son of Didumos, and for the aforesaid area called Achenes' on the south the areas called after Chousous owned by Psenkebkis son of Pakebkis, on the north the aforesaid entrance and exit into which the aforesaid Tamarres and her assigns and heirs shall open a door from the an entrance and exit leading from, and the said Tamarres and her assigns and heirs shall enter and go out through the exit leading to the north and east, on the west a public road, on the east the house of the aforesaid Marsisouchos son of N.N. Each of the contracting parties therefore and their assigns and heirs shall possess and own the shares which each has received from the present day forever and neither shall proceed against the other on any account in respect of the shares which each of them has received. If either of the contracting parties violates any of the aforesaid provisions, the breaker of the contract shall forfeit to the party abiding by it twice the amount of the damage and expenses and as a fine 200 drachmas of silver, and to the Treasury a like sum, and the contract shall be no less valid. The wife of Marepsemis, Thomsais daughter of Marepsemis, aged about 30, having a scar on her right, with Marepsemis himself as guardian, consents to this division, and neither brings nor will bring any accusation, nor will any representative of hers do so . . .'

28 See also house division of the Tebtynis house in *P.Tebt.* II 533 (between 156 and 161 CE).

29 Property in full is also sold on between men and women. For instance, in *P.Tebt.* II 510 (114/15 CE) Herakleides sells his house to Didyme.

30 See Tacoma 2006. The nature of what we mean by 'elite' in the context of urban life in Roman Egypt is exemplified by the uncertainty over the precise nature of membership of both gymnasial and metropolitan groups in Hellenized metropoleis: Montevecchi 1975; Sijpesteijn 1976; Ruffini 2006; Yiftach-Firanko 2010; Leon 2012.

31 Most recently, and controversially, Huebner 2007; Clarysse and Thompson 2008; Rowlandson and Takahashi 2009.

32 Notably, census data in Bagnall and Frier 2006: 145-Ar-19, 145-Ar-20, 173-Pr-10 (marriages without children); 103-Ar-3, 187-Ar-8, 187-Ar-12, 173-Ar-21, 173-Ar-9, 103-Ar-5, 103-Ar-1, 187-Ar-23, 173-Ar-2, 131-He-4, 173-Pr-5, 117-Ar-1, 131-Ar-3, 187-Ar-22, 159-Ar-26 (marriages with children); 145-Ar-9, 159-Ar-11, 187-Ar-4 (multiple generations of close-kin marriages). Notable divorce agreement: *P. Kron.* 52 = *P.Mil.Vogl.* 85 (138 CE). Notable *epikrisis*

document: *P.Oxy.* XII 1452 (127–28 CE). Notable birth declaration: *P.Oxy.* XXXVIII 2858 (171 CE). Notable literary references: Diodorus I 27, 1–2; Philo *De spec. leg.* 3.22–25; Theocrytus *Idyll* XVII; Athenaeus Deinosophistae 620–21a; Seneca *Apocolocyntosis* 8; Pausanias I VII 1; Sextus Empirius *Outlines of Pyrrhonism* I 152, III 205, III 234; *Gnomon of the Idios Logos* (*BGU* V 1210) 23; Plutarch *Roman Questions* 6.

33 As Rowlandson and Takahashi 2009 argue convincingly, this is the reason why brother–sister marriage is an attractive option, but it is also the case that the cultural background to the phenomenon is important in creating a framework in which the 'incest taboo' is not a barrier to the widespread practice of this marriage strategy.

34 *P. Tebt.* II 351 (2nd century CE) 'Eudaimonis daughter of Apollonios has paid the tax upon the present of a house in the village of Tebtynis given to her by her mother Taorsenouphis daughter of Kronion on her marriage with her brother on the mother's side Kronion son of Harpokrates, 4 drachmas. Written by Alexander son of Hermias.'

35 *P.Mil.Vogl.* II 54 in which Kronion finishes paying off years of arrears on the land.

36 See especially Tacoma 2006: *passim*.

37 See Alston 1997: esp. 35, who argues that 25 per cent of leases of shares of houses were between neighbours. Sales of houses between neighbours may also be evident, for example *SB* XVIII 13792 (2nd century CE).

38 *P.Mil.Vogl.* III 143 (170/1 CE).

39 *P.Fam. Tebt.* 31 (144 CE).

40 *P.Kron.* 53 (114 CE).

41 *P.Lips.* I 16 (138 CE).

42 See Alston 1997: 26–27.

43 *P.Tebt.* II 372 (141 CE). '... to Areios son of Herakleios, greeting. We wish to lease to you for a period of 6 years from the first day of Thoth of the coming 5th year of Antoninus the lord the house and court belonging to us jointly at the village of Tebtynis, with the existing doors and keys, at a total rent for the 6 years of 152 drachmas of silver, which we, the party of Geminus, have received in advance from you, Areios, on condition that Areios shall have the right of domicile whether for himself or others and of [. . .] in the aforesaid house; and we, the party of Geminus, shall not be permitted to lease it to others or to use it ourselves within the stated term; and after its expiration Areios shall deliver to us, the party of Geminus, the house free of all damage with the doors as they stand and the keys. (2nd hand) We, Geminus and Pasis and N.N., have leased to Areios the house and court aforementioned for six years from the day aforementioned, and we have received in advance the hundred fifty two drachmas for the rent of the six years aforementioned, we having no power to sublet or use it ourselves as stated above. I, N.N., have written for them, because they do not know letters. The fourth year (the 4th year) of Imperator Caesar

Titus Aelius Hadrianus Antoninus Augustus Pius, in the month Kaisareios on the 4th of the intercalary days.'

44 Such as *P.Mich.* II 121 v. (42 CE). See also *P.Mich.* XXI 36, VII 41, V 31, XIV 25, XV 16 for sales of house, and for division of houses see *P.Mich.* XIV 23, XII 20, VII 25. Transfer of ownership *P.Mich.* IV 10.

45 See also Hobson 1984: 385.

46 Muhs 2008: 198.

47 Though of course this would not have been the only, nor the most common or preferable, means of achieving this end.

48 Nevett 2011: 27.

49 Muhs 2008: 189.

References

Alston, R. (1997). Houses and households in Roman Egypt. In R. Laurence and A. Wallace-Hadrill, eds., *Domestic Space in the Roman World: Pompeii and Beyond*. Portsmouth, RI: Journal of Roman Archaeology, 25–39.

   (2007). Some theoretical considerations and a Late Antique house from Roman Egypt. In R. Westagate, ed., *Building Communities: House, Settlement and Society in the Aegean and Beyond*. Athens: British School at Athens Studies 15, 373–78.

Bagnall, R. S. (2011). *Everyday Writing in the Graeco-Roman East*. Berkeley: University of California Press.

Bagnall, R. S. and Davoli, P. (2011). Archaeological work on Hellenistic and Roman Egypt, 2000–2009. *American Journal of Archaeology* 115(1), 103–57.

Bagnall, R. S. and Frier, B. W. (2006). *The Demography of Roman Egypt*, 2nd ed. Cambridge: Cambridge University Press.

Bagnall, R. S., Frier, B. W. and Rutherford, I. C. (1997). *The Census Register P.Oxy. 984: The Reverse of Pindar's Paeans*. Papyrologica Bruxellensia 29. Brussels.

Baird, J. A. (2014). *The Inner Lives of Ancient Houses: An Archaeology of Dura Europos*. Oxford: Oxford University Press.

Blouin, K. (2014). *Triangualar Landscapes: Environment, Society, and the State in the Nile Delta under Roman Rule*. Oxford: Oxford University Press.

Boak, A. E. R. (1935). *Soknopaiou Nesos: The University of Michigan Excavations at Dimê in 1931–32*. Ann Arbor: University of Michigan Press.

Boak, A. E. R. and Peterson, E. (1931). *Karanis: Topographical and Architectural Report of Excavations during the Seasons 1924–31*. University of Michigan Humanistic Series, vol. 25

Clarysse, W. and Thompson, P. (2008). *Counting the People in Hellenistic Egypt*. Cambridge: Cambridge University Press.

Cuvigny, H. (2009). The finds of papyri: the archaeology of papyrology. In R. S. Bagnall, ed., *The Oxford Handbook of Papyrology*. Oxford: Oxford University Press, 30–58.

Davoli, P. (1998). *L'archeologia urbana nel Fayum di eta ellenistica e romana.* Naples: Missioni congiunta delle Università di Bologna e di Lecce in Egitto 1.

(2005). New excavations at Soknopaiou Nesos: the 2003 season. In S. Lippert and M. Schentuleit, eds. *Tebtynis und Soknopaiu Nesos: Leben im römerzeitlichen Fajum. Akten des Internationalen Symposions vom 11. Bis 13, Dezember 2003 in Sommerhausen bei Würzburg.*

(2008). Nuove risultati delle campagne di scavo 2004–2006 a Soknopaiou Nesos (Egitto). In S. Lippert and M. Schentuleit, eds., *Graeco-Roman Fayum: Texts and Archaeology. Proceedings of the Third International Fayum Symposion, Freudenstadt, May 29 – June 1, 2007.* Wiesbaden, 75–92.

(2010). Archaeological research in Roman Soknopaiou Nesos: results and perspectives. In K. Lembke, M. Minas-Nerpel and S. Pfeiffer,, eds., *Tradition and Transformation: Egypt under Roman Rule. Proceedings of the International Conference, Hildesheim, Roemer- and Pelizaeus-Museum, 3–6 July 2008.* Leiden and Boston: Culture and History of the Ancient Near East 41, 53–77.

(2011). Reflections on urbanism in Graeco-Roman Egypt: a historical and regional perspective. In E. Subías, P. Azara, J. Carruesco, I. Fiz, and R. Cuesta, eds., *The Space of the City in Graeco-Roman Egypt: Image and Reality.* Tarragona: Institut Catalá d'Arqueologia Clássica, 69–92.

(2012). The archaeology of the Fayum. In C. Riggs, ed., *The Oxford Handbook of Roman Egypt.* Oxford: Oxford University Press, 152–70.

De Maria, S., Campagnoli, P., Giorgi, E. and Lepore, G. (2006). Topografia e urbanistica di Soknopaiou Nesos. *Fayum Studies* 2, 23–90.

Fischer-Bovet, C. (2014). *Army and Society in Ptolemaic Egypt.* Cambridge: Cambridge University Press.

Gallazzi, C. (1999). Further surprises from Tebtynis. *Egyptian Archaeology* 14, 16–17.

Gallazzi, C. and Hadji-Minaglou, G. (2000). *Tebtynius I : La reprise des fouilles et le quartier de la chapelle d'Isis-Thermouthis.* Cairo: Institut française d'archéologie orientale.

Hadji-Minaglou, G. (2007). *Les habitations à l'est du temple de Soknebtynis.* Cairo : Fouilles de l'Institut Français d'Archéologie Orientale du Caire 56 – Fouilles franco-italiennes Tebtynis 4.

Hobson, D. W. (1985). House and household in Roman Egypt. *Yale Classical Studies* 28, 211–29.

Huebner, S. (2007). Brother–sister marriage in Roman Egypt: a curiosity of human-kind or a widespread family strategy? *Journal of Roman Studies* 97, 21–49.

(2013). *The Family in Roman Egypt: A Comparative Approach to Intergenerational Solidarity and Conflict.* Cambridge: Cambridge University Press.

Husselman, E. M. (1979). *Karanis Excavations of the University of Michigan in Egypt 1928–1935: Topography and Architecture. A Summary of the Reports of the Director, Enoch E. Peterson.* Ann Arbor: Kelsey Museum of Archaeology Studies, vol. 5.

Langellotti, M. (2020). *Village Life in Roman Egypt: Tebtunis in the First Century AD.* Oxford: Oxford University Press.

Langellotti. M. and Rathbone, D. W. (2020). Introduction. In M. Langellotti and D. W. Rathbone, eds., *Village Institutions in Egypt in the Roman to Early Arab Periods.* Oxford: Oxford University Press, 1–19.

Leon, D. W. (2012). An *epikrisis* document from Oxyrhynchus (P.Mich. inv. 261). *Bulletin of the American Society of Papyrologists* 49, 95–108.

Lippert, S. L. and Schentuleit, M., eds. (2008). *Tebtynis und Soknopaiu Nesos: Leben im römerzeitlichen Fajum. Akten des Internationalen Symposions vom 11. bis 13. Dezember 2003 in Sommerhausen bei Würzburg.*

Monson, A. (2012). *From the Ptolemies to the Romans: Political and Economic Change in Egypt.* Cambridge: Cambridge University Press.

Montevecchi, O. (1975). L'epikrisis dei Greco-egizi. *Proceedings of the XIV International Congress of Papyrologists,* 227–32. Oxford: Egypt Exploration Society.

Muhs, B. (2008). Fractions of Houses in Ptolemaic Hawara. In S. L. Lippert and M. Schentuleit, eds., *Graeco-Roman Fayum: Texts and Archaeology. Proceedings of the Third International Fayum Symposion, Freudenstadt, May 29 – June 1, 2007,* 187–97. Wiesbaden.

Nevett, L. (2011). Family and household, ancient history and archaeology: a case study from Roman Egypt. In B. Rawson, ed., *A Companion to Families in the Greek and Roman World.* Oxford: Blackwell Companions to the Ancient World, 15–31.

Pudsey, A. (2011). Nuptiality and the life cycles of families in Roman Egypt. In C. Holleran and A. Pudsey, eds., *Demography and Society in the Graeco-Roman Worlds: New Insights and Approaches.* Cambridge: Cambridge University Press, 60–98.

(2012). Death and the family: widows and divorcées in Roman Egypt. In L. Larsson Lovén and M. Harlow, eds., *Families in the Roman and Late Antique Roman Worlds.* London: Continuum, 157–80.

(2013). Children in early Roman Egypt. In J. Evans Grubbs and T. G. Parkin, eds., *Handbook of Children and Education in the Greco-Roman World.* Oxford: Oxford University Press, 484–509.

(2015). Children and the family in late Roman Egypt: everyday life in a monastic context. In C. Laes, K. Mustakallio and V. Vuolanto, eds., *Children and Family in Late Antiquity: Life, Death and Interaction.* Leuven: Peeters, 215–34.

Rathbone, D. W. (1996). Towards a historical topography of the Fayum. In D. M. Bailey, ed., *Archaeological Research in Roman Egypt.* Ann Arbor: Journal of Roman Archaeology Supplement 19, 50–56.

(2001). Mapping the south-west Fayum: sites and texts. *Atti del XXII Congresso Internazionale di Papiriologia, Firenze 1998 Istituto Papirologico 'G. Vitelli'.* Florence, 1109–17.

Rowlandson, J., ed. (1988). *Women and Society in Graeco-Roman Egypt: A Sourcebook.* London: Routledge.

Rowlandson, J. and Takahashi, R. (2009). Brother–sister marriage and inheritance strategies in Graeco-Roman Egypt. *Journal of Roman Studies* 99, 104–39.

Ruffini, G. (2006). Genealogy and the gymnasium. *Bulletin of the American Society of Papyrologists* 43, 71–99.

Sijpesteijn, P. (1976). Some remarks on the Epicrisis of οἱ ἀπὸ γυμνασίου in Oxyrhynchus. *Bulletin of the American Society of Papyrologists* 13, 181–90.

Tacoma, R. (2006). *Fragile Hierarchies: The Urban Elites of Third Century Roman Egypt.* Leiden: Brill.

Takahashi, R. (2021). *The Ties That Bind: The Economic Relationships of Twelve Tebtunis Families in Roman Egypt.* London: Bulletin of the Institute of Classical Studies Supplements.

Vandorpe, K. (2009). Archives and dossiers. In R. S. Bagnall, ed., *Oxford Handbook of Papyrology*, Oxford: Oxford University Press, 216–55.

van Minnen, P. (1994). House-to-house enquiries: an interdisciplinary approach to Roman Karanis. *Zeitschrift für Papyrologie und Epigraphik* 100, 227–51.

Yiftach-Firanko, U. (2003). *Marriage and Marital Agreements: A History of the Greek Marriage Document in Egypt, 4th Century BCE–4th Century CE.* Munich: C. H. Beck Publishing House.

(2010). A gymnasial registration report from Oxyrhycnhos. *Bulletin of the American Society of Papyrologists* 47, 45–66.

10 | The Elusive *vestibulum*

SIMON SPEKSNIJDER

In late Republican and early Imperial literature, we find that houses
(*domus*) at Rome were entered through a *vestibulum*, something which
the 2nd-century author Aulus Gellius defined as a 'vacant place before the
entrance, midway between the door of the house and the street'.[1] In this
chapter, I offer a study of Italic domestic *vestibula* described or built
between *c.* 200 BCE and 200 CE on the basis of both literary and archaeological sources in order to further our understanding of the form and
function of the *vestibulum* and, by extension, Roman elite housing. Even
though we have an abundance of textual evidence, *vestibula* have been
remarkably hard to locate in the archaeological record. We are faced with a
significant mismatch that has not been recognized in previous scholarship
but which stems from a fact that plagues all studies on Roman domestic
space: in general, ancient literary texts offer information on spaces which
differs from what has been preserved archaeologically.

In the first part of this chapter, I provide a set of defining characteristics
of *vestibula* on the basis on the literary sources. This investigation is based
on a word search in the online *Library of Latin Texts*.[2] Using the *Thesaurus
Linguae Graecae*, I also searched for the word *prothuron* in Greek texts, as
this word is used as a synonym for *vestibulum*.[3] Except for metaphorical
vestibula and a few *vestibula* mentioned in epics, we can assume that all
vestibula mentioned were real architectural spaces (that is, not fictional).
Collectively, the literary sources provide coherent information on the form
and function of domestic *vestibula*,[4] but a full analysis of these sources has
been lacking. This has led to misconceptions about the appearance of
vestibula and where they were located relative to the *domus* they belonged
to—misconceptions this chapter seeks to correct.[5]

The archaeological sources are the focus of the second section of the
chapter. On the basis of the defining characteristics found in the written
sources, I review spaces labelled *vestibula* by other scholars and argue that
the word *vestibulum* has all too easily been used as a label for very diverse
sets of material remains.[6] In fact, very few material remains correspond to
the descriptions in the literary sources. In highlighting the persistent
misuse of the label *vestibulum*, this chapter adopts an argument put

forward by several scholars who have critically examined previous studies on Roman housing. Among others, Penelope Allison and Lisa Nevett have argued that both historians and archaeologists have used 'labels' (like *atrium* or *tablinum*) found in Vitruvius and other textual sources uncritically and indiscriminately in order to define the material remains of domestic spaces and the activities that took place within them.[7]

In the second section I also attempt to identify some spaces that seemingly fit the literary characterizations of *vestibula*, an approach condemned by scholars such as Allison.[8] However, such a search is warranted for a number of reasons. Firstly, only literary sources can help us to envisage the physical appearance and uses of domestic *vestibula*; inscriptions offer no help.[9] Secondly, the literary sources offer unambiguous descriptions of *vestibula*, leaving little doubt as to what it is we should look for in the archaeological record.[10] Lastly, it is significant if a space can be identified as a *vestibulum*. As we will see, *vestibula* primarily served as waiting areas for guests who came to the ritualized morning greeting or *salutatio* of the owner of the house, the *dominus*.[11] These guests were, by virtue of the fact that they showed up, tied to the host on the basis of an (often unequal) exchange relationship.[12] In other words, if a *domus* featured a *vestibulum*, this implies that its owner received a fair number of clients in the morning and that he was a high-standing citizen, probably a magistrate. To identify a *vestibulum* archaeologically tells us not only something about the use of Roman domestic space, but also about social relations and hierarchies in the Roman world.

The final section of this chapter is dedicated to the question why we have few archaeological remains that fit the literary descriptions. I propose ways forward in our search for *vestibula* but also for future research on Roman domestic spaces. Since literary sources on the *domus* inform us mostly about Rome yet the material evidence is not from Rome, more care is needed in separating 'Roman' (that which is found at or relates to the city of Rome) from 'non-Roman' evidence.

The Literary Sources

Aulus Gellius and Macrobius provide full descriptions on the appearance and location of *vestibula*, partly relying on a now-lost text by Aelius Gallus, a 1st-century BCE grammarian or jurist.[13] They are primarily interested in the meaning and etymology of the word *vestibulum*, since, according to Gellius, some men in his time were unsure about the meaning of the word (more on this presently). In dozens of other texts, domestic *vestibula* are mentioned only in passing. Far from being 'second-rate' sources, these texts provide valuable information on *vestibula* in their own right.

The textual evidence is skewed towards the *domus* of the senatorial and equestrian elite resident at Rome.[14] The evidence on public buildings certainly suggests that *vestibula*, at least conceptually, were to be found all through the Roman world.[15] Domestic *vestibula* could also be far from Rome. In Apuleius' *Florida* we find that one of the 'nobles' (*proceres*) of Thebes had a house 'graced by a large *vestibulum*' (*domus amplo ornata vestibulo*) while a *prothuron* full of people features in a speech by Dio Chrysostom.[16] These *vestibula* were (imagined to be) in places under Roman rule. Livy also writes about much earlier domestic *vestibula* at Syracusa and Carthage during the Second Punic War and Pliny thought that Chauci had *vestibula* too; in these cases, one cannot escape the idea that Roman ideas on *domus* were projected onto other peoples and times.[17] In this first section, I will also make use of literary sources describing the imperial residences on the Palatine. However 'public' these may have been, they nonetheless fulfilled a domestic purpose, and more importantly, the descriptions of palatial *vestibula* are completely consistent with those of other domestic *vestibula*.

Location

Where was the *vestibulum* located, relative to the *domus* it belonged to? The sources are unanimous in stating that it was outside and in front of the house. Gellius (relying on Aelius Gallus) states:

> The *vestibulum* is not in the house itself, nor is it a part of the house, but is an open place before the door of the house, through which there is approach and access to the house from the street, while on the right and left the door is hemmed in by buildings extended to the street and the door itself is at a distance from the street, separated from it by this vacant space.[18]

Macrobius writes that 'it is agreed that *vestibulum* is the name given to the space which separates a house from the street'.[19] Much earlier, Varro defined a *vestibulum* as a space 'that is before the house' (*vestibulum, quod est ante domum*).[20] In other texts, both in Latin and Greek, we find that the *vestibulum* is explicitly contrasted to the interior of a house or (in Philo) that that the *prothuron* was outside (*exō*) of a house.[21] Elsewhere, *vestibulum* is contrasted with the front door (*ianua*) or threshold (*limen*), or more implicitly with the doorkeepers.[22] A *vestibulum* was thus located before the front door and was never the actual entrance to a *domus*. Also, there is no evidence that a *vestibulum* was a part of the street (or pavement), as these are mentioned in opposition to each other; Macrobius explicitly notes that those in *vestibula* were 'neither standing in the street nor actually within the house'.[23]

The location of the *vestibulum* relative to the *domus* is consistent with what we know of *vestibula* of other buildings.[24] Moreover, it is echoed in the other uses we find for the word in Latin literature. As the *Oxford Latin Dictionary* (second edition) notes, a *vestibulum* could be 'the space in front of the living quarters, natural or artificial, of any creatures'. For instance, beehives, chicken pens and spider's nests had *vestibula*.[25] A *vestibulum* could also be the entrance or approach to any place or region.[26] Lastly, *vestibulum* could be used metaphorically as the entry to a topic or the introduction of a speech.[27]

Cassius Dio reveals something on the location of imperial *vestibula* when he states that Commodus would not even allow those wanting to greet him at his *salutatio* to stand in his *prothuron* (at his winter palace at Nicomedia), so they had to wait outside (*exō*).[28] We should not take this to mean that the *prothuron* was inside, but simply that it was within the palace 'precincts'. Otherwise, there is only Suetonius, who records that Caligula 'extended a part of the palace right into the Forum, taking over the temple of Castor and Pollux as his own *vestibulum*. Often he would stand between the divine brothers displaying himself for worship by those visiting the temple.'[29] This is an anomaly: nowhere else do we find a whole and separate structure functioning as a *vestibulum* for another building. It surely was anomalous to near-contemporaries also, as Suetonius notes this in the part of Caligula's biography that describes him 'as a monster' (*de monstro*).[30]

Gellius implies that the location of domestic *vestibula* changed around, or shortly before, his lifetime (mid-2nd century CE): 'I have observed that some men who are by no means without learning think that the *vestibulum* is the front part of the house, which is commonly known as the *atrium*.' He contrasts his own age, when apparently some could no longer distinguish the *vestibulum* from the *atrium*, with 'early times' (*antiquitus*), when people surely did know the difference.[31] However, Gellius himself still defined its form and function on the basis of the aforementioned Aelius Gallus; other authors writing in the 2nd century also take a *vestibulum/prothuron* as something that was in front of a house (or figuratively

an 'entry' to a topic).[32] I therefore see no evidence to support Xavier
Lafon's claim that *vestibula* had 'moved inside' and were fully covered
by the 1st century BCE.[33] Later on, this might indeed have happened: for
example, Servius (in his commentary on the *Aeneid*) equates *vestibula* with
atria and *ianua* in the late 4th or early 5th century.[34] Yet the same Servius
appears in Macrobius' *Saturnalia* as interlocutor discussing *Aeneid*
6.273–74. These lines describe Aeneas' view of Orcus or the underworld:
'just before the *vestibulum*, within the very jaws (*fauces*) of Orcus / Grief
and avenging Anxiety have set their bed.'[35] Servius/Macrobius states that
Aeneas saw both spaces standing from the road: 'when he sees the *fauces*
and the *vestibulum* of the house of the wicked he is not inside the house . . .
but it is from the road that he sees places that are situated between the
road and the house.'[36] The late antique evidence is contradictory and
remains inconclusive, but it is evident that, before the mid-2nd century
CE, *vestibula* were located in front of and outside the *domus* they gave
access to.

Appearance, Size and the Absence of Roofs

The location of *vestibula* ensured that they were directly accessible and
visible from both the street and the house.[37] Gellius makes the general
statement that 'on the right and left the door is hemmed in by buildings
extended to the street'.[38] In between, one would find the *vestibulum*, open
to the street, with all except one side being enclosed by protruding 'wings'
of the house and the facade. This is confirmed by Cicero when he writes
that he and some followers 'retreated into the *vestibulum*' (*discessimus in
vestibulum*) of a man called Tettius Damio when Cicero was attacked. His
helpers could then easily hold off the attackers, aided by the walls of the
domus protecting them on most sides.[39] Cicero's remark also reveals that a
vestibulum was part of someone's property and formed an integral part of
the *domus* it gave access to, both physically and conceptually. The space
itself was deemed to be 'empty' – Gellius characterizes it as *locus vacuus* or
area vacanti.[40] It was only empty in architectural terms, for a *vestibulum*
could be lavishly decorated and contain trees and as well as statues, *spolia*
(weapons and *rostra*), or, in the case of Augustus, a *corona civica* and above
the door the inscription that he had been proclaimed *Pater Patriae* (see
below for visual evidence of his *vestibulum*).[41] In short, *vestibula* resembled
what we would now call a courtyard or forecourt and were decorated with
the prized possessions of the owner of the house.[42]

Regarding the size of *vestibula*, Gellius and Macrobius inform us that they were large (*spatia grandia/loci grandes*).[43] But how large exactly? Firstly, Cicero stipulates that *vestibula* had to be 'proportionally sized': 'just as with *vestibula* and entrances that are added to the house and temples, the prologue that is put before a case must be proportionate to the subject matter itself'.[44] A comparable dictum is found in Vitruvius, who states that it is appropriate to have 'suitable and elegant *vestibula* matching magnificent interiors', for if the entrances are insignificant (*humiles*) and shabby (*inhonestos*), they are not *cum decore*.[45] Although Vitruvius does not mention size explicitly, *humilis* can also mean 'small' or 'diminutive'.

Secondly, the sources on things placed inside *vestibula* give an indication of their size. For example, Juvenal mentions a *vestibulum* that was so large that it contained a *quadriga* (with horses that were *alti*, tall) and an equestrian statue of the owner.[46] On imperial *vestibula*, Suetonius records that Vespasian once dreamt about seeing scales placed in the 'middle part' (*media parte*) of his *vestibulum*, with, on the one side, Claudius and Nero, and, on the other, himself with his sons.[47] Both *vestibula*, however imaginary, were invoked as being spacious enough to contain such large statues and leave room for groups of visitors to stand and walk past.

Thirdly, numerous sources offer information on the number of people present in *vestibula*, waiting there to be admitted to greet the owner of the house during his *salutatio*. The size of these groups of visitors surely varied, but the word most often used is *turba*, 'a multitude'. Although we cannot tell how many people made up a *turba*, we repeatedly find that a crowd of *salutatores* could fill up *vestibula* and *atria*, even those that were spacious (*ampla*).[48] Indeed, so many people went to *salutationes* that Seneca saw 'the streets beset with a huge throng of people and the ways jammed with the crowds of those passing in both directions.'[49] The spaciousness of the *vestibulum* of the Domitianic *Domus Flavia* is confirmed by Gellius: 'in the *vestibulum* of the palace on the Palatine a large number of men (*multitudo*) of almost all ranks had gathered together, waiting for an opportunity to pay their respects to Caesar [Antoninus Pius].'[50] Only once do we find an exact number of people: Livy writes that 306 soldiers (the 'whole *gens*' of the Fabii) were present in a consul's *vestibulum*, though this (supposedly) happened roughly 450 years before his time.[51] Summarizing, the sources present *vestibula* as spacious and large enough to contain sizeable groups of dozens if not hundreds of visitors, as well as space-consuming statues.

The last question on the form of *vestibula* concerns both their appearance and construction: did they have roofs? Above, we have already seen that the *vestibulum* was located 'outside' and, more importantly, contrasted to the rest of the house as not belonging to the covered part. This dichotomy is most explicit in Cicero's *Pro Caecina*: 'I ask you [Gaius Piso], if, this day, when you are returning home, men collected in a body, and armed, not only prevent you from crossing the threshold and from coming under the roof of your own house, but keep you off from approaching it – from even entering the *vestibulum* – what will you do?'[52] Other evidence on roofs is more indirect but no less convincing. Firstly, while some statues might have fitted under a roof, the size of the colossus (120 feet) in the *vestibulum* of Nero's *Domus Aurea* effectively rules out that this palatial *vestibulum* was covered.[53] Also, altars could be set in *vestibula*, which made them *sub dio* (i.e. uncovered).[54] According to Pliny, the Chauci collected rainwater in pits (*scrobibus*) in their *vestibula*.[55] Lastly, at least some *vestibula* held trees; one (fabulous) palatial *vestibulum* in Catullus has trees that offer shade.[56]

Lafon has argued that *vestibula* were covered already in the 1st century BCE, on the basis of Vitruvius who writes that 'for those of moderate income, magnificent *vestibula*, *tablina* and *atria* are unnecessary', while for 'the most prominent citizens [i.e. magistrates] . . ., *vestibula* should be constructed that are lofty (*alta*) and lordly (*regalia*)'.[57] In other words, we find that *vestibula* were somehow comparable to *atria* and *tablina*.[58] But this does not imply that *vestibula*, like *atria*, had roofs: Vitruvius refers only to the (relative) size and decoration of *vestibula* and does not comment on any technical matters concerning its construction.[59] In short, all evidence suggests that *vestibula* were uncovered, at least before the mid-2nd century CE.

Function

Why did some Romans have large uncovered spaces before their *domus*? As noted above, *vestibula* are generally described as waiting areas used by those who wanted to greet a *dominus* during his morning *salutatio*. Gellius and Macrobius both conclude (following Aelius Gallus) that *vestibulum* was probably derived from the verb *stare* (to stand). Gellius writes: 'therefore from that standing in a large space, and as it were from a kind of "standing place" (*stabulatio*), the name *vestibulum* was given to the great places left, as I have said, before the doors of houses, in which those who had come to call stood, before they were admitted to the house'.[60]

Macrobius agrees: 'in this place those who had come to pay their respects to the master of the house used to stand before they were admitted ....'.[61] Many other sources confirm the general function of *vestibula* as waiting areas.[62] The public nature – in terms of both access and visibility – of *vestibula* was crucial in this regard.[63] Having large groups of visitors augmented the prestige of the *dominus*: the more visitors one received, the better.[64] To have them waiting in full view of the city allowed onlookers to see how many clients the *dominus* had. As with decorative and honorific objects, *domini* put their *salutatores* on display in the *vestibulum*.[65]

Imperial *vestibula* also served as waiting areas for those wanting to greet the emperor.[66] Gellius and Cassius Dio give first-hand accounts of their experiences during such *salutationes*, including their time waiting in a *vestibulum*.[67] Elsewhere, Gellius notes that he waited for the emperor's *salutatio* in the *Area Palatina*.[68] This space is poorly understood and it is quite possible that both spaces functioned as waiting areas, but also that the *vestibulum* was part of the *Area Palatina* or even that they were one and the same.[69]

There are three unique uses of *vestibula* in the literary sources. First, Vitruvius notes that 'those who deal in farm products have stables and sheds in their *vestibula*'.[70] He arguably refers to *villae rusticae* and not *domus*, and we cannot expect *salutatores* to have visited such a 'working farm'. Suetonius records that Augustus' body was placed inside the *vestibulum* of his house.[71] This must have been the Roman equivalent of 'lying in state'; the open nature and large size of *vestibula* enabling many to see their *princeps* for the last time. Lastly, there is the confusing remark by Cassius Dio's on senatorial banquets that were held in the *vestibula* of senatorial *domus* during the time of Augustus, something which not even the author himself could understand.[72]

All in all, from literary sources we learn that domestic *vestibula* had the following characteristics: they were located in front of the *domus* (or palace) to which they belonged, visible but separate from the street. Even though they were 'empty' and uncovered, conceptually they did form part of the *domus*. *Vestibula* could be large, in some cases at least large enough to accommodate significant groups of people and sizeable statues. The appearance of *vestibula* remains more nebulous, but they were partially enclosed and habitually decorated with statues, trees and, probably less often, *spolia*. In short, to look for *vestibula* in the archaeological record means to look for spaces outside and in front of a *domus* or palace, large in both absolute and relative terms (i.e. large enough to hold groups of people and proportionate to the building it belonged to), and with the potential to function as waiting areas.

The Archaeological Sources

In studies on Roman housing, countless excavated rooms or spaces in Ostia Pompeii, Rome and elsewhere in the empire have been labelled as *vestibula*.[73] Below, I argue that very few (if any) excavated spaces conform to the characteristics of *vestibula* as found in the literary sources. The constraints of space and time make it impossible to discuss all spaces labelled *vestibula* individually. Therefore, they are grouped together in different types in order to distinguish between those proposed *vestibula* that do or do not seem to conform to the literary descriptions. The first group of architectural spaces discussed is made up of rooms inside *domus*, followed by so-called *fauces-vestibula* and porticos. I conclude with a discussion of the few spaces that arguably might have been or functioned as *vestibula*.

Spaces inside the Domus

Could internal rooms, located behind the threshold, be *vestibula*? This idea contradicts all basic information we have gathered from the literary sources, yet we find many internal spaces labelled as such on archaeological plans, even in studies by those who advocate a cautious approach to using labels found in the written sources.[74]

The most vocal supporter of this position has been Eleanor Leach, who proposes to consider 'atrium A' of the Pompeiian House of Iulius Polybius (IX 13,1–3) as a *vestibulum*.[75] She argues that it was a *vestibulum* partly because it lacked an *impluvium* (and was hence not an *atrium*) and partly because of the 'stately' wall paintings. However, the absence of an *impluvium* in a 3rd-century BCE *domus* does not necessarily mean that the room was not an *atrium* since early Roman *domus* often featured covered (i.e. testudinate) *atria*.[76] Second, we do not have evidence for wall paintings in *vestibula* in the literary sources. Most importantly, the space is fully covered and could only be reached through a narrow hallway and thus did not border the street. Therefore, on the basis of its form and location we should not see 'atrium A' as a (possible) *vestibulum*.[77] When it comes to function, however, we cannot rule out the possibility that it was actually a waiting area or perhaps a reception room. The modern word 'vestibule' might be a suitable designation for spaces just behind the front door that were arguably not *atria*.[78] In any case, internal rooms were not *vestibula*.

Fauces-Vestibula

In an archaeological commentary on the 'villa-letters' by Pliny the Younger (*Ep.* 2.17 and 5.6), Reinhard Förtsch has listed some spaces which he dubbed '*fauces-vestibula*'.[79] These *fauces-vestibula* can be best described as relatively small areas in front of the door of a *domus*, roughly as wide as the narrow entranceways (i.e. those spaces usually labelled *fauces*) lying behind.[80] In most cases, the front door was set back in a 'niche' a couple of metres from the outer wall, which left an area before the door, open to the street but enclosed on three sides. Förtsch's *fauces-vestibula* are all covered by the roof of the house, though at the so-called Villa of San Marco at Stabiae a small porch was built in front of the *fauces-vestibulum*.

This space (3.55 × 3.45 m, Figure 10.1) at Stabiae, and other spaces labelled *fauces-vestibula*, conform to some of the characteristics found

Figure 10.1 Entrance area of the Villa of San Marco, Stabiae, reproduced from https://commons.wikimedia.org/wiki/File:Main_entrance_Villa_San_Marco_Stabiae.jpg, licensed under the Creative Commons Attribution-Share Alike 3.0

in literary sources.[81] The spaces are outside, between the door and the street, and rather empty apart from (in some cases) benches along the walls. These benches could serve as seats for waiting visitors, although they were probably constructed to be used by more than just *salutatores*.[82]

However, if the *fauces-vestibula* functioned as waiting areas, the number of visitors these spaces could contain was very limited, which does not conform to what we know about visitor numbers at *salutationes*. They also were not large enough to be decorated with statues, trees or anything else than wall paintings. Moreover, the average size of these areas hardly made them 'proportionate' to the rest of the house.[83] For example, the *fauces-vestibulum* of the Pompeiian House of D. Octavius Quartio (II 2.1–3.5–6) is 1.90 × 2.80 m (Figure 10.2), yet the whole *domus* measured around 1,000 m².[84] Other *fauces-vestibula* are equally small compared to the *domus* they gave access to, both in absolute and relative terms.[85] Somewhat of an exception is the so-called Casa di Giove Fulminatore in Ostia, a *domus* built in the Augustan era measuring no more than 550 m².[86] This house features an uncovered forecourt (*c.* 3.90 × 2.80 m) before the door, partially enclosed by walls but open to the street (Figure 10.3).

Figure 10.2 Area before the door of the House of Octavius Quartio, Pompeii. Photo by author. By permission Ministero per i Beni e le Attività Culturali e per il Turismo – Parco Archeologico di Pompei

Figure 10.3 Entrance area of the Casa di Giove Fulminatore, Ostia. Photo by author. The possible *vestibulum* is located between the threshold (centre) and the road (top). By permission Direzione Generale Musei, Parco Archaeologico di Ostia Antica

On the basis of the fact that the *fauces-vestibula* were covered, too small to be suited as waiting areas for large groups of visitors and hardly proportionate to the houses they gave access to, we should discard the *fauces-vestibula* as 'proper' *vestibula*. Nevertheless, it is possible that they were built to resemble and perhaps fulfil (on a very different scale) the same function as 'proper' and much larger *vestibula* before grand *domus* in the city of Rome (see below); this seems particularly plausible for the uncovered space before the Casa di Giove Fulminatore.

Porticos

Very small porches or porticos (<5 m^2) have been labelled *vestibula*, such as those that gave access to the Villa of Diomedes just outside Pompeii, the so-called Villa of Rabato on Malta, or a villa excavated near Pula, but these should be discarded on the basis of their size.[87] More interesting are grand porticos, for example those excavated at Sirmione and at the Villa of Publius Fannius Synistor in Boscoreale (Figure 10.4, space 'B').[88] As the former can only be partially reconstructed, the latter deserves special attention. It was an exterior yet covered space that gave access to a leisure villa, closed on three sides (the walls on these sides were covered with wall paintings) and completely open on the fourth. Its dimensions (*c.* 4.5×12 m) provided ample waiting space for even large groups of visitors. The fact that it is a podium does not necessarily mean that it was not a *vestibulum*. In one of Seneca's letters we find the expression *vestibula suspensa*: *suspensus* can mean a number of things, including 'raised', which makes it possible that some *vestibula* were podium-like structures reachable only by a flight of stairs.[89] Evidently, porticos are by their very nature covered, but in other aspects (above all, size and location) the portico found at Boscoreale shares some characteristics with *vestibula* described in the literary sources.

Possible Vestibula?

The final spaces discussed are quite diverse, but for the most part conform to the characteristics of *vestibula* laid out by the texts. Most importantly, they are significantly larger than the spaces discussed so far, which makes them more suitable as waiting areas and hence more likely to have been named, or to have functioned, as *vestibula*.

In its first conception, the Villa dei Misteri in Pompeii featured an entrance area of *c.* 3×4 m in front of the main door.[90] It was partly covered by an arch, open to the street, and had benches along the walls. When the villa was enlarged, two 'wings' on either side were added, which created an uncovered forecourt of at least 3×8 m (Figure 10.5; its full dimensions are unknown as it has not been completely excavated). The space was fully incorporated into the building and enclosed on three sides. One can easily imagine visitors waiting here before being admitted into the villa.

Rather different is the Pompeiian house of M. Epidius Rufus or the Casa dei Diadumeni (IX 1,20; Figure 10.6).[91] The house features a podium ($19 \times 1.5 \times 1.5$ m) running along the whole facade of the house with two flights

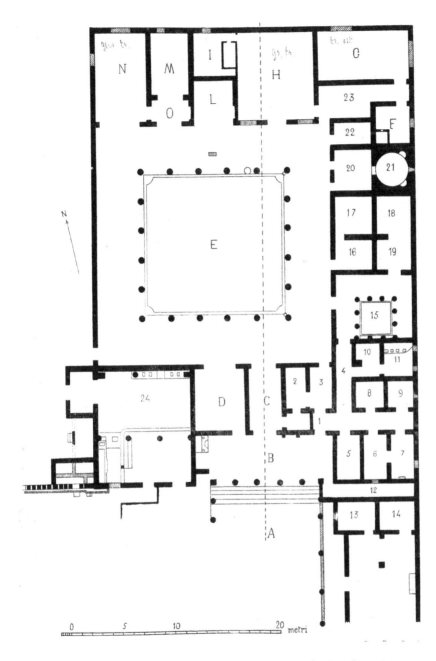

Figure 10.4 Plan of the Villa of P. Fannius Synistor, Boscoreale. Barnabei 1901.

of steps at both ends. As such, the podium was an integral part of the house yet outside and uncovered, and potentially provided space to stand and wait before admission into the house. The structure is unparalleled in Pompeii and (as far as I know) elsewhere in the Roman world.

Figure 10.5 Entrance area of the Villa of the Mysteries, Pompeii. Photo by author. By permission Ministero per i Beni e le Attività Culturali e per il Turismo – Parco Archeologico di Pompei

Figure 10.6 Podium of the house of M. Epidius Rufus or Casa dei Diadumeni, Pompeii. Photo by author. By permission Ministero per i Beni e le Attività Culturali e per il Turismo – Parco Archeologico di Pompei

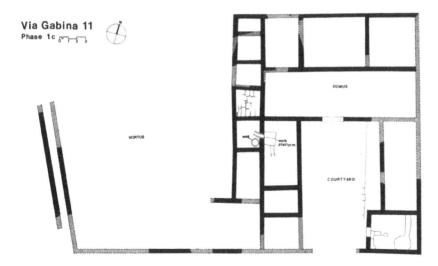

Figure 10.7 Plan of the villa excavated along the Via Gabina, Rome. By kind permission of Professor Walter Wildrig

The final architectural space discussed here is the court of a 'working villa' excavated along the Via Gabina, some 10 km east of the Porta Maggiore in Rome (Figure 10.7).[92] The villa underwent major changes in its plan and use, but in its first phase (from roughly the 3rd century BCE until the early Imperial period) it had a U-shaped plan. This left an open and large forecourt (*c.* 12 × 6 m) that gave access to both the working and domestic areas of the villa, respectively the 'arms' and the 'base' of the U. This building is quite possibly an example of the *vestibula* of those 'who deal in farm products' mentioned by Vitruvius, although no traces of any structures like 'stables and sheds' survive.[93] As far as I am aware, no other domestic buildings with a comparable U-shaped ground plan have been excavated.[94]

These last three spaces discussed at fit the literary descriptions of *vestibula* to some degree, even though none was very large, there is no evidence that they were decorated by statues or other sizeable objects, and only the courtyard of the villa along the Via Gabina may have held trees. It therefore must remain doubtful whether any of the spaces were indeed *vestibula*.

The *Vestibulum* on the Palatine

We can only make educated guesses on whether the *domus* and villas discussed above featured *vestibula*, yet we know for certain that the imperial dwellings on the Palatine featured *vestibula*. Not all of these have been preserved – the massive *vestibulum* of Nero's palace was already destroyed in antiquity – or can be securely located, but it is possible to reconstruct and even identify some of these.

There are no archaeological remains identified as Augustus' *vestibulum*, not least because there is disagreement on where it was located (most probably directly north-east of the temple of Apollo).[95] However, there is visual evidence of its appearance. A coin struck in 12 BCE shows the doors of his *domus* flanked by two laurel trees with the *corona civica* above it.[96] More detailed information can be derived from one side of the so-called 'Sorrento base' (side C, Figure 10.8) which shows the same crown above opened doors but flanked by an Ionic colonnade.[97] Without a doubt, both the coin and the base depict the *vestibulum* of Augustus' house. The colonnade suggests that the *vestibulum* was a large and uncovered space, especially if the temple depicted on side A of the base is the temple of Vesta on the Palatine that was dedicated in 12 BCE (meaning that this temple was inside Augustus' *vestibulum*).[98]

On the basis of the archaeological remains it is thought that Caligula could have used the temple of Castor and Pollux as his *vestibulum*, as reported by Suetonius.[99] The excavated structures reveal that the temple had become an integral part of the structure on the Palatine, which at least does not contradict Suetonius' words. Sadly, the walls of the cella are gone, which makes it impossible to see how a connection between the palace and the temple was executed architecturally, though a wooden bridge seems the most plausible solution.[100]

The large rectangular palace on the Palatine constructed in the time of Domitian comprised two 'sectors', of which the so-called *Domus Flavia* was the more public sector.[101] Finsen suggested an octagonal room (roughly in the middle of the western facade of the complex) as the palace's *vestibulum* and public entrance.[102] Even if we disregard the fact that the room was inside and covered, it seems it was too small and too peripheral to have functioned as the waiting space for imperial *salutationes*. Furthermore, to reach it, visitors had to walk around the north-western corner of the palace where the so-called *Aula Regia* (Figure 10.9) was located, arguably the principal venue for imperial *salutationes*.[103] A *vestibulum* on the northern side of the complex makes more sense, as this was the direction from which visitors would have come, having made their way up the *Clivus Palatinus* from the Forum.[104] The badly preserved courtyard on the north-eastern end (Figure 10.9) was the first palatial space reached from this road.

Figure 10.8 The 'Sorrento base', showing the *vestibulum* of the *domus* of Augustus. By kind permission, Deutsches Archäologisches Institut Rom, Negative number 65.1251

Although it can only be partially reconstructed it is clear that it was enclosed on three sides, uncovered and very spacious (*c.* 50 × 30 m), and as such conforms to the characteristics of *vestibula* in general. It must have been a fitting palatial *vestibulum* from which the audience chambers could be easily reached.

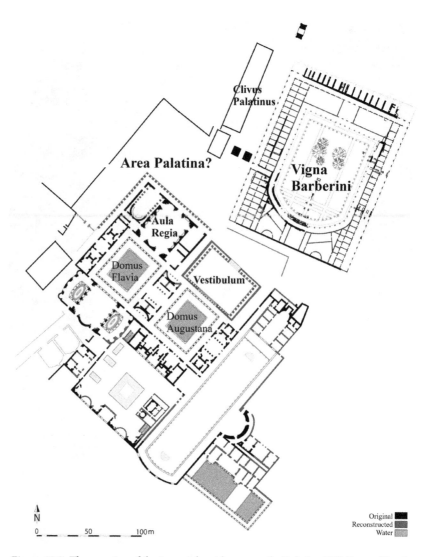

Figure 10.9 The remains of the imperial residences on the Palatine Hill, Rome. Plan by Jens Pflug and Ulrike Wulf-Rheidt, after École française de Rome (Vigna Barberini) and Architekturreferat DAI Zentrale, Berlin (Flavian Palace). Courtesy of Jens Pflug and Architekturreferat DAI Zentrale, Berlin.

Connecting the Literary and Material Sources

In the first part of this chapter the form and function of *vestibula* were laid out as described in the literary sources. In the second part, I have tried to link the information extracted from the literary sources with the archaeological remains of excavated rooms and spaces. However, the number of (partially) 'matching' remains is very small, and even those spaces – apart from the *Domus Flavia* on the Palatine – seem insignificant in comparison to the spacious and monumental forecourts described in the literary sources. How can we explain this mismatch, and how can we possibly find more *vestibula* in the future?

First of all, I suggest a new way of looking for *vestibula*. Given that a *vestibulum* was an 'empty' space before and outside a *domus*, it is not easily archaeologically recoverable, unless the remains of the *domus* itself would reveal a space or forecourt between extending 'wings' or outer walls. But even then, few would deem this worthy of exploration; it is telling that the forecourt of the Villa dei Misteri was left partially unexcavated. To locate *vestibula*, we should not only pay attention to the ground plan of a building, but also its relation to the other buildings and particularly its relation to any street. How could this work in practice? Let us look again at the plan of the Villa of P. Fannius Synistor found at Boscoreale. Above, I have suggested that the material remains of portico 'B' (Figure 10.4) partially fit the literary descriptions of *vestibula*. However, the area in front of the portico (space 'A') might just as well have been a *vestibulum*.[105] This space cannot be fully reconstructed, but it was evidently large, in front of the building, uncovered and at least partially enclosed. It seems to have been a vacant area, which existed not so much physically but rather conceptually.

Secondly, there is a fundamental problem which haunts any study on Roman housing. The literary sources which form the starting point of this chapter are, as noted above, biased, since they are written by elite men (senators and some equestrians) living in Rome. On the other hand, material remains of Roman housing are not strictly 'Roman' at all, since material remains of *domus* are few and far between at Rome, with the exception of late antique dwellings.[106] Until recently, what is actually Pompeiian or Ostian was often presented as simply 'Roman'.[107] Now, after decades with 'a lack of a research agenda', some recent publications on houses in Rome are starting to provide a glimpse of what elite domestic spaces might have looked like.[108] Yet a study of *vestibula* shows that there is still a major gap to be bridged. The domestic world of the late Republican and early Imperial elite at Rome, seemingly familiar to us on the basis of literary texts, remains distant as long as it cannot be connected to a corpus of material remains.

This is all the more pertinent for a study on *vestibula*, since it seems that only houses of the Rome-based elite were the kind of *domus* that featured *vestibula*. Gellius and Macrobius mention that *vestibula* were part of *amplas domos*, that is, spacious or large houses.[109] Owning a *domus* was out of reach for the majority of the Roman population, but owning a large *domus* (or a suburban villa) was surely limited to only a tiny fraction of the population. Also, we have seen that *vestibula* were waiting areas for *salutatores.* In Goldbeck's study of *salutationes* we find that these morning greetings were hosted by a very select group of people: for the Republican period, we only find senatorial *domini* receiving morning guests; during the imperial period, a few powerful *equites*, lower-ranking men belonging to the imperial family and some senatorial women also organized *saluta-tiones.*[110] As a result, *salutationes* were usually held at Rome, which fits with the fact that the overwhelming majority of the *vestibula* described in our sources were located at Rome.[111] The literary evidence on *salutationes* makes it quite possible that very few domestic *vestibula* were ever built, and that we should look for them in Rome.[112]

Ultimately, this suggests that none of the archaeological remains dis-cussed above can be labelled as a *vestibulum*, with the exception of the *Domus Flavia*. Only Vitruvius hints that *vestibula* could be part of non-elite *domus* (outside Rome?), since he writes that, 'for those of moderate income', 'magnificent *vestibula*' are unnecessary, which allows for the construction of 'normal' *vestibula* for those of 'moderate income'.[113] Perhaps the *fauces-vestibulum* of the Casa di Giove Fulminatore in Ostia and the spaces in front of the Pompeiian Casa dei Diadumeni or the Villa dei Misteri should be regarded as such normal or (perhaps more fittingly) 'aspirational' *vestibula*.

Until we make a conscious effort to look for *vestibula* while excavating and we have a significant corpus of remains found at Rome, we should be very cautious about using the label *vestibulum*. The persistent misuse of this label has created the false impression that *vestibula* were ubiquitous. It is imperative that the mismatch between literary and archaeological sources on *vestibula* is recognized, and that we exercise great care when trying to identify *vestibula* in the archaeological record, just as with any other Roman domestic space.

Notes

1 Gellius 16.5.8: *locum ante ianuam vacuum . . . qui inter fores domus et viam medius esset.*

2 *Vestibula* are mentioned 156 times in practically all genres of Latin literature between 200 BCE and 200 CE by thirty authors in fifty-one works. This count does not include Macrobius' *Saturnalia*, which was included for this investigation.

3 Vitruvius 6.7.5: '*prothura* in Greek are *vestibula* before the entrance doors' (*prothura graece dicuntur, quae sunt ante ianuas vestibula*). More importantly, the characteristics of *prothura* correspond to those of *vestibula*: Hellmann 1992: 348–49.

4 At least seventy-five domestic *vestibula* are mentioned in Latin and Greek texts by roughly thirty authors. An exact count is impossible: sometimes the nature of a building featuring a *vestibulum* is unclear.

5 The first collection is found in Marquardt 1864: 227–32. Leach 1993 and Lafon 1995 are the only studies of *vestibula*, but I am not in agreement with their conclusions. Timothy Wiseman discusses *vestibula* on the Palatine hill in a number of studies: Wiseman 1982; 1987; 2011; 2012; 2013.

6 'Vestibule'/'vestibolo' is used as a synonym for *vestibulum* by e.g. Pesando and Guidobali 2006 and Proudfoot 2013, yet present-day vestibules are internal rooms and *vestibula* were, as we will see, external spaces.

7 Allison 1997; 2001; 2004: 176–77; Nevett 1997; 2010: 89–118.

8 Allison 2001: 185–92; 2004: 177; cf. Leach 1997: 50.

9 Four inscriptions mention *vestibula*, but all concern public or unknown buildings: *AE* 1989, 168 and Solin 1989; *CIL* III 2072 = *ILS* 8340 and Cambi 1987, 265–68; *CIL* VIII 2654/18104; and lastly *AE* 2005, 1102.

10 In contrast to e.g. *cubicula*: Allison 2001: 183–84, based on Riggsby 1997.

11 On *salutationes*, see above all Goldbeck 2010; see also Badel 2007 and Speksnijder 2015.

12 See Saller 1982: 127–29 and Goldbeck 2010: 246–81 on patronage and *salutationes*.

13 Gellius 16.5; Macrobius 6.8.14–23. Note that Macrobius partly copied Gellius' text.

14 Only two sources mention Italic villas with *vestibula*: Pliny, *Ep.* 2.17.15 and Valerius Maximus 2.10.2b.

15 See eg. Cicero, *Against Verres* 2.2.160 (Syracusa); Dio Chrysostom 36.33–34 (Pontus); *CIL* VIII 2654/18104 (Numidia) and *AE* 2005, 1102 (Switzerland).

16 Apuleius, *Florida* 22 and Dio Chrysostom, 77/78.34–35. The latter was not composed at Rome: von Arnim 1898: 254.

17 Livy 24.21.8, 33.48.9 and 39.51.7; Pliny, *Natural History* 16.4 on the Chauci.

18 Gellius 16.5.3: . . .*vestibulum esse dicit non in ipsis aedibus neque partem aedium, sed locum ante ianuam domus vacuum, per quem a via aditus accessus que ad aedis est, cum dextra sinistra que ianuam tecta que sunt viae iuncta atque ipsa ianua procul a via est area vacanti intersita.* Cf. 16.5.8: see note 1.

19 Macrobius 6.8.23: . . .*vestibulum constat aream dici quae a via domum dividit.*

20 Varro, *LL* 7.81.

21 E.g. Cicero, *Pro Caecina* 35 and 89; Livy 1.40.5; Vitruvius 6.7.5; Philo, *Virt.* 89 with Deuteronomy 24:10.

22 E.g. Aelius Aristides, *Plato in Def. Four* (=3 Behr) 667–68; Cicero, *De oratore* 1.200, *Pro Milone* 75; Plautus, *Mosellaria.* 795 and 817 (*pace* Leach 1993: 24 on Plautus).

23 Macrobius 6.8.20: . . . *neque in via stabant neque intra aedes erant* . . . Cf. Gellius 16.5.3 and Macrobius 6.8.23 (notes 18–19); Livy 24.21.8;

Nicolaus, Fr. 97 (=FGrH 90 F 130.26) and (more indirectly) Cicero, *Letters to Atticus* 4.3.3.

24 E.g. Vitruvius 7.*praef*.17, who envisages a *vestibulum* located *ante* and *in fronte* of a temple.

25 Beehive: e.g. Columella 9.7.4 (book 9 is filled with *vestibula*) and Vergil, *Georgics* 4.20. Chicken pens: Varro, *De re rustica* 3.9.7. Spider's nest: Pliny the Elder, *Natural History* 11.80.

26 Cicero, *Against Verres* 2.5.170: Messina is the *vestibulum* of Sicily. See also e.g. Curtius Rufus 7.4.14 and Livy 36.22.11.

27 See e.g. Cicero, *De Oratore* 2.230 and *Or.* 50; Seneca, *Natural Questions* 7.30.6.

28 Cassius Dio 78(77).17.3.

29 Suetonius, *Caligula* 22.2: ... *partem Palatii ad forum usque promovit, atque aede Castoris et Pollucis in vestibulum transfigurata, consistens saepe inter fratres deos, medium adorandum se adeuntibus exhibebat* ... Cf. Cassius Dio 59.28.5, although he does not explicitly label the temple as *prothuron*.

30 Claudius 'returned' the temple to the people: Cassius Dio 60.8.

31 Gellius 16.5.1–2 and 8: *animadverti enim quosdam haudquaquam indoctos viros opinari vestibulum esse partem domus primorem, quam vulgus 'atrium' vocat* ... *qui domos igitur amplas antiquitus faciebant, locum ante ianuam vacuum relinquebant, qui inter fores domus et viam medius esset.*

32 Compare Gellius 4.1.1 and 19.13.1 with Fronto, *Ad M. Caes.* 4.3.1 and Cassius Dio, 78(77).17.1–3. The same goes for earlier 2nd-century authors: Juvenal 1.132 and 7.125–28; Suetonius, *Caligula* 22 and 42, *Nero* 31, *Tiberius* 26, *Vespasian* 25; Tacitus, *Annals* 2.31 and 11.25, *Histories* 1.86. Quintilian, at the end of the 1st century, explicitly juxtaposes the *vestibulum* and the *atrium*: *Inst. Or.* 11.2.20–23.

33 Lafon 1995, 414.

34 Servius 1.726, 2.469 and 6.273; cf. Nonius Marcellus, *De Prop. Serm* 75, cited by Wiseman 2011, 73. Tertullian, *Paen.* 7 is the only 3rd-century Latin text to mention *vestibula*.

35 Vergil, *Aeneid* 6.273–74: *vestibulum ante ipsum primis in faucibus Orci / Luctus et ultrices posuere cubilia Curae* ...

36 Macrobius 6.8.23: *cum videt fauces atque vestibulum domus impiorum, non est intra domum* ... *sed de via videt loca inter viam et aedes locata.* In the *Aeneid* itself the threshold (*limen*) is mentioned after the *vestibulum* (6.279) as are the doors (*fores*, 6.286); see 6.552–56 for another *vestibulum* before a door. Cf. Gellius 16.5.12. *Fauces* is now usually used as the label for narrow entranceways behind the front door of a *domus*: Leach 1997, 53–54. Given the text of Vergil and the commentaries by Gellius and Macrobius, we should perhaps reconsider this label too.

37 Philostratus the Younger, *Imagines* 877.3; Tacitus, *Annals* 2.31.

38 Gellius 16.5.3, see note 18.

39 Cicero, *Letters to Atticus* 4.3.3.

40 Gellius 16.5.3 and 16.5.8. *Area* in itself can mean 'empty space' and the word is used twice in Latin literature as a synonym for *vestibulum*: Macrobius 6.8.23 and Pliny, *Pan.* 52.3 (a *vestibulum* of a temple). Cf. Velleius Paterculus 2.14.3, on which see Cooper 2007, 11 n. 25.

41 *Spolia*: Ovid, *Tristia* 3.33–34 and Pliny *Natural History* 35.7; cf. Wiseman 1987 nn. 5–6 for less explicit sources. *Rostra*: Cicero, *Phil.* 2.68. *Corona civica*: Cassius Dio 53.16, Ovid, *Fasti* 1.614 and 4.953; Valerius Maximus 2.8.7; cf. Suetonius, *Tiberius* 26 and *Claudius* 17 and Zanker 1988, 92–94. *Pater patriae*: Augustus, *Res Gestae* 35. On trees, see below.

42 Cf. Wiseman 2013, 261.

43 Gellius 16.5.9; Macrobius 6.8.20.

44 Cicero, *De Oratore* 2.320: . . .*oportet, ut aedibus ac templis vestibula et aditus, sic causis principia pro portione rerum praeponere.*

45 Vitruvius 1.2.6: . . .*cum aedificiis interioribus magnificis item vestibula convenientia et elegantia erunt facta.*

46 Juvenal 7.122–28. On statues see also Cassius Dio 46.33.1–2; Pliny the Elder, *Natural History* 34.29; Tacitus, *Annals* 11.35.

47 Suetonius, *Vespasian* 25.

48 E.g. Cicero, *De Oratore* 1.200; Seneca, *Cons. Ad Marc.* 10 (mentioning *vestibula ampla*), *Cons. Ad Pol.* 4.2 and *Ep.* 84.12; Statius, *Silvae* 4.4.39–42.

49 Seneca, *De Beneficiis* 6.34.4–5: *obsessos ingenti frequentia vicos et commeantium in utramque partem catervis itinera compressa.* Cf. Goldbeck 2010: 131–34 on visitor numbers.

50 Gellius, 4.1.1: *in vestibulo aedium Palatinarum omnium fere ordinum multitudo opperientes salutationem Caesaris constiterant* . . . Cf. Gellius 19.13.1.

51 Livy, 2.49.2–4.

52 Cicero, *Caec.* 35: *quaero, si te hodie domum tuam redeuntem coacti homines et armati non modo limine tectoque aedium tuarum sed primo aditu vestibuloque prohibuerint, quid acturus sis.* Cf. *Caec.* 89: the *vestibulum* did not belong to the 'inner part' (*interiore aedium parte*) of a house.

53 Suetonius, *Nero* 31 and Pliny, *Natural History* 34.45–46. See Lega 1989–1990, 348–52.

54 Lafon 1995: 408 on altars; cf. Dio Chrysostom 36.33–34.

55 Pliny, *Natural History* 16.4. Wiseman 2012 suggests that an altar for Vesta was placed in Augustus' *vestibulum* on the basis of Ovid, *Fasti* 6.299–304; cf. Coarelli 2012: 399–420.

56 Catullus 64.292–94; see also e.g. Cassius Dio 53.16.4; Ovid, *Tristia* 3.39–40; Valerius Maximus 1.8.2.

57 Lafon 1995: 414 and Vitruvius 6.5.1–3: *qui communi sunt fortuna, non necessaria magnifica vestibula nec tabulina neque atria* . . . *nobilibus vero,* . . . *faciunda sunt vestibula regalia alta, atria et peristylia amplissima* . . .

58 Cf. Seneca, *Cons. Ad Marc.* 10.1.

59 Moreover, Vitruvius 1.2.6 (note 45) explicitly contrasts *interioribus aedificiis* with *vestibula*.

60 Gellius 16.5.9–10: *ab illa ergo grandis loci consistione et quasi quadam stabulatione vestibula appellata sunt spatia, sicuti diximus, grandia ante fores aedium relicta, in quibus starent, qui venissent, priusquam in domum intromitterentur.*

61 Macrobius 6.8.20: *in eo loco qui dominum eius domus salutatum venerant priusquam admitterentur consistebant* . . . What follows is basically copied from Gellius.

62 Appian, *Bella Civilia* 3.14; Cicero, *De Oratore*. 1.200; Seneca, *Ep.* 84.12 and (much later) Nonius Marcellus, *De Prop. Serm.* 75 explicitly confirm this. Implicit are Cicero, *Letters to Atticus* 4.3.5; Dio Chrysostom 77/78.34–35; Seneca, *Cons. Ad Marc.* 10 and *Cons. Ad Pol.* 4.2; Statius, *Silvae* 4.4.39–42; Vitruvius 6.5.1–3. Cf. Livy 33.48.9 on Hannibal's *vestibulum*.

63 Wallace-Hadrill 1994 first discussed 'public' and 'private' spaces within (Pompeiian) *domus*. Lauritsen 2011, Proudfoot 2013 and most recently Berry 2016 have since stressed that (visual) access to even 'public' domestic spaces was controlled; cf. Speksnijder 2015 on control during *salutationes*.

64 See eg. Cicero, *Sulla* 73; Seneca, *Ep.*, 76.12; Tacitus, *Dialogue on Oratory* 6.1–4.

65 Cf. Speksnijder 2015: 94–95 and Hartnett 2017: 207–209.

66 See Winterling 1999: 117–44 on imperial *salutationes*.

67 Gellius 4.1.1 and 19.13.1; Cassius Dio 78(77).17.1–3 (on the winter palace at Nicomedia); cf. Epictetus, *Diss.* 1.30.6–7.

68 Gellius 20.1.1–2: *in area Palatina cum salutationem Caesaris opperiremur,* cf. 20.1.5. Cf. Torelli 1993 and Royo 1999: 138–41.

69 Any option is possible: Gellius 20.1.1 is our only literary source on this area, and *vestibulum* and *area* were used as synonyms: note 40. Wiseman 2013: 253–54 and 263 takes the *Area Palatina* and the *vestibulum* of Augustus' house to be different but adjacent spaces, as do I: see below.

70 Vitruvius 6.5.2: *qui autem fructibus rusticis serviunt, in eorum vestibulis stabula, tabernae* . . .

71 Suetonius, *Divus Augustus* 100.

72 Cassius Dio 51.22.9.

73 Many spaces are labelled *vestibula* in, for example, the Laterza archaeological guides of Ostia (Pavolini 2006) and Pompeii and Herculaneum (Pesando and Guidobaldi 2006); see e.g. Hales 2003: 172–80 and Carucci 2007 on *domus* in southern France and northern Africa respectively. Förtsch 1993: 127–34 and 181–84; Leach 1993; Lafon 1995; and Proudfoot 2013 are four studies (partially) dedicated to search for *vestibula* in the archaeological record.

74 E.g. Leach 1993; Wallace-Hadrill 1994: 231 (who equates *vestibulum* with 'entrance lobby'); Allison 2004: 64 (*fauces* and *vestibulum* are part of the 'front hall area' and formed the 'main entranceway') with 163; Clarke

2013: 344 ('authors other than Vitruvius' use *vestibulum* to refer to the principal entry, 'a narrow, tunnel-like, ramping space', named *fauces* by Vitruvius).

75 Leach 1993. On the house in general, see De Franciscis 1988. Förtsch 1993: 182–83 (no. XI 10–17) and Lafon 1995: 416 list some internal '*vestibula*'.

76 Wallace-Hadrill 1997.

77 Leach quotes Wiseman 1982: 28, who writes that a *vestibulum* is a 'substantial rectangular area outside, open to the street', yet argues that this internal space 'answers to Wiseman's specifications': Leach 1993: 23.

78 See rooms suggested by Förtsch 1993: 182 (no. XI 12–13): the entrance hall of the early imperial 'palace' at Fishbourne (Cunliffe 1971, 119–23) and a T-shaped entrance room of a villa at Francolise (Cotton and Métraux 1985: 42).

79 Förtsch 1993, 181–82 (no. XI 1–6). Cf. Proudfoot 2013 for a study of comparable Pompeiian spaces dubbed (duly avoiding ancient terminology) 'entrance vestibules'.

80 Such spaces were already labelled *vestibula* in the 19th century: Mau 1899: 241 fig. 110.

81 See Pesando and Guidobaldi 2006: 423–27 on the villa, with further bibliography.

82 Allison 2004: 163; see more generally Hartnett 2008 on Pompeiian benches; cf. Hartnett 2017: 195–223. There is no literary evidence on *salutatores* being seated in front of a house: Hartnett 2017: 208 n. 44.

83 The average size of the *fauces–vestibula* listed by Förtsch 1993: 181–82 is 10 m^2 and all give access to houses/villas (significantly) larger than 1,000 m^2.

84 On the house, see Pesando and Guidobaldi 2006: 138–40.

85 E.g. the late Republican villa at Settefinestre, which had a *pars urbana* of around 1,200 m^2 and a *fauces–vestibulum* of around 5 m^2: Carandini et al. 1985: 259 (no. 43) and 187. Compare two seemingly spacious villas found close to Rome: De Franceschini 2005: 241 (no. 84) and Lugli 1915: 263–80 (the 'vestibolo' is mentioned at 271).

86 Lorenzatti 1998: esp. 85; not mentioned by Förtsch 1993.

87 Villa of Diomedes: Pesando and Guidobaldi 2006: 266–67 with further bibliography. Villa of Rabato: Ashby and Rushforth, 1915: 34–48. Pula: Förtsch 1993: 182 (no. XI 9) and De Franceschini 1998: 591–92. Cf. Wiseman 2013: 261: 'a *vestibulum* is not a porch'.

88 Sirmione: Ruffia 2005. Boscoreale: listed by Förtsch 1993: 184 (no. XI 20) and first published by Barnabei 1901, who labels the portico 'androne o vestibolo' on 14 n. 11; see also Bergmann *et al.* 2010.

89 Seneca, *Ep.* 84.12: *magno adgestu suspensa vestibula* can be translated as 'the raised *vestibula* [beset] with a huge throng'. The Loeb translation is equally correct: 'the *vestibula* rendered hazardous by the huge throng'.

90 See Förtsch 1993: 183 (XI 7) on the *vestibulum*. On the villa see e.g. Dickmann 1999: 170–76 and Pesando and Guidobaldi 2006: 267–73.

91 Förtsch 1993: 183 (XI 18); cf. Leach 1993: 23 and Lauter 2009 (*non vidi*).

92 Förtsch 1993: 183 (XI 19). On the villa in general, see Widrig 1980.

93 'Farm products': Vitruvius, 6.5.2.

94 The excavators note that to the best of their knowledge this is the only U-shaped Italic villa: Widrig 1980: 122–23.

95 Wiseman 2013: 260–62, with further references.

96 *Roman Imperial Coinage* I 419; now at the British Museum, inv. no. 1867,0101.596.

97 See Cecamore 2004 and Coarelli 2012: 399–420 on the base and architectural setting, with further references.

98 See note 55.

99 Hurst 1988: 17; cf. Van Deman 1924 and Tamm 1964. See notes. 28–29 for the literary sources.

100 Hurst 1988; cf. Tamm 1964: 163–64.

101 On the *Domus Flavia*, see e.g. Finsen 1962; 1969; Royo 1999: 303–68; Zanker 2002; Mar 2009.

102 Finsen 1969: 9–10.

103 On the reception rooms, see Zanker 2002: 110–14.

104 Cf. Zanker 2002: 115–16; Mar 2009; Coarelli 2012: 487–91 and Wiseman 2013: 262.

105 See Barnabei 1901: 14 and 18, who thinks it was a peristyle.

106 Cf. Guidobaldi 2000: 133–34 Wallace-Hadrill 2001: 128–30; Hales 2003: 11.

107 Cf. Allison 2001: 189–92; Guilhembet 2007.

108 The quotation is from Wallace-Hadrill 2001: 130. Recent studies on *domus* at Rome include the publications of Jean-Pierre Guilhembet (too many to list here); Carandini 2010, though see Wiseman 2012 on Carandini's speculative work; and now Platts 2018.

109 Gellius 16.5.8; Macrobius 6.8.19.

110 Goldbeck 2010: 60–73.

111 Goldbeck 2010: 88–89; cf. Eck 1997 on the need for senators to live in Rome. See notes 14–15 for *vestibula* outside Rome.

112 Marquardt 1864: 229 already noted that 'in gewöhnlichen Bürgerhäusern in Rom wie in Municipalstädten wäre ein *vestibulum* ohne Zweck gewesen …'; cf. Dyer 1871: 253.

113 Vitruvius 6.5.1: see note 57.

References

Allison, P. M. (1997). Artefact distribution and spatial function in Pompeian houses. In B. Rawson and P. Weaver, eds., *The Roman Family in Italy.* Oxford: Clarendon Press, 321–54.

(2001). Using the material and written sources: turn of the millennium approaches to Roman domestic space. *American Journal of Archaeology* 105, 181–208.

(2004). *Pompeian Households: An Analysis of the Material Culture*. Los Angeles: Cotsen Institute of Archaeology.

Arnim, H. von (1898). *Leben und Werke des Dio von Prusa*. Berlin: Weidmann.

Ashby, T. and Rushforth, G. R. (1915). Roman Malta. *Journal of Roman Studies* 5, 23–80.

Badel, C. (2007). L'audience chez les sénateurs. In J. Caillet and M. Sot, eds., *L'audience: rituels et cadres spatiaux dans l'Antiquité et le Haut Moyen Age*. Paris: Picard, 141–64.

Barnabei, F. (1901). *La villa Pompeiana di P. Fannio Sinistore scoperta presso Boscoreale*. Rome: Tipografia della R. Accademia dei Lincei.

Bergmann, B. A. *et al.* (2010). *Roman Frescoes from Boscoreale: The Villa of Publius Fannius Synistor in Reality and Virtual Reality*. New York: Metropolitan Museum of Art.

Berry, J. (2016). Boundaries and control in the Roman house. *Journal of Roman Archaeology* 25, 125–41.

Cambi, N. (1987). Salona und seine Nekropolen. In H. von Hesberg and P. Zanker, eds., *Römische Gräberstrassen: Selbstdarstellung, Status, Standard. Kolloquium in München vom 28. bis 30. Oktober 1985*. Munich: Beck, 251–80.

Carandini, A. (2010). *Le case del potere nell'antica Roma*. Rome: Laterza.

Carandini, A. *et al.* (1985). *Settefinestre: una villa schiavistica nell'Etruria romana*. Modena: Panini.

Carucci, M. (2007). *The Romano-African* Domus: *Studies in Space, Decoration and Function*. BAR International Series 1731. Oxford: BAR.

Cecamore, C. (2004). Le figure e lo spazio sulla base di Sorrento. *Mitteilungen des Deutschen Archäologischen Instituts, Römische Abteilung* 111, 105–41.

Clarke, J. R. (2013). *Domus*/single family house. In R. B. Ulrich and C. K. Quenemoen, eds., *A Companion to Roman Architecture*. Malden, MA: Wiley-Blackwell, 342–62.

Coarelli, F. (2012). *Palatium: il Palatino dalle origini all'impero*. Rome: Edizioni Quasar.

Cooper, K. (2007). Closely watched households: visibility, exposure and private power in the Roman *domus*. *Past & Present* 197, 3–33.

Cotton, M. A. and Métraux, G. P. R. (1985). *The San Rocco villa at Francolise*. London: British School at Rome and Institute of Fine Arts, New York University.

Cunliffe, B. (1971). *Fishbourne: A Roman Palace and Its Garden*. London: Society of Antiquaries of London.

De Franceschini, M. (1998). *Le ville romane della X Regio (Venetia et Histria): catalogo e carta archeologica dell'insediamento romano nel territorio, dall'età repubblicana al tardo impero*. Rome: L'Erma di Bretschneider.

(2005) *Ville dell'agro romano*. Rome: L'Erma di Bretschneider.

De Franciscis, A. (1988). La casa di C. Iulius Polybius. *Rivista di Studi Pompeiani* 2, 15–36.

Dickmann, J. A. (1999). *Domus frequentata: anspruchsvolles Wohnen im pompejanischen Stadthaus*. Munich: Verlag Dr. F. Pfeil.

Dyer, T. H. (1871). *Pompeii: Its History, Buildings, and Antiquities*, 3rd ed. London: Bell.

Eck, W. (1997). Rome and the outside world: senatorial families and the world they lived in. In B. Rawson and P. Weaver, eds., *The Roman Family in Italy*. Oxford: Clarendon Press, 73–99.

Finsen, H. (1962). *Domus Flavia sur le Palatin: Aula Regia – Basilica*. Munksgaard: Hafniae.

   (1969). *La résidence de Domitien sur le Palatin*. Copenhagen: Analecta Romana Instituti Danici. Supplementum 5.

Förtsch, R. (1993). *Archäologischer Kommentar zu den Villenbriefen des jüngeren Plinius*. Mainz: Zabern.

Goldbeck, F. (2010). *Salutationes: die Morgenbegrüßungen in Rom in der Republik und der frühen Kaiserzeit*. Berlin: Akademie.

Greenough, J. B. (1890). The *fauces* of the Roman house. *Harvard Studies in Classical Philology* 1, 1–12.

Guidobaldi, M. P. (2000). Le abitazioni private e l'urbanistica. In A. Giardina, ed., *Storia di Roma dall'antichità a oggi: Roma antica*. Rome: Laterza, 133–61.

Guilhembet, J.-P. (2007). Normes romaines et résidences pompéiennes: remarques historiographiques. In M. O. Laforges, ed., *La norme à Pompéi. Ier s. avant – Ier s. après J.-C., colloque de Lyon 17/11/2004* (*Contributi di Archeologia Vesuviana* III). Rome: L'Erma di Bretschneider, 93–107.

Hales, S. (2003). *The Roman House and Social Identity*. Cambridge: Cambridge University Press.

Hartnett, J. (2008). *Si quis hic sederit*: streetside benches and urban society in Pompeii. *American Journal of Archaeology* 112, 91–119.

   (2017). *The Roman Street: Urban Life and Society in Pompeii, Herculaneum, and Rome*. Cambridge: Cambridge University Press.

Hellmann, M. C. (1992). *Recherches sur le vocabulaire de l'architecture grecque, d'après les inscriptions de Délos*. Paris: Diffusion De Boccard.

Hurst, H. (1988). Nuovi scavi nell'area di Santa Maria Antiqua. *Archeologia Laziale* 9, 13–17.

Lafon, X. (1995). Dehors ou dedans? Le *vestibulum* dans les *domus* aristocratiques à la fin de la République et au début de l'Empire. *Klio* 77, 405–23.

Lauritsen, M. T. (2011). Doors in domestic space at Pompeii at Herculaneum: a preliminary study. In D. Mladenović and B. Russell, eds., *TRAC 2010: Proceedings of the Twentieth Annual Theoretical Roman Archaeology Conference*. Oxford: Oxbow, 59–75.

Lauter, H. (2009). *Die Fassade des Hauses IX 1,20 in Pompeji: Gestalt und Bedeutung*. Mainz: Philipp von Zabern.

Leach, E. W. (1993). The entrance room in the house of Iulius Polybius and the nature of the Roman *vestibulum*. In E. M. Moormann, ed., *Functional and Spatial Analysis of Wall Painting: Proceedings of the Fifth International Congress on Ancient Wall Painting, Amsterdam, 8–12 September 1992.* Leiden: Stichting Babesch, 23–28.

(1997). *Oecus* on Ibycus: investigating the vocabulary of the Roman house. In S. E. Bon and R. Jones, eds., *Sequence and Space in Pompeii.* Oxford: Oxbow, 50–72.

Lega, C. (1989–90). Il Colosso di Nerone. *Bullettino della Commissione Archeologica Comunale di Roma* 93, 339–378.

Lorenzatti, S. (1998). La *domus* di Giove Fulminatore. *Bolletino di Archeologia* 49–50, 79–98.

Lugli, G. (1915). Le antiche ville dei Colli Albani prima della occupazione domizianea. *Bullettino della Commissione Archeologica Comunale di Roma* 42, 251–316.

Mar, R. (2009). La *Domus Flavia*, utilizzo e funzioni del palazzo di Domiziano. In F. Coarelli, ed., *Divus Vespasianus: il bimillenario dei Flavi.* Milan: Electa, 250–63.

Marquardt, J. (1864). *Römische Privatalterthümer (erste Abteilung).* Leipzig: Weidmann.

Mau, A. (1899). *Pompeii: Its Life and Art.* New York: Macmillan & Co. Ltd.

Nevett, L. (1997). Perceptions of domestic space in Roman Italy. In B. Rawson and P. Weaver, eds., *The Roman Family in Italy.* Oxford: Clarendon Press, 281–98.

(2010) *Domestic Space in Classical Antiquity.* Cambridge: Cambridge University Press.

Pavolini, C. (2006). *Ostia (Guide archeologische Laterza).* Rome: Laterza.

Pesando, F. and Guidobaldi, M. P. (2006). *Pompei, Oplontis, Ercolano, Stabiae (Guide archeologische Laterza).* Rome: Laterza.

Platts, H. (2018). The development and role of the Roman aristocratic *domus*. In C. Holleran and A. Claridge, eds., *A Companion to the City of Rome.* London: Wiley Blackwell, 299–316.

Proudfoot, E. (2013). Secondary doors in entranceways at Pompeii: reconsidering access and the 'view from the street'. In A. Bokern *et al.*, eds., *TRAC 2012: Proceedings of the Twenty-Second Annual Theoretical Roman Archaeology Conference.* Oxford: Oxbow, 91–115.

Riggsby, A. M. (1997). 'Public' and 'private' in Roman culture: the case of the *cubiculum*. *Journal of Roman Archaeology* 10, 36–56.

Royo, M. (1999). *Domus imperatoriae: topographie, formation et imaginaire des palais impériaux du Palatin.* Rome: École Française de Rome.

Ruffia, E. (2005). *Le 'Grotte di Catullo' a Sirmione: guida alla visita della villa romana e del museo.* Milan: Edizioni ET.

Saller, R. P. (1982). *Personal Patronage under the Early Empire*. Cambridge: Cambridge University Press.

Solin, H. (1989). Iscrizioni inedite nel Museo Campano. *Epigraphica* 51: 47–66.

Speksnijder, S. A. (2015). Beyond 'public' and 'private': accessibility and visibility during *salutationes*. In K. Tuori and L. Nissin, eds., *Public and Private in the Roman House and Society*. Journal of Roman Archaeology Supplementary Series 102. Portsmouth, RI: JRA, 87–99.

Sutherland, C. H. V., Carson, R. A. G., Carradice, I., Buttrey, T.V., Mattingly, H., Amandry, M. and A. Burnett, A. (1984). *The Roman Imperial Coinage*, 2nd ed. London: Spink and Son.

Tamm, B. (1964). Ist der Castortempel das *vestibulum* zu dem Palast des Caligula gewesen? *Eranos* 62, 146–69.

Torelli, M. (1993). s.v. "Area Palatina", *Lexicon Topographicum Urbis Romae (Volume Primo, A–C)*, ed. E. M. Steinby. Rome: Edizioni Quasar, 119.

Van Deman, E. B. (1924). The House of Caligula. *American Journal of Archaeology* 28, 368–98.

Wallace-Hadrill, A. (1994). *Houses and Society in Pompeii and Herculaneum*. Princeton: Princeton University Press.

(1997). Rethinking the Roman atrium house. In R. Laurence and A. Wallace-Hadrill, eds., *Domestic Space in the Roman World: Pompeii and Beyond*. Journal of Roman Archaeology Supplementary Series 22. Portsmouth, RI: JRA, 219–40.

(2001). Emperors and houses in Rome. In S. Dixon, ed., *Childhood, Class and Kin in the Roman World*. London: Routledge, 128–43.

Widrig, W. M. (1980). Two sites on the ancient Via Gabina. In K. Painter, ed., *Roman Villas in Italy: Recent Excavations and Research*. London: British Museum, 119–40.

Winterling, A. A. (1999). *Aula Caesaris: Studien zur Institutionalisierung des römischen Kaiserhofes in der Zeit von Augustus bis Commodus (31 v. Chr.–192 n. Chr.)*. Munich: R. Oldenbourg.

Wiseman, T. P. (1982). *Pete nobiles amicos*: poets and patrons in Late Republican Rome. In B. Gold, ed., *Literary Patronage in Greece and Rome*. Chapel Hill: University of North Carolina Press, 29–49.

(1987). *Conspicui postes tectaque digna deo*: the public image of aristocratic and imperial houses in the Late Republic and Early Empire. In *L'Urbs: espace urbain et histoire (Ier siècle av. J.-C. – IIIe siècle ap. J.-C.). Actes du colloque international organisé par le Centre national de la récherche scientifique et l'École française de Rome (Rome, 8–12 mai 1985)*. Rome: Ecole française de Rome, 393–413.

(2011). Vesta and *vestibulum*: an Ovidian etymology. *Scholia* 20, 72–79.

(2012). Where did they live (e.g., Cicero, Octavius, Augustus)? *Journal of Roman Archaeology* 25, 656–72.

(2013). The Palatine, from Evander to Elagabalus. *Journal of Roman Studies* 103, 234–68.

Zanker, P. (1988). *The Power of Images in the Age of Augustus*. Ann Arbor: University of Michigan Press.

(2002). Domitian's palace on the Palatine and the imperial image. In A. K. Bowman H. M. Cotton, M. Goodman and S. Price, eds., *Representations of Empire: Rome and the Mediterranean World*. Oxford: Oxford University Press, 105–30.

11 | Living in the Liminal

Lares Compitales Shrines, Freedmen and Identity in Delos

CRYSTA KACZMAREK

Outside the entrances of houses in the residential districts of Delos are remains of altars interpreted as shrines of the Roman cult of the *lares compitales*. An analysis of these shrines, incorporating archaeological, epigraphic and literary data, and taking the meanings of the location and practices of the cult into consideration, enables us to reach a more nuanced understanding of the *lares compitales* cult on Delos. Not only does this shed light on the potential meanings of this cult for its members in the 2nd and 1st centuries BCE, but it also illuminates how the *lares* shrines, and more generally, domestic space, may have functioned as a means of social identity expression and negotiation in ancient Greek and Roman societies. In keeping with the theme of the volume, this chapter is the result of a study which integrates textual and archaeological data in order to reach a deeper and more nuanced understanding of domestic space in the ancient world.

Identification of the *lares* shrines on Delos took place during the course of the excavations conducted by the École Française d'Athènes (EfA) on the residential districts in the late 19th and early 20th centuries, the results of which are published in the *Exploration Archéologique de Délos* (*EAD*).[1] The explicit study of the Delian *lares* shrines began in 1926 with Marcel Bulard, who compiled a catalogue of fifty-four shrines from Delos, twenty-three of which contained reconstructable traces of religious themed paintings. However, he erroneously identified the cult as the *lares familiares*, on the basis of similarities to the domestic shrines in the houses of Pompeii.[2] In his 1970 publication, Philippe Bruneau corrects Bulard's misattribution and demonstrates that the Delos shrines were a closer parallel, not to the shrines within the houses of Pompeii, but rather to the twenty-three shrines (ten of which are identified with certainty) found at crossroads in the residential neighbourhoods.[3] In addition, Bruneau added another four examples to the Delian repertoire.[4] With four additional examples reported by Bezerra de Meneses and Sarian in 1970 and 1973,[5] a total of thirty houses with shrines formed the basis for the first comprehensive study on the Delian *lares compitales* shrines, completed in 2003 by Claire Hasenohr.

Although Hasenohr's study marked an important step in the examination of the wall paintings associated with the *lares* shrines, it only included shrines with visible remains of painting, leaving out any examples whose paintings could not be reconstructed.[6] Although other scholars have engaged with the evidence from Delos, these shrines appear mostly as minutiae in comparative studies of domestic space.[7] The remaining studies of the *lares* concentrate predominantly on their manifestations in other parts of the Roman world, namely central and southern Italy and Spain.[8] Furthermore, while many scholars assert that the cult is particularly associated with enslaved people and freedmen, no one has yet attempted to determine why the *lares compitales* cult was attractive to these participants. By bringing together the literary, epigraphic and contextual archaeological data into a cohesive study it is possible to investigate the cultural role and meanings of the cult for its participants.[9]

This chapter includes all securely identified Delian *lares* shrines, and as such contributes to the current corpus of knowledge of the Delian *lares* and the role of Roman domestic cult more generally, by focusing the analysis on two aspects of the *lares* cult that have not yet been explored: the role of the *lares* shrines as a medium for the expression and negotiation of social identity; and the meaning of the cult for its members, particularly freedmen. In order to achieve this, I will begin by presenting the archaeological and epigraphic data, then place the data within the wider context of *lares* worship in the Roman world. I will finish by focusing discussion of the shrines on the potential significance of the cult to freedmen.

In addition to the thirty-one examples of *lares* shrines found in thirty different houses that Hasenohr included in her 2003 study,[10] I have identified another fifteen, giving a total dataset of forty-five houses with shrines (see Table 11.1). Since 1970, when Bruneau attributed the shrines to the cult of the *lares compitales*, *lares* shrines have been identified by the presence of certain characteristics and elements: the presence of an altar or niche, or just a wall, usually near the entrance to the house on an external wall,[11] with accompanying paintings carrying specific sets of images representing the celebration of the *Compitalia* (see Figure 11.1).[12]

One of the unique features of the Delian shrines, in contrast to other parts of the Roman world such as Pompeii, is the addition of depictions of deities and heroes such as Hercules and Mercury.[13] Although depictions of Hercules appear occasionally in Pompeian *lares* shrines,[14] they appear far more frequently in Delos. Furthermore, unlike the Pompeian *lares* shrines, the Delian examples do not include depictions of the *genius*, the individual

Table 11.1. *Catalogue of shrines of the* Lares compitales *on Delos*

Shrine no.	House	Identifying characteristic	References
Bulard 1926b, no. 1 and 2	Maison du lac	Paintings left of door west of the court	Bruneau 1970: 404–405; Bulard 1926a: 59–60, fig. 23; Hasenohr 2003: no. 1 and 2; Tang 2005: 241
Bulard 1926b, no. 3	House west of the Maison du lac	Paintings on wall both sides of door	Hasenohr 2003: no. 3; Tang 2005: 242
Bulard 1926b, no. 4	House I and II, îlot des bronzes	Paintings flanking entrance door EA (Bulard 1926a: 64–69)	Hasenohr 2003: no. 4; Siebert 2001: 55–73, pl. III; Bruneau 1970: 591, 599; Tang 2005: 229–30
Bulard 1926b, no. 5	House north of the Poseidoniasts of Berytos	Paintings flanking door; altar opposite side of road facing door	Bruneau 1970: 594; Chamonard 1924: 441–42; Tang 2005: 229
Bulard 1926b, no. 6 and 7	Magasin aux colonnes	Painting and niche beside door	Hasenohr 2003: no. 6 and 7
Bulard 1926b, no. 9	Shop (magasin delta) of House opening onto the north road	Paintings flanking NW door; altar right of NE door	Hasenohr 2003: no. 9,
Bulard 1926b, no. 10	Magasin XIX	Paintings and altar right of NW door, altar right of NE door	Hasenohr 2003: no. 10
Bulard 1926b, no. 11	Theatre House II B	Paintings and niche, side of walled door	Chamonard 1924: 29–31 pls. III–IV; Hasenohr 2003: no. 11; Tang 2005: 259–60
Bulard 1926b, no. 12	Theatre II D	Paintings flanking entrance, south wall of room a	Bruneau 1970: 404–405, 594–95; Hasenohr 2003: no. 12; Chamonard 1924: 32, pls. III–IV; Tang 2005: 260–61
Bulard 1926b, no. 13	Theatre III F	Paintings and altar, side of door	Chamonard 1924: 32; pls. V–VI; Hasenohr 2003: no. 13; Tang 2005: 265
Bulard 1926b, no. 14	House at Theatre III intersection of street 2 and alley ζ	Paintings and altar, left of door	Hasenohr 2003: no. 14; Tang 2005: 273
Bulard 1926b, no. 17	Theatre VI G	Paintings and altar, side of door	Bruneau 1970: 594–96; Hasenohr 2003: no. 17, Tang 2005: 265
Bulard 1926b, no. 18	Theatre VI H	Paintings right of door	Bruneau 1970: 404–405; Chamonard 1924: 56–58 pls. III–IV; Hasenohr 2003: no. 18; Tang 2005: 279
Bulard 1926b, no. 19	Theatre VI I (Maison du Dionysos)	Paintings left of the door on façade of Theatre Road	Bruneau 1970: 640; Chamonard 1924: 486–562, pls. III–IV; Hasenohr 2003: no. 19; Tang 2005: 279–80; Trümper 1998, plan 1 301–303, 333 fig. 65, no. 80.

Bulard 1926b, no. 20	House north-east of Theatre Insula II	Paintings and altar right and left of door	Tang 2005: 284; Hasenohr 2003: no. 20
Bulard 1926b, no. 21	House opposite DelT6 (Theatre II E)	Painted altars flanking door	Hasenohr 2003: no. 21; Tang 2005: 284
Bulard 1926b, no. 22	Maison des dauphins	Painting and altar flanking door	Bruneau 1970: 404–405; Chamonard 1924: 401–10, 475–86; pls. XXIII–XXVI;
Bulard 1926b, no. 23	House west of la Maison des dauphins	Paintings, side of door	Bruneau 1970: 594–96; Hasenohr 2003: no. 23.
Bulard 1926b, no. 24	Stadium I B or House east of I B	Paintings and altar right of stairway entrance	Hasenohr 2003: no. 24; Tang 2005: 245
Bulard 1926b, no. 25 and 26	Stadium 1 C (House of Q. Tullius)	Paintings and altar beside walled door on south exterior wall	Bruneau 1970: 404–405, 594–95; Hasenohr 2003: no. 25 and 26; Rauh 1993: 200–202; Tang 2005: 243
Bulard 1926b, no. 27	Stadium I D	Paintings and altar and niche, side of door	Bruneau 1970: 595–96; Hasenohr 2003: no. 27; Tang 2005: 243–44
Bulard 1926b, no. 34	Theatre Rue 1, no. 5 en face de l'extremité Ouest de l'analemma Nord du théâtre	Altar, side of door	Chamonard 1924: pls. V, VI
Bulard 1926b, no. 35	Theatre II E	Paintings, east face of house flanking entrance at room a	Chamonard 1924: 270, pls. III–IV; Tang 2005: 261
Bulard 1926b, no. 38	Theatre VI B	Painted room vestibule A	Chamonard 1924: 53, pls. III–IV; Tang 2005, 276
Bulard 1926b, no. 40	Theatre VI J	Altar and niche, SE angle of courtyard d	Chamonard 1924, 59–60, pls. III–IV; 5; Tang 2005, 280–1;
Bulard 1926b, no. 42	Stadium 1 E	Paintings and altar beside west entrance	Tang 2005: 244–45; Trümper 1998: 218–22, fig. 22, no. 28
Bulard 1926b, no. 43	Stadium II A	Paintings and altar, east of entrance	Tang 2005: 245; Trümper 1998: 222–23, fig. 24, no. 29
Bulard 1926b, no. 44	Inopus House B	Altar at intersection of road at corner of house	Chamonard 1924: 435–37, pl. XXVIII; Rauh 1993: 203; Tang 2005: 253–54
Bulard 1926b, no. 46	Theatre II A (Maison du trident)	Painting and altar in vestibule (a)	Chamonard 1924: 27–29, pls. III–IV; Tang 2005: 259
Bulard 1926b, no. 48	House across from Maison du lac, SW corner of North Palaestra	Paintings both sides of door	Rauh 1993: 210, fig. 37; Bruneau 1970: 643; Tang 2005: 242
Bulard 1926b, no. 51	House on the corner of Theatre III, ruelle δ	Niche and painting, side of door	Chamonard 1924: 252, pls. V, VI

Table 11.1. (*cont.*)

Shrine no.	House	Identifying characteristic	References
Bulard 1926b, no. 54	The eastern house (Aphrodision II)	Painting and niche beside door	Tang 2005: 284
Hasenohr 2003 no. 55	House west of the Maison de la colline	Painting and altar, right of door	Bruneau 1970: 591–92; 1975: 292; Bezerra de Meneses and Sarian 1973; Tang 2005: 241
Hasenohr 2003 no. 56	Maison aux frontons	Paintings in room X	Bezerra de Meneses, 1970: 191–93; Bruneau 1970: 590; Tang 2005: 237
Hasenohr 2003 no. 57	Intersection of west and north roads of the Ilôt des bronzes	Paintings and altar, NW corner of insula by room FQ	Bruneau 1970: 640–41; Siebert 2001: 78–80, pl. III, Tang 2005: 231
Hasenohr 2003 no. 58	House VII, Ilôt des bronzes	Painting, west of entrance	Bruneau 1970: 591; Siebert 2001: 81–84, pl. III; Tang 2005: 231–32
Hasenohr 2003 no. 59	House II, Ilôt des bijoux	Painting west of main entrance of vestibule J' and staircase	Siebert 2001: 23–31, pl. 1; Tang 2005: 233
Hasenohr 2003 no. 60	House III, Ilôt des bijoux	Paintings and altar east of door	Siebert 2001: 31–35, pl. 1; Tang 2005: 233–34
Hasenohr 2003 no. 61	Maison de l'Hermes	Paintings beside door	Rauh 1993: 219–30; Tang 2005: 252
Hasenohr 2003 no. 62	Maison defFourni	Painting flanking stairs leading to the court	Bruneau 1970: 590, 592, 633; Bruneau and Ducat 1983: 166; Tang 2005: 286–87
Bruneau no. 63	Inopus C (maison a une seule colonne)	Niche and paintings with altar space beside door	Chamonard 1924: pl. XXVIII, 437–38; Bruneau 1972: 218–21, 223; 1973: 113–19, 126; Tang 2005: 254
Bruneau no. 64	Maison des masques (House B)	Painted west of entrance (a)	Bruneau 1972: 239–60: Tang 2005: 256–57
Bruneau no. 65	House C (Ilôt de la Maison des masques)	Painted at entrance (a) to east	Bruneau 1972: 260; Tang 2005: 257
Bruneau no. 66	Maison des comédiens, middle part of the Ilôt de la Maison des comédiens	Niche, painted room	Bezerra de Meneses 1970: pl. A; Bruneau 1972: 172–7; Tang 2005: 237–38
Bruneau no. 67	Maison de la colline	Paintings flanking main entrance	Bezerra de Meneses and Sarian 1973: 90–110; Chamcnard 1924: 411–16, pls. XIV–XVII; Bruneau 1972: 182–83; Tang 2005: 240–41

Figure 11.1 Example of *Lares* shrine flanking the door of a house. EfA/Bulard 1926b: fig. 41. École Française d'Athènes/M. Bulard.

protector deity of male Roman citizens, nor of serpents.[15] Another important aspect of the Delian *lares compitales* cult was its dual nature: not only did cult practice take place outside the individual houses, but also in a more public context, by means of dedications made at the so-called Agora of the Compitaliastai (or Agora of the Hermiastai, as it is also known).[16]

Lares shrines on Delos were usually placed on the external wall of a home, on one or both sides of, or across the street from, a doorway (see Figure 11.1).[17] Thirty-eight of forty-five examples conform to this rule, with the remaining seven being found inside the home.[18] In the cases where altars are present, twenty-two of the forty-five examples, a variety of materials and construction methods are used: they are quadrangular, circular or semicircular built altars constructed from stuccoed rubble masonry of gneiss or poros stone, earth and mortar, or more rarely, monolithic marble.[19] In nine cases, niches replace or accompany an altar.[20] Evidence of several coats of paint suggests that participants refurbished and reused the shrines regularly.[21] Of the forty-five shrines, forty-two presented traces of paint, although eight of these are not well enough preserved to permit the reconstruction of the images.[22]

Of the shrines that include reconstructable paintings, the most commonly depicted scene, with sixteen attestations, is pugilistic contests, interpreted as part of the *ludi* celebrated at the *Compitalia* (see Figure 11.2).[23] The second most common scene, appearing on twelve shrines,[24] consists of one or more individuals performing a ritual offering on an altar (Figures 11.3 and 11.4).[25] The majority of these scenes depict individuals identified tentatively as Roman, since they are clothed in togas and perform the ritual *velato capite* (with head covered).[26] This is, however, a rather simplistic identifier and could reflect an iconographic tradition rather than Roman identity of the participants. Despite this, given the fact that the *lares* represent one of the traditional cults of the Romans, it is perhaps not a stretch to suggest that the figures depicted *velato capite* are intended to depict Roman practitioners and members of their extended *familia*, including slaves and freedmen.[27] There is a single occurrence (at the House west of the Maison de la Colline) where the individuals depicted perform the sacrifice in Greek fashion with heads wreathed, rather than covered in Roman style (Figure 11.5).[28] Interestingly, this shrine also includes inscriptions in both Latin and Greek, as will be discussed in more detail below.[29]

The main individual performing the sacrifice usually has a hand outstretched over, or stands near, the altar.[30] The items sacrificed consist of pork joints, fruit and incense.[31] In addition to the individual(s) performing the sacrifice, one or more other figures often accompany the scene. Some are dressed in short garments, often preparing a sacrificial pig or holding other items for sacrifice,[32] and are identified as slaves or attendants (see Figures 11.3–11.7).[33] One or more *aulos* players may also accompany this scene (see Figure 11.3),[34] as do prizes: an amphora, a palm, a crown or a ham.[35] Other images on or surrounding the altars include depictions of gods such as Mercury,[36] or heroes such as Hercules.[37] The cult of Hercules in the Roman world has a long history of association with the enslaved population, starting with its maintenance being entrusted to public slaves in the 4th century BCE.[38]

Thirteen depictions of the *lares* occur in seven different houses.[39] They are dressed in short tunics, sometimes with a mantle attached at the neck or floating from the back, wear either Phrygian caps or are wreathed with garlands, and hold a *rhyton*, a *patera* or a *situla* in an upraised hand (Figure 11.8).[40] These attributes of the *lares* are not particular to the Delos examples, but are part of an iconographic tradition that is remarkably consistent across the Roman world.[41]

At the House west of the Maison de la Colline, THEOGIPIASON was painted in Latin on a scene of three men with heads wreathed in Greek ritual fashion performing a sacrifice at an altar; interpreted to represent three names Theog[. . .], [H]ip[. . .] and Iason (Figure 11.5).[42] Here we have

Figure 11.2 Example of pugilistic contest. EfA/ Bezerra de Meneses and Sarian 1973: fig. 23. École Française d'Athènes / H. Sarian and Bezerra de Meneses.

Figure 11.3 Painted reconstruction of sacrifice scene, from Magasin XIX. EfA/ Bulard 1926b: PL. XIX. École Française d'Athènes / M. Bulard

Figure 11.4 Painted reconstruction of sacrifice scene, from Stadium I D. EfA/ Bulard 1926b: PL. XXIV. École Française d'Athènes / M. Bulard

Figure 11.5 Sacrifice scene with wreathed participants, from the House west of the Maison de la Colline. EfA/ Bezerra de Meneses and Sarian 1973: fig. 22. École Française d'Athènes / H. Sarian and Bezerra de Meneses

three Greek names, written in Latin on a shrine of a Roman cult, with depictions of participants sacrificing in Greek fashion. In Stadium house I C, three slaves or freedmen of Quintus Tullius dedicated a statue to their patron, inscribed with a dedication in both Latin and Greek (*ID* 1802).[43] One of these individuals, the freedman Q. Tullius Q. l. Heracleo / Κόιντος Τύλλιος Ἡρακλέων, is confirmed in the lists from the Agora of the Compitaliastai, to which I will later return, as a magistrate in 98/97 BCE (*ID* 1761).[44] Although this inscription does not appear directly on the altar, it confirms that freedmen were present in this house and adds more support to the connection between this cult with slaves and freedmen. On the shrine outside of Stadium house 1D the names Crusipus Heliod[...] (or Heliofo[...]), Παρμ[ε]ν[ίων] and Ἀγατ[...] were written in either Latin or Greek.[45] All of these names are of Greek origin, but there is no Roman cognomen associated and therefore they do not provide

Figure 11.6 Painted reconstruction of attendants preparing sacrificial pig, from Stadium 1 D.EfA/ Bulard 1926b: PL. XXV.1. École Française d'Athènes / M. Bulard

determinative evidence about the ethnic identity of these members. Four Greek names appear, but only one is written in Greek. Bruneau suggests that this shrine demonstrates mixed nationality since the individuals bear names of Greek origin but the figures depicted on the shrine are in togas *velato capite*.[46] The images present on the *lares compitales* shrines, however, may represent a set generic iconographic repertoire belonging to this cult. It seems more likely, as proposed by other scholars[47] and suggested by the presence of Greek-style wreathed individuals on the shrine of the House west of the Maison de la Colline, that these individuals represent various members of the household who are participating in the rituals.

In every case where inscriptions on a shrine name depicted individuals, the names suggest that they are freedmen or slaves of Roman families. With the exception of one instance in Stadium I C, no Roman *nomina* or *cognomina* are associated with the Greek personal names appearing on the shrines and therefore there is no confirmation from this source of this hypothesis. Since so few shrines had inscriptions naming participants, it is necessary to turn to another source of information on the *lares compitales* cult of Delos, the public dedications of the Compitaliastai.

Figure 11.7 Attendant preparing sacrificial pig. EfA/ Bulard 1926b: PL. XXV.2. École Française d'Athènes / M. Bulard.

Figure 11.8 The *lares*, from the House west of the Maison de la Colline. EfA/ Bezerra de Meneses and Sarian 1973: PL. 1.2. École Française d'Athènes/ Bezerra de Meneses and H. Sarian.

Dedications to various gods were found in the Agora of the Compitaliastai (also called the Agora of the Hermiastai), a civic building, interpreted as the location of an association of slaves and freedmen of Italian families, on the basis of the discovery of these inscriptions (*ID* 1760–1771). Written in Greek, dating to the late 2nd and early 1st centuries BCE,[48] these inscriptions are addressed to the gods (θεοί), interepreted as representing the *lares*. The dedicants are listed and explicitly referred to as Κομπεταλιασταί.[49] The actual function of this college and its associated buildings has not been conclusively determined,[50] however, it seems to be a public, communal manifestation of the cult practised in the residential districts.[51] What is clear is that when the civic status of the participants can be determined, they overwhelmingly represent slaves and freedmen of Roman families;[52] most of them individuals having Greek *praenomen* and the *nomen* or *cognomen* of a Roman family.[53]

The evidence from the inscriptions on the shrines and from the Agora of the Compitaliastai points to the particular importance of this cult for the slaves and freedmen of Delos. In order to identify any detectable patterns that could account for the presence or absence of a *lares* shrine in a given type of house, I have analysed the available architectural and archaeological data, asking, for example, if these shrines occur in rich or poor houses, large or small ones. In order to accomplish this, after selecting ninety-six houses with adequate data from Monika Trümper's 1998 catalogue, I calculated the mean house size and number of rooms for the total sample. I then selected the houses with *lares* shrines (thirty-three of the ninety-six houses with floor plan data), and calculated the mean house size and number of rooms for the total sample, the houses with *lares* shrines and those without. The mean house size includes ground floor measurements, including the courtyard, in order avoid the bias due to houses having separate occupants for each level. The mean house size of the total sample is 240.6 m². It was immediately apparent that houses with *lares* shrines are generally larger than the total population with a mean house size of 299.7 m², while houses with no shrines are significantly smaller at a mean of 197.3 m². The same trend holds true for number of rooms, with the total population having a mean of 9.25 rooms, houses with *lares* 11.34, and houses without 8.02.

Further, a chi-squared test and a cluster analysis were performed to determine whether there was any correlation between the presence of *lares* shrines and prestige goods (namely marble architectural elements, peristyles, mosaic floor treatments – *opus tessellatum* and *vermiculatum* – wall painting, and sculpture). Because it can be used to determine whether there is a statistically significant association between variables in a wide range of situations, the chi-squared test is commonly used by archaeologists in many fields.[54] A chi-squared test calculates the expected frequency of given variables if the distribution were evenly distributed across the populations (the null hypothesis), and tests this against the actual presence of these variables in order to determine whether a statistically significant relationship exists. A positive value of 16.07 was found for the chi-square test, measuring the correlation between the presence of *lares* shrines and the number of prestige goods, meaning that there is a positive relationship between the presence of prestige goods and the presence of *lares*.

Cluster analysis is a classification method that is concerned with defining groups within a dataset, based on the concept that members of a group are more similar to one another than to members of another group.[55] This analysis is designed to take ungrouped data and discover patterns based on similarity and differences in the parameters set by the investigator.[56] While there are several methods of cluster analysis, the most common, and the one used here, is the hierarchical agglomerative cluster analysis, which separates all data and then builds groups by starting with the most similar items and continuing at increasingly smaller levels of similarity until all units are grouped together at the lowest level of similarity.[57] The results of my cluster analysis conformed to the results of the chi-square test. At level five, the highest level of similarity, mosaics, marble columns, marble thresholds and sculpture are grouped together, revealing that these items most frequently occur together. At level four, *lares* shrines, peristyles, wall painting, and columns made from materials other than marble, join the items from level five.

The results of the statistical analyses suggest that there are indeed identifiable patterns in terms of the contexts in which the *lares* shrines occur. Houses with *lares* shrines are more likely to be larger and have more rooms than houses without shrines. Additionally, *lares* shrines are more likely to occur in association with prestige goods such as marble architecture, peristyles, mosaics, wall painting and columns. These results could be interpreted to mean that wealthy, free citizens are more likely to own the houses with *lares* shrines, and it is their dependants, either freedmen or slaves, who are associated with the practice of the *lares* cult.[58] It is, however, entirely possible that wealthy freedmen could have owned at least some of the houses with shrines. Unfortunately, the attribution of property owners to individual houses is impossible, and therefore these results are not able to tell us more than the fact that the shrines are located in larger, more elaborately decorated homes. If we now turn to the literary sources, we can place the Delos shrines within the wider context of the worship of the *lares*, and begin to reach an understanding of the potential significance that this cult may have had for the participants.

The nature of the *lares*, and their cult, is far from clear and is plagued with difficulties of reconstruction due to the fact they are rarely mentioned in the ancient sources. Complicating matters even further is the fact that the *lares* have several known manifestations: the *lares familiares* (of the household), the *lares viales* (of the roads),[59] the *lares permarini* (of ocean voyages),[60] the *lares militares* (of the soldiers), the *lares praestites* (guardians of the city),[61] the *lares semitales* (of the footpaths or byways), the *lares ludentes* (of the games) and the *lares compitales* (of the cross roads).[62] Inscriptions dating from the Republican to the late Imperial period from various parts of the Roman world attest to these names.[63] They, along with the literary sources, provide little information about how or why the *lares* are divided into different forms.[64] Early discussions, primarily between Waites and Wissowa, focused on their origins as either related to ancestors or protectors of places.[65] There is something of a consensus among scholars that the common characteristic of the different forms of the *lares* is their protective and productive nature.[66] The remainder of this chapter will concentrate on the *lares* in the form of the *compitales*.

The literary sources that specifically mention the *lares compitales* give some detail about their role and about the practices of their associated cult.[67] The earliest known reference comes from the poet Naevius in the 3rd century BCE, who mentions a man named Theodotus painting *lares ludentes* on altars for the *Compitalia*.[68] Because he does not mention the location, nature or function of the cult, this reference only tells of its existence at that time. Ovid tells of the mythical birth of the *lares* twins, stating that they protect the crossroads and forever keep watch in their city (*qui compita servant et vigilant nostra semper in urbe, lares*).[69] Pliny the Elder remarks that the city of Rome was divided into fourteen districts with 265 crossroads of the *lares* (*compita larum cclxv*).[70] Horace and Propertius state that on the day of the festival, at the end of December or beginning of January at the winter solstice, honey cakes and pork were sacrificed and games (*ludi compitalicii*) are celebrated in the streets.[71] The performance of sacrifices is supported archaeologically by the depictions of scenes of sacrifices of pork on the Delian altars. Furthermore, it is likely that the depictions of pugilists, as well as prizes, represent games associated with the practice of the cult. While this chapter does not seek to use archaeological data to confirm or contradict literary evidence, the convergence of the sources allows us to assume with relative certainty that sacrifices took place at the *lares* shrines and games were played in celebration.

Dionysos of Halicarnassus also mentions the *lares compitales*, and gives much greater detail. He states that the festival and cult originated under Servius Tullius, and was celebrated at καλιάδες (shrines or chapels) set up by inhabitants of houses for the ἥρωες προνώπιοι (heroes of the façades) in all of the στενωποί (roads or alleys), the ceremonies being performed ἐν τοῖς προνωπίοις (in front of the façades) and access being limited to slaves.[72] The locations of the shrines in Delos seem to support this testimony. Dionysos of Halicarnassus is the only source that states that the worship of *lares* is limited to slaves. While the epigraphic evidence from Delos does indicate that slaves and freedmen likely participated in this cult, neither the archaeological nor the epigraphic data support the assertion that only slaves participated in the cult. Cato states that the *vilicus* of a villa should perform no religious rites except at the *Compitalia* at the crossroads (*in compito*) or the hearth (*in foco*)[73]; it is never indicated that no other members of the household may participate. In fact, Macrobius and Festus mention explicitly how the night before the *Compitalia* the participants attached woollen dolls, one for each free member of the household, and woollen balls, one for each slave, to the *compita*, or doors.[74] Perhaps what Dionysos of Halicarnassus meant is that religious and ritual participation by slaves was limited to this cult. If this was the case, it would hardly be surprising that freedmen continued to participate in this cult, if it was the only one in which they had personal involvement. Cato also provides additional evidence for why the cult may have been important for slaves, mentioning that they should receive a double portion of wine on the day of the festival.[75] These sources converge once again with the archaeological data, further corroborating the theory that this cult was of particular importance to the enslaved population. It is therefore not unfitting to assume that it would continue to be so as slaves were freed and left their servile status behind them.

When taken together, the literary, archaeological and epigraphic data identify a number of trends in the location, nature and practices of the *lares compitales* cult on Delos. The shrines are located at the doors of houses, where the cult practices would have taken place during the festival of the *Compitalia* when sacrifices were made by slaves and freedmen associated with this cult in the sources. It should be noted, however, that it is not slaves who were depicted performing sacrifices on the shrines at Delos, but what appear to be free Roman male citizens wearing togas *velato capite*. It is not possible to identify whether these individuals are citizens or perhaps freedmen, but it does suggest that it was not only slaves who participated in the practice of this cult. Statistical analyses demonstrate that the shrines occurred predominantly in houses that are larger, have more rooms, and have larger quantities of decorations and prestige goods. Despite the fact that these analyses do not allow us to determine whether free or freed individuals owned these houses, the results do not exclude the association of these shrines with slaves and freedmen. In fact, it is not unreasonable to assume that these larger houses were owned by free citizens with slaves and/or freedmen within their household.[76]

It is by taking the information retrieved from various sources on the *lares compitales* cult on Delos, and interpreting it within an appropriate theoretical framework that concentrates on its construction through the communal repetition of rituals, that we can reach an understanding of what meaning the *lares compitales* cult may have had for its members. This will in turn allow a better understanding of the role of household and civic religion as a medium for social identity expression and negotiation and, much like the other contributions in this volume, domestic space in general.

The following theory of religious practice and construction of meaning was originally developed by the sociologist Pierre Bourdieu and elaborated by Louis Althusser,[77] and since then the theory has been adapted and applied in studies of ancient religious practices.[78] This theory states that the actions and rituals involved in religious practice have social weight because individuals, both those who participate in the action and those who do not, assign value to the practices.[79] Repetition of these practices confirms and reinforces their social significance, and because they are considered socially valuable the repetition constructs the overarching ideas, meanings, concepts, purposes and goals of the religion.[80] These constructed meanings in turn inform the practices and actions of the participants, so that there is a reciprocal influence and reinforcement of social value between the practice and constructed meanings.[81] Shared participation in the practices and constructed meanings, which have social value, also function to create and maintain group bonds and solidarity.[82] Those participating are separated from those who are not, creating a sense of identity and otherness.[83] Using this theoretical perspective to interpret the Delian evidence, I believe, provides useful tools to shed light on the potential constructed meanings embedded in the practice of the *compitales* cult.

As a socially valued religious practice, in which Romans were accustomed to participate, the presence of the *lares compitales* cult on Delos where there was a large Roman population, because of its role as a trade port, is not surprising. Although it is possible that originally this cult was limited to Romans, the evidence from Delos shows that individuals with personal names of Greek origin also took part. It is not clear whether they are of Greek origin however, and the most one can say is that the iconography suggests that the majority of the participants performed the rituals associated with the cult in Roman fashion, despite the fact that we know of participants with Greek names.

In order to determine why these individuals chose to participate in the cult and what potential meanings it had for its members, we must look at the values associated with the practices of this cult, as well as the physical location that structured these practices. The *lares compitales* are associated with physical boundaries, they are worshipped at points of transition, and the cult is practised at the doors of houses, a physical boundary between the household and outside world. Physical boundaries are often imbued with symbolic and social meaning and this is certainly the case in both Greek and Roman cultures, where physical boundaries are frequently given religious and symbolic significance, for example at a temple or sanctuary.[84] The border or *temenos* of the sanctuary is a boundary between the sacred and profane, it is physical yet symbolic.[85] In addition to the *lares*, other Roman deities involved boundaries. Ovid reports that Terminus, the boundary stone, is worshipped at the divisions of fields in order to prevent strife between neighbours and war between states.[86] In addition, Livy states that the fetial priests concerned with declarations of war and peace treaties, followed a ritual which was performed at fixed boundaries (at the boundary line of the city, when entering the town gate, and when entering the marketplace).[87] If we add other deities such as Janus, Hercules and Mercury, who all have associations with doors and therefore boundaries, as well as festivals, such as *Saturnalia* and *Terminalia*,[88] it is clear that Roman religious practice places a general importance on boundaries and transitions.

In the case of the *lares compitales* of Delos, the cult operates at the physical boundary between the house and the outside world, and at the symbolic boundary between public and private. The door is a mediating space which both separates the private from the public outside world and allows transition between the two. The timing of this festival, shortly after the Saturnalia at the end of December or the beginning of January,[89] contributed to the liminal quality of the cult, since the month of January was intimately related to the location of the cult, doorways. Janus, the Roman god after whom January is named, is the quintessential deity of *transitiones perviae*,[90] the guardian of doorways, 'the embodiment of a boundary'.[91] Furthermore, the shrines of Delos frequently include images of both Hercules and Mercury, both of whom serve, at least in part, as protectors of doorways.[92] The relationships, therefore, between the *lares*, the location of the cult's practice, the timing of the festival, and the additional deities associated with the cult, all relate to boundaries: between the inside and outside, public and private, and between years.

This liminal character of the cult can be taken one step further and another symbolic boundary can be inferred. The literary references to the *lares compitales* associate them especially with slaves. In 64 BCE, the Senate suppressed the *ludi compitalicii* and the associated *collegia*, formed primarily of slaves and freedmen, for fear of subversion and riots.[93] The epigraphic evidence from the Agora of the Compitaliastai on Delos, documenting participants in the cult, displays a preponderance of slaves and freedmen (*ID* 1760–71). It can then be said that the cult of the *lares compitales* operates within the social boundary between the free and the enslaved. During the period when the *lares compitales* cult was being practised at Delos, the mid- to late 2nd and mid -1st centuries BCE, in the Roman world an increasing number of slaves were achieving freedom creating an essentially new social class.[94] Freedmen, no longer having servile status, fully belong neither among the slave or citizen class, but rather represent a liminal zone between the two categories. Crossing of the social boundaries between slave and free was accompanied by a transference of status and the abandonment of one identity for another.

By communally participating in a religious practice that gives value to boundaries, freedmen create and maintain group bonds with others participating in the same rituals.[95] Through the creation of group bonds these individuals are negotiating their place in their social world by expressing, and placing value on, their social identity. Through setting up shrines, or by participating in the rituals associated with them, individuals express their social identity as participating members of the cult, and are accepted as valid participants by other members. By participating in a cult which is associated with boundaries – physical and symbolic – the individual constructs meaning, and since the experience is communal, it gives a shared sense of identity to those participating. It is possible that the *lares compitales* cult, as a religious practice concerned with boundaries, was attractive and easily elaborated by freed individuals who crossed this social boundary. By expressing their sense of belonging as a member of a social boundary group, in the domestic context (at the doors of houses), as well as in a more public setting (the Agora of the Compitaliastai), membership is materially reified, not only by the household, but by the wider community as well. This ability of the *Lares compitales* to encourage social cohesion may have been one of the prime motivations for Augustus' reform of the cult and institution of new shrines throughout the *vici* of Rome.[96] Augustus not only reorganized the city of Rome into fourteen regions consisting of several hundred *vici*, but also ordered that the *lares* be wreathed twice a year, and combined the cult with his own *genius* and the *lares augusti*.[97] By associating the worship of the *genius augusti* with the cult of the *lares*, Augustus was able to effectively communicate the new imperial power to a large portion of the general population, legitimizing its existence.[98]

Furthermore, by participating in a long-standing religious action, the members of the cult express a shared identity with other members of a socially accepted and valued religious practice, in turn reinforcing the legitimacy of the social hierarchy. Through the dual public and private rituals, through its liminal quality and its social inclusiveness, the *lares compitales* cult had the potential to legitimize the basic structure of Roman society. The household, and therefore the Empire, included not only free Roman citizens but slaves and freedmen as well, and therefore their participation in the cult was permitted. The participation of all members of a household, of varied social statuses, in a cult with roots early in Roman history confirms the validity of society's hierarchy and encourages social cohesion. In fact, Dionysius of Halicarnassus (IV 14, 3–4) reports that these shrines caused sufficient fear, due to their role as centres of religious and social congregation, that in 64 BCE the *ludi compitalicii* were abolished by order of the senate because of the dangers presented by their ability to unite the masses.[99]

Although the level of involvement of free citizens is unclear, in both the archaeological and textual data, it is possible that if they participated it was because the *lares* were a traditional Roman cult, since by doing so they confirmed their social status as free citizens. Furthermore, for free citizens, practice in this cult may have been primarily concerned with the protection and well-being of the household as a whole, including free, enslaved and freed individuals. If individuals of different social statuses all participated in the *lares compitales* cult, as seems to be the case, it follows that a variety of constructed meanings associated with the practice of the cult existed, representing the interests of different participants. Free individuals participating in the same cult meant sharing in an ancestral custom, while for freedmen the *lares* cult may have responded to a need for a sense of group belonging with other individuals with similar social identities, as well as a desire to identify themselves as no longer belonging to the servile class. In the case of slaves, it is possible that their participation in the cult reflects a desire or aspiration towards moving upwards through social boundaries.

As the number of freed slaves was increasing, the possibility for a slave to move upwards in the social hierarchy increased. Regardless of the desires to which this cult responded, the fact that it included individuals of all social statuses meant that it reinforced the wider societal hierarchy and legitimized it, not only through the association with gods and a cult, but also with gods and a cult deeply rooted in the early history of Rome. By practising this cult both in a public location (the Agora of the Compitaliastai) and in front of private residences in the neighbourhoods of Delos, members collectively performed rituals passed down through generations, forming social bonds and reifying societal hierarchies at both the household and the wider societal level. Participants of different social statuses, through the building of shrines and the communal practice of rituals, expressed their membership in the cult and in consequence their membership of Roman society, in locations that would be seen and recognized by other members of the cult and probably by the community as a whole.

It is only through having investigated this aspect of domestic space in Delos using both archaeological and textual data that it was possible to advance these theories on the potential meanings of this cult to its participants. It is through investigating domestic space in creative ways incorporating multiple lines of evidence that we are able to contribute to a better understanding of the role of domestic space in the ancient world. As is evident from the wide-ranging subjects investigated in this volume, these types of studies have the potential to illuminate the ways in which domestic space interacted with, was influenced by, and influenced socio-cultural, religious, economic and political aspects of society.

Notes

1 Thirty-eight volumes from 1909 to 2007.
2 Bulard 1926a; 1926b; Hasenohr 2003: 168–69.
3 Bakker 1994: 125–27.
4 Bruneau 1970: 590ff.; 1. Maison de fourni; 2. Maison des comédiens; 3. Ilot des bronzes at the intersection of west and north roads; 4. House west of the Maison de la colline.
5 1. Maison aux frontons; 2. Maison de l'Hermès; 3. House II, Îlot des bijoux; 4. House III, Îlot des bijoux.

6 Hasenohr 2003 does not include the examples in Bulard 1926b: 161–98 of monuments with no remains of paint, nos. 5, 8, 15, 16 and 28 through 54, in her analysis.

7 Trümper 1998; Burke 2000; Tang 2005.

8 Bakker 1994; Pérez Ruiz 2008; Stek 2008; Anniboletti 2011; Santos Yanguas 2012.

9 Since this chapter was originally written, Flower 2017 has published a monograph focusing on the *lares* throughout the Roman world, a chapter of which is dedicated to Delos.

10 Hasenohr 2003 includes shrines nos. 1 through 27, excluding 5, 8, 15 and 16 of Bulard 1926b and 55 through 62 from Bezerra de Meneses 1970: 191–93 (no. 56); Bruneau 1970: 590–91 (nos. 56–58 and 62); 1975: 292–93 (no. 61); Bezerra de Meneses and Sarian 1973 (no. 55); and Siebert 2001: 106, 152 (nos. 57–60). Note also that Hasenohr and Bulard's nos. 6 and 7 are from the same location.

11 See Table 11.1.

12 Bulard 1926b: 9.

13 Bulard 1926b: 9.

14 See Hasenohr 2003: no 85.

15 Bruneau 1970: 598; Hasenohr 2003: 203.

16 Bodel 2008: 248; for the Agora of the Compitaliastai (or Hermiastai) see Bruneau and Ducat 1983; Rauh 1993.

17 Bulard 1926b: 8.

18 The seven shrines located inside houses are: 1. House north of the Poseidoniasts of Berytos; 2. Ilôt des bronzes – intersection of west and north roads of the Ilôt des bronzes; 3. Maison aux frontons; 4. Theatre House II A (Maison du trident); 5. Theatre House VI B; 6. Theatre House VI J; 7. Maison des comédiens.

19 See Bulard 1926a, 1926b; Bruneau 1970; Hasenohr 2003.

20 1. House on the corner of Theatre III, ruelle δ; 2. House across from Maison du Lac; 3. the Eastern House (Aphrodision II); 4. Theatre VI J; 5. Theatre II B; 6. Inopus House C (maison a une seule colonne); 7. Magasin aux colonnes; 8. Magasin δ of House opening onto the north road of Inopus Insula; 9. Stadium I D; 10. Stadium 1 C (House of Q. Tullius); 11. Maison des comédiens.

21 Chamonard 1924: 411–16, pls. XIV–XVII; Bruneau 1970: 597; Trümper 1998: 211–12: no. 22 fig. 16; Hasenohr 2003: 171; Tang 2005: 240–41.

22 The shrines with no traces of paint are: 1. Théâtre Rue 1, no. 5 en face de l'extremité Ouest de l'analemma Nord du théâtre; 2. House across from Maison du lac, SW corner of North Palaestra; 3. Theatre VI J; 4.

The shrines that preserve traces of paint or undercoats but do not allow reconstruction are: 1. House north of the Poseidoniasts of Berytos; 2. Theatre II E; 3. Theatre VI B; 4. Stadium 1 E; 5. Stadium II A; 6. Inopus House B; 7. Theatre II A (Maison du trident); 8. House on the corner of Theatre III, ruelle δ.

23 Bulard 1926b: nos. 2, 4, 9, 10, 12, 17, 18, 20, 21, 22, 23, 25, 27; Bezerra de Meneses and Sarian 1973; Hasenohr 2003: nos. 55, 57, 58.

24 Bulard 1926b: nos. 4, 10, 12, 14, 17, 23, 25, 27; Hasenohr 2003: nos. 55, 56, 58, 62.

25 1. House D west of the building of the Poseidoniasts of Berytos; 2. Magasin XIX; 3. Theatre II D; 4. Theatre III, intersection of street 2 and alley ζ; 5. Theatre VI G; 6. House west of la Maison des dauphins; 7. Stadium I C; 8. Stadium I D; 9. House I, Ilôt des bronzes, and House II, Ilôt des bronzes; 10. House across from Maison du lac, SW corner of North Palaestra; 11. House on the corner of Theatre III, ruelle δ; 12. the Eastern House (Aphrodision II).

26 Bruneau 1970: 599–600; Hasenohr 2003: 172.

27 Bruneau 1970: 599–600

28 Daux 1966: 989–91; Bruneau 1970: 404–405, 590–94 ; Bezerra de Meneses and Sarian 1973: 79–97.

29 Bruneau 1970: 599–600.

30 Bulard 1926a: 40–47; 1926b: no 27; Hasenohr 2003: 173.

31 Bulard 1926b: nos. 2, 10 and 27; Hasenohr 2003: 172.

32 Bulard 1926b, no. 27.

33 Bulard 1926b: 57–96.

34 Bulard 1926b: nos. 4, 10 and 27.

35 Bulard 1926b: no. 25; Hasenohr 2003: 172, 174, 176–79.

36 Bulard 1926b: no. 12, Bezerra de Meneses and Sarian 1973; Hasenohr 2003, no. 55.

37 Bulard 1926b: nos. 2, 12, 18, 22, 25, 27; Bezerra de Meneses and Sarian 1973; Hasenohr 2003, no. 55.

38 Livy I.7.12–14; Beard et al. 1998: II: 19.

39 1. Maison du lac; 2. Shop (Magasin δ) of House opening onto the north road; 3. House west of la Maison des dauphins; 4. Stadium 1 C (House of Q. Tullius) 5. Stadium I D; 6. House west of the Maison de la colline; 7. Theatre VI H.

40 Bulard 1926b: nos. 1, 2, 9, 18, 23, 26, 27; Bezerra de Meneses and Sarian 1973: no. 55, figs. 28–30; Hasenohr 2003: 174–75, no. 55.

41 Bodel 2008: 260–61.

42 Daux 1966: 989–91; Bruneau 1970: 404–405, 590–94; Bezerra de Meneses and Sarian 1973: 79–97; Hasenohr 2003: 174.

43 Rauh 1993: 202.

44 Tang 2005: 56.

45 Daux 1966: 989–91; Bruneau 1970: 404–405, 590–94; Bezerra de Meneses and Sarian 1973: 79–97; Hasenohr 2003: 174.

46 Bruneau 1970: 599.

47 Bulard 1926b, nos. 23, 27; Bruneau 1970: 599; Bezerra de Meneses and Sarian 1973: 90; Hasenohr 2003: no. 55.

48 Bruneau 1970: 615–19; Tang 2005: 53.

49 ID 1760–66, 1768–71.

50 See Flower 2017: 175–91, for a recent discussion of the role of this association on Delos.

51 Hasenohr 2003: 169.

52 Bruneau 1970: 615–20; Hasenohr 2003: 211; Tang 2005: 53.

53 Bruneau 1970: 6; Tang 2005: 53.

54 Shennan 1997: 65.

55 Shennan 1997: 195.

56 Shennan 1997: 195.

57 Shennan 1997: 195–98, 201.

58 Flower 2017: 176 associates these houses with Roman citizens not resident on Delos for most of the year, their households being run by freedmen and slaves.

59 Varro, *Ling*, 625; Plautus, *Merc.* 865.

60 Livy, 40.53.

61 Ovid, *Fasti*: 127–42.

62 Lang 1921: 133; Orr 1978: 1566–67.

63 *CIL* II 4320, II 2417, II 2518, VI 36810, VI 36811, VI 36812, VI 36813, XI 3079, XIV 4547.

64 Orr 1978: 1566–67.

65 Wissowa 1912; Waites 1920; Lang 1921; Orr 1972.

66 Wissowa 1912; Waites 1920; Orr 1972: 5–7;Anniboletti 2010: 69–70; Chaniotis 2011: 30–31.

67 For multiple discussions of the literary references see Orr 1972; 1978; Hasenohr 2003; Bodel 2008; Stek 2008.

68 ap. Festus 230M.

69 Ovid, *Fasti* II 614–17.

70 Pliny the Elder, *Natural History* 3.30.

71 Horace (*Odes* III 23, 3–4); Propertius *El.* IV 1, 23; Hasenohr 2003: 168.

72 Dionysus of Halicarnassus, *Roman Antiquities* IV 14.3–4.

73 Cato, *De agricultura* 5.3.

74 Festus, *Laneae Effigies;* Macrobius, *Saturnalia* 1, 7, 34.

75 Cato, *De agricultura* 57, 2.

76 Bodel 2008: 265.

77 See Joas and Knöbl 2013: 1–32.

78 See, for example, Stowers 2008; Chaniotis 2011; Katajala-Peltomaa and Vuolanto 2013.

79 Stowers 2008: 8, 13–14; Joas and Knöbl 2013: 9–19.

80 Stowers 2008: 8, 13–14; Joas and Knöbl 2013: 9–19.

81 Joas and Knöbl 2013: 9–19.

82 Stowers 2008: 14.

83 Katajala-Peltomaa and Vuolanto 2013: 13, 15.

84 Anttonen, 2005: 187–89; Pedley 2005: 29.

85 Pedley 2005: 29.

86 Ovid, *Fasti* II.639–46; Beard *et al.* 1998: II: 3–4.

87 Livy, I.32.6–14; Beard *et al.* 1998: II: 7–8; Hasenohr 2003: 199–200.
88 Beard *et al.* 1998: II: 19.
89 Dionysus of Halicarnassos. *Roman Antiquities* 4.14.4; Cicero, *Against Piso* 8; *Letters to Atticus* 7.7.3.
90 Cicero, *De natura deorum* 2.67.
91 Taylor 2000: 1.
92 Bulard 1926b, nos. 2, 11, 18, 22, 25; Bruneau, 1970, 404–407; 604–605; Bezerra de Meneses and Sarian 1973, no. 55; Hasenohr 2003: 182–83.
93 Stek 2008: 238.
94 See López Baria de Quiroga 1995: 326–48 and Mouritsen 2011 for detailed discussion of freedmen.
95 Katajala-Peltomaa and Vuolanto 2013: 13, 15.
96 Beard *et al.* 1998: I: 139; Bodel 2008: 263; Suetonius, *De vita Caesarum, Augustus* 31.
97 Suetonius, *De vita Caesarum, Augustus* 31; Bakker 1994: 130–31; Bodel 2008: 260–62.
98 Beard *et al.* 1998: I: 185; Stek 2008: 238–39.
99 Beard *et al.* 1998: I: 139; Hasenohr 2003: 168.

References

Anniboletti, L. (2010). Compita Vicinalia a Pompei: Testimonianze del Culto. *Vesuviana* 2, 77–138.

   (2011). Compita Vicinalia di Pompei e Delo: Testimonianze arceologiche del culto domestico. In F. Ghedini and M. Bassani, eds., *Religionem significare. Aspetti storico-religiosi, strutturali, iconografiche e materiali dei Sacra Privata. Atti dell'incontro di studio (Padova 8–9 giugno 2009)*. Rome: Quasar.

Anttonen, V. (2005). Space, body and the notion of boundary: a category-theoretical approach to religion. *Temenos* 41(2), 185–201.

Bakker, J. Th. (1994). *Living and Working with the Gods: Studies of Evidence for Private Religion and Its Material Environment in the City of Ostia (100–500 AD)*. Amsterdam: J.C. Gieben.

Beard, M., North J. and Price S. (1998). *Religions of Rome*, vols. 1 and 2. Cambridge: Cambridge University Press.

Bezerra de Meneses, U. (1970). Le revêtement mural. In U. Bezerra de Meneses, P. Bruneau and C. Vatin, eds., *L'Îlôt de la Maison des Comédiens. Exploration archéologique de Délos*, 27. Paris: Éditions E. de Boccard.

Bezerra de Meneses, U. andSarian H. (1973). Nouvelles peintures liturgiques de Délos. *Bulletin de correspondance hellénique Supplément* 1(1), 77–109.

Bodel, J. (2008). Cicero's Minerva, *Penates*, and the mother of the *Lares*: an outline of Roman domestic religion. In J. Bodel and S. M. Olyan, eds., *Household and Family Religion in Antiquity: Contextual and Comparative Perspectives*. Oxford: Wiley-Blackwell.

Bruneau, P. (1970). *Recherches sur les cultes de Délos à l'époque hellénistique et à l'époque impériale.* Série Athènes, 217. Bibliothèques de l'Ecole française d'Athènes et de Rome. Paris: Boccard. (1972). *Exploration archéologique de Délos. Fasc. xxix. Les mosaïques.* Paris: De Boccard.

(1973). Le quartier de l'Inopus à Délos et la fondation du S dans un 'lieu plein d'ordure'. *Bulletin de correspondance hellénique Supplément* 1(1), 111–36.

(1975). Deliaca [n° 1–15]. *Bulletin de correspondance hellénique* 99, 267–311.

Bruneau, P. and Ducat, J. (1983). *Guide de Délos.* Athens: École française d'Athènes.

Bulard, M. (1926a). *La religion domestique dans la colonie italienne de Délos: D'après peintures murales et les autels historiés.* Paris: E. de Boccard.

(1926b). *Descriptions des revêtements peints à sujets religieux. Exploration archéologique de Délos 8.* Paris: E. de Boccard.

Burke, S. (2000). *Delos: Investigating the notion of privacy within the ancient Greek house* (PhD thesis, University of Leicester).

Chamonard, J. (1924). *Le Quartier du théâtre. Exploration Archéologique de Délos 7 (1e et 2e partie).* Paris: E. de Boccard.

Chaniotis, A. (2011). Emotional community through ritual: initiates, citizens, and pilgrims as emotional communities in the Greek World. In A. Chaniotis, ed., *Ritual Dynamics in the Ancient Mediterranean: Agency, Emotion, Gender, Representation.* Stuttgart: Steiner.

Daux, G. (1966). Chronique des fouilles et découvertes archéologiques en Grèce en 1965. *Bulletin de correspondance hellénique* 90(2), 715–1019.

Flower, H. I. (2017). *The Dancing Lares and the Serpent in the Garden: Religion at the Roman Street Corner.* Princeton: Princeton University Press.

Hasenohr, C. (2003). Les compitalia à Délos. *Bulletin de correspondance hellénique* 127, 167–249.

Joas, H, and Knöbl, W. (2013). Between structuralism and theory of practice: the cultural sociology of Pierre Bourdieu. In S. Susen and B. S. Turner, eds., *The Legacy of Pierre Bourdieu: Critical Essays.* London: Anthem Press, 1–32.

Katajala-Peltoma, S. and Vuolanto, V. (2013). Religious practices and social interaction in the Ancient and Medieval world. In S. Katajala-Peltoma and V. Vuolanto, eds., *Religious Participation in Ancient and Medieval Societies: Rituals, Interaction and Identity.* Rome: Acta Instituti Romani Finlandiae 41.

Laing, G. (1921). The origin of the cult of the *Lares. Classical Philology* 16, 124–40.

López, Barja de Quiroga, P. (1995). Freedmen social mobility in Roman Italy. *Historia: Zeitschrift für AlteGeschichte* 44(3), 326–48.

Mouritsen, H. (2011). *Freedmen in the Roman World.* Cambridge: Cambridge University Press.

Orr, D. G. (1972). *Roman domestic religion: a study of the Roman household deities and their shrines at Pompeii and Herculaneum* (PhD thesis, University of Maryland, College Park).

(1978). Roman domestic religion: the evidence of the household shrines. *Aufstieg und Niedergang der Romischen Welt,* II 16(2), 1557–91.

Pedley, J. (2005). *Sanctuaries and the Sacred in the Greek World.* Cambridge: Cambridge University Press.

Pérez Ruiz, M. (2008). Un caso singular de estatuta Romana de culto domestic. *Archivo Español de Arqueología* 81, 273–87.

Rauh, N. K. (1993). *The Sacred Bonds of Commerce: Religion, Economy and Trade Society at Hellenistic Roman Delos, 166–87 B.C.* Amsterdam: J. C. Gieben.

Santos Yanguas, N. (2012). El culto a los Lares Viales en Asturias. Ilu. *Revista de Ciencias de las Religiones* 17, 173–84.

Shennan, S. (1997). *Quantifying Archaeology.* Edinburgh: Edinburgh University Press.

Siebert, G. (2001). *Exploration archéologique de Délos – Fascicule XXXVIII – L'Îlot des Bijoux, L'Îlot des Bronzes, La Maison des Sceaux 1. Topographie et Architecture. Fascicule 1 et 2.* Paris: École française d'Athènes.

Stek, T. D. (2008). *Sanctuary and society in central-southern Italy (3rd to 1st centuries BC): a study into cult places and cultural change after the Roman conquest of Italy.* (PhD thesis, Instituut voor Cultuur en Geschiedenis (ICG), University of Amsterdam.)

Stowers, S. (2008). Theorizing religion of ancient households and families. In J. Bodel and S. M. Olyan, eds., *Household and Family Religion in Antiquity: Contextual and Comparative Perspectives.* Oxford: Wiley-Blackwell, 5–19.

Tang, B. (2005). *Delos, Carthage Ampurias: The Housing of Three Mediterranean Trading Centres.* Rome: L'Erma di Bretschneider.

Taylor, R. (2000). Watching the skies: Janus, Auspication, and the shrine in the Roman forum. *Memoirs of the American Academy in Rome* 45, 1–40.

Trümper, M. (1998). *Wohnen in Delos. Eine baugeschichtliche Untersuchung zum Wandel der Wohnkultur in hellenistischer Zeit.* Internationale Archäologie 46. Rahden: Verlag Marie Leidorf.

Waites, M. (1920). The nature of the *Lares* and their representation in Roman art. *American Journal of Archaeology* 24, 241–61.

Wissowa, G. (1912). *Religion und Kultus der Römer.* Munich: C.H. Beck.

12 | Experiencing Sense, Place and Space in the Roman Villa

HANNAH PLATTS

At the far end of the terrace, the arcade and the garden is a suite of
rooms which are really and truly my favourites, for I had them built
myself. Here is a sun-parlour facing the terrace on one side, the sea on
the other, and the sun on both. There is also a room which has folding
doors opening on to the arcade and a window looking out on the sea.
Opposite the intervening wall is a beautifully designed alcove which
can be thrown into the room by folding back its glass doors and
curtains, or cut off from it if they are closed: it is large enough to hold a
couch and two arm-chairs, and has the sea at its foot, the neighbouring
villas behind, and the woods beyond, views which can be seen
separately from its many windows or blended into one. Next to it is a
bedroom for use at night which neither the voices of my household, the
sea's murmur, nor the noise of any storm can penetrate, any more than
the lightning's flash and light of day unless the shutters are open. This
profound peace and seclusion are due to the dividing passage which
runs between the room and the garden so that any noise is lost in the
intervening space. A tiny furnace-room is built on here, and by a
narrow outlet retains or circulates the heat underneath as required.
Then there is an ante-room and a second bedroom, built out to face the
sun and catch its rays the moment it rises, and retain them until after
midday, though by then at an angle. When I retire to this suite I feel as
if I have left my house altogether and much enjoy the sensation:
especially during the Saturnalia when the rest of the roof resounds with
festive cries in the holiday freedom, for I am not disturbing my
household's merrymaking nor they my work.

Pliny, Epistulae II.17

The last forty years has seen increased interest in Roman domestic space.
Andrew Wallace-Hadrill's investigations of Pompeii and Herculaneum, in
particular, presented an insightful examination of Roman housing and its
articulation of social identity on the Italian peninsula.[1] This paved the way
for other investigations into personal display in the domestic realm including considerations of architecture and landscape, decoration, statuary
collections as well as how housing provided a means of displaying an
individual's understanding of being Roman.[2]

Evidence for Roman housing is multifaceted: textual recollections of specific dwellings, such as the above extract from Pliny, are examined in combination with archaeological remains. Yet this breadth of information presents scholars with significant epistemological concerns in combining literary and documentary evidence with archaeological material such as house plans, decor and other related assemblages. In particular, questions should be raised as to how to draw together various types of evidence that often present differing, and sometimes contradictory, impressions.[3]

This chapter explores the Roman villa of mainland Italy during the early Empire and the alternative ways in which scholars might study the diverse evidence types found therein. It is concerned particularly with how multi-sensory experiences within, and responses to, Roman villas in literary evidence might also be interpreted from extant archaeological remains. To do so it examines the Villa of Diomedes through a multisensory lens and, in doing so, also employs the philosophical underpinnings behind recent human sensory experience investigations. This villa, built around two peristyle gardens, was located on the western outskirts of Pompeii on the Bay of Naples and was destroyed in the eruption of Vesuvius in 79 CE. By studying the possible human physical experiences of this Roman villa, this chapter explores how far and why individuals, either owners or occupants, attempted to control a visitor's sensory engagement with their extra-urban domain.[4] Whilst some studies have considered aspects of vision and its function in the Roman domestic realm, research into the role of sight combined with other senses remains underexplored.[5] It is hoped that using a multisensory approach we might develop a deeper understanding of the construction of elite Roman identities through sensory display and manipulation.[6]

Reading or 'Reading' Ruins?

It is necessary to outline the methods and problems of engaging with ancient evidence, before focusing on literary and archaeological examples of Roman villas. We should also consider how such approaches have influenced the interpretation of the bodily senses within the academic fields of social sciences and humanities.

Interpretation of literary material varies significantly from examining tangible artefacts. Texts 'speak out' to the reader and influence understanding according to the author's wishes whilst archaeological remains offer individuals the immediacy of physically 'experiencing' rather than merely 'viewing' them. Consequently, combining diverse evidence to develop insight into Roman domesticity is complex since scholars must explore the relationship between the domestic realm portrayed in text and what emerges from the archaeology and often they need to balance substantial discrepancies between the two.[7]

Of the traditionally recognized five senses in the Western sensorium, sight has been understood as the most significant and this apparent supremacy poses a substantial problem for archaeologists examining the material remains of ancient cultures.[8] Moreover, vision's continued pre-eminence becomes clearer when we consider attempts to promote the other senses through scholarly interpretations of human expression, experience and material culture, for these have similarly failed to challenge the perceived importance of sight.

Let us consider, for example, the significant attempts over the last half-century to encourage scholars to re-engage with studying bodily experience and the array of human senses through which the world is perceived. Of particular importance here was the work of the French philosopher Merleau-Ponty from the middle of the 20th century.[9] Key to his approach of interpreting visual, physical, dramatic and literary experiences of human life was his emphasis on the ability to 'read' different types of evidence. Thus he suggested that the study of music, religious ritual, dance or the visual and dramatic arts employed a relatively standardized approach similar to that used to study texts.[10]

Although Merleau-Ponty's methodology aimed to develop engagement with the varied sensory aspects of human experience, the consequence of 'reading' the evidence it promoted inherently emphasized vision whilst allowing other sensory responses of touch, sound, smell and taste to fade into insignificance. Recently scholars have criticized the logocentric bias of his philosophy, questioning whether examining human action based purely around a linguistic study of human experience should be considered reductive. One of the severest critics of Merleau-Ponty's logocentric approach to 'reading' human experience was Michel Serres, who saw Merleau-Ponty's insistence on understanding all human experience as verbal expression and language as condensing the nature of human worldly engagement to a one-dimensional, inflexible interpretation that left its audience's comprehension incomplete.[11] Accordingly Serres proposed an alternative approach that aimed to rehabilitate the body's sensory perceptions as a central facet of understanding the world and human interaction within it.[12] Whilst Merleau-Ponty attempted to rehabilitate the full human sensorium in 1962, it was only from ensuing criticism and developments into exploring the range of corporeal experience from scholars such as

Serres that considerations of the olfactory, auditory, haptic, gustatory as well as the ocular have begun to feature within academic disciplines.[13]

Yet the sensory revolution and its attempt to restore the whole human sensory realm to studies in social sciences and humanities remains incomplete. Within archaeology, attempts to take advantage of increasing interest in sensory approaches across numerous scholarly disciplines have started to encourage the development of new questions and frameworks for studying the tangible remains of ancient societies.[14] The discipline, however, remains dominated by the visual, with the last few decades seeing attempts to reconstruct imagined journeys through Rome taking into consideration changing views as individuals moved through the city's streets.[15] More recently, analysis of interconnecting street networks and their surrounding urban environments has been developed to explore how the vision and movement of these journeys, combined with the other sensory experiences of sound, smell and taste, affect an individual's interpretation of location.[16]

It is not just our understanding of ancient cities that has been dominated by sight. When it comes to the archaeology of the ancient domestic realm, here again vision has controlled proceedings. Given the nature of the two-dimensional plans used to map the size, shape and surroundings of houses, an emphasis on sight defining how we understand the domestic realm is unsurprising. However, investigations into spatial conditions, street networks and their environments as outlined above do not preclude smaller-scale sensory analysis of the relation of buildings to the street, to next-door properties and indeed even within individual buildings. Yet whilst floor plans, axial views through buildings, the size and shape of objects are emphasized in archaeological reports, the effects of smells and sounds, of texture and light on individuals and their responses to their surroundings are rarely considered, even when, as we shall see below, literary descriptions of buildings are fully immersed in the body's complete sensory experience.

Approaching a Sensory Methodology to Ancient Domestic Space

Over the last two decades, research into Roman domestic space has witnessed a growing interest in the examination of sightlines within and outside houses as well as movement and access within the house.[17] In particular, work has focused increasingly on the spatial layout of ancient residences.[18] Applying theories of space syntax proposed by Hillier and

Hanson to the area of *regio* VI of Pompeii, Mark Grahame has examined the organization of space in residences and its effect on social encounters and levels of privacy and visibility. He argued that buildings can be understood through their walls and boundaries, irrespective of interior decor, artefacts and people, although he also points out that it is not just a building's footprint that is important but rather, 'A study of other aspects of the built environment, such as, decoration and artefacts will enable increasing levels of meaning to be reached. Consequently, there is a *limit* to what can be learned from the walls alone.'[19]

Grahame raises important points regarding the study of Roman housing; however his approach is not without difficulties. In particular, issues arise from his suggestion that buildings can be read in a manner similar to that of texts and that the architectural space within buildings is governed by rules that order the space itself in a manner similar to the syntaxes that dictate word order to produce coherent sentences.[20] His proposals for how we 'read' space see parallels between the way text seeks to fix speech and how architecture tries to 'fix' the 'contextuality' of space, in other words the social encounters within it.[21] Significantly, Grahame notes that text actually fails in its endeavour to 'fix' speech, because as he rightly comments 'Texts are consequently open to numerous readings because what is inscribed into them is not the actuality of speech, but rather an interpretation of it. Likewise architecture tries to "fix" social interaction, but also fails.'[22] It is, however, in his further discussion of this that concerns arise.

> Built space, as Bourdieu reminds us, is analogous to a 'book' that is read through 'displacements' of 'the body' (1977: 89-90). However, just like a written text, once the 'text' of space has been read, the knowledge inscribed in that text becomes available to the 'reader', making continuous readings unnecessary. Only when changes are made to the built environment does it become necessary to read it again.[23]

By arguing that once a text has been read there is no need to revisit it Grahame seems to ignore his earlier argument that texts can be read in numerous ways. Yet though words are fixed when written in terms of their order and letters, the context in which they are read can constantly alter how they are interpreted.[24] Moreover, his comment about changes to the built environment requires further thought. When structures are altered, the manner in which they are understood will change; however, we also need to consider that interpretation of a building can also be altered without modification to the structure itself but by changes in the sensory landscape or within the individual experiencing it. Alterations to a building's temperature, lighting, sounds, smells, the time of day or year, can affect how a building is perceived, as can any physical or emotional changes in a person experiencing a building, such as ageing, pregnancy, fear and depression.[25] Consequently such transformations within a building's space, even though temporary, can lead to the need to 'read it again'.

What is important to emphasize here is that just like texts, buildings are open to multiple simultaneous interpretations – all of which can be affected by numerous factors including viewer/visitor status or background, time of day/season, weather. Imperative within our attempts to understand text and building, then, is the context in which the printed word or building is approached. It is not just when visible changes are made to a written word or to the structure of a building that we need to consider how interpretation and/or use might change – though these undeniably can alter perception. Rather when approaching any written page or any building's space and structure we should ask how the non-visual senses might affect its audience. If prose or a poem is read aloud, will the listener's response be the same as if they had read it themselves? Similarly, if a person stands in a room, will their response to the space be the same as when viewing the space on an architectural plan? To read a building as a text is to respond to it in a one-dimensional fashion that relies on vision over other senses and fails to allow an understanding of the changes to a space when other corporeal responses are also taken into account. The justified access-maps, which Grahame's approach to mapping domestic space employs, remain popular for visually plotting the accessibility of spaces.[26] Through this method of mapping building location or room distribution, however, networks of movement and vision continue to be emphasized, since these access-maps are merely another way of representing a space and its subdivisions in a two-dimensional form rather like a floor or archaeological plan. There is, then, a significant gap between the physical experience of a space and the manner in which it can be represented on the page, and justified access-maps serve as a means of further highlighting this disparity.[27]

Literary descriptions of Roman villas highlight interest not just in the views and sightlines of residences, but also concern with other sensorial responses elicited within and by the dwelling. Let us return to the extract from Pliny: there has been considerable discussion as to whether Pliny's letters depict real residences.[28] Irrespective of whether they are real dwellings or not, vision and vistas clearly play a vital role in the portrayal of his Laurentine villa. From Pliny's descriptions of the views of sea and neighbouring villas to those that he experiences within the villa, the sensory experience of sight is fundamental to how he perceives his villa and how he wants others to understand it.[29] 'The sea-front gains much from the pleasing variety of the houses built either in groups or far apart; from the sea or shore these look like a number of cities.'[30] Closer examination of this letter, however, emphasizes the importance of other senses within his villa description. Aural senses, for example, are emphasized in his discussion of the effect of the closing or opening of shutters when he writes, 'this is the winter-quarters and gymnasium of my household for no winds can be heard there except those which bring the rain clouds'.[31]

As well as sight and sound, however, this letter is full of a range of olfactory and haptic references. Thus at his Laurentine villa he describes the 'terrace scented with violets', the 'western breezes' which ensure 'the atmosphere is never heavy with stale air', the ball court basking in the 'full warmth of the setting sun' and the rooms that are organized to take advantage of the seasonal climate.[32] All these aspects of his villa depiction present a residence overflowing with pleasurable corporeal experience for both owner and visitor. We find even gustatory references in Pliny's description of fishing from the sea nearby, 'The sea has admittedly few fish of any value, but it gives us excellent soles and prawns.'[33]

Pliny's picture of his villa abounds with multisensory descriptions that aim to bring his residence to life for his reader in what appears to be an almost ekphrastic portrayal of his residence. Whilst the term *ekphrasis* has been commonly used to describe the literary or rhetorical depiction of works of art, it has more recently been used to explain more broadly all types of description, which were 'usually characterised by the common feature of vividness (*enargeia* in Greek; *evidentia* or *perspicuitas* in Latin)'.[34] Moreover whilst vision remains key in ekphrasis, as Elsner has pointed out 'even at its most visual – when words grope to represent images – it [ekphrasis] finds itself straying to the evocative resonances of the other senses: sound, smell, taste, and touch. We can try to imagine an 'ekphrasis degree-zero', perhaps, but this would come dangerously close to a litany of colors, shapes, bumps, ridges, textures . . .'.[35] If, as Chinn explains, we can see ekphrasis within Pliny's villa description V.6, then seeing at least the influence of an ekphrastic literary style, with its emphasis on a plethora of senses beyond that of the visual, within his other villa depictions (for example II.17) becomes less surprising. It perhaps explains why it is possible to draw so much sensory information from just the text of Pliny.[36]

It is at the start and end of his letter that we learn why Pliny explains his residence so thoroughly to his friend, Gallus. The letter opens with the following lines, 'You may wonder why my Laurentine place . . . is such a joy to me, but once you realise the attractions of the house itself, the amenities of its situation, and its extensive sea-front, you will have your answer.' He closes with the comment,

> And now do you think I have a good case for making this retreat my haunt and home where I love to be? You are too polite a townsman if you don't covet it! But I hope you will, for then the many attractions of my treasured house will have another strong recommendation in your company.[37]

Little is known about Gallus, the addressee of this letter. Its opening and closing sections raise the question as to whether Gallus was familiar with Pliny's Laurentine villa, for they suggest that Pliny was keen to acquaint Gallus with the residence. Without knowing more about Gallus, we cannot confirm whether or not he was a regular visitor to Pliny's villa or indeed if he had ever visited. Gallus is not a regular contact within the *Letters* so it might be argued that Pliny is introducing his dwelling to someone unfamiliar with it. Whatever the answer to that uncertainty, we know Pliny wrote his letters for publication.[38] They were written to be read by a wider audience, not all of whom would be familiar with his villa. Thus, the letter to Gallus might be a way to depict his extramural home to a friend (whether or not he was familiar with it) but it was certainly a method of extolling the glories of his residences, together with his other successes and achievements, to his other readers. Pliny was using his *Epistle* to present to Gallus the splendours of his villa and at the same time persuading others of this.

Pliny's description of his Tuscan villa to Domitius Apollinaris also draws on significant multisensory experiences. Sight is highlighted through references to vistas and views with comments such as 'Picture yourself in a vast amphitheatre' and 'My house is on the lower slopes on a hill but commands as good a view as if it were higher up.'[39] Yet the reader is also encouraged to imagine the full physical experience of the residence, as haptic, aural, olfactory and gustatory senses are portrayed as well as changes in light and seasons. References to 'the sun's kindly warmth', the temperature of certain rooms or colonnades in the winter and summer, the streams and fountains that can be heard throughout the villa, together with the implied scents of 'the clear sky and pure air' and the roses growing in the riding-ground, the promised taste of the food on dishes which float around the dining table on 'vessels shaped like birds or little boats', or the fruit trees alternating with box shrubs, all combine to emphasize the immediacy and reality of this imagined visit to Pliny's Tuscan villa.

As with Pliny's letter to Gallus, the opening and closing lines of his epistle to Domitius Apollinaris imply that the addressee was perhaps not entirely familiar with the residence and its multisensory splendours. Pliny seeks to dispel an inaccurate belief that the Tuscan villa was unhealthy in the summer. 'So to rid you of all your fears on my account, let me tell you about the climate, the countryside, and the lovely situation of the house...'.[40] Irrespective of how well acquainted Domitius Apollinaris was with this Tuscan dwelling, Pliny ensured he depicted his home for all to experience its full sensory glory. Pliny's success in narrating the wonders of his villa(s) to all was predicated around making the residence(s) come alive for his readers – the only way to manage this was complete human corporeal immersion in the dwelling(s).

Pliny was not alone in this: Statius, writing around the same time as Pliny, and Seneca the Younger, a generation earlier, are equally rich in multisensory villa images.[41] Bergmann's investigation of Statius' poem on the villa of Pollio Felix examines in considerable depth the role of vistas within this residence: the villa's architectural structures were a means for imposing order on the land and allowing nature to be 'shaped into perfect views'.[42] Statius also calls on other bodily sensations with descriptions of various veined marbles (lines 83–97), the damp beach (line 19) the sodden locks of Cymadoce (lines 24–25), the glasslike sea (line 65), all of which are highly tactile. References to the smoking bathhouse (line 22), the bitter sea (line 23) and the 'exhausted seas' laying aside their fury and the gentler breath of the 'mad winds' (lines 33–35) draw on senses of smell, taste and hearing respectively.

Similarly Seneca's comparison of Scipio's 2nd-century BCE villa with those of his own times calls upon a plethora of sensory responses. Seneca portrays Scipio as smelling of 'the camp, the farm and heroism' and bathing irregularly in the murky, dirty dark and in cold water. By comparison, Seneca's perfumed peers faced vitriolic criticism for bathing daily in sunlit marbled baths with glittering glass ceilings, filled with hot water crashing from different heights.[43] Indeed close consideration of Varro's *Rerum Rusticarum*, written in 37–36BCE, suggests that even at this considerably earlier date there was an increasing interest not just in the role of sight within villa residences but also in the importance of other physical experiences.[44] Varro describes fruit and produce of some residences as well as artworks and marble to encourage gustatory and haptic responses respectively,[45] whilst his account of Lucullus' aviary/dining-room combination (an architectural failure because of the unpleasant odours diners experienced inside) underlined the role of the complete sensory realm within the villa.[46]

The above examples of literary accounts emphasize the need to look beyond vision and vistas in order to gain a clearer understanding of the complex social and cultural phenomenon that is the Roman villa. From Varro's early descriptions to those from Pliny the Younger, it is evident that for many of Rome's elite, extramural residences were places for a range of sensorial experiences for both themselves and their visitors. Yet the corporeal immersion that occurred within these dwellings required careful control on the part of the villa owner in order to ensure that he remained in charge of the image of himself and his household that he wished to portray. The competitive nature of ancient Roman society and the manner in which Rome's elite sought to construct and control the image they presented to their peers has been widely examined.[47] Using the work of the anthropologist Eric Wolf, I have discussed elsewhere that the desire of individuals to control the possible field of action of others presented an important way to display to contemporaries the nature and level of one's power and social standing.[48] Monumental building, such as terracing and tunnelling, presented a dramatic way for villa owners to demonstrate power through large-scale display of controlling Nature, but I also suggest that careful control and manipulation of multisensory experiences within the domestic realm presented a crucial way in which Rome's elite attempted to parade themselves to contemporaries.[49] Such displays did risk going wrong, as we can see from Lucullus and his dining-room-cum-aviary; however, the potential for success and the kudos this could bring was arguably worth the gamble.

With this in mind, we need to consider whether controlling and manipulating multiple senses within the villa realm as has been indicated within literary descriptions is reflected within the archaeological evidence. In her investigation of multisensory movement within the city of Rome, Betts rightly emphasizes that the public sphere of Rome was a rich tapestry of sensorial stimulation; however, she underplays the potential importance of multisensory experience and bodily immersion within the private sphere, for she implies that the sensory experience to be had within the home is one that is familiar and expected. Using Porteous' understanding of the habituation effect on sensory perception as the means by which individuals become accustomed to certain sensory experiences, Betts implies that corporeal experiences that occur within the domestic realm are habituated, or familiar, to those who encounter them.[50]

> Home [is] an intimate locale, where familiar, habituated smells and
> sounds in particular, but also the repeated experiences of other senses
> interweave to create a sense of place ... In the most private spheres, the
> familiar is physiologically apprehended by the senses, but is not necessar-
> ily consciously experienced, particularly smell, a result of habituation.[51]

Yet to assume that all sensory occurrences within the home are familiar
and 'habituated' or can be perceived as 'the repeated experiences of other
senses [which] interweave to create a sense of place' is questionable, for it
groups together a wide variety of individuals who might experience the
sensory occurrences of the home, irrespective of age, gender, status, time of
day, season, and the extent to which they are, or are not, familiar with the
residence in question. As Porteous goes on to state, 'In everyday terms,
one's house has a characteristic smell readily perceived by visitors but
apparent to the occupant only after having been away from home for
sometime.' The multisensory perception of one visitor to a home will be
different from that of its owner, and indeed of other visitors, and will vary
according to the visitor's particular familiarity (or lack of it) with the
dwelling.[52] Thus, whilst the domestic sphere undoubtedly presents a
narrower sensory realm to be experienced than that of the public sphere
of a city, it cannot be assumed that all sensory responses that occur will be
expected and familiar, or habituated, to all individuals within the house, be
they insiders or outsiders to the household.

What follows are some possible new approaches and necessary considerations in exploring multisensory responses within Roman villas, through
their extant archaeological remains. My focus, on the Villa of Diomedes
located on a main road leading into Pompeii, the Via Ercolanense, offers an
introductory approach to multisensory investigations of the archaeology of
Roman villas. It does not purport to present the exhaustive and final insight
into multisensory experience in the villa. Rather, having highlighted the
problems of ocular and logocentricity in archaeology, which filter into all
aspects of archaeological exploration including that of the domestic realm,
I have aimed to promote exploration of the Roman villa beyond that of
vistas and sight in order to enable a deeper comprehension of the villa as a
highly complex phenomenon through which Rome's elite attempted to
articulate social and cultural belonging.[53]

When looking at plans of the Villa of Diomedes (Figure 12.1), the
sightlines between rooms can clearly be observed, thus enabling understanding of who and what could be seen within the villa. Questions might,
however, be raised as to the extent to which sounds and smells, for example

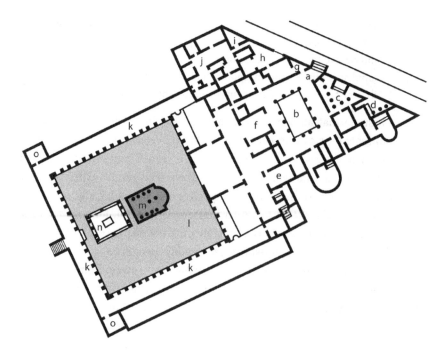

Figure 12.1 Villa of Diomedes. Reproduced by kind permission,
Bloomsbury Publishing

within the villa or from the street outside, might filter into the residence,
thereby affecting (or even dictating) reaction and response to the dwelling
and thus a visitor's perception of the villa owner.

Interaction Between Villa, Street and the Surrounding Landscape

The Villa of Diomedes is located on the western outskirts of Pompeii
(Figure 12.2). Leaving the town via the Herculaneum gate, one walks down
the Via dei Sepolcri, where extramural dwellings are interspersed with
shops and monumental tombs on both sides of the road.[54] Before reaching
the Villa of Diomedes, one would have passed on the left the sizeable Villa
of Cicero (remains now reburied), the entrance of which was well set back
from the road up a narrow path. A little further down on the right-hand
side of the Via dei Sepolcri, past some monumental tombs, was the Villa of
the Mosaic Columns, set back from the road and accessible via one of two
entrances located between shops and connected to the villa by narrow, long
passageways. Approximately 175 metres from the Herculaneum Gate, as

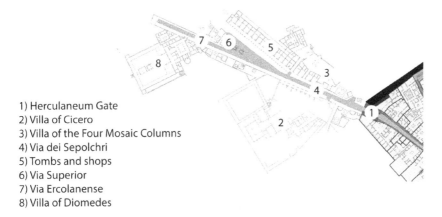

1) Herculaneum Gate
2) Villa of Cicero
3) Villa of the Four Mosaic Columns
4) Via dei Sepolchri
5) Tombs and shops
6) Via Superior
7) Via Ercolanense
8) Villa of Diomedes

Figure 12.2 Detail of the plan of Pompeii, showing the location of the Villa of Diomedes. Reproduced by kind permission, Bloomsbury Publishing

the road divides into the Via Ercolanense and the Via Superior, is the entrance to the Villa of Diomedes, located on the Via Ercolanense.

The Villa of Diomedes was substantial. This villa, and so too the Villa of Cicero, the Villa of the Four Mosaic Columns and the Villa of Mysteries, was larger than surrounding buildings and monuments in the vicinity of the Herculaneum Gate.[55] As such one might imagine that it would visually dominate the surroundings, but when we consider its entrance in relation to the street, and the way in which visitors might have experienced this, a more complex image develops.

Whilst the Villa of the Four Mosaic Columns and the Villa of Cicero were set back from the street, the Villa of Diomedes was situated directly on the Via Ercolanense. The Villa of Diomedes had two entrances. The main entrance required the visitor to walk up about eight steep steps, which led directly onto a small peristyle garden. The front section of the villa was about a metre above street level. The layout of the villa, with its raised entrance and front section, and its considerably lower rear section, reflected the sharp drop in ground level between the two sections of the residence. Yet it is likely that such organization also played an important role in manipulating how visitors physically experienced the residence, particularly those unfamiliar with it. The need to climb the stairs from street level to access the interior of the residence was a physical action by which visitors bodily raised themselves up to reach the owner's or occupier's level.

That external noises in cities disturbed residents in their homes is highlighted in textual evidence. Thus Juvenal complains of the carts, cattle and people shouting in the streets, which 'deprive a Claudius of sleep', whilst Seneca rails about the sounds emanating from the baths below his digs, which disturb his writing.[56] Such objections to unwanted disturbances by noises in the street outside filtering indoors provide an interesting comparison to the peace and solitude that we have seen Pliny the Younger strove to achieve whilst in his Laurentine villa. It would seem that, at least for our elite literary sources, having to experience loud and uncontrolled noises particularly in or near one's home was perceived negatively.

Being so close to the street at the Villa of Diomedes, it is likely that the front section of the villa would have experienced some level of noise from the traffic of carts and people moving into and out of the city, particularly at those times of the day when the town's waste was being removed or deliveries were being made. Here we must note that the loudest sound to be experienced in the Roman period would have been thunder at 120 decibels (dB).[57] Few sounds above 75 dB – equivalent to a human shout at a distance of 1 m – would have regularly been heard.[58] Given the proximity of the small peristyle courtyard to the Via Ercolanense, the sound of human conversation, shouts and carts would probably be heard within the front section of the villa, even though the villa's substantial walls and relatively small entrance would have helped to reduce some noise of the bustling street. Indeed it should, of course, be realized that sound attenuation is not merely affected by distance from the source of a sound. Sound is a movement of energy that travels in waves. When sound waves hit a surface, some of their energy is absorbed by the surface with which they make contact and some of it is reflected away. Different materials have varying levels of absorption and reflection. Likewise, the frequency of a sound (whether high- or low-pitched) also impacts upon levels of sound absorption or reflection by materials. Thus there are numerous factors that affect the transmission of sound within a residence from outside including the level of sound from source (in dB), its pitch, the distance and the materials through which it must travel.[59] In addition to this, the specific location of the Villa of Diomedes must also be considered. The situation of the dwelling's entrance being 1 metre higher than the street outside will also have deflected some of the noise from the road outside, thereby reducing slightly the level of sound reaching into the house. Finally, we should remember the role that doors, curtains and furniture play in reducing the transmission of sound waves. Whilst we cannot be sure, for example, whether doors to this residence would have been shut or remained open, it is likely that this would alter according to the time of day (closing the doors at night) and perhaps season (closing the doors in the winter to protect from any cold). Thus closed doors would have helped to diminish sounds from the street, although the lack of a roof over the courtyard would have allowed more noise to filter in than if the entire area had been covered.[60]

Bearing in mind the impact of these varying factors upon the transmission of sounds inside the house from outside, the deeper into the villa a visitor was admitted, the harder it would have been to hear the sounds from the street outside. Not only will the distance from the sound source have increased, but the travelling sound waves will have hit more surfaces that will have absorbed and reflected sound energy from the waves and these levels of sound absorption and reflection themselves will be affected by the original pitch of the sound. By the time a visitor was reclining and dining in the triclinium (n on fig. 12.1), located in the large colonnaded garden in the back section of the residence, he or she was approximately 65 metres from the Via Ercolanense. Even with no sound-absorbing or -reflecting obstacles, such as doors, walls or curtains, and no other noise-emitting objects such as fountains between a shout of 75 dB in the street and the diner reclining in the triclinium, the sound that would be heard would be reduced to that of quiet conversation.[61] If we take into consideration that between the garden triclinium and the front entrance are numerous walls, not to mention possible curtains and doors which no longer exist, as well as the sound of the fountain located directly in front of the dining area and the rustling of leaves from the trees planted in the garden, it becomes evident that the deeper into the building one is taken, the more control the owner has over the visitor's aural experience. This therefore gave the villa owner or occupier the ability to order and manipulate a visitor's auditory impression of the villa according to the standing of the visitor and the image of himself that he wished to present. By leading them through to the back section of his villa, he could immerse visitors in a world of trees rustling, fountains flowing and birds twittering. Conversely, by leaving them in the front of his dwelling they were likely to be constantly reminded of the reality of the world outside. The difference in noises heard by guests then could be varied according to their location within the villa. Moreover the function of particular parts of the dwelling equally might alter according to time of day, season of year, standing of guest together with the impression of himself that the owner/occupier wanted to impart to the visitor in question. Once inside the small peristyle court a multitude of sensory encounters, beyond that of vision, awaited the visitor and all helped construct, or destroy, the image that the owner wanted to portray. Regulation by the owner, not just over the views that the visitor experiences, but the smells, sounds and cutaneous sensations, was therefore vital.

On entering the residence, directly behind the visitor was a wall with a doorway leading to a small pool in a triangular colonnaded courtyard (c on fig. 12.1). To the left of this was the rest of the bathing suite, which included an apodyterium, a tepidarium and a *caldarium*, and accessed by a narrow corridor that led off the plunge-pool courtyard was a kitchen where a little stove was discovered next to which was a toilet (d on fig. 12.1).[62] Perhaps this little kitchen was used to provide hot drinks and light food as well as easy toilet access to the bathers. In visual terms, this bathing/kitchen/toilet area was carefully organized in order to reduce unpleasant sights. Thus, the back wall of the plunge pool was decorated with painted fish, and on either side of this fish-scape were garden scenes depicted as though they were views through windows onto a garden beyond.[63] In reality, behind these depictions was the busy Via Ercolanense. The access corridor to the kitchen, likewise, acted as a visual barrier, for it was narrow and enclosed whilst the triangular shape of the kitchen beyond ensured the bathers could see very little of its interior.

The ocular experiences to be had in this section of the residence were not, however, the only sensations manipulated by the owner. The distance of the kitchen from the plunge pool was approximately 6 metres, which means a human shout from the kitchen of 75 dB would only be reduced to some 63 dB. Further architectural organization or features, however, acted to reduce further the noise from the kitchen into the courtyard and vice versa. The narrowness of the access corridor and the transition from the enclosed corridor into the more open space of the plunge pool with its two-sided colonnaded portico would have produced an acoustic effect, referred to as an *aural cut-out*, which would have significantly diminished the sounds from the kitchen being heard in the bathing area, whilst still enabling relatively easy access to the kitchen for slaves or bathers.[64] Moreover, in the middle of the painted-fish scene was located a fountain, shaped like a mask, through which water poured into the pool below, helping to mask further any unwanted noise from the kitchen.[65]

In addition to regulation of sights and sounds experienced in the triangular courtyard, the owner also aimed to manipulate the visitor's olfactory and cutaneous sensations in order to promote a positive personal impression. The pool, although not under the cover of the triangular colonnade, had its own sloping roof fixed onto the back wall and supported by two further columns. Thus whilst bathers could feel a breeze or the warm air on their skin, they were sheltered from excessive heat or rain by the pool's roof. Residual warmth from the stove in the kitchen might also have helped to maintain temperate conditions in this outside bathing area. Likewise, the location of the stove on the far wall away from the access corridor together with the separation of the kitchen by the narrow corridor would perhaps help to diminish smells emanating from the small kitchen/toilet.[66] Of course for any slaves working in the small kitchen next to the toilet, the smells, sights and sounds must have been pretty terrible as they mingled together. As well as being hot, noisy and cramped, it is worth remembering that it was the typical layout of Roman houses to locate toilets in the kitchen, which were not always connected to the main sewers. In Pompeii at least, toilets were connected to cesspits where human and food waste would sit and rot for periods of time.[67] Thus any nice smells of food being cooked were likely to blend with the lingering stench of excrement and urine at least for those in the kitchen area. Even, then, for a slave to move from the kitchen to the triangular courtyard, or indeed beyond into the heart of the dwelling, would likely have stimulated a multitude of changing physical sensations as smells of food, bodily waste and the items being cooked on the stove, together with the noise of clattering pans and voices and high temperature conditions, diminished.

When in use, then, this bathing/kitchen/toilet area would have accorded a range of physical sensations that would have benefited from monitoring by the owner to safeguard as positive an impression as possible. Moreover, given the proximity of this area to the peristyle garden as the first area of the owner's realm that most visitors experienced, care was also required to ensure that sensations of the baths and kitchen were restricted to that area. Thus the triangular courtyard was separated from the peristyle garden by a large wall and a small doorway.

Further careful architectural planning within this villa offered the owner opportunities to control a visitor's sensory experience. A separate, lower entrance from the street was situated to the right of the main entrance and led into the main service area of the residence (h, i, j on fig. 12.1). This service area was also accessible via a narrow stairway located to the right of the monumental entrance. The situation of the villa's service area at a lower level in the residence's front half worked to moderate unpleasant sensory disturbances filtering into the residence's reception areas. Not only was this section of the villa removed from a visitor's vision, but the location of another kitchen area on this lower level (i on fig. 12.1), together with other service rooms, slave quarters and a place to house carts, would have further helped restrict the seepage into the peristyle garden at (b) of cooking smells and the sound of slaves and clattering cooking equipment. Sound and smells operate in rather different directional planes from the body than sight, for they occupy a spherical experiential field, whilst vision is broadly restricted to a forward-facing plane.[68] Since the kitchen on the lower level was only about 25 metres away from the peristyle garden, some sounds and smells from the service quarters are likely still to have been experienced in the front half of the dwelling, for example the scent of cooking meat.[69] If we take into consideration both the distance sounds and smells must travel, however, and the presence of walls and temporary barriers such as closed doors and curtains possibly located between the service area and the peristyle garden, we can again understand how the villa owner/occupier might have modified the multiple sensory experiences of his guests. Indeed, as with the case of sounds from the street, the further into the residence the visitor was admitted the less he or she would encounter smells or sounds from the villa's service quarters. It is important to bear this in mind when we think about the rear section of the villa and the location of the two dining rooms (e and n on fig. 12.1). Whilst (e) was the winter triclinium for the residence, (n) acted as the summer dining area. Both dining rooms, and particularly (n), were located at some distance from the service sections of the residence. Indeed in the case of (e), which was a little closer to both kitchen and service areas of the dwelling as well as the Via Superior, the room's entrance was situated facing away from the service sections with its back wall acting as a sort of barrier to any unpleasant smells, sounds or sights. The locations of these dining rooms in the archaeological evidence is particularly important to bear in mind if we consider that at an elite Roman meal the slaves were meant to ensure that the diners did not know what course or delicacy was coming to the table next.[70] At the very least, from ancient literary evidence, it was only the lower classes who had contact with or interest in the smell of cooking food.[71] Potter suggests that such location of the toilets in the kitchen area was perhaps a consequence of trying to keep unpleasant smells together in the same area of the house. It could also be added here that if this is the case, this would also make it easier to close off (or open up) the respective sections of the residence as required.[72]

Other reception areas were carefully located throughout the residence in order that the owner could provide an optimum multisensory experience for visitors. Whilst discussions remain over the specific use of certain rooms within the dwelling, some rooms and their functions have been identified. Of particular interest is the tablinum located on the west side of the peristyle garden (f on fig. 12.1), for whilst this room had two modes of access located opposite one another, at least one entrance closest to the rear garden could be closed off. Hence the owner could severely restrict the views of a visitor standing in the peristyle garden at (b) to that of the peristyle garden at (b) alone. The placing of walls of rooms on the western side of the peristyle garden at (b) meant that if the rear entrance to the tablinum was closed off, no view into the back half of the villa could be had from the front part of the villa. As well as controlling a visitor's visual experience of the villa, closing or opening the rear of the tablinum would also restrict the seepage of sound and smells from the rear of the residence to the front and vice versa. Furthermore, closing the tablinum's rear wall would affect the cutaneous sensations of a visitor standing in the peristyle as it would prevent strong winds blowing from the back garden into the villa's front section, and would thus provide shelter from inclement weather.

The final area of the villa that suggests the owner's interest in manipulating his visitor's corporeal responses can be found on the western portico of the rear section. On either corner of this portico were covered turrets, which only had windows looking out across the sea (o on fig. 12.1). These towers were at the furthest point within the villa from the Via Superior and the villa's own peristyle garden at (b) and service quarters (at h, i, j on fig. 12.1) where much of the hubbub of life within the villa would occur. The significant distance between the villa's entrance and the two belvederes, together with the orientation of their only windows towards the sea, the entrances to these rooms facing each other, and the likelihood of obstructions to the dispersal of sounds and smells from the front section of the villa, suggests these towers acted in a similar fashion to the suite of rooms of which Pliny is so proud at his Laurentine villa, which enabled complete sensorial isolation from the rest of the residence.[73]

Conclusion

In the 19th century the German architect Gottfried Semper emphasized the importance of a multisensory approach to housing when he wrote: 'To complete the image of an oriental residence one has to imagine the costly furnishings of gold-plated couches and chairs, divans, candelabras, all kinds of vases, carpets, and the fragrance of incense.'[74] Yet it has only been from the second half of the 20th century that philosophical studies into the interpretation of sensory information, by scholars such as Merleau-Ponty and Lefebvre, have emphasized the central role of senses and the body in one's experience of the world. Indeed it was the work of Serres in the 1980s that developed an understanding of the plurality and overlap in sensory responses to the world by emphasizing that in understanding our surroundings we do not employ our senses individually but rather in combination.

A criticism raised against sensory archaeology's phenomenological approach is that there has been a tendency to emphasize study into the ritual rather than mundane. Whilst not focusing on the 'mundane' life as potentially experienced by slaves (although some attempts to draw possible distinctions between slave and owner/occupier are pointed out above), this chapter considers the possible complexities of daily life and experience in the villa domain for members of the elite as they try to present themselves, in architectural form, to their peers and rivals. In presenting a possible view of the lived experience of the villa, this chapter addresses some of the recently raised criticisms of sensory archaeology.[75] Whether we are considering Pliny's idyllic descriptions of his villas or Seneca's description of Scipio's supposedly basic villa in comparison with opulent contemporary examples, or Statius' panegyrical villa poems, it is evident that authors realized that these complex residences had the potential to effect a plethora of sensorial responses – not just those of a visual nature. By placing vision and movement at the forefront of studies of ancient living space, at the expense of the other senses, we limit our understanding of life in the ancient Roman domestic realm. This chapter has investigated the villa through a multisensory lens and as such develops a new method of 'reading' and mapping the physical experience of the ancient domestic realm with which our literary evidence is imbued. Whilst sightlines into and around dwellings and justified access-maps are potentially useful for understanding at face value the relationship of one room to another, or the ways one might move around a house, they rely on a two-dimensional reading of space. This chapter highlights the crucial importance of reading between the lines of the text or floorplan in order to allow the residence and how it might have been experienced to speak for itself. It is only then that we can hope to develop our understanding of the villa's role as a place for displaying an owner's standing and his power to control a visitor's experience and response to the domestic sphere.

Notes

1 Wallace-Hadrill 1988. Cf. Wallace-Hadrill 1994.
2 On the architecture and landscape of Roman domestic space see e.g. Bergmann 1994; 2002; Platts 2011; Zarmakoupi 2014; on the decoration of Roman housing see, e.g., Clarke 1991; Bergmann 1994; Leach 2004. On statuary collections of Roman housing see e.g. Neudecker 1988; Mattusch 2005. On displaying Roman identity in the domestic realm see Hales 2003.

3 See Baird, Chapter 13 in this volume, on differences between text and material sources. On problems of using text to explore space see Lefebvre 1991. For a detailed discussion of Lefebvre see Alston, Chapter 14 in this volume.

4 This chapter concerns the role of owners or occupants of residences who had the wherewithal to organize space and/or decor. Slaves and children as inhabitants would experience the dwelling sensorially in considerably different ways from any elite adult inhabitants (see, for example, brief references to how slaves might have experienced the Villa of Diomedes below). The ability of either group, however, to control the arrangement and use of space in the villa is questionable. Consequently these groups do not form the focus of this chapter.

5 On vision and sightlines in Roman domestic space see, e.g., Clarke 1991; Grahame 1997, 2000; Bergmann 2002; Leach 2004; Klynne 2005; Platts 2011. On multisensory experience in houses of Rome, Pompeii and Herculaneum, see Platts 2016, 2019.

6 Recent years have seen increasing interest in the sensory realm within archaeology. For edited collections on sensory archaeology see, e.g., Hamilakis *et al.* 2002; Day 2013; Betts 2017. On tactile aspects of buildings see, e.g., MacGregor 1999; Cummings 2002. On the development of acoustic archaeology see, e.g., Lawson and Scarre 2006; cf. Watson and Keating 1999 on the acoustic analysis of megalithic monuments in prehistoric Britain. Archaeology of smell is not common; however, see Insoll 2007: 49–53 for a possible methodology – cf. Hamilton and Whitehouse 2006a on measuring olfactory senses in Neolithic villages of Italy; Derrick 2017 on smellscapes of Vindolanda; Day 2013 on smell in Minoan society, and 2017 on smell in Roman entertainment. Closely connected with smell is taste and this, like smell, has received considerably less investigation. For research into taste see Hamilakis 1998, 1999, 2008; Fox 2008; Hamilakis and Sherratt 2012; Hopwood 2013. Recently there have been approaches to archaeological sites which investigate a combination of senses – see, e.g., Weddle 2017 on touch and taste in Graeco-Roman animal sacrifice; Betts 2011 on the possible sounds and smells of ancient Rome; Houston and Taube 2000 on sight, smell and sound in Mesoamerica. For broad overviews of full sensory responses to archaeological sites see, e.g.. Skeates 2010; Hamilakis 2013; Platts 2016, 2019.

7 For recent examinations of the relationship between text and physical remains see, e.g., Storey 1999; Allison 2001; papers in Sauer 2004; cf. Baird, Chapter 13, and Alston, Chapter 14, in this volume.

8 For chronological accounts of ocularcentrism in the West see, e.g., Synnott 1991; Classen 1993: 15–36; 1997; Howes 2003; Smith 2007; Hamilakis 2013: 24–34.

9 Merleau-Ponty 1962 [1945]: 219–20. Merleau-Ponty responded to theories of Cartesian dualism that proposed a division between mind and body, placing

greater importance on the mind's perception of the world than on the body's experience. For Descartes, the senses' fallibility meant that only the mind's perception of the world was accurate. On Merleau-Ponty as a response to Descartes see Synnott 1991: 70; cf. Hamilakis 2013: 28.

10 Howes 2005: 1. Proponents of the linguistic turn include Merleau-Ponty 1962 [1945]; Ricouer 1970; Barthes 1982.

11 Serres 1995 [1990]: 131–32. According to Serres' critique, Merleau-Ponty's *Phenomenology of Perception* was 'tragically stripped of any tangible experience. Lots of phenomenology and no sensation – everything via language.' Cf. Evans and Lawlor 2000: 15; Day 2013: 5 on the logocentricity of Merleau-Ponty's philosophy.

12 Serres 1995: 71. Lefebvre 1991 has likewise raised in depth questions of how to interpret space and the importance of the bodily experience of it.

13 See, e.g., Howes 2005; Day 2013; Hamilakis 2013 for general bibliographies of sensory studies. For specific focus on individual senses, see the volumes from the Sensory Formations series (e.g. Bull and Back 2004) and Routledge's series on Senses in Antiquity. For a temporal approach to sensory history see the Cultural History of the Senses series.

14 See note 6.

15 Favro 1996; Purcell 1987; Vout 2007.

16 Betts 2011.

17 See note 5.

18 See, e.g., Grahame 1993, 1997, 1998, 2000. For a review of Grahame 2000, see George 1999.

19 Grahame 2000: 98.

20 Grahame 2000: 24–28, cf. 3–4. But see Lefebvre 1991: 7, 27 on the problems of applying the 'codes' used for reading text to 'read' space. See also Lefebvre 1991: 7, 27 on the reductive nature of 'reading' space like a text, cf. Serres 1995 [1990]: 131–32. On Lefebvre's critique of 'reading' space see Alston, Chapter 14 in this volume.

21 Grahame 2000: 27. For a more detailed discussion of Grahame's concept of 'contextuality' of space, see Grahame 2000: 11.

22 Grahame 2000: 27.

23 Grahame 2000: 28, citing Bourdieu 1977: 89–90.

24 Context here means the location, time and person reading the text in question. If any of these alter, how the text is understood can change. Thus, even being read by the same person at different times or in different locations can affect a text's interpretation.

25 See, e.g., Nevett 2010 on changes in time and season affecting room use in Pompeian houses; cf. Foxhall 2000 on changes in time and season in Greek housing. On marking and measuring of time in the Graeco-Roman world, see Hannah 2009. The situation in 2020 of enforced lockdown due to COVID-19 has highlighted an increasing need to explore our changing

relationships with our dwellings and the impact they can have upon our emotional well-being. In particular, reports (e.g. Graves 2020) on gender imbalances in domestic roles and home-schooling, and increasing levels of domestic abuse in some homes emphasize how perceptions of buildings can shift.

26 See, e.g., Stöger 2011 on analysis of the distribution of *scholae* in Ostia using justified access-maps; Grahame 1993, 1997, 1998, 2000 on spatial analysis of Pompeian residences using justified access-maps. Cf. Hillier and Hanson 1984; Hanson 2003; Robertson *et al.*, 2006 for further examples of the use of justified access-maps in archaeology and architecture.

27 Cf. Williams 2013: 208, citing Lefebvre 1991: 39. For criticisms regarding Hillier and Hanson's space syntax analysis see Lawrence 1990: 75. On criticisms of Grahame's space syntax analysis study of Pompeian residences see George 2002: 239.

28 See, e.g., Sherwin-White 1966; Förtsch 1993; Du Prey 1994: xxxi–xxii.

29 Bergmann 1994, 2002 on the importance of views within villas.

30 Pliny, *Epistulae*, II.17.

31 Pliny, *Epistulae* II.17. cf. the aural references in the extract at the start of this chapter regarding the noise of his slaves during Saturnalia not disturbing him whilst he works.

32 Pliny, *Epistulae* II.17.

33 Pliny, *Epistulae* II.17. Taste is also implied in Pliny's references to the garden, which he says 'is thickly planted with mulberries and figs, trees which the soil bears very well'.

34 On ekphrasis in Pliny's letters, see Chinn 2007. On the traditional definition of ekphrasis as only connected to rhetorical or literary descriptions of works of art see Chinn 2007: 265 esp. n. 1. On the problems associated with such a narrow interpretation of the term see Chinn 2007: 265 n. 2. Cf. Elsner 2007: 20.

35 Elsner 2007: ii

36 Chinn 2007: 265.

37 Pliny, *Epistulae* II.17.

38 Pliny, *Epistulae* I.1.

39 Pliny, *Epistulae* V.6.

40 Pliny, *Epistulae* V.6.

41 Sen. *On Scipio's Villa*; Statius *Silvae* II.2.

42 Bergmann 1994: 66.

43 Sen., *On Scipio's Villa*.

44 On the date of Varro's *De re rustica* see Linderski, 1985: 248–54; 1989: 105–27.

45 Varro, *De re rustica* I.II.10; I.LIX.

46 Varro, *De re rustica* III.IV.2.

47 See, e.g., Talbert 1984; Beacham 1992, 1999; Bell 2004.

48 Platts 2011, 2019. Cf. Wolf 1990: 586 for a detailed discussion of this notion of 'structural power', which employed Michael Foucault's interpretation of power as being the ability 'to structure the possible field of action of others'.

49 On maritime villas as symbols of human control over the natural world, see Marzano 2007: 21.

50 Porteous 2006: 90 comments, 'The perceived intensity of a smell declines rapidly after one has been exposed to it for some time. Not that the smell disappears, but the perceiver becomes habituated to it.'

51 Betts 2011: 122–23.

52 On the individual nature of sensory perception see Hamilakis 2013: 10; cf. Day 2013: 4.

53 My focus here is on owner manipulation of aural, olfactory, visual and cutaneous responses in the Villa of Diomedes. This chapter does not consider all possible means of physical response manipulation; for example I do not explore the use of different textures, lighting and tastes within the residence as a means of influencing a visitor's impression of the owner.

54 On tombs outside the Herculaneum gate see Kockel and Weber 1983; Cooley and Cooley 2004; Cormack 2007.

55 The Villa of Diomedes measured 1,229 m^2, the Villa of Cicero measured 5,549 m^2, the Villa of the Four Mosaic Columns measured 2,932 m^2, the Villa of Mysteries measured 2,895 m^2.

56 Juvenal, *Sat.* III. 236–38; Seneca, *Epistulae* LVI.

57 Betts 2011:125.

58 Speaking measures around 60 dB, whilst rainfall is around 50 dB. When distance is doubled from a sound source, sound levels drop by 6 dB. Thus, if a sound is 75 dB at 1 metre from source, at 2 metres from source the sound will measure 69 dB and at 4 metres it will measure 63 dB. Measurements obtained from http://ele.aut.ac.ir/~wind/en/tour/env/db/dbdef.htm. Information on the inverse square law obtained from www.nonoise.org/hearing/noisecon/noisecon.htm.

59 On the acoustic properties of spaces see Veitch 2017.

60 For discussion of entrance doors to residences being open or closed see Platts 2019: 80ff.

61 At 64 metres from source, a 75 dB shout is reduced to 39 dB, which is a little less than the noise level produced from an average residence.

62 With the small stove was also found a pot, a pan with two handles that were blackened by smoke, a grill and several earthen pots.

63 Jashemski 1993: 280 citing Dyer 1868: 486.

64 According to Mongelluzzo 2013: 101, 'movement from inside to outside spaces caused an acoustical effect known as the cut out. This effect is a sudden drop in intensity of sound . . . Cut out effects can mark transitions between spaces; for example they can occur upon entering a room or crossing a courtyard.' Cf. Augoyard and Torgue 2006, and Plin. II.17 cited in the extract at the start of this chapter on the important role of a small passageway in his Laurentine villa

which ensured silence and isolation whilst his slaves revelled during the Saturnalia.

65 Jashemski 1993: 280 citing Dyer 1868: 486.

66 According to Hamilton and Whitehouse 2006a: 178 the smell of meat cooking in an enclosed outdoor area travels a minimum of 17 metres and a maximum distance of 122 metres. We cannot be sure what was cooked in this kitchen; however pleasant, or unpleasant, smells produced here would be marginally diminished by the architectural layout of this area.

67 Platts 2019: 206–207. On possible slave experiences of kitchens as being hot, cramped, smelly and noisy, see Platts 2019: 195–198.

68 Betts 2011: 123.

69 See note 65 on the distances cooked meat smells travel.

70 Potter 2014: 127.

71 Martial *Epigrams* 1.92.9; Juvenal *Satires* 5.162–68; Horace *Satires* 2.38.8; Petronius Satyricon 2.1; 70.11, cf. Potter 2014: 127; Schmeling 2011: 5, 290.

72 On masking smells from kitchens and toilets using a variety of methods including architecture, obstacles and burning of herbs, see Platts 2019: 193–230.

73 See extract from Pliny Epistulae II.17 at the start of this chapter.

74 Semper, 1984: 85.

75 Day 2013: 7. I note Day's criticism that in attempting to highlight the experience of the individual, often the white, Western male academic's sensory experience is foregrounded. Due to the dominance of elite men in Roman society, the above investigation focuses on how an elite male villa owner might manipulate a visitor's experience of his residence. Future investigations might consider how female owners might influence the sensory realm of their residences. Moreover, studies might also foreground how different visitors or inhabitants might respond to the dwelling. Cf. Hamilton and Whitehouse 2006b: 33, 35.

References

Allison, P. M. (2001). Using the material and written sources: turn of the millennium approaches to Roman domestic space. *American Journal of Archaeology* 105, 181–208.

Augoyard, J. F. and Torgue, H. (2006). *Sonic Experience: A Guide to Everyday Experience*. Montreal: McGill-Queen's University Press.

Barthes, R. (1982). *Empire of Signs*, trans. R. Howard. New York: Hill and Wang.

Bartsch, S. and Elsner, J. (2007). Introduction: eight ways of looking at an ekphrasis. *Classical Philology* 102, i–vi.

Beacham, R. (1992). *The Roman Theatre and Its Audience*. Cambridge, MA: Harvard University Press.

(1999). *Spectacle Entertainments of Early Imperial Rome*. New Haven: Yale University Press.

Bell, A. (2004). *Spectacular Power in the Greek and Roman City*. Oxford: Oxford University Press.

Bergmann, B. (1994). Painted perspectives of a villa visit. In E. Gazda, ed., *Roman Art in the Private Sphere*. Ann Arbor: University of Michigan Press, 49–70.

(2002). Art and nature at Oplontis. In T. McGinn *et al.*, *Pompeian Brothels, Pompeii's Ancient History, Mirrors and Mysteries, Art and Nature at Oplontis, & The Herculaneum 'Basilica'*. Portsmouth, RI : Journal of Roman Archaeology, 87–122.

Betts, E. (2011), Towards a multisensory experience of movement in the city of Rome. In R. Laurence and D. Newsome, eds., *Rome, Ostia and Pompeii: Movement and Space*. Oxford: Oxford University Press, 118–32.

(2017). *Senses of the Empire*. Abingdon: Routledge.

Bourdieu, P. (1977). *Outline of a Theory of Practice*. Cambridge: Cambridge University Press.

Bull, M. and Back, L., eds. (2004). *The Auditory Culture Reader*. Oxford: Berg.

Chinn, C. M. (2007). Before your very eyes: Pliny Epistulae 5.6 and the ancient theory of ekphrasis. *Classical Philology* 102(3), 265–80.

Clarke, J. (1991). *The Houses of Roman Italy, 100BC–250AD: Ritual, Space and Decoration*. Berkeley: University of California Press.

Classen, C. (1993). *Worlds of Sense: Exploring the Senses in History and across Cultures*. London: Routledge.

(1997). Foundations for an anthropology of the senses. *International Social Science Journal* 153, 401–12.

Cooley, A. and Cooley, M. (2004). *Pompeii: A Sourcebook*. London: Routledge.

Cormack, S. (2007). Tombs at Pompeii. In J. J. Dobbins and P. W. Foss, eds., *The World of Pompeii*. London: Routledge, 585–606.

Cummings, V. (2002). Experiencing texture and transformation in the British Neolithic. *Oxford Journal of Archaeology* 21(3), 249–61.

Day, J., ed. (2013). *Making Senses of the Past: Towards a Sensory Archaeology*. Carbondale: Illinois University Press.

Day. J. (2017). Scents of place and colours of smell: fragranced entertainment in ancient Rome. In E. Betts, ed., *Senses of the Empire: Multisensory Approaches to Roman Culture*. Abingdon: Routledge, 176–92.

Derrick, T. (2017). Sensory archaeologies: a Vindolanda smellscape. In E. Betts, ed., *Senses of the Empire: Multisensory Approaches to Roman Culture*. Abingdon: Routledge, 71–85.

Du Prey, P. de la R. (1994). *The Villas of Pliny from Antiquity to Posterity*. Chicago: University of Chicago Press.

Dyer, T. (1868). *Pompeii: Its History, Buildings and Antiquities*. London: Bell & Daldy.

Elsner, J. (2007). Viewing Ariadne: from ekphrasis to wall painting in the Roman world. *Classical Philology* 102(1), 20–44.

Evans, F. and Lawlor, L., eds. (2000). *Chiasms: Merleau-Ponty's notion of the flesh.* Albany: State University of New York Press.

Favro, D. (1996). *The Urban Image of Augustan Rome.* Cambridge: Cambridge University Press.

Förtsch, R. (1993). *Archäologischer Kommentar zu den Villenbriefen des jüngeren Plinius. Beiträge zur Erschliessung hellenistischer und kaiserzeitlicher Skulptur und Architektur 13.* Mainz am Rhein: Zabern.

Fox, R. (2008). Tastes, smells and spaces: sensory perceptions and Mycenean palatial feasting. In L. Hitchcock, R. Laffineur and J. Crowley, eds. *DAIS. The Aegean Feast.* Liège and Austin, University of Liège and University of Texas at Austin: 133–40.

Foxhall, L. (2000). The running sands of time: archaeology and short term time scales. *World Archaeology* 31, 484–98.

George, M. K., ed. (1999). *Constructions of Space IV: Further Developments in Examining Social Space in Ancient Israel.* LHBOTS 569. New York and London: Bloomsbury.

George, M. (2002). Review of *Reading Space: Social Interaction and Identity in the Houses of Roman Pompeii* by Grahame, M. *Journal of Roman Studies* 92: 238–39.

Grahame, M. (1993). Reading the Roman house: the social interpretation of spatial order. In A. Lesley, ed., *Theoretical Roman Archaeology & Architecture: The Third Conference Proceedings.* Glasgow: Cruithne Press, 48–74.

  (1997). Public and private in the Roman house: the spatial order of the Casa del Fauno. In R. Laurence and A. Wallace-Hadrill, eds., *Domestic Space in the Roman World: Pompeii and Beyond. Journal of Roman Archaeology* Supplementary Series 22. Portsmouth, RI: JRA, 137–64.

  (1998). Material culture and Roman identity: the spatial layout of Pompeian houses and the problem of ethnicity. In J. Berry and R. Laurence, eds., *Cultural Identity in the Roman Empire.* London: Routledge, 156–78.

  (2000). *Reading Space: Social Interaction and Identity in the Houses of Roman Pompeii (A Syntactical Approach to the Analysis and Interpretation of Built Space).* Oxford: Archaeopress.

Graves, L. (2020). Women's domestic burden just got heavier with the coronavirus. *Guardian*, 16 March.

Hales, S. (2003). *The Roman House and Social Identity.* Cambridge: Cambridge University Press.

Hamilakis, Y. (1998). Eating the dead: mortuary feasting and the political economy of memory in the Bronze Age Aegean. In K. Branigan, ed., *Cemetery and Society in the Aegean Bronze Age.* Sheffield: Sheffield Academic Press, 115–32.

  (1999). Food technologies/technologies of the body: the social context of wine and oil production and consumption in Bronze Age Crete. *World Archaeology* 31, 38–54.

(2008). Time, performance and the production of a mnemonic record: from feasting to an archaeology of eating and drinking. In L. A. Hitchcock, R. Laffineur and J. Crowley, eds., *DAIS: The Aegean Feast*. Liège and Austin: University of Liege, and University of Texas at Austin, 3–20.

(2013). *Archaeology and the Senses: Human Experience, Memory and Affect*. Cambridge: Cambridge University Press.

Hamilakis, Y., Pluciennik, M. and Tarlow, S., eds. (2002). *Thinking through the Body: Archaeologies of Corporeality*. New York: Kluwer Academic/Plenum Publishers.

Hamilakis, Y. and Sherratt, S. (2012). Feasting and the consuming body in Bronze Age Crete and Early Iron Age Cyprus. In G. Cadogan, M. Iakovou, K. Kopaka and J. Whitley, eds., *Parallel Lives: Ancient Island Societies in Crete and Cyprus*. London: British School at Athens, 187–07.

Hamilton, S. and Whitehouse, R. (2006a). Three senses of dwelling: beginning to socialise the Neolithic ditched villages of the Tavoliere, Southeast Italy. In V. Jorge *et al.*, eds., *Approaching 'Prehistoric and Protohistoric Architectures' of Europe from a 'Dwelling Perspective'. Proceedings of the TAG session, Sheffield 2005*. Journal of Iberian Archaeology 8. Porto: Association for the Improvement of Cooperation in Iberian Archaeology, 159–84.

(with Brown, K., Combes, P., Herring, E. and Seager Thomas, M.) (2006b). Phenomenology in practice: towards a methodology of a 'subjective' approach. *European Journal of Archaeology* 9(1), 31–71.

Hannah, R. (2009). *Time in Antiquity*. London: Routledge.

Hanson, J. (2003). *Decoding Homes and Houses*. Cambridge: Cambridge University Press.

Hillier, B. and Hanson, J. (1984). *The Social Logic of Space*. Cambridge: Cambridge University Press.

Hopwood, M. (2013). Sustenance, taste, and the practice of community in Ancient Mesopotamia. In J. Day, ed., *Making Senses of the Past: Towards a Sensory Archaeology*. Carbondale: Center for Archaeological Investigations, Southern Illinois University Carbondale and Southern Illinois University Press, 222–42.

Houston, S. and Taube, K. (2000). An archaeology of the senses: perception and cultural expression in ancient Mesoamerica. *Cambridge Archaeological Journal* 10, 261–94.

(2003). *Sensual Relations: Engaging the Senses in Culture and Social Theory*. Ann Arbor: University of Michigan Press.

(2005). *Empire of the Senses: The Sensual Culture Reader*. Oxford: Berg.

Insoll, T. (2007). *Archaeology: The Conceptual Challenge*. London: Duckworth.

Jashemski, W. (1993). *The Gardens of Pompeii, Volume II: Appendices*. New York: Caratzas Brothers.

Klynne, A. (2005). The laurel grove of the Caesars: looking in and looking out. In A. Klynne, and B. Santillo Frizel, eds., *Roman Villas around the Urbs:*

Interaction with Landscape and Environment. Proceedings of a Conference held at the Swedish Institute in Rome, September 17–18, 2004. Rome: Swedish Institute at Rome.

Kockel, V. and Weber, B. F., eds. (1983). Die Villa delle colonne a mosaico in Pompeji. *Mitteilungen des Deutschen Archäologischen Instituts, Römische Abteilung* 90(1), 51–89.

Laurence, R. and Newsome, D., eds. (2011). *Rome, Ostia, Pompeii: Movement and Space.* Oxford: Oxford University Press.

Lawrence, R. (1990). Public collective and private space: a study of urban housing in Switzerland. In S. Kent, ed., *Domestic Architecture and the Use of Space: An Interdisciplinary, Cross-Cultural Study.* Cambridge: Cambridge University Press, 73–91.

Lawson, G. and Scarre, C., eds. (2006). *Archaeoacoustics.* Cambridge: McDonald Institute for Archaeological Research.

Leach, E. W. (2004). *The Social Life of Painting in Ancient Rome and on the Bay of Naples.* Cambridge: Cambridge University Press.

Lefebvre, H. (1991). *The Production of Space*, trans. D. Nicholson Smith. Oxford and Cambridge, MA: Blackwell.

Linderski, J. (1985). The dramatic date of Varro, *De Re Rustica*, Book III and the elections in 54. *Historia* 34, 248–54.

   (1989). Garden parlors: nobles and birds. In R. I. Curtis, ed., *Studia Pompeiana et classica in Honor of Wilhelmina F. Jashemski, II.* New Rochelle, NY: Aristide D. Caratzas, 105–27.

MacGregor, G. (1999). Making sense of the past in the present: a sensory analysis of carved stone balls. *World Archaeology* 31, 258–71.

Marzano, A. (2007). *Roman Villas in Central Italy: A Social and Economic History.* Leiden and Boston: Brill.

Mattusch, C. C. with Lie, H, (2005). *The Villa dei Papiri at Herculaneum: Life and Afterlife of a Sculpture Collection.* Los Angeles: Getty Publications.

Merleau-Ponty, M. (1962 [1945]). *Phenomenology of Perception*, trans. C. Smith. London: Routledge.

Mongelluzzo, R. (2013). Maya palaces as experiences: ancient Maya royal architecture and its influence on sensory perception. In J. Day, *Making Senses of the Past: Toward a Sensory Archaeology.* Carbondale: Center for Archaeological Investigations, Southern Illinois University Carbondale and Southern Illinois University Press, 90–112.

Neudecker, R. (1988). *Die Skulpturenausstattung Römischer Villen in Italien*, Mainz am Rhein: Zabern.

Nevett, L. C. (2010). *Domestic Space in Classical Antiquity.* Cambridge: Cambridge University Press.

Platts, H. (2011). 'Keeping up with the Joneses': competitive display within the Roman villa landscape. In N. Fisher and H. Van Wees, eds., *Competition in the Ancient World.* Swansea: Classical Press of Wales, 239–79.

(2016). Approaching a lived experience of ancient domestic space. In S. Griffiths and A. von Lünen, eds., *Spatial Cultures: Towards a New Social Morphology of Cities*. Abingdon: Routledge, 43–53.

(2019). *Multisensory Experience in Ancient Rome: Power and Space in Roman Houses*. London: Bloomsbury.

Porteous, J. D. (2006). Smellscape. In J. Drobnik, ed., *The Smell Culture Reader*. Oxford: Berg, 89–106.

Potter, D. (2014). The scent of Roman dining. In M. Bradley, ed., *Smell and the Ancient Senses*. New York: Routledge, 120–32.

Purcell, N. (1987). Town in country and country in town. In E. B. Macdougall, ed., *Ancient Roman Villa Gardens. Dumbarton Oaks Colloquium on the History of Landscape Architecture 10*. Washington, DC: Dumbarton Oaks, 185–203.

Ricouer, P. (1970). The model of the text: meaningful action considered as a text. *Social Research* 38, 529–62.

Robertson, E. C., Seiber, J. D., Fernandez, D. C. and Zender, M. U. (2006). *Space and Spatial Analysis in Archaeology*. Calgary: University of Calgary Press.

Sauer, E., ed. (2004). *Archaeology and Ancient History: Breaking down the Boundaries*. London and New York: Routledge.

Schmeling, G. (2011). *A Commentary on the Satyrica of Petronius*. Oxford: Oxford University Press.

Semper, G. (1984). Structural elements of Assyrian–Chaldean architecture. In *Gottfried Semper: In Search of Architecture*, trans. W. Herrmann. Cambridge, MA: MIT Press.

Serres, M. with Latour, B. (1995 [1990]). *Conversations on Science, Culture and Time*, trans. R. Lapidus. Ann Arbor: University of Michigan Press.

Sherwin-White, A. N. (1966). *The Letters of Pliny. A Historical and Social Commentary*. Oxford: Clarendon Press.

Skeates, R. (2010). *An Archaeology of the Senses: Prehistoric Malta*. Oxford: Oxford University Press.

Smith, M. (2007). *Sensing the Past: Seeing, Hearing, Smelling, Tasting, and Touching in History*. Berkeley: University of California Press.

Stöger, H. (2011). The spatial organization of the movement economy: the analysis of Ostia's *Scholae*. In R. Laurence and D. Newsome, eds., *Rome, Ostia and Pompeii: Movement and Space*. Oxford: Oxford University Press, 215–42.

Storey, G. R. (1999). Archaeological and Roman society: integrating textual and archaeological data. *Journal of Archaeological Research* 7(3), 203–48.

Synnott, A. (1991). Puzzling over the senses: from Plato to Marx. In D. Howes, ed., *The Varieties of Sensory Experience: A Sourcebook in the Anthropology of the Senses*. Toronto: University of Toronto Press, 61–76.

Talbert, R. (1984). *The Senate of Imperial Rome*. Princeton: Princeton University Press.

Veitch, J. (2017). Soundscape of the street: architectural acoustics in Ostia. In E. Betts, ed., *Senses of the Empire*. Abingdon: Routledge, 54–70.

Vout, C. (2007). Sizing up Rome, or theorizing the overview. In D. H. J. Larmour and D. Spencer, eds., *The Cites of Rome: Time, Space, Memory*. Oxford: Oxford University Press, 295–322.

Wallace-Hadrill, A. (1988). The social structure of the Roman house. *Papers of the British School at Rome* 56, 43–97.

(1994). *Housing and Society in Pompeii and Herculaneum*. Princeton: Princeton University Press.

Watson, A. and Keating, D. (1999). Architecture and sound: an acoustic analysis of megalithic monuments in Prehistoric Britain. *Antiquity* 73, 325–36.

Weddle, C. (2017). Blood, fire and feasting: the role of touch and taste in Graeco-Roman animal sacrifice. In E. Betts, ed., *Senses of the Empire*. Abingdon: Routledge, 104–19.

Williams, J. (2012). Musical space and quiet space in medieval monastic Canterbury. In J. Day, ed., *Making Senses of the Past: Towards a Sensory Archaeology*. Carbondale: Illinois University Press, 196–221.

Wolf, E. R. (1990). Facing power – old insights, new questions. *American Anthropologist* 82, 586–96.

Zarmakoupi, M. (2014). *Designing for Luxury on the Bay of Naples: Villas and Landscapes (c.100 BCE–79 CE)*. Oxford: Oxford University Press.

13 | Houses and Time

Material Memory at Dura-Europos

J. A. BAIRD

Written and material sources can be employed to be complementary in understandings of the ancient world, but they are not equal: this inequality is not a matter of subservience or superiority, but rather a less value-laden one of differing qualities. One of the places the differing qualities of written and material sources are perhaps most clear is in their temporal aspects. For example, ancient documents related to houses, such as parchments and papyri which record mortgages and house sales, were produced in a particular moment, within official constraints of documentary practices, and their content is often explicitly placed within formal structures of time, such as the year a particular man held a certain priesthood or a specific ruler was in power.[1] Such evidence is rich, but by contrast, the life cycles of material houses tend to pivot around human – and less formal – scales of generational time, the biological life cycles of individual people, the life cycles of families, and the temporal qualities inherent in the built structures and their upkeep: the length of time a coat of plaster remained tight against the rain, or the way a house was divided between heirs by blocking up doors with mudbrick. Archaeological houses hold the material memory of such cycles, physically recording the rhythms of daily life, of kinship as it was spatially enacted, and the maintenance and transformations of the house as a bounded unit.[2] This chapter examines the ways the material form of the house can hold these different forms of time, and explores the way archaeological time frames can disrupt other ways of conceptualizing the past, for instance, the time frames provided by historical periodization.[3] With reference to the houses of Dura-Europos, the chapter questions the differing temporalities of the diverse forms of evidence and asks how these might be used together, avoiding the urge to force them to align, to paint a richer picture of ancient houses and ancient lives.

In recent years, a more detailed approach to objects has revealed some micro- and short-term aspects of Roman period houses, for instance in the use of objects at particular times of the day, and the identification of the flexible use of space through the analysis of objects. Necessarily, such studies have tended to focus on a particular moment in the use of the house, generally its final phase or abandonment.[4] House plans, too, tend to be considered at the end point of the house's life, as that is what is usually recorded and published in archaeological state plans, because it is what is generally most accessible and recoverable when buildings are excavated. Examination of the changes in the use of houses over the longer term has tended to rely on the evidence of architectural phasing, and less on object approaches, again due to the character of the evidence and the nature of archaeological recording. Phasing of architecture, in turn, tends to be tethered to historical chronologies, whether as absolute date ranges or historical ones (e.g. 'the Hellenistic houses of Delos', or 'houses in Roman Athens'), which themselves are used analogously as cultural and social markers. Thus, temporally complicating factors are not limited to the archaeological evidence of houses themselves but also extend to the way in which it is recorded, categorized and represented.

The temporal qualities of the house, as far as they are understood in the present, have thus been shaped by a range of factors, including ancient use and subsequent formation processes, but also disciplinary practices and representations: how we excavate, record and represent those houses, and how we understand and practise phasing and periodization. All of these factors inherently shape interpretations. This chapter seeks to question what might be learned from interrogating the evidence of time perspectives as they relate to houses and households in more detail. It also examines the relationship between archaeological time conventions, historical time frames, and different time concepts in the ancient world. It explores the different time perspectives of the evidence of the houses at Dura-Europos, both material and textual.[5]

The site now known by the modern amalgam Dura-Europos (hereafter, Dura) lies on the edge of the Syrian steppe, on a naturally fortified promontory overlooking the Euphrates river. It was excavated in the 1920s and 1930s by a joint expedition by Yale and the French Academy. Dura began as a Hellenistic military colony, in the late 4th century BCE. The town seems to have taken shape initially around its citadel, and an orthogonal grid of streets was probably laid out later in the Hellenistic period, in the 2nd century BCE. In the late 2nd century the city came under Arsacid, or Parthian, control. During this time many Hellenic civic institutions seem to have continued, and an urban elite continued in their control of these. The site came under Roman control around 165 CE, and by the late 2nd–early 3rd century CE a Roman military garrison had been installed within the city walls, taking up much of the north side of the town. About 256, Dura was taken by the Sasanians, and was never substantially reoccupied.[6]

Dura has a complicated history of study, in part precisely because its material form did not map easily onto historical paradigms: Dura was a site with what might be called a hybrid vernacular built environment and material culture which did not slot easily into understandings of 'Roman', 'Parthian' and 'Greek' historical periods and cultural standards.[7] Similarly, because Dura did not feature, except in passing, in the surviving corpus of Classical authors, it was necessary to use the site's own material and textual evidence to slot it into existing historical narratives, which has not been without its own difficulties.[8]

Representing Time

Archaeological plans are one of the key ways in which we understand and represent ancient houses. Figure 13.1 is a plan, made in the 1930s by one of the site's architects, Henry Pearson, to represent an idealized form of a house at Dura-Europos.[9] The illustration brings together features found in houses across the site, where over 100 such structures were excavated, and represents them as a single building, literally drawing together Pearson's extensive expertise. Even more than a conventional plan, this drawing compresses time and space into a single place and moment. The shading, putting the light source at the upper left, casts shadows into a house and inside its rooms, giving us a sense of a building that has no roof – it is the house as an idealized archaeological object, an archaeological object which can be peered into as if it were a dollhouse.

The chief architect working at Dura was A. H. Detweiler, who made the site plan and was later head of the American Schools of Oriental Research and then Dean of the Architecture School at Cornell. He, like Pearson, was a perceptive architect, and other plans from Dura do have some elements of phasing, showing earlier walls or abutments indicating relative chronological sequences (Figure 13.2). Overall, though, at Dura as at so many other archaeological sites, our archaeological representations, both in drawing and photography, depict houses as frozen moments that preserve a particular past, a moment in time when we consider the archaeological remains to be most representative of past reality (Figure 13.3). Archaeological photographs in some ways replicate cleaned-up, ordered, architectural drawings, presenting an empty stage set onto which the past can be projected, as can also be seen in reconstruction drawings, peopled by still, faceless figures (Figure 13.4).[10]

The architectural plan as it is understood in the contemporary world is a starting point, the design for something to be built in the future: the

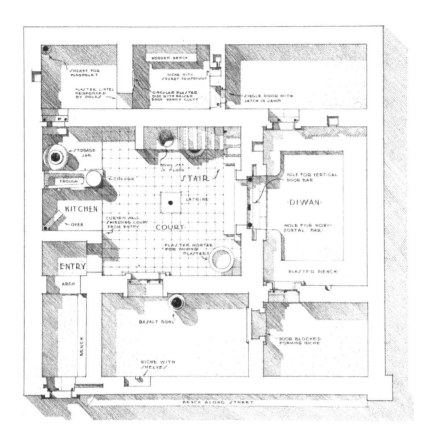

Figure 13.1 Idealized plan of house at Dura by H. Pearson. Yale University Art Gallery (YUAG) Dura archive

archaeological plan is its temporal opposite, a plan of an 'end point' of architecture when no longer in use. This is one of the reasons that our means of representing archaeological traces, whether in drawing or photography, can never quite hold the temporal qualities of archaeological evidence, which are material, messy and imprecise, have a duration and do not match up neatly with other forms of representation or time measurement.[11] Houses bring together different timescales, from the duration of the physical structure and its relationship to long-term cultural practices (at Dura, for instance, the courtyard house form and offset entrance), to momentary actions like the writing of a graffito or the lighting of a lamp. So, while the excavated houses at Dura were aggregate archaeological traces (palimpsests, even) of years and decades of occupations and modifications, their archaeological representations are usually only able to convey a moment of this. The moment we see on the archaeological page is not that

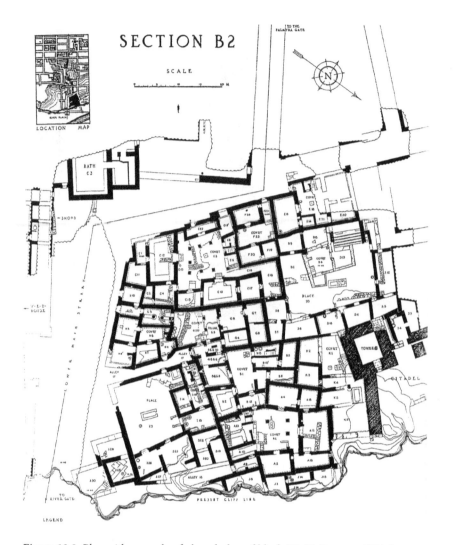

Figure 13.2 Plan with example of phased plan of block B2. H. Pearson, YUAG Dura archive

of abandonment, but a cleaned-up 'scientific' tableau of disciplinary practice as enacted through visual paradigms inherited from architectural drawing.

Of course, ancient Dura had its own systems of time measurement. Historical representations of time in Dura's past included its famed Roman military *feriale*, a 3rd-century document recording Augustan festivals.[12] Inside a house converted for use by the Roman military, a parapegma was scratched onto a wall.[13] Measured time at Dura is attested in a host of ways, from the use of the Seleucid era and eponymous priesthoods

Figure 13.3 Photograph of house D1, the 'House of Lysias'. YUAG Dura archive k327.

in documents and inscriptions, to a sundial for measuring the time within the day.[14] In modern narratives, Dura's history has been divided into Seleucid (*c.* 303–113), Parthian (*c.* 113–65), and Roman (165–256) periods, but in fact none of these dates is certain, and some are very problematic indeed.[15] Even the documentary record at Dura was not so clear-cut in its periodization, for instance with the Seleucid calendar continuing to be used (or again being used) in the Roman period, alongside other formal time-keeping practices.[16]

On another alignment are the material chronologies, which generally do not match neatly with historical ones, although they are tethered at some moments: for instance in an inscription which records an earthquake in 160 CE as having happened in a certain hour of the day, in a rare but precise link with geological time.[17] Our time problem is made trickier by the use of chronological terms for material culture which are also cultural (or implicitly ethnic) markers. For instance, the presence of 'Roman' material culture (including items like brooches and coins) precedes Roman hegemony in the region, and 'Parthian' pottery (green-glazed fineware) long outlasts Parthian rule.[18] In the same way, houses at Dura transcend tidy historical periodization, with some outlasting empires and others being transformed by new rulers, and never conforming to received

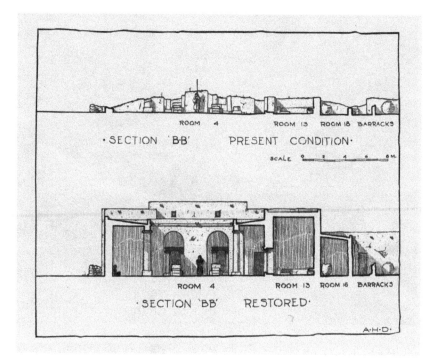

Figure 13.4 Isometric drawing by A. H. Detweiler, of the building known as the Dolicheneum and adjoining 'barracks' housing. In this figure the 'scale' human figure, holding a drawn scale in the top drawing becomes a dark-clad figure in the reconstruction of the past, in the lower one. YUAG Dura archive Y597b.

ideas of what a Greek, Parthian, or Roman house should look like.[19] What we can say is that for most of Dura's houses their last period of occupation was the mid-3rd century, when the site was under Roman control and had been for several generations, and a Roman garrison had been within the city walls for (at least) several decades.

Houses that Hold Time: Durene Houses and Chronologies

Archaeological evidence, it has been argued, has a particularly strong relationship with the long-term, because it tends to be seen as an aggregate (or palimpsest) more easily understood in relationship to environmental or social processes.[20] The houses of Dura can be used as such evidence, to examine long-term social structures and processes at the site. For instance, we might consider the continuity of building practice, house form or property ownership. This highlights a problem, however. For example, taking into account the drawings above, one of the ways in which archaeological representations so often fail us is in their inability to represent *duration*. There is a tendency to associate the concept of a house plan or 'design' with an 'original' house structure, and to treat changes and modifications over time as corruptions of that original form (archaeology, it might be argued, never ceases its quest for origins).[21] At Dura, many houses were continually occupied over generations and many decades, if not for more than a century. This is attested in the archaeology, from the many floor levels in houses and plaster coats on walls, and from graffiti and other texts at the site which contain absolute dates, as well as stratigraphic records. The architectural plans made by archaeologists, then, represent the end point of this occupation – at Dura, this was about 256 CE when the city was taken by the Sasanians.[22] The duration of the houses, however, bridges their inception and construction, over centuries of their occupation (or the continued use of a house plot or boundaries) and their survival into the present time.[23]

Houses do not fit easily within Dura's historical periodization – unlike, for instance, public architecture (such as Dura's city walls, the public archives building of the Chreophylakeion, or the triumphal arch of Trajan outside the site), they do not relate directly to the power structures of polis and empire.[24] The times that houses hold are not fixed or even linear. For example, while Dura was a Hellenistic foundation, taken next by the Parthian empire and then the Roman, there are not 'Greek', nor 'Parthian' or 'Roman' phases to the houses. Rather, houses are tied to cycles of time within the day, the seasons, and the generations of the household. The social and material entity of the house cuts across these different timescales, and does not always slot easily into historical systems of time measurement. Material phases do not map neatly onto historical ones. The structure of the house itself could span multiple generations, archaeological objects might give us evidence for shorter-term activities that took place only at a certain time of day, and textual evidence of graffiti and papyri elucidates activities which have not been recovered, or recognized, materially.

In many parts of the city, the fabric of houses held the evidence of earlier times: in the agora, the exterior walls of many of the houses were made up of large blocks of dressed stone, reused from the walls that had made up what was probably a large Seleucid public building, not the usual plastered rubble and mudbrick of Durene domestic architecture. These remains were not 'beneath' the Roman houses of the 3rd century, but formed part of their visible fabric (e.g. in block G5, see Figure 13.5).[25] Similarly, on the interior

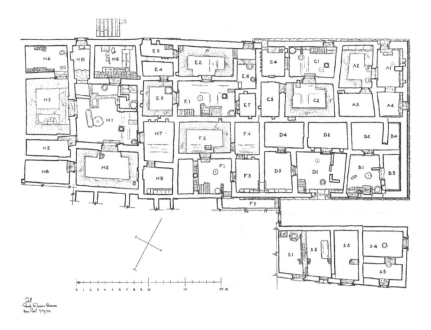

Figure 13.5 Working plan of G5 and G7 by Frank Brown. Left edge of wall missing as excavation of the block was not completed. Reused stone walls indicated by drawn second lines around either side of exterior walls on top, right, and bottom sides of the block. YUAG Dura archive.

of other houses, there was the use of living rock as house walls on the terraced slopes of the city which had been formed by the quarries of earlier periods (those which probably supplied the large stone blocks of the monumental structures), where the marks of early stoneworking labour remained visible.[26] Rising street levels, particularly in the agora, forced doorways to become raised and steps to be made down into buildings from the exterior; and in some places, what had been the ground floor level became the cellar as the superstructure buildings rose to accommodate the change.[27] Near the city gate, windows were plastered over, probably so privacy could be maintained as street levels rose to the level where passers-by could have glanced into the dwelling.[28] Such longer-term changes were things that could be seen and experienced in the houses: they were not 'phases' which were erased and rewritten in later periods, like a manuscript scraped of ink in preparation for a new text, but continuous uses which were rewrought and legible in the urban fabric, akin to annotations and corrections between the lines. House walls also held other durations, related to kinship and the maintenance of the house as a conceptual unit, as will be discussed below.

While archaeological evidence as a whole may be useful for looking at long-term processes and structures, the short-term is nonetheless also in evidence, often structuring the nature of deposition within houses.[29] Similarly, archaeologies of the longer term ignore to a certain extent human times, lived experience and agency.[30] The material nature of the archaeological record in fact bridges these scales, with everyday actions repeated to form structures with longevity, the way the earth floor of a house is made up of thousands of residues of short-lived actions. The archaeological methods of the 1920s and 1930s, when most of the known houses of Dura were excavated, were not conducive to the recognition of the short-term within houses. Fragments are nevertheless visible. The short term is in evidence in the houses of Dura in single actions whose repetition made them apparent, for instance in the polished interiors of the 'coolers' found in many houses, which seem to have been a type of large mortar in which something was repeatedly ground.[31] Graffiti clustered in entrance vestibules where visitors awaited admittance to houses.[32] Objects can also give evidence of short-term activities, even if it is difficult to fasten these activities to particular spaces within the house due to the nature of archaeological recording.[33] Cooking pots, for instance, generally had a short use-life because of their repeated exposure to heat, and while Dura's houses mostly lack permanent cooking installations, the remains of burnt cooking pots reveal these activities nonetheless.[34] Other objects were a hedge against misfortune, a hope for a longer-term future than certain individuals (in the event) experienced, as for instance coin hoards which were deposited in some houses, but never retrieved.[35]

Houses hold a range of evidence for activities and processes which array from the momentary to the *longue durée*, and rather than being a mere reflection of those activities and processes, the binding of different times is one of a house's features.[36] The construction of the house had elements, like mudbrick that used chaff and needed to dry in the sun, which depended on seasonal weather.[37] Visible changes in houses, signs of occupation and modification such as the subdivision of rooms, or the expansion of a house plot, are not simply changes which occur over time, but are one way in which time is lived out and perceived by the house's inhabitants. Wholesale transformation in the use of materials and use of space within houses came, at Dura, only with the occupation of some houses by the Roman military garrison and the absolute disruption of the tempo of previous life at the site that went alongside this.[38]

We need to ask (at Dura and elsewhere) not just what archaeologically visible architectural changes to houses mean, but what the continued occupation and modification of such structures can tell us about the experience of living in those buildings. One of the most interesting things about ancient houses, and modern ones for that matter, is their duration, and the way that houses *hold time* in a way that was visible to and had an impact upon those who occupied the house.[39] In the block G5–G7 pictured in Figure 13.5, for example, a blocked door between rooms H5 and H6 in the lower left corner remained visible (as did others, like that between rooms C3 and C4)[40]; the interior and exterior walls of much of the block had visible monumental stone walls of the Seleucid period incorporated into their fabric (as marked by the scalloped line around the interior and exterior walls of right side of the block on the drawing), and the north exterior wall of the block revealed its gradual construction in being slightly out of alignment.

If the most characteristic aspect of the everyday is its ceaselessness, houses themselves embody this, and transcend the difference in scale between the short- and long-term.[41] The different resolutions or scales of data available from the excavation of houses, from the reiterative mainten-ance of buildings, to the urban scale of a site like Dura, allow us to look not only at individual actions of everyday life, but the structures which generate that action.[42] Changes to houses accommodate changing household rela-tionships and structures, but their continued use coincides with (and represents) the fundamental continuity of the household and patriarchal structures of inheritance over time.[43] The long-term occupation evidenced by the archaeological traces of Dura's houses thus is the material record of the longevity of its social units. By this I do not mean that every house with a long record was the residence of different generations of branches of the same household, although that seems to have been the case in some (see below), but rather, simply, that the continuity of property, of house form, of specific materials, of decoration, use, access, etc., all would indicate that a particular *way of living* was maintained.[44] The reverse is also true, and the houses themselves and their duration over time enabled the maintenance of a particular way of living.

That way of living in Dura's houses is implied by their form. Virtually every house, from the smallest to the largest, shares three features: an entranceway directly off the street which isolates the house from the exterior, a courtyard, and a principal room off the courtyard in which reception activities could take place. These commonalities were the things recognized by Pearson in his idealized house (Figure 13.1), and all suggest the importance of the interiority of the house. The external façade was not a characteristic that was elaborated. This inwardness of the houses is also demonstrated by the fact that many houses also had a cistern in their courtyard, and so direct access to water was a concern at a household level. The isolation of the house unit from others, and a level of self-sufficiency, were thus integral to a household's self-definition and function; however, many houses also share internal party walls, so the isolation of the household with regard to circulation between dwellings or the visual access into a dwelling from the street did not extend to the need for the house to be physically/structurally independent.

The relationship *between* houses and the way these changed over time was also something which was physically recorded in the fabric of the houses. The polycentric houses of Dura, many of which had multiple courtyards, suggest multiple family households were resident. Such households were one strategy by which property holding (both in terms of houses and probably also related to agricultural landholding outside the city) could be maintained over time. The longevity of the house as a physical entity may be read over the long term as a social and economic strategy for the maintenance of property over time in the face of changing imperial powers, as for example can be seen in the palatial 'House of Lysias' (Figure 13.6), the largest house excavated in the city, occupying an entire city block, which can be linked by textual graffito to an elite family which held the hereditary position of *strategos* in the city.[45] That is, the continued power of Lysias and his family in the city over time is demonstrated by the

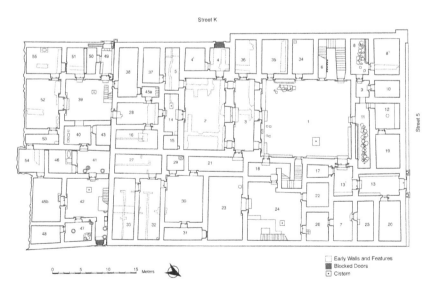

Figure 13.6 Block D1, the 'House of Lysias'. Author after van Knox in YUAG Dura archive.

duration of their house, and reciprocally the house was a means by which that power could be maintained, demonstrated and enacted. Power relationships held in the house go beyond those of the family of Lysias, though: the use of materials and house form tied into long-term local traditions of vernacular architecture in Mesopotamia and northern Syria.[46] Similarly, the continued respect for the lines of the orthogonal road system at Dura, which was probably laid down in the 2nd century BCE and not encroached upon by later domestic buildings, is probably indicative of a continued civic authority, again despite changing imperial regimes.[47] This system of urban circulation was markedly changed only when the Roman army took control of the city and installed a garrison on the north side of the city in the 3rd century, and it was with the military control of the city's roads and gates that the tempo of life, and the control of that tempo, would have radically altered.[48]

Houses that Remember: House History and Household Memory

At Dura, the houses' fabric, of mudbrick and plaster, was inherently adaptable and changeable. Their maintenance and modification held and displayed time: for instance, when doors were blocked with mudbricks and plaster to reconfigure the space, the door frame was often left visible, and continued to have a visual presence in the space even though it was not in use (Figure 13.7). Sometimes, this space was converted into wall niches or a tall recess within the room. The duration of the houses was also apparent in the build-up of plaster on house walls over the seasons. Windows which had been high in house walls were blocked, perhaps as they ceased to afford sufficient privacy as street levels rose, and thresholds wore down. In this way, a window or door may have gone out of use, but it could continue to have a presence within a house. As I will argue below, that presence could perhaps continue, too, to have a meaning to the occupants.

At Dura, the preserved texts included many graffiti on house walls. The graffiti also included pictorial examples, and among the texts were a variety of forms, frequently including lists and accounts, as well as those of the *mnesthe* formula, asking that a person be remembered.[49] Graffiti were one way information could be both recorded *and* displayed. Lists which were graffitied onto walls included those that may have been a household inventory, and accounts, receipts and tabulations.[50] Drawings included hunting scenes, animals and religious imagery.[51] These texts and images

Figure 13.7 Image of blocked door in house D5-G, as preserved in 2007. Photo by author.

have both authors and audience; they record a text made at a particular moment in time, but unlike a parchment, sealed and filed away in the archive for possible consultation in the future, these remained on display, and could have an active physical presence. Graffiti may have been ignored or forgotten, but they could be read at any time, and even spoken aloud. Many that covered the walls of house B8-H, also called the 'house of the archives' on account of the large number of graffiti, served as receipts and records for financial transactions that were displayed – and presumably, consulted. Rather than seeing these texts only as an archive from which economic information might be extracted,[52] we might also use them to reconstruct the activities within particular parts of the house over time.[53]

All archaeological traces are traces of memory, and just as our memory brings the past into the present, traces of earlier changes in houses allow the memory of those changes a continued presence, both in the ancient past and today.[54] House walls held memories – sometimes in a literal sense – as we can see in the graffiti which seek remembrance. As I have argued elsewhere, these graffiti are not graffiti in the modern sense of being somehow subversive or disruptive. It seems to have been perfectly normal at Dura to use your house walls to carve a little dedication to the gods or make an inventory of household goods. Graffiti in modern houses is so prohibited that the excavators had assumed the graffiti were a sign of abandonment or neglect, without really considering what they actually said or how they might have been used.[55] The *mnesthe* texts, in particular, explicitly call for remembrance of a named individual, and in houses such as the 'House of Lysias' in block D1, it seems that these were made by visitors to the house, as they awaited admittance, asking for the remembrance of the head of the household himself.[56] Such graffiti then are both acclamations, and indicators of social relationships (between visitors and the head of household) and how these were enacted spatially (in the act of waiting, sitting on a bench, scratching a little graffito, perhaps in hopes that whatever favour you have come to request is fulfilled). The texts could have been scratched relatively quickly, but that they cluster and are added over time indicates they were allowed to remain in place, and perhaps read by others.[57] Texts within houses, like the houses themselves, are multi-scalar, and when read in context can bridge the short- and longer-term house histories, moving from individual agency (in the making of a single graffito) to larger power structures (the remembrance of a powerful local individual and one's relationship to him, the act of waiting as a social enactment of power relationships in which the person waiting is the one with less power), to the maintenance of those structures over time (the addition of more graffiti and the lack of removal of the texts, and their display for others). In the same structure, the House of Lysias, human bodies were buried beneath a floor. These remains beneath floors, unique amongst Dura houses, whether victims of murder or even evidence of an ancestor cult (a well-known phenomenon in earlier periods in Mesopotamia), could in either case be an example of how houses can embody memory, with bodies of earlier generations interred beneath floors like telltale hearts.[58]

The continued presence of such earlier times contributes to the construction of a sense of 'place', in which remembered events happened and the past has a continued, if subtle, material presence in the everyday.[59] These are not the official memory practices of public inscriptions, or of ancestor veneration,[60] but the mundane, embodied and personal ones. Relationships are what make up a *household*; while the physical *house* is usually considered as a separate conceptual entity, there are deep entanglements between the physical structure and the human relationships. House is conceptual entity in and of itself, a socially constructed place. Houses were not only places into which people are born and live out their lives, but the means by which they live: in the simple form of providing shelter, but

also structuring and being structured by social relationships and interactions with other people, whether members of the household or visitors.
The sense of place was perhaps much stronger *within* the houses, and
Dura's houses did much to focus their energies on the interior space while
presenting a blank facade to those on the street.

Houses changed over time for a number of reasons: adjacent property
might be acquired into which a house could expand, for example. This
modification records part of the household's economic history. Houses
were also modified in order to meet the needs of changing family structures. As I have argued elsewhere, an archival document from Dura's
Parthian era which discusses the distribution of house property between
brothers, apparently at the time of their father's death (*P. Dura* 19),
demonstrates the link between the configuration of houses and changes
to their physical structure being linked to kinship structures.[61] In this case,
the physical house underwent significant adaptations at a significant time
in the life of the family – here, the death of the head of the household. No
archaeologically excavated house at Dura matches, perfectly, that described
in this document. However, in describing the link that might exist between
the house form and its residents' changing relationship to each other, the
document perhaps indirectly decodes other structures for us. There is no
direct match between words and walls, but if we consider the evidence of
both, we head towards a more nuanced idea of ancient houses.

P. Dura 19 describes the division of a house between male siblings, the
sons of one Polemocrates, and details their responsibilities in this division.[62] Each son owned a particular part of the house – and in order to
make their own part contiguous they had to block some doors, open other
ones. They were jointly responsible for party walls, and certain areas, like
the entrance and courtyard, were to be used in common. Changing house
configuration could thus in some cases be linked directly to the changing
kinship configuration of its residents and their relationships to each other.
The physical house, and the changes that were visible, were something that
could be read by people within it. Both the material form of the walls, the
blocked doors, the communal entrance, could hold memories, as could the
shape of the rooms or the spaces within the house. Just as walls stabilized
and reified relationships and social bonds, we might think of houses
themselves as 'a container of both families and memories'.[63]

P. Dura 19 was a 'double-document'; part of it was sealed for verification
purposes while a copy was open and could be consulted. It had been lodged
in an archive, and was found with other archival documents dumped in a
city tower, probably with the mass movement of earth to shore up the city

walls against the Sasanian incursion.[64] So, while the legal document of *P. Dura* 19 recorded their responsibilities and was a safeguard against property infraction within the brothers' family, the material house was a physical expression of the brothers' relative statuses and relationship to each other, one in which daily life was lived out. While no archaeological house plan at Dura matches precisely the layout described in *P. Dura* 19, this document can enable us to understand the way in which we might read generational time from archaeological houses, by examining modifications and the changing circulation patterns within them.

P. Dura 19 records three generations – that of the sons inheriting the property at the time the document was made, the earlier inheritance of their father and his brother, and their paternal grandfather. The ways in which the physical house was transformed upon the death of Polemocrates is recorded in detail, and so the house itself was transformed by and marked generational time. Each of the named heirs of Polemocrates is described as owning a vertical space within the structure, off the courtyard, and the house was reconfigured so that they can have contiguous access to the rooms they own within this. Similarly, access between the brothers' spaces is recorded in the document as being blocked, despite the shared external entrance and use of a communal courtyard. Because the upper-floor ownership then mirrored that on the ground floor, an inhabitant or visitor did not need access to the entire structure in order to read the grammar of the architecture which denoted the control of different parts of the structure by different brothers. The communal courtyard held the memory of an earlier family configuration; the brothers' separate dwellings within a single former structure were a later configuration, but both were simultaneously evident within the house.[65] At Dura, we can also use this sort of document to help us understand the material on the ground. The preserved archaeological houses are the end points of hundreds of years of transformation, but armed with documents such as *P. Dura* 19 we can get an idea of how they came to be that shape, and how kinship structures were enacted via the house and framed everyday practice.

P. Dura 19 is a Parthian-era document, but the type of transformation of house it describes is visible all over the city well into the Roman period, and it perhaps reveals a much more densely occupied urban space than had previously been thought, as it had previously been assumed the houses represented 'nuclear' family dwellings.[66] Houses are differently transformed only when the Roman military installed themselves within the city walls in the 3rd century – we then get an entirely different character of use, for example in block E8 which was transformed into military

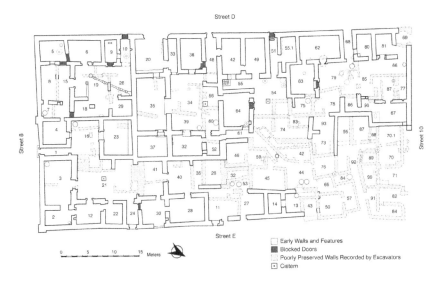

Figure 13.8 Plan of block E8. Author after Pearson in YUAG Dura archive.

accommodation: courtyards, not integral to the military way of living as they had been to the previous occupants, were subdivided (Figure 13.8). Entranceways were opened up along exterior walls which allow direct access from the street, as the visual isolation of those inhabiting the dwelling is no longer pertinent. Materially, fired brick and other materials were introduced into house structures.

Links between houses as property and as kinship can also be seen elsewhere in the form of the houses – for instance, in the House of Lysias, which remained undivided as a large house, probably in line with the endogamous practices which were part of the ruling family's strategy of holding onto power over a long period of time.[67] The property of the house, and the house as a locus and display of family power over others in the city, were another way the elite of Dura negotiated their place under Roman rule, alongside (e.g.) Roman naming practices or cooperation with the Roman military.

These material pasts of the houses of Dura could be 'read' and understood by inhabitants, and were a past that was more present in the activities of daily life than were the official documents of the past stored carefully away in the city archive. The continuity and maintenance of house forms under the occupation of successive empires is not only evidence of an efficient local form of mudbrick courtyard house, but also one aspect of cultural memory that was being held on to. Perhaps we need to consider the long-term curation of houses in the same terms as we do the long-term curation of objects, having biographies which stretch over generations and continue to exist in representations and into the material present.

Olivier has written that 'duration is the physical expression of memory', and in the inhabitation and modification of the houses, the structures hold the memory and traces of the changing shape of their resident groups over time.[68] The forms of houses are not just about change (modifications) or continuity (lack of modifications, or continued maintenance), but the continued perceptible traces of both of these over time (e.g. the existence of a blocked door, as noted above – both physically and in terms of their conceptual resonance – in the lives of later occupants). The physical form of the house was also related to rootedness and generational scales in their ability to 'anchor' time in the material presence of the home.[69] The materiality of these other forms of time and of duration allows us to move away from event-based histories more familiar from the Classical world, of famous men and great battles, to that grounded in lived experience and everyday life.[70] Such forms of time can be read alongside the profound changes of how time was experienced under imperial rule.[71]

It is useful to consider how the forms of material memory perhaps held in Dura's houses are connected with other memorial practices at the site. For example, while a few painted portraits survive, all from sanctuary contexts, there is generally speaking no tradition of private portraiture in sculpture recorded at Dura. Likewise, the funerary portraits so familiar at the Syrian site of Palmyra have no Durene equivalent. This is probably in part to do with local forms of artistic production: the local gypsum could not be finely carved, although sculpture at Dura was common enough.[72] What does this 'lack' of personal portraiture and commemoration through portraits say about memorial practices at Dura? Family histories were visible in painted depictions in some sanctuaries, if not commemorated in the usual funerary sense,[73] and remembrance graffiti were a more informal if ubiquitous practice throughout the site. Perhaps the houses themselves, in the visible ways in which they were reconfigured and changed and occupied, were a form of local memory practice.

Conclusion

Palimpsests are a virtue of archaeology. A palimpsest is not a document which is completely erased and rewritten (if it was, how would we know of its past?), but rather one in which the past is reused, effaced, on a material that accumulated those iterative changes. Palimpsests are a material document in which the past is transformed into something else, but in which the past persists beneath that new guise. These stratifications of meaning build up over time.[74] The accumulation and transformation of houses over time preserves different notions of historicity, but might be similarly legible under careful scrutiny.[75] Changes might belong to a time in the past (like a door that was blocked up with mudbrick) but could be visible into later periods and hence a material way of remembering for the later inhabitants of the house (to whom the blocked door, perhaps, reshaped the circulation of their dwelling after the death of the former head of the household). Collective identities coalesce around shared pasts. At Dura, these shared pasts were not only those of old priesthoods which perhaps continued over centuries, as attested in the documents, but also shared pasts of families, embodied in houses.

Houses hold time. Changes in houses hold the memory of the moment when those changes were made, and they hold onto and display their older forms which no longer exist (the frame of the door is still visible: we know it was once a door and that it is no longer). From parchments such as *P. Dura* 19, we know that such visible and material changes could relate to important moments in a family's history, such as the death of the head of the household and the reshaping of the physical house to accommodate the changed shape of the family units left behind. The impact of such things on daily life is perhaps subtle but formative, reminding inhabitants of family structures and power, of relationships past and present.[76]

Notes

1 Even these conventions themselves could of course lack fixity: Hannah 2009; Salzman 2013. The texts of the papyri could of course relate complex temporal issues, and were themselves material documents (although they tend not to be treated as such): on the differing taphonomies which affect our knowledge through such documents, Bagnall 2011: 27–28.

2 On material memory: Olivier 2011.

3 On the relationship between time concepts and the understanding of the past, and on time perspectivism in archaeology, Murray 1999a, 1999b.

4 Using Allison's assemblages at Pompeii, Allison 2004; Nevett 2010: 115; and for e.g. the study of the final phase of a block of houses at Dura through its objects (which identify a military use of civilian housing), see Baird 2012a. Evidence of the even more 'micro' level comes from the microarchaeological analysis of house floors, which are tied less to abandonment levels; see e.g. Ullah 2012. Microstratigraphic analysis remains rarely undertaken, however, in Classical

contexts, although it is designed into e.g. the new work being undertaken at Olynthos: Nevett *et al.* 2017 and 2020.

5   On time perspectivism, 'the belief that different timescales bring into focus different sorts of processes, requiring different concepts and different sorts of explanatory variables', see especially Bailey 1983, 1987, 2007. Definition from Bailey 1987: 7. For critique of and responses to Bailey, Shanks and Tilley 1987: 118–136; Murray 1999b.

6   For an overview of the site and the history of its excavation, Baird 2018.

7   On the historiography and complications of cultural ascriptions at Dura, see Baird 2014: 256–62.

8   For a useful reappraisal of Dura's chronology, see Edwell 2008: 93–148.

9   This plan is actually a detail from a larger drawing which has examples of different elements of Durene domestic architecture, including, for example, different types of stairways at the site. It seems to have been a preliminary study for a larger work by Pearson which was never completed. It appeared in the published preliminary report, but reproduced at such a small scale that it was all but illegible: Rostovtzeff 1934: plate VI.

10 Baird 2011a.

11 McFadyen 2011. On the inadequacies of archaeological recording for understanding housing, see also Platts, Chapter 12, this volume.

12 Fink *et al.* 1940; Gilliam 1954; Fishwick 1988; Reeves 2005.

13 Rostovtzeff *et al.* 1936: no. 622; Lehoux 2007: 170–71.

14 On time measurements used in the parchments and papyri, Welles *et al.* 1959: 10. On the sundial, Baird 2014: 161–62.

15 The precise dating of these phases is the topic of some debate; see Edwell 2008. There was also apparently a brief Roman occupation under Trajan, virtually unattested save for the inscription on the arch just outside the city, although see now also James 2015 for previously unidentified camps.

16 For example. *P. Dura* 25, 180 CE deed recording the sale of a slave, which includes official Roman dating, four eponymous priests, and the Seleucid date, denoted as being 'of the former reckoning'. It begins: 'In the consulship of Bruttius Praesens for the second time and of Julius Verus for the second time, in the twentieth year of the principate of Imperator Caesar Lucius Aurelius Commodus, Augusti, and 491 of the former reckoning, on the fourth of the month of Peritius, in Europos towards Arabia. In the year when Lysanias, son of Zenodotus and grandson of Heliodorus, was priest of Zeus; Theodorus, son of Athenodotus and grandson of Artemidorus, was priest of Apollo; Heliodorus, son of Diocles and grandson of Heliodorus, was priest of the Ancestors; and Danymus, son of Seleucus and grandson of Danymus, was priest of King Selecus Nicator. . .', translation Welles *et al.* 1959: 129.

17 The 160 CE earthquake inscription was set up in the 'Temple of Bel' and records an altar set up to Zeus Megistos: 'The ninth day of the month of Dios about the fourth hour of the day, when the earthquake occurred

throughout the region the city set up this altar to the Greatest Zeus.' Baur and Rostovtzeff 1931: 86–87, no. H.2. On the identification of the 'Temple of Bel', Kaizer 2016.

18 On brooches, Frisch and Toll 1949; Baird 2016a; on coins, Bellinger 1949; Clark 1978.

19 This lack of conformity to ideals is perhaps why the houses of Dura have been excluded from histories of Graeco-Roman domestic architecture and dismissed as strange and 'random': Sartre 2007: 27. Further on this problem, Baird 2014: 32.

20 Bailey 2007.

21 This obsession with the 'original' form of houses extends to the form of ancient cities as well, as evidenced in the concern with the concept of 'town planning'. On the trouble with 'design' and drawing and reading plans of archaeological structures, see McFadyen 2012.

22 On dating the end of Dura, James 1985; MacDonald 1986; Baird 2012b.

23 On the preoccupation with identifying an 'original' house design, see e.g. Saliou 2004.

24 In the Roman West, this relationship is discussed by Revell 2009.

25 On the early phases of the agora and 'bazaar', see Brown in Rostovtzeff *et al.* 1944: 3–27. Brown, here and elsewhere (e.g. in his work on block E4), implies a stratigraphy in the building with his written descriptions 'Beneath the structures of later periods . . .' for the structures discussed here (Rostovtzeff *et al.* 1944, 3), which does not exist. Rather, these walls remained present and reused. There was a stratigraphy excavated by Brown in the adjacent streets and floor levels, but he seems to lack the language to adequately describe the phasing of the built, standing, structures. Earlier, monumental walls such as these were also incorporated into the houses in block D3/4.

26 E.g. in block C3. On the placement of houses within former quarries and the relationship to urban power structures, Baird 2012c.

27 E.g., G1-G.

28 E.g., The window in the north wall of M7-W7.

29 Foxhall 2000.

30 Gardner 2012.

31 Baird 2014: 93–94.

32 Baird 2016b: 22.

33 As discussed by Foxhall 2000: 491–95. Foxhall also discussed the way in which the 'archaeological event' is actually an agglomeration of small-scale and short-term activities Foxhall 2000: 486; for a more detailed examination of the problem of scale and the archaeological event, Lucas 2008.

34 Baird 2014: 171.

35 Not all coin groups classified as 'hoards' at Dura were such deposits: some were apparently foundation deposits, others simple losses, see discussion in Baird 2012b, 316.

36 That is, time as both process and representation: Bailey 1983: 166.

37 On the mudbrick and other building materials at Dura, Bessac et al. 1997; Dandrau 1997; Gelin 2000; Bessac 2004.

38 Roman military interventions in houses included taking over several blocks of housing for use by military personnel, and, in those structures, the reconfiguration of space, introduction of new materials (including the use of fired brick) and different structural elements (e.g. hypocausts, which do not otherwise appear in Durene houses). Further, see Baird 2014: 111–54.

39 Just as many of us now live in Victorian houses built with different practices of living in mind, these buildings not only reflect but shape social relations within them: we continue to live in them both in spite of and because of their age, due to a variety of factors including the economic (that is, what is economical, and the availability of 'housing stock'), the aesthetic (the 'original features' of estate agents' brochures), that which Bourdieu called habitus (we live in houses, with, e.g., bedrooms because that's how we've 'always' done it, and other ways of living seem so unnatural as to be virtually inconceivable), and the social (the inheritance of a property, the size of a household), etc.

40 NB: G5-C is the house which seems to have been used as a 'brothel'; see Baird 2007; 2014: 196–200.

41 The ceaselessness of the everyday: Highmore 2002: 21.

42 Lucas 2010.

43 I draw heavily on Olivier 2011: 174, 'This contradictory relationship generates history'; that is, the relationship between changes and the fact that the underlying thing remains the same (e.g. new houses in a city centre may be built, but fundamentally people still want to live there . . .).

44 At Dura, the houses seem to have had a relatively stable form (with much minor variation) in the 2nd and 3rd centuries CE. Earlier phases are not well known for a number of reasons, both owing to the type of excavation and the character of the site.

45 Cf Alston, Chapter 14, this volume, and similar strategies used at Palmyra. On this House of Lysias, see also de Pontbriand 2012.

46 Baker 2007: 70ff.; 2010.

47 See, for continued respect for the road system by private property boundaries, e.g., block L5: Baird 2014: 43. On the date of the road system, see Leriche 1996; 2003.

48 Further on the town plan, Leriche 1996, 2003; James et al. 2012. On the tempo of urban life at Dura and the control of the city gates and roads by the military, James 2019.

49 On graffiti at Dura, Baird 2011b; on graffiti in Durene houses, Baird 2016; on remembrance graffiti in Durene sanctuaries, Stern 2012.

50 Household inventories: C7-F, no. 295; C7-G^3, nos. 300 and 301, published in Baur et al. 1933; accounts, e.g. those of B8-H, the 'House of Nebuchelus', Baur et al. 1933: 79–145.

51 Durene pictorial graffiti compiled in Goldman 1999; Langner 2001.

52 Ruffing 2000.

53 Baird 2016b.

54 Olivier 2011.

55 E.g. Baur *et al.* 1933: 136.

56 Baird 2016b. On the formula at Dura, Baird 2011b.

57 Frye *et al.* 1955: 147–51.

58 Bodies beneath floors in the Mesopotamian world are usually interpreted as those of ancestors – although in the Greek world they are sometimes interpreted as murder victims. Dura lies between these spheres, and the poor recording of the inhumations (only a photograph and a few field notes) makes it difficult to be definitive about the purpose of interring the remains beneath the house. Further on these human remains, Baird 2014: 295.

59 For an archaeological overview of theories of place- and memory-making, Van Dyke and Alcock 2003.

60 At Dura, one of the eponymous priests was that of the ancestors: see *P. Dura* 25 (as quoted in note 14). The *P. Dura* series of documents was published in Welles *et al.* 1959.

61 Baird 2014. On *P. Dura* 19 see also Saliou 1992.

62 Other, more fragmentary documents also record the division of houses as inheritances, e.g. the 1st-century *P. Dura* 16. Other property (a slave and vineyard) divided between brothers, probably upon inheritance, in *P. Dura* 25.

63 Morton 2007: 159.

64 Welles *et al.* 1959: 104.

65 The same way we might understand former warehouses which have been converted into apartments or flats (with both the former and current use being easily legible to visitors) in modern European cities. Or, indeed, the way Victorian terrace houses in central London are converted into university offices (such as the one in which I write this chapter) which continue to structure and enable hierarchies different to those initially intended, with academic offices in the former servants' quarters accessible via labyrinthine stairways while university administrators are situated in sprawling street-level suites.

66 Will 1988.

67 Baird 2014: 285ff.

68 Olivier 2001: 61.

69 Tuan 1977: 187; Dietler and Herbich 1993: 252–53.

70 On lack of attention by archaeologists to *longue durée* or microhistorical (as opposed to event-based) approaches, Olivier 2011: 188.

71 Gardner 2012: 161.

72 The sculpture of Dura was catalogued in Downey 1969: 1977.

73 On the 'private' nature of some cults at Dura, Dirven 2004; see also Elsner 2001.

74 Olivier 1999: 127.

75 Lucas 2005: 37; Bailey 2007: 203.

76 Today, the houses of Dura continue, bearing the new wounds of more recent empires. On the destruction of the site, see e.g. images in Casana and Jakoby Laugier 2017.

References

Allison, P. M. (2004). *Pompeian Households: An Analysis of the Material Culture*. Los Angeles: Cotsen Institute of Archaeology.

Bagnall, R. S. (2011). *Everyday Writing in the Graeco-Roman East*. Vol. 69. Berkeley: University of California Press.

Bailey, G. (1987). Breaking the time barrier. *Archaeological Review from Cambridge* 6, 5–20.

(2007). Time perspectives, palimpsests and the Archaeology of time. *Journal of Anthropological Archaeology* 26, 198–223.

Bailey, G. N. (1983). Concepts of time in Quaternary Prehistory. *Annual Review of Anthropology* 12, 165–92.

Baird, J. A. (2007). Shopping, eating and drinking at Dura-Europos: reconstructing contexts. In L. Lavan, E. Swift and T. Putzeys, eds., *Objects in Context, Objects in Use: Material Spatiality in Late Antiquity*. Leiden: Brill, 413–37.

(2011a). Photographing Dura-Europos, 1928–1937: an archaeology of the archive. *American Journal of Archaeology* 115(3), 427–46.

(2011b). The graffiti of Dura-Europos: a contextual approach. In. J. A. Baird and C. Taylor, eds., *Ancient Graffiti in Context*. New York and London: Routledge, 49–68.

(2012a). Re-excavating the houses of Dura-Europos. *Journal of Roman Archaeology* 25, 146–69.

(2012b). *Dura Deserta*: the death and afterlife of Dura-Europos. In N. Christie and A. Augenti, eds., Urbes extinctae: *Archaeologies of Abandoned Classical Towns*. Aldershot: Ashgate, 307–29.

(2012c). Constructing Dura-Europos, ancient and modern. In K. Lafrenz Samuels and D. Totten, eds., *Making Roman Places, Past and Present*. Portsmouth, RI: JRA Supplemental Series, 34–49.

(2014). *The Inner Lives of Ancient Houses: An Archaeology of Dura-Europos*. Oxford: Oxford University Press.

(2016a). Everyday life in Roman Dura-Europos: the evidence of dress practices. In T. Kaizer, ed., *Religion, Society and Culture at Dura-Europos*. Cambridge: Cambridge University Press, 30–56.

(2016b). Private graffiti? Scratching the walls of houses at Dura-Europos. In R. Benefiel and P. Keegan, eds., *Inscriptions in Private Places*. Brill Studies in Greek and Roman Epigraphy. Leiden: Brill, 13–31.

(2018). *Dura-Europos*. London: Bloomsbury.

Baker, H. D. (2007). Urban form in the first millennium BC. In G. Leick, ed., *The Babylonian World*. London: Routledge, 66–77.

(2010). The social dimensions of Babylonian domestic architecture in the Neo-Babylonian and Achaemenid periods. In J. Curtis and St J. Simpson, eds., *The World of Achaemenid Persia: History, Art and Society in Iran and the Ancient Near East*. London: I.B. Tauris, 179–94.

Baur, P. V. C. and Rostovtzeff, M. I., eds. (1931). *The Excavations at Dura-Europos conducted by Yale University and the French Academy of Inscriptions and Letters. Preliminary Report of Second Season of Work, October 1928–April 1929*. New Haven: Yale University Press.

Baur, P. V. C., Rostovtzeff, M. I. and Bellinger, A. R., eds. (1933). *The Excavations at Dura-Europos Conducted by Yale University and the French Academy of Inscriptions and Letters. Preliminary Report of Fourth Season of Work, October 1930–March 1931*. New Haven: Yale University Press.

Bellinger, A. R. (1949). *The Excavations at Dura-Europos. Final Report VI: The Coins*. New Haven: Yale University Press.

Bessac, J.-C. (2004). Carrières et topographie à Doura-Europos. In P. Leriche and M. Gelin, eds., *Doura Europos-Études V, 1994—1997*. Beirut: IFAPO, 247–58.

Bessac, J.-C., Abdul Massih, J. and Valat, Z. (1997). De Doura-Europos à Aramel: étude ethno-archaéologique dans des carrières de Syrie. In P. Leriche, M. Gelin and A. Dandrau, eds., *Doura Europos Études IV*. Paris: Librairie Orientaliste Paul Geuthner, 159–97.

Casana, J., and Jakoby Laugier, E. J. (2017). Satellite imagery-based monitoring of archaeological site damage in the Syrian Civil War. *PLOS ONE* 12(11), 1–31.

Clark, J. R. (1978). Measuring changes in the ease of trade with archaeological data: an analysis of coins found at Dura Europus in Syria. *Professional Geographer* 30(3), 256–63.

Dandrau, A. (1997). Gypse, plâtre et djousse. In *Doura-Europos Études IV*, 155–57. Beirut: IFPO.

de Pontbriand, S. (2012). La résidence de Lysias à Europos-Doura. Un première approche. In P. Leriche, S. de Pontbriand, and G. Coqueugniot, eds., *Europos-Doura Varia* 1, 77–92.

Dietler, M. and Herbich, I. (1993). Living on Luo time: reckoning sequence, duration, history and biography in a rural African society. *World Archaeology* 25(2), 248–60.

Dirven, L. (2004). Religious competition and the decoration of sanctuaries. The case of Dura-Europos. *Eastern Christian Art* 1, 1–19.

Downey, S. B. (1969). *The Excavations at Dura-Europos conducted by Yale University and the French Academy of Arts and Letters, Final Report 3, Part 1, Fascicle 1. The Heracles Sculpture*. New Haven: Yale University Press.

(1977). *Excavations at Dura-Europos, Final Report Volume 3, Part 1, Fasc. 2, The Stone and Plaster Sculpture*. Los Angeles: Institute of Archaeology, University of California.

Edwell, P. M. (2008). *Between Rome and Persia: The Middle Euphrates, Mesopotamia and Palmyra under Roman Control*. London: Routledge.

Elsner, J. (2001). Cultural resistance and the visual image: the case of Dura-Europos. *Classical Philology* 96(3), 269–304.

Fink, R. O., Hoey, A.S. and Snyder, W.S., eds. (1940). *The Feriale Duranum*. Yale Classical Studies 7. New Haven: Yale University Press.

Fishwick, D. (1988). Dated inscriptions and the Feriale Duranum. *Syria* 115, 349–61.

Foxhall, L. (2000). The running sands of time: archaeology and the short-term. *World Archaeology* 31, 484–98.

Frisch, T. and Toll, N. (1949). *The Excavations at Dura-Europos. Final Report Volume 4, Part 4, The Bronze Objects. Fascicle 1: Pierced Bronzes, Enameled Bronzes, and Fibulae*. New Haven: Yale University Press.

Frye, R. N., Gilliam, J. F., Ingholt, H. and Welles, C. B. (1955). Inscriptions from Dura-Europos. *Yale Classical Studies* 14, 123–213.

Gardner, A. (2012). Time and empire in the Roman world. *Journal of Social Archaeology* 12(2), 145–66.

Gelin, M. (2000). *Histoire et urbanisme d'une ville à travers son architecture de brique crue: L'exemple de Doura-Europos (Syrie orientale helléenistique, Parthe et Romaine)*. Paris 1.

Gilliam, J. F. (1954). The Roman military Feriale. *Harvard Theological Review* 47, 183–96.

Goldman, B. (1999). Pictorial graffiti of Dura-Europos. *Parthica* 1, 19–106.

Hannah, R. (2009). *Time in Antiquity*. London and New York: Routledge.

Highmore, B. (2002). *Everyday Life and Cultural Theory: An Introduction*. London: Routledge.

James, S. (1985). Dura-Europos and the chronology of Syria in the 250s AD. *Chiron* 15, 111–24.

(2015). Of colossal camps and a new Roman battlefield: remote sensing, archival archaeology and the 'conflict landscape' of Dura-Europos, Syria. In D. J. Breeze, R. Jones and I. A. Oltean, eds., *Understanding Roman Frontiers*. Edinburgh: John Donald, 328–45.

(2019). *The Roman Military Base at Dura-Europos, Syria: An Archaeological Visualisation*. Oxford: Oxford University Press.

James, S., Baird, J. A. and Strutt K. (2012). Magnetometry survey of Dura's Roman military base and vicinity. In P. Leriche, G. Coqueugniot and S. du Pontbriand, eds., *Europos-Doura Varia* 1, 111–16.

Kaizer, T. (2016). Revisiting the "Temple of Bêl" at Dura-Europos: A Note on the Fragmentary Fresco from the Naos. In M. K. Heyn and A. I. Steinsapir, eds., *Icon, Cult, and Context: Sacred Spaces and Objects in the Classical World*. Los Angeles: Cotsen Institute of Archaeology, 35–46.

Langner, M. (2001). *Antike Graffitizeichnungen. Motive, Gestaltung und Bedeutung*. Wiesbaden: L. Reichert.

Lehoux, D. (2007). *Astronomy, Weather, and Calendars in the Ancient World: Parapegmata and Calendars in the Ancient World.* Cambridge: Cambridge University Press.

Leriche, P. (1996). Le Chreophylakeion de Doura-Europos et la mise en place du plan hippodamien de la ville. In M.-F. Boussac and A. Invernizzi, eds., *Archives et sceaux du monde Hellénistique,* 157–69. Paris: Bulletin de Correspondance Hellenique Supplément 29.

(2003). Europos-Doura Hellénistique. In *TOPOI Supplément 4, La Syrie Hellénistique.* Lyon. 171–91.

Lucas, G. (2005). *The Archaeology of Time.* London: Routledge.

(2008). Time and the archaeological event. *Cambridge Archaeological Journal* 18(1), 59–65.

(2010). Time and the archaeological archive. *Rethinking History* 14(3), 343–59.

MacDonald, D. (1986). Dating the fall of Dura-Europos. *Historia* 35, 45–68.

McFadyen, L. (2011). Practice, drawing, writing and object. In T. Ingold, ed., *Redrawing Anthropology.* Farnham: Ashgate, 33–43.

(2012). The time it takes to make: design and use in architecture and archaeology. In W. Gunn and J. Donovan, eds., *Design and Anthropology. Anthropological Studies of Creativity and Perception.* Farnham: Ashgate, 101–20.

Meskell, L. (2003). Memory's materiality: ancestral presence, commemorative practice and disjunctive locales. In R. M. Van Dyke and S. E. Alcock, eds., *Archaeologies of Memory.* Oxford: Blackwell, 34–55.

Morton, C. (2007). Remembering the house: memory and materiality in Northern Botswana. *Journal of Material Culture* 12(2), 157–79.

Murray, T. (1999a). Introduction. In T. Murray, ed., *Time and Archaeology.* London: Routledge, 1–7.

(1999b). A return to the 'Pompeii premise'. In T. Murray, ed., *Time and Archaeology.* London: Routledge, 8–27.

Nevett, L. C. (2010). *Domestic Space in Classical Antiquity.* Cambridge: Cambridge University Press.

et al. (2017). Towards a multi-scalar, multidisciplinary approach to the classical Greek city: the Olynthos project. *Annual of the British School at Athens* 112, 155–206.

et al. (2020). Constructing the 'urban profile' of an ancient Greek city: evidence from the Olynthos project. *Annual of the British School at Athens* 115, 329–78.

Olivier, L. (1999). The Hochdorf 'princely' grave and the question of the nature of archaeological funerary assemblages. In T. Murray ed., *Time and Archaeology.* London: Routledge, 109–38.

(2001). Duration, memory, and the nature of the archaeological record. In H. Karlsson, ed., *It's about Time. The Concept of Time in Archaeology.* Gothenburg: Bricoleur Press, 61–70.

(2011). *The Dark Abyss of Time: Archaeology and Memory*. Lanham, MD: AltaMira Press.

Reeves, M. B. (2005). *The Feriale Duranum, Roman Military Religion, and Dura-Europos: A Reassessment*. Buffalo: State University of New York Press.

Revell, L. (2009). *Roman Imperialism and Local Identities*. Cambridge: Cambridge University Press.

Rostovtzeff, M. I., ed. (1934). *The Excavations at Dura-Europos conducted by Yale University and the French Academy of Inscriptions and Letters. Preliminary Report of Fifth Season of Work, October 1931–March 1932*. New Haven: Yale University Press.

Rostovtzeff, M. I., Bellinger, A. R., Brown, F.E. and Welles, C. B., eds. (1944). *The Excavations at Dura-Europos conducted by Yale University and the French Academy of Inscriptions and Letters. Preliminary Report on the Ninth Season of Work, 1935–1936. Part 1, The Agora and Bazaar*. New Haven: Yale University Press.

Rostovtzeff, M. I., Bellinger, A. R., Hopkins, C. and Welles, C. B., eds. (1936). *The Excavations at Dura-Europos conducted by Yale University and the French Academy of Inscriptions and Letters. Preliminary Report of Sixth Season of Work, October 1932–March 1933*. New Haven: Yale University Press.

Ruffing, K. (2000). Die Geschäfte des Aurelios Nebuchelos. *Laverna* 11, 71–105.

Saliou, C. (1992). Les quatre fils de Polémocratès (P. Dura 19). *Doura-Europos Études 1990 [Syria LXIX]*, 65–100.

(2004). La forme d'un îlot de Doura-Europos . . . l'îlot C7 revisité. In P. Leriche, M. Gelin and A. Dandrau, eds., *Doura-Europos Etudes V, 1994–1997*, Paris: Librairie Orientaliste Paul Geuthner, 65–78.

Salzman, M. R. (2013). Structuring time: festivals, holidays and the calendar. In P. Erdkamp, ed., *The Cambridge Companion to Ancient Rome*. Cambridge: Cambridge University Press.

Sartre, M. (2007). Domestic architecture in the Roman Near East. In K. Galor and T. Waliszewski, eds., *From Antioch to Alexandria: Recent Studies in Domestic Architecture*. Warsaw: Institute of Archaeology, University of Warsaw, 25–35.

Shanks, M. and C. Tilley (1987). *Social Theory and Archaeology*. Albuquerque: University of New Mexico Press.

Stern, K. (2012). Tagging sacred space in the Dura-Europos Synagogue. *Journal of Roman Archaeology* 25, 171–94.

Tuan, Y.-F. (1977). *Space and Place*. Minneapolis: University of Minnesota Press.

Ullah, I. (2012). Particles of the past: microarchaeological spatial analysis of ancient house floors. In C. P. Foster and B. J. Parker, eds., *New Perspectives on Household Archaeology*. Winona Lake, IN: Eisenbrauns, 123–38.

Van Dyke, R. M. and Alcock, S. E. (2003). Archaeologies of memory: an introduction. In *Archaeologies of Memory*. Malden, MA: Blackwell, 1–13.

Welles, C. B., Fink, R. O. and Gilliam, J. F. (1959). *The Excavations at Dura-Europos conducted by Yale University and the French Academy of Inscriptions and Letters, Final Report V, Part I, The Parchments and Papyri*. New Haven: Yale University Press.

Will, E. (1988). La population de Doura-Europos: Une évaluation. *Doura-Europos Études 1988 [Syria, tome LXV]*, 315–21.

14 | Spaces of Desire

Houses, Households and Social Reproduction in the Roman World

RICHARD ALSTON

This chapter considers how spatial theory might help us engage in different ways with the ancient house. Whereas archaeologists and ancient historians are forced to work from the material remains towards social structures, this analysis reverses that movement, starting from social structures to understand the processes that lead to the production of domestic space. This duality reflects a central problem in the analysis of domestic space; we accept that the spatial arrangements within a society are intimately linked with social structures, yet do we give analytical priority to the material (the space) or the intellectual (social structures)?[1] The problem is a particular version of the familiar and fundamental issue of the relationship between the material world and intellectual formations. In this paper, I follow Pierre Bourdieu (see below) and Antony Giddens (etc.) in arguing that social structures must be continuously imagined and performed in order to have effect. Such structures rest not in an externalized memory trace of learnt rules but in an internalized 'practical consciousness' which is closely related to an individual's identity.[2] This relationship of social structures and identity works through a social imaginary, a network of ideas which locates individuals within a social (and cosmological) order. The social imaginary provides individuals with the practical knowledge to function within a society and, simultaneously, with the narratives of identity that allow individuals to make rational sense of their place in the world.[3] It is thus both a social technology and an ideological system.

The social imaginary is imbued with power relations. These stem largely from material relations. The social imaginary is thus in a dialectical relationship with the material distribution of resources. This relationship may work directly, through a performed distribution of resource within a network that reflects social power (one person is given more resource than another or gives resource directly to another), or indirectly, through symbols, which require and reproduce ideology (one person has more significant material goods than another). The built environment, which comes into being through discrete acts of production, both reflects the distribution of resources within a social system (material differences) and locates an individual within a socially meaningful spatial distribution (ideological signifiers).

In what follows, I trace the dialectics of built environment and social ideologies. I focus on the processes by which social actors transition from words to walls and from walls to words. I begin with an extended consideration of the dialectics of space and society and the position of the house in such dialectics. I argue for a focus on the micro-dynamics of social formations and the fluidity of social formations operating within particular networks of power. According to this argument, the house/household is always in dynamic relations with other social elements. In the second section, I examine Henri Lefebvre's meditations on the production of space to argue that although space is subject to certain organizing principles, there is always a capacity for individual agency and resistance. In the third and fourth sections, I explore briefly the implications for our study of housing in the Roman world arguing that decisions on housing were always localized, dependent on individual agents, their desires and aspirations, and intimately involved in the perceived requirements of social and material reproduction. It follows that house forms always had the potential to change within particular social and temporal locations.

House, Space, Society

In much contemporary thinking, the house has been given a central place in this dialectical relationship between the social imaginary and the built environment.[4] The extent of the possible relationship can be seen from Pierre Bourdieu's famous and much-cited ethnographic description of a Kabyle house.[5] Bourdieu sees the house as a central element in *habitus*, the structured environment through which social rules are inculcated and reproduced. *Habitus* operates through arrangements of architecture, domestic artefacts and behaviours within the house to represent and normalize an entire cosmology (including gender relations, social status, temporal understandings and a divine order). Bourdieu's discussion is a radical instance of a contemporary perception of the domestic as *the* fundamental and formative space in society in which the individual experiences social disciplines and acquires the behaviours that enable social participation (see the discussion of Lefebvre below). In much modern social and anthropological thought, the house is seen as a key location in the processes of social reproduction, and consequently house and family have been central political concerns since the mid-19th century.[6]

Yet, it is less clear that ancients shared this emphasis on the domestic.[7] When compared with all the ancient theoretical literature on the city (and especially religious aspects of city society), the ancient house is comparatively lightly treated.[8] In Cicero, *De officiis*, 1.54, for instance, the state is treated as an outgrowth of the family, but this seems of no practical or theoretical importance.[9] In Vitruvius, *De architectura*, the extraordinary myth of architectural invention depicts housing as the initial form of architectural design, but sets the myth in a communal, proto-urban society in which social competition and interaction leads to civilizational (and social) development.[10] In Aristotle's *Politics*, the *polis* is given primacy over the family, even if the earlier stage of political development (the monarchy) is seen as an outgrowth of householder politics.[11] In these reflections, the house is neither seen as a primary location in the reproduction of social relations nor oppositional to the public realm.[12]

The modern emphasis on the domestic relates to a polarity between public and private. This polarity underpins considerations of the limits of the state and is foundational of liberal political philosophy. The house has been seen as the realm in which the citizen is sovereign in contrast to the realm of the state (city) in which sovereignty is given up by the citizen and tenure is public. The freedom of the individual and rights over private property are fundamental tenets of liberal capitalism. For that reason, contemporary historians tend to draw a clear distinction between ancient and modern understandings of the private. In its modern separation from the public, the house can be seen as the space of freedom, the space of repose, the place of individualism, the space of family, and the non-space in which the interests of the state cannot/should not run.[13] In its ancient form, the domestic is seen as implicated in the space of the city, the place of the citizen in which public and private blend to inform a unitary spatial and political culture.[14]

Yet, such an ancient–modern dichotomy has little to recommend it. As ancient historians have investigated the complexities of the public–private divide in ancient housing, so modern critics have considered the multifaceted nature of public and private in modernity. Hannah Arendt explored the emergence of a 'public' in modernity that is both distinct from the state and separate from the domestic. For Arendt, this public provided the social location of ideological practices: structures of thought that in her view depend on 'mass societies' and are distinct from the discursive practices of the state, the home and, indeed, the ancient state.[15] In a similar vein, Jürgen Habermas argued that modernity saw the emergence of a bourgeois 'public' opposed to the sphere of the court (aristocratic society), which exercised its authority through the discourses of newspapers and other mass media. This had the effect of bringing into being the public sphere and creating a powerful new and complex 'public' composed of multiple agents and voices that was neither located in the domestic nor the state, but affected both.[16]

Habermas' emphasis on discourses parallels the historical investigations of Michel Foucault, with their stress on the intimate life of moderns (though he never considered the formation of 'the domestic'). Notably, however, Foucault found similar patterns in the formation of discourses in the antique and modern worlds.[17] Specific spatial and ideological values will vary from society to society, but there seems no obvious reason to assume that the manner in which those values were formed will have differed in an ancient city from the similar processes in modernity.[18]

We may then suppose that societies influence the processes of societal reproduction that are conducted within the house and we may assume that the processes of domestic social reproduction influence society as a whole. The houses of modernity and antiquity (overloaded with symbolic value as they were), existed in a complex and negotiated relationship between individual, family and wider social powers. Even if the house is the primary space of social reproduction (as referenced in Bourdieu's conception of *habitus*), houses and house-residents cannot exist even in theoretical autarky: indeed, Aristotle sees the primacy of the *polis* as resulting partly from its being the smallest political organization that could be autarkic.[19] Social reproduction, then, occurs in multiple locations, associated with the domestic, public and, ultimately, the global (imperial).

Integrating these scenes of reproduction – and here I reference the work of Homi K. Bhabha – entails a hybridization of space (and culture).[20] As Clifford Geertz has shown, even isolated local societies (beloved by anthropologists) are in flux and subject to internal and external contention.[21] Such hybridization works against cultural and social essentialism, rendering the 'Indian', the 'Greek', the 'Roman' house problematic as conceptions, but perhaps more controversially for ancient historians similarly undermining the 'Ancient' city: all such spaces are (useful) fictions that attempt to give normative status to particular socio-spatial aggregations. Hybridization, in contrast, historicizes sociocultural structures, seeing them as generated by particular and shifting conjunctions of social power rather than as being relatively 'timeless' and stable structures identifiable with long-lasting political–state institutions (the Greek *polis*; the Roman Empire) or ethnic groups.

As space is a multi-levelled aggregation, so society is similarly formed. Social structures are ideological and are thus produced at the level of the individual but are also recognizably replicated across extended territories. This cannot result from a 'top-down' imposition of values from a polity (the state), since it is difficult to imagine a state (ancient or modern) quite so powerful, but must emerge from the reproduction of social codes by individual social actors.[22] Those social codes are precisely those identified by Arendt and Habermas as existing within a public sphere. Individuals adhere to those social codes in a localized engagement and perform the values of society in their everyday behaviours. Such behaviours are not however a passive acceptance of social order. Instead they involve an active engagement with social regulations. Their adherence to social norms can only be explained if social agents perceive those norms as personally beneficial.

Individuals' interest in adherence to social codes is ensured by the operation of power. This power may be repressive (policing power), but is often enabling in providing access to social resources necessary for social reproduction. Social codes are maintained for as long as individuals recognize contingent advantage in adherence to such codes or as long as the acquiescence in such codes provides associated social benefits or as long as disciplinary mechanisms effectively marshal the population. The system is not, however, unstable since the associated social benefits include the provision of a symbolic system through which social exchange can take place. Every society and every individual within a society requires social exchange. The social necessity for a symbolic economy makes the costs of radical social change (revolution) very high and provides considerable benefit for those who adhere to societal norms. The ideologies and behaviours associated with a symbolic economy are generated and performed repeatedly and frequently in everyday transactions, in the context of power relations which are most intimate at the local (household) level but can extend to state levels. In parallel, the ideologies of social relations have multiple articulations (symbolic and verbal), at levels from the household to the imperial.

This understanding of the formation of and adherence to social ideologies enhances the role of the individual and the local by pointing to the microdynamics of social formation and reproduction. In such a context, 'society' is a problematic but useful portmanteau term since it collates a mass of individual social transactions, rather as 'economy' is the sum of multiple economic transactions. It is, nevertheless, more pragmatic to think of a society as multiple networks of social relations. These are structured through social power and formed by social actors exercising choice in their engagements with particular networks. In reality, of course, the choices of social actors are constrained by the material requirements for social reproduction:

social power enables us to achieve our social needs (our requirements for biological sustenance and reproduction) and desires (what we wish for additional to our social needs). But, crucially, such constraints allow scope for individual agency and manipulation of social norms. Social formations operate as fluid, agonistic, enabling (and repressive) networks. It is through such networks that the various levels of political power from the state to the household are integrated and mutually influential.

The spatial–societal dialectic requires that we see the house as always embedded within wider sociological and spatial frameworks and caught within those agonistic, fluid relationships between individual and social formations. The house can never determine social formations, nor can it be determined by social formations: social formations are simply too dynamic to allow such fixity.

Spatial Order, Agency, Social Change

Towards the end of his life, Henri Lefebvre, the French geographer–philosopher, took to musing on the traffic outside his Parisian flat. He noted that the city had rhythm to it. Each individual went about her or his own business in his or her own time. There should have been anarchy, but instead there was order. The urban rhythm was generated by the conditions of production and consumption. People went to work, school, shops, bars, restaurants, homes. The streets were cleaned and serviced to a complex choreography.[23] If the juxtaposition of people made possible potentially disruptive chance encounters, the delicate rhythms of the city ensured order: the association of chaos and urbanism is the view from outside; from the inside, cities are disciplined.[24]

Lefebvre was an unorthodox Marxist. In the *Production of Space*, he integrated the spatial into Marxist critique.[25] He set himself both against the reliance on historicism within conventional Marxist thought and the increasing emphasis on the linguistic and the textual within the emergent postmodernism of Derrida and Kristeva (and perhaps Foucault).[26] His approach was innovative because of a focus on space rather than time. Lefebvre argued that spatial practice located the individual within a set of social and economic parameters, which determined behaviour. Through the spatial, Lefebvre was attempting to solve a central problem of materialist philosophy: the relationship between economic structures (seen as determining historical progress) and ideology (seen as determining individual actions).[27] Whereas Gramsci and Althusser found ideology embedded within discourses which were at least one step removed from the determining structures of economic life (among intellectuals or within 'Ideological State Apparatuses'), Lefebvre saw the spatial as working more intimately than discourses (codes) in shaping ideology.[28] Consequently, he argued that social change could not be achieved without spatial change.[29]

Lefebvre insisted that the world is experienced through the body and thus it followed that ideologies must be reproduced in the body. The arrangements of bodies in space ensured the continuity of production (the economy) and reproduction (the household).[30] As a consequence, radical change must start from the body.[31] He argued that the different levels of spatial analysis (local–regional–global) are integrated,[32] but the effects of spatial order on the individual warrant a particular focus on the domestic as the scene of reproduction (biological and social):

> As a substitute for the monumentality of the ancient world, housing, under the control of the state which oversees both production and reproduction, refers us from a cosmic 'naturalness' (air, water, sun, 'green space'), which is at once arid and fictitious, to genitality – to the family, the family unit and biological reproduction ... Shattered by a host of separations and segregations, social unity is able to reconstitute itself at the level of the family unit.[33]

In modern societies (in what must surely be a false opposition to the ancient world), the space of politicization is not the public environment of the city, with its class struggle, differential group interests and hyper-competitive capitalism, but the house. The house appears to be a space of resistance to modernity and its characteristic alienation. Yet, the mass production of houses (under the supervision of the state or economic forces) points to the impossibility of separating the domestic from wider societal influences. Such separations are, for Lefebvre, illusory since neo-capitalism constructs houses as it constructs cities as it constructs the geography of global inequality. Nevertheless, since we experience the world through our bodies primarily, any ordering of society must begin with the individual and the domestic. This emphasis on the individual provides a capacity for resistance to the hegemonic system and the possibility of social innovation. In spite of the overwhelming and globalized power that animates the socio-economic system, Lefebvre allowed for individual agency, innovation and the revolutionary potential of resistance. Such resistance needed space and in the Lefebvrean dynamic the scenes of the most intense politicization and thus potential for conflict were those spaces closest in, the body and, secondarily, the house.

Lefebvre offered a tripartite scheme of spatial analysis: spatial practice, representations of space, and representational space. The first of these is the space of the everyday and consists of people inhabiting space in particular ways. The second is the space of design and space as a material good: it is what architects, builders, urbanists, politicians and social engineers pro- duce. The third is representational space, which is the space of inhabitants, of the clandestine, of the artistic. This last is space as understood by those who inhabit that space.[34] The implications of this triad are twofold. In a negative formulation, space is too complex to reduce to a pattern of language or of signs (which map representations of space). Although Lefebvre may have overly downplayed the importance of discourse/text in framing social life, his critique is persuasive:

> When codes worked up from literary text are applied to spaces – to urban
> spaces, say – we remain . . . on the purely descriptive level. Any attempt to
> use such codes as a means of deciphering social space must surely reduce
> that space itself to the status of a *message*, and the inhabiting of it to the
> status of a *reading*. This is to evade both history and practice.[35]

The reduction of space to language conceals the processes by which social space is produced and creates an illusion of transparency (that space can be simply read rather than lived).[36] Treating space as text is a 'theoretical error' since it fails to comprehend the details of the lived experience of space and ignores the power relations enacted in the spatial form.[37] But it also simplifies the nature of space since:

> Social space can in no way be compared to a blank page upon which a
> specific message has been inscribed . . . Both natural and urban spaces are,
> if anything, 'over-inscribed': everything therein resembles a rough draft,
> jumbled and self-contradictory. Rather than signs, what one encounters
> here are directions – multifarious and overlapping directions.[38]

Lefebvre reacted against writers such as Bachelard who, in finding the historico-poetic resonances of his furniture, diverged considerably from any form of lived reality and instead posited an interpretation of space in nostalgic, perhaps even obsessive, contrariness to the everyday.[39] Lefebvre's multiplicity of signs on the palimpsest of (domestic) space offers scope for individual agency in determining which, if any, of those directions to follow.

A second issue relates to the role of agency in the production of space. Lefebvre argued that 'every society – and hence every mode of production with all its subvariants . . . – produces a space, its own space', which, stripped of its Marxist content, would mean that every social formation would have a distinctive spatial form.[40] Further, Lefebvre asserted that every social group must, in order to recognize themselves or be recognized by others, generate (or produce) a space.[41] Thus, different social agents or groups will compete to express their identity within space and perhaps deploy different strategies of self- or group-assertion. It follows that spatial arrangements in most societies will be agonistic and complex. Further, since most societies will have multiple modes of production, they will exhibit multiple spatial forms. Therefore, spaces of production and reproduction will at the very least exhibit multiplicity and in that multiplicity there is the possibility of choice and innovation. Such choice might entail a conservative rejection of newer forms or a deliberate engagement with non-traditional spatial to either advertise difference or, indeed, attempt a new way of living.[42]

To take an example, Bourdieu's Kabyle house would seem embedded within a particular and fixed mode of social reproduction. Through the house (*akham*) Bourdieu offers a unitary vision of Kabyle society, but that society had to a large extent already disappeared by 1960. As Bourdieu and his colleagues well knew, his vision of the *akham* (house) was a recreation of a structure that was being reimagined in new economic and social conditions in cities and diasporic contexts. If it had ever existed, Bourdieu's *akham* had been swept aside by economic change, urbanization and political transformation and was being remade as a nostalgic political choice reinforcing nationalistic cultural identities.[43] In a society of multiple and competing agents with diverse and conflicting interests, it was open to an individual to adopt a variety of strategies with regard to social reproduction and social space.

This emphasis on the multiplicity of agents offers a more radical means of understanding social space. Lefebvre's approach to space contrasted notably with that adopted by Foucault. Notoriously, Foucault employed spatial metaphors extensively (such as the Panopticon of social science) without ever engaging with the science of space (geography).[44] For Foucault, discourse largely determined the spatial. Equally notably, there is little agency in the Foucauldian social dynamic: authors reflect, replicate and advance the social discourses in which they are implicated.[45] Part of Foucault's scheme is to show how only particular discourses were authorized. Lefebvre, however, followed Gramsci in offering a much wider conception of the intellectual class responsible for the formation and propagation of ideologies. Every social agent has a capacity for innovation, even if that innovation is simply to adopt codes unfamiliar from his or her traditions.[46]

Lefebvre wrote that 'space is . . . populated by visible crowds of objects and invisible crowds of needs'.[47] We can understand these needs as being those of social groups (however defined) from the level of the imperial to the individual and everything in between. Those needs (desires) are socially constrained and in the agonistic interplay of desires and restraints some desires will not be met. Yet, the desiring subjects are multiple and not merely the scions of a literate intellectual class. Such multiplicity has the potential for social unrest if social desires are not met, and social change if social desires are met en masse.[48] In the context of an invisible crowd of unmet desires, it makes sense to talk of the city having an unconscious which is present in the representational element of Lefebvre's spatial triad.[49]

In a focus on desire, we may reverse Lefebvre's reading of contemporary housing bringing state power to the level of 'genitality'. Instead, we can argue that the needs and desires that are enacted in biological/social reproduction are in themselves productive of space. Politically, such desires drove the democratic state interventions in housing that Lefebvre noted, and the desire for certain kinds of familial reproduction provided the commercial impetus for modern suburban housing. The politics of desire worked to disrupt a prior hegemonic bio-politics.[50] The result was not, of course, utopia or freedom, but the substitution of one spatial–political regime for another. There was repression in such a productive process, be it the repression of individuals within the domestic community or of the community of the house in relationship to the wider social body. Further, the development of a new bio-political mode necessitated the suppression of an older form, and there is no reason to believe that this was an entirely consensual process or that no one grieved for the old order. But in the interplay of desire and repression, there was the possibility of widespread social and spatial change, which in modernity caused and was made possible by shifts in political and economic structures.

The tension between change and continuity plays into power dynamics *within* the household. As the house is the scene of biological and social reproduction (of genitality in the Lefebvrean phrase), control of the house enables supervision of those processes of reproduction and the representation of those processes to a wider community. The house contains all the interests, desires and power relations within a collective community (the family/household), and the results of the play of those individual desires depend heavily on the status and power of particular individuals (men and women, servile and free, adult and child), but will also reference the wider community where, in large part, status differentials are asserted. To take an

example, a man's power *in* the house may be authorized by social convention and recognition of that power within a social formation. But the power
of the household lies in the pooling of the collective desires and resources of
its community.

In modernity, although capitalist production is mostly spatially divorced
from the house, social reproduction continues in most instances to focus on the
house. The house is essential to the organization of labour and social reproduction on which the continued working of the capitalist system depends since
it enables the (re)production of the workforce who animate the social system.
Since the house community is in itself dependent upon that capitalist system
for its continued reproduction, the modern house and advanced capitalism
exist in symbiosis. In this way, a house is and always has been a machine for
living, a piece of social technology that enables social reproduction.

In antiquity, there was less separation of economic production and
social reproduction. The economic requirements for social reproduction
could only be fulfilled through the house community. The residents had to
ensure the replication of a certain economic mode and the power relations
inherent in that mode so as to secure the continued economic viability of
their way of life. In economic modes in which, for instance, production
depends on the pooling of labour resources, a house would, we might
expect, provide for larger households and associated economic functions
(large courts, room for animals, perhaps multiple flexible dwelling spaces
within the house). By contrast, production which depends on individual
and alienated labour (perhaps typically urban) requires different perhaps
more flexible spatial and domestic configurations.[51]

The social location of the house in this pivotal (liminal) location
between wider social practices and the individual and the function of the
house in production and reproduction mean that the house was central to
antique social formations. Setting the local (houses in this case) within the
global (imperial in this case) allows us to explore the relationship between
local and imperial political structures. Seeing the house as a product of
multiple desires allows us to focus on the role of individual agents, who
were themselves negotiating those political levels, in changing or maintaining housing and social formations. Such approaches may allow us to think
more subtly about issues of social inequality and gender in household
formation and the possibility of marginal understandings and subversions
of domestic space.[52] The interplay of desires intersects with requirements
for biological, economic and social reproduction. The house is thus a
material representation of the material needs for reproduction and the

symbolic desires of the residents for social status and recognition. It is a location in which the material and the ideological engage profoundly and in the production of which the individual and the societal are combined. The space of the house is thus produced by manifold social pressures, but also, and somewhat contrary to Lefebvre, by the desiring subject in engagement with his or her requirements and desires for social and material reproduction. It is these desires that have the potential to make manifest social change.

In the next sections, I look briefly at two issues relating to housing and social reproduction. In the first instance, I examine the strategies of social reproduction in elite housing and how those strategies affected the relationship between the individual and the house and the house and the city. In the second example, I consider change and continuity in rural housing in relation to issues of acculturation (as a desire of the provincial house owner) and the significance of continuities in architectural and economic modes.

Household, Villa, Estate

It seems likely that in the early Imperial period Roman males delayed marriage and tended to marry significantly younger women. The literary evidence is anecdotal and mostly unreliable, with examples such as Junius Mauricus, a man in his mid-thirties, who appears to have contracted a first marriage to a virginal girl (aged about seventeen).[53] Pliny the Younger married a girl who may have been more than twenty-five years younger than him (though it was not his first marriage).[54] The epigraphic evidence, which is probably more representative of general social patterns, suggests that the norm was for men to marry in their late twenties in most regions of the West, with the majority of men marrying by thirty-four and with majority of women marrying between the ages of twenty and twenty-four. The conclusion is drawn from a comparison of commemorators and age of the deceased on tombstones and a notable shift from parents to spouses which can be associated with particular age groups.[55] The explanation for delayed male marriage is likely to be economic.[56] Since marriage tended to lead to the formation of new households, the resources necessary for the formation of those new households needed to be available.[57] The desire for some measure of economic independence created a dynamic in which young men required land to found a family, but also gave parents the power to delay male marriage by not releasing resource and thus to continue to exploit the labour of young adult males.

Before the mid-2nd century BCE, Italian rural housing appears to have been mostly small-sized farms suitable for maintaining small families.[58] From the 2nd century BCE onwards, we see the gradual development of the luxury villa.[59] This development was not a 'natural' outgrowth of improved economic circumstances but a change in the way in which wealth was expressed. These villas represented new desires (*luxuria*), central to Rome's cultural revolution, and were an insurgent power within the Roman spatial order.[60] Consequently, the new villas both caused anxiety among the traditional elite and were desired by members of that elite as signifying membership of this new group.[61]

The impact of that desire is hinted at in discussions of the premier villa builder of the late Republic, Lucullus. The Lucullan villa was explicitly an escape from traditional spatial and moral disciplines related to his withdrawal from curia and Forum. Lucullus' self-differentiation resulted in his ironic identification as Xerxes Togatus, which referenced Lucullus' imperial escapades.[62] It is unlikely that his villa even alluded to Persian art, yet the expropriation of Greek artistic traditions inserted the villa aristocracy within a new imperial geography, reflected in the exoticism of art and building materials, which extracted the aristocrats from a traditional spatial and moral order. Consequently, new desires could be played out within the villa and, whether or not we believe the stories, these desires find their most obvious expression in the imperial villas of Tiberius and Gaius and the Golden House of Nero with their associated legends of illicit sexual activity. Thus, we have a powerful association of house (villa), sexual desire and tyranny.

By the mid- to late 1st century, there was an established villa literature, exemplified in the villa poetry of Statius and the villa descriptions of Pliny.[63] One of the more notable features of these literary villas, which must have had extensive servile establishments, is emptiness. In Statius, *Silvae* 1.3, for instance, the villa of Manilius Vopsicus is described in the most soporific terms, with all life at rest. The household of Pliny's Laurentine villa appears only at the Saturnalia and then at the other end of the house while the Tuscan villa, though set in a productive countryside, appears to contain Pliny and, possibly, a topiarist.[64] Pliny's isolated grottoes, his villa-lakes (and one can compare Hadrian's villa at Tivoli), his working of nature to his demands were expressions of a power over nature and of a desire for individualistic power unchallenged by social convention.[65]

Such power depended on an accumulation of wealth not just sufficient to build these grandiose monuments, but also to give some reality to the autarkic pretensions of the villa. The early Imperial period saw the rich get richer. This was not just a process confined to the high Imperial aristocracy, but the lesser aristocracy seem also to have benefited from the Imperial peace and to have extended their property holdings.[66] Such prosperity might have provided more economic niches for households, which would have led to the formation of new families and population growth (meeting a desire for reproduction). Instead, the Roman elite concentrated resources in more powerful households, adopting a strategy in which the family attempted to maintain or improve status over generations by retaining wealth.

Larger houses reflect a desire for social status. Such status could only be achieved within households that avoided, whenever possible, partition of resources (and status) and this was a powerful incentive to adopt family limitation strategies. The rise of the household as a means of status competition carried implications for the status of wives: their status depended less upon their birth family than on the households formed with their husbands. The commitment of these wives to their new households created a closer identification with the conjugal couple, who shared desires, status and increasingly elaborate space. Such an identification allowed women to represent their households, but also subsumed their individual identities into the disciplinary and economic structures of those households. The so-called new conjugality of the 1st century CE can be seen to depend on the shifting modes of economic and social reproduction.[67]

This dynamic continued into late antiquity.[68] The injunctions of Cassiodorus to the Symmachi make obvious the blurring of lines between city and estate.[69] The power of the great estates led to them taking on at least some of the architectural language of the city, as well as absorbing some of the political functions previously carried out by urban collectives.[70] The wealth of the great villas allowed their owners flights of architectural and artistic fancy, which led, among other things, to the great flourishing of mosaic art through late antiquity, but at the same time rendered the individuals dependent on the household for social reproduction. As households became larger, so the capacity of even the most powerful individuals to act independently of the household was reduced. Rather than an assertion of individuality against the community, villa culture once located within a wider economic environment begins to look more like an accession of power and status to the household. The difficulties Melania the Younger faced in her attempts to dissolve her aristocratic household, for instance, suggest that she was not in any sense we would recognize the owner of her property. Instead, she was a member of a household which was a major political and economic institution in 5th-century Rome.[71] Melania's investing of her identity in Christianity may be seen as a radical attempt to resist the hegemonic politics of the household. Her desire to dissolve her familial estates undermined the economic and social reproductive capacity of the house as her desire for celibacy was to lay claim on her body and reproductivity.

Farm, Village, Empire

Across the Roman Empire, there was a considerable diversity of rural domestic architectural types which would seem to reflect a multitude of different social formations. In most antique rural environments, the key to social reproduction was control over land and labour. Different communities solved that problem in different ways and as a result the processes of household formation and, indeed, the architectural forms adopted varied considerably. The Egyptian rural household, for instance, appears to have been strongly virilocal with average age at first marriage for men being significantly lower than in the West, perhaps in the early twenties rather than the early thirties.[72] Rural household structures appear also to have been different from what can be understood of Western households (which is very little), with *frérèches* (households formed around brothers) being a common form.[73] Since households were not neo-local and *frérèches* could contain multiple conjugal units, marriage of males did not require a significant partition of household resources. Marriage would entail acquiring a dowry (which mostly did not have land associated) and the labour of the new wife. Although households could survive on very small plots of land, pooling resources allowed more flexibility and diversity, and probably improved the status of the family.[74]

Although we do not have the documentary material and thus cannot assess the ages of marriage, there were similar patterns at play in Roman Syria. There, the village houses follow distinctive patterns, with often very large courtyards (with evidence of agricultural production) and residential structures (sometimes multiple) located within the enclosure. The pattern can be seen very obviously at Umm el-Jimal and in the various surveys of village settlements through the high lands of Syria.[75] Domestic architecture suggests some form of extended family households manipulating perhaps relatively large landholdings and thereby diversifying and reducing risk in a harsh agricultural environment.

There are likely to have been several ways of solving the particular economic and environmental challenges set in these regions, but once particular economic modes were established, they shaped residential patterns, family structures and domestic architecture. Such residential patterns were anything but timeless: many of the rural areas of the Syria jebels saw extensive sedentary settlement only during the Roman period and were subsequently sites of considerable agricultural innovation and settlement growth.[76] Yet, departing from established patterns of residential and economic organization entailed risk. The particular modes of household organization were such as to ensure (as best anyone knew) the social and economic reproduction of the household; the house provided the necessary social spaces for such reproduction. Any new housing or household form risked disrupting those processes.

Secondly, in the Syrian case, status and identity are likely to have been heavily invested in the houses: they tended to be well-built structures and set within settlements which frequently lacked significant public spaces or obvious public institutions. The large houses in the small village settlement of Kafr Shams, for example, were clearly centres of agricultural activity. The rooms are grouped around courtyards, with the roofed areas being semi-discrete suites of rooms (though upper storeys are only partially preserved). The houses themselves may have evolved into separate entities over generations (*Maison 5* appears to 'borrow' space from *Maison 2*, suggesting a close relationship between the two households). The houses show considerable evidence of architectural ornamentation, some of which at least was outward-facing.[77] Such houses represented wealth and were a significant material resource in themselves, which would have discouraged the partition of household resources. Further, the decision-makers within households, those who might consider a new strategy of reproduction, were likely to be those most heavily invested in the current reproductive modes: change would not necessarily be in their individual, local interests. It seems very likely that the residences housed extended families.

Nevertheless, we can say little or nothing about any 'sense of belonging' from such evidence nor indeed about the 'impact of Rome'. The requirements for economic and social reproduction and local desires for status may have exercised a conservative influence on domestic architectural forms, but there is no reason to believe that such conservatism was a means of transmitting a message about Imperial cultural and political identities: the house was just too important to be reduced to a message board.

Nevertheless, many regions of the Empire did see significant change in housing, particularly in north-west Europe.[78] The adoption of certain 'codes' from exotic (imperial) cultures, as in the case of villas, signified an engagement with a wider cultural and economic geography, but acquired significance within a local cultural environment. Adopting exogenous architectural codes was a heavy investment in a form of identity politics (especially in comparison with cheaper possible signifiers, such as wine or clothing). Such an investment needs to be read as a local play for status.[79] The cultural result was necessarily hybrid. Such hybridity allows for the possibility that traditional patterns of social reproduction were maintained.[80]

Conversely, if provincials saw advantages in the adoption of new economic modes or forms of social reproduction, for instance commercial farming or slave labour, the technological requirements of such modes would likely require the production of new spaces. In adopting such modes, the household integrated with imperial economic modes and social formations, an integration that we would expect to be reflected in architecture. We might expect new economic modes to produce new architectural forms (though we might recall the nostalgic and conscious conservatism of the 'Kabyle house'), but exogenous architectural forms in themselves cannot be taken to signify new modes of social reproduction.

Accustomed as we are to 'national' cultures and societies, the discussion of the Roman provincial house allows us to rethink the dynamic of acculturation. If social formations are generated locally in communication with other spatial levels, the location of culture must be multiple. The association of a particular identities with particular modes of economic exploitation, production and reproduction is questionable: to assert oneself as Roman required a particular ideological association with the Roman Empire, but the means by which that ideological stance found representation in domestic culture (if indeed it did) or economic activities must have varied and are potentially obscure to us. The risk factors in shifting house and household productive arrangements were comparatively high, especially in harsh environmental or economic circumstances. The risk factors in adopting a symbol of the Imperial culture, a mosaic floor, for instance, were very low.

Nevertheless, the Imperial formation did have the capacity to inculcate fundamental social change by providing new sources of social power, new economic and cultural modes and, potentially, new desires. Empire provided options, though, and of course, those options had embedded within them a variety of structural inequalities of wealth and power. Change in the fundamentals of social reproduction was a possible response to Empire, but could not be a 'top-down' process: it needed to be generated at the domestic level and with the individual and was a response to calculations of social risk, benefit and ambition.

Conclusion

This odyssey begins and ends in the house. Bachelard and Bourdieu, in their very different ways, found the world in the house. Lefebvre showed how that might be, exploring the multilayered nature of spatial production and its linkage with social reproduction. My emphasis on social formations allows us to focus on the processes of production and reproduction. My effort is to bring social (spatial) analysis to the level of the individual and to put the desiring subject at the centre of social production. In ancient societies (and probably most modern societies) social reproduction depended heavily on the domestic community. In my brief outline of ancient examples, we see how the desires of householders drove social and architectural change, notably in the development of the luxury villa, and how the requirements to maintain the villa-household operated eventually to limit the social power of the individual. In other forms of rural housing, we see varied responses to the requirements of social and economic reproduction. These responses can only be understood on the basis of local decision-making, not notably in reference to the dynamics of cultural assimilation into imperial forms, but in the tight constraints of the needs for social reproduction. Such desires did not operate in dialectical relations with the symbolic economy of the various ancient communities, since the relationship was actually closer. Desires were structured by that symbolic economy, and existed and had meaning only within that symbolic economy. Consequently, those desires reproduced that symbolic economy in their realization. The symbolic economy was affected by Imperial level interventions, but the agency that drove key decision-making was always of necessity local. The production of household space is not the manifestation of globalized or Imperial spatial arrangements or resistance thereto, but is inextricably hybrid, between walls and words, individuals and society.

The household is the community in which we engage most intimately and which makes possible our identities and the living of our lives. Even as the global influences our lives, we live locally and we generate our domestic spaces in a dialectic with other spatial forms. Social reproduction must begin in the house, but the house is always engaged in wider spatial forms. Similarly, to understand social formations ancient and modern, we must begin and end with the house as the realm of reproduction and desire, but take account of all the spaces encountered in the social odyssey through which we attempt to fulfil our needs and individual desires.

Notes

1 There is a long and honourable academic tradition of geographical and spatial determinism. For a radical instance in housing studies, see Hillier and Hanson 1984. The view has underpinned town and environmental planning since the beginning of the 20th century. See Geddes 1949 and the discussion in Welter 2002 and Alston 2012.

2 See Giddens 1984. See also, for comparison, Althusser 2008 for the performative aspects of social ideology.

3 See Taylor 2002. Taylor built on the work of Anderson 2006 in which Anderson stressed the necessity of invention and cultural symbolism in the formation of group consciousness.

4 In addition to the works cited above and below, see Rapaport 1969 and Habermas 1991, for his consideration of the emergence of a public sphere and a domestic sphere in modern spatial awareness. See also Sennett's detailed study of house and society in Sennett 1984.

5 Bourdieu 1979, reprinted in Bourdieu 1990.

6 See Tosh 1999, on the invention of the domestic in Victorian England. See also Hill 1875; Barnett and Barnett 1915 [1888]. See also Arendt 1958, who argues that in modernity 'society' absorbs the domestic. Here, I argue for more agency in relation to society, but Arendt points to a political concern with the domestic.

7 See Milnor 2005 who argues for 'an invention' of the domestic under Augustus, by which she means that the domestic became a fundamental element in Augustan ideology.

8 One may compare the modern anthropologically informed perspective of the Roman city growing out of networks of kin. See the discussion in Saller 1997.

9 Cicero, De officiis 1.21; 50–51. Cicero also speculates that primitive communism was the original form of social organization, but contemporary Rome was hardly communist.

10 Vitruvius, De architectura 2.1–7.

11 Aristotle, Politics 1.1252a–53b. Xenophon, Oeconomicus argues for household management and agriculture as a primary activity of moral value which provides disciplines useful for the polis, which demonstrates a linkage between oikos and polis.

12 See the discussion in Thomas 1996.

13 Such concerns animate a range of debates from American libertarianism to privacy law (see the UK Human Rights Act (1998), Art. 8, incorporating the European Convention on Human Rights).

14 See, most influentially, Wallace-Hadrill 1988. Concentrating on Roman examples, see (exempli gratia) Hales 2003: 1 who notes 'The Roman's house, it

might be said, was his *forum*'; Bradley 1991: esp. 6–11 Ruggiu 1995; Riggsby 1997. For the Greek world, see Nevett 1999, and the papers collected in Westgate *et al.* 2007, for discussions of the complex and gendered nature of public and private.

15 Arendt 1958.

16 Habermas 1991 built on the work of Norbert Elias, notably Elias 2000.

17 See Foucault 1986, 1981, 1998. For an analysis of Foucault's use of the Classical see Alston 2017: 8–30.

18 I take the integration of the domestic and the *polis* in ancient and modern considerations of the *polis* as utopian and unrealistic. The Greek city had a 'public' in a different way from that imagined by Habermas and Arendt for modern societies, but it was still a profoundly ideological formation. See my discussion in Alston 2010.

19 Aristotle, *Politics* 1.1252b–53a.

20 Bhabha 2012.

21 Geertz 1975.

22 The gap between pervasive social rules and limited state authority informs Foucault's distinction between power (which lies in all social interaction) and sovereignty: see Foucault 1976 [1991]: 88–89; 1997.

23 Lefebvre 1996.

24 See Chakrabarty's account of the rhythm of garbage collection in Indian cities, Chakrabarty 1992. This argument runs contrary to de Certeau 1984.

25 Lefebvre 1991.

26 See, for example, Lefebvre 1991: 5–6 and 102–42. The radical nature of his enterprise is less obvious four decades after the original French publication and in a world in which the internal Marxist intellectual debates seem at best sophistic.

27 Issues of ideology sit at the heart of Marx's philosophical engagement with and rejection of Hegelianism, Marx and Engels 1964.

28 See the collection of essays in Althusser 2008; see Gramsci 1968. The 'gap' between the material relations of production and ideology in Gramsci and Althusser is such that it raises questions as to whether ideology is, in the last instance, determined by economic relations.

29 Lefebvre 1991: 54. 'A revolution that does not produce a new space has not realised its full potential: indeed, it has failed in that it has not changed itself, but has merely changed ideological superstructures, institutions, or political apparatuses. A social transformation, to be truly revolutionary in character must manifest a creative capacity in its effects on daily life, in language, and in space.'

30 For the corporeal see Lefebvre 1991: 162, and esp., 207–17. The emphasis on the bodily stems from a reaction to existentialism, though Sartre is not mentioned. For spaces of production and reproductions see Lefebvre 1991: 32: 'Social space contains – and assigns ... appropriate places to – (1) the social relations of

reproduction ... and (2) the relations of production ... These two sets of relations, productive and reproductive, are inextricably bound up with one another... [T]he two interlocking levels of biological reproduction and socio-economic production together constitute societal reproduction – that is to say, the reproduction of society as it perpetuates itself generation after generation.'

31 Lefebvre 1991: 166. 'Any revolutionary "project" ... whether utopian or realistic, must, if it is to avoid hopeless banality, make the reappropriation of the body, in association with the reappropriation of space, into a non-negotiable part of its agenda.'

32 Lefebvre 1991: 86, 412.

33 Lefebvre 1991: 232. We might wish to substitute 'economy' or 'market' for 'state'.

34 Lefebvre 1991: 33–36. See also Soja 1996: 1–82, for a reworking of what Soja calls the 'trialectics' of Lefebvre, and de Certeau 1984 for a consideration of the everyday spatial practices.

35 Lefebvre 1991: 7.

36 Lefebvre 1991: 27.

37 Lefebvre 1991: 94.

38 Lefebvre 1991: 142.

39 Lefebvre 1991: 102; Bachelard 1994.

40 Lefebvre 1991: 31.

41 Lefebvre 1991: 416–17.

42 See Alston forthcoming for a discussion of the adoption of the symbols of Romanization in Egyptian domestic space.

43 Silverstein 2004: 553–78.

44 See Crampton and Elden 2007. See also, from among a range of engagements with the spatial, Foucault 1976 [1991]. For Foucault's explicit discussion of geography, see Crampton 1976, 1977.

45 Issues of liberty and resistance are deeply problematic in Foucault's thought. Resistance is seemingly ever-present, but liberty never present. See Taylor 1984.

46 Foucault 1984: 32–50 argues that characteristic of modernity is the urge 'to face the task of producing' the self, which occurs in aesthetics (cultural codes). Foucault keeps the analysis at the level of the individual, but once whole populations take on the role of self-fashioning, the result would be transformative.

47 Lefebvre 1991: 394.

48 See Hardt and Negri 2004 for the revolutionary potential of global population movements and multiple desires.

49 Lefebvre 1991: 36.

50 See Stavrakis 1999 and the works of Žižek, indicatively, Žižek 1999, 2008: 1–55 in which he explores the link between ideology, desires, and the unconscious.

51 Ancient historians are comfortable with economic demands requiring extended households, but it also seems likely that the demands of a capitalist economy would render smaller, more flexible households advantageous. See Engels 1940.

52 The potentially subversive memories of place account for the interest of cultural geography in the ways in which the socially marginal or the subaltern understand space. See Gregory 1994; Soja 1996.

53 Pliny, *Epistulae* 1.14. Lelis *et al.* 2003 collate the literary evidence, but fail to consider contextual factors. See the response from Scheidel 2007: 389–402.

54 See Alston and Spentzou 2011: 124–31.

55 Saller 1987: 21–34. Some of the samples are very small, and even later marriage in Africa and Spain may be a statistical quirk.

56 See Herlihy and Klapsich-Zuber 1985: 87 for dramatic changes in age at first marriage for men, rising from 23.8 to 29.6, in response to economic change over the century from 1372 to 1470 for the city of Prato.

57 Plutarch, *Crassus* 1, notes the exceptional circumstance of Crassus and his three adult brothers living under the same roof even when two of those brothers were married.

58 See the survey in Rathbone 2008. Volpe 1990 produces a regional survey of small farms. Carandini 1985: 106–107 and Carandini and Cambi 2002: 140–42 look at colonial farmhouses. Goodchild 2007: 64, 118 models smallholdings in the Tiber as excavated by Jones 1963; Ward-Perkins *et al.* 1986.

59 For surveys, see Lafon 2001; Marzano 2007.

60 Wallace-Hadrill 2008: *passim*, but in summary on p. 450 he writes 'the growth of luxury is not about wealth alone, but about the relationships between wealth and status recognition'.

61 See, *exempli gratia*, Plutarch, *Lucullus* 38–41; Sallust, *Cattaline*, 11–13; Cicero, *Letters to Atticus* 1.19; 1.20.

62 Pliny, *Natural History* 9. 170; Velleius Paterculus 2.33; See also Jolivet 1987 and Evans 2008: 104–108

63 Pliny, *Epistulae* 2.17; 5.6; 9.7; 9.36; 9.40. See also Statius, *Silvae* 1.3; 2.2; 3.1.

64 Pliny, *Epistulae* 2.17; 5.6.

65 Such power borders on the imperial and the divine, see Statius, *Silvae* 2.2 and 3.11, in which the villa has a divine presence.

66 Champlin 1981; Duncan-Jones 1990: 121–42.

67 Veyne 1987: 1–234, see 36: 'In the first century B.C. a man was supposed to think of himself as a citizen who had fulfilled all his civic duties. A century later he was supposed to think of himself as a good husband.' Veyne depends on Foucault 1986. See also the dynamic outlined in van Bremen 1996.

68 See Vera 1995.

69 Cassiodorus, *Variae* 3.51

70 Mazza 2001, outlines the development of the great *oikoi* in Egypt, institutions that performed governmental functions while being households of extended

families. For late villa typologies in Italy, see Sfameni 2006. For villas as 'public buildings', see Lavan 2001. See also the survey by Ellis 2007.

71 Gerontius, Life of Melania the Younger 10–14.

72 Bagnall and Frier 1994: 111–22. Epigraphic evidence is mostly urban, but the discussion here focuses on rural households. For further discussion of the Egyptian rural household, see Alston forthcoming. For a discussion of the micro-dynamics of family structure, see Hübner 2013.

73 See Pudsey 2011.

74 See the discussion in Alston 2005, arguing for varied strategies of family formation in Roman Egypt, but with an emphasis on the nuclear unit as the primary social and legal group. The argument is developed in Alston forthcoming which argues that the importance of households for social reproduction meant that the household retained considerable authority over its members, but that the social group of the household extended beyond the community resident in any one house.

75 Tchalenko 1953; Hirschfeld 1986; Tate 1992; Sodini 1995; 1997; De Vries 1998; Magness 2003.

76 Decker 2009.

77 Clauss-Balty 2008: 41–103; Dentzer-Feydy 2008.

78 There is a vast bibliography on the villa, see Percival 1976; Hingley 1989; Scott 1993 [1976]; Smith 1997.

79 See the discussion in Habermehl 2013.

80 See the discussion of the multilocational nature of culture above, p. 000.

References

Alston, R. (2005). Searching for the Romano-Egyptian family. In M. George, ed., *The Roman Family in the Roman Empire: Rome, Italy and Beyond*. Oxford: Oxford University Press, 129–57.

(2010). Post-politics and the ancient Greek city. In R. Alston and O. van Nijf, eds., *Political Culture in the Greek City after the Classical Age*. Leuven, Paris and Walpole, MA: Peeters, 307–36.

(2012). Class cities: Classics, utopianism, Classics and urban planning in early-twentieth-century Britain. *Journal of Historical Geography* 38, 263–72.

(2017). Introduction: Foucault's Rome. In S. Bhatt and R. Alston, eds., *Foucault's Rome (Foucault Studies 22)*, 8–30.

(forthcoming). Modes of production and reproduction in Roman-era Egyptian villages. In C. E. Barrett, ed., *Households in Context: Dwelling in Ptolemaic and Roman Egypt*. Ithaca, NY: Cornell University Press.

Alston, R. and Spentzou, E. (2011). *Reflections of Romanity: Discourses of Subjectivity in Imperial Rome*. Columbus: Ohio State University Press.

Althusser, L. (2008). *On Ideology*. London and New York: Verso.

Anderson, B. (2006). *Imagined Communities: Reflections on the Origin and Spread of Nationalism*. London and New York: Verso.

Arendt, H. (1958). *The Human Condition*. Chicago and London: University of Chicago Press.

Bachelard, G. (1994). *The Poetics of Space*, trans. M. Jolas. Boston: Beacon Press.

Bagnall, R. S. and Frier, B. W. (1994). *The Demography of Roman Egypt*. Cambridge: Cambridge University Press.

Barnett, S. A. and Barnett, H. O. (1915 [1888]). *Practical Socialism*. London: Longmans.

Bhabha, H. K. (2012). *The Location of Culture*. London: Routledge.

Bourdieu, P. (1979). The Kabyle house or the world reversed. In P. Bourdieu, *Algeria 1960*, trans. R. Nice. Cambridge: Cambridge University Press, 133–53. Reprinted in Bourdieu, P. (1990). *The Logic of Practice*. Cambridge: Polity, 271–83.

Bradley, K. R. (1991). *Discovering the Roman Family: Studies in Roman Social History*. Oxford: Oxford University Press.

Carandini, A. (1985). *La romanizzione dell' Etruria: il territorio di Vulci*. Milan: Regione Toscana.

Carandini, A. and Cambi, F., eds. (2002). *Paesaggi d' Etruria: Valle dell' Albegna, Valle del Oro, Valle del Chiarone, Valle del Tafone*. Rome: Edizioni di Storia e Letteratura.

Chakrabarty, D. (1992). Of garbage, modernity, and the citizen's gaze. *Economic and Political Weekly* 27(10–11), 541–47, reprinted in Chakrabarty, D. (2002) *Habitations of Modernity: Essays in the Wake of* Subaltern Studies. Chicago: University of Chicago Press, 65–79.

Champlin, E. (1981). Owners and neighbours at Ligures Baebiani. *Chiron* 11, 115–46.

Clauss-Balty, P. (2008). Maisons romano-byzantines dans les villages de Batanée: Missions 2002–2004. In P. Clauss-Balty, ed., *Hauran III: L'habitat dans les campagnes de Syrie du Sud aux époques classique et médiévale*. Beirut: Institut français du Proche Orient, 41–103.

Crampton, J. W. (1976). Des questions de Michel Foucault à *Hèrodote*. *Hèrodote* 3, 9–10.

    (1977). Des résponses aux questions de Michel Foucault. *Hèrodote* 6, 3–23.

Crampton, J. W. and Elden, S., eds. (2007). *Space, Knowledge, Power: Foucault and Geography*. Aldershot: Taylor and Francis.

de Certeau, M. (1984). *The Practice of Everyday Life*, trans. S. Rendall. Berkeley: University of California Press, 91–110.

De Vries, B. (1998). *Umm el-Jimal: A Frontier Town and Its Landscape in Northern Jordan I*. JRA Suppl 26. Portsmouth, RI: Journal of Roman Archaeology.

Decker, M. (2009). *Tilling the Hateful Earth: Agricultural Production and Trade in the Late Antique East*. Oxford: Oxford Univesity Press.

Dentzer-Feydy, J. (2008). Le décor architectural des maisons de Batanée. In P. Clauss-Balty, ed., *Hauran III: L'habitat dans les campagnes de Syrie du Sud aux époques classique et* médiévale. Beirut: Institut français du Proche Orient, 183–231.

Duncan-Jones, R. (1990). *Structure and Scale in the Roman Economy*. Cambridge: Cambridge University Press.

Elias, N. (2000). *The Civilizing Process: Sociogenetic and Psychogenetic Investigations*. Oxford and Malden, MA: Wiley-Blackwell.

Ellis, S. (2007). Late Antique housing and the uses of residential buildings: an overview. In L. Lavan, L. Özgenel and A. Sarantis, eds., *Housing in Late Antiquity: From Palaces to Shops*. Leiden: Brill, 1–22.

Engels, F. (1940). *The Origins of the Family, Private Property and the State in the Light of the Research of Lewis H. Morgan*. London: Lawrence and Wishart.

Evans, R. (2008). *Utopia Antiqua: Readings of the Golden Age and Decline at Rome*. London and New York: Routledge.

Foucault, M. (1976 [1991]). *Discipline and Punish: The Birth of the Prison*. London: Penguin.

(1984). What is Enlightenment? In P. Rabinow, ed., *The Foucault Reader*. Harmondsworth: Penguin, 32–50.

(1986). *The History of Sexuality: III: The Care of the Self*. London: Penguin.

(1981). *The History of Sexuality: I: The Will to Knowledge*. London: Penguin.

(1997). *"Society Must Be Defended": Lectures at the Collège de France, 1975–76*, ed. M. Bertani and A. Fontana, trans. D. Macey. New York: Picador.

(1998). *The History of Sexuality: II: The Use of Pleasure*. London: Penguin.

Geddes, P. (1949). *Cities in Evolution: An Introduction to the Town Planning Movement and to the Study of Civics*. London: Williams and Norgate.

Geertz, C. (1975). *The Interpretation of Cultures: Selected Essays*. London: Hutchinson.

Giddens, A. (1984). *The Constitution of Society: Outline of the Theory of Structuration*. Cambridge: Polity.

Goodchild, H. (2007). *Modelling Roman Agricultural Production in the Middle Tiber Valley, Central Italy*. (PhD thesis, University of Birmingham.)

Gramsci, A. (1968). *The Modern Prince and Other Writings*. New York: Lawrence and Wishart.

Gregory, D. (1994). *Geographical Imaginations*. Cambridge, MA, and Oxford: Blackwell.

Habermas, J. (1991). *The Structural Transformation of the Public Sphere: An Inquiry into a Category of Bourgeois Society*, trans. Thomas Burger with the assistance of Frederick Lawrence. Cambridge, MA: Massachusetts Institute of Technology.

Habermehl, D. (2013). *Settling in a Changing World: Villa Development in the Northern Provinces of the Roman Empire*. Amsterdam Archaeological Studies, 19. Amsterdam: Amsterdam University Press.

Hales, S. (2003). *The Roman House and Social Identity*. Cambridge: Cambridge University Press.

Hardt, M. and Negri, A. (2004). *Multitude: War and Democracy in the Age of Empire*. London: Hamish Hamilton.

Herlihy, D. and Klapsich-Zuber, C. (1985). *Tuscans and Their Families: A Study of the Florentine Catasto of 1427*. New Haven and London: Yale University Press.

Hill, O. (1875). *Homes of the London Poor*. London: Macmillan.

Hillier, B. and Hanson, J. (1984). *The Social Logic of Space*. Cambridge: Cambridge University Press.

Hingley, R. (1989). *Rural Settlement in Roman Britain*. London: Seaby.

Hirschfeld, Y. (1986). *Dwelling Houses in Roman and Byzantine Palestine*. Jerusalem: Franciscan Printing Press.

Hübner, S. R. (2013). *The Family in Roman Egypt: A Comparative Approach to Intergenerational Solidarity and Conflict*. Cambridge: Cambridge University Press.

Jolivet, V. (1987). Xerxes Togatus: Lucullus en Campanie. *Mélanges de l'école française de Rome* 99, 875–904.

Jones, G. D. B. (1963). Capena and the Ager Capenas: Part II. *Papers of the British School at Rome* 31, 100–158.

Lafon, X. (2001). *Villa maritima: recherches sur les villas littorales de l'Italie romaine (IIIe siècle av. J.-C. / IIIe siècle ap. J.-C*. Rome: Ecole française de Rome.

Lavan, L. (2001). The *praetorium* of civil governors in Late Antiquity. In L. Lavan and W. Boden, eds., *Recent Research in Late Antique Urbanism*. JRA Suppl. 42. Portsmouth, RI: Journal of Roman Archaeology, 39–56.

Lefebvre, H. (1991). *The Production of Space*, trans. D. Nicholson Smith. Oxford and Cambridge, MA: Blackwell.

(1996). Seen from the window. In R. Kafman and E. Lebas, eds. and trans., *Writings on Cities*. Malden, MA, Carlton MN, and Oxford: Blackwell, 219–27.

Lelis, A. A., Percy, W. A., Beert, C. and Verstraete, W. (2003). *The Age of Marriage in Ancient Rome*. Lewiston, ME and Lampeter: Edwin Mellen Press.

Magness, J. (2003). *The Archaeology of Early Islamic Settlement in Palestine*. Winona Lake, IN: Eisenbrauns.

Marx, K. and Engels, F. (1964). *The German Ideology*. Moscow: Marx–Engels Institute.

Marzano, A. (2007). *Roman Villas in Central Italy; A Social and Economic History*. Columbia Studies in the Classical Tradition, 30. Leiden and Boston: Brill.

Mazza, R. (2001). *L'Archivio degli Apioni: terra, lavoro e proprietà senatoria nell'Egitto tardoantico*. Bari: Edipuglia.

Milnor, K. (2005). *Gender, Domesticity, and the Age of Augustus: Inventing Private Life*. Oxford: Oxford University Press.

Nevett, L. (1999). *House and Society in the Ancient Greek World*. Cambridge: Cambridge University Press.

Percival, J. (1976). *The Roman Villa: A Historical Introduction*. London: Batsford.

Pudsey, A. (2011). Nuptiality and the demographic life cycle of families in Roman Egypt. In C. Holleran and A. Pudsey, *Demography and the Graeco-Roman World: New Insights and Approaches*. Cambridge: Cambridge University Press, 60–98.

Rapaport, A. (1969). *House Form and Culture*. Englewood Cliffs: Prentice Hall.

Rathbone, D. W. (2008). Poor peasants and silent sherds. In L. de Ligt and S. Northwood, eds., *People, Land, and Politics: Demographic Developments and the Transformation of Roman Italy 300 BC–AD 14* (*Mnemosyne* Suppl. 303). Leiden and Boston: Brill, 305–32.

Riggsby, A. M. (1997). 'Public' and 'private' in Roman culture: the case of the Cubiculum. *Journal of Roman Archaeology* 10, 35–66.

Ruggiu, A. Z. (1995). *Spazio privato e spazio pubblico nella città romana*. Rome: École française de Rome.

Saller, R. P. (1987). Men's age at marriage and its consequences in the Roman family. *Classical Philology* 82, 21–34.

   (1997). Roman kinship: structure and sentiment. In B. Rawson and P. Weaver, eds., *The Roman Family in Italy: Status, Sentiment, Space*. Oxford: Oxford University Press, 7–34.

Scheidel, W. (2007). Roman funerary commemoration and the age at first marriage. *Classical Philology* 102, 389–402.

Scott, E. (1993 [1976]). *A Gazetteer of Roman Villas in Britain*. Leicester: School of Archaeological Studies, University of Leicester.

Sennett, R. (1984). *Families against the City: Middle Class Homes of Industrial Chicago, 1872–1890*. Cambridge, MA, and London: Harvard University Press.

Sfameni, C. (2006). *Ville residenziali nell' Italia tardoantica*. Bari: Edipuglia.

Silverstein, P. A. (2004). Of rooting and uprooting: Kabyle habitus, domesticity, and structural nostalgia. *Ethnography* 5, 553–78.

Smith, J. T, (1997). *Roman Villas: A Study in Social Structure*. London: Routledge.

Sodini, J. P. (1995). Habitat de l'Antiquité Tardive. *Topoi* 5, 151–218.

   (1997). Habitat de l'Antiquité Tardive (2). *Topoi* 7, 435–577.

Soja, E. W. (1996). *Thirdspace: Journeys to Los Angeles and Other Real and Imagined Places*. Malden, MA, Oxford and Carlton, ME: Blackwell.

Stavrakis, P. J. (1999). *Moscow and Greek Communism, 1944–1949*. Ithaca, NY: Cornell University Press.

Tate, G. (1992). *Les Campagnes de la Syrie du Nord au IIe au VIIe siècle I*. Paris: Librairie orientaliste Paul Geuthner.

Taylor, C. (1984). Foucault on freedom and truth. *Political Theory* 12(2), 152–83.

   (2002). Modern social imaginaries. *Public Culture* 14(1), 91–124.

Tchalenko, G. (1953). *Villages antiques de la Syrie du Nord: le massif de Bélus à l'époque romaine.* Paris: Institut français d'archéologie de Beyrouth.

Thomas, Y. (1996). Fathers as citizens of Rome, Rome as a city of fathers (second century BC – second century AD). In A. Burguière, C. Klapisch-Zuber, M. Segalen and F. Zonabe, eds., *A History of the Family I: Distant Worlds, Ancient Worlds.* Cambridge: Polity, 228–69.

Tosh, J. (1999). *A Man's Place: Masculinity and the Middle Class Home in Victorian England.* New Haven: Yale University Press.

van Bremen, R. (1996). *The Limits of Participation: Women and Civic Life in the Greek East in the Hellenistic and Roman Periods.* Dutch Monographs on Ancient History and Archaeology. Amsterdam: Gieben.

Vera, D. (1995). Dall "villa perfecta" alla villa di Palladio: sulle trasformazioni del sistema agrario in Italia fra Principato e Dominato. *Athenaeum* 83, 189–211, 331–56.

Veyne, P. (1986). Le Dernier Foucault et sa morale. *Critique* 471–472, 933–41.

(1987). The Roman Empire. In P. Veyne ed., *A History of Private Life: I: From Pagan Rome to Byzantium.* Cambridge, MA, and London: Harvard University Press.

Volpe, G. (1990). *La Daunia nell' età della romanizzazione: paesaggio agrario, produzione scambi.* Bari: Edipuglia.

Wallace-Hadrill, A. (1988). The social structure of the Roman house. *Papers of the British School at Rome* 56, 43–97.

(2008). *Rome's Cultural Revolution.* Cambridge: Cambridge University Press.

Ward-Perkins, B., Mills, N., Gadd, D. and Delano Smith, C. (1986). Luni and the Ager Lunensis: the rise and fall of a Roman town. *Papers of the British School at Rome* 54, 81–146.

Welter, V. (2002). *Biopolis: Patrick Geddes and the City of Life.* Cambridge, MA: Harvard University Press.

Westgate, R., Fisher, N. and Whitley, J., eds. (2007). *Building Communities: House, Settlement and Society in the Aegean and Beyond.* London: British School at Athens.

Žižek, S. (1999). *The Ticklish Subject: The Absent Centre of Political Ontology.* London: Verso.

(2008). How did Marx invent the symptom? In S. Žižek, ed., *The Sublime Object of Ideology.* London: Verso, 1–55.

15 | A Response: 'Using the Material and Written Sources' Revisited

PENELOPE ALLISON

The interrelatedness, not only of 'words and walls', the title of the conference in which many of these papers were initially presented,[1] but also of the full range of material culture found within, and comprising, these 'walls' and these 'words', has long been a concern of mine. As a response to the chapters in this volume I will revisit, in particular, my article, 'Using the material and the written sources: turn-of-the-millennium approaches to Roman domestic space', published two decades ago.[2] I will use the arguments in that article as a means for assessing the progress this volume represents, since the turn of the millennium, in terms of more critically informed approaches to the interrelatedness of available written and material evidence for better understandings of domestic practice in the ancient world. Firstly, I will outline the background to the earlier article, its objectives and reactions to it, to demonstrate scholarly perspectives at that time. I will then use the specific themes in my article – 'the (nature of the) data', 'analytical and interpretative procedures' and 'asking appropriate questions of diverse data' – to assess how the current volume demonstrates the progress made in the last two decades, in particular in more critical use of the material record for better understandings of household behaviour in the Greek and Roman worlds. I will also refer to themes in my 1999 introduction to *The Archaeology of Household Activities*,[3] as relevant to the chapters in this volume. I include quotations from the works of other scholars at the turn of the millennium to assess the extent to which their concerns have also been met, or might be considered outmoded, by this volume.

Turn-Of-The-Millennium Approaches to Ancient Domestic Space

Since the early 1990s, I have argued that the archaeological evidence for household behaviour in the ancient world is under-explored and that this evidence, and particularly the artefactual evidence, needs to be foregrounded with more critical approaches to past interpretations that have used textual analogy imprecisely to interpret such remains.[4] I have argued that material remains from the ancient world have frequently been misrepresented because they have often been interpreted by past scholars who have inappropriately labelled them through written evidence that is not necessarily and not precisely related.[5] Past emphases on the written sources, and on the interpretation of the material record through these textual sources, have led to an entrenched perception that the written texts are the true arbiters of ancient domestic practice, while the archaeology was a mess.[6] These arguments and this research led scholars such as Andrew Wallace-Hadrill to acknowledge the important role of artefactual evidence in writing Pompeii's social history,[7] and Eleanor Leach to take a more critical 'view from the texts' and a more holistic approach to the uses of names for spaces in Roman houses, across a wide range of these texts.[8] Leach's analyses demonstrated the need for a more equal and interrogative approach to the material and the textual evidence.

Such research also led to Beryl Rawson and Paul Weaver to stress the need to 'use new evidence and new approaches to take the study of [the Roman] family in new directions' and to argue that contributors to their volume, *The Roman Family in Italy: Status, Sentiment and Space*, had not 'discard[ed] the solid body of literary evidence which has long been known: they use[ed] it extensively and critically but [did] not let it dominate or distort what the material evidence might tell us. They [tried] to discover what relationships there might be between the two bodies of evidence.'[9]

My 2001 article essentially critiqued approaches to the archaeological evidence for Roman houses that often saw this evidence as an illustration of the textual evidence. My aim was to highlight the need for 'exploring relationships between the material evidence and other sources',[10] and for 'the development of methods to reveal relationships between the social and the material in the past'.[11] My principal argument was that many of the houses we excavate around the Roman world were not built or lived in by the writers of the ancient texts, or their peers, and so their writings are not strictly applicable to these remains. I introduced the types of data relevant to investigating Roman domestic space and commented, often quite critically, on the analytical procedures and interpretative processes being used to investigate these data and their interrelationships. I suggested approaches to the material remains by which they might be more rigorously analysed for more situated perspectives on ancient domestic practice.[12]

Reactions to this article were immediate and also diverse. Rawson called it 'a magisterial critique setting out, for the future, methodological and theoretical approaches to Roman material culture',[13] and Bettina

Bergmann acknowledged that 'we had reached an important moment in the study of the Roman house … with scholars approaching domestic space down different disciplinary and methodological avenues'.[14] However, Bergmann warned that the recriminations in my article would 'signal a heated backlash, at least from some'.[15] Indeed, Andrew Riggsby wrote that I 'retain an absolutist position'[16] and Ray Laurence that my article 'reads like a manifesto as to why ancient historians and archaeologists should study their separate but entwined disciplines without reference to each other's evidence or interpretations'.[17] Given my long-standing concern for 'the necessity for an assessment of the relationship between archaeological and textual evidence for Roman room function'[18] and my call to foreground archaeological evidence and disentangle it from past interpretations of it, these reactions seemed rather surprising. Rolf Tybout also wrote that 'artefacts found in situ and seemingly at variance with the main function of a room type, as attested in literature, do not warrant profound scepticism concerning the essential validity of the literary evidence'.[19] His perspective here exemplified the then scholarly acceptance of the validity of past interpretations of material evidence through the textual, particularly the labels applied to excavated spaces, as well as deep-seated prejudices against our abilities to interpret the material, and particularly artefactual, evidence independently of written sources, despite this being an essential, and successful, approach in prehistoric archaeology.[20]

The question now is, to what extent are the chapters in this current volume successful in taking forward the study of ancient houses and households, and in providing more appropriately integrated approaches to all available and relevant data?

The Data

In my 2001 article I outlined the main types of data used by scholars studying domestic behaviour in the Roman world as being the writings of ancient authors, epigraphy, and material culture, and emphasized that the latter usually comprised domestic structures, and sometimes their decoration, rather than their contents. The more specific question here, then, is whether the authors in this volume have been more successful in choosing appropriate types of available data, and also in integrating them appropriately, for the specific aims of their studies.

I had argued that '[v]ery little of the fragmentary remains of Roman written works [of the ancient authors] … pertain to domestic practices and their physical settings' or 'provide useful information on the spatial aspects of household behaviour',[21] as outlined in the introduction to this volume. It is notable that chapters in this volume generally do not use ancient texts as their only data, or use material remains uncritically to illustrate such texts, although some advocate a more critical and comprehensive use of the text evidence. For example, Janett Morgan's 'view from the texts' argues for a more holistic interrogation of ancient Greek texts for more informed interpretations of the use of space in excavated Athenian houses. This stance was demonstrated by Andrew Wallace-Hadrill in the 1990s for Roman houses,[22] but perhaps needs to be emphasized for the Greek world. Simon Speksnijder's examination of the textual term *'vestibulum'* and his conclusions that this term applies principally to élite houses in Rome and is inappropriate for interpreting most of the archaeological record of Roman houses illustrates my earlier argument about the need to consider the specific context and agenda of these diverse sets of data.[23]

Other chapters take more specifically integrated approaches to textual and material evidence, with varying levels of success. For example, Maeve McHugh examines the types and distribution of ancient Greek 'farmsteads', in the archaeological record, and also the descriptions of several Greek authors on the accessibility of their farms from urban centres, although her conclusions are driven by the textual evidence. Hannah Platts also commences with the physical remains, those of the Villa of Diomedes, outside Pompeii. She integrates analyses of the writings of Pliny the Younger with those of this dwelling's location, layout and to a minor extent its elevation, and a certain amount of speculation, to postulate the sensory experiences within this residence. Lisa Nevett takes up these earlier calls with a refreshing approach to integrating textual and material-cultural evidence by using the material-cultural evidence as the framework to interrogate critically the textual evidence. Similarly, Emily Varto critiques previous positivist approaches that used Homer to illuminate the archaeological remains of Mycenean palaces, and demonstrates that more careful reading of the text shows closer links between this text and extant remains of later Iron Age Greek houses. Amy Smith integrates ancient Greek authors' references to marriages and the illumination of these ceremonies in Greek vase-paintings to critique some of the myths in modern scholarship about the marriage process. Essentially, therefore, most chapters in this volume demonstrate more critical approaches to the interrelatedness of the writings of ancient authors and the physical evidence for houses, and greater sensitivity to the complexity of the relationships between different

bodies of data, than was common at the turn of the millennium.[24] Details
of these approaches are further examined below.

In 2001 I had argued that epigraphical evidence was more useful for
'investigations of the composition of households than for the study of the
social use of space',[25] referring mainly to inscriptions and the practice of
decontextualizing them.[26] Particularly notable in this volume, then, is the
use of the papyri and graffiti for more contextualized analyses of domestic
practice that go beyond concerns for family structure. Both Inge
Uytterhoeven and April Pudsey use the rich papyrus remains from the
Fayum as their main data. Uytterhoeven integrates these epigraphical data
and the structural evidence of Graeco-Roman houses from this region –
their layout, materials and decoration – for a 'more detailed picture of the
physical appearance of houses and their socio-economic and cultural
implications'. Pudsey uses papyri from the villages of Karanis, Tebtynis
and Soknopaiou Nesos to identify changing family and household structures that could provide a framework for interpreting the layouts of houses
in Roman Tebtynis. She makes only passing reference to the latter, though,
noting that the usefulness of the archaeological evidence at these Fayum
villages for any detailed analyses is restricted by its recording methods.
Two further chapters make good use of epigraphical evidence in the form
of graffiti. Much of the focus of Jen Baird's paper is on the graffiti from the
houses in Dura-Europos, which she contextualizes within these houses, to
some extent. Crysta Kaczmarek analyses the locations of the structural
remains of *Lares* shrines, their associated decoration and graffiti naming
individuals, and relevant textual references, to demonstrate the sociocultural significance of the *Lares compitales* cult in Delos. While there are
some analytical problems with these chapters using epigraphical evidence,
discussed below, they exemplify the much greater and more effective use of
such evidence for household studies than two decades ago.

As mentioned above, in 2001 I also argued that 'the extensive material
evidence for housing' comprises not just structural remains but also decoration and artefacts.[27] Most of the chapters in this volume integrate textual
or epigraphical data with mainly structural remains, rather than with
decorative and artefactual evidence, as per the original conference title.
Both Uytterhoeven and Kaczmarek do make use of the decorative evidence
to identify the status and functions of the structures they are investigating,
although not artefactual data, no doubt because of the nature of the
excavations and recording of their case studies – a major problem for
many domestic sites in the ancient world, as highlighted by Pudsey,
Nevett and Morgan and exemplified by Casper Meyer. However, some of

the sites studied by Uytterhoeven would appear to have a greater range of more recently excavated and recorded data. On the other hand, pottery assemblages provide important datasets for McHugh's farmsteads, for which few 'walls' are preserved. Artefacts displayed in museums are Meyer's data, and Katerina Volioti considers extant remains of so-called *lekythoi*, as well as some of their archaeological contexts and textual information on this vase type.

It is notable that most chapters in this volume use, at most, two different types of the three main data types. Richard Alston's chapter is perhaps an exception here, engaging with textual, epigraphical and material (be it mainly structural) data to demonstrate more theorized approaches to social production and to identify household organization and family relationships. Here he uses ancient authors for élite housing, and epigraphical evidence from Egypt and structural and decorative evidence from Syria for understanding 'rural domestic architectural types'. However, he does not assess the actual epigraphical data and structural and decorative data in his analyses which are based largely on secondary interpretations and which, particularly in the Syrian case, lack presentation of the actual data (the 'walls') to fully substantiate his case.

Nevertheless, it is significant that most of the chapters have indeed integrated more than one type of data into their arguments. Some have deliberately taken more specifically material-cultural approaches while two have used textual and epigraphical evidence to set frameworks for investigating the material. To some extent these latter two reiterate turn-of-the-millennium approaches although in different contexts. In general, these chapters demonstrate more awareness of and more rigorous approaches to such integration and give less, uncritical, primacy to the textual evidence.[28]

As I argued in 2001, more interrogative integration of textual and material-cultural evidence is important for 21st-century investigations of the ancient world, in which ancient world archaeologists have developed greater concern for social practice and ancient historians have paid more attention to the role of material culture in their interpretations of social practice.[29] Indeed the training of a new generation of ancient world scholars has ostensibly bridged this disciplinary divide.[30] However, contributors to Sauer's volume have stressed the difficulty of critically integrating different types of imprecisely related data for an interpretation that is critically aware of the full significance of the primary data and of any lack of fit between the different types.[31] The question now is, are we more successful at interrogating these diverse sets of data in our investigations of domestic behaviour, two decades on?

Analytical and Interpretive Frameworks

My particular concern in 2001 was for the development of more rigorous methodological and theoretical frameworks for reading material culture to investigate social practice. I will, therefore, examine in more detail the analytical and interpretative processes these chapters employ, according to the sections in my 2001 paper, and, where appropriate, as discussed in my 1999 introduction to *The Archaeology of Household Activities*.[32]

Labelling as Textual Analogy

In the early 1990s I had argued that we needed to move away from 'the obsession with taking names from the texts and applying them to archaeo-logically excavated spaces'.[33] Wallace-Hadrill also admonished the practice of 'ransacking' ancient texts for labels for excavated spaces, as a process by which to explain them.[34] I further argued that 'the relationship between text and material culture was often analogical' and that using nomenclature found in the texts to label extant architectural forms and thereby ascribe a function to them often constitutes a compromise of the evidence.[35] Riggsby took a comparably critical approach to room-labels in the written sources to demonstrate how the term '*cubiculum*' could not be associated with a specific function.[36] Importantly, Rawson warned of the 'danger that we will treat the labels as part of the archaeological primary source and prejudice the function of that space'.[37]

Most chapters in this volume avoid this type of labelling of structural forms for identifying their functions, with the exception of Speksnijder's chapter. In his attempt to tie the term '*vestibulum*' to the archaeological evidence for Roman houses, Speksnijder argues that 'very few (if any) excavated spaces conform to the characteristics found in the literary sources'. He is probably correct in his critique of Leach's earlier approach to '*vestibula*' here[38] but, as indicated above, the problem is not with each individual case but with this blanket approach to integrating textual nomenclature with material-cultural evidence.[39] Speksnijder notes such integration needs to be much more specific in terms of the precisely similar contexts of both the textual terminology and the archaeological evidence. As I had argued, cases where 'both written and material remains ... are inextricably linked are extremely rare'.[40] Riggsby had also argued that 'the application of these terms to particular spaces in archaeological contexts can be problematic, even when the philology is not'.[41] And he acknowledged that some scholars had already questioned 'the accuracy (or more precisely the utility) with which labels derived from literary texts (but assigned to specific spaces only in the last two centuries) are assigned to rooms in surviving houses'.[42]

The uncritical and positivistic labelling of artefacts with textual nomenclature has also long been an analytical approach in ancient world studies against which I have warned,[43] and Morgan reiterates this warning here. Such labels are often used as conventions and some indeed would seem appropriate for particular artefact forms. Volioti uses the textual label *lekythoi* as primary evidence for identifying the function of the vessels known archaeologically, and labelled *lekythoi* on the basis of their shape. Indeed fabric and decoration often mark out the different types of so-called *lekythoi* discussed by Volioti. While Volioti provides some interesting observations we could perhaps be more critical of this assumed vessel name for all vessels found of this particular shape, or shapes, not least because she draws to our attention a so-called *aryballos* whose owner called it a *lekythos*!

Architectural Typology

In my 2001 paper I had argued that typology, and particularly structural typology, was used more heavily to interpret spatial function in houses in parts of the ancient world that lacked apparent recourse to textual analogy to label domestic spaces.[44] Many of the studies in this volume involve such regions of the ancient world and use structural typologies to identify social behaviour. Uytterhoeven bases her social classification of Fayum houses on a former structural typology of house types in the Fayum. While this is a useful approach, as I had argued in 2001, architectural typology can 'make only a limited contribution to better understandings of domestic spatial behavior and status, without recourse to other evidence or theoretical frameworks'.[45] That is, house layouts do not, in themselves, identify household behaviour and traditional 'common-sense' approaches can lead to anachronistic and culturally insensitive interpretations.[46] Here Platts is rightly critical of Mark Grahame's admitted 'myopic' approach to the complex dataset of Pompeian houses in which he used layout alone of a single house to understand social practice. Alston also uses the 'architectural types' of rural houses in Syria to identify the types of families they housed and their socio-economic structure. Because of his use of secondary sources and their interpretations the analytical processes by which he has reached his interpretations of these remains are not fully transparent.[47] Without a more explicit reading, and demonstration, of these 'rural domestic architectural types' and their proposed inhabitants, I am sceptical about his admittedly interesting arguments. I also feel that Pudsey has perhaps missed a trick by not actually demonstrating the extent to which the papyrus evidence from Roman Tebtynis can provide a framework for more detailed interrogative analyses of the physical remains of houses and house layouts at this site, however poorly recorded, to identify physical evidence of house sharing.

Architectural Typology Combined with Labelling

Speksnijder's analyses involve a structural typology 'grounded in [textual] nomenclature', which, I had argued, can be a problematic approach.[48] To some extent Uytterhoeven has also done this, with her focus on the so-called 'peristyle house' as the nomenclature for an élite house form, an approach privileging Vitruvian terminology and its association with house status.[49] However, as noted above, most papers here avoid this kind of labelling. As Wallace-Hadrill demonstrated in the 1990s, and as Morgan advocates in this volume, the texts provide much more than merely labels by which the functions of structural forms in the physical record can be identified. Indeed Varto successfully argues that the expression '*en mega-roisi*' does not refer to activities physically located in the Bronze Age structural remains which scholars have labelled *megaroi*, but to the more social conception of being 'at home' as opposed to being engaged in activities, such as warfare, away from the household. She also argues that the term was in use during later periods.

Decorative Typologies, Iconographies and Pictorial Analogy

Decorative typologies for understanding the use of domestic space (see Allison 2001: 192) are not evident in this volume, more because of the types of analyses rather than a specific rejection of this approach. Uytterhoeven alludes to decorative evidence to support her typological associations but does not use decorative typologies or any assessment of levels of decoration and social status,[50] perhaps because the evidence is insufficient for such analyses. Iconography plays a part in Kaczmarek's paper, but iconographic analyses have a more important role in the chapters by Meyer, Volioti and Smith, dealing with painted Greek vases. These analyses are essentially pictorial analogy and differ from the approaches I discuss in my 2001 article, concerning Roman wall painting, but resonate with those discussed in my 1999 introduction.[51] For example, Volioti, following Oakley,[52] uses the depiction of a plain black *lekythos* in the funerary iconography on Attic white-ground *lekythoi* as the background to her argument that *lekythoi* were household items used as oil containers for foodways rather than for perfume. This essentially art-historical approach itself is not so different from those at the turn of the millennium,[53] but is used more critically and comprehensively by Volioti. Meyer argues that the iconography on Greek vases has been used in museum display, in the absence of any contextual information, as a 'false analogy' and a 'seemingly neutral presentation of historical reality'. Through his critique of past 'household archaeology' approaches to the significance of 'genre' scenes of Greek vases he contributes to the continued exposure of ongoing biases in understandings of concepts of 'public' and 'private' and of gendered roles in the ancient Greek world,[54] and, importantly, the need to consider the intended destination, or context, of many of these vases, with their imagery.

Modern and Ethnographic Analogy

In 2001 I warned against uncritical, and often subconscious, use of modern analogy and against a concept of 'common sense', in studying domestic behaviour, stressing their normalizing effect.[55] This critique is taken up here by Meyer in his exposure of museums' use of 'modern-day ... categories of interpretation' and his demonstration of how their displays have compromised the historicity of the artefacts' meaning. Modern analogy has played only a very small part in the analyses in the chapters in this volume, though. Nevertheless it can be very useful for our investigations when used in a critically interrogative and cross-cultural manner to test our assumptions rather than to validate them.[56] This is well put in Alston's theoretical discussion concerning modern housing, in which he argues against an 'ancient–modern dichotomy' in the perceived polarity of the public and the private in modernity, and stresses the need to consider the 'multifaceted nature' of the modern world in this regard.

In 1999 I discussed the use of ethnographic analogy as an analytical tool in household archaeology and stressed Wylie's warning about the appropriateness of the 'analytical inference' for the particular data.[57] McHugh takes a suitably critical approach to past uses of ethnographic analogy to identify the sizes of farms associated with ancient farmsteads and Morgan proposes more rigorous approaches to using ethno-historical analogy to infer house types and the use of domestic space, stressing that textual evidence is also a valuable form of ethnographic material, to be used cautiously in interpreting archaeological evidence.

Contextualized Artefact Assemblages

In 2001 I argued that the movable, and particularly the more mundane, contents of Roman houses are generally removed from their domestic contexts during excavation and recording, and that only rarely have their 'provenance, distribution or quantification ... been used to throw light on domestic behaviour', in which regard ancient world archaeology was out of step with the rest of the archaeological discipline.[58] For some of the chapters in this volume this still seems to be the case, although this is not necessarily the fault of the authors. As Pudsey notes,[59] this situation is in large part because many of the sites being analysed here were excavated before more contextualized recordings of such movable remains were being carried out. This, no doubt, is at least one reason why Kaczmarek did not consider artefact assemblages in her study of *Lares* shrines and wealthy houses in Delos, despite the contribution such evidence might have made to her study. As Meyer argues, the removal from their archaeological contexts of the artefacts with which many classical archaeologists deal – that is, removal of 'works of art' to museums – was a 'compromise ... between historical explanation ... and idealization of ... art'. Uytterhoeven claims that the study of house layout and ornamentation can be complemented by analyses of house contents (artefacts and bioarchaeological remains) from the more recent excavations at numerous sites in the Fayum, from which she selected her data. However, she focuses, in a rather traditional manner, on the structural and epigraphical remains, perhaps because of the initial conference title, 'Between Words and Walls', or the nature of the artefactual evidence.

While, one might indeed argue that a volume initially concerned with 'words and walls' is not essentially concerned with contextualized artefactual, or ecofactual, evidence, some of the chapters do consider contexualized artefact assemblages. Nevett alludes to her own analyses, and that of Nicholas Cahill's,[60] of artefact assemblages at Olynthos for greater understandings 'of the organization of housing and the use of space'. Morgan surveys how house contents recording, in both texts and in archaeological excavations, can be used in studies of the Classical Greek house, but, as outlined above, warns against simplistic assumptions about the interrelatedeness of these two sets of data. More positively here, pottery scatters identified through archaeological survey, and the nature of these assemblages, provide one of McHugh's principal criteria for identifying farmsteads, and potentially, their specific character.[61] Volioti also considers contextualized artefact assemblages. Following Lynch,[62] she uses the discovery of *lekythoi* in what are likely to have been domestic contexts, in Athens and beyond, to argue that these were domestic containers rather than purely funerary objects. While her argument is well supported by her analysis of the precise shapes of these *lekythoi*, the quality of excavation recording has again meant that she has not been able to do a comprehensive analysis of so-called *lekythoi* in domestic contexts to support her typological analyses. Here Volioti reiterates Lynch's argument that plain black and black-figured *lekythoi* were used in the domestic realm. It would appear that, to date, no white-ground *lekythoi* have been found in domestic contexts, as argued by Lynch. Volioti's discussion on the role of these artefacts within the social context of the family could be further substantiated by presentation of spatial analyses.[63]

Interdisciplinary Approaches

In my 2001 paper, I argued that '[i]nterdisciplinary borrowing . . . [has] almost become *di rigeur* for an investigator of Roman domestic space' (Allison 2001: 198). An apparent lack of explicit interdisciplinary borrowing in most of the chapters in this volume, therefore, seems somewhat surprising. The main exception is Alston who argues for the primary understanding of concepts of social structure through which to investigate textual and material evidence. Some of the particular studies of social theorists which Alston proposes can provide such social structure have already been proposed and used as such frameworks in previous studies of domestic space in the ancient world.[64] While Antony Giddens' theory of structuration, Clifford Geertz's cultural interpretations, and Michael Foucault's spatial metaphors, to take some examples, have had important input into post-processual archaeology more broadly since the 1980s,[65] this is perhaps less true for studies of domestic spaces in the ancient Mediterranean world.[66] Thus, Alston's theoretical standpoint takes up existing approaches in archaeology more broadly and urges ancient world scholars to think more critically about how such theorists provide us with ways of thinking about ancient domestic behavior and related social structures.

While I did not specifically address gender and space in my 2001 paper, my 1999 introduction stressed the important lens that feminist and gender theory provide for a more critical investigation of ancient households, incidentally critiquing Bourdieu here.[67] Engagement with feminist and gender theory is implicit in many current studies of ancient households and this underpinning is apparent, if not explicit, in many of these chapters. Particularly notable is Meyer's critique of the simplistic associations in museum displays of the men and women depicted in Greek vase paintings. This underpinning is also found in Pudsey's paper, on female ownership of property and in Varto's warning of unjustified gendered dichotomies in past studies of evidence for domestic space in Homer. These chapters indeed contribute to our understandings of the historicity of gendered practice, and also ought to remind us that social status is often a more important criterion in the ancient world than gender or rather sex, per se.[68]

Under this 'Interdisciplinary Approaches' heading I include modes of inquiry that also stem from social science approaches to space and households. For example, in my 2001 article I argued that '[house o]ccupancy has often been studied atheoretically', and stressed the importance of investigating ancient households as 'systems of membership'.[69] Most chapters in this volume implicitly accept that ancient households comprise more than the male 'householder'. In several chapters the authors discuss, unproblematically, both men and women in their studies of domestic social structure, demonstrating more gendered perspectives and greater awareness of the visibility and roles of both in this arena. Less evident, though, is discussion on other even less visible members of these households, such as slaves and children, although these household members are more 'visible' in the chapters in this volume than they were in the scholarship of two decades ago. Uytterhoeven considers the range of people, including children and other 'non-kin dependants', who made up the likely numbers of such household members in Fayum households. Other authors refer more explicitly to slaves, freedmen and children as household residents or members of family groups, and some, in particular, give these other household members more specific consideration in their analyses (e.g. Morgan, Kaczmarek, Platts, Pudsey and Varto).

Another mode of inquiry that is becoming relatively widespread in archaeology since the turn of the millennium is consideration for 'the body' and particularly its sensory experiences.[70] Platts investigates how occupants of, and visitors to, the so-called Villa of Diomedes, outside Pompeii, would have experienced the various parts of this house, particularly in terms of smells and noise, to 'flesh out' our interpretations of Roman villas.

Temporality

In 1999 I discussed temporality and the difficulty of understanding the daily life cycle of the household, and the life cycle of the house itself, through the archaeological record.[71] The difficulty of isolating a single household in the past and the concept of household series were articulated by Smith in the early 1990s.[72] Baird has made an important contribution to reading time in the archaeological record in her discussion of the different temporalities of the seemingly contemporary but different types of evidence, namely the temporal inequalities evident between the structural remains and the associated texts. While the concept of temporal disjuncture itself is not new, interesting here are the overlapping stories, and memories, that would seem to 'reside' with texts like graffiti, 'between' the physical structure and human behaviour within it.

Symbolism and Ritual

In 1999 I argued that 'studies of household archaeology have tended to ignore the roles of ritual and symbolism in household behaviour'.[73] Many of these chapters allude to the symbolic value of ancient houses to their occupants. Nevett focuses specifically on the 'symbolic manipulation of domestic space', in terms of monumentality and decoration, to articulate social aspirations even if the spaces in question, here the so-called *andrones*, may not actually have functioned as might be expected. A related type of symbolism is evident in, and has been acknowledged for, Roman houses.[74] To my knowledge, though, this has been a less investigated aspect of the remains of Greek houses. Household rituals are also mentioned in a number of chapters (e.g. the *salutatio* in Speksnijder's chapter, funerary rituals in Varto's chapter), and Morgan discusses the main rituals for Classical Greek households and their often temporary impact on domestic space. Specific household rituals are the subject of both Kaczmarek's and Smith's chapters, although interestingly these rituals take place, at least in part, outside house walls, extending the concept of domestic space into supposedly public space, but still inside 'social habituation and protocols of identity' as articulated by Meyer. Volioti argues against the specific ritual significance of *lekythoi*, although, as outlined above, I am not convinced that she has successfully argued this for white-ground *lekythoi* which are more strongly linked to funerary ritual.

Asking Appropriate Questions of Diverse Data

In 2001 I argued for the need to 'follow lines of inquiry to which particular evidence is best suited' and stressed the importance for studies of ancient housing of re-examin[ing] 'old evidence' in new light'.[75] I argued that 'current [research] questions ... require much more sensitive interaction between readings of the ancient texts, readings of the complete material record, social theory, and critical appraisals of the biases inherited from past generations of Roman historians and archaeologists'.[76] Speksnijder's analyses and conclusions demonstrate, in part, the importance of such arguments.

Thus, I had cautioned against examining 'previous interpretations of the data rather than the original data', and against not 'taking into account the often already interpretative nature of the available information' – that is the 'factoids' that pervade the long-investigated subject of ancient housing, and that have often become so entrenched in modern scholarship that they are confused with the primary data.[77] Stephen Dyson similarly stressed the need for critical assessment of the assumptions of 19th-century scholars about relationships between excavated houses and texts, and also that, for example, many of the supposed 'literary references' to Pompeii (e.g. Vitruvius) are indeed secondary interpretations from 19th-century perspectives (i.e. from August Mau).[78] This is successfully demonstrated here by Varto for early Greek houses.

Appropriate Evidence

Obviously, selection of data and analytical procedures depends on the types of questions each author wants to address. In this volume investigating 'Housing in the Ancient Mediterranean World', most chapters use more than one type of data, as discussed above, and have essentially used appropriate data in an adequately comprehensive manner. That said, and as intimated above, while Pudsey argues for an abstract approach, using only papyri, in '...examin[ing] ... the processes of changes in house use in both social and material terms', I do think some analyses of the material remains at Tebtynis, or at least a presentation of these structural remains for the reader to assess (i.e. some house plans) would have been useful here, to 'observe practices in which houses morph in shape and structure along with changing family and household structures', or indeed to argue that this is not evident. Similarly, Platts' archaeological case study is perhaps an odd choice given its early excavation and poor state of preservation and recording, and its rather dubious classification as a 'villa sub-urbana', a stone's throw from Pompeii's Herculaneum Gate. She might have been better served to have chosen another Campanian 'villa', that was not excavated over 200 years ago and has been more recently investigated (e.g. the villas at Stabiae or Oplontis), for a more comprehensive use of available material evidence.

Reinterpretation of Old Data, Not Old Interpretations

A notable feature of this volume, with the possible exception of Uytterhoeven's chapter, is the re-examination of material rather than the presentation of new material, which is common practice in recent, more social, approaches to the ancient Mediterranean world. It is notable that most chapters here consciously engage with the actual data rather than its interpretation. Again, Alston is the main exception here, in his interpretations of epigraphical and archaeological evidence for rural household structures without presenting the evidence itself.

Appropriate Analytical Methods

Is it also notable that several chapters take more explicit material-cultural approaches to their research question (e.g. Nevett, McHugh) and more critical and comprehensive approaches to the use of ancient texts (e.g. Morgan, Varto). Also notable here is a greater use of scientific analytical methods for studies of ancient households than was evident at the turn of the millennium. For example, McHugh uses GIS and spatial analysis in her analyses of essentially geographical data and Kaczmarek uses quantitative analyses to demonstrate effectively the strong association of *Lares* shrines with the larger houses in Delos.

Conclusions

The above discussion outlines some of the strengths and weaknesses within and among the chapters in this volume, with particular reference to the themes I discussed at the turn of the millennium. At that time, and indeed into the first decade of this millennium, there had been discussion on boundaries between studies of ancient history and of the archaeology of the Greek and Roman worlds.[79] I had argued that a fuller understanding of the nature of the data and a better understanding of their analytical possibilities were needed, and especially for material culture, to reach meaningful interpretations that take a critical approach to past interpretations of these data. I wrote that '[T]hrough more stringent assessment of the relationship of these [archaeological] data to textual data a more holistic and reliable understanding of [ancient] domestic life can be developed'[80] and 'that the kind of information which we can glean from archaeological data is often in a very different form from that which we can glean from written texts ... and the relationship between them is often difficult to grasp.'[81] David Mattingly wrote that 'the reality of the Pompeian evidence rarely comes close to the supposed normative model derived from study of literary sources'.[82]

These arguments, in many ways, reiterated one from over 150 years ago when Thomas Dyer wrote:

> the *atrium* and the *cavaedium* ... appear to signify the same thing ... some commentators on Vitruvius ... deny this ... no wonder that so much obscurity and difference of opinion prevail on these subjects, since almost all our knowledge is derived from the scant account of Vitruvius; and it is obvious that whatever general rules might be recognised by architects, they must have been modified in innumerable instances by the caprice or convenience of individuals. It is dangerous, therefore, to attempt to wrest the text of an author, to make it square with some 'specimen' which has been preserved or described; for we can never be sure that the two were even meant to coincide ...[83]

And, fifty years ago, Birgitta Tamm also argued for the need to 'abandon old [Vitruvian] points of departure in the discussion about [extant remains of] Roman houses'.[84] Essentially there is a strong association between archaeological and the textual remains from the ancient world, but the relationships between these sets of evidence is more complex than is often presented. The aim of my 2001 paper had been to highlight, yet again, the need for an awareness, and the implementation, of processes by which diverse types of evidence could be analysed and meaningful interpretations are formulated. I had stressed how the original evidence had often been obliterated by the interpretative processes used by past scholars.

All the chapters in this volume show, to varying degrees, consideration of the need to think more critically about how these diverse sets of data might be related. Equally they highlight that there are not just two diverse bodies of evidence, but that there is a range of data types, written and material and both, that can be analysed by a range of different methods. Indeed, this volume amply demonstrates that we have moved on from debates that were dominating studies of ancient domestic space at the turn of the millennium, and notably those concerning a disciplinary divide. The authors are cognizant of the difference types of evidence and, in general, of their interpretative possibilities and limitations. Broadly speaking, the authors show rigorous interrogative approaches to the different bodies of data, resulting in many interesting and thought-provoking ideas. It is inevitable that different scholars with different training and differing skills sets have different approaches to reading and negotiating the various types of evidence – some are obviously more specific and some more general and wide-reaching. It is notable here that most authors, whatever their training, have attempted, often very successfully, to take a more rigorous approach to the analyses of these diverse types of data. Evident here are greater understandings, than two decades ago, that the primary data for some questions concerning ancient domestic behaviour are textual, for others they are archaeological, and that there is a difference between these primary data and the secondary interpretations of them.

Significant across all these chapters is that the material-cultural record stands on an equal footing with the textual, and that analyses of this record engage with more material-cultural approaches rather than use it as an illustration of the textual evidence. Housing in the ancient Mediterranean world is one of the most fruitful areas where different types of evidence inform on different aspects of domestic life differently. The task of understanding the relationships between these diverse types of data, though, is not as easy as past scholars have thought. The volume demonstrates that considerable advances have been made in the last two decades and that we are moving in the right direction, with a range of analytical approaches for investigating diverse types of data for a greater, and more nuanced, understanding of the ancient domestic life that underpinned all other aspects of ancient society.

In our desire for comparative analyses to assess social practice within physical or documentary evidence, and to avoid anecdotal approaches to lived space we need values (or data) which are comparable. But it is important that we avoid generalizing from the particular by overlaying different types of data whose relationships are often rather tenuous. In particular, we need to take more critical methodological, rather than speculative, approaches to material remains and to take more holistic and more critically analytical approaches to all bodies of evidence, including artefactual evidence, to consider lived space, not just constructed space. While investigating artefactual evidence from past excavations can be a hard ask, if we can demonstrate the need for consideration of the possibilities for such evidence, however poor, this can inspire excavators and

excavation report writers to pay more attention to their spatial contexts
and to socially oriented questions.[85] And continued critical engagement
with social theory can assist us in developing even more rigorously interrogative material and textual approaches to housing in the ancient
Mediterranean world.

Notes

1 'Between Words and Walls: Material and Textual Approaches to Housing in
   the Graeco-Roman World', conference held at Birkbeck College, London,
   29–30 August 2013, at which I was a session responder and discussant.
2 Allison 2001a.
3 Allison 1999a.
4 E.g. Allison 1992a: 15–17; 1993; 1997a; 1997b; 1999a; 1999b.
5 See also Foxhall 2004.
6 See Allison 1992b: 49.
7 Wallace-Hadrill 1994: 87–90.
8 Leach 1997: 53, 67. See also Leach 2004: acknowledgements.
9 Rawson and Weaver 1997: 5.
10 Allison 2001a: 203.
11 Allison 2001a: 183.
12 See Allison 2001a: 203.
13 Rawson 2003: 124.
14 Bergmann 2001: 56.
15 Bergmann 2001: 57.
16 Riggsby 2003: 170 n. 8.
17 Laurence 2004: 104.
18 Allison 1993: 7.
19 Tybout 2001: 43.
20 See e.g. Ciolek-Tiorello 1984. See also Schiffer 1987; LaMotta and Schiffer 1999.
21 Allison 2001a: 183–84.
22 Wallace-Hadrill 1990: 145–148; 1994: 3–7.
23 E.g. Allison 1997a: 323.
24 See Allison 2001a: 185–188.
25 Allison 2001a: 184.
26 See also Allison 2001b.
27 Allison 2001a: 184.
28 Cf. Allison 2001a: 185.
29 Allison 2001a:203. Wallace-Hadrill has not, as argued by Platts in this volume,
   'paved the way' for scholars such as Leach and Clarke, not to mention
   numerous other archaeologists, in their investigations of Roman art and society
   through material-cultural evidence, and especially through display in Roman

houses (see e.g. Clarke 1991; Gazda 1991; Leach 1993). As I argued at the turn of the millennium, Wallace-Hadrill's main influence has been on the engagement of more text-based scholars with such, more archaeological, scholarship.

30 See Sauer 2004.

31 See esp. Foxhall 2004; Hoffmann 2004.

32 Allison 1999a.

33 Allison 1993: 7.

34 Wallace-Hadrill 1994: 6.

35 Allison 2001a: 185–188. See also Allison 1999a: 12–13.

36 Riggsby 1997. Although to my mind not critical enough in that he assumed this label to be evidence in Pompeian houses as part of the primary evidence, rather than being a secondary interpretation (Allison 2001a: 188).

37 Rawson 2003: 124.

38 Leach 1993.

39 See also Allison 2008: 1454.

40 Allison 2001a: 185.

41 Riggsby 2003: 170.

42 Riggsby 1997: 43 n. 41.

43 Allison 1999b: esp. 59–65.

44 Allison 2001a: 188.

45 Allison 2001a: 189.

46 See Whitley 1998: 9; Allison 2001a: 197.

47 Cf. Allison 2001a: 183.

48 Allison 2001a: 190.

49 See Leach 1997; Allison 2001a: 191.

50 See Wallace-Hadrill 1994: 149–74.

51 See Allison 1999a: 13. See also Allison 1992c.

52 Oakley 2004.

53 E.g. Goldberg 1999.

54 See Allison 1999a: 11.

55 Allison 2001a: 194–195.

56 See Allison 2001a: 202; 2008: 1454 and fig. 2.

57 Allison 1999a: 12–13; Wylie 1985.

58 Allison 2001a: 195.

59 Reiterating Allison 2001a: 196.

60 Cahill 2002.

61 See also Foxhall 2004.

62 Lynch 2011.

63 See e.g. Cougle 2008.

64 E.g. Bourdieu (although see Allison 1999a: 1, 9–10 and 2001: 198, following vom Bruck (1997); see also George 2004) and Lefebvre (Laurence 1997; cf. Allison 2001a: 199).

65 E.g. Wylie 1989. See also Wylie 2002; Harris and Cipolla 2017: 26, 43–44 *passim*.

66 In the introduction to this volume the editors also refer to microhistory, micro-archaeology, important for investigations of domestic contexts (see Allison 2020, esp. 7–8). Here they give a nod to New Materialism and the 'material turn' in history (e.g. Schouwenberg 2015).

67 Allison 1999a: 9–10. See also Allison 2015: 104–106.

68 See Allison 2015.

69 Allison 2001a: 199 and 202; see also Allison 1999a: 2.

70 E.g. Joyce 2005; Skeates 2010; see also Hamilakis 2013.

71 Allison 1999a: 12.

72 Smith 1992.

73 Allison 1999a: 11.

74 E.g. Hales 2000 on Cicero, *De domo sua*.

75 Allison 2001a: 202.

76 Allison 2001a: 202.

77 Allison 2001a: 201.

78 Dyson 1997: 153.

79 E.g. Sauer 2004; Caraher *et al.* 2008.

80 Allison 1997a: 322.

81 Allison 1997a: 354; see also Foxhall 2004.

82 Mattingly 1997: 215–216.

83 Dyer 1867: 253, footnote.

84 Tamm 1973: 55.

85 See Cool 2007: 54–55; Allison 2013: esp. 36–39. See also Allison *et al.* 2018.

References

Allison, P. M. (1992a). *The distribution of Pompeian house contents and its significance* (PhD thesis, University of Sydney. Ann Arbor, MI: UMI Dissertation Services no. 9400463, 1994).

(1992b). Artefact assemblages: not the Pompeii Premise. In E. Herring, R. Whitehouse and J. Wilkins, eds., *Papers of the Fourth Conference of Italian Archaeology, London 1990*, 3, pt I. London: Accordia Research Centre, 49–56.

(1992c). The relationship between decoration and room type in Pompeian houses: a case study of the Casa della Caccia Antica. *Journal of Roman Archaeology* 5, 235–49.

(1993). How do we identify the use of space in Roman housing? In E. Moorman, ed., *Functional and Spatial Analysis of Wall Painting*. Bulletin Antieke Beschaving, Annual papers in Classical Archaeology 3. Leiden: Babesch, 1–8.

(1997a). Artefact distribution and spatial function in Pompeian houses. In B. Rawson and P. Weaver, eds., *The Roman Family in Italy: Status, Sentiment and Space*. Oxford: Oxford University Press, 321–54.

(1997b). Roman households: an archaeological perspective. In H. M. Parkins, ed., *Roman Urbanism: Beyond the Consumer City*. London and New York: Routledge, 112–46.

(1999a). Introduction. In P. M. Allison, ed., *The Archaeology of Household Activities*. London and New York: Routledge, 1–18.

(1999b). Labels for ladles: interpreting the material culture of Roman households. In P. M. Allison, ed., *The Archaeology of Household Activities*. London and New York: Routledge, 57–77.

(2001a). Using the material and the written sources: turn of the millennium approaches to Roman domestic space. *American Journal of Archaeology* 105, 181–208.

(2001b). Placing individuals: Pompeian epigraphy in context. *Journal of Mediterranean Archaeology* 14(1), 54–75.

(2008). Household archaeology. In D. Pearsall, ed., *Encyclopedia of Archaeology*. London: Elsevier, 1449–58.

(2013). *People and Spaces in Roman Military Bases*. Cambridge: Cambridge University Press.

(2015). Characterising Roman artefacts for investigating gendered practices in contexts without sexed bodies. *American Journal of Archaeology* 119(1), 103–23.

(2020). *Who Came to Tea at the Old Kinchega Homestead: Tablewares and Teawares and Social Interaction at an Australian Outback Homestead*. British Archaeological Reports, International Series 2964. Oxford: Archaeopress.

Allison, P. M., Pitts, M. and Colley, S., eds. (2018). Special issue: Big Data on the Roman Table: New Approaches to Tablewares in the Roman World. *Internet Archaeology* 50.

Bergmann, B. (2001). House of cards: a response to R. A. Tybout. *Journal of Roman Archaeology* 14, 56–57.

Cahill, N. (2002). *Household and City Organization at Olynthus*. New Haven and London: Yale University Press.

Caraher, W. R., Hall, L. J. and Moore , R. S. (2008). Introduction: A tribute to Timothy E. Gregory. In W. R. Caraher and L. J. Hall, eds., *Archaeology and History in Roman, Medieval and Post-medieval Greece: Studies on Method and Meaning in Honor of Timothy E. Gregory*. Burlington: Ashgate.

Ciolek-Tiorello, R. S. (1984). An alternative model for room function from the Grasshopper Pueblo, Arizona. In H. J. Heitala, ed., *Intrasite Spatial Analysis in Archaeology*. Cambridge: Cambridge University Press, 127–53.

Clarke, J. R. (1991). *The Houses of Roman Italy 100 BC – AD 250: Ritual, Space and Decoration*. Los Angeles: University of California Press.

Cool, H. E. M. (2007). Telling stories about Brougham, or the importance of the specialist report. In R. Hingley and S. Willis, eds., *Roman Finds: Context and Theory*. Proceedings of a conference held at the University of Durham. Oxford: Oxbow, 54–58.

Cougle, L. (2008). Dress and social identities: the role of GIS in mapping social structure in the central Italian Iron Age cemetery of Osteria dell'Osa. In P. M. Allison, ed., Dealing with Legacy Data. *Internet Archaeology* 24.

Dyer T. H. (1867). *Pompeii: Its History, Buildings and Antiquities*. London: Bell and Dawdy.

Dyson, S. L. (1997). Some random thoughts on a collection of papers on Roman archaeology. In S. E. Bon and R. Jones, eds., *Sequence and Space in Pompeii*. Oxford: Oxbow, 150–57.

Foxhall, L. (2004). Field sports: engaging Greek archaeology and history. In E. Sauer, ed., *Archaeology and Ancient History: Breaking down the Boundaries*. London and New York: Routledge, 76–84.

Gazda, E., ed., (1991). *Roman Art in the Private Sphere: New Perspectives on the Architecture and Décor of the* Domus, Villa *and* Insula. Ann Arbor: University of Michigan Press.

George, M. (2004). Domestic architecture and household relations: Pompeii and Roman Ephesos. *Journal for the Study of the New Testament* 27(1), 7–25.

Goldberg, M. Y. (1999). Spatial and behavioural negotiation in Classical Athenian city houses. In P. M. Allison, ed., *The Archaeology of Household Activities*. London and New York: Routledge, 142–61.

Hales, S. (2000). At home with Cicero. *Greece and Rome* 47, 44–55.

Hamilakis, Y. (2013). *Archaeology and the Senses: Human Experience, Memory, and Affect*. Cambridge: Cambridge University Press.

Harris, O. and Cipolla, C. (2017). *Archaeological Theory in the New Millennium: Introducing Current Perspectives*. London and New York: Routledge.

Hoffmann, B. (2004). Tacitus, Agricola and the role of literature in the archaeology of the first century AD. In E. Sauer, ed., *Archaeology and Ancient History: Breaking down the Boundaries*. London and New York: Routledge, 151–65.

Joyce, R. (2005). Archaeology and the body. *Annual Review of Anthropology* 34, 139–58.

LaMotta, V. M. and Schiffer, M. B. (1999). Formation processes of house floor assemblages. In P. M. Allison, ed., *The Archaeology of Household Activities*. London and New York: Routledge, 19–29.

Laurence, R. (1997). Space and text. In R. Laurence and A. Wallace-Hadrill, eds., *Domestic Space in the Roman World: Pompeii and Beyond*. Journal of Roman Archaeology Supplement 22. Portsmouth, RI: Journal of Roman Archaeology, 7–14.

(2004). The uneasy dialogue between ancient history and archaeology. In E. Sauer, ed., *Archaeology and Ancient History: Breaking down the Boundaries.* London and New York: Routledge, 99–113.

Leach, E. (1993). The entrance room in the House of Iulius Polybius and the nature of the Roman vestibulum. In E. Moorman, ed., *Functional and Spatial Analysis of Wall Painting.* Bulletin Antieke Beschaving, Annual Papers in Classical Archaeology 3. Leiden: Babesch, 23–33.

Leach, E. W. (1997). Oecus on Ibycus: investigating the vocabulary of the Roman house. In S. E. Bon and R. Jones, eds., *Sequence and Space in Pompeii.* Oxford: Oxbow, 50–72.

(2004). *The Social Life of Painting in Ancient Rome and on the Bay of Naples.* Cambridge: Cambridge University Press.

Lynch, K. M. (2011). *The Symposium in Context. Pottery from a Late Archaic House near the Athenian Agora.* Hesperia Supplement 46. Princeton: American School of Classical Studies at Athens.

Mattingly, D. J. (1997). Beyond belief: drawing a line beneath the consumer city. In H. M. Parkins, ed., *Roman Urbanism: Beyond the Consumer City.* London and New York: Routledge, 210–18.

Oakley, J. H. (2004). *Picturing Death in Classical Athens: The Evidence of the White Lekythoi.* Cambridge: Cambridge University Press.

Rawson, B. (2003). The Roman family in recent research: state of the question. *Biblical Interpretation* 11(2), 119–38.

Rawson, B. and Weaver, P., eds. (1997). *The Roman Family in Italy: Status, Sentiment and Space.* Oxford: Oxford University Press.

Riggsby, A. (1997). 'Private' and 'public' in Roman culture: the case of the *cubiculum. Journal of Roman Archaeology* 10, 36–56.

(2003). Pliny in space and time. *Arethusa* 36, 167–86.

Sauer, E. W., ed., (2004). *Archaeology and Ancient History: Breaking down the Boundaries.* London and New York: Routledge.

Schiffer, M. B. (1987). *Formation Processes in the Archaeological Record.* Albuquerque: University of New Mexico (republished 1996, Salt Lake City).

Schouwenberg, H. (2015). Back to the future? History, material culture and new materialism. *International Journal of History, Culture and Modernity* 3(1), 59–72.

Skeates, R. (2010). *An Archaeology of the Senses: Prehistoric Malta.* Oxford: Oxford University Press.

Smith, M. (1992). Braudel's temporal rhythms and chronological theory in archaeology. In A. B. Knapp, ed., *Archaeology, Annales, and Ethnohistory.* Cambridge: Cambridge University Press, 23–34.

Tamm, B. (1973). Some notes on Roman houses. *Opuscula Romana* IX.6, 53–60.

Tybout, R. A. (2001). Roman wall-painting and social significance. *Journal of Roman Archaeology* 14, 33–56.

Vom Bruck, G. (1997). A House Turned Inside Out: Inhabiting Space in a Yemini City. *Journal of Material Culture* 2, 139–72.

Wallace-Hadrill, A. F. (1990). The social spread of Roman luxury: sampling Pompeii and Herculaneum. *Papers of the British School at Rome* 58, 145–92.

(1994). *Houses and Society in Pompeii and Herculaneum.* Princeton: Princeton University Press.

Whitley, D. (1998). New approaches to old problems. In D. Whitley, ed., *Reader in Archaeological Theory: Post-processual and Cognitive Approaches.* London: Routledge, 1–28.

Wylie, A. (1985). *Reactions against Analogy.* Advances in Archaeological Method and Theory 8. New York: Springer, 63–111.

(1989). Archaeological cables and tacking: the implications of practice for Bernstein's 'Options beyond objectivism and relativism'. *Philosophy of the Social Sciences* 19, 1–18.

(2002). *Thinking from Things: Essays in the Philosophy of Archaeology.* Berkeley, Los Angeles and London: University of California Press.

Index

CPSIA information can be obtained
at www.ICGtesting.com
Printed in the USA
LVHW061818100922
728077LV00003B/67